CENTRAL LIBRARY
MARKET SQUARE
PRESTON 53191

SYSTEM COPY

D1348830

PPTR   W'GEAC   X

                                             X

PRESTON THE
LOCAL LANCASHIRE
STUDIES LIBRARY

HARRIS PUBLIC LIBRARY
PRESTON ✓

FOR REFERENCE
WITHDRAWN FROM
LANCASHIRE LIBRARIES
ONLY

OOP
retain
05-05-05

PPR

AUTHOR	CLASS
COOK, C.	R 941·06
TITLE	No.
BRITISH HISTORICAL	03431047
FACTS, 1688-1760.	
1988	

THE LANCASHIRE LIBRARY 30/1/89
LIBRARY HEADQUARTERS, 143 CORPORATION STREET, PRESTON PR1 8RH

a30118 034310478b

MACMILLAN HISTORICAL AND POLITICAL FACTS

* ENGLISH HISTORICAL FACTS, 1485–1603 (Ken Powell and Chris Cook)

* ENGLISH HISTORICAL FACTS, 1603–88 (Chris Cook and John Wroughton)

* BRITISH HISTORICAL FACTS, 1688–1760 (Chris Cook and John Stevenson)

* BRITISH HISTORICAL FACTS, 1760–1830 (Chris Cook and John Stevenson)

* BRITISH HISTORICAL FACTS, 1830–1900 (Chris Cook and Brendan Keith)

* BRITISH POLITICAL FACTS, 1900–85 (David Butler and Gareth Butler)

MACMILLAN EUROPEAN POLITICAL FACTS

* EUROPEAN POLITICAL FACTS, 1789–1848 (Chris Cook and John Paxton)

* EUROPEAN POLITICAL FACTS, 1848–1918 (Chris Cook and John Paxton)

* EUROPEAN POLITICAL FACTS, 1918–84 (Chris Cook and John Paxton)

Series Standing Order

If you would like to receive future titles in this series as they
are published, you can make use of our standing order
facility. To place a standing order please contact your
bookseller or, in case of difficulty, write to us at the address
below with your name and address and the name of the
series. Please state with which title you wish to begin your
standing order. (If you live outside the UK we may not have
the rights for your area, in which case we will forward your
order to the publisher concerned.)

Standing Order Service, Macmillan Distribution Ltd,
Houndmills, Basingstoke, Hampshire, RG21 2XS, England.

Also by Chris Cook and John Stevenson

THE SLUMP: Society and Politics during the Depression

THE LONGMAN ATLAS OF MODERN BRITISH HISTORY, 1700–1970

THE ATLAS OF MODERN WARFARE

THE LONGMAN HANDBOOK OF MODERN BRITISH HISTORY, 1714–1980

THE LONGMAN HANDBOOK OF MODERN EUROPEAN HISTORY,
1763–1985

Other books by Chris Cook

* THE AGE OF ALIGNMENT: ELECTORAL POLITICS IN BRITAIN, 1922–29

* A SHORT HISTORY OF THE LIBERAL PARTY, 1900–84

* BY-ELECTIONS IN BRITISH POLITICS (ed. with John Ramsden)

*THE POLITICS OF REAPPRAISAL, 1918–39 (ed. with Gillian Peele)

*THE DECADE OF DISILLUSION (ed. with David McKie)

*CRISIS AND CONTROVERSY: Essays in Honour of A. J. P. Taylor
(ed. with Alan Sked)

*SOURCES IN BRITISH POLITICAL HISTORY, 1900–51 (6 vols)
(with Philip Jones et al.)

POST-WAR BRITAIN: A Political History (with Alan Sked)

*TRENDS IN BRITISH POLITICS (ed. with John Ramsden)

*SOURCES IN EUROPEAN POLITICAL HISTORY (3 vols) (ed. with
Geoff Pugh et al.)

Other books by John Stevenson

SOCIAL CONDITIONS IN BRITAIN BETWEEN THE WARS

POPULAR DISTURBANCES IN ENGLAND, 1700–1870

LONDON IN THE AGE OF REFORM

POPULAR PROTEST AND PUBLIC ORDER (ed. with R. Quinault)

HIGH AND LOW POLITICS (ed. with M. Bentley)

BRITISH SOCIETY, 1914–45

ORDER AND DISORDER IN EARLY MODERN ENGLAND (ed. with
A. J. Fletcher)

* Also published by Macmillan

BRITISH
HISTORICAL FACTS,
1688–1760

CHRIS COOK

*Head of the Department of History, Philosophy and European Studies,
Polytechnic of North London*

and

JOHN STEVENSON

Reader in History, University of Sheffield

**MACMILLAN
PRESS**

PPR **03431047**

© Chris Cook and John Stevenson 1988

All rights reserved. No reproduction, copy or transmission
of this publication may be made without written permission.

No paragraph of this publication may be reproduced, copied
or transmitted save with written permission or in accordance
with the provisions of the Copyright Act 1956 (as amended),
or under the terms of any licence permitting limited copying
issued by the Copyright Licensing Agency, 33–4 Alfred Place,
London WC1E 7DP.

Any person who does any unauthorised act in relation to
this publication may be liable to criminal prosecution and
civil claims for damages.

First published 1988

Published by
THE MACMILLAN PRESS LTD
Houndmills, Basingstoke, Hampshire RG21 2XS
and London
Companies and representatives
throughout the world

Printed in Hong Kong

British Library Cataloguing in Publication Data
Cook, Chris
British historical facts, 1688–1760.
1. Great Britain—Social conditions—
17th century   2. Great Britain—Social
conditions–18th century
I. Title   II. Stevenson, John, *1946–*
941   HN385
ISBN 0–333–17232–9

CONTENTS

PREFACE

This volume has attempted to present, within a single medium-sized book, a reference work on English history from 1688 to 1760 that will be of value to teachers, to students and to research workers in this important period of modern history. Within this book we have attempted to bring together as many of the important historical facts as can be reasonably assembled. Inevitably, however, no book of this type can be entirely comprehensive. In some areas the data is unreliable or indeed non-existent. Reasons of space also dictate the amount of information that can be presented.

In any book of this sort, the compilers owe a deep debt both to existing published works and to individual scholars who have offered help and advice, in particular to Stephen Brooks who compiled the chapter on the armed forces.

Finally, we would like to appeal to scholars and others working in this field to point out any omissions or errors in this book, so that the volume may be expanded or enlarged in future editions.

14 November 1987
CHRIS COOK
JOHN STEVENSON

ACKNOWLEDGEMENTS

The authors and publishers wish to thank the following who have kindly given permission to reproduce copyright material:

Cambridge University Press for tables from *Abstract of British Historical Statistics*, 2nd edn, by B. R. Mitchell and P. Deane (Cambridge University Press, 1971).

Longman for permission to use a table from *Religion and Society in Industrial England* by A. D. Gilbert (Longman, 1976).

Oxford University Press for a table from *The Population of Ireland, 1750–1845* by K. H. Connell (Oxford University Press, 1950).

1 THE MONARCHY

BIOGRAPHICAL DETAILS OF MONARCHS AND THEIR ISSUE

WILLIAM III

Born 4 Nov 1650, the son of William II, Prince of Orange and Mary Stuart, daughter of Charles I. On 13 Feb 1689 William and Mary were made King and Queen for their joint and separate lives. William had married Mary, the daughter of James II on 4 Nov 1677.

ANNE

Born 6 Feb 1665, the daughter of James II and Anne Hyde. She acceded to the throne 8 Mar 1702 and died 1 Aug 1714. On 28 July 1683 she married Prince George, the son of Frederick III of Denmark. The marriage produced:

William Born 24 July 1689. Created Duke of Gloucester, 27 July, he died on 30 July 1700.

Her other children were still-born or died in infancy.

GEORGE I

Born 28 May 1660, the son of Ernest Augustus, Elector of Hanover and Sophia, daughter of Frederick, the Elector Palatine. He acceded to the throne 1 Aug 1714 and died on 11 Jun 1727. On 21 Nov 1682 he married Sophia Dorothea, daughter of George William, Duke of Luneberg-Celle. The marriage produced the following children:

1. **George**   later George II (q.v.). Born 30 Oct 1683.
2. **Sophia Dorothea** Born 16 Mar 1687. Died 28 June 1757. On 17 Nov 1706 she married Frederick William, later King of Prussia.

George I's illegitimate children (by the Duchess of Kendal) were Petronille Melusine (born 1693) and Margaret Gertrude (born 1703).

GEORGE II

Born 30 Oct 1683, the son of George I and Sophia Dorothea. He acceded to the throne on 11 Jun 1727, and died 25 Oct 1760. On 22 Aug 1705 he married Caroline, the daughter of John Frederick, Margrave of Brandenburg-Anspach. The marriage produced the following children:

1.	**Frederick**	Born 20 Jan 1707. Died 20 March 1751. Created Prince of Wales 7 Jan 1729.
2.	**Anne**	Born 22 Oct 1709. Died 12 Jan 1759. On 14 March 1734 she married Prince William IV of Orange.
3.	**Amelia (Emily)**	Born 30 May 1711. Died 31 Oct 1786.
4.	**Caroline Elizabeth**	Born 30 May 1713. Died 28 Dec 1757.
5.	**George William**	Born 2 Nov 1717. Died in infancy.
6.	**William Augustus**	Born 15 Apr 1721. Died 31 Oct 1765. Created Duke of Cumberland 27 July 1726.
7.	**Mary**	Born 22 Feb 1723. Died 16 Jan 1772. On 8 May 1740 she married Frederick, later Landgrave of Hesse-Cassel.
8.	**Louisa**	Born 7 Dec 1724. Died 8 Dec 1751. On 27 Oct 1743 she married Frederick, later King of Denmark.

GEORGE III

Born 24 May 1738, the son of Frederick, Prince of Wales, and Augusta, daughter of Frederick II, Duke of Saxe-Gotha. He acceded to the throne on 25 Oct 1760 and died on 29 Jan 1820. On 8 Sep 1761 he married Charlotte, daughter of Charles Louis, Duke of Mecklenburg-Strelitz. Because of his insanity, the Prince of Wales became regent on 5 Feb 1811.

His marriage produced the following children:

1.	**George**	Later George IV. Born 12 Aug 1762. Died 26 Jun 1830.
2.	**Frederick**	Born 16 Aug 1763. Created Duke of York 29 Nov 1784. Died 5 Jan 1827.
3.	**William**	Later William IV. Born 21 Aug 1765. Died 20 June 1837.
4.	**Charlotte**	Born 29 Sep 1766. Died 5 Oct 1828. Married, 18 May 1797, Frederick Charles, later King of Wurttemberg.
5.	**Edward**	Born 2 Nov 1767. Created Duke of Kent 24 Apr 1799. Died 23 Jan 1820.
6.	**Augusta**	Born 8 Nov 1768. Died 22 Sep 1840.
7.	**Elizabeth**	Born 22 May 1770. Died 10 Jan 1840. Married, 7 Apr 1818, Frederick Joseph, Prince of Hesse-Homburg.
8.	**Ernest Augustus**	Born 5 June 1771. Died 18 Nov 1851. Created Duke of Cumberland, 24 Apr 1799. Succeeded as King of Hanover 20 June 1837.
9.	**Augustus**	Born 27 Jan 1773. Died 21 Apr 1843. Created Duke of Sussex 27 Nov 1801.

10.	**Adolphus**	Born 24 Feb 1774. Died 8 July 1850. Created Duke of Cambridge 27 Nov 1801.
11.	**Mary**	Born 25 Apr 1776. Died 30 Apr 1857. Married, 22 July 1816, William, Duke of Gloucester.
12.	**Sophia**	Born 3 Nov 1777. Died 27 May 1848.
13.	**Octavia**	Born 23 Feb 1779. Died 3 May 1783.
14.	**Alfred**	Born 22 Sep 1780. Died 26 Aug 1782.
15.	**Amelia**	Born 7 Aug 1783. Died 2 Nov 1810.

Allowances to Members of the Royal Family in 1760

Grantees, with their Relationship to the Sovereign

		£
Dowager Princess of Wales	Mother	60 000
Duke of York	Brother	12 000
Duke of Gloucester (Wm. Henry)	Brother	8000
Duke of Cumberland (Hy. Fredk.)	Brother	8000
Princess Amelia	Aunt	12 000
Duke of Cumberland (son of Geo. II)	Uncle	15 000

ROYAL ABSENCES

WILLIAM III

11 Jun–6 Sep 1690	Ireland
16 Jan–13 Apr 1691	United Provinces
2 May–19 Oct 1691	United Provinces – Netherlands
5 Mar–18 Oct 1692	United Provinces – Netherlands
31 Mar–29 Oct 1693	United Provinces – Netherlands
6 May–9 Nov 1694	United Provinces – Netherlands
12 May–10 Oct 1695	United Provinces – Netherlands
6 May–6 Oct 1696	United Provinces – Netherlands, Cleves
26 Apr–14 Nov 1697	United Provinces – Netherlands
20 Jul–3 Dec 1698	United Provinces
2 Jun–18 Oct 1699	United Provinces
5 Jul–18 Oct 1700	United Provinces
4 Jul–4 Nov 1701	United Provinces

GEORGE I

1 Aug–18 Sep 1714	Hanover

7 Jul 1716–18 Jan 1717	Hanover
11 May–14 Nov 1719	Hanover
15 Jun–10 Nov 1720	Hanover
5 Jun–28 Dec 1723	Hanover and Brandenburg
4 Jun 1725–23 Jan 1726	Hanover
3 Jun–11 Jun 1727	Hanover

GEORGE II

22 May–11 Sep 1729	Hanover
7 Jun–26 Sep 1732	Hanover
17 May–26 Oct 1735	Hanover
24 May 1736–14 Jan 1737	Hanover
23 May–13 Oct 1740	Hanover
7 May–20 Oct 1741	Hanover
11 May–15 Nov 1743	Hanover and the German campaign
10 May–31 Aug 1745	Hanover
19 May–23 Nov 1748	Hanover
17 Apr–4 Nov 1750	Hanover
6 Apr–18 Nov 1752	Hanover
28 Apr–15 Sep 1755	Hanover

TABLE OF REGNAL YEARS
1688–1760

WILLIAM AND MARY

1	13 Feb 1689 12 Feb 1690	WILLIAM III	
2	13 Feb 1690 12 Feb 1691	7	28 Dec 1694 27 Dec 1695
3	13 Feb 1691 12 Feb 1692	8	28 Dec 1695 27 Dec 1696
4	13 Feb 1692 12 Feb 1693	9	28 Dec 1696 27 Dec 1697
5	13 Feb 1693 12 Feb 1694	10	28 Dec 1697 27 Dec 1698
6	13 Feb 1694 27 Dec 1694	11	28 Dec 1698 27 Dec 1699

| 12 | 28 Dec 1699
27 Dec 1700 | 14 | 28 Dec 1701
8 Mar 1702 |
| 13 | 28 Dec 1700
27 Dec 1701 | | |

ANNE

1	8 Mar 1702 7 Mar 1703	8	8 Mar 1709 7 Mar 1710
2	8 Mar 1703 7 Mar 1704	9	8 Mar 1710 7 Mar 1711
3	8 Mar 1704 7 Mar 1705	10	8 Mar 1711 7 Mar 1712
4	8 Mar 1705 7 Mar 1706	11	8 Mar 1712 7 Mar 1713
5	8 Mar 1706 7 Mar 1707	12	8 Mar 1713 7 Mar 1714
6	8 Mar 1707 7 Mar 1708	13	8 Mar 1714 1 Aug 1714
7	8 Mar 1708 7 Mar 1709		

GEORGE I

1	1 Aug 1714 31 July 1715	8	1 Aug 1721 31 July 1722
2	1 Aug 1715 31 July 1716	9	1 Aug 1722 31 July 1723
3	1 Aug 1716 31 July 1717	10	1 Aug 1723 31 July 1724
4	1 Aug 1717 31 July 1718	11	1 Aug 1724 31 July 1725
5	1 Aug 1718 31 July 1719	12	1 Aug 1725 31 July 1726
6	1 Aug 1719 31 July 1720	13	1 Aug 1726 11 June 1727
7	1 Aug 1720 31 July 1721		

GEORGE II

1	11 June 1727 10 June 1728	18	11 June 1744 10 June 1745
2	11 June 1728 10 June 1729	19	11 June 1745 10 June 1746
3	11 June 1729 10 June 1730	20	11 June 1746 10 June 1747
4	11 June 1730 10 June 1731	21	11 June 1747 10 June 1748
5	11 June 1731 10 June 1732	22	11 June 1748 10 June 1749
6	11 June 1732 10 June 1733	23	11 June 1749 10 June 1750
7	11 June 1733 10 June 1734	24	11 June 1750 10 June 1751
8	11 June 1734 10 June 1735	25	11 June 1751 10 June 1752
9	11 June 1735 10 June 1736	26	11 June 1752 10 June 1753
10	11 June 1736 10 June 1737	27	11 June 1753 10 June 1754
11	11 June 1737 10 June 1738	28	11 June 1754 10 June 1755
12	11 June 1738 10 June 1739	29	11 June 1755 10 June 1756
13	11 June 1739 10 June 1740	30	11 June 1756 10 June 1757
14	11 June 1740 10 June 1741	31	11 June 1757 10 June 1758
15	11 June 1741 10 June 1742	32	11 June 1758 10 June 1759
16	11 June 1742 10 June 1743	33	11 June 1759 10 June 1760
17	11 June 1743 10 June 1744	34	11 June 1760 25 Oct 1760

CONTEMPORARY EUROPEAN SOVEREIGNS
1688–1760

BAVARIA (Electors)

1679	Maximilian II
1726	Karl Albrecht I
1745	Maximilian III
1777	Karl Theodor I

BRANDENBURG (Electors of)

1640	Frederick William (The Great Elector)
1688–	Frederick III (became King Frederick I
1713	of Prussia in 1701)

DENMARK

1670	Christian V
1699	Frederick IV
1730	Christian VI
1746	Frederick V
1766	Christian VII

FRANCE

1643	Louis XIV
1715	Louis XV
1774	Louis XVI

HOLY ROMAN EMPIRE

1658	Leopold I
1705	Joseph I
1711	Charles VI
1740	Charles VII of Bavaria
1745	Francis I
1765	Joseph II

OTTOMAN EMPIRE

1687	Suleiman II
1691	Ahmed II
1695	Mustafa II

1703	Ahmed III
1730	Mahmud I
1754	Osman III
1757	Mustafa III
1773	Abdul Hamid I

THE PAPACY

1676	Innocent XI
1689	Alexander VIII
1691	Innocent XII
1700	Clement XI
1721	Innocent XIII
1724	Benedict XIII
1730	Clement XII
1740	Benedict XIV
1758	Clement XIII
1769	Clement XIV

POLAND

1674	John Sobieski
1697	Augustus II
1704	Stanislaw Leszczynski
1709	Augustus II (again)
1733	Stanislaw Leszczynski (again)
1734	Augustus III
1764	Stanislaw Poniatowski

PORTUGAL (Braganza dynasty)

1683	Pedro II
1706	John V
1750	Joseph
1777	Pedro III

PRUSSIA (Kings from 1701; prior to 1701, see under Brandenburg)

1701	Frederick I
1713	Frederick William I
1740	Frederick II
1786	Frederick William II

RUSSIA (Romanov dynasty)

1682	Peter I (The Great)
1725	Catherine I
1727	Peter II
1730	Anne
1740	Ivan VI
1741	Elizabeth
1762	Peter III
1762	Catherine II (The Great)
1796	Paul

SAXONY

1680	John George III
1691	John George IV
1694	Frederick Augustus I
1733	Frederick Augustus II

SPAIN

1665	Charles II
1700	Philip V of Anjou
1724	Louis I
1724	Philip V of Anjou
1746	Ferdinand VI
1759	Charles III
1788	Charles IV

SWEDEN

1660	Charles XI
1697	Charles XII
1718	Ulrica Eleonora
1720	Frederick I
1751	Frederick Adolphus
1771	Gustavus III

THE JACOBITE LINE

JAMES II

Born 14 Oct 1633, the son of Charles I and Henrietta Maria. He acceded to the throne on 6 Feb 1685, fled the kingdom on 23 Dec 1688 and died on 6

Sep 1701. He married twice: Anne Hyde, on 3 Sep 1660 (she died 31 Mar 1671), and Mary of Modena, on 30 Sep 1673. The children of James II were as follows:

1.	**Mary**	Born 30 Apr 1662, the daughter of Anne Hyde; married William, Prince of Orange. Proclaimed joint Sovereign with her husband on 13 Feb 1689; died on 28 Dec 1694.
2.	**Anne**	Born on 6 Feb 1665, the daughter of Anne Hyde, acceded to the throne on 8 Mar 1702; died on 1 Aug 1714.
3.	**James Francis Edward**	The 'Old Pretender' or James III; born on 10 June 1688, the son of Mary of Modena. Styled James III in 1701 by Louis XIV; attainted in 1702, he died in Rome on 1 Jan 1766.
4.	**Louisa Maria Theresa**	Born on 28 Jun 1692, the daughter of Mary of Modena; died on 18 Aug 1712.

CHARLES EDWARD STUART

Also known as the 'Young Pretender' or 'Bonnie Prince Charlie', born 31 Dec 1720, the grandson of James II and son of James Francis Edward, the 'Old Pretender'. He landed in Scotland on 25 Jul 1745 to lead the Jacobite forces on behalf of the claims of his father to the throne of Great Britain. Following the decisive defeat of the Jacobite armies at Culloden on 16 Apr 1746, he spent several months as a fugitive in Scotland before escaping to France in September 1746. He died in exile in Rome on 31 Jan 1788.

HENRY BENEDICT MARIA CLEMENT, CARDINAL YORK

Born March 1725, the second son of James, the 'Old Pretender' or James III. He came to England to support his brother Charles Edward in 1745, but on return to Italy became bishop of Ostia and prefect of St. Peter's Rome; Cardinal (1747), archbishop of Corinth (1759), and bishop of Tusculum (1761). Assumed title Henry IX of England, 1788, but accepted gift of money from George III after his residence sacked by the French in 1799. Died at Frascati, August 1807.

2 CHRONOLOGY

THE GLORIOUS REVOLUTION, 1685–1689

1685

6 February   Accession of James II.

16 February   Lawrence Hyde, Earl of Rochester, appointed Lord Treasurer and Lord President of the Council (18 February).

April   Meeting of Scottish Parliament expresses loyalty to James.

11 May   James orders Lord Treasurer to stop recovery of fines from specified 'loyal' recusants.

19 May   Parliament meets; James granted 'for life' the revenues conferred on Charles II. Earl of Danby released from the Tower.

26 May   House of Commons grand committee on religion passes two resolutions pledging them to defend the 'reformed religion' and calling for the enforcement of the laws against all dissenters. After the King displays his anger the Commons rejects the resolutions and accepts the royal pledge to defend the Church of England.

11 June   Outbreak of Monmouth rebellion. Parliament votes new duties on tobacco, sugar, French linen, brandies, calicoes and wrought silks, as well as restoring duties on wine and vinegar which had expired in 1681, against the security of which the King was empowered to raise £400 000.

30 June   Earl of Argyll executed for rising in support of Monmouth.

6 July   Defeat of Monmouth's army at Sedgemoor and capture of Monmouth.

15 July   Monmouth executed at Tower Hill.

September   Judge Jeffreys presides over 'Bloody Assizes' in the West Country.

28 September   Jeffreys appointed Lord Chancellor.

12–19 November   Parliament grants James a further £700 000 on the basis of new duties, but the King's request for Catholic officers to be permitted in the army provokes opposition. James prorogues Parliament (20 November).

4 December   Earl of Sunderland appointed Lord President of the Council.

1686

March   Duke of Queensbury removed as Scottish Treasurer and office placed in commission.

June   In the collusive action of Godden v. Hales the Court of King's Bench ruled that James II had the right to dispense with the Test Act for particular cases. James proceeds to introduce further Roman Catholics into the army, and into the universities, Anglican Church, and Privy Council.

14 June   Scottish Parliament prorogued after refusal to grant indulgence to Catholics.

July   James sets up a Court of Ecclesiastical Commission to control the church.

10 December   Earl of Rochester dismissed as Treasurer.

1687

12 February   Declaration of Indulgence issued to Roman Catholics and Quakers in Scotland.

4 April   James II granted extensive indulgence in England to Protestant dissenters and Roman Catholic recusants.

April   James orders Magdalen College, Oxford, to elect Anthony Farmer, a reputed Catholic. When the Fellows refused the College was ordered to set aside their own choice and a visitation of ecclesiastical commissioners was sent to install him.

28 June   Second Declaration of Indulgence in Scotland.

2 July   Parliament, prorogued since 20 November 1685, was dissolved.

3 July   D'Adda publicly received as papal nuncio.

July–August   James begins purge of office-holders, gathering pace in winter of 1687–8. Many Tory Anglicans dismissed from municipal corporations and replaced by nonconformists and Catholics. Many Lord and Deputy Lieutenants removed for showing unwillingness to repeal Test Acts. Scottish burghs ordered to cease elections and await royal nomination.

14 November   Official confirmation of Queen's pregnancy.

1688

3 May   Republication of the Declaration of Indulgence.

4 May   James II orders Anglican clergy to read the Declaration from the pulpit on two consecutive Sundays and Bishops required to see to it that copies distributed.

18 May Archbishop of Canterbury, Sancroft, and six other Bishops personally petition the King to be excused from reading the Declaration, arousing the King's anger.

8 June The 'Seven Bishops' are arrested on a charge of seditious libel and committed to the Tower.

10 June Birth of son to James II and Mary of Modena, providing for a Catholic succession, and alleged by Protestants to be a child smuggled into the palace in a warming pan.

29–30 June Trial and acquittal of the Seven Bishops.

30 June Leading Whigs and Tories led by Danby, Shrewsbury, Devonshire, Compton, Sidney, Lumley and Russell invite William of Orange to invade England in defence of 'Liberties'.

30 September William of Orange accepts invitation to invade England and issues a declaration denouncing the 'evil counsellors' who had subjected the country 'in all things relating to their consciences, liberties and properties to arbitrary government' and calling for 'a free and lawful parliament' to be assembled 'as soon as possible'.

1 November William and the Dutch invasion fleet successfully set sail for England.

5 November William of Orange lands at Torbay with 15 000 Dutch troops.

14 November Earl of Abingdon and Lord Cornbury join William's forces.

15 November Risings in the North and Midlands in support of William.

19 November James joins his army at Salisbury.

21 November William begins march on London.

22 November Northern and Midland 'rebels' issue a declaration from Nottingham setting forth their 'innumerable grievances' and calling on 'all good protestants and subjects' to support William.

After a Council of War, James decides to retreat with his forces to London. Churchill and Grafton leave James, followed by increasing elements of the royal army.

24 November James's army begins retreat to London.

26 November James reaches London and summons a Great Council to meet on the 27th.

27 November　At a Great Council in Whitehall attended by nine bishops and between thirty or forty peers, James is urged to dismiss Catholics from his service, issue a general pardon and call a new Parliament. Writs issued for a new Parliament on 15 January (28th), followed by a Proclamation promising free elections and immunity for all peers and members of the Commons.

29 November　James issues orders for his son to be sent to France.

30 November　*London Gazette* announces that Halifax, Nottingham and Godolphin were to treat with William on the King's behalf.

7–9 December　William meets royal commissioners at Hungerford and terms are arranged for an armistice while Parliament assembled.

10 December　James learns from the commissioners confirmation of William's terms. Meanwhile James secures the Great Seal, burns writs summoning Parliament and annuls those already sent out.

Mary of Modena and the royal heir flee to France.

11 December　James, having disposed of the Great Seal in the Thames, attempts to escape to France but is intercepted at Sheerness and forced to return to London (16th). Widespread anti-Catholic rioting in London and elsewhere. Meeting of peers and bishops at Guildhall issues Guildhall Declaration for a free Parliament to enact 'effectual securities for our religion and laws'. The City of London calls on William to enter London.

12 December　Commander of the fleet, Dartmouth, puts it under William's control. Provisional government under the presidency of Halifax established by the peers in London.

16 December　William summons the fleet to the Nore.

17 December　William summons a meeting of peers at Windsor to advise him on what to do about the King's return. It was decided that the King should go to Ham on the Thames.

18 December　James requests to go to Rochester, upon which William enters London.

20 December　William summons peers to meet him on the 21st to advise on calling 'a free parliament'.

23 December　James leaves for France.

26 December　William summons all those who had sat in Parliament in Charles II's time and a deputation from the City of London to advise him.

28 December　William accepts the invitation of both peers and commons to take charge of the civil administration and to summon a convention.

1689

22 January   Meeting of Convention Parliament.

28 January   The Commons declares that James II had abdicated and that the throne was vacant and against a 'popish prince'.

8 February   Commons approve draft of Declaration of Rights, vesting the throne in William and Mary and the line of succession through Anne.

13 February   Parliament offers the crown to William and Mary who are proclaimed King and Queen for their joint and separate lives, accompanying the offer with a Declaration of Rights. This asserted the 'true, ancient and indubitable rights of the people of this realm' and contained the following provisions: (i) that the making or suspending of law without consent of Parliament is illegal; (ii) that the exercise of the dispensing power is illegal; (iii) that the ecclesiastical commission court and other such like courts are illegal; (iv) that levying money without consent of Parliament is illegal; (v) that it is lawful to petition the sovereign; (vi) that the maintenance of a standing army without the consent of Parliament is illegal; (vii) that it is lawful to keep arms; (viii) that elections of members of Parliament must be free; (ix) that there must be freedom of debate in Parliament; (x) that excessive bail should never be demanded; (xi) that juries should be impanelled and returned in every trial; (xii) that grants of estates as forfeited before conviction of the offender are illegal; (xiii) that parliament should be held frequently.

William and Mary were declared King and Queen for life, the chief administration resting with William; the crown was next settled on William's children by Mary; in default of such issue, on the Princess Anne of Denmark and her children; and in default of these, on the children of William by any other wife.

Parliamentary Committee begins preparation of Declaration into a draft Bill of Rights.

1 March   Oaths of allegiance and supremacy taken to William and Mary, some peers and members of the lower house, as well as six bishops and 400 clergymen refuse, marking the beginning of the non-juror schism.

5 March   Earl of Nottingham made Secretary of State.

12 March   Landing of James II at Kinsale in Ireland opens his campaign to recapture the throne (see p. 155). Meeting of Scottish Convention.

11 April   Coronation of William and Mary.

11 May   William and Mary accept Claim of Right of Scottish Convention Parliament, asserting the constitutional liberties of the Kingdom.

24 May   Toleration Act exempts dissenters who had taken the oaths of allegiance and supremacy from penalties for non-attendance on the services of the established church.

POLITICAL CHRONOLOGY, 1689–1760

1689

January   Meeting of Convention Parliament (22nd). Throne declared vacant (28th) by the Commons.

February   William and Mary proclaimed King and Queen for life (13th). Declaration of Rights drawn up, determining line of succession. Toleration Bill introduced in the Lords (28th).

March   Oaths of allegiance and supremacy (1st), refused by over 400 non-jurors.
Earl of Nottingham made Secretary of State (5th). Bill of Comprehension introduced in Lords (11th). Landing of James II at Kinsale (12th).

April   Coronation of William and Mary (11th). Scottish Convention passes 'Articles of Grievance' (13th).

May   William and Mary accept crown of Scotland: Toleration Act passed by Parliament (24th); comprehension proposals dropped.

June   Scottish Convention meets as Parliament (5th).

December   Bill of Rights enacted, determining the line of succession and prohibiting a Catholic from succeeding to the throne, as well as reiterating the provisions of the Declaration of February (see p. 15).

1690

February   Convention Parliament dissolved (6th). Sancroft, five Bishops and 400 clergy deprived of their living for refusing to take the oath to William and Mary.

March   Second Parliament of William and Mary meets (20th). Act of recognition affirms the legality of the acts of the Convention Parliament.

May   Act of Grace gives indemnity to all supporters of James II, except those in treasonable correspondence with him (20th). Resignation of Shrewsbury and Halifax. Prorogation of Parliament and appointment of a council of nine to advise Mary during the

King's absence (23rd).
Lords of Articles abolished in Scotland (8th).

June   William leaves for Ireland (14th).

July   Battle of the Boyne (1st), defeat of James and his army.

1691

July   Defeat of French and Irish forces at Aughrim (12th).

August   William offers indemnity to all Highland clans still in rebellion
              if they will take oath of allegiance by end of year.

October   Treaty of Limerick effectively ends Irish war. Irish soldiers and
              officers offered free transportation to France; Irish Catholics to
              retain religious liberties as under Charles II (later repudiated by
              Irish Parliament).

1692

January   Earl of Marlborough (John Churchill) dismissed for communi-
              cating with James II (10th).

February   Massacre of Glencoe (13th).

March   Earl of Nottingham becomes sole Secretary of State.

May   Marlborough imprisoned in the Tower but released shortly
              afterwards.

1693

March   Lord Somers leads Whig 'Junto' as Lord Keeper.

November   Dismissal of Earl of Nottingham, Tory Secretary of State.

1694

March   Earl of Shrewsbury, member of Whig Junto, becomes Secretary
              of State.

May   Removal of leading Tories from government, apart from Danby
              and Godolphin, leaves power largely in the hands of the Whig
              Junto, consisting of Somers, Shrewsbury, Wharton, Russell and
              Montagu.

July   Charter of the Governor and Company of the Bank of England for the raising of a loan of £1 200 000 to finance the siege of Namur.

December   Triennial Act passed (3rd), providing for a new Parliament to be elected every three years; receives royal assent (22nd). Queen Mary dies of smallpox (28th).

Expiration of the licensing act and effective end to press censorship.

1695

May   Duke of Leeds (formerly Earl of Danby) forced to resign as Lord President of Council (6th).

October   Dissolution of Parliament (11th).

November   Meeting of third Parliament of the reign, supported by a large Whig majority.

Recoinage act.

1696

February   Plot to kill the King uncovered led by Sir John Fenwick and Jacobites (14th); Oath of Association to defend William and Protestant succession promulgated throughout England and Wales.

1697

January   Execution of Sir John Fenwick (21st).

April   Lord Somers made Lord Chancellor (22nd); charter of Bank of England renewed.

May   Resignation of Godolphin as First Lord of the Treasury; appointment of Montagu (1st).

September   Treaty of Ryswick signed, ending War of the League of Augsburg.

December   Robert Harley's motion to disband all forces raised since 1680 approved by both houses of Parliament; resignation of Earl of Sunderland. Parliament established a civil list not exceeding £700 000 a year for the support of William himself and the civil administration. William III recognised by Louis XIV as King of England.

1698

August	William III commits England to Partition Treaty with Holland (19th), dividing Spanish possessions, without consulting ministers or Parliament.
December	Meeting of William's fourth Parliament (6th).

1699

January	Parliament forces William to reduce drastically the size of the English army and disband his Dutch guards.
	Act for preventing growth of popery; all persons who refuse oaths of allegiance and supremacy to lose estates. Catholic school-teachers and priests liable to imprisonment for life.

1700

March	Second Partition Treaty with France and Holland ratified (14th). Scottish colonists forced to withdraw from Darien.
April	Parliament prorogued (11th). William forced to dismiss Somers as Lord Chancellor (17th).
July	Death of Duke of Gloucester, last of Anne's children.
December	Godolphin rejoins ministry as Treasurer.

1701

February	Parliament resumes sitting (6th); Harley elected Speaker of the Commons.
April	Commons begin impeachment proceedings against Whig ministers Somers, Orford, and Montagu for failure to consult Parliament over Partition Treaties.
June	Act of Settlement passed determining that the Protestant succession should pass through the electress Sophia of Hanover, granddaughter of James I, next in line after Princess Anne (12th). The Act also declares that the sovereigns of Great Britain should be Protestant and not leave the kingdom without the consent of Parliament; that the country should not be involved in war for the defence of the foreign possessions of the sovereigns; that no foreigner should receive a grant from the crown or hold office, civil or military; that ministers to be responsible for the acts of

their sovereigns; that judges to hold office for life unless guilty of misconduct.

September   Death of James II; James Edward proclaimed King of Great Britain and Ireland by Louis XIV.

November   Parliament dissolved (11th).

December   Sixth Parliament of William III (30th).

1702

February   Act for attainder against the Pretender, James Edward Stuart (20th); Act of Abjuration of Pretender, requiring oath of loyalty to King and heirs according to Act of Settlement (24th).

March   Death of William III; Queen Anne succeeds to the throne (8th). Marlborough made Captain-General of armed forces (24th).

April   Coronation of Queen Anne.

May   Declaration of war against France and Spain (4th). Godolphin appointed Lord Treasurer.

June   Scottish Parliament proclaims Anne Queen of Scotland and nominates commissioners to treat for Union with England.

October   Meeting of Anne's first Parliament (20th).

1703

January   Tory bill against occasional conformity defeated in the Lords.

March   Queen persuades the Earls of Nottingham and Rochester to dismiss several Whig Lord and Deputy Lieutenants, sheriffs and justices of the peace.

August   Scottish Parliament passes Act of Security claiming right to name Protestant successor to Queen Anne and safeguard Scottish Parliament, trade and religion from English domination. Refused royal assent.

November   Establishment of Queen Anne's Bounty.

December   Second bill against occasional conformity defeated in the Lords after Commons approval (7th).

1704

April   Henry St John becomes Secretary at War (20th).

May   Robert Harley made Secretary of State (18th).

August   Marlborough's victory at Blenheim (13th).

             Amended version of Scottish Act of Security given royal assent.

December   Further attempt to restrict occasional conformity defeated in Parliament (14–15th).

1705

April   Dissolution of Anne's first Parliament (5th).

September Scottish Parliament approves Act for appointment of commissioners to negotiate union with England.

October   Second Parliament of Anne's reign meets (25th).

1706

April   Scottish commissioners meet English commissioners at Westminster (16th).

May   Victory at Ramillies (23rd).

July   Articles of Union signed between English and Scottish Commissioners (22nd).

December   3rd Earl of Sunderland appointed Secretary of State (3rd).

1707

January   Scottish Parliament ratifies Articles of Union (16th).

March   Act of Union joins kingdoms of England and Scotland under name of Great Britain (6th). The Act provides that the princess Sophia of Hanover and her Protestant heirs should succeed to the crown of the United Kingdom; that there would be one Parliament at Westminster to which Scotland should send 16 elective peers and 45 members of the commons; that no more Scottish peers be created; that Scottish law and legal administration remain unchanged; that the Episcopal church in England and Presbyterian in Scotland be unchanged; and for the adoption of a common flag – the Union Jack, a common coinage, and free Anglo-Scottish and colonial trade.

April   Final dissolution of Scottish Parliament (28th).

May   Union of England and Scotland comes into effect (1st).

October   Second Parliament of Anne reconvenes as first Parliament of Great Britain.

1708

February   Harley and St John dismissed from the Cabinet; Robert Walpole appointed Secretary at War (25th).

March   James Edward, the old Pretender, lands in Scotland; but a French fleet sent to assist him was repulsed by Admiral Byng and he soon returned to France.

July   Battle of Oudenarde (11th).

November   The third Parliament of Queen Anne's reign meets (16th).

1709

September   Battle of Malplaquet (11th).

October   Townshend's Barrier treaty (29th). Copyright Act.

November   Dr Henry Sacheverell preaches a sermon at St Pauls Cathedral, condemning the toleration of nonconformists and praising divine right of monarchy (5th).

December   Dr Sacheverell impeached by House of Commons (13th).

1710

Feb–Mar   Trial of Dr Sacheverell (27 Feb–20 Mar); Dr Sacheverell suspended from preaching for three years (23 Mar); during trial pro-Sacheverell riots occur in which London mobs sack several leading nonconformist meeting houses.

June   Sunderland dismissed as Secretary of State, South (14th).

August   Godolphin and Whig ministry dismissed by the Queen; Robert Harley, as Chancellor of Exchequer, and Henry St John, form Tory ministry (8th).

September   Dissolution of Parliament followed by election (21st).

November   Fourth Parliament of Anne meets with Tory majority (25th).

1711

February   Property Qualification Act passed, county MPs must own property worth £600 and borough MPs property worth £300 per annum.

March   Robert Harley made Lord Treasurer (29th).

May   Harley created Earl of Oxford (23rd).

December   Bill against occasional conformity introduced in the Lords by Nottingham (15th); Duke of Marlborough dismissed as Commander-in-Chief. Duke of Ormond becomes Commander-in-Chief.

1712

January   Anne creates twelve new Tory peers to ensure success of government peace initiative in Lords (1st); Robert Walpole imprisoned in Tower for alleged corruption as Secretary at War.

July   Henry St John created Viscount Bolingbroke.

1713

April   Peace of Utrecht (11th).

August   Anne's fourth Parliament dissolved, followed by elections. Earl of Mar appointed Secretary of State for Scotland (8th).

1714

February   Fifth Parliament of Queen Anne meets (16th)

May   Schism Act passed. No person allowed to keep a school unless a member of the Anglican Church.

July   Henry St John (Bolingbroke) secures dismissal of the Earl of Oxford and begins attempt to pack administration with Jacobite sympathisers. Severe illness of Queen Anne forces calling of Privy Council. Pro-Hanoverian Duke of Shrewsbury appointed Lord Treasurer in place of Oxford (30th).

August   Death of Queen Anne (1st); George I proclaimed King in London and leading cities. Bolingbroke dismissed from office.

September   George I arrives in England (18th). *Whig administration formed under Lord Stanhope.* Principal figures: Lord Stanhope (Secretary of State); Lord Halifax (First Lord of the Treasury); Lord Townshend (Secretary of State); Earl of Nottingham (Lord

President of the Council); Lord Sunderland (Lord Lieutenant of Ireland).

October   Coronation of George I (20th).

1715

March   Meeting of first Parliament of George I with large Whig majority (17th).

June   Bolingbroke, Ormond and Oxford impeached. Flight of Bolingbroke and Ormond; Oxford committed to the Tower. Widespread rioting followed by Riot Act strengthening power of magistrates by making many riots a capital offence.

September Jacobite rising in Scotland under the Earl of Mar.

October   Robert Walpole appointed First Lord of the Treasury.

November   Jacobites defeated at Sheriffmuir and Preston.

December   Pretender (James III) arrives in Scotland (22nd).

1716

February   Pretender flees Scotland after failure of England to rise in support (10th). Impeachment of Jacobite leaders; execution of Derwentwater and Kenmure.

May   Septennial Act extends maximum duration of parliaments to seven years.

December   Lord Townshend dismissed as Secretary of State for opposing French alliance favoured by George I.

1717

January   Triple Alliance formed between England, France and Holland to uphold the Treaty of Utrecht (4th).

February   Convocation of the Church of England ceased to meet regularly.

April   Walpole resigns from administration, succeeded as First Lord by Stanhope. Addison and Sunderland become Secretaries of State.

July   Oxford released from the Tower (1st).

1718

March   Sunderland remodels ministry: Sunderland becomes First Lord
of the Treasury, Stanhope Secretary of State, and Aislabie
Chancellor of the Exchequer.

August   Quadruple Alliance formed between England, France, the
Emperor and Holland.

December   War between England and Spain.

1719

January   Repeal of the Schism and Occasional Conformity Acts.

April   Peerage Bill to fix the number of peers in the House of Lords
defeated.

December   Peerage Bill, reintroduced by the Duke of Buckingham, defeated
in the Commons.

1720

January   Spain joins Quadruple Alliance, ending hostilities with England.

February   House of Commons accepts South Sea Company's scheme for
taking over part of the National Debt in return for exclusive
trade in the South Seas.

April   Royal assent given to Act empowering South Seas Company to
manage National Debt (7th). Stocks begin a sharp rise.

June   Robert Walpole and Charles Townshend return to office as
Paymaster-General and Lord President of the Council respectively.

Oct–Nov   'South Sea Bubble' begins to burst, with panic selling and the
ruin of many investors.

December   Walpole begins restoration of public credit. Secret Committee
appointed to investigate the affairs of the South Sea Company.
The Company's directors are detained and those holding
government posts dismissed and expelled from the House of
Commons. Aislabie, Chancellor of the Exchequer, and Earl of
Sunderland implicated.

1721

February   Death of Stanhope (5th); Townshend becomes Secretary of State
in place of Stanhope.

March   House of Commons votes Aislabie guilty of fraud, expels him from the House and commits him to the Tower. Sunderland acquitted on charges of corruption but eventually resigns.

April   *Walpole administration formed.* Principal figures: Robert Walpole (First Lord of the Treasury and Chancellor of the Exchequer); Lord Townshend (Secretary of State); Lord Carteret (Secretary of State).

1722

April   Death of Sunderland.

May   Atterbury plot by Jacobites uncovered. Leading Jacobite sympathisers arrested.

October   Meeting of George I's second Parliament (9th). Habeas Corpus suspended; penal taxes levied on Catholics and non-jurors; Francis Atterbury (Bishop of Rochester) exiled.

1723

May   Lord Bolingbroke pardoned and returns to England in June.

June   System of bonded warehouses established to prevent smuggling and increase revenues on tea and coffee.

1724

April   Carteret dismissed as Secretary of State and becomes Lord Lieutenant of Ireland; Thomas Pelham Holles, Duke of Newcastle, appointed Secretary of State and his brother, Henry Pelham, Secretary at War.

1725

April   City Elections Act regulating conduct of elections in London increases power of Court of Aldermen and leads to strong opposition to Walpole in the City.

July   Riots against malt tax in Scotland.

September   Treaty of Hanover between England, France and Prussia.

1726

November   Publication of *The Craftsman*, edited by Bolingbroke and Pulteney, attacking Walpole and his foreign policy.

1727

February   Hostilities break out between Britain and Spain.

June   Death of George I; succession of George II. Walpole reappointed First Lord of the Treasury and Chancellor of the Exchequer. Civil List raised to £800 000 per annum.

July   George I's second Parliament formally dissolved.

1729

November   Treaty of Seville with Spain; confirmation of *assiento* treaty allowing limited trade with Spanish colonies; Gibraltar ceded to England.

1730

May   Lord Harrington replaces Townshend as Secretary of State.

1731

March   Treaty of Vienna; Austrian Emperor agrees to disband Ostend East India Company.

1733

March   Widespread opposition to Walpole's Excise Bill.

April   Walpole's majority in House of Commons reduced to 16 on Excise proposals; Walpole offers resignation to the King. Though remaining in office, Walpole postpones discussion of the Bill until June, effectively dropping the scheme.

May   Walpole narrowly staves off defeat in the House of Lords over handling of South Sea Company affairs.

1734

March   Motion to repeal Septennial Act defeated.

April   Dissolution of Parliament, followed by elections (16th).

1735

January   Second Parliament of George II meets (14th), the Walpole administration having lost seats but still commanding a substantial majority.

1736

March	Repeal of Test Act defeated 251 to 123 in Commons. Gin Act passed, taxing spirits and imposing licences for selling them, to come into force on 29 September.
July	Anti-Irish and Gin Act disturbances in London.
September	Porteus Riots in Edinburgh. Fine levied on the city.

1737

September	Frederick, Prince of Wales, quarrels with his father and sides openly with the opposition to Walpole.
November	Death of Queen Caroline (20th).

1738

January	Spanish attacks on British shipping denounced by the opposition in the Commons and the City of London.
March	Examination by Commons Committee of Captain Jenkins who alleged ill-treatment at hands of Spanish Guardas Costas in 1731. Carteret succeeds in passing resolutions in House of Lords condemning Spanish right to search British ships in Spanish American waters.

1739

January	Convention of Pardo agreed between Britain and Spain over trade disputes.
March	Address approving Pardo Convention carried in the Commons by Walpole by only 28 votes against the opposition of William Pitt and the 'Patriots'.
October	Walpole forced to accede to demand for war with Spain – the 'War of Jenkin's Ear'.
November	Capture of Porto Bello by Admiral Vernon.

1740

February   Motion to investigate the Convention of Pardo rejected by 247 votes to 196.

April   Argyll dismissed from his military appointments, because of increasing antipathy to Walpole. Hervey's replacement of Godolphin as Lord Privy Seal offends the Duke of Newcastle who threatens resignation.

June   Death of Sir William Wyndham, chief leader of the Tories.

October   George Dodington loses his post as Commissioner of the Treasury and moves into opposition to Walpole.

1741

February   Motion for Walpole's dismissal defeated by 184 votes.

April   King's Speech invites Parliament to support the Pragmatic Sanction: £300 000 voted in subsidies for Queen Maria Theresa of Austria. Parliament dissolved (25th). In ensuing election Walpole's majority reduced to under 20 seats by defeats in Cornwall and Scotland.

December   Parliament reassembles and Walpole defeated in seven divisions.

1742

February   Walpole decides to resign after defeat over Chippenham election petition (11th). *Carteret administration* formed. Principal figures: John Carteret (Secretary of State); Earl of Wilmington (First Lord of the Treasury).

1743

August   Henry Pelham becomes First Lord of the Treasury in place of Earl of Wilmington.

1744

March   France declares war on Britain.

November   Carteret resigns after increasing disagreement in the Cabinet and Parliament about his foreign policy. *Pelham administration* formed. Principal figures: Henry Pelham (First Lord of the

Treasury); Earl of Harrington (Secretary of State); Duke of Bedford (First Lord of the Admiralty).

1745

May   Battle of Fontenoy. Marshal Saxe defeats Duke of Cumberland.

July   Second Jacobite rebellion. The Young Pretender, Charles Edward Stuart, lands in Scotland and proclaims his father as James VIII of Scotland and James III of England (23rd). Highland clans rise in support.

September   The Pretender enters Edinburgh with 2000 men (11th); Jacobite victory at Prestonpans (21st).

December   Pretender reaches Derby, but decides to retreat to Scotland because of lack of support in England (4th).

1746

February   Pelham, Newcastle, Hardwicke and Harrington resign after disagreements with the King over foreign policy. Bath and Granville attempt to form an administration. *Pelham administration* reformed. Principal figures: H. Pelham (First Lord of the Treasury); Earl of Harrington (Secretary of State); Duke of Newcastle (Secretary of State); William Pitt, the Elder (Vice-Treasurer of Ireland).

April   Defeat of Young Pretender and Jacobite forces at battle of Culloden (16th).

May   Pitt becomes Paymaster-General of the forces.

September   Flight of the Young Pretender to France.

1748

October   Treaty of Aix-la-Chapelle ends War of Austrian Succession.

1751

May   Act passed for adoption of the reformed (Gregorian) calendar in England and the colonies. Year to begin from January 1 instead of March 25; 11 days to be omitted from the calendar between 3 and 14 September 1752.

1753

June   Jewish Naturalisation Act passed, but repealed the following year because of the popular opposition (December 1754).

1754

March   Death of Pelham. *Newcastle administration* formed. Principal figures: Duke of Newcastle (First Lord of the Treasury); Earl of Holderness (Secretary of State); Henry Fox (Secretary at War); William Pitt (Paymaster).

1755

May   Admiral Boscawen fails to prevent French reinforcements reaching North America. Subsidy treaties agreed with Hesse-Cassel and Russia to provide troops in the event of war.

November   Henry Fox becomes Secretary of State; Pitt dismissed.

1756

January   Treaty between Britain and Prussia (16th).

May   Britain declares war on France (17th).

June   Loss of Minorca after failure of Admiral Byng to defeat French invasion fleet.

October   Henry Fox announces intention to resign after severe criticism of the conduct of the war in the House of Commons. Newcastle resigns; King asks Fox to form an administration, but refuses. Devonshire agrees to form an administration with Pitt (29th).

November   *Pitt–Devonshire administration formed.* Principal figures: Duke of Devonshire (First Lord of the Treasury); William Pitt (Secretary of State).

1757

April   King demands Pitt's resignation after failure to achieve success in the war. George Grenville (Treasurer of the Navy) and Legge (Chancellor of the Exchequer) resign with Pitt. Widespread popular support shown for Pitt.

July   After considerable negotiations *Pitt–Newcastle administration* formed. Principal figures: William Pitt (Secretary of State); Duke of Newcastle (First Lord of the Treasury); Henry Fox (Paymaster).

Militia Act remodels militia with members chosen by ballot; widespread rioting provoked (Aug–Sep).

October	Failure of Rochefort expedition; news of defeats in India and Canada leads to criticism of the conduct of the war in Europe.
November	Victory for Britain's ally, Frederick the Great, at Rossbach.
December	Victory of Frederick at Leuthen.

1758

April	At Second Treaty of Westminster, Prussia and Britain pledged themselves not to make a separate peace. Frederick granted an annual subsidy of £670 000.
July	Capture of Louisburg in North America (26th).
November	Occupation of Fort Duquesne by Colonel Forbes.

1759

May	Capture of Guadeloupe.
June	Capture of Fort Niagara in North America.
July	Bombardment of Le Havre thwarts French plans for invasion of Britain.
August	Boscawen's defeat of French fleet at Lagos (Cape St Vincent).
September	Wolfe's victory at Battle of the Plains of Abraham (13th) and capture of Quebec (18th).
November	Defeat of French fleet by Admiral Hawke at Quiberon Bay (20th).

1760

September	Surrender of Montreal to the British; virtual loss of Canada by the French.
October	Death of George II (25th); accession of George III.

3 ADMINISTRATIONS AND POLITICAL BIOGRAPHIES

MINISTRIES AND ADMINISTRATIONS*

CHRONOLOGICAL LIST

Date of formation	Name	Years Covered
May 1702	Godolphin–Marlborough	1702–10
Aug 1710	Harley	1710–14
Sep 1714	Stanhope	1714–17
Apr 1717	Stanhope–Sunderland (remodelled 1718)	1717–21
Apr 1721	Walpole	1721–42
Feb 1742	Carteret	1742–4
Nov 1744	Pelham	1744–6
Feb 1746	Bath	1746
Feb 1746	Pelham	1746–54
Mar 1754	Newcastle	1754–6
Nov 1756	Pitt–Devonshire	1756–7
July 1757	Pitt–Newcastle	1757–61

GODOLPHIN–MARLBOROUGH, 1702–10

Ld Treas.	Sidney Godolphin, Ld Godolphin	8 May 02 (dism. 8 Aug 10)
Chanc. Exch.	Henry Boyle	29 Mar 01
	John Smith	11 Feb 08

*Note: The formation of administrations ultimately depended upon the power of appointment to major public offices and to the royal household by the Crown. Although such appointments were made throughout this period, and prior to it, it was only gradually with the development of parliamentary government as a regular feature of political life that wholesale changes in office holders can be identified which relate to changes in royal favour or in the parliamentary situation. While it would be possible to suggest putative titles and dates of administrations prior to 1702, it was with the accession of Anne that the pattern of more readily identifiable ministries and administrations became more clearly evident.

Ld Pres.	Thomas Herbert, E of Pembroke and E of Montgomery	9 July 02
	John Somers, Ld Somers	25 Nov 08
D. Lanc.	Sir John Leveson-Gower	12 May 02
	James Stanley, E of Derby	1 June 06
Master-Gen. of Ordnance	John Churchill, D of Marlborough	1 July 02
Sec. of State (*South*)	Daniel Finch, E of Nottingham	2 May 02 (vac. c. 22 Apr 1704)
	Sir Charles Hedges	18 May 04 (dism. Dec 06)
	Charles Spencer, E of Sunderland	3 Dec 06 (dism. 13–14 June 10)
	William Legge, Ld Dartmouth	15 June 10 (vac. 6–13 Aug 13)
Sec. of State (*North*)	Sir Charles Hedges	2 May 02
	Robert Harley	18 May 04 (vac. 13 Feb 08)
	Henry Boyle	13 Feb 08 (vac. Sept 10)
P.S.	John Sheffield, M. of Normanby (D of Buckinghamshire and Normanby, 1703)	27 Apr 02
	John Holles, D of Newcastle-Upon-Tyne (died 15 July 11)	21 Mar 05
B.O.T.	Thomas Thynne, Vt Weymouth	12 June 02
	Thomas Grey, E of Stamford	25 Apr 07
Admir.	Prince George of Denmark	20 May 02
	Queen Anne (Lord High Admiral)	28 Oct 08
	Thomas Herbert, E, of Pembroke	29 Nov 08
	Edward Russell, E of Oxford	8 Nov 09

Sec. at War	George Clarke	3 Mar 92
	Henry St John	20 Apr 04
	Robert Walpole	25 Feb 08
Treas. of the	Sir Thomas Littleton	29 May 99
Navy	Robert Walpole	21 Jan 10
Pay.-Gen.	John Howe	4 Jan 03
	Charles Fox	4 Jan 03
	James Brydges	07

HARLEY, 1710–14 (formed August 1710)

Ld Treas.	John Poulett, Earl Poulett	11 Aug 10
	Robert Harley, E of Oxford	29 Mar 11
	Charles Talbot, D of	
	Shrewsbury (vac. Oct 1714)	30 July 14
Chanc. Exch.	Robert Harley	10 Aug 10
Ld Pres.	Laurence Hyde, E of	21 Sept 10
	Rochester	(d. 21 May 11)
	John Sheffield, D of	
	Buckinghamshire and of	
	Normanby	14 June 11
D. Lanc.	William Berkeley,	
	Ld Berkeley	21 Sept 10
Master-Gen. of	John Churchill, D of	
Ordnance	Marlborough	1 July 02
	Richard Savage, Earl Rivers	1 Jan 12
	James Douglas, D of Hamilton	
	and Brandon (died 15 Nov 12)	1 July 12
Sec. of State (South)	William Legge, Ld Dartmouth	15 June 10
	(E of Dartmouth, 1711)	(vac. 6–13 Aug. 1713)
	Henry St John,	17 Aug 13
	Vt Bolingbroke	(dism. 31 Aug 14)
Sec. of State (North)	Henry St John,	
	Vt Bolingbroke	21 Sept 10
	William Bromley	17 Aug 13
		(dism. Sept 14)
P.S.	John Holles, D of Newcastle-	
	Upon-Tyne (died 15 July 11)	21 Mar 05

	John Robinson, Bp of Bristol	31 Aug 11
	William Legge, E of	
	Dartmouth	21 Aug 13
B.O.T.	Thomas Grey, E of Stamford	25 Apr 07
	Charles Finch, E of	
	Winchilsea	12 June 11
	Francis North, Ld Guildford	15 Sept 13
Admir.	Edward Russell, E of Oxford	8 Nov 09
	Sir John Leake	4 Oct 10
	Thomas Wentworth, E of	
	Strafford	30 Sept 12
Sec. at War	George Granville	28 Sept 10
	Sir William Wyndham	28 June 12
	Francis Gwyn	21 Aug 13
Treas. of the Navy	Robert Walpole	21 Jan 10
	Charles Caesar	8 June 11
Pay.-Gen.	James Brydges	…07
	Thomas Moore	…13
	Edward Nicholas	…13

STANHOPE, 1714–17 (formed Sep 1714)

1st Ld Treas.	Charles Montagu, E of	
	Halifax	11 Oct 14
	Charles Howard, E of	
	Carlisle	23 May 15
	Robert Walpole	10 Oct 15
Chanc. Exch.	Richard Onslow	13 Oct 14
	Robert Walpole	12 Oct 15
Ld Pres.	Daniel Finch, E of	
	Nottingham	22 Sept 14
	William Cavendish, D of	
	Devonshire	6 July 16
Ld Chanc.	William Cowper,	
	Lord Cowper	21 Sept 14
P.S.	Thomas Wharton,	
	Earl Wharton	27 Sept 14
	(Seal in commission 30 Apr–	
	2 Sep 15)	

	Charles Spencer, E of Sunderland	2 Sept 15
	Evelyn Pierrepoint, D of Kingston-Upon-Hull	19 Dec 16
D. Lanc.	Heneage Finch, E of Aylesford	4 Nov 14
	Richard Lumley, E of Scarborough	12 Mar 16
Master-Gen. of Ordnance	John Churchill, D of Marlborough	1 Oct 14
Sec. of State (South)	James Stanhope	27 Sept 14
	Paul Methuen	22 June 16
Sec. of State (North)	Charles Townshend, Vt Townshend	17 Sept 14
	James Stanhope	12 Dec 16
Sec. for Scotland	James Graham, D of Montrose	24 Sept 14
	John Ker, D of Roxburghe	13 Dec 16
Pay.-Gen.	Robert Walpole	17 Sept 14
	E of Lincoln	Oct 15
Admir.	Edward Russell, E of Oxford	14 Oct 14
Sec. at War	William Pulteney	Sept 14
B.O.T.	Francis North, Ld Guildford	15 Sept 13
	William Berkeley, Ld Berkeley	13 Dec 14
	Henry Howard, E of Suffolk	12 May 15
Ld Lt of Ireland	Charles Spencer, E of Sunderland	4 Oct 14
	Charles Townshend, Vt Townshend	13 Feb 17

STANHOPE–SUNDERLAND, 1717–18 (formed April 1717)

1st Ld Treas.	James Stanhope, Vt Stanhope	12 Apr 17
Chanc. Exchq.	James Stanhope, Vt Stanhope	15 Apr 17
Ld Pres.	Vacant from 30 Mar 17	

Ld Chanc.	William Cowper, Ld Cowper	21 Sept 14
Sec. of State (South)	Joseph Addison	15–16 Apr 17
Sec. of State (North)	Charles Spencer, E of Sunderland	15–16 Apr 17
Sec. for Scotland	John Ker, D of Roxburghe	13 Dec 16
P.S.	Evelyn Pierrepoint, D of Kingston-Upon-Hull	19 Dec 16
D. Lanc.	Richard Lumley, E of Scarborough	12 Mar 16
	Nicholas Lechmere	19 June 17
Pay.-Gen.	E of Lincoln	Oct 15
Admir.	James Berkeley, E of Berkeley	16 Apr 17
B.O.T.	Henry Howard, E of Suffolk	12 May 15
	Robert Darcy, E of Holdernesse	31 Jan 18
Lt Lt of Ireland	Charles Powlett, D of Bolton	27 Apr 17

RECONSTRUCTED STANHOPE–SUNDERLAND, 1718–21 (March 1718)

1st Ld Treas.	Charles Spencer, E of Sunderland	21 Mar 18
Ld Pres.	Charles Spencer, E of Sunderland	16 Mar 18
	Evelyn Pierrepoint, D of Kingston-Upon-Hull	6 Feb 19
	Charles Townshend, Vt Townshend	11 June 20
Ld Chanc.	Thomas Parker, Ld Macclesfield	12 May 18
Sec. of State (North)	James Stanhope, Earl Stanhope (died 4 Feb 21)	18–21 Mar 18
	Charles Townshend, Vt Townshend	10 Feb 21
Sec. of State (South)	James Craggs (died 16 Feb 21)	16 Mar 18

Chanc. Exch.	John Aislabie	20 Mar 18
P.S.	Evelyn Pierrepoint, D of	
	Kingston-Upon-Hull	19 Dec 16
	Henry Grey, D of Kent	14 Feb 19
	Evelyn Pierrepoint, D of	
	Kingston-Upon-Hull	13 June 20
Pay.-Gen.	Earl of Lincoln	Oct 15
	Robert Walpole	11 June 20
B.O.T.	Robert Darcy, E of	
	Holdernesse	31 Jan 18
	Thomas Fane, E of	
	Westmorland	11 May 19
Ld Lt of Ireland	Charles Pawlett, D of Bolton	27 Apr 17
	Charles, D of Grafton	8 June 20
Sec. of Scotland	John Ker, D of Roxburghe	13 Dec 16
Admir.	James Berkeley, E of	
	Berkeley	16 Apr 17

WALPOLE 1721–42 (formed April 1721)

1st Ld Treas.	Robert Walpole	4 Apr 21
Chanc. Exch.	Robert Walpole	3 Apr 21
Ld Chanc.	Thomas Parker,	
	Ld Macclesfield	
	(Seal in Commission Jan 25)	12 May 18
	Peter King, Ld King	1 June 25
	Charles Talbot, Ld Talbot	
	of Hensol (died 14 Feb 33)	29 Nov 33
	Philip Yorke, Ld Hardwicke	21 Feb 37
Ld Pres.	Charles Townshend,	
	Vt Townshend	11 June 20
	Henry Boyle, Ld Carleton	25 June 21
	William Cavendish, D of	
	Devonshire (died 4 Jun 29)	27 Mar 25
	Thomas Trevor, Ld Trevor	
	of Bromham (died	
	19 June 30)	8 May 30
	Spencer Compton, E of	
	Wilmington	31 Dec 30

P.S.	Evelyn Pierrepoint, D of Kingston-Upon-Hull (died 5 Mar 26)	13 June 20
	Thomas Trevor, Ld Trevor of Bromham	10 Mar 26
	Spencer Compton, E of Wilmington (Seal in Commission 1 Jan 31)	8 May 30
	William Cavendish, D of Devonshire	12 June 31
	Henry Lowther, Vt Lonsdale	8 May 33
	Francis Godolphin, E of Godolphin	15 May 35
	John Hervey, Ld Hervey of Ickworth	29 Apr 40
Admir.	James Berkeley, E of Berkeley	16 Apr 17
	George Byng, Vt Torrington	29 July 27
	Charles Wager	25 Jan 33
D. Lanc.	Nicholas Lechmere (Ld Lechmere, 1721)	19 June 17
	John Manners, D of Rutland	24 July 27
	George Cholmondeley, E of Cholmondeley	17 May 36
Sec. of State (South)	John Carteret, Ld Carteret	4 Mar 21
	Thomas Pelham-Holles, D of Newcastle	6 Apr 24
Sec. of State (North)	Charles Townshend, Vt Townshend (vacated office 16 May 30)	10 Feb 21
	William Stanhope, Ld Harrington	19 June 30
B.O.T.	Thomas Fane, E of Westmorland	11 May 19
	Benjamin Mildmay, Earl Fitzwalter	14 May 35
	John Monson, Ld Monson	27 June 37
Ld Lt of Ireland	Charles, D of Grafton	8 June 20
	John Carteret, Ld Carteret	6 May 24
	Lionel Cranfield, E of	

	Dorset	23 June 30
	William Cavendish, D of	
	Devonshire	9 Apr 37

CARTERET, 1742–4 (formed Feb 1742)

1st Ld Treas.	Spencer Compton, E of	
	Wilmington	16 Feb 42
	Henry Pelham	27 Aug 43
Chanc. Exch.	Samuel Sandys	12 Feb 42
	Henry Pelham	12 Dec 43
Sec. of State (North)	John Carteret, Ld Carteret	12 Feb 42
Sec. of State (South)	Thomas Pelham-Holles,	
	D of Newcastle-Upon-Tyne	6 Apr 24
Ld Pres.	William Stanhope, E of	
	Harrington	13 Feb 42
Ld Chanc.	Philip Yorke, Ld Hardwicke	21 Feb 37
P.S.	John Hervey, Ld Hervey	
	of Ickworth	29 Apr 40
	John Leveson-Gower,	
	Ld Gower	13 July 42
	George Cholmondeley,	
	E of Cholmondeley	12 Dec 43
D. Lanc.	George Cholmondeley,	
	E of Cholmondeley	17 May 36
	Richard Edgcumbe,	
	Ld Edgcumbe of Mount	
	Edgcumbe	22 Dec 43
B.O.T.	John Monson, Ld Monson	27 June 37
Admir.	Sir Charles Wager	25 Jan 33
	Daniel Finch, E of	
	Winchilsea and E of	
	Nottingham	19 Mar 42
Ld Lt of Ireland	William Cavendish, D of	
	Devonshire	9 Apr 37

PELHAM, 1744–6 (formed Nov 1744)

1st Ld Treas.	Henry Pelham	27 Aug 43

Chanc. Exch.	Henry Pelham	12 Dec 43
Sec. of State (North)	William Stanhope, E of Harrington	24 Nov 44
Sec. of State (South)	Thomas Pelham-Holles, D of Newcastle-Upon-Tyne	6 Apr 24
Ld Pres.	William Stanhope, E of Harrington	13 Feb 42
	Lionel Cranfield Sackville, D of Dorset	3 Jan 45
Ld Chanc.	Philip Yorke, Ld Hardwicke	21 Feb 37
P.S.	George Cholmondeley, E of Cholmondeley	12 Dec 43
	John Leveson-Gower, Ld Gower	26 Dec 44
D. Lanc.	Richard Edgcumbe, Ld Edgcumbe of Mount Edgcumbe	22 Dec 43
B.O.T.	John Monson, Ld Monson	27 June 37
Admir.	Daniel Finch, E of Winchelsea	19 Mar 42
	John Russell, D of Bedford	27 Dec 44
Ld Lt of Ireland	William Cavendish, D of Devonshire	9 Apr 37
	Philip Dormer Stanhope, E of Chesterfield	8 Jan 45

BATH, 1746 (Feb 1746)

On 6 February 1746, George II asked the Earl of Bath (William Pulteney) and Earl Granville (John Carteret) to form a new administration, taking the offices of First Lord of the Treasury and Secretary of State (North) respectively. Henry Pelham, the Duke of Newcastle, the Earl of Harrington and Lord Hardwicke resigned office. Although Bath and Granville took office for a few days, the King was forced to reappoint the previous administration.

PELHAM, 1746–54

1st Ld Treas.	Henry Pelham	14 Feb 46

Chanc. Exch.	Henry Pelham	12 Dec 43
Sec. of State (North)	William Stanhope, E of Harrington (vacated 28 Oct 46)	14 Feb 46
	Philip Dormer Stanhope, E of Chesterfield (vacated 6 Feb 48)	29 Oct 46
	Thomas Pelham-Holles, D of Newcastle-Upon-Tyne	6–12 Feb 48
Sec. of State (South)	Thomas Pelham-Holles, D of Newcastle-Upon-Tyne	14 Feb 46
	John Russell, D of Bedford (vacated 13 June 51)	6–12 Feb 48
	Robert Darcy, E of Holderness	18 June 51
Ld Pres.	Lionel Cranfield Sackville, D of Dorset	3 Jan 51
	John Carteret, E of Granville	17 June 51
P.S.	John Leveson-Gower, Ld Gower	26 Dec 44
D. Lanc.	Richard Edgcumbe, Ld Edgcumbe	22 Dec 43
B.O.T.	John Monson, Ld Monson	27 June 37
	George Montagu, E of Halifax	1 Nov 48
Admir.	John Russell, D of Bedford	27 Dec 44
	John Montagu, E of Sandwich	20 Feb 48
	George Anson, Ld Anson	22 June 51

NEWCASTLE, 1754–6 (formed Mar 1754)

1st Ld Treas.	Thomas Pelham-Holles, D of Newcastle-Upon-Tyne	16 Mar 54
Chanc. Exch.	Sir William Lee	8 Mar 54
	Henry Bilson Legge	6 Apr 54
	Sir George Lyttleton	25 Nov 55

Ld Pres.	John Carteret, E of Granville	17 June 51
P.S.	John Leveson-Gower, Ld Gower (d. 25 Dec 54)	26 Dec 44
	Charles Spencer, D of Marlborough	9 Jan 55
	Granville Leveson-Gower, Earl Gower	22 Dec 55
D. Lanc.	Richard Edgcumbe, Ld Edgcumbe	22 Dec 43
Sec. of State (North)	Robert Darcy, E of Holderness	23 Mar 54
Sec. of State (South)	Sir Thomas Robinson (vacated Oct 55)	23 Mar 54
	Henry Fox (vacated 13 Nov 56)	14 Nov 55
B.O.T.	George Montagu, E of Halifax	1 Nov 48
Admir.	George Anson, Ld Anson	22 June 51
Ld Lt of Ireland	Lionel Cranfield, D of Dorset	15 Dec 50
	William Cavendish, D of Devonshire	2 Apr 55

PITT–DEVONSHIRE, 1756–7 (formed Nov 1756)

1st Ld Treas.	William Cavendish, D of Devonshire	16 Nov 56
Chanc. Exch.	Henry Bilson Legge	16 Nov 56
	William Murray, Ld Mansfield	13 Apr 57
P.S.	Granville Leveson-Gower, Earl Gower	22 Dec 55
D. Lanc.	Richard Edgcumbe, Ld Edgcumbe	22 Dec 43
Sec. of State (South)	William Pitt (Dismissed 6 Apr 57)	4 Dec 56

Sec. of State (*North*)	Robert Darcy, E of Holderness (vacated 9 Jun 57)	23 Mar 54
B.O.T.	George Montagu, E of Halifax	1 Nov 48
Admir.	Richard Grenville, Earl Temple	19 Nov 56
	Daniel Finch, E of Nottingham	6 Apr 57
Treas. of Navy	George Grenville	25 Nov 56
Ld Lt of Ireland	William Cavendish, D of Devonshire	2 Apr 55
	John Russell, D of Bedford	3 Jan 57

PITT–NEWCASTLE, 1757–61 (formed July 1757)

1st Ld Treas.	Thomas Pelham-Holles, D of Newcastle	29 June 57
Chanc. Exch.	Henry Bilson Legge	2 July 57
	William Wildman Barrington-Shute, Vt Barrington	19 Mar 61
Ld Pres.	John Carteret, E of Granville	17 June 51
P.S.	Richard Grenville-Temple, Earl Temple	5 July 57
Ld Keeper	Sir Richard Henley	30 June 57
D. Lanc.	Richard Edgcumbe, Ld Edgcumbe	22 Dec 43
	Thomas Hay, E of Kinnoull and Ld Hay	24 Jan 58 (renewed 27 Feb 60)
Sec. of State (*South*)	William Pitt	27 June 57
Sec. of State (*North*)	Robert Darcy, E of Holderness	23 Mar 54
	John Stuart, E of Bute	25 Mar 61

B.O.T.	George Montagu, E of Halifax	1 Nov 48
Admir.	George Anson, Ld Anson	2 July 57
Treas. of Navy	George Grenville	25 Nov 56
Sec. at War	William Wildman Barrington-Shute, Vt Barrington	14 Nov 55
	Charles Townshend	18 Mar 61
Pay.-Gen.	Henry Fox	July 57
Ld Lt of Ireland	John Russell, D of Bedford	3 Jan 57

MINISTERIAL BIOGRAPHIES

The following names include the major holders of office in the period. Peers are listed under the last title they held, e.g. for Carteret, see Granville. Usually only major offices are included.

ADDISON, JOSEPH (1672–1719)

MP, Lostwithiel 1708; Malmesbury 1709–19. Secretary of State 1717–18; previously Under-Secretary of State 1706; secretary to Wharton when Lord Lieutenant of Ireland, 1709. Distinguished essayist and poet, contributed to Steele's *Tatler* 1709–11, and produced with Steele the *Spectator* 1711–12; contributor to *Guardian* 1713 and revived *Tatler* in 1714.

BATH, E OF   WILLIAM PULTENEY (1684–1764)

MP Hedon 1705–34; Middlesex 1734–42. Secretary at War 1714–17; resigned with Walpole but moved into opposition after failing to secure office under his premiership. Later wrote for *The Craftsman* and joined 'the patriots'. Declined invitation to form administration after the fall of Walpole and refused office, although a member of Cabinet under Wilmington. Created Earl of Bath 1742; failed in attempt to form an administration at behest of George II in 1746.

BEDFORD, 4TH D OF   JOHN RUSSELL (1710–71)

First Lord of the Admiralty 1744–8; Lord Justice of Great Britain 1745,

1748 and 1750; Secretary of State 1748–51; Lord Lieutenant of Ireland 1756–7; Privy Seal 1761–3; Lord President 1763–5.

BOLINGBROKE, 1ST VT HENRY ST JOHN (1678–1751)

MP, Wooton Bassett 1701–10; Berkshire 1710–12; Secretary at War 1704–8; Secretary of State 1710–13, 1713–14. Took charge of peace negotiations of Utrecht, 1713. Dismissed from office by George I in 1714 for his support for the Pretender. Motion for his impeachment carried, bill of attainder passed against him and name erased from roll of peers, 1714; fled to France and became Secretary of State to the Pretender; dismissed from his service 1716. Pardoned 1723; returned to England 1725. Contributed to *The Craftsman* and author of several political works, notably, *The Idea of a Patriot King*, 1738.

BROMLEY WILLIAM (1664–1732)

MP, Warwickshire 1690–1702; Oxford University 1702–32. Speaker of the House of Commons 1710; Secretary of State 1713–14.

CARLETON, 1ST B HENRY BOYLE (d. 1725)

MP, Tamworth 1689–90; Cambridge University 1692–1705; Westminster 1705–10. Chancellor of the Exchequer 1701; Lord Treasurer of Ireland 1704–10; Secretary of State 1708–10; Lord President 1721–5.

CARLISLE, 3RD E OF CHARLES HOWARD (1674–1738)

MP, Morpeth 1690–2; First Lord of the Treasury 1701–2, 1715. Commissioner for Scottish Union.

CHATHAM, 1ST E OF WILLIAM PITT 'the elder' (1707–78)

MP, Old Sarum 1735–47; Seaford 1747–54; Aldborough 1754–6; Oke-hampton 1756–7; Bath 1757–66. Vice-Treasurer of Ireland 1746; Paymaster-General 1746–55; Secretary of State 1756–7, 1757–61; Privy Seal (Prime Minister) 1766–8. Leader of the House of Commons 1756–61.

CHESTERFIELD, 4TH E OF PHILIP DORMER STANHOPE (1694–1773)

MP, St Germans 1715–22; Lostwithiel 1722–5. Privy Councillor 1727; Lord Steward 1730–3; Secretary of State 1746–8.

CRAGGS, JAMES (1686-1721)

MP, Tregony 1713-21. Secretary at War 1717-18; Secretary of State 1718-21. Implicated in the South Sea Company scandal.

DARTMOUTH, 1ST E OF WILLIAM LEGGE (1672-1750)

Privy Councillor 1702; Secretary of State 1710-13; Privy Seal 1713-14.

DEVONSHIRE, 4TH D OF WILLIAM CAVENDISH (1720-64)

MP, Derbyshire 1741-51. Styled Marquis of Hartington until 1755; Baron Cavendish of Hardwicke, 1751; Duke of Devonshire 1755. Lord Lieutenant of Ireland 1755-6; First Lord of the Treasury (Prime Minister) 1756-7; Lord Chamberlain 1757-62.

GODOLPHIN, 1ST E OF SIDNEY GODOLPHIN (1645-1712)

MP, Helston 1668-79; St Mawes 1679-81. A Lord of the Treasury, 1679; Secretary of State 1684; Commissioner of the Treasury 1687; head of the Treasury 1690-6. Lord Justice 1695, 1700-1. Lord High Treasurer 1702-10.

GRANTHAM, 1ST B THOMAS ROBINSON (1695-1770)

MP, Thirsk 1727-34; Christchurch 1748-61. Diplomatist, English representative at Congress of Soissons, 1728-9; ambassador at Vienna 1730-48, joint-plenipotentiary of England in negotiations of Aix-la-Chapelle 1748. Privy Councillor 1750; Secretary of State and leader of the House of Commons 1754-5, joint postmaster-general 1765-6.

GRANVILLE, 1ST E JOHN CARTERET (1690-1763)

Took seat in House of Lords, 1711. Envoy to Sweden 1719; negotiated peace between the Baltic powers 1719-20. Secretary of State 1742-4; failed to form an administration, 1746; Lord President of the Council 1751-63.

HALIFAX, 1ST E OF CHARLES MONTAGU (1661-1715)

MP, Maldon 1689-95; Westminster 1695-1700. Clerk of the Privy Council 1689; a Lord of the Treasury 1692. Chancellor of the Exchequer 1694-9; Privy Councillor 1694. Proposed formation of National Debt, 1692; introduced bill establishing Bank of England, 1694; introduced Recoinage Bill 1695. First Lord of the Treasury 1697-9; auditor of the Exchequer, 1699-1714.

Impeached by House of Commons, 1701 for corruption, but charges dismissed. First Lord of the Treasury 1714–15.

HARRINGTON, 1ST E OF   WILLIAM STANHOPE (1690–1756)

MP, Derby 1715–22, 1727–30. Diplomatist and statesman; envoy to Madrid 1717–18; Turin 1718; ambassador in Spain 1719–27. Vice-Chamberlain 1727–30; Privy Councillor 1727–30. Secretary of State 1730–42; Lord President 1742–5; Secretary of State 1744–6, again 1746; Lord Lieutenant of Ireland 1746–51.

HEDGES, SIR CHARLES (d. 1714)

MP, Oxford 1698–1700; Dover 1701; Malmesbury 1701, Calne 1702; West Looe, 1705, 1708, 1710; East Looe, 1713–14. Secretary of State 1700–1; 1702–6.

HOLDERNESS, 4TH E OF   ROBERT D'ARCY (1718–78)

Ambassador to Vienna 1744–6; minister plenipotentiary at the Hague 1749–51. Secretary of State 1751–61; Privy Councillor 1751.

HOLLAND, 1ST B   HENRY FOX (1705–74)

MP, Hindon 1735–41; Windsor 1741–61; Dunwich 1761–3. Lord of the Treasury 1743; Secretary at War 1746–54; Secretary of State 1755–6; Paymaster-General 1757–65; Leader of the House of Commons 1762–3.

LONSDALE, VT   JOHN LOWTHER (1655–1700)

MP, Westmorland 1676–96. Vice Chamberlain 1689–94; Privy Councillor 1689. First Lord of the Treasury 1690–2; Privy Seal 1699–1700. Active supporter of exclusion of Duke of York from the succession and of William III's invasion in 1688.

MANCHESTER, 1ST D OF   CHARLES MONTAGU (1660–1722)

Ambassador extraordinary at Venice 1697; Paris 1699; Venice, again, 1707. Secretary of State 1702.

METHUEN, PAUL (1672–1757)

MP, Devizes 1708–10, Brackley 1713–47. Envoy to the King of Portugal 1697–1705; Minister to Turin 1705; ambassador to Portugal 1706–8. Lord of the Admiralty 1714–17; Secretary of State 1717. Ambassador to Spain and Morocco and Privy Councillor 1714. Comptroller of the Household 1720–5.

NEWCASTLE, 1ST D OF THOMAS PELHAM-HOLLES (1693–1768)

Lord Chamberlain 1717–24. Secretary of State 1724–46, 1746–54. First Lord of the Treasury 1754–6, 1757–62. Lord Privy Seal, July 1765 to Aug 1766. Created Earl of Clare and Duke of Newcastle 1715.

NOTTINGHAM, 2ND E OF AND 6TH OF WINCHILSEA DANIEL FINCH (1647–1730)

Privy Councillor 1680; succeeded to his father's title 1682; First Lord of the Admiralty 1681–4; in 1688–9 proposed a regency to fill the gap after the flight of James II. Secretary at War 1688–93; Secretary of State 1702–4; Lord President of the Council 1714–16.

ORFORD, 1ST E OF ROBERT WALPOLE (1676–1745)

MP, Castle Rising 1700–1; Kings Lynn 1702–12, 1713–42. Secretary at War 1708–11; Paymaster of the Forces 1714–17, 1720–1. Privy Councillor 1714. First Lord of the Treasury and Chancellor of the Exchequer 1715–17, 1721–42. Order of the Bath 1725; Knight of the Garter 1726; Earl of Orford 1742.

OXFORD, 1ST E OF ROBERT HARLEY (1661–1724)

MP, Tregony 1689–90; New Radnor 1690–1711. Speaker of the House of Commons 1701–5; Secretary of State 1704–8; Chancellor of the Exchequer 1710–1; Lord Treasurer 1711–14. Created Baron Harley, Earl of Oxford and Mortimer 1711; Knight of the Garter 1712. Effective leader of strong Tory administration from 1710; obtained dismissal of Marlborough and helped to force through the peace of Utrecht, but supplanted by Bolingbroke and dismissed from office in 1714. Movement of impeachment against him dismissed, 1717.

PELHAM, HENRY (1695–1754)

MP, Seaford 1717–22; Sussex 1722–54. Secretary at War 1724–30; Paymaster-General 1730–43; First Lord of the Treasury and Chancellor of the Exchequer 1743–54.

PETERBOROUGH, 3RD E OF AND 1ST E OF MONMOUTH CHARLES MORDAUNT (1658–1735)

Privy Councillor 1689; First Lord of the Treasury 1689–90; joint-commander of expeditionary force to Spain 1705; recalled to England 1707 to face enquiry into his conduct. Knight of the Garter 1713; ambassador extraordinary to Italian princes 1713–14.

POULETT, 1ST E   JOHN POULETT (1663–1743)

Privy Councillor 1702; created Earl Poulett 1706. First Lord of the Treasury 1710–11; Knight of the Garter 1713.

ROMNEY, E OF   HENRY SIDNEY OR SYDNEY (1641–1704)

MP, Bramber 1679–81; Tamworth 1689. Envoy to The Hague 1679–81 and General of British regiments in Dutch service 1681–5. Carried invitation to William III and accompanied him to England. Created Privy Councillor and Viscount Sydney 1689. Secretary of State 1690–1; Lord Lieutenant of Ireland 1692–3; Master General of Ordnance 1693–1702. Created an earl 1694; a Lord Justice 1697; Groom of the Stole 1700–2.

SHREWSBURY, 1ST D OF   CHARLES TALBOT (1660–1718)

Accompanied William III to England 1688; Secretary of State 1689–90, 1694–8. Knight of the Garter 1694; accused of complicity in Jacobite intrigues and withdrew temporarily from public affairs. Ambassador to France 1712–13; Lord Lieutenant of Ireland 1713–14. Lord Treasurer 1714 (July–Oct), ensuring Hanoverian succession. Lord Chamberlain 1714–15.

SOMERS, B   JOHN SOMERS (1651–1716)

MP, Worcester 1689–93. Junior Counsel for the Seven Bishops; negotiated with William III preceding his invasion; in Convention Parliament asserted that James II had abdicated; presided over the drafting of the Declaration of Rights. Solicitor-General 1689–93; Lord-Keeper 1693–7; Lord High Chancellor 1697–1700. Created Baron Somers 1697. Impeached in 1700, but acquitted of charges. Lord President 1708–10.

STANHOPE, 1ST E   JAMES STANHOPE (1673–1721)

MP, Newport (I. of Wight) 1715–17. British minister in Spain 1706; appointed commander of British forces in Spain 1708. Secretary of State 1714–17, 1718–21. Took leading part in securing Hanoverian succession; carried impeachment of Ormonde and directed measures for suppressing Jacobite rising of 1715. Lord Treasurer and Chancellor of the Exchequer 1717–18. Defeated on Peerage Bill and compromised by South Sea Bubble question.

SUNDERLAND, 3RD E OF   CHARLES SPENCER (1674–1722)

MP, Tiverton 1695–1702. Envoy extraordinary to Vienna 1705. Secretary of State, 1706–10. Lord Lieutenant of Ireland 1714–17; Lord Privy Seal 1715–16. First Lord of the Treasury 1718–21. Disgraced and forced to resign following South Sea Bubble.

TANKERVILLE, E OF   FORDE GREY (d. 1701)

Succeeded as third Baron Grey 1675. Forced into exile on discovery of Rye House Plot 1683; commanded Monmouth's horse at Sedgemoor, but restored to his title 1685. Supported William III; created Earl of Tankerville 1695; Privy Councillor 1695. Commissioner of Trade 1696; first Commissioner of the Treasury 1699. Lord Privy Seal 1700–1.

TOWNSHEND, 2ND VT   CHARLES TOWNSHEND (1674–1738)

Succeeded to the peerage 1687; negotiator of treaty of union 1706; Privy Councillor 1707; plenipotentiary to Netherlands 1709, but recalled 1711 on change of administration and vote of censure passed against him. Secretary of State 1714–16. Lord Lieutenant of Ireland, 1717; Lord President of the Council 1720–1; Secretary of State, 1721–30. Knight of the Garter, 1724. Resigned following disagreements with Walpole on foreign policy.

TRENCHARD, SIR JOHN (1640–95)

MP, Taunton 1678–81; Dorchester 1688; Thetford 1689–90; Poole 1690–5. Supporter of the Exclusion Bill and implicated in the Rye House Plot; arrested and later fled abroad. Pardoned by James II; knighted 1689. Secretary of State 1692–5.

TRUMBULL, SIR WILLIAM (1639–1716)

MP, East Looe 1685–7; Oxford University 1695–8, knighted 1684; envoy to France 1685; ambassador to Turkey 1686–91; governor of Hudson's Bay and Turkey companies; Lord of the Treasury 1694; Secretary of State, Privy Councillor and Secretary to Lords Justices 1695.

VERNON, JAMES (1646–1727)

MP, Cambridge University 1678–9; Penryn 1695–8; Westminster 1698–1702; Penryn 1705–10. Political agent in Holland 1672; attached to the Paris embassy 1673; secretary to the Duke of Monmouth 1674–8; editor *London Gazette* 1678–89; a commissioner of prizes 1693–1705. Secretary of State 1697–1702; teller of the Exchequer 1702–10.

WILMINGTON, 1ST EARL OF   SPENCER COMPTON (1673–1743)

MP, Eye 1698–1710; East Grinstead 1713–15; Sussex 1715–22; East Grinstead 1722; Sussex 1722–8. Chairman of Committee of Privileges and Elections 1705–10. Speaker of the House of Commons 1715–27; Paymaster-General 1722–30. Knight of the Bath 1725; created Baron Wilmington 1728; and Earl 1730. Lord Privy Seal 1730; Lord President 1730–42; First Lord of the Treasury 1742–3.

4 SELECTED HOLDERS OF MAJOR PUBLIC OFFICE

FIRST LORD OF THE TREASURY

Oct	14	E of Halifax
May	15	E of Carlisle
Oct	15	Robert Walpole
Apr	17	Earl Stanhope
Mar	18	E of Sunderland
Apr	21	Robert Walpole[1]
Feb	42	E of Wilmington
Aug	43	Henry Pelham
Feb	46	E of Bath[2]
Feb	46	Henry Pelham
Mar	54	D of Newcastle
Nov	56	D of Devonshire
Jul	57	D of Newcastle
May	62	E of Bute

LORD CHANCELLOR

1689–93		In commission
Mar	93	Ld Somers
May	00	Sir Nathan Wright (Ld Keeper)
Oct	05	Ld Cowper
Sep	08	In commission
Oct	10	Ld Harcourt
Sep	14	Ld Cowper
May	18	E of Macclesfield
Jan	25	In commission

[1] No office of Prime Minister existed in this period, but it is customary to regard Walpole as the first to wield Prime Ministerial authority. It was also to become common for such authority to be combined with the post of First Lord of the Treasury, but not in every case. See the list of administrations (pp. 33–46) for the offices held by the leading politicians in successive administrations.

[2] For the interruption of Henry Pelham's tenure of office in February 1746 see p. 42.

Jun	25	Ld King
Nov	33	Ld Talbot
Feb	37	E of Hardwicke
Nov	56	In commission
Jun	57	E of Northington
Jul	66	Ld Camden

LORD PRESIDENT OF THE COUNCIL

Feb	89	D of Leeds
May	99	E of Pembroke
Jan	02	D of Somerset
Jul	02	E of Pembroke
Nov	08	Ld Somers
Sep	10	E of Rochester
Jun	11	D of Buckinghamshire
Sep	14	E of Nottingham
Jul	16	D of Devonshire
Mar	18	E of Sunderland
Feb	19	D of Kingston
Jun	20	Vt Townshend
Jun	21	Ld Carleton
Mar	25	D of Devonshire
May	30	Ld Trevor
Dec	30	E of Wilmington
Feb	42	E of Harrington
Jan	45	D of Dorset
Jun	51	E of Granville
Sep	63	D of Bedford

LORD PRIVY SEAL

Mar	89	M of Halifax
Feb	90	In commission
Mar	92	E of Montgomery
May	99	Vt Lonsdale
Nov	00	E of Tankerville
Jun	01	In commission
Apr	02	D of Buckinghamshire
Mar	05	D of Newcastle
Aug	11	John Robinson
Aug	13	E of Dartmouth
Sep	14	M of Wharton
Apr	15	In commission

Sep	15	E of Sunderland
Dec	16	D of Kingston
Feb	19	D of Kent
Jun	20	D of Kingston
Mar	26	Ld Trevor
May	30	E of Wilmington
Jan	31	In commission
Jun	31	D of Devonshire
May	33	Vt Lonsdale
May	35	E of Godolphin
Apr	40	Ld Hervey
Jul	42	Ld Gower
Dec	43	E of Cholmondeley
Dec	44	Ld Gower
Jan	55	D of Marlborough
Dec	55	Earl Gower
Jul	57	Earl Temple
Oct	61	In commission

SECRETARY OF STATE FOR THE NORTHERN DEPARTMENT

Oct	88	Vt Preston
Mar	89	E of Nottingham
Dec	90	Vt Sydney
Mar	93	Sir John Trenchard
Mar	94	D of Shrewsbury
May	95	Sir William Trumbull
Dec	97	James Vernon
Nov	00	Sir Charles Hedges
Jan	02	James Vernon
May	04	Sir Charles Hedges
May	04	Robert Harley
Feb	08	Hon Henry Boyle
Sep	10	Henry St John (Vt Bolingbroke)
Aug	13	William Bromley
Sep	14	Vt Townshend
Dec	16	Vt Stanhope
Apr	17	E of Sunderland
Mar	18	Earl Stanhope
Feb	21	Vt Townshend
Jun	30	E of Harrington
Feb	42	Earl Granville
Nov	44	E of Harrington
Feb	46	Earl Granville

Feb	46	E of Harrington
Oct	46	E of Chesterfield
Feb	48	D of Newcastle
Mar	54	E of Holderness
Mar	61	E of Bute

SECRETARY OF STATE FOR THE SOUTHERN DEPARTMENT

Feb	89	E of Shrewsbury
Dec	90	E of Nottingham
Mar	93	E of Nottingham (again)
Mar	94	Sir John Trenchard
Apr	95	D of Shrewsbury
May	99	E of Jersey
Nov	00	James Vernon
Jan	02	E of Manchester
May	04	Sir Charles Hedges
Dec	06	E of Sunderland
Jun	10	Ld (E of) Dartmouth
Aug	13	Vt Bolingbroke
Sep	14	Vt Stanhope
Jun	16	Paul Methuen
Apr	17	Joseph Addison
Mar	18	James Craggs
Mar	21	Ld Carteret
Apr	24	D of Newcastle
Feb	48	D of Bedford
Jun	51	E of Holderness
Mar	54	Sir Thomas Robinson
Nov	55	Henry Fox
Dec	56	William Pitt
Apr	57	E of Holderness
Jun	57	William Pitt
Oct	61	E of Egremont

CHANCELLOR OF THE EXCHEQUER

Apr	89	Ld Delamere
Mar	90	Richard Hampden
May	94	C. Montagu
Jun	99	J. Smith
Mar	01	Hon H. Boyle
Apr	08	J. Smith
Aug	10	Robert Harley

Jun	11	R. Benson
Aug	13	Sir W. Wyndham
Oct	14	Sir Richard Onslow
Oct	15	Robert Walpole
Apr	17	Earl Stanhope
Mar	18	John Aislabie
Feb	21	Sir John Pratt
Apr	21	E of Orford
Feb	42	Ld Sandys
Dec	43	Henry Pelham
Mar	54	Sir William Lee
Apr	54	Henry Bilson Legge
Nov	55	Ld Lyttelton
Nov	56	Henry Bilson Legge
Apr	57	Ld Mansfield
Jul	57	Henry Bilson Legge
Mar	61	Vt Barrington

FIRST LORD OF THE ADMIRALTY

(* = Ld High Admiral)

Feb	89	E of Torrington*
Jan	90	E of Pembroke
Mar	92	Ld Cornwallis
Apr	93	Anthony Carey (Vt of Falkland)
May	94	E of Orford
May	99	E of Bridgwater
Apr	01	E of Pembroke*
May	02	Prince George of Denmark
Oct	08	Queen Anne*
Nov	08	E of Pembroke
Nov	09	E of Orford
Oct	10	Sir John Leake
Sep	12	E of Strafford
Oct	14	E of Orford
Apr	17	E of Berkeley
Jul	27	Vt Torrington
Jan	33	Sir Charles Wager
Mar	42	E of Winchilsea and Nottingham
Dec	44	D of Bedford
Feb	48	E of Sandwich
Jun	51	Ld Anson
Nov	56	Earl Temple
Apr	57	E of Winchilsea and Nottingham

| Jul | 57 | Ld Anson |
| Jun | 62 | E of Halifax |

PRESIDENT OF THE BOARD OF TRADE (since 1696)

May	96	E of Bridgwater
Jun	99	E of Stamford
Jun	02	Vt Weymouth
Apr	07	E of Stamford
Jun	11	E of Winchilsea
Sep	13	Ld Guildford
Dec	14	Ld Berkeley
May	15	E of Suffolk and Bindon
Jan	18	E of Holderness
May	19	E of Westmorland
May	35	Earl Fitzwalter
Jun	37	Ld Monson
Nov	48	E of Halifax
Mar	61	Ld Sandys

CHANCELLOR OF THE DUCHY OF LANCASTER

May	87	Robert Phelipps
Mar	89	D of Ancaster and Kesteven
May	97	E of Stamford
May	02	Ld Gower
Jun	06	E of Derby
Sep	10	Ld Berkeley
Nov	14	E of Aylesford
Mar	16	E of Scarborough
Jun	17	Ld Lechmere
Jul	27	D of Rutland
May	36	E of Cholmondeley
Dec	43	Ld Edgcumbe
Jan	58	E of Kinnoull
Dec	62	Ld Strange

LORD LIEUTENANT OF IRELAND (since 1700)

Dec	00	E of Rochester
Feb	03	D of Ormond
Apr	07	E of Pembroke
Dec	08	E of Wharton
Oct	10	D of Ormond

Sep	13	D of Shrewsbury
Oct	14	E of Sunderland
Feb	17	Vt Townshend
Apr	17	D of Bolton
Jun	20	D of Grafton
May	24	Ld Carteret
Jun	30	D of Dorset
Apr	37	D of Devonshire
Jan	45	E of Chesterfield
Nov	46	E of Harrington
Dec	50	D of Dorset
Apr	55	D of Devonshire
Jan	57	D of Bedford
Apr	61	E of Halifax

CHIEF SECRETARY FOR IRELAND

Feb	88	Patrick Tyrrell
Sep	92	Sir Cyril Wyche
May	95	Sir Richard Aldworth
Dec	00	Francis Gwyn
Feb	03	Edward Southwell
Apr	07	George Dodington
Dec	08	Joseph Addison
Oct	10	Edward Southwell
Sep	13	Sir John Stanley
Oct	14	Joseph Addison
Apr	17	Edward Webster
Jun	20	Horatio Walpole
Aug	21	Edward Hopkins
May	24	Thomas Clutterbuck
Jun	30	Walter Cary
Apr	37	Sir Edward Walpole
May	39	Thomas Townshend
Oct	39	Henry Bilson Legge
Jun	41	Vt Duncannon
Jan	45	Richard Liddell
Jul	46	Sewallis Shirley
Nov	46	Edward Weston
Dec	50	Ld George Sackville
Apr	55	Henry Seymour Conway
Jan	57	Richard Rigby
Apr	61	William Gerard Hamilton

SECRETARY AT WAR

Mar	92	George Clarke
Apr	04	Henry St John (Vt Bolingbroke)
Feb	08	Robert Walpole
Sep	10	Ld Lansdowne
Jun	12	Sir William Wyndham
Aug	13	Francis Gwyn
Sep	14	William Pulteney (E of Bath)
Apr	17	James Craggs
Mar	18	Vt Castlecomer
May	18	Robert Pringle
Dec	18	George Treby
Apr	24	Hon Henry Pelham
May	30	Sir William Strickland
May	35	Sir William Yonge
Jul	46	Henry Fox
Nov	55	Vt Barrington
Mar	61	Hon Charles Townshend
Nov	62	Welbore Ellis

PAYMASTER-GENERAL

	13	Thomas Moore and Edward Nicholas
Sep	14	Robert Walpole
Oct	15	E of Lincoln
Jun	20	Robert Walpole
Apr	21	Ld Cornwallis
	22	Hon Spencer Compton
May	30	Hon Henry Pelham
	43	Sir Thomas Winnington
May	46	William Pitt
Nov	55	{ E of Darlington { Vt Dupplin
Jun	57	Henry Fox

MASTER-GENERAL OF THE ORDNANCE

	81	Ld Dartmouth
	89	D of Schomberg
	93	E of Romney
Jul	02	D of Marlborough
Jan	12	Earl Rivers

Jul	12	D of Hamilton and Brandon (d. Nov 12)
Oct	14	D of Marlborough
Jul	22	Earl Cadogan
Jul	25	D of Argyll and Greenwich
Jul	40	D of Montagu
	42	D of Argyll
	43	D of Montagu
Jan	56	D of Marlborough
Jul	59	Earl Ligonier
Jul	63	D of Rutland

TREASURER OF THE NAVY

Oct	14	John Aislabie
Mar	18	Richard Hampden
Oct	20	Vt Torrington
Apr	24	Hon Pattee Byng
Apr	34	Arthur Onslow
May	42	Hon Thomas Clutterbuck
Dec	42	Sir Charles Wager
Dec	43	Sir John Rushout
Dec	44	George Bubb Dodington (Ld Melcombe)
May	49	Hon Henry Bilson Legge
Apr	54	Hon George Grenville
Jan	56	George Bubb Dodington (Ld Melcombe)
Jun	62	Vt Barrington

MASTER OF THE MINT

	85	Thomas Neale
	99	Isaac Newton (Sir Isaac, 1705)
		Major Wyvil (York)
	27	John Conduit
	37	Hon Richard Arundel
	44	Hon William Chetwynd (later Vt Chetwynd)

ATTORNEY-GENERAL

Feb	89	Henry Pollexfen
May	89	George Treby
May	92	John Somers
Jun	95	Thomas Trevor
Jun	01	Edward Northey

Apr	07	Simon Harcourt
Oct	08	James Montagu
Sep	10	Simon Harcourt
Oct	10	Sir Edward Northey
Mar	18	Sir Nicholas Lechmere
May	20	Sir Robert Raymond (Ld Raymond)
Feb	24	Sir Philip Yorke (Ld Hardwicke)
Jan	34	Sir John Willes
Jan	37	Sir Dudley Ryder (Ld Ryder)
May	54	Hon William Murray (Ld Mansfield)
Nov	56	Sir Robert Henley (Ld Northington)
Jun	57	Sir Charles Pratt (Earl Camden)
Jan	62	Hon Charles Yorke

SOLICITOR-GENERAL

Feb	89	George Treby
May	89	John Somers
May	92	Thomas Trevor
Jun	95	John Hawles
Jun	02	Simon Harcourt
Apr	07	James Montagu
Oct	08	Robert Eyre
May	10	Robert Raymond
Oct	14	Nicholas Lechmere
Dec	15	John Fortescue Aland
Jan	17	William Thomson
Mar	20	Philip Yorke
Feb	24	Clement Wearg
Apr	26	Charles Talbot
Jan	34	Dudley Ryder
Jan	37	John Strange
	42	William Murray
May	54	Richard Lloyd
Nov	56	Hon Charles Yorke
Jan	62	Fletcher Norton

UNDER SECRETARIES OF STATE FOR THE NORTHERN DEPARTMENT

1692	William Bridgeman
	James Vernon
	Thomas Hopkins (*vice* Vernon)
1697	Thomas Hopkins
	John Ellis (*vice* Bridgeman)

1700	John Ellis
	John Tucker (*vice* Hopkins)
1704	Richard Warr
	Erasmus Lewis
1710	George Tilson
	Horatio Walpole
1717	George Tilson
	Charles Delafaye
1724	George Tilson
	Thomas Townshend
1730	George Tilson
	Edward Weston
1740	Thomas Stanhope (*vice* Tilson)
1742	Edward Weston
	J. A. Balaguier
1745	Edward Weston
	W. R. Chetwynd
1746	W. R. Chetwynd
	John Potter
1748	Andrew Stone
	Thomas Ramsden
1750	Claudius Amyand
	Hugh Valence Jones (*vice* Ramsden)
1751	James Wallis (*vice* Amyand)
	Andrew Stone
1754	James Wallis
	Richard Pottinger (*vice* Stone)
1760	Michael Peter Morin (*vice* Pottinger)
	William Fraser (*vice* Wallis)

UNDER SECRETARIES OF STATE FOR THE SOUTHERN DEPARTMENT

1689	Richard Warr
	John Isham
1699	Robert Yard
	Matthew Prior
1702	Richard Warr
	William Aglionby
1704	John Isham (*vice* Aglionby)
1707	John Tucker
	Joseph Addison
1710	Thomas Hopkins
	Robert Pringle
1714	Robert Pringle (cont.)

	Charles Stanhope
1717	Temple Stanian
	Thomas Tickell
1718	Corbiere
	Charles Delafaye
1724	Charles Delafaye
	Temple Stanian
1735	John Couraud (*vice* Stanian)
	Andrew Stone (*vice* Delafaye)
1743	Thomas Ramsden (*vice* Couraud)
1748	Richard Nevill Aldworth
	John Potter
	Hon Richard Leveson-Gower (*vice* Potter)
1751	Claudius Amyand
	Richard Pottinger
1754	Claudius Amyand
	James Rivers
1755	Claudius Amyand
	James Rivers
	Henry Rivers
1756	Robert Wood
	James Rivers

JUNIOR COMMISSIONERS OF THE TREASURY

Apr	89	Vt Mordaunt
		Ld Delamere
		Ld Godolphin
		Hon Sir H. Capel
		R. Hampden
May	90	Sir J. Lowther
		R. Hampden
		Sir S. Fox
		T. Pelham
Nov	90	Ld Godolphin
		Sir J. Lowther
		R. Hampden
		Sir S. Fox
		T. Pelham
Mar	92	Ld Godolphin
		R. Hampden
		Sir S. Fox

Sir E. Seymour
C. Montagu

Dec 01   E of Carlisle

May 94   Ld Godolphin   Sir S. Fox
            Sir S. Fox   Hon H. Boyle
            C. Montagu   R. Hill
            Sir W. Trumbull   T. Pelham
            J. Smith
                        Feb 02   E of Carlisle
Nov 95   Ld Godolphin   Sir S. Fox
            Sir S. Fox   Hon H. Boyle
            C. Montagu   R. Hill
            J. Smith   T. Pelham

May 96   Ld Godolphin   May 02   Ld Godolphin
            Sir S. Fox
            C. Montagu   Jun 07   E of Godolphin
            J. Smith
            Sir T. Littleton Aug 10   Earl Poulett
                                         R. Harley
May 97   C. Montagu   Hon H. Paget
            Sir S. Fox   Sir T. Mansell
            J. Smith   R. Benson
            Sir T. Littleton
            T. Pelham   May 11   E of Oxford

                             Jul 14   D of Shrewsbury
Jun 99   C. Montagu
            E of Tankerville Oct 14   Ld Halifax
            Sir S. Fox   Sir R. Onslow
            J. Smith   Sir W. St Quintin
            Hon H. Boyle   E. Wortley Montagu
                                         P. Methuen
Nov 99   E of Tankerville
            Sir S. Fox   May 15   E of Carlisle
            J. Smith   Sir R. Onslow
            Hon H. Boyle   Sir W. St Quintin
            R. Hill   E. Wortley Montagu
                                         P. Methuen
Dec 00   Ld Godolphin
            Sir S. Fox   Oct 15   R. Walpole
            J. Smith   Sir W. St Quintin
            Hon H. Boyle   P. Methuen
            R. Hill   Ld Finch
                                         Hon T. Newport
Mar 01   Ld Godolphin
            Sir S. Fox   Jun 16   R. Walpole
            Hon H. Boyle   Sir W. St Quintin
            R. Hill   P. Methuen

		Ld Torrington			W. Clayton
		R. Edgcumbe			Sir W. Yonge
Apr	17	J. Stanhope	May	35	Sir R. Walpole
		Ld Torrington			G. Dodington
		J. Wallop			Sir G. Oxenden
		G. Baillie			W. Clayton
		T. Micklethwaite			E of Cholmondeley
Mar	18	E of Sunderland	May	36	Sir R. Walpole
		J. Aislabie			G. Dodington
		J. Wallop			Sir G. Oxenden
		G. Baillie			Ld Sundon
		W. Clayton			T. Winnington
Jun	20	E of Sunderland	Jun	37	Sir R. Walpole
		J. Aislabie			G. Dodington
		G. Baillie			Ld Sundon
		Sir C. Turner			T. Winnington
		R. Edgcumbe			G. Earle
Apr	21	R. Walpole	Oct	40	Sir R. Walpole
		G. Baillie			Ld Sundon
		Sir C. Turner			T. Winnington
		R. Edgcumbe			G. Earle
		Hon H. Pelham			G. Treby
Apr	24	R. Walpole	Apr	41	Sir R. Walpole
		G. Baillie			Ld Sundon
		Sir C. Turner			G. Earle
		W. Yonge			G. Treby
		G. Dodington			T. Clutterbuck
May	25	Sir R. Walpole	Feb	42	E of Wilmington
		Sir C. Turner			S. Sandys
		Sir W. Yonge			Hon G. Compton
		G. Dodington			Sir J. Rushout
		Sir W. Strickland			P. Gybbon
Jul	27	Sir R. Walpole	Aug	43	Hon H. Pelham
		Sir C. Turner			S. Sandys
		G. Dodington			Hon G. Compton
		Sir G. Oxenden			Sir J. Rushout
		W. Clayton			P. Gybbon
May	30	Sir R. Walpole	Dec	43	Hon H. Pelham
		G. Dodington			Hon G. Compton
		Sir G. Oxenden			P. Gybbon

E of Middlesex
H. Fox

Dec 44   Hon H. Pelham
E of Middlesex
H. Fox
Hon R. Arundel
G. Lyttleton

Jun 46   Hon H. Pelham
E of Middlesex
G. Lyttleton
Hon H. Bilson Legge
J. Campbell

Jun 47   Hon H. Pelham
G. Lyttleton
Hon H. Bilson Legge
J. Campbell
G. Grenville

Apr 49   Hon H. Pelham
G. Lyttleton
J. Campbell
G. Grenville
Hon H. Vane

Mar 54   D of Newcastle
Sir G. Lyttleton
J. Campbell
Hon G. Grenville
Ld Barnard

Apr 54   D of Newcastle
E of Darlington
Hon H. Bilson Legge
Vt Dupplin

R. Nugent

Nov 55   D of Newcastle
E of Darlington
Sir G. Lyttleton
Vt Dupplin
R. Nugent

Dec 55   D of Newcastle
Sir G. Lyttleton
R. Nugent
P. Wyndham O'Brien
H. Furnese

Nov 56   D of Devonshire
Hon H. Bilson Legge
R. Nugent
Vt Duncannon
Hon J. Grenville

Jul 57   D of Newcastle
Hon H. Bilson Legge
R. Nugent
Vt Duncannon
Hon J. Grenville

Jun 59   D of Newcastle
Hon H. Bilson Legge
R. Nugent
Hon J. Grenville
Ld North

Dec 59   D of Newcastle
Hon H. Bilson Legge
Hon J. Grenville
Ld North
J. Oswald

SENIOR (PARLIAMENTARY) SECRETARIES TO THE TREASURY

Apr	89	W. Jephson	Apr	52	J. West
Jun	91	H. Guy	Nov	56	N. Hardinge
Mar	95	W. Lowndes	Apr	58	J. West
Jan	24	J. Scrope	May	62	S. Martin

JUNIOR (FINANCIAL) SECRETARIES TO THE TREASURY (since 1711)

Jun	11	T. Harley	Jul	42	H. Furnese
Nov	14	J. Taylor	Nov	42	J. Jeffreys
Oct	15	H. Walpole	May	46	J. West
Apr	17	C. Stanhope	Apr	52	N. Hardinge
Apr	21	H. Walpole	Nov	56	S. Martin
Jun	30	E. Walpole	Jul	57	J. West
Jun	39	S. Fox	May	58	S. Martin
Apr	41	Hon H. Legge	May	62	J. Dyson

CLERK OF THE TREASURY

(by)	1689	W. Lowndes	Oct	1713	W. Thomas
		S. Langford	Nov	1714	W. Glanville
		R. Squibb	Nov	1714	H. Kelsall
		W. Glanville	Jan	1718	W. Lowndes
		J. Evelyn	Feb	1724	M. Frecker
			Dec	1738	T. Bowen
(by)	1693	W. Shaw	Aug	1742	H. Fane
		R. Aldworth	Nov	1752	P. Leheup
		R. Powys	Jul	1755	C. Lowndes
		J. Taylor	Jul	1757	E. Burnaby
			Jul	1759	J. Postlethwaite
	c.1697	C. Tilson	Jul	1759	R. Yeates

COMMISSIONERS OF CUSTOMS FOR ENGLAND AND WALES

1688	14 Jan	Sir Nicholas Butler
		Sir Dudley North
		Sir John Werden
		Thomas Chudleigh
		William Culliford
1688	28 Feb	Sir Nicholas Butler
		Henry Browne
		Sir Dudley North
		Sir John Werden
		William Culliford
1689	20 Apr	George Booth
		Sir Richard Temple
		Sir John Werden
		Sir Robert Southwell
		Sir Robert Clayton

		Sir Patience Ward
		Thomas Pelham
1691	24 Mar	George Booth
		Sir Richard Temple
		Sir John Werden
		Sir Robert Southwell
		Sir Robert Clayton
		Sir Patience Ward
		Henry Guy
1691	3 Jul	George Booth
		Sir Richard Temple
		Sir John Werden
		Sir Robert Southwell
		Sir Patience Ward
		Sir Robert Clayton
		Charles Godolphin
1694	14 Aug	Sir Robert Clayton
		Sir Patience Ward
		Sir Robert Southwell
		Charles Godolphin
		Sir Walter Young
		James Chadwick
		Samuel Clarke
1696	14 Apr	Sir Robert Clayton
		Sir Patience Ward
		Sir Robert Southwell
		Charles Godolphin
		Sir Walter Young
		James Chadwick
		Samuel Clarke
		Benjamin Overton
1697	21 June	Charles Godolphin
		Sir Walter Young
		Samuel Clarke
		Benjamin Overton
		Sir Henry Hobart
		Sir John Austin
		Robert Henley
1698	22 Nov	Charles Godolphin
		Sir Walter Young
		Samuel Clarke
		Benjamin Overton
		Sir Henry Hobart
		Sir John Austin

		Robert Henley
		Sir William St Quintin
1699	22 Nov	Charles Godolphin
		Sir Walter Young
		Samuel Clarke
		Benjamin Overton
		Robert Henley
		Sir William St Quintin
		Hon Thomas Newport
1701	18 Dec	Charles Godolphin
		Samuel Clarke
		Benjamin Overton
		Robert Henley
		Thomas Newport
		Arthur Maynwaring
		William Culliford
1703	14 Jul	Charles Godolphin
		Samuel Clarke
		Thomas Newport
		Arthur Maynwaring
		William Culliford
		Sir John Werden
		Richard Bretton
1705	15 May	Charles Godolphin
		Samuel Clarke
		Thomas Newport
		William Culliford
		Sir John Werden
		Richard Bretton
		Thomas Hall
1706	6 June	Charles Godolphin
		Samuel Clarke
		Thomas Newport
		William Culliford
		Sir John Werden
		Thomas Hall
		Sir Matthew Dudley
1708	4 May	Charles Godolphin
		Samuel Clarke
		Thomas Newport
		William Culliford
		Sir John Werden
		Sir Matthew Dudley
		Sir John Stanley

1708	23 Dec	Charles Godolphin
		Thomas Newport
		William Culliford
		Sir John Werden
		Sir Matthew Dudley
		Sir John Stanley
		John Shute
1711	25 Jan	Charles Godolphin
		Sir John Werden
		Sir John Stanley
		Matthew Prior
		John Bridges
		Robert Williamson
		Edward Gibbons
1714	17 May	Sir John Werden
		Sir John Stanley
		Matthew Prior
		John Bridges
		Robert Williamson
		Edward Gibbons
		Charles Godolphin
		Sir David Nairne
1714	4 Dec	Sir Walter Young
		Sir Matthew Dudley
		Sir John Stanley
		Robert Williamson
		John Pulteney
		Thomas Walker
		Sir Charles Peers
1715	17 Mar	Sir Walter Young
		Sir Matthew Dudley
		Sir John Stanley
		John Pulteney
		Thomas Walker
		Sir Charles Peers
		Sir Thomas Frankland
1718	2 Jan	Sir Walter Young
		Sir Matthew Dudley
		Sir John Stanley
		John Pulteney
		Thomas Walker
		Sir Charles Peers
		Robert Baylis
1720	1 Oct	Sir Walter Young

		Sir Matthew Dudley
		Sir John Stanley
		John Pulteney
		Thomas Walker
		Sir Charles Peers
		Robert Baylis
1721	4 Sept	Sir Walter Young
		Sir John Stanley
		John Pulteney
		Thomas Walker
		Sir Charles Peers
		Robert Baylis
		Sir John Evelyn
1722	27 Mar	Sir Walter Young
		Sir John Stanley
		Thomas Walker
		Sir Charles Peers
		Robert Baylis
		Sir John Evelyn
		Thomas Maynard

COMMISSIONERS OF CUSTOMS FOR GREAT BRITAIN

Fourteen commissioners were appointed, seven to reside in London, five in Edinburgh, and two to attend the outports.

1723		Sir Walter Young
		Sir John Stanley
		Thomas Walker
		Sir Charles Peers
		Robert Baylis
		Sir John Evelyn
		Thomas Maynard
		Sir James Campbell
		Humphry Brent
		John Campbell
		Brian Fairfax
		Henry Hale
		George Drummond
		John Hill
1727	18 Oct	Sir Walter Young
		Sir John Stanley
		Thomas Walker

Sir Charles Peers
Sir John Evelyn
Thomas Maynard
Sir James Campbell
Humphry Brent
John Campbell
Brian Fairfax
Henry Hale
George Drummond
John Hill
Allan Broderick

1728   19 Jul   Sir Walter Young
Sir John Stanley
Thomas Walker
Sir Charles Peers
Sir John Evelyn
Sir James Campbell
Humphry Brent
John Campbell
Brian Fairfax
Henry Hale
George Drummond
John Hill
Allan Broderick
Gwynn Vaughan
Thomas Maynard

1730   21 Sept   Sir Walter Young
Sir John Stanley
Thomas Walker
Sir Charles Peers
Sir John Evelyn
Sir James Campbell
John Campbell
Brian Fairfax
Henry Hale
George Drummond
John Hill
Gwynn Vaughan
George Ross (aft. Ld Ross)

1731   14 May   Sir Walter Young
Sir John Stanley
Thomas Walker
Sir Charles Peers
Sir John Evelyn

		Sir James Campbell
		John Campbell
		Brian Fairfax
		Henry Hale
		George Drummond
		John Hill
		Gwynn Vaughan
		George Ross
		Wardel George Westby
1731	28 Aug	Sir John Stanley
		Thomas Walker
		Sir Charles Peers
		Sir John Evelyn
		Sir James Campbell
		John Campbell
		Brian Fairfax
		Henry Hale
		George Drummond
		John Hill
		Gwynn Vaughan
		George Ross
		Wardel George Westby
		Sir Robert Baylis
1732	2 Jan	Sir John Stanley
		Sir Charles Peers
		Sir John Evelyn
		Sir James Campbell
		John Campbell
		Brian Fairfax
		Henry Hale
		George Drummond
		John Hill
		Gwynn Vaughan
		George Ross
		Wardel George Westby
		Sir Robert Baylis
		Edward Trelawney
1735	24 May	Sir John Stanley
		Sir Charles Peers
		Sir John Evelyn
		Sir James Campbell
		John Campbell
		Brian Fairfax
		George Drummond

		John Hill
		Gwynn Vaughan
		George Ross
		Wardel George Westby
		Sir Robert Baylis
		Edward Trelawney
		Sir Robert Corbett
1737	15 Oct	Sir John Stanley
		Sir John Evelyn
		John Campbell
		Brian Fairfax
		John Hill
		Gwynn Vaughan
		George Ross
		Wardel George Westby
		Sir Robert Baylis
		Sir Robert Corbett
		Richard Chandler
		Beaumont Hotham
		Richard Somers
		Colin Campbell
1741	29 June	Sir John Stanley
		Sir John Evelyn
		John Campbell
		Brian Fairfax
		John Hill
		George Ross (now Ld Ross)
		Wardel George Westby
		Sir Robert Baylis
		Richard Chandler
		Beaumont Hotham
		Richard Somers
		Colin Campbell
		Edward Riggs
		Isaac Leheup
1742		Sir John Stanley
		Sir John Evelyn
		John Campbell
		Brian Fairfax
		John Hill
		Wardel George Westby
		Sir Robert Baylis
		Richard Chandler
		Beaumont Hotham

                  Richard Somers
                  Colin Campbell
                  Gwynn Vaughan

At this time, the commission for Great Britain was divided, and nine commissioners were appointed for England and Wales, and five for Scotland.

COMMISSIONERS OF CUSTOMS FOR ENGLAND AND WALES

1742	Sep	Sir John Stanley
		Sir John Evelyn
		Brian Fairfax
		John Hill
		Sir Robert Baylis
		Richard Chandler
		Wardel George Westby
		Beaumont Hotham
		Samuel Mead
1744		Sir John Evelyn
		Brian Fairfax
		John Hill
		Sir Robert Baylis
		Richard Chandler
		Wardel George Westby
		Beaumont Hotham
		Samuel Mead
		Gwynn Vaughan
1747		Sir John Evelyn
		Brian Fairfax
		Sir Robert Baylis
		Richard Chandler
		Wardel George Westby
		Beaumont Hotham
		Samuel Mead
		Gwynn Vaughan
		William Levinz
1748		Sir John Evelyn
		Brian Fairfax
		Richard Cavendish
		Wardel George Westby
		Beaumont Hotham
		Samuel Mead
		Gwynn Vaughan
		William Levinz

	Edward Hooper
1750	Sir John Evelyn
	Sir Miles Stapleton
	Richard Cavendish
	Wardel George Westby
	Beaumont Hotham
	Samuel Mead
	Gwynn Vaughan
	William Levinz
	Edward Hooper
1752	Sir John Evelyn
	Richard Cavendish
	Wardel George Westby
	Beaumont Hotham
	Samuel Mead
	Gwynn Vaughan
	William Levinz
	Edward Hooper
	Thomas Tash
1756	Sir John Evelyn
	Richard Cavendish
	Beaumont Hotham
	Samuel Mead
	Gwynn Vaughan
	William Levinz
	Edward Hooper
	Thomas Tash
	Claudius Amyand
1758	Sir John Evelyn
	Richard Cavendish
	Beaumont Hotham
	Samuel Mead
	William Levinz
	Edward Hooper
	Thomas Tash
	Claudius Amyand
	Henry Pelham
1761	Sir John Evelyn
	Beaumont Hotham
	Samuel Mead
	William Levinz
	Edward Hooper
	Thomas Tash
	Claudius Amyand

Henry Pelham
John Frederick

POSTMASTER-GENERAL

1687	Philip Fowde (for D of York)
1690	Sir Robert Cotton
	Thomas Frankland
1708	Thomas Frankland
	Sir John Evelyn
1715	Ld Cornwallis
	Jason Craggs
1720	Edward Carteret
	Galfridus Walpole
1725	Edward Carteret
	Edward Harrison
1732	Edward Carteret (sole)
1733	Edward Carteret
	Ld Lovel (later Vt Coke and Earl of Leicester)
1739	Sir John Eyles
	Ld Lovel
1744	E of Leicester (sole)
1745	E of Leicester
	Sir Everard Faulkener
1758	E of Leicester (sole)
1759	E of Besborough
	Hon Robert Hampden

SURVEYOR-GENERAL OF THE LAND REVENUES OF THE CROWN

1682	William Harbord	1726	Phillips Gybbon
1692	William Tailer	1730	Exton Sayer
1693	Samuel Travers	1732	Thomas Walker
1710	J. Manley	1750	Vt Galway
1714	Alexander Pendarves	1751	Robert Herbert
1715	H. Chomeley	1769	Peter Burrell
1722	J. Poulteney		

SURVEYOR-GENERAL OF WOODS, FORESTS, PARKS AND CHASES

1688	Philip Riley	1716	Edward Younge
1701	Thomas Hewett	1720	Charles Whithers
1702	Edward Wilcox	1736	Francis Whitworth
1714	Thomas Hewett	1742	Henry Legge

1745   John Phillipson
1756   John Pitt
1763   Sir Edmond Thomas

JUDGE ADVOCATE GENERAL

1684	George Clarke	1734	Sir Henry Hoghton
1705	Thomas Byde	1741	Thomas Morgan
1715	Edward Hughes		

LORD ADVOCATE (SCOTLAND)

1709	Sir David Dalrymple	1742	Robert Craigie
1720	Robert Dundas	1746	William Grant
1725	Duncan Forbes	1754	Robert Dundas
1737	Charles Areskin	1760	Thomas Miller

SECRETARY OF STATE FOR SCOTLAND

Feb	09	D of Queensberry
Sep	13	E of Mar
Sep	14	D of Montrose (dis Aug 15)
Dec	16	D of Roxburghe (dis Aug 25)
Feb	42	M of Tweeddale (res Jan 46)

UNDER SECRETARY OF STATE FOR SCOTLAND*

Feb	09	J. Montgomery	Sep	14	C. Kennedy
Feb	09	N. Rowe	Dec	16	T. Scott
Sep	13	W. Strahan	Feb	42	A. Mitchell

LORD CHANCELLOR: IRELAND

1710   Sir Constantine Phipps
1714   Alan Brodrick (Vt Midleton)
1725   Richard West
1726   Thomas Wyndham (Ld Wyndham)
1739   Robert Jocelyn (Vt Jocelyn)
1757   John Bowes (Ld Bowes)

---

* Queensberry, the first Secretary of State for the Scottish Department, appointed two Under Secretaries in 1709; his successors, however, employed only one.

ATTORNEY-GENERAL: IRELAND

Dec	86	Sir Richard Nagle
Oct	90	Sir John Temple
May	95	Robert Rochfort
Jun	07	Alan Brodrick
Dec	09	John Forster
Jun	11	Sir Richard Levinge
Nov	14	George Gore
May	20	John Rogerson
May	27	Thomas Marlay
Sep	30	Robert Jocelyn
Sep	39	John Bowes
Dec	41	Stephen George Caulfield
Aug	51	Warden Flood
Jul	60	Philip Tisdall

SOLICITOR-GENERAL: IRELAND

Jul	60	Sir John Temple
Jan	89	Sir Theobald Butler (rem 25 July)
Nov	90	Sir Richard Levinge
May	95	Alan Brodrick
Apr	04	Sir Richard Levinge
Sep	09	John Forster
Dec	09	William Whitsed
Jun	11	Francis Bernard
Nov	14	John Rogerson
Apr	27	Robert Jocelyn
Sep	30	John Bowes
Sep	39	Stephen George Caulfield
Dec	41	Warden Flood
Aug	51	Philip Tisdall
Jul	60	John Gorp

LORD HIGH STEWARD

1689	E of Devonshire (coronation of William III and Mary)
1692	M of Carmarthen (trial of Ld Mohun)
1699	Ld Somers (trials of E of Warwick and Holland, and of Ld Mohun)
1702	D of Devonshire (coronation of Queen Anne)
1714	D of Grafton (coronation of George I)

1716   Ld Cowper (trials of E of Derwentwater, Ld Widdrington, E of Nithsdale, E of Carnwath, Vt Kenmure and Ld Nairne; again in March for trial of E of Wintoun)
1717   . Ld Cowper, again (trial of E of Oxford and Earl Mortimer)
1725   Ld King (trial of E of Macclesfield)
1727   D of Dorset (coronation of George II)
1746   Ld Hardwicke (trials of E of Kilmarnock, E of Cromarty and Ld Balmerino)
1747   Ld Hardwicke again (trial of Ld Lovat)
1760   Ld Henley (trial of Earl Ferrers)
1761   Earl Talbot (coronation of George III)

LORD GREAT CHAMBERLAIN

1666   (3rd) E of Lindsey
1701   (4th) E of Lindsey (M of Lindsey, 1707 and D of Ancaster and Kesteven, 1715)
1723   (2nd) D of Ancaster and Kesteven
1742   (3rd) D of Ancaster and Kesteven
1778   (4th) D of Ancaster and Kesteven

LORD STEWARD

1689   E (D) of Devonshire
1707   2nd D of Devonshire
1710   D of Buckinghamshire
1711   Earl Paulet
1714   2nd D of Devonshire (again)
1716   D of Kent
1718   D of Argyll
1725   D of Dorset
1730   E of Chesterfield
1733   3rd D of Devonshire
1737   D of Dorset (again)
1744   3rd D of Devonshire (again)
1749   D of Marlborough
1755   D of Rutland
1761   E of Talbot

LORD CHAMBERLAIN

1689   E of Dorset and Middlesex
1695   E of Sunderland
1699   D of Shrewsbury

1700   E of Jersey
1704   E (M, D) of Kent
1714   D of Shrewsbury
1715   D of Bolton (resigned, Jul 15)
1715–17 vacant
1717   D of Newcastle
1724   D of Grafton
1757   D of Devonshire
1762   D of Marlborough

VICE-CHAMBERLAIN

1689   Sir John Lowther (Vt Lonsdale)
1690   Hon Peregrine Bertie
1706   Thomas Coke (Ld Lovel, E of Leicester)
1727   William Stanhope (E of Harrington)
1730   Ld John Hervey
1740   Ld Sydney Beauclerk
1742   Hon William Finch
1765   George Bussy (Vt Villiers, E of Jersey)

TREASURER OF THE CHAMBER

1689   Sir Rowland Gwin
1692   E of Orford
1702   Vt Fitzharding
1713   Ld De La Warr
1714   E of Radnor
1720   Henry Pelham
1722   Charles Stanhope
1727   Ld Hobart (E of Buckinghamshire)
1744   Sir John Hinde Cotton
1746   Hon Richard Arundel
1747   Ld Sandys
1755   E of Hillsborough
1756   Charles Townshend
1761   Sir Francis Dashwood (Ld Le Despencer)

MASTER OF THE HORSE

1689   Henry de Nassau d'Auverquerque
1702   D of Somerset
1715   { Hon Conyers D'Arcy
         { Francis Negus   –Commissioners

1717   Henry Berkeley *vice* D'Arcy. Negus then sole commissioner until 1727.

1727   E of Scarborough

1734   {Hon James Lumley
           {Hon Henry Berkeley –Commissioners

1735   D of Richmond
1751   M of Hartington (D of Devonshire)
1755   D of Dorset
1757   Earl Gower
1760   E of Huntingdon
1761   D of Rutland

TREASURER OF THE HOUSEHOLD

1689   Ld Newport (E of Bradford)
1708   E of Cholmondeley
1712   Ld Lansdowne of Bideford
1714   E of Cholmondeley (again)
1725   (Sir) Paul Methuen
1730   Ld Bingley
1731   Ld (E) De La Warr
1737   Earl Fitzwalter
1755   Ld Berkeley of Stratton
1756   Vt Bateman
1757   E of Thomond
1761   E of Powis

COMPTROLLER OF THE HOUSEHOLD

           1689   Hon Thomas Wharton (Ld, E and M of Wharton)
           1702   Sir Edward Seymour
           1704   Sir Thomas Mansell (Ld Mansell)
(May)   1708   E of Cholmondeley
(Oct)   1708   Sir Thomas Felton
(Jun)   1709   Sir John Holland
           1711   Sir Thomas Mansell (again)
           1712   Ld Lansdowne of Bideford
           1713   Sir John Stonehouse
           1714   Hugh Boscawen (Vt Falmouth)
           1720   (Sir) Paul Methuen
           1725   Ld Finch (E of Winchilsea & Nottingham)
           1730   Hon Sir Conyers D'Arcy
           1754   E of Hillsborough

	1755	Ld Hobart (E of Buckinghamshire)
	1756	Hon Richard Edgcumbe (Ld Edgcumbe)
	1761	E of Powis

CAPTAIN OF THE CORPS OF GENTLEMEN PENSIONERS

c.	1689	Ld Lovelace
	1693	E (D) of Montagu
	1695	D of St Albans
	1712	D of Beaufort
	1714	D of St Albans (again)
	1726	M of Hartington (D of Devonshire)
	1731	E of Burlington and Cork
	1734	D of Montagu
	1740	D of Bolton
	1742	Ld (E) Bathurst
	1745	Ld Hobart (E of Buckinghamshire)
	1756	Ld Berkeley of Stratton
	1762	E of Lichfield

CAPTAIN OF THE YEOMEN OF THE GUARD

1702	M of Hartington (D of Devonshire)
1707	Vt Townshend
1714	Ld Paget (E of Uxbridge)
1715	E of Derby
1723	Ld Stanhope (E of Chesterfield)
1725	E of Leicester
1731	Ld (E of) Ashburnham
1733	E of Tankerville
1737	D of Manchester
1739	E of Essex
1743	Ld Berkeley of Stratton
1746	Vt Torrington
1747	Vt Falmouth
1782	D of Dorset

COFFERER OF THE HOUSEHOLD

c.	1688	Ld Herbert of Chirbury
	1702	Sir Benjamin Bathurst
	1704	Hon Francis Godolphin (E of Godolphin)
	1711	Samuel Masham (Ld Masham)
	1714	E of Godolphin (again)

1723	William Pulteney (E of Bath)
1725	E of Lincoln
1730	Horace Walpole (Ld Walpole)
1741	Sir William Yonge
1743	Ld Sandys
1744	Edmond Waller
1746	E of Lincoln (D of Newcastle)
1754	Sir George Lyttelton (Ld Lyttelton)
1755	D of Leeds
1761	Hon J. Grenville

LORD HIGH CONSTABLE

(officiated at coronations on dates given below)

11	Apr	1689	D of Ormond
13	Apr	1702	D of Bedford
20	Oct	1714	D of Montagu
11	Oct	1727	D of Richmond, Lennox and Aubigny
22	Sep	1761	D of Bedford

MASTER OF THE GREAT WARDROBE

1685	E of Arran (D of Hamilton)
1689	Ld (E, D of) Montagu
1709	D of Montagu
1750	Sir Thomas Robinson (Ld Grantham)
1754	William Wildman (Vt Barrington)
1755	Ld Grantham (again)
1760	Earl Gower

GROOMS OF THE STOLE

1685	E of Peterborough
1689	E of Portland
1699	E of Romney
1704	Duchess of Marlborough
1710	Duchess of Somerset
1714	E (D) of Dorset and Middlesex
1719	E of Sunderland
1723	E of Godolphin
1735	E of Pembroke
1750	E of Albemarle
1755	E of Rochford

1760   E of Bute
1761   E of Huntingdon

THE ORDERS OF KNIGHTHOOD

KNIGHTS COMPANION OF THE BATH

*(from the revival of the Order by George I, May 1725)**

George I (all invested 27 May 1725 and installed 17 June 1725)

Prince William Augustus, D of Cumberland
2nd D of Montagu (Great Master)
6th D of Richmond (not invested)
2nd D of Manchester
E of Burford (D of St Albans)
6th E of Leicester
2nd E of Albermarle
1st E of Delorain
2nd E of Halifax
E of Sussex
1st E of Pomfret
Lord Paulet (son of D of Bolton)
1st Vt Torrington
Vt Malpas (E of Cholmondeley)
Vt Glenorchy (E of Breadalbane)
Ld (1st E) De La Warr
Ld (E) of Clinton
Robert Walpole (2nd E of Orford)
E of Wilmington
William Stanhope
Conyers D'Arcy
Hon Thomas Saunderson (3rd E of Scarborough)
Paul Methuen
Sir Robert Walpole (1st E of Orford)
Robert Sutton
Lt Gen Charles Willis

*The Order is of very ancient origin. After some time in abeyance, it was revived and remodelled by George I by statute dated 18 May 1725. After this date, the Order consisted of the Sovereign, a Great Master and 36 Companions. In 1815, the Order was again remodelled and very much enlarged – partly to reward services in the campaigns against Napoleon.

Sir John Hobart (Ld Hobart, E of Buckinghamshire)
Sir William Gage
Robert Clifton
Michael Newton
William Yonge
Thomas Watson Wentworth (E of Malton, M of Rockingham)
John Monson (Ld Monson)
William Morgan
Thomas Coke (Ld Lovell, Vt Coke, E of Leicester)
4th E of Inchiquin**
Vt Tyrconnell**

**Invested 28 May 1725.

George II

1732	12 Jan	Henry Brydges (M of Carnarvon, 2nd D of Chandos)
		1st Vt Bateman
		Sir George Downing
1732	17 Jan	Charles Gunter Nicol
1742	26 Jun	Sir Thomas Robinson (Ld Grantham)
1743	12 Jul	Lt-Gen Philip Honywood
		Lt-Gen Hon James Campbell
		Lt-Gen John Cope
		Fl Marshal Sir John Ligonier (Earl Ligonier)
1744	28 May	6th Vt Fitzwilliam
		Sir Charles Hanbury Williams
		Henry Calthorpe
		Thomas Whitmore
		Sir William Morden Harbord
1747	29 May	Rear Admiral Peter Warren
1747	14 Nov	Vice-Admiral Edward Hawke (Ld Hawke)
1749	2 May	Lt-Gen Hon Charles Howard
		General Sir John Mordaunt
		Maj-Gen Charles Armand Powlett
		John Savile (Ld Pollington, E of Mexborough)
1752	12 Mar	3rd Ld Onslow
1753	27 Aug	Edward Walpole (son of Robert Walpole)
		Lt-Gen Charles Paulet (5th D of Bolton)
		Edward Montagu (Ld, then Earl, Beaulieu)
		Lt-Gen Hon Richard Lyttelton
1753	12 Dec	Admiral Sir William Rowley
1754	23 Sep	Benjamin Keene
1756	27 Nov	Lt-Gen William Blakeney (Ld Blakeney)

KNIGHTS OF THE GARTER

Creations, 1689–1760

William III

1689	3 Apr	1st D of Schomberg
	14 May	4th E (1st D) of Devonshire
1690	30 Dec	Frederick III, Elector of Brandenburg (King Frederick I of Prussia)
		D of Brunswick and Lüneburg Zell
1692	2 Feb	George IV, Duke of Saxony
		E of Dorset (1st E of Middlesex)
1694	25 Apr	1st D of Shrewsbury
1696	6 Jan	Prince William, D of Gloucester (son of Queen Anne)
1697	19 Feb	1st E of Portland
1698	30 May	D of Newcastle
1700	14 May	8th E of Pembroke (and 5th E of Montgomery)
1701	18 Jun	Elector of Hanover (later King George I of England)
		D of Queensberry (and D of Dover)

Queen Anne

1702	14 Mar	2nd D of Bedford
		E (1st D) of Marlborough
1703	12 Aug	3rd D of Schomberg (and 1st D of Leinster)
1704	6 Jul	1st Ld (1st E of) Godolphin
1706	4 Apr	Elector, Prince of Hanover (King George II of England)
1710	22 Mar	2nd D of Devonshire
		D of Argyll (E, then D, of Greenwich)
1712	25 Oct	4th D of Hamilton (1st D of Brandon)
		D of Kent
		1st Earl Poulett
		21st E of Oxford (and Earl Mortimer)
		3rd E of Strafford
1713	4 Aug	3rd E of Peterborough

George I

1714	16 Oct	2nd D of Bolton
		2nd D of Rutland
		10th E (1st D) of Dorset and Middlesex
		1st E of Halifax

1717	3 Jul	Prince Frederick Lewis (D of Gloucester, D of Edinburgh, Prince of Wales)
		Ernest Augustus (Bp of Osnaburg and D of York)
1718	31 Mar	1st D of St Albans
		2nd D of Montagu
		4th D of Newcastle
		3rd E of Berkeley
1719	29 Apr	1st D of Kingston
		4th E of Sunderland
1721	27 Mar	2nd D of Grafton
		19th E of Lincoln
1722	10 Oct	3rd D of Bolton
		3rd D of Rutland
		1st D of Roxburghe
1724	9 Jul	2nd E of Scarborough
		2nd Vt Townshend
1726	26 May	7th D of Richmond and Lennox
		Sir Robert Walpole (E of Orford)

George II

1730	18 May	William Augustus, D of Cumberland
		5th E of Chesterfield
		3rd E of Burlington and Cork
1733	12 Jun	William of Nassau, Prince of Orange
		3rd D of Devonshire
		E of Wilmington
1738	20 Feb	23rd E of Essex
		1st Earl Waldegrave
1741	20 Mar	Frederick III, Prince (later Landgrave) of Hesse-Cassel
		2nd D of St Albans
		3rd D of Marlborough
		2nd D of Kingston
		2nd D of Portland
1741	2 May	Frederick III, D of Saxe-Gotha
1745	24 Apr	John Adolphus, D of Saxe-Weissenfels
1749	22 Jun	George William Frederick, Pr of Brunswick-Lüneburg (King George III)
		Charles William Frederick, Margrave of Brandenburg-Anspach
		4th D of Leeds
		7th D of Bedford

		14th E of Albemarle
		2nd Earl Granville
1752	13 Mar	Edward Augustus, Pr of Brunswick-Lüneburg
		(D of York and Albany)
		William of Nassau, Prince of Orange
		21st E of Lincoln (2nd D of Newcastle)
		8th E of Winchilsea (E of Nottingham)
		4th E of Cardigan (3rd D of Montagu)
1756	18 Nov	4th D of Devonshire
		7th E of Carlisle
		15th E (3rd D) of Northumberland
		16th E (4th M) of Hertford
1757	30 Jun	2nd E Waldegrave
1759	16 Aug	Ferdinand, Prince of Brunswick-Bevern
1760	4 Feb	2nd M of Rockingham
		Earl Temple

KNIGHTS OF THE THISTLE

(from the revival and restoration in 1703 to 1760)*

Queen Anne

1704	4 Feb	2nd D of Argyll
1704	7 Feb	1st D of Atholl
		1st M of Annandale
		E of Dalkeith
		6th E of Orkney
		1st E of Seafield (E of Findlater)
1705	30 Oct	2nd M of Lothian
		4th E of Orrery
1706	10 Aug	23rd E of Mar
		3rd E of Loudoun
1710	25 Mar	2nd E of Stair
1713	17 Jan	1st E of Portmore

*On 29 May 1687, James II ordered Letters Patent to be made out for 'reviving and restoring the Order of the Thistle to its full glory, lustre and magnificency'. The earlier history of the Order remains obscure. During the reign of William and Mary the Order remained in abeyance. It was revived again by Anne on 31 December 1703. These 1703 statutes were later modified on 17 February 1715 by George I and on 8 May 1827 by George IV. By this last modification the number of Knights of the Order was extended from 12 to 16.

George I

1716	22 June	1st E of Cadogan
		16th E of Sutherland
1717	1 Mar	6th E of Haddington
1721	28 Mar	2nd E of Tankerville
1725	2 Mar	23rd E of Essex
		E of Dalkeith (2nd D of Buccleuch)
		2nd E of Marchmont
1726	23 Sep	5th D of Hamilton (2nd D of Brandon)

George II

1730	16 May	3rd E of Tankerville
1731	10 Dec	19th E of Moray
1732	2 Jan	2nd E of Portmore
1734	11 Feb	2nd D of Atholl
		3rd M of Lothian
1738	10 Jul	15th E of Morton
		1st E of Hopetoun
		3rd E of Bute
1739	7 Jun	4th E of Berkeley
1741	23 Feb	21st E of Moray
1742	22 Jun	3rd E of Hyndford
1743	29 Mar	4th E of Dysart
1747	10 Feb	3rd D of Gordon
1752	11 Mar	5th E of Dumfries
1753	29 Mar	10th E of Rothes
		1st Earl Brooke (Earl of Warwick)
1755	18 Mar	6th D of Hamilton (and 3rd D of Brandon)

5 PARLIAMENT

HOUSE OF COMMONS

SPEAKERS OF THE HOUSE OF COMMONS, 1688–1760

Date of Election	Name	Constituency
19 May 1685	Sir John Trevor (1637–1717)	Denbigh
22 Jan 1689	Henry Powle (1630–92)	Windsor
20 Mar 1690	Sir John Trevor (1637–1717)	Yarmouth (I. of W.)
14 Mar 1695	Paul Foley (1645–99)	Hereford
6 Dec 1698	Sir Thomas Littleton (1647–1710)	Woodstock
10 Feb 1701	Robert Harley (1661–1724)	New Radnor
25 Oct 1705	John Smith (1655–1723)	Andover
16 Nov 1708	Sir Richard Onslow (1654–1717)	Surrey
25 Nov 1710	William Bromley (1664–1732)	Oxford University
16 Feb 1714	Sir Thomas Hanmer (1677–1746)	Suffolk
17 Mar 1715	Sir Spencer Compton (1673–1743)	Sussex
23 Jan 1728	Arthur Onslow (1691–1768)	Surrey
3 Nov 1761	Sir John Cust (1718–70)	Grantham

CHAIRMEN OF WAYS AND MEANS

28 Mar 1715	William Farrer	
3 Feb 1728	Sir Charles Turner	
9 Feb 1739	Francis Fane	
19 Nov 1754	Job Staunton Charlton	
17 Nov 1761	Marshe Dickinson	

CLERKS OF THE HOUSE

1683	Paul Jodrell
1727	Edward Stables

1732   Nicholas Hardinge
1748   Jeremiah Dyson
1762   Thomas Tyrwhitt

PARLIAMENTARY SESSIONS

Year	Date of assembly	Dates of sessions	Date of dissolution
1689*	22 Jan 1689	22 Jan–20 Aug 1689	
		19 Oct 1689–27 Jan 1690	6 Feb 1690
1690	20 Mar 1690	20 Mar–23 May 1690	
		2 Oct 1690–5 Jan 1691	
		22 Oct 1691–24 Feb 1692	
		4 Nov 1692–14 Mar 1693	
		7 Nov 1693–25 Apr 1694	
		12 Nov 1694–3 May 1695	11 Oct 1695
1695	22 Nov 1695	22 Nov 1695–27 Apr 1696	
		20 Oct 1696–16 Apr 1697	
		3 Dec 1697–5 Jul 1698	7 Jul 1698
1698	24 Aug 1698	6 Dec 1698–4 May 1699	
		16 Nov 1699–11 Apr 1700	19 Dec 1700
1701	6 Feb 1701	6 Feb–24 Jun 1701	11 Nov 1701
1701	30 Dec 1701	30 Dec 1701–23 May 1702	2 Jul 1702
1702	20 Aug 1702	20 Oct 1702–27 Feb 1703	
		9 Nov 1703–3 Apr 1704	
		24 Oct 1704–14 Mar 1705	5 Apr 1705
1705	14 Jun 1705	25 Oct 1705–21 May 1706	
		3 Dec 1706–24 Apr 1707	
		23 Oct 1707–1 Apr 1708	3 Apr 1708
1708	8 Jul 1708	16 Nov 1708–21 Apr 1709	
		15 Nov 1709–5 Apr 1710	21 Sep 1710
1710	25 Nov 1710	25 Nov 1710–12 Jun 1711	
		7 Dec 1711–8 Jul 1712	8 Aug 1713
1713	12 Nov 1713	16 Feb–9 Jul 1714	
		1 Aug–25 Aug 1714	15 Jan 1715

*This was a Convention. The assembly declared itself a Parliament on 20 February 1690 and this declaration received the royal assent on 23 February 1689

1715	17 Mar 1715	17 Mar 1715–26 Jun 1716	
		20 Feb–15 Jul 1717	
		21 Nov 1717–21 Mar 1718	
		11 Nov 1718–18 Apr 1719	
		23 Nov 1719–11 Jun 1720	
		8 Dec 1720–29 Jul 1721	
		31 Jul–10 Aug 1721	
		19 Oct 1721–7 Mar 1722	10 Mar 1722
1722	10 May 1722	9 Oct 1722–27 May 1723	
		9 Jan–24 Apr 1724	
		12 Nov 1724–31 May 1725	
		20 Jan–24 May 1726	
		17 Jan–15 May 1727	
		27 Jun–17 Jul 1727	5 Aug 1727
1727	28 Nov 1727	23 Jan–28 May 1728	
		21 Jan–14 May 1729	
		13 Jan–15 May 1730	
		21 Jan–7 May 1731	
		13 Jan–1 Jun 1732	
		16 Jan–13 Jun 1733	
		17 Jan–16 Apr 1734	17 Apr 1734
1734	13 Jun 1734	14 Jan–15 May 1735	
		15 Jan–20 May 1736	
		1 Feb–21 Jun 1737	
		24 Jan–20 May 1738	
		1 Feb–14 Jun 1739	
		15 Nov 1739–29 Apr 1740	
		18 Nov 1740–25 Apr 1741	27 Apr 1741
1741	25 Jun 1741	1 Dec 1741–15 Jul 1742	
		16 Nov 1742–21 Apr 1743	
		1 Dec 1743–12 May 1744	
		27 Nov 1744–2 May 1745	
		17 Oct 1745–12 Aug 1746	
		18 Nov 1746–17 Jun 1747	18 Jun 1747
1747	13 Aug 1747	10 Nov 1747–13 May 1748	
		29 Nov 1748–13 Jun 1749	
		16 Nov 1749–12 Apr 1750	
		17 Jan–25 Jan 1751	
		14 Nov 1751–26 Mar 1752	
		11 Jan–7 Jun 1753	
		15 Nov 1753–6 Apr 1754	8 Apr 1754

1754   31 May 1754   31 May–5 Jun 1754
                            14 Nov 1754–25 Apr 1755
                            13 Nov 1755–27 May 1756
                             2 Dec 1756–4 Jul 1757
                             1 Dec 1757–20 Jun 1758
                            23 Nov 1758–2 Jun 1759
                            13 Nov 1759–22 May 1760
                            26 Oct 1760–29 Oct 1760
                            18 Nov 1760–19 Mar 1761   20 Mar 1761

COMPOSITION OF THE HOUSE

Period	England	Wales	Scotland	Ireland	County	Borough	Univ.	Total
1688–								
1707	489	24			92	417	4	513
1707–								
1800	489	24	45		122	432	4	558
1801–								
1826	489	24	45	100	186	467	5	658
1826–								
1832	489	24	45	100	188	465	5	658

Prior to 1707, the House of Commons returned 513 members, 489 from England and 24 from Wales. The counties returned 92 members, the boroughs 417 and the ancient universities 4.

During the period 1707–60, after the addition of the Scottish members, the House of Commons returned 558 members, representing 314 constituencies. The detailed breakdown of these figures was as follows:

England, 489 members, 245 constituencies:
   40   counties, returning 2 members each;
  196   boroughs, returning 2 members each;
    2   boroughs (London and the combined constituency of Weymouth and Melcombe Regis), returning 4 members each;
    5   boroughs (Abingdon, Banbury, Bewdley, Higham Ferrers and Monmouth), returning 1 member each;
    2   universities (Oxford and Cambridge) returning 2 members each.

Wales, 24 members, 24 constituencies:
  12   12 counties, returning 1 member each;
  12   boroughs, returning 1 member each.

Scotland, 45 members, 45 constituencies:
  27   counties, returning 1 member each;
   3   pairs of counties, 1 county in each pair alternating with the other in returning 1 member;

1   burgh (Edinburgh), returning 1 member;
14   groups of burghs, each returning 1 member.

This representation remained the same until 1800, when as a result of the Act of Union, total membership of the House of Commons increased to 658, with Ireland returning exactly 100 members.

HOUSE OF LORDS

CLERKS OF THE PARLIAMENTS

1660–91	John Browne	1716–40	William Cowper
1691–1716	Matthew Johnson	1740–88	Ashley Cowper

CLERK ASSISTANT

1660–64	John Throckmorton	1715–23	Matthew Johnson, ju
1664–82	John Walker, sen.	1724–52	James Merest
1682–1715	John Walker, jun.	1753–65	Joseph Wight

GENTLEMAN USHER OF THE BLACK ROD

1683	T. Duppa	1710	Sir W. Oldes
1694	Sir F. Sheppard	1747	Hon H. Bellenden
1698	Sir D. Mitchell	1761	Sir S. Robinson

YEOMAN USHER OF THE BLACK ROD

1660	J. Whynyard	1717	J. Incledon
1690	B. Coling	1754	R. Quarme
1702	J. Phillips	1787	R. Quarme
1709	D. Davis		

SERJEANT-AT-ARMS

1673	{ Sir G. Charnock	1713	C. Stone
	{ R. Charnock	1747	R. Jephson
1697	R. Persehouse	1789	W. Watson
1713	S. Goatley		

DEPUTY SERJEANT-AT-ARMS

By 1730	T. Hollinshead	by 1776	F. Macklay

COMPOSITION OF THE HOUSE

Date	Sovereign and regnal year	Remarks	Dukes	Marquises	Earls	Viscounts	Barons	Representing Scotland	Archbishops and Bishops	Total
1714	1 George I	After the Union with Scotland in 1707	23	2	74	11	67	16	26	219
1727	1 George II		31	1	71	15	62	16	26	222
1760	1 George III		25	1	81	12	63	16	26	224

SCOTTISH REPRESENTATIVE PEERS

The provisions for electing the Scottish representative peers were contained in the Scottish Union with England Act 1707 (1706, c. 7) and the Union with Scotland Act 1707 (6 Ann c. 78). Later legislation, in 1847 and 1851, introduced certain changes.

There were 16 Scottish representative peers, elected for the period of each Parliament, with by-elections held when necessary to fill such vacancies as occurred. Elections were held in Edinburgh, with peers entitled to vote either in person, or by proxy, or by sending a signed list. The Lord Clerk Register (or the Clerks of Session) acted as Returning Officers.

THE LORD CLERK REGISTER

1705–8	Sir James Murray
1708–14	E of Glasgow
1714–16	E of Ilay
1716	D of Montrose
1716–33	Ld Polwarth (E of Marchmont)
1733–9	E of Selkirk
1739–56	M of Lothian
1756–60	Alexander Hume Campbell
1760–8	E of Morton

ELECTIONS OF SCOTTISH REPRESENTATIVE PEERS

Date			General or by-election	Numbers of peers present
1708	17	Jun	G	57
1710	10	Nov	G	49
1712	14	Aug	B	32
1713	13	Jan	B	25
	8	Oct	G	36
1715	3	Mar	G	43
1716	28	Feb	B	18
1721	1	Jun	B	22
1722	21	Apr	G	42
	15	Aug	B	18
1723	13	Jun	B	13
1727	20	Sep	G	33
1730	17	Nov	B	23
1731	19	Feb	B	17
1732	28	Jan	B	17

1733	21	Sep	B	37
1734	4	Jun	G	60
1736	22	Oct	B	33
1737	14	Apr	B	21
1738	14	Mar	B	21
1739	22	Mar	B	20
1741	13	Jun	G	37
1742	30	Apr	B	24
1744	12	Oct	B	17
1747	1	Aug	G	33
1750	15	Mar	B	25
1752	9	Jul	B	26
	16	Nov	B	23
1754	21	May	G	36

Except for June 1734 (when the place was the Burgh Room) and for June 1741 (when the place was the Court of Exchequer), all elections took place in the Palace of Holyrood House. The Returning Officers were the two Clerks of Sessions.

GROWTH OF THE CONSTITUENCIES

Summary 1509–1707

	Counties	Boroughs	Universities	Progressive total
In existence in 1509	74	222		296
Henry VII				
Prerogative Charters		14		
Acts of Parliament	16	15		341
Edward VI				
Prerogative Charters		34		375
Mary I				
Prerogative Charters		23		398
Elizabeth I				
Prerogative Charters		62		460
James I				
Prerogative Charters		11		
Resolutions of the House of Commons		12	4	487
Charles I				
Resolutions of the House of Commons		20		507
Charles II				
Acts of Parliament	2			513
Prerogative Charters		2		513
James II				
Anne				
Union with Scotland	30	15		558

No further changes occurred until the Union with Ireland in 1800.

THE FRANCHISE

England and Wales   By a statute of 1430 (18 Hen. VI c.7), in the counties the voting qualification was the possession of freehold property valued for the land tax at 40 shillings per annum – the 40s freeholder. In the boroughs various qualifications applied. The main types were:

Scot and Lot (SL)   right of voting vested in inhabitant householders paying poor rate.
Householder (H)   also known as 'potwalloper' franchise. Right of voting vested in all inhabitant householders not receiving alms or poor relief.
Burgage (B)   franchise attached to property in the borough.
Corporation (C)   right of voting confined to the corporation.
Freeman (FM)   right of voting belonged to the freemen of the borough (in the City of London in the livery, rather than in the freemen as a whole).
Freeholder (FH)   right of voting lay with the freeholders.

Scotland   In the Scottish counties the franchise belonged to freeholders possessing land valued at 40s 'of old extent' or to owners of land rated at £400 Scots (c. £35 sterling). In Sutherland the vote also extended to tenants of the Earl of Sutherland. The Scottish boroughs, or burghs, were combined in groups for the purpose of electing MPs by a process of indirect election. Voting was vested in the small burgh councils.

CLASSIFICATION OF ENGLISH BOROUGHS, 1760

Electors	SL	H	B	C	FM	FH	Total
Over 5000	1	1			5		7
1001 to 5000	6	2			24	4	36
601 to 1000	7	5			9	1	22
301 to 600	10	1			13		24
101 to 300	8	5	10	1	11	1	36
51 to 100	4		10	2	5		21
50 or fewer	2		15	26	13		56
Total	38	14	35	29	80	6	202

THE CONSTITUENCIES, 1688–1760

ENGLISH COUNTIES

Constituency	MPs	Constituency	MPs
Bedfordshire	2	Lincolnshire	2
Berkshire	2	Middlesex	2
Buckinghamshire	2	Monmouthshire	2
Cambridgeshire	2	Norfolk	2
Cheshire	2	Northamptonshire	2
Cornwall	2	Northumberland	2
Cumberland	2	Nottinghamshire	2
Derbyshire	2	Oxfordshire	2
Devon	2	Rutland	2
Dorset	2	Shropshire	2
Durham	2	Somerset	2
Essex	2	Staffordshire	2
Gloucestershire	2	Suffolk	2
Hampshire	2	Surrey	2
Herefordshire	2	Sussex	2
Hertfordshire	2	Warwickshire	2
Huntingdonshire	2	Westmorland	2
Kent	2	Wiltshire	2
Lancashire	2	Worcestershire	2
Leicestershire	2	Yorkshire	2

ENGLISH BOROUGHS

Constituency	Type of seat	MPs
Abingdon	SL	1
Aldborough	SL	2
Aldeburgh	FM	2
Amersham	SL	2
Andover	C	2
Appleby	B	2
Arundel	SL	2
Ashburton	B	2
Aylesbury	H	2
Banbury	C	1
Barnstaple	FM	2
Bath	C	2

Constituency	Type of seat	MPs
Bedford	FM	2
Bere Alston	B	2
Berwick-on-Tweed	FM	2
Beverley	FM	2
Bewdley	FM	1
Bishop's Castle	FM	2
Bletchingly	B	2
Bodmin	C	2
Boroughbridge	B	2
Bossiney	FM	2
Boston	FM	2
Brackley	C	2
Bramber	B	2
Bridgnorth	FM	2
Bridgwater	SL	2
Bridport	SL	2
Bristol	FM	2
Buckingham	C	2
Bury St Edmunds	C	2
Callington	SL	2
Calne	C	2
Cambridge	FM	2
Camelford	FM	2
Canterbury	FM	2
Carlisle	FM	2
Castle Rising	FM	2
Chester	FM	2
Chichester	SL	2
Chippenham	B	2
Chipping Wycombe	FM	2
Christchurch	C	2
Cirencester	H	2
Clitheroe	B	2
Cockermouth	B	2
Colchester	FM	2
Corfe Castle	SL	2
Coventry	FM	2
Cricklade	FH	2
Dartmouth	FM	2
Derby	FM	2
Devizes	C	2

Constituency	Type of seat	MPs
Dorchester	SL	2
Dover	FM	2
Downton	B	2
Droitwich	C	2
Dunwich	FM	2
Durham	FM	2
East Grinstead	B	2
East Looe	FM	2
East Retford	FM	2
Evesham	FM	2
Exeter	FM	2
Eye	SL	2
Fowey	SL	2
Gatton	SL	2
Gloucester	FM	2
Grampound	FM	2
Grantham	FM	2
Great Bedwyn	B	2
Great Grimsby	FM	2
Great Marlow	SL	2
Great Yarmouth	FM	2
Guildford	FM	2
Harwich	C	2
Haslemere	FH	2
Hastings	FM	2
Hedon	FM	2
Helston	C	2
Hereford	FM	2
Hertford	FM	2
Heytesbury	B	2
Higham Ferrers	FM	1
Hindon	H	2
Honiton	H	2
Horsham	B	2
Huntingdon	FM	2
Hythe	FM	2
Ilchester	H	2
Ipswich	FM	2
King's Lynn	FM	2
Kingston-upon-Hull	FM	2
Knaresborough	B	2

Constituency	Type of seat	MPs
Lancaster	FM	2
Launceston	FM	2
Leicester	FM	2
Leominster	SL	2
Lewes	SL	2
Lichfield	FM	2
Lincoln	FM	2
Liskeard	FM	2
Liverpool	FM	2
London	FM	4
Lostwithiel	C	2
Ludgershall	FH	2
Ludlow	FM	2
Lyme Regis	FM	2
Lymington	FM	2
Maidstone	FM	2
Maldon	FM	2
Malmesbury	C	2
Malton	B	2
Marlborough	C	2
Midhurst	B	2
Milborne Port	SL	2
Minehead	H	2
Mitchell	SL	2
Monmouth	FM	1
Morpeth	FM	2
Newark	SL	2
Newcastle-under-Lyme	FM	2
Newcastle-upon-Tyne	FM	2
Newport	B	2
Newport (I of W)	C	2
New Romney	C	2
New Shoreham	SL	2
Newton	C	2
Newtown (I of W)	B	2
New Windsor	SL	2
New Woodstock	FM	2
Northallerton	B	2
Northampton	H	2
Norwich	FM	2
Nottingham	FM	2

Constituency	Type of seat	MPs
Okehampton	FM	2
Old Sarum	B	2
Orford	FM	2
Oxford	FM	2
Penryn	SL	2
Peterborough	SL	2
Petersfield	B	2
Plymouth	FM	2
Plympton Erle	FM	2
Pontefract	B	2
Poole	FM	2
Portsmouth	FM	2
Preston	H	2
Queensborough	FM	2
Reading	SL	2
Reigate	FH	2
Richmond	B	2
Ripon	B	2
Rochester	FM	2
Rye	FM	2
St Albans	FM	2
St Germans	H	2
St Ives	SL	2
St Mawes	FM	2
Salisbury	C	2
Saltash	C	2
Sandwich	FM	2
Scarborough	C	2
Seaford	SL	2
Shaftesbury	SL	2
Southampton	FM	2
Southwark	SL	2
Stafford	FM	2
Stamford	SL	2
Steyning	SL	2
Stockbridge	SL	2
Sudbury	FM	2
Tamworth	SL	2
Taunton	H	2
Tavistock	FH	2
Tewkesbury	FM	2

Constituency	Type of seat	MPs
Thetford	C	2
Thirsk	B	2
Tiverton	C	2
Totnes	FM	2
Tregony	H	2
Truro	C	2
Wallingford	SL	2
Wareham	SL	2
Warwick	SL	2
Wells	FM	2
Wembley	B	2
Wendover	H	2
Wenlock	FM	2
Westbury	B	2
West Looe	FM	2
Weymouth and Melcombe Regis	FH	4
Whitchurch	B	2
Wigan	FM	2
Wilton	C	2
Winchelsea	FM	2
Winchester	FM	2
Wootton Bassett	SL	2
Worcester	FN	2
Yarmouth (I of W)	C	2
York	FM	2

UNIVERSITIES

	MPs
Cambridge	2
Oxford	2

WELSH COUNTIES

Anglesey	1
Breconshire	1
Cardiganshire	1
Carmarthenshire	1
Carnarvonshire	1

Denbighshire	1
Flintshire	1
Glamorganshire	1
Merionethshire	1
Montgomeryshire	1
Pembrokeshire	1
Radnorshire	1

WELSH BOROUGHS

Constituency	Type of seat	MPs
Beaumaris	C	1
Brecon	FM	1
Cardiff Boroughs	FM	1
Cardigan Boroughs	FM	1
Carmarthen	FM	1
Carnarvon Boroughs	FM	1
Denbigh Boroughs	FM	1
Flint Boroughs	SL	1
Haverfordwest	FM	1
Montgomery	FM	1
New Radnor Boroughs	FM	1
Pembroke Boroughs	FM	1

SCOTTISH COUNTIES

Constituency	MPs		
Aberdeenshire	1	Lanarkshire	1
Argyllshire	1	Linlithgowshire	1
Ayrshire	1	Orkney and Shetland	1
Banffshire	1	Peebleshire	1
Berwickshire	1	Perthshire	1
Dumfriesshire	1	Renfrewshire	1
Dunbartonshire	1	Ross-shire	1
Edinburghshire	1	Roxburghshire	1
Elginshire	1	Selkirkshire	1
Fife	1	Stirlingshire	1
Forfarshire	1	Sutherland	1
Haddingtonshire	1	Wigtownshire	1
Inverness-shire	1		
Kincardineshire	1	Buteshire ⎫	1
Kirkcudbright Stewartry	1	Caithness ⎭ *	1

Clackmannanshire ⎱ *	1	Dumfries Burghs	1
Kinross-shire ⎰	1	Dysart Burghs	1
		Edinburgh	1
Nairnshire ⎱ *	1	Elgin Burghs	1
Cromartyshire ⎰	1	Glasgow Burghs	1
		Haddington Burghs	1
		Inverness Burghs	1
SCOTTISH BURGHS†		Linlithgow Burghs	1
		Perth Burghs	1
Aberdeen Burghs	1	Stirling Burghs	1
Anstruther Easter Burghs	1	Tain Burghs	1
Ayr Burghs	1	Wigtown Burghs	1

DISBURSEMENT OF SECRET SERVICE MONEY, 1728–60

	£		
1728	45 744	1745	24 000
1729	57 880	1746	22 000
1730	53 391	1747	41 000
1731	63 918	1748	33 000
1732	73 781	1749	38 000
1733	87 470	1750	29 000
1734	117 140	1751	32 000
1735	66 630	1752	40 000
1736	95 313	1753	35 000
1737	61 999	1754	50 000
1738	72 828	1755	40 000
1739	74 250	1756	38 000
1740	80 116	1757	50 000
1741	80 977	1758	40 000
1742	64 949	1759	30 000
1743	54 300	1760	40 000
1744	34 970		

Source L. B. Namier, *The Structure of Politics at the Accession of George III* (London, 1929), p. 242.

*In alternate Parliaments one of each pair of counties was represented.

†*An indirect system of election operated in all the Scottish burghs except Edinburgh, where the 33 members of the Town Council elected one MP directly. In the other burghs, the Town Councils nominated one delegate each, a majority of electors in each district electing one MP.

6 ELECTIONS

ELECTIONS AND ELECTION RESULTS, 1689–1761

Introduction

An accurate return of election results in this period is fraught with difficulty. It must be noted at the outset that no general election in this period was in fact general, the number of contests ranging from high points such as 1710 and 1722 to the much lower numbers for elections such as 1747 and 1761 (see pp. 118–19). Even at the most heavily contested elections, a very large number of seats remained uncontested. Moreover, in spite of strong party feeling at some points in this period, notably in the reign of Queen Anne, the classification of MPs by party labels is a matter of some contention. Hence, unlike a modern election where almost all seats are contested by candidates standing under a clear party label, this period has both a fluctuating number of contests and uncertain party allegiances. None the less, scholars have attempted to estimate in general terms both the results of the contests that took place at elections and the resulting impact upon representation in the House of Commons. It should be noted that the result of an election was only one factor in determining the composition of the House of Commons: challenges on election petitions subsequent to an election, the allegiance of MPs returned from uncontested seats, and shifts in allegiance at, or shortly following, the sitting of a new Parliament must also be taken into consideration. As a result, allegiance at the opening of a session did not necessarily reflect solely or even primarily the outcome of the last general election. Historians have therefore turned both to contemporary estimates of support and to division lists for estimates of groupings at the opening of a new parliament. Neither source, however, supplies completely reliable indications of allegiance and a degree of imprecision has to be accepted in any estimates so derived. Finally, the role and definition of political groupings and the importance of party allegiance remains a subject of much debate. 'Court and Country' divisions and Namierite analysis of political activity have considerably modified consideration of the importance of party labels for much of this period, although these views have also been subject to criticisms in their turn. The following summary of elections and their results must be viewed in the light of these qualifications.

1689

In the aftermath of the flight of James II, elections were called in January 1689 for the 'Convention Parliament'. Contests took place in nine counties

111

and forty-one boroughs. Although party divisions were not expressed strongly in the mood of national emergency and *de facto* interregnum, Parliament began to divide on partisan issues after the vesting of the throne in William and Mary. One hundred and fifty-one 'hard core' Tories have been identified from the vote against the throne being declared vacant on 5 February 1689, while the 174 members who voted in January 1690 for the Sacheverell clause have been identified as committed Whigs. Nearly 200 members, new and previously elected, can be considered as uncommitted in the Commons as a whole.

1690

The 'Convention Parliament' was prorogued on 27 January 1690 and dissolved ten days later because of William's dissatisfaction with the Whigs' attempt to monopolise office and the Tories' offer of a more favourable settlement of the Revenue. In the absence of division lists for the period 1690–6 a precise delineation of election results is not possible, but there were notable losses by the Whigs and early divisions saw substantial Tory majorities in the Commons, although these were to be eroded in the course of the Parliament with the rise of the Whig 'Junto'.

1695

William's decision to dissolve Parliament was taken before he left England to conduct the military campaigns on the Continent which concluded in the fall of Namur. The election results in the autumn saw significant Tory losses, including six in the City of London and in Westminster, although it was not until early 1696 that the various Whig factions were able to establish a clear majority in the House of Commons.

1698

An election was due in the summer of 1698 under the provisions of the Triennial Act. Parliament was prorogued on 5 July and dissolved two days later, elections taking place in July and August. Analysis of the election results suggests that the Whig 'Junto' lost its majority in the Commons with Tory candidates making significant gains in both county and borough seats.

1700

The instability of the existing Ministry following the election of 1698 led to a major reconstruction of the administration in the autumn of 1700, creating a virtually Tory Ministry with only one Whig remaining in an important office. Dissolution of Parliament did not take place for a further six weeks, partly as a result of the news of the death of Charles II of Spain and its diplomatic repercussions. Eventually Parliament was dissolved on 19

December 1700. The resulting election led to substantial Tory gains with at least thirty former Whigs failing to be returned. Although not in itself sufficient to ensure a Tory majority in the Commons, subsequent divisions showed that the new Parliament contained a significant majority prepared to support the Tories.

1701

As early as September 1701 William III sought to go to the country to obtain a more favourable House of Commons, although the dissolution was not proclaimed until 11 November. In the subsequent election, although the Tories lost seats and some prominent members, the Whig gain was sufficiently small to leave both sides claiming a majority. The Whigs estimated a gain of 30 seats, but modern research has estimated that the new Parliament still contained a nominal Tory majority of 289 Tories to 224 Whigs. After Parliament met, however, the Tory majority was decreased by William's movement towards the Whigs and poor attendance on the part of Tory members. The first divisions were extremely close, the Speakership being carried for the Whigs by only four votes. By the end of February 1702, the Whigs were generally able to obtain a somewhat precarious majority in the divisions with uncommitted members taking the Whig side. Further clarification of the party situation was prevented by the death of William on 8 March 1702.

1702

The formation of a new administration containing many Tories, by Queen Anne, was followed by a general election in the summer, announced by a dissolution on 3 July. The election witnessed at least 87 contests in England and Wales. The election has been estimated at returning a Tory majority of over 130 seats in the new Parliament, reflected in Tory majorities of that order in the divisions of the autumn.

1705

Parliament was prorogued on 14 March 1705 and a dissolution followed shortly under the provisions of the Triennial Act. The election which followed was one of the most bitterly fought of the eighteenth century with over 100 contests in England alone, including 26 counties. According to modern calculations 267 Tories and 246 Whigs were returned, yielding a Whig gain of 60 seats over the previous administration.

1708

The election of 1708 marked the first election for the Parliament of Great Britain following the Act of Union with Scotland, signed the previous year, which entitled 45 Scottish MPs to sit at Westminster. Parliament was prorogued on 1 April and the elections took place in May. It has been suggested that the Whigs gained some 30 seats in England and Wales, producing 291 Whigs and 222 Tories returned. With most of the new Scottish MPs also voting in their favour, the Whigs were able to go on to win most of the votes on election petitions. Sunderland declared it 'the most Whig Parliament [there] has been since the Revolution'.

1710

Following a widespread replacement of the Whig administration in the spring and summer of 1710 with the filling of most of the important ministerial posts by Tories, and a strong tide of anti-Whig feeling in the country, the general election in the autumn produced widespread Tory gains, with contemporary estimates of at least two Tories elected for every Whig returned. Modern estimates suggest that 332 Tories and 181 Whigs were returned for England and Wales, with a Whig majority in Scotland somewhat mitigating the Tory landslide.

1713

The general election which took place in August and September 1713 occurred when both public opinion and the influence of the Court were still predisposed in favour of the Tories, resulting in a large Tory majority in England and Wales only somewhat diminished by a clear Whig majority in Scotland. *The History of Parliament* provides the following breakdown of results:

	Tories	Whigs
England	323	166
Wales	21	3
Scotland	14	31
Total	358	200

Decisions on election petitions, decided overwhelmingly in favour of the Tories, increased the nominal Tory majority to an estimated 372 Tories as opposed to 185 Whigs. This majority, however, proved less conclusive than it appeared as Parliament did not meet to conduct serious business until almost six months later on 2 March 1714, when parliamentary allegiance was beginning to be affected by the question of the Hanoverian succession, much reducing the effective Tory strength in divisions in the House of Commons.

1715

By the time of the death of Queen Anne on 1 August 1714, the Hanoverian succession had been largely secured by pro-Hanoverian appointments to the

Privy Council. Parliament, which had been prorogued on 9 July 1714, met again on 5 August, but was prorogued once more on 25 August awaiting a fresh election, meeting again only to transact the formal business of further prorogation. The dismissal of Bolingbroke at the end of August and George I's arrival in the country on 19 September was followed by the construction of a Whig administration. When Parliament was formally dissolved in January 1715 the election took place in a climate which was flowing strongly against the Tories, who were being widely associated by Whig propaganda as opposing the Protestant succession and as betrayers of British policy interests in the Treaty of Utrecht. The election resulted in an almost complete reversal of party fortunes in 1713. *The History of Parliament* gives the following post-election returns:

	Tories	Whigs
England	195	294
Wales	15	9
Scotland	7	38
Total	217	341

Moreover, as was customary, election petitions were decided in favour of the majority party: of 46 Tory and 41 Whig petitions, no Tory petition was successful but 31 Tories were unseated. As a result, post-petition party strength altered to 372 Whigs to 186 Tories.

1722

Under the provisions of the Septennial Act passed in 1716, an election was due early in 1722 and Parliament was dissolved on 10 March. Against the background of the South Sea scandal and Walpole's increasing supremacy in the House of Commons, the Tories were eclipsed, making the election in some areas, like Scotland, more of a contest between rival groups of Whigs. In all there were more than 150 contests, a larger number than at any other election in the period 1688–1760 and at least 30 more than in 1715. Most of the returns for the English boroughs came in by the end of March, with the results for the English counties, Cornwall, Wales, and Scotland coming in during April.

The results were 379 Whigs returned against 178 Tories, representing a Whig gain of almost 40 seats on the result in 1715. After election petitions had been heard the composition of the House of Commons has been estimated at 389 Whigs to 169 Tories.

1727

The general election which followed the death of George I witnessed 118 contests. Walpole, having secured the continuity of his administration after a brief period of uncertainty, was able to erode further the number of his opponents. Wales which had produced a steady Tory majority hitherto, returned a Whig majority of 14 members, while the English boroughs moved ever more firmly under Whig control. The returns produced 427 Whigs and 131 Tories. Sixty-one petitions followed the elections, 24 of which were heard, resulting in three further Whig gains. The resulting House of Commons therefore consisted of 415 Whig ministerialists, an opposition Whig group of 15 led by Pulteney, and 128 Tories, a nominal majority of 272.

1734

The general election of 1734, called under the provisions of the Septennial Act, took place against the recent background of Walpole's controversial Excise Bill, which he had been forced to withdraw in April of the previous year in the face of bitter opposition and falling majorities. At the dissolution of Parliament in April 1734 the House of Commons has been estimated at containing 342 Whig supporters of the administration, 86 opposition Whigs, and 130 Tories, representing a government majority of 126. The election witnessed 135 contests and was fiercely contested with some Tory successes in the English counties. The election returns were as follows:

Ministerial Whigs	326
Opposition Whigs	83
Tories	149

The government made a further four gains on election petitions, producing a House of Commons consisting of 330 ministerial supporters, 83 opposition Whigs, and 145 Tories.

1741

Parliament was dissolved on 27 April 1741. Following the increasing difficulties of Walpole's administration, the government majority had fallen to around 50 seats, reflecting a considerable defection of ministerial supporters to the ranks of the opposition. The elections witnessed 94 contests but were not fought in a particularly excitable atmosphere. The administration lost seats in two areas of traditional support, Scotland, where the influence of the Duke of Argyll was committed against it, and in Cornwall where the Prince of Wales lent his support to the opposition. As a result, the Ministry lost 21 seats in these two areas alone. The results produced were as follows:

Ministerial Whigs	286
Opposition Whigs	31
Tories	136

Five seats were left unfilled as a result of double returns, leaving a much reduced theoretical majority for the administration of 19.

However, when Parliament met on 1 December 1741, some 23 seats were vacant by death and double returns, reducing the nominal government majority still further to 16 (276 government supporters, 124 opposition Whigs, and 135 Tories). In January and February 1742 the combined opposition sought further to reduce the government majority by contesting election returns. After several close votes, including a number of ministerial defeats, Walpole resigned after losing the determination of the election of Chippenham by 16 votes (241 to 225) on 2 February 1742.

1747

Parliament was dissolved on 18 June 1747. The re-establishment of the Pelham administration, following the unsuccessful attempt by Bath and Granville to form a new administration in February 1746, left a strong government majority of around 160. In a relatively quiet election with only 60 contests, the administration was able to exercise more of the customary influence in places such as Scotland and Cornwall than Walpole had been able to do in 1741. As a result the number of opposition MPs returned for Scotland was reduced from 26 to 10 (out of 45) and in Cornwall from 29 to 19 compared with 1741. Moreover, the seats in the metropolitan area which had often proved a centre of opposition support were largely taken by the ministry. The general election resulted in the following return:

Ministerial Whigs	338
Opposition Whigs	97
Tories	117

Election petitions resulted in the overturn of seven opposition MPs and the government was also successful in six double returns, giving a total when Parliament met of 351 ministerial supporters, 92 opposition Whigs, and 115 Tories, a majority of 144.

1754

Henry Pelham died on 6 March 1754 while preparations were in train for a general election under the provisions of the Septennial Act. At least 62 constituencies went to the poll in 1754 with the influence of the Duke of Newcastle organising the government interest. According to a contemporary listing, the government was estimated to have gained a further 11 seats. The returns were as follows:

Government	368
Opposition Whigs	42
Tories	106
Doubtful	26

1761

Parliament was dissolved on 20 March 1761 and elections were held in circumstances which were somewhat unusual in the eighteenth century, in that there was no organised opposition in the House of Commons and, coming after the accession of George III, under his instructions that no government money should be used to assist the election of the administration's supporters. In the event, the election saw only 53 contests, the lowest number in the period 1688–1761. The election of 113 Tories, including 21 new members, scarcely diminished a substantial government majority.

Sources The compilation of the above summary owes an enormous debt to the pioneering efforts of the *History of Parliament* project, notably the volumes edited by R. Sedgewick, *The History of Parliament: The House of Commons, 1715–1754* (OUP, 1970) and Sir Lewis Namier and John Brooke, *The History of Parliament: The House of Commons, 1754–1790* (HMSO, 1964). Valuable additional information for the period prior to 1715 has been obtained from W. A. Speck, *Tory and Whig: The Struggle in the Constituencies, 1701–1715* (London, 1970) and B. W. Hill, *The Growth of Parliamentary Parties, 1689–1742* (London, 1976) and *British Parliamentary Parties, 1742–1832* (London, 1985).

GENERAL ELECTIONS, 1701–1761: NUMBER OF CONTESTS

There is no completely reliable return of the number of contests available for this period. In general, this list follows the standard authorities, primarily the volumes of the *History of Parliament* for 1715–54 and 1754–90. Until the volumes dealing with the period prior to 1715 are complete it is not possible to provide an equivalent guide to the period 1688–1715. However, this list is supplemented for 1701 to 1715 by the valuable additional material contained in J. Cannon, *Parliamentary Reform, 1642–1832* (Cambridge, 1973), Appendix 3, and W. A. Speck, *Tory and Whig: The Struggle in the Constituencies* (London, 1970), Appendix E.

	England	Wales	Scotland
1701	89 (18)	2	
1702	85 (18)	2	
1705	108 (26)	2	
1708	92 (14)	5	NA
1710	127 (23)	4	NA
1713	97 (12)	3	NA
1715	111 (17)	8	9

1722	127 (17)	9	20
1727	96 (12)	13	9
1734	107 (13)	8	20
1741	65 (4)	11	18
1747	51 (3)	2	7
1754	60 (5)	4	2^1
1761	46 (4)	2	6

Notes: figures in brackets denote county contests
^{1} Scottish counties only
NA Not Available

7 RELIGION

THE ANGLICAN CHURCH

1688   Archbishop Sancroft and six Bishops protest against James II's Delaration of Indulgence, suspending laws against Catholics and dissenters. Tried for seditious libel, but acquitted.

1689   Toleration Act allows dissenters to worship publicly on taking an oath and permits Quakers to affirm, but excludes Catholics and Unitarians. Attempt to alter the Prayer Book in order to attract the dissenters back to the Church of England fails owing to opposition of Convocation. Archbishop Sancroft, five Bishops and more than 400 clergy, the non-jurors, refuse to take oaths of supremacy and allegiance to William and Mary and are deprived of their livings.

1695   Locke's *Reasonableness of Christianity* published.

1698   The Society for Promoting Christian Knowledge is founded.

1701   Mission branch of the Society for Promoting Christian Knowledge is founded as the Society for the Propagation of the Gospel.

1703   Bill to prevent Occasional Conformity passes the House of Commons but is rejected by the Lords.

1704   Queen Anne's Bounty: Queen Anne surrenders the claim of the throne to first fruits and tenths to endow poorer clergy.

1707   Act of Security of Church of England excludes Presbyterians from holding office in England.

1709   Dr Sacheverell impeached after preaching against toleration of dissenters and denouncing the Whig Ministers as traitors to the Church.

1710   Trial of Dr Sacheverell at Westminster Hall leads to rioting in London and attacks on dissenting chapels. Lords order Sacheverell's sermon to be burnt and silence him for three years.

1711   Occasional Conformity Act passed against Protestant dissenters. Parliament votes £350000 to build 52 churches in London.

1713   Bishop Gibson produces the *Codex Juris Ecclesiastici Anglicani*, a comprehensive study of the legal rights and duties of the English clergy and of the constitution of the Church.

1714 Schism Act introduced, forbidding nonconformists to teach.

1716 Negotiations between non-jurors and Greek Church for reunion.

1717 Convocation prorogued as a consequence of its censure of Hoadly, Bishop of Bangor, for his sermon declaring against tests of orthodoxy. Convocation does not reassemble again until 1852. Hoadly replies to the censure and 'Bangorian controversy' ensues.

1719 Repeal of Occasional Conformity and Schism Acts.

1723 Francis Atterbury, Bishop of Rochester, exiled for part in pro-Jacobite plot.

1727 First annual Indemnity Act introduced to cover breaches of the Test Act.

1729 John Wesley, junior Fellow of Lincoln College, Oxford, becomes leader of a strict religious society, dubbed Methodists.

1730 Tindal's *Christianity As Old As the Creation* declared that Christ merely confirmed the law revealed by the light of Nature.

1733 Hoadly's *Plain Account of the Lord's Supper*, describing the ceremony as purely memorial, attacked.

1736 Warburton's *Alliance of Church and State* argues for the necessity of an Established church and a test on dissenters.

1739 George Whitefield starts open-air preaching near Bristol.

1745 Many of the non-jurors implicated in the Jacobite rebellion.

1746 SPCK produces Welsh Bible and Prayer Book.

1749 George Whitefield becomes chaplain to Lady Huntingdon.

1753 Lord Hardwick's Marriage Act: clergy to be heavily punished for performing marriage ceremonies without previous publication of banns or production of licence.

1757 Publication of Hume's *Natural History of Religion*.

REVENUES FROM BISHOPRICS, 1760

See	Revenue p.a.
Canterbury	£7000
Durham	£6000
Winchester	£5000
York	£4500

London	£4000
Ely	£3400
Worcester	£3000
Salisbury	£3000
Oxford	£500 (+ £1800)
Norwich	£2000
Bath and Wells	£2000
Bristol	£450 (+ £1150)
Exeter	£1500
Chester	£900 (+ £600)
Rochester	£600 (+ £900)
Lincoln	£1500
Lichfield and Coventry	£1400
St Asaph	£1400
Bangor	£1400
Chichester	£1400
Carlisle	£1300
Hereford	£1200
Peterborough	£1000
Llandaff	£500 (+ £450)
Gloucester	£900 (+ rich Durham prebend)
St Davids	£900 (+ two livings)

Source   A list of the Archbishops, Bishops, Deans and Prebendaries in England and Wales in His Majesty's Gift, with the Reputed Yearly Value of Their Respective Dignities (1762)

ARCHBISHOPS AND BISHOPS

PROVINCE OF CANTERBURY: ENGLAND

Canterbury

1678	William Sancroft	1737	John Potter
1691	John Tillotson	1747	Thomas Herring
1695	Thomas Tenison	1757	Matthew Hutton
1716	William Wake	1758	Thomas Secker

London

1676	Henry Compton	1723	Edmund Gibson
1714	John Robinson	1748	Thomas Sherlock

Winchester

1684	Peter Mew(s)	1723	Richard Willis
1707	Jonathan Trelawney	1734	Benjamin Hoadly
1721	Charles Trimnell		

Bath and Wells

1685	Thomas Ken(n)	1727	John Wayne
1691	Richard Kidder	1743	Edward Willes
1704	George Hooper		

Bristol

1685	Jonathan Trelawney	1733	Charles Cecil
1689	Gilbert Ironside	1735	Thomas Secker
1691	John Hall	1737	Thomas Gooch
1710	John Robinson	1738	Joseph Butler
1714	George Smalridge	1750	John Conybeare
1719	Hugh Boulter	1756	John Hume
1724	William Bradshaw	1758	Philip Yonge

Chichester

1685	John Lake	1722	Thomas Bowers
1689	Simon Patrick	1724	Edward Waddington
1691	Robert Grove	1731	Francis Hare
1696	John Williams	1740	Matthias Mawson
1709	Thomas Manningham	1754	William Ashburnham

Ely

1684	Francis Turner	1723	Thomas Greene
1691	Simon Patrick	1738	Robert Butts
1707	John Moore	1748	Thomas Gooch
1714	William Fleetwood	1754	Matthias Mawson

Exeter

1689	Jonathan Trelawney	1724	Stephen Weston
1708	Offspring Blackall	1742	Nicholas Claget
1717	Lancelot Blackburn	1747	George Lavington

Gloucester

1681	Robert Frampton	1731	Elias Sydall
1691	Edward Fowler	1735	Martin Benson
1715	Richard Willis	1752	James Johnson
1721	Joseph Wilcocks	1760	Williams Warburton

Hereford

1662	Herbert Croft	1721	Benjamin Hoadly
1691	Gilbert Ironside	1724	Henry Egerton
1701	Humphrey Humphries	1746	James Beauclerk
1713	Philip Bisse		

Lichfield

1671	Thomas Wood	1717	Edward Chandler
1692	William Lloyd	1731	Richard Smalbroke
1699	John Hough	1750	Frederick Cornwallis

Lincoln

1675	Thomas Barlow	1716	Edmund Gibson
1692	Thomas Tenison	1723	Richard Reynolds
1695	James Gardiner	1744	John Thomas
1705	William Wake		

Norwich

1685	William Lloyd	1727	William Baker
1691	John Moore	1733	Robert Butts
1708	Charles Trimnell	1738	Thomas Gooch
1721	Thomas Green	1748	Samuel Lisle
1723	John Leng	1749	Thomas Hayter

Oxford

1688	Timothy Hall	1715	John Potter
1690	John Hough	1737	Thomas Secker
1699	William Talbot	1758	John Hume

Peterborough

1685	Thomas White	1729	Robert Clavering
1691	Richard Cumberland	1747	John Thomas
1718	White Kennett	1757	Richard Terrick

Rochester

1684	Thomas Sprat	1731	Joseph Wilcocks
1713	Francis Atterbury	1756	Zachary Pearce
1723	Samuel Bradford		

Salisbury

1667	Seth Ward	1723	Benjamin Hoadly
1689	Gilbert Burnet	1734	Thomas Sherlock
1715	William Talbot	1748	John Gilbert
1721	Richard Willis	1757	John Thomas

Worcester

1683	William Thomas	1717	John Hough
1689	Edward Stillingfleet	1743	Isaac Maddox
1699	William Lloyd	1759	James Johnson

PROVINCE OF CANTERBURY: WALES

Bangor

1673	Humphrey Lloyd	1723	William Baker
1689	Humphrey Humphries	1728	Thomas Sherlock
1702	John Evans	1734	Charles Cecil
1716	Benjamin Hoadly	1738	Thomas Herring
1722	Richard Reynolds	1743	Matthew Hutton

1748   Zachary Pearce
1756   John Egerton

Llandaff

1679	William Beaw	1739	Matthias Mawson
1706	John Tyler	1740	John Gilbert
1724	Robert Clavering	1749	Edward Cressett
1729	John Harris	1755	Richard Newcome

St Asaph
1680   William Lloyd
1692   Edward Jones
1703   George Hooper
1704   William Beveridge
1708   William Fleetwood
1715   John Wynne
1727   Francis Hare
1732   Thomas Tanner
1736   Isaac Maddox
1743   John Thomas (elected December 1743 but translated before
        consecration)
1744   Samuel Lisle
1748   Robert Hay Drummond

St David's

1687	Thomas Watson	1731	Elias Sydall
	[vacant 1699–1705]	1732	Nicholas Claggett
1705	George Bull	1743	Edward Willes
1710	Philip Bisse	1744	Richard Trevor
1713	Adam Ottley	1753	Anthony Ellis
1724	Richard Smallbrooke		

PROVINCE OF YORK

York

1688	Thomas Lamplugh	1743	Thomas Herring
1691	John Sharp	1747	Matthew Hutton
1714	William Dawes	1757	John Gilbert
1724	Lancelot Blackburn		

Durham

1674	Nathaniel Crew	1750	Joseph Butler
1721	William Talbot	1752	Richard Trevor
1730	Edward Chandler		

Carlisle

1684	Thomas Smith	1723	John Waugh
1702	William Nicolson	1735	George Fleming
1718	Samuel Bradford	1747	Richard Osbaldeston

Chester

1686	Thomas Cartwright	1714	Francis Gastrell
1689	Nicholas Stratford	1726	Samuel Peploe
1708	William Dawes	1752	Edmund Keene

Sodor and Man

1684	Baptist Levinz
1698	Thomas Wilson
1755	Mark Kildesley

SCOTLAND

(Although episcopal government in the Church of Scotland was abolished in 1689, some bishops continued to exercise their functions; dates of the death of Bishops are given in parentheses).

Aberdeen
1682   George Haliburton (d. 1715)

Argyll
1688   Alexander Monro (not consecrated; d. 1698)

Brechin
1684   James Drummond (d. 1695)

Caithness
1680   Andrew Wood (d. 1695)

Dunblane
1684   Robert Douglas (d. 1716)

Dunkeld
1686   John Hamilton (d. 1689)

Edinburgh
1687   Alexander Rose (d. 1720)

Galloway
1688   John Gordon (d. 1726)

Glasgow
1687   John Paterson (d. 1708)

The Isles
1680   Archibald Graham (or MacIlvernock), (d. 1702)

Moray
1688   William Hay (d. 1707)

Orkney
1688   Andrew Bruce (d. 1699)

Ross
1696   James Ramsay (d. 1696)

St Andrews
1684   Arthur Rose (d. 1704)

Note: dates given are those of consecration or, in the case of translation from another see, confirmation of new appointment.

SCOTLAND

1688   News of William III's landing leads to the beginning of restoration of Presbyterianism.

1689   Episcopal clergy ejected and Presbyterianism restored. All acts supporting episcopacy rescinded and episcopacy abolished, though some of the Scottish Bishops perpetuate themselves and are still strongly supported in the east and north-east.

1690   Lay patronage abolished and Act of Supremacy rescinded. Ejected ministers restored and General Assembly meets.

1695   First Catholic Bishop appointed for Scotland.

1698   Aikenhead executed for blasphemy at Edinburgh.

1700   Estimate that out of 900 parishes, ministers in 165 adhered to the Episcopal Church.

1707   Act of Union gives full rights to the Presbyterian Church of Scotland.

1711   Greenshields, an Episcopalian, is condemned by the Court of Session for using the English liturgy in Edinburgh, but the decision reversed by the House of Lords.

1712   Toleration Act for Scotland. Right of nominating ministers restored to laymen, unless Roman Catholics, thereby depriving kirk sessions of the right of electing ministers. Strict Presbyterians refuse to recognise the Act restoring lay patronage.

1725   'Holy Bounty' granted to protestantise the Highlands.

1730   Glas attacks the civil establishment of the Church and forms the Glassite Sect, later developed by his son-in-law Sandeman.

1733   Secession from Church of Scotland led by Ebenezer Erskine in protest at lay patronage, the growth of toleration, and the threatened abolition of penal statutes against witchcraft.

1746   Following the Jacobite rebellion, the Scottish episcopal clergy are persecuted. Meetings of more than five are forbidden; public services are banned and made illegal to have churches or chapels. Some clergy resign their orders and others go into exile.

1747   Erskine's secession Church splits into Burghers, led by Erskine, and anti-Burghers.

1752   A compromise reached on lay patronage; presbytery could satisfy itself on life, learning and doctrine of patron's nominee.

PROTESTANT DISSENTERS

1688   James II orders a Declaration of Indulgence, suspending laws against Catholics and dissenters, to be read in all churches.

1689   Toleration Act allows dissenters to worship publicly on taking an oath, and permits Quakers to affirm, but excludes both Catholics and Unitarians. Protestant dissenters allowed to build chapels. Attempts to alter the Prayer Book to attract the dissenters back to the Church fails owing to opposition of Convocation.

1694   George Fox's *Journal* published.

1696   Toland's *Christianity not Mysterious* founding the Deist movement in England is burnt by the public hangman.

1697   Lord Mayor of London, a dissenter, openly practices Occasional Conformity.

1702   Defoe's *Short Way with Dissenters* satirises the sentiments of extreme High Churchmen.

1703   A bill to prevent Occasional Conformity passes the House of Commons but defeated in the Lords by the opposition of Whig peers.

1709   Dr Sacheverell preaches against toleration of dissenters.

1710   Trial of Dr Sacheverell leads to attacks on dissenting chapels in London.

1711   Occasional Conformity Act passed.

1714   Bolingbroke introduces the Schism Act, forbidding nonconformists to teach.

1715 Widespread attacks on dissenting meeting houses especially in London, the North-West and the Midlands.

1716 Dr Williams founds the Dr Williams Library.

1718 Act of quieting and establishing corporations. Dissenters could retain seat without taking sacrament if not challenged within six months.

1719 Repeal of Schism and Occasional Conformity Acts. Meeting of Presbyterians at Salters Hall protests against the need to subscribe to a belief in the Trinity by the clergy, beginning a major shift towards Unitarianism.

1727 Walpole introduces the first annual bill of indemnity for neglect of the Test and Corporation Acts, enabling dissenters to take the sacrament after, not before election.

Ministers of Presbyterian, Independent and Baptist congregations around London form General Body of Protestant Dissenting Ministers.

1728 Moravian mission established in England.

1729 Doddridge establishes a Presbyterian Academy at Market Harborough.

1732 Organisation of Protestant dissenting deputies to act as pressure group for dissenters.

1736 Attempt to relieve Quakers from tithes fails.

DISSENTERS' PLACES OF WORSHIP, 1691–1760
(all denominations)

	Permanent	Temporary
1691–1700	32	1247
1701–10	41	1219
1711–20	21	875
1721–30	27	448
1731–40	24	424
1741–50	27	502
1751–60	55	703

Source A. D. Gilbert, *Religion and Society in Industrial England: Church, Chapel and Social Change, 1740–1914* (London: Longman, 1976), p. 34.

THE METHODIST MOVEMENT

1729   John Wesley, junior Fellow of Lincoln College, Oxford, becomes leader of a strict religious society formed by his brother Charles Wesley and dubbed 'Methodists'.

1738   John Wesley returns from America, falls under the influence of Peter Böhler, a Moravian, and is converted in Aldersgate on 24 May. George Whitefield undertakes missionary work in America.

1739   George Whitefield starts open-air preaching at Kingswood, Bristol. John Wesley follows Whitefield's example of preaching in the open air. Methodist Society meets in Old Foundry, Moorfields, London.

1740   Wesley severs his connection with the Moravians. He begins to employ lay preachers and build chapels. Wesley and Whitefield agree to differ over the doctrine of predestination.

1743   Methodists produce rules for 'classes'. Welsh Calvinistic Methodist body founded by Whitefield. Serious anti-Methodist rioting in Wednesbury.

1744   First Methodist Conference held at Foundry Chapel, London, consisting of John and Charles Wesley, four clergy and four lay preachers. Resolves that Bishops are to be obeyed 'in all things indifferent', canons to be observed 'as far as can be done with a safe conscience' and 'societies to be formed where the preachers go'.

1747   Methodist societies grouped into circuits. First of John Wesley's visits to Ireland.

1749   Calvinists under Whitefield desert Wesley; Whitefield becomes chaplain to Lady Huntingdon.

1756   Wesley's *Twelve Reasons Against a Separation from the Church* attempts to restrain breakaway tendencies among his followers.

1760   Wesley's lay preachers take out licences as dissenting teachers; some begin to administer the sacraments.

ROMAN CATHOLICISM

In 1685, England was divided into four districts by the Papacy – London, Midland, Western, Northern – in each of which a papal vicar exercised the authority normally possessed by the ordinary (bishop). In law Roman Catholic priests faced the penalties of high treason for saying Mass; unlicensed teachers could be fined 40s a day; laymen refusing to take an oath denying the spiritual authority of the Pope, were guilty of recusancy. This meant they could not hold any office, keep arms, go to Italy, travel more than five miles without licence, or be executor, guardian, doctor or lawyer. They could not sit in Parliament nor on corporations. The nearest protestant kin could claim lands from a Roman Catholic heir. Roman Catholics were also subject to double land tax.

In practice the treatment of Roman Catholics was not so severe as the laws allowed: few were punished for saying or hearing Mass and magistrates seldom tendered the recusancy oath except in times of national emergency.

1688   James II orders a Declaration of Indulgence to be read in all churches, suspending laws against both Catholics and dissenters. Widespread attacks on Catholic property in London, York, Norwich, Newcastle, Cambridge, Oxford, Bristol and elsewhere (continuing into January 1689), following on the birth of James II's heir. Flight of James II effectively ends his attempt to reimpose Catholicism in England.

1689   Roman Catholics excluded from terms of Toleration Act.

1695   Act passed 'for preventing growth of popery'. Priests forbidden to exercise their functions and Catholics prevented from inheriting or buying land or sending their children abroad, unless they abjured their religion.

1714   Ultramontane Roman Catholics refuse to abandon claims of Pope Sixtus V to release subjects of a heretic monarch from oath of fealty.

1716   Recusancy laws enforced in many counties as a consequence of the Jacobite rising.

1717   Pope burning processions held in London and Oxford to celebrate George I's return from Hanover.

1723   Levy of £100 000 placed on Roman Catholics as a result of Atterbury plot.

1746   Attacks on Catholic chapels in Liverpool and Sunderland following Jacobite rising.

1747   Duke of York, the brother of Charles Edward Stuart, created a cardinal (d. 1805).

1760   Pitt obtains from the Theological Faculties of the Sorbonne, Louvain and other universities, a declaration that the Pope has no civil authority in England, that he cannot absolve from the Oath of Allegiance, and that faith must be kept with heretics.

8 TREATIES AND DIPLOMACY

PRINCIPAL TREATIES 1688–1760

Date signed		Place Signed
1689		
Apr 20	Treaty with the Netherlands concerning the fitting out of a fleet	Whitehall
Aug 15	Treaty with Denmark	Copenhagen
Aug 22	Convention with the Netherlands concerning prohibition of commerce with France	London
Aug 24	Treaty of friendship and alliance with the Netherlands	Whitehall
Oct 22	Treaty with the Netherlands concerning ships taken from the enemy	Whitehall
Dec 9	Accession of Great Britain to Grand Alliance between the Emperor and the Netherlands (12 May 1689)	—
1690		
May 16	Treaty of alliance with Elector of Brandenburg	Westminster
Nov 3	Treaty of defensive alliance with Denmark and the Netherlands	Copenhagen
1691		
Jun 30	Convention with Denmark and the Netherlands touching the commerce in France	Copenhagen
Oct 22	Treaty with the Netherlands concerning vessels captured and recaptured	Whitehall
1692		
Oct 31	Convention with Spain and the Netherlands for the fleet in the Mediterranean	The Hague
Dec 22	Subsidy treaty with the Netherlands and Elector of Hanover	The Hague
1693		
Feb 20	Treaty of subsidy with Elector of Saxony	Dresden

| Mar | 2 | Instrument of England and the Netherlands for payment of 150 000 dollars to Elector of Saxony | Dresden |

1694

| May | 23 | Treaty of subsidy with the Netherlands and Elector of Saxony | Dresden |
| Oct | 11 | Additional articles with Tripoli | Tripoli |

1695

| Mar | 18 | Convention with the Emperor, the Netherlands and Bishop of Munster | The Hague |
| Apr | 5 | Renewal of articles of peace with Algiers of 1686 | Algiers |

1696

| Dec | 3 | Treaty with Denmark and the Netherlands | The Hague |

1697

| Sep | 20 | Articles of peace with France | Ryswick |

1698

May	14	Convention with Sweden and the Netherlands for entering into a defensive triple league	The Hague
Jun	28	Renewal of articles of peace with Algiers of 1686	Algiers
Sep	24/Oct 11	Treaty with France and the Netherlands concerning settlement of succession of Spain on the Electoral Prince of Bavaria (First Partition Treaty)	Loo/The Hague

1699

| May | 16 | Articles of peace with Tunis | Tunis |

1700

Jan	16	Treaty with Sweden	London
Jan	23–30	Treaty of alliance with Sweden and the Netherlands	The Hague/London
Mar	3–25	Treaty with France and the Netherlands for settling succession of Crown of Spain (Second Partition Treaty)	London/The Hague
Aug	17	Treaty of peace and commerce with Algiers	Algiers

1701

| Jan | 20 | Treaty of Alliance with Denmark and the Netherlands | Odensee |

Jun 15	Treaty between Denmark and Britain, and the Netherlands	Copenhagen
Aug 10	Additional articles with Algiers	Algiers
Sep 7	Treaty with the Emperor and the Netherlands (Accessions: Prussia 18 Feb 1702; Wolfenbuttel 21 Apr 1702; Treves 22 Jun 1702; Elector of Mainz and Margrave of Brandenburg in the name of the Circle of Franconia 24 Jun 1702; the Bishop of Constance and Duke of Württemburg in the name of the Circle of Suabia 4 Aug 1702; Elector of Mainz in his own name and that of the Circle of the Rhine Sep 1702; the Bishop of Munster 18 Mar 1703; Mecklenburg 14 Sep 1703; Savoy by Treaty with Britain 4 Aug 1704; the Bishop of Munster and Paderborn 1 Mar 1710)	The Hague
Oct 7	Convention between Britain and the Netherlands, and Sweden confirming previous treaties	The Hague
Nov 11	Particular and perpetual alliance with the Netherlands	The Hague

1702

30 Dec 1701– 20 Jan 1702	Treaty of alliance with Prussia and the Netherlands	The Hague/London
30 Dec 1701– 20 Jan 1702	Treaty of subsidy between Britain and the Netherlands, and Prussia	The Hague/London
Feb 7/13	Convention with the Netherlands and Landgrave of Hesse-Cassel	The Hague/London
Apr 12	Articles with the Netherlands concerning the Pretender	The Hague
Apr 18	Agreement with the Empire and the Netherlands for declaring war with France and Spain on the same day	The Hague
May 8	Convention with the Netherlands and Elector of Treves	The Hague
May 6–17	Convention with the Netherlands and Elector of Treves	The Hague/London
Jun 21	Convention with Brunswick Luneburg for a supply of 10 000 men	The Hague
Nov 16	Convention with Brunswick Luneburg (with separate article 12 Dec 1702–2 Jan 1703)	The Hague

1703

Mar 13	Convention with the Netherlands and Bishop of Munster	The Hague

Mar	15	Convention with the Netherlands and Duke of Holstein	The Hague
Mar	15	Convention with the Netherlands to employ 20 000 additional troops in 1703	The Hague
Mar	27	Convention with the Netherlands and Duke of Saxe-Gotha	The Hague
Mar	31	Convention with the Netherlands and Landgrave of Hesse-Cassel	The Hague
Apr	11	Treaty with the Emperor and the Netherlands prohibiting commerce with France	The Hague
May	16	Treaty of defensive alliance between Britain, the Empire and the Netherlands, and Portugal	Lisbon
May	17	Convention with the Netherlands and Elector Palatine	The Hague
Jun	20	Treaty with the Netherlands for renewal of former treaties	Westminster
Aug	16	Treaty of stricter alliance and for the tranquillity of Europe with Sweden and the Netherlands	The Hague
Oct	28	Treaty of peace and commerce with Algiers	Algiers
Nov	20–Dec 24	Convention with Elector of Brunswick	London/The Hague
Dec	27	Treaty of commerce with Portugal	Lisbon

1704

Aug	4	Treaty with Savoy (with separate article Nov 18)	Turin
Nov	28	Treaty with King of Prussia	Berlin
Dec	30	Convention with Elector of Brunswick and Duke of Zell	London

1705

Feb	20	Treaty with Portugal concerning post office	London
Jun	20	Treaty of alliance with Principality of Catalonia	Genoa
Dec	3	Treaty with Prussia renewing treaty of 1704	Berlin
Dec	8	Convention with Elector of Hanover	Hanover

1706

| May | 20 | Convention with the Netherlands and Landgrave of Hesse-Cassel (further treaty 25–27 Mar 1701) | Cassel |

May 26	Convention with the Netherlands and Elector Palatine	The Hague
Oct 22	Treaty of commerce with Danzig	Danzig
Nov 18	Convention with Elector of Brunswick Lüneburg	The Hague
Nov 24	Treaty with Prussia (further treaty 19 Apr 1708)	The Hague
	Treaty with the Netherlands for securing Protestant succession	

1707

Jul 10	Treaty of peace and commerce with Spain	Barcelona

1708

Apr 14	Convention with the Emperor for 4000 Imperialists to be sent from Italy to Catalonia	The Hague
Apr 14	Convention with Elector of Hanover	The Hague
Mar 10–Apr 17	Convention with the Netherlands and Landgrave of Hesse-Cassel	Brussels/The Hague

1709

Jan 14	Convention with Elector of Brunswick	The Hague
Feb 22	Convention with the Netherlands and Elector of Saxony (renewed 7 May 1710 and 24 Mar 1711)	The Hague
Mar 31	Treaty with the Netherlands and Prussia	The Hague
Apr 12	Treaty with Prussia	The Hague
May 28	Articles preliminary to the treaties of a general peace (of 1713) between Britain, the Empire and the Netherlands, and France	The Hague
Oct 29	Treaty with the Netherlands for securing the succession to the Crown of Great Britain, and for settling a barrier for the Netherlands against France	The Hague
Nov 7	Convention with Elector of Treves	The Hague
Nov 8	Convention with Elector of Brunswick	The Hague

1710

Mar 31	Convention with the Netherlands and the Emperor concerning Imperial neutrality (renewed Aug 4)	
May 30	Treaty with Poland for two battalions	Camp before Douay

Oct 29	Military convention between Marlborough and Prince Eugene	The Hague
Oct 15	Convention with Elector of Brunswick	The Hague
Nov 30	Convention with Elector of Treves	The Hague
Dec 7	Military convention between Marlborough and Prince Eugene	The Hague

1711

May 27	Military treaty between Marlborough and Prince Eugene	The camp at Warde
Sep 27	Preliminary articles for a treaty of peace with France	London
Dec 22	Confirmation of treaties with the Netherlands	London
Dec 28	Convention with Elector of Brunswick	London

1712

Jan 14	Convention with Elector of Treves	The Hague
Jan 25	Convention with the Netherlands and Elector of Brunswick	The Hague
Mar 24	Convention with Elector of Saxony	The Hague
Aug 19	Treaty of suspension of arms with France (prolonged Dec 7–14)	Paris

1713

Jan 29–30	Treaty with the Netherlands guaranteeing Protestant succession to Crown of Great Britain and the barrier of the Netherlands	Utrecht
Mar 8	Declaration of commerce and navigation with the Two Sicilies	Utrecht
Mar 14	Convention with the Emperor for evacuating Catalonia	Utrecht
Mar 14	Convention with France for evacuating Catalonia	Utrecht
Mar 26	The Asiento with Spain for supplying slaves to the Spanish West Indies	Madrid
Mar 27	Preliminary treaty of peace with Spain	Madrid
Apr 11	Treaty of peace and friendship with France	Utrecht
Apr 11	Treaty of navigation and commerce with France (additional articles 9 May)	Utrecht
Jul 13	Treaty of peace and friendship with Spain	Utrecht
Jul 26	Provisional regulation of trade in the Spanish Low Countries between Britain and the Netherlands	Utrecht

| Dec 9 | Treaty of navigation and commerce with Spain | Utrecht |

1714

| Jul 22 | Treaty of peace, friendship and commerce with Morocco | Tehuan |

1715

Jul 26	Convention with Austrian Netherlands concerning import of British woollen cloths	London
Nov 15	Treaty with United Provinces and Charles VI for restoration of Austrian Netherlands, to Charles, except for the barrier given to the United Provinces (Barrier Treaty)	Antwerp
Dec 14	Treaty of commerce with Spain	Madrid

1716

Feb 6	Treaty with the Netherlands (with Separate Article Apr 3)	London
May 25	Treaty of alliance with Emperor (Additional Article 1 Sep 1717)	London
May 26	Convention with Philip V of Spain for explaining the articles of the Assiento (1713)	Madrid
Jul 19	Treaty of peace with Tripoli	Tripoli
Aug 30	Treaty of peace and commerce with Tunis	Tunis
Oct 29	Treaty of peace and commerce with Algiers	Algiers

1717

| Jan 4 | Treaty of alliance with France and the Netherlands | The Hague |

1718

Jul 18	Convention with France for bringing about peace between the Emperor and the Kings of Spain and Sicily	Paris
Jul 18	Convention with France for settling separate and secret articles of Quadruple Alliance	Paris
Aug 2	Quadruple Alliance with Charles VI, France and the Netherlands (Accession: King of Sardinia Nov 8)	London
Dec 22	Convention with Charles VI and the Netherlands concerning the Barrier Treaty of 1715	The Hague

1719

Feb	8	Convention with Hamburg concerning the herring trade	Hamburg
Apr	14	Capitulation for the Dutch troops	The Hague
Aug	4	Treaty with Prussia	Berlin
Aug	29	Preliminary convention with Sweden	Stockholm
Oct	27	Convention between Sweden and Denmark (signed by Lord Carteret and the Swedish Minister)	Stockholm
Oct	30	Convention with Denmark	Copenhagen
Nov	18	Convention with Emperor and France, excluding sons of Philip of Spain and Elizabeth Farnese from succession to Tuscany, Parma and Piacenza	The Hague

1720

Jan	21	Treaty with Sweden	—
Feb	16	Accession of Spain to convention between France and Britain of 18 Jul 1718	The Hague
Feb	17	Accession of Spain to Treaty of London of 2 Aug 1718	The Hague
Feb	29	Convention for armistice by sea with France and Spain	The Hague.
Mar	18	Instrument of admission of King of Sardinia to Act of Accession of King of Spain to Treaty of London, signed by Britain, France, Spain, Sardinia and the Empire	The Hague
Apr	2	Convention for suspension of arms by sea with France, Spain, Sardinia and the Empire	The Hague

1721

Jan	23	Treaty of peace and commerce with Morocco	Fez
Jun	13	Treaty with Spain	Madrid
Jun	13	Treaty of defensive alliance with France and Spain	Madrid
Sep	27	Act of guarantee with France concerning the renunciations by the Emperor and the King of Spain	Paris

1722

Aug	27	Act of guarantee with France of the Kingdom of Sardinia	Versailles

1723

Oct	10	Treaty with Prussia	Charlottenbourg

1724

Jan	24	Act of guarantee with France	Cambrai

1725

Sep	3	Defensive treaty of alliance with France and Prussia	Hanover

1726

Aug	9	Act of accession of the Netherlands to Treaty of Hanover	The Hague

1727

Mar	12	Convention with Hesse-Cassel	London
Mar	14	Accession of Sweden to Treaty of Hanover	Stockholm
Apr	16	Treaty of alliance with France and Denmark	Copenhagen
May	31	Preliminary articles between the Emperor and the Allies of Hanover	Paris
Nov	25	Treaty with Duke of Wolfenbuttel	London

1728

Jan	14	Articles of peace and commerce with Morocco (Additional Articles Jul 1729)	Mequinez
Mar	6	Convention with the Emperor, Spain and the Netherlands concerning the execution of the Preliminaries of 31 May 1727	The Pardo
May	27	Renewal of former treaties with the Netherlands	London

1729

Mar	18	Treaty of peace with Algiers	Algiers
Sep	6/8	Convention agreeing to mediation over differences with Prussia	Berlin
Nov	9	Treaty of peace and friendship with France and Spain	Seville
Nov	21	Accession of the Netherlands to treaty of Nov 9	Seville

1730

Mar	31	Articles of peace and commerce with Tripoli	Tripoli

1731

Mar	16	Treaty of peace and alliance with the Emperor, in which the Netherlands are included	Vienna
Jul	22	Treaty with Spain and the Emperor (Accession: Tuscany Sep 21)	Vienna

Oct	17	Convention with Bremen concerning the herring trade	Bremen
Oct	31	Regulation signed by plenipotentiaries of Britain and Spain for introduction of Spanish garrisons into Tuscany	Leghorn

1732

Feb	20	Act of concurrence of the Netherlands to the Treaty of Vienna of 16 Mar 1731	The Hague
Feb	20	Article with the Netherlands concerning the East India Company at Ostend	The Hague

1734

Sep	30	Treaty and secret articles with Denmark	London
Dec	2	Treaty of commerce with Russia	St Petersburg
Dec	15	Treaty of peace with Morocco	—

1738

Sep	9	Convention with Spain	London

1739

Jan	14	Convention with Spain	The Pardo
Mar	14	Treaty with Denmark	Copenhagen

1740

May	9	Treaty with King of Sweden, as Landgrave of Hesse-Cassel	London

1741

Apr	3	Treaty with Russia	St Petersburg
Jun	24	Convention with Queen of Hungary	Hanover

1742

Feb	23	Cartel for exchange of prisoners with Spain	Paris
Jun	25	Convention with Queen of Hungary	London
Nov	18	Treaty of defensive alliance with Prussia	London
Dec	11	Treaty with Russia	Moscow

1743

Feb	15	Treaty with Austria-Hungary	London
Sep	13	Definitive treaty of peace, union, friendship and mutual defence with Hungary and Sardinia	Worms

1744

Feb	10	Convention with Austria-Hungary	London

Apr	27	Treaty of alliance with Elector of Cologne	London
May		Treaty of alliance with Elector of Mainz (prolonged Jun 1747)	—
Jul	4	Treaty with the Netherlands and the Elector of Cologne	The Hague
Aug	11	Treaty with Queen of Austria-Hungary	London
Sep	18	Convention with the Netherlands	London

1745

Jan	8	Treaty of alliance with Queen of Hungary, Poland and the Netherlands	Warsaw
Apr	2	Treaty with Queen of Hungary	London
May	21	Treaty granting £60 000 to Sardinia	London
Jun	1	Convention with Queen of Hungary	At the quarters of General de Lapines
Jun	8	Convention with Queen of Hungary	Hanover
Jun	16	Treaty with King of Sweden, as Landgrave of Hesse-Cassel	Hanover
Aug	26	Preliminary convention with Prussia (with further declaration signed in London 12 Sep)	Hanover

1746

Jun	10	Convention with Queen of Hungary	London
Jun	10	Treaty with Sardinia	London
Jul	21	Subsidiary treaty with the Netherlands and Bavaria	Munich
Aug	30	Provisional convention of subsidy between Britain and the Netherlands, and Queen of Hungary	The Hague

1747

Jan	12	Convention for the campaign of 1747 with Austria-Hungary, the Netherlands and Sardinia	The Hague
Jun	12	Convention with Russia	St Petersburg
Nov	19	Convention between Britain and the Netherlands, and Russia for passage of Russian troops across Germany	St Petersburg
Nov	27	Convention with Russia	St Petersburg

1748

Jan	26	Convention for the campaign of 1748 with Austria-Hungary, the Netherlands and Sardinia (Additional Convention May 3)	The Hague

Feb	1	Subsidiary convention with the Netherlands and Duke of Wolfenbuttel	The Hague
Apr	30	Preliminary articles of peace with France and the Netherlands	Aix-la-Chapelle
Oct	18	Treaty of Aix-la-Chapelle with France and the Netherlands (Accessions: Spain Oct 20; Austria-Hungary Oct 23; Modena Oct 25; Genoa Oct 28; Sardinia Nov 7)	Aix-la-Chapelle

1750

Jan	15	Treaty of peace with Morocco (Additional Articles Feb 1751)	Fez
Aug	22	Alliance with Austria-Hungary and Bavaria	Hanover
Aug	22	Alliance with the Netherlands and Bavaria	Hanover
Oct	5	Treaty of commerce with Spain	Madrid
Oct	30	Alliance with Russia and Austria-Hungary	St Petersburg

1751

Jun	3	Additional article with Algiers	Algiers
Sep	13	Alliance with the Netherlands and Poland	Dresden
Sep	19	Treaty of peace and commerce with Tripoli	Tripoli
Oct	19	Treaty of peace and commerce with Tunis	Bardo

1753

May	11	Alliance with the Empire, Hungary and Modena	Vienna

1755

Jun	18	Treaty with Landgrave of Hesse-Cassel	Hanover
Sep	30	Treaty with Russia	St Petersburg

1756

Jan	16	Treaty with Prussia	London

1758

Apr	11	Treaty with Prussia	London
Dec	7	Convention with Prussia	London

1759

Jan	17	Convention with Landgrave of Hesse-Cassel	London
Nov	9	Convention with Prussia	—

1760

Jan	14	Treaty with Duke of Brunswick	Marburg

Apr	1	Convention with Hesse-Cassel	London
Jul	28	Treaty of peace and commerce with Morocco	Fez
Dec	12	Convention with Prussia	—
1761			
Jan	28	Renewal of peace with Tripoli	Tripoli
Mar	3	Protocol with Hesse	London
Aug	10	Convention with Brunswick for troops	Brunswick

PRINCIPAL BRITISH DIPLOMATIC REPRESENTATIVES,* 1688–1760

Abbreviations of Diplomatic Rank: Amb: Ambassador; Env: Envoy; Ex: Extraordinary; In Ch of Aff: In Charge of Affairs; Mil: Military; Min: Minister; Miss: Mission; Plen: Plenipotentiary; Res: Resident; Sec: Secretary; Spec: Special.

BAVARIA

George Stepney	1704	No special rank
Seigneur de St Saphorin	1725	No special rank
Isaac Leheup	1726	No special rank
Sir Thomas Robinson (Baron Grantham)	1745	Env Ex + Plen
Onslow Burrish	1746–58	Min
Fulke Greville	1764–70	Env Ex

DENMARK

Robert Molesworth (Vt Molesworth)	1689–92	Env Ex
Hugh Greg	1692–1701	In Ch of Aff
	1701–2	Min Res
Robert Sutton (Baron Lexington)	1693	Env Ex
James Cressett	1699–1700	Env Ex
James Vernon	1702–6	Env Ex
Daniel Pulteney	1706–15	Env Ex
Lord Polwarth	1716–20	Env Ex
	1720–1	Amb Ex
Baron Glenorchy	1720–31	Env Ex
Adm. Sir John Norris	1727	Env Ex
Brig. Richard Sutton, MP	1729	Spec Mil Miss

British Diplomatic Representatives, 1689–1789, D. B. Horn, Camden 3rd Series, vol. *XLVI*, 1932, London.

Walter Titley	1729–30	Sec in Ch of Aff
	1731–9	Min Res
	1739–68	Env Ex

THE EMPIRE

Baron Paget	1689–92	Env Ex
George Stepney	1693	Sec or Agent
Baron Lexington	1694–7	Env Ex
Robert Sutton	1697–1700	Sec, later Res
George Stepney	1701–5	Env Ex
	1705–6	Env Ex + Plen
Charles Whitworth (Baron Whitworth)	1703–6	In Ch of Aff
Earl of Sunderland	1705	Env Ex
Duke of Marlborough	1705	No special rank
Baron Raby (Earl of Strafford)	1706	Env Ex + Plen
Earl of Manchester	1707	No special rank
Sir Philip Meadowe	1707–9	Env Ex
Maj-Gen. Francis Palmes	1707–8	Env Ex
	1709–11	Env Ex
Earl of Peterborough	1711	No special rank
Abraham Stanyan	1712–13	No special rank
James Stanhope (Earl Stanhope)	1714	No special rank
Baron Cobham	1714–15	Env Ex + Plen
Maj-Gen. William Cadogan (later Earl Cadogan)	1715	rank unknown
Abraham Stanyan, MP	1716–18	Env Ex + Plen
Seigneur de St Saphorin	1718–21	rank unknown
	1721–7	Env Ex + Plen
Earl Cadogan	1719–20	Amb Ex + Plen
Charles Harrison	1724–5	Min
Lord (Earl 1729) Waldegrave	1727–31	Amb Ex + Plen
Thomas Robinson, MP	1730	Min
	1730–50	Min Plen
Thomas Villiers	1742–3	Min Plen
Robert Keith	1748–53	Min
	1753–7	Min Plen

FLANDERS

John Eckhart	1689–92	Res
Robert Wolseley	1692–6	Env Ex
Richard Hill	1696–9	Env Ex
Marmande	1699–1701	Sec

George Stepney	1706–7	Env Ex + Plen
John Lawes	1707–8	In Ch of Aff
Lt-Gen. William Cadogan	1707–11	Env Ex + Plen
Earl of Orrery	1711–12	Env Ex
	1712–13	Env Ex + Plen
John Lawes	1712–14	Act Min Plen
Lt-Gen. William Cadogan	1714–15	Env Ex + Plen
William Leathes	1715–17	Sec at Brussels
	c. 1718–24	Res
Robert Daniel	1722–45	In Ch of Aff
Onslow Burrish	1742–4	Sec
	1744	Res
Solomon Dayrolle	1752–7	Min

Diplomatic relations suspended 1757–63

FRANCE

Earl of Portland	1697–8	Env + Amb Ex
Matthew Prior	1698–9	Sec
Earl of Jersey	1698–9	Amb Ex
Earl (Duke) of Manchester	1699–1701	Amb Ex

1701–13 Rupture of diplomatic relations

Matthew Prior	1712–15	Plen
Duke of Shrewsbury	1712–13	Amb Ex
Earl of Peterborough	1713–14	Amb Ex
General Charles Ross	1714	Env Ex
Earl of Stair	1714–15	Min
Earl of Stair	1715	Env Ex
Earl of Stair	1715–20	Amb Ex
Col William Stanhope, MP	1719	Plen
Sir Robert Sutton	1720–1	Amb + Plen
Sir Luke Schaub	1721–4	Amb
Thomas Crawford	1722–4	Res
Horatio Walpole	1723	No special rank
	1724	Env Ex
	1724–7	Amb Ex
	1727–30	Amb Ex + Plen
Lord Waldegrave	1725	Env Ex
	1727–8	No special rank
	1730–40	Amb Ex + Plen
Anthony Thompson	1740–4	In Ch of Aff

Diplomatic relations suspended 1744–8

Earl of Albemarle	1749–54	Amb Ex + Plen

Diplomatic Relations suspended 1755–63

GERMANY *see under* THE EMPIRE

NETHERLANDS *see under* UNITED PROVINCES OF THE NETHERLANDS

OTTOMAN EMPIRE *see under* TURKEY

POLAND

George Stepney	1698	No special rank
Sir William Browne	1700	Res
Rev John Robinson	1702–7	Env Ex
Earl of Stair	1709–10	Env Ex
George Mackenzie	1710–14	Sec in Ch of Aff
Charles Whitworth (Baron Whitworth)	1711	Amb Ex + Plen
James Scott	1711–15	Env Ex
Sir Richard Vernon	1715–18	Env Ex
Lt-Gen. Francis Palmes	1718–19	Env Ex + Plen
James Scott	1719–22	Min, later Env Ex
Edward Finch	1725–7	Min Plen
George Woodward	1728–31	Res
Sir Luke Schaub	1730–1	Spec Miss
George Woodward	1732–5	Env Ex
Denton Boate	1735–8	Sec in Ch of Aff
Thomas Villiers	1738–43	Env Ex
Edward Finch	1740	Min Plen
Sir Thomas Villiers	1744–6	Env Ex + Plen
Sir Charles Hanbury Williams, MP	1747–9	Env Ex
	1750	Min
	1751–5	Env Ex + Plen
Viscount Stormont	1756–63	Env Ex

PORTUGAL

John Methuen	1692–7	Env Ex
Paul Methuen	1697–1706	Env Ex (In Ch of Aff, 1694–6)
John Methuen	1703–6	Amb Ex + Plen
John Milner	1706	In Ch of Aff
Paul Methuen	1706–8	Amb Ex
Earl of Galway	1707–10	Amb Ex + Plen
George Delaval	1710–14	Env Ex
Henry Worsley	1713–19	Env Ex

Henry Worsley	1719–22	Env Ex + Plen
Thomas Lumley (Sir Thomas	1722–4	Env Ex
Saunderson, KB from 1723)	1724–5	Env Ex + Plen
Brig. James Dormer	1725–7	Env Ex
Baron Tyrawly	1728–41	Env Ex
Adm. Sir John Norris	1735–7	Min Plen
Hon Charles Compton	1741–2	In Ch of Aff
	1742–5	Env Ex
Benjamin Keene	1745–50	Env Ex + Plen
Abraham Castres	1749–57	Env Ex
Baron Tyrawly	1752	Min Plen
Hon Edward Hay	1757–62	Env Ex

PRUSSIA

Baron Lexington	1689	Env Ex
James Johnston	1690–2	Env Ex
George Stepney	1692	In Ch of Aff
George Stepney	1698–9	Env Ex
Philip Plantamour	1699–1703	In Ch of Aff
Count von Friesen	1700	Env Ex (appt cancelled)
James Cressett	1700	Env Ex
Baron Raby	1701	rank uncertain
	1703–5	Env Ex
	1705–11	Amb Ex
Charles Whitworth (Baron)	1711	no spec rank
Brig. William Breton	1712–14	Env Ex
Earl of Forfar	1715	Env Ex
Baron Polwarth	1716	Env Ex + Plen
Charles Whitworth (Baron)	1716–17	Env Ex + Plen
	1719–22	Min Plen
James Scott	1722–4	Min
Col (Brig 1727) Charles du Bourgay	1724–30	Env Ex
Captain Melchior Guy Dickens	1730–40	Sec
	1740–1	Min
Thomas Robinson	1741	Spec Miss
Earl of Hyndford	1741–4	Env Ex + Plen
Thomas Villiers	1746	Min Plen
Henry Bilson Legge, MP	1748	Env Ex + Plen
Sir Charles Hanbury Williams, KB	1750–1	Env Ex + Plen
Andrew Mitchell	1756–60	Min

RUSSIA

Charles Goodfellow	1699–1712	Min + Con-Gen
Charles Whitworth (Baron)	1704–9	Env
Charles Whitworth (Baron)	1709–11	Amb Ex
Charles Whitworth (Baron)	1711–12	Amb Ex + Plen
George Mackenzie	1714–15	Min Res
James Haldane	1716–17	Min Res
Adm. Sir John Norris	1717	Env Ex + Plen
Charles Whitworth	1717	No special rank
Capt. James Jefferyes	1718–21	Min Res

Diplomatic relations suspended 1719–30

Thomas Ward	1728–30	Consul-General
	1730–1	Min Res
Claudius Rondeau	1730–1	Consul-General
	1731–9	Min Res
Lord Forbes	1733–4	Min Plen
Edward Finch, MP	1740–2	Env Ex + Plen
Sir Cyril Wich, Bart	1741–2	Env Ex
	1742–4	Env Ex + Plen
Baron Tyrawly	1743–5	Env Ex + Plen
Earl of Hyndford	1744–5	Min Plen
	1745–9	Amb Ex + Plen
Lt-Col Melchior Guy Dickens	1749–55	Env Ex + Plen
Baron Jakob Wolff	1744–50	Consul-General
	1750–9	Min Res
Sir Charles Hanbury Williams, KB, MP	1755–7	Amb + Plen
Robert Keith	1757–62	Env Ex + Plen

SARDINIA AND SAVOY

Edmund Poley	1691–3	Env Ex
William Aglionby	1693–4	Env Ex
Earl of Galway	1693–6	Env Ex
Richard Hill	1699	Env Ex
Richard Hill	1703–6	Env Ex
John Chetwynd (Vt)	1705–6	No special rank
Paul Methuen	1706	Env Ex
John Chetwynd (Vt)	1706–13	Env Ex
Maj-Gen. Francis Palmes	1708–10	Env Ex
Earl of Peterborough	1710–11	No special rank
Abraham Stanyan	1712–13	Spec Mission
Earl of Peterborough	1712	Min Plen
Earl of Peterborough	1713	Amb + Ex Plen

George St John	1714	Env Ex
John Molesworth (Vt 1725)	1720–5	Env Ex + Plen
John Hedges	1726–7	Env Ex
Earl of Essex	1731–2	Min Plen
	1732–6	Amb
Arthur Villettes	1734–41	Sec
	1741–9	Res
Lt-Gen. Thomas Wentworth	1747	No special rank
Lt-Gen. James St Clair	1748	No special rank
Earl of Rochford	1749–55	Env Ex + Plen
Earl of Bristol	1755–8	Env Ex
James Stewart Mackenzie	1758–60	Env Ex

SPAIN

Alexander Stanhope	1689–99	Env Ex
Francis Schonenberg	1690–1702	Env Ex
William Aglionby	1692 & 1700–1	No special rank
Col Mitford Crowe	1705–6	No special rank
Col Mitford Crowe	1706	Env Ex + Plen
Paul Methuen	1705–6	Env Ex
Brig (Earl) Stanhope	1706	Env Ex
Brig (Earl) Stanhope	1706–7	Env Ex + Plen
Brig (Earl) Stanhope	1708–10	Env Ex + Plen
Earl of Peterborough	1706–7	Amb Ex + Plen
Henry Worsley, MP	1708	Env Ex
James Craggs	1708–11	Res Env Ex
Duke of Argyll	1711	Amb Ex + Plen
Baron Lexington	1712–13	Amb Ex + Plen
Baron Bingley	1714	Amb Ex
Paul Methuen, MP	1715	Amb Ex + Min Plen
George Bubb	1715–17	Env Ex + Plen
Col William Stanhope	1717–18	Env Ex + Plen
Earl Stanhope	1718	No special rank

Diplomatic relations suspended 1718–20

Col William Stanhope	1720–1	Env Ex + Plen
	1721–7 & 1729	Amb Ex + Plen
Benjamin Keene	1727–34	Min Plen
	1734–9	Env Ex + Plen
Abraham Castres	1739	Plen

Diplomatic relations suspended 1739–46

Sir Benjamin Keene (KB 1754)	1746–57	Amb Ex + Plen
Earl of Bristol	1758–61	Amb Ex + Plen

SWEDEN

William Duncombe	1689–92	Env Ex
Rev. John Robinson	1692–6	In Ch of Aff/Agent
Rev. John Robinson	1696–1702	Min Res
Rev. John Robinson	1702–9	Env Ex
George Stepney	1702	Env Ex
Robert Jackson	1710–17	Min Res
Robert Jackson	1719–29	Min Res
Capt. James Jefferyes	1711–15	Res or Min
Lord Carteret	1719–20	Amb Ex + Plen
William Finch, MP	1720–4	Env Ex
Adm. Sir John Norris	1720	Plen
Stephen Poyntz	1724–7	Env Ex + Plen
	1727	Amb Ex
Vice-Adm. Sir Charles Wager	1726	Plen
Isaac Leheup, MP	1727	Env Ex + Plen
Edward Finch, MP	1728–39	Env Ex
Lt-Col Melchior Guy Dickens	1742–8	Min

Diplomatic relations suspended 1748–1763 apart from abortive mission in 1757

SWITZERLAND (including Geneva and the Grison Leagues)

Thomas Coxe	1689–92	Env Ex
Baron de Heunniguen	1689–90	Env Ex
	1692–1702	Env Ex
Marquis d'Arsellières	1695–1710	'generally employed'
William Aglionby	1702–5	Env Ex
Abraham Stanyan	1705–14	Env Ex (& to the Grisons from 1707)
Francis Manning	1708–9	In Ch of Aff
	1709–13	Sec to the Grisons
Francis Manning	1716–22	Res
James Dayrolle	1710 & 1715–17	Res at Geneva
Comte de Marsay	1717–34 &	In Ch of Aff, or
	1734–9	Min Res to Helvetic Republic & to the Grison Leagues
	1739–62	Min at Geneva
John Burnaby	1743–50	Min
Jérôme de Salis	1743–50	Env Ex to Grison Leagues
Arthur Villettes	1749–62	Min

TURKEY

Sir William Trumbull	1687–91	Amb
Sir William Hussey	1690–1	Amb
Thomas Coke	1691–3	In Ch of Aff
William Harbord	1691–2	Amb
William Paget (Baron)	1692–1702	Amb
Sir James Rushout	1697–8	Amb
George Berkeley (Earl)	1698–9	Amb
Sir Robert Sutton	1700–17 & 1718	Amb
Edward Wortley-Montagu	1716–18	Amb
Abraham Stanyan	1717–30	Amb
Earl of Kinoull	1729–36	Amb
Sir Everard Fawkener	1735–46	Amb
James Porter	1746–62	Amb

UNITED PROVINCES OF THE NETHERLANDS

Earl of Pembroke	1689	Amb Ex
Vt Dursley	1689–94	Env Ex
William Harbord	1690	Amb
Matthew Prior	1694–7	Sec
Vt Villiers (Earl of Jersey)	1695–7	Env Ex (+ Plen)
Sir Joseph Williamson	1697–9	Amb Ex
Alexander Stanhope	1700–6	Env Ex
Earl (Duke) of Marlborough	1701	Amb Ex + Plen
	1702–12	Amb Ex + Plen
James Dayrolle	1706–12	Res
George Stepney	1706–7	Env Ex + Plen
Lt-Gen. William Cadogan	1707–11	Env Ex + Plen
Charles Townsend (Vt)	1709–11	Amb Ex + Plen
Horatio Walpole (Baron)	1709–11	Sec of Embassy
Earl of Orrery	1711	Env Ex + Plen
Baron Raby (E of Strafford)	1711–14	Amb Ex + Plen
Lt-Gen. William Cadogan	1714–16	Env Ex + Plen
(Baron 1716, Earl 1718)	1716–21	Amb Ex + Plen
Horatio Walpole	1715 & 1715–16	Min & Plen
William Leathes	1717	Res
Charles Whitworth (Baron Whitworth 1721)	1717	Env Ex
	1717–21	Min Plen
James Dayrolle	1717–39	Res
Horatio Walpole	1722	Min Plen

William Finch	1724–8	Env Ex + Plen
Earl of Chesterfield	1728–32	Amb Ex + Plen
William Finch	1733–4	Min Plen
Horatio Walpole	1734	Min
	1734–7 & 1739	Amb Ex + Plen
Robert Trevor	1736–9	Sec
	1739–41	Env Ex
	1741–7	Env Ex + Plen
Earl of Stair	1742–3	Amb Ex + Plen
Earl of Chesterfield	1745	Amb Ex + Plen
Earl of Sandwich	1746–9	Min Plen
Solomon Dayrolle	1747–52	Res
Earl of Holderness	1749–51	Min Plen
Sir Joseph Yorke, KB	1751–61	Min Plen

9 THE ARMED FORCES

OUTLINES OF BRITISH CAMPAIGNS*

WAR OF THE GRAND ALLIANCE 1688–1697

1688	Sep 25	Louis XIV invaded the Palatinate.
1689	May 12	Treaty between the Emperor and the Netherlands signed at Vienna; the accession of England (on 9 Dec), Spain, Savoy, Brandenburg, Saxony, Hanover and Bavaria established the Grand Alliance.
	Aug 25	Battle of Walcourt – Prince George Frederick of Waldeck, with an English contingent of 8000 men under Marlborough, defeated the French.
1690	Jul 1	Battle of **Fleurus** – French under Duc de Luxembourg defeated the allies.
	Jul 10	Battle of **Beachy Head** – Admiral de Tourville with 78 ships defeated Torrington's Anglo-Dutch fleet of 73.
1691	Apr 8	Mons fell to the French.
	Sep 20	Waldeck defeated at the battle of Leuze.
1692	May 29– Jun 3	Battle of **La Hogue** – Admirals Russell and Rooke led an Anglo-Dutch fleet of 96 ships to victory over de Tourville with 44.
	Aug 3	Battle of Steenkerke – William III attacked Luxembourg's strong defensive position; he was repulsed, but the French were unable to pursue.
1693	Jun 27–28	Battle of **Lagos** – de Tourville attacked a Smyrna convoy, and, after beating off Rooke's escorting squadron, he destroyed 100 ships.
	Jul 29	William sent 20000 men to relieve Liège, and stood with the rest of his army at **Neerwinden**, where he was attacked and defeated by Luxembourg.
	Oct 11	French captured Charleroi.

*Where the name of a battle is given in bold type further details can be found in the section Principal Battles 1688–1763'.

1695	Jan	Luxembourg dies, and was replaced by the Duc de Villeroi.
	Sep 1	Namur surrendered to William.
1696	Jun 8	Assault on Brest a failure.
1697	Sep 20	Treaty of Ryswick – Louis XIV restored his conquests, and recognised William III as King of England.

REVOLUTION OF 1688 AND THE WARS IN SCOTLAND AND IRELAND 1688–1691

1688	Nov 5	William of Orange landed at Torbay and advanced on London; James II fled to France (see pp. 13–16).
1689	Feb 13	William and Mary proclaimed joint sovereigns of England.
	Mar 22	James II landed in Ireland at Kinsale with 5000 French soldiers. He marched with the Jacobite Earl of Tyrconnel to the north, where the Protestants had declared for William III.
	Apr 29	Londonderry besieged. An English naval force under Capt Leake raised the siege on 9–10 Aug. After local forces under Col Wolseley defeated the Jacobites the siege of Enniskillen was lifted, and William's army overran the whole of Ulster.
	Jul 17	In Scotland a Royalist army was routed at **Killiecrankie** by Jacobites led by Viscount Graham of Claverhouse and Dundee. He was killed in the battle, however, and the rising collapsed.
1690	Jun 14	William landed in Ireland and advanced on Dublin.
	Jul 1	James was defeated at the battle of the **Boyne**, and fled to France.
	Sep–Oct	Marlborough took Cork and Kinsale.
1691	Jul 12	Jacobites defeated at the battle of **Aughrim.**
	Oct 13	Limerick surrendered on the signing of a treaty bringing the Irish war to a close.

WAR OF THE SPANISH SUCCESSION, 1701–1713

(a) **Flanders**

| 1700 | Nov | Death of Charles II of Spain; Louis XIV's grandson becomes Philip V. |

1701	Sep 7	Treaty between England, the Netherlands and the Emperor.
1702	Mar 8	Death of William III.
	May 15	England declared war on France.
	Jun–Jul	Marlborough advanced into the Spanish Netherlands, but the Dutch deputies vetoed plans to bring the French to battle.
	Sep–Oct	Marlborough besieged the Meuse fortresses and captured Venlo, Roermond and Liège.
1703	May	Marlborough invaded the electorate of Cologne and took Bonn, but failed in his plan to seize Antwerp.
1704		Marlborough's intention was to concentrate the allied forces in the Danube Valley to save Vienna, drive the French out of Germany and eliminate Bavaria from the war.
	May	Marlborough began the march to the Danube.
	Jun	Marlborough met Prince Eugène and Louis of Baden at Mondelsheim, continuing with Louis to the Danube.
	Jul 2	Marlborough captured **Donauwörth**, forcing the French to retreat southwards.
	Aug 6	Marlborough and Eugène joined forces, while Louis of Baden was sent to besiege Ingolstadt.
	Aug 13	As the French and Bavarians advanced, Marlborough and Eugène attacked and decisively defeated them at **Blenheim**.
1705		Stalemate in the Low Countries. Marlborough pierced the French lines at Tirlemont on 18 Jul, but Dutch caution prevented him from exploiting this.
1706	May 23	Villeroi, marching towards Liège, was heavily defeated by Marlborough at **Ramillies,** and driven back to Courtrai.
	Jun–Oct	Marlborough captured Antwerp, Dunkirk, Menin, Dendermonde and Ath, firmly establishing his hold on the Spanish Netherlands.
1707		Vendôme, who had replaced Villeroi, held the Flanders front.
1708	Jul 4–5	French army took the offensive, and captured Ghent and Bruges.
	Jul 11	Marlborough defeated Vendôme at **Oudenarde**.
	Jul 12	Vendôme checked the pursuing Allies at Ghent.

Marlborough's plan for the invasion of France was not accepted. Instead Lille was besieged and fell on 22 Oct.

1709	Jan	Ghent and Bruges fell to the Allies.
	Jul 29	Allies captured Tournai, and besieged Mons. Villars was ordered to defend Mons, so advanced and entrenched at Malplaquet threatening the besiegers.
	Sep 11	Marlborough and Eugène defeated the French at **Malplaquet**, but suffered very heavy casualties.
	Oct 26	Mons surrendered.
1710		Marlborough captured Douai on 10 Jun and Béthune on 30 Aug.
1711		Marlborough succeeded in breaking the French 'ne plus ultra' defensive lines in Aug, but was dismissed from his command on 31 Dec.
1712	Jul 24	After the English contingent had been withdrawn, Eugène was defeated by Villars at **Denain**.
1713	Apr 11	Treaty of Utrecht – The French ceded Newfoundland, Nova Scotia, St Kitts and the Hudson Bay territory to England, and undertook to demolish the fortifications at Dunkirk. They also recognised the Protestant Succession, and agreed not to help the Stuarts.

(b) Spain and the Mediterranean

1702	Aug–Sep	Anglo-Dutch force of 50 ships and 15 000 men under Admiral Rooke and the Duke of Ormonde repulsed at Cadiz.
	Oct 12	Rooke destroyed the Spanish treasure fleet in Vigo Bay.
1703	May 16	Portugal joined the alliance.
1704	Feb	Rooke landed the Archduke Charles with 2000 English and Dutch troops at Lisbon.
	Aug 4	Rooke captured Gibraltar.
	Aug 24	French navy under the Count of Toulouse defeated by Rooke in battle of **Malaga**.
1705	Mar 10	Admiral Sir John Leake defeated a French squadron under Admiral de Pointis in battle of **Marbella**, and the siege of Gibraltar was lifted.

	Jun	Allied troops under Admiral Sir Cloudesley Shovell and Lord Peterborough landed in Catalonia.
	Oct 3	Allies captured Barcelona, but were besieged by the French.
1706	Apr 30	French lifted the siege of Barcelona when Lord Henry Galway led an invasion of Spain from Portugal.
	Jun 26	Galway captured Madrid, but the French retook it in Oct.
	Jun–Sep	English fleet under Leake captured Cartagena, Alicante and the Balearic Islands of Mallorca and Ibiza.
1707	Apr 25	Galway's advance on Madrid was halted by the French under the Duke of Berwick at the battle of **Almanza**.
	Jul–Aug	Prince Eugène besieged Toulon, with the support of the allied fleet under Shovell, but was unsuccessful, although the French had scuttled 50 ships in the harbour in case the city fell.
1708	Aug	Admiral Leake captured Sardinia.
	Sep	General James Stanhope captured Minorca.
1710	May	Stanhope advanced on Madrid, but had to retreat, pursued by Vendôme.
	Dec 10	Stanhope was defeated and captured at **Brihuega**.
1714	Sep 11	French captured Barcelona.
1715	Feb	Spain and Portugal made peace by the treaty of Madrid.

JACOBITE REBELLIONS, 1715 & 1745 (see p. 155 for Scotland in 1688–9)

1. 'The Fifteen'

1715	Sep 6	Earl of Mar raised Stuart standard at Braemar. A Jacobite army advanced to Preston, but was forced to surrender there on 13 Nov. On the same day Mar fought an inconclusive battle with government troops led by the Duke of Argyll at **Sheriffmuir**.
	Dec 22	James Edward, the Pretender, landed at Peterhead, but returned to France Feb 1716, as Jacobites dispersed before advancing government forces. Attempts by the Duke of Ormonde to land in Devon Oct–Dec 1715 found no support.

2. 'The Forty-Five'

1745	Jul 23	Charles Edward, the Young Pretender, landed in Scotland.
		His army of Highlanders entered Edinburgh Sep 17, and routed an English army under Sir John Cope at **Prestonpans** Sep 21.
	Dec 4	Jacobite army reached Derby, but then began to retreat, pursued by the Duke of Cumberland. Jacobites won battles of Penrith, 18 Dec, and Falkirk 17 Jan 1746, but were decisively defeated at **Culloden** 16 Apr.
1746	Sep	Charles Edward escaped to France.

WAR OF THE QUADRUPLE ALLIANCE, 1718–1720

1717	Jan 4	England, France and Holland formed Triple Alliance to oppose Spanish ambitions in France and Italy. Spain occupied Sardinia Nov 1717, and Sicily Jul 1718.
1718	Aug 2	Austria joined the Triple Alliance, and an English fleet landed Austrian troops near Messina, which surrendered Oct 1719.
	Aug 11	Admiral Byng destroyed Spanish fleet off **Cape Passaro.**
1719		Failure of Spanish expedition to Scotland. French army invaded Spain, and British amphibious forces captured Vigo and Pontevedra.
	Dec 5	Spanish prime minister, Alberoni, dismissed.
1720	Feb 17	Treaty of The Hague concluded the war. The succession to Tuscany, Parma and Piacenza was assured to Charles, eldest son of Philip of Spain and Elizabeth Farnese, while Philip renounced his claims in France and Italy. Sardinia was given to Victor Amadeus of Savoy in place of Sicily, which was made over to Austria.

A further conflict broke out in 1727, when England and France sought to prevent Charles from taking over the Italian Duchies. After brief hostilities, negotiations were opened, and peace was made at the Treaty of Seville 9 Nov 1729, in which Charles' claims were recognised.

WAR OF THE AUSTRIAN SUCCESSION, 1739–1748

1739	Oct 19	England declared war on Spain after prolonged commercial disputes (War of Jenkins' Ear).
		Admiral Vernon captured Porto Bello Nov 1739. But attacks on Cartagena, Cuba and Panama failed, and Vernon and General Wentworth were recalled in 1742.
		1740–4 Anson carried out his circumnavigation, raiding Spanish South American possessions.
1740	Oct	The death of Emperor Charles VI, the succession of Maria Theresa, and Frederick the Great's invasion of Silesia in December brought on the general European conflict, the War of the Austrian Succession.
1741	Sep	George II concluded a treaty with France neutralising Hanover.
1742		After Walpole's resignation in Feb, Carteret persuaded George II to end Hanover's neutrality, and sent an army of English, Hanoverians and Hessians (Pragmatic Army) under Lord Stair to the Low Countries.
1743		Joined by Dutch and Austrian troops, led by George II, the Pragmatic Army advanced and defeated the French at **Dettingen** 27 Jun. Attempts to invade France were unsuccessful.
1744	Mar	France formally declared war on England, and a French army led by Marshal de Saxe invaded the Low Countries.
		A Franco-Spanish plan for an invasion of England came to nothing. A drawn naval engagement took place off Toulon in Feb.
1745		Saxe besieged Tournai, and defeated a relieving army at **Fontenoy** 11 May. Tournai fell 22 May.
	Jun 16	In North America an expedition captured Louisburg from the French.
1746		Saxe completed the conquest of the Austrian Netherlands, taking Brussels in Feb, Antwerp in Jun, and defeating the allies at **Roucoux** 11 Oct.
1747		Saxe invaded Holland, and defeated Cumberland at **Lauffeld** 2 Jul.

Admirals Anson and Hawke won decisive naval victories off **Cape Finisterre** in May and Oct.

1748   Oct 18   Treaty of Aix-la-Chapelle concluded the war. The main points were that Prussia retained Silesia and Glatz. Parma, Piacenza and Guastalla were ceded to Don Philip of Spain. France evacuated the Austrian Netherlands, restored the barrier fortresses to the Dutch and recognised the Hanoverian succession in England. Louisburg was exchanged for Madras, captured by the French in 1746.

SEVEN YEARS' WAR, 1756–1763

(a) **Europe**

1756   Aug 29   Frederick the Great's invasion of Saxony began the conflict in Europe (Britain and France had been at war since May 1756).

1757   Jul   A French army invaded Hanover. Cumberland was defeated at **Hastenbeck,** and signed the Convention of Kloster-Seven 8 Sep, disbanding his army.

    Nov 5   Frederick the Great's victory at Rossbach. The Convention was repudiated, and Ferdinand of Brunswick was given command of the allied army.

1758   Apr   British subsidies to Frederick by the Treaty of London. Ferdinand launched an offensive against the French, pushing them across the Rhine 27 Mar, and defeating them at Krefeld 23 Jun. The French replied by invading Hesse.

1759   Apr 13   Ferdinand defeated by Broglie at **Bergen.**

    Aug 1   Ferdinand defeated the French at **Minden**; they retreated from Hesse.

1760   Broglie was victorious at Korbach 10 Jul, but this was offset by Ferdinand's victory at **Warburg** 31 Jul. Hanover was saved, but a diversion on the lower Rhine was defeated by the French at **Kloster Kamp** 16 Oct.

1761   Ferdinand's advance from Westphalia was defeated by Broglie near Grünberg 21 Mar. A French counter-thrust was defeated at **Vellinghausen** 15 Jul.

	Oct 5	Pitt resigned, and Bute refused to renew the subsidy treaty with Frederick.
1762	Jan 5	Death of Empress Elizabeth of Russia.
	May 5	Treaty of St Petersburg – peace between Prussia and Russia.
	May 22	Peace between Prussia and Sweden.
1763	Feb 15	Treaty of Hubertusburg signed by Prussia, Austria and Saxony, restoring the *status quo ante bellum*.

(b) North America

1754	Jul 3	A Virginian force led by George Washington was forced to surrender to the French at Fort Necessity.
1755	Jul 9	Braddock's expedition to attack Fort Duquesne was destroyed at the **Monongahela River**.
1756	Aug	Montcalm captured Forts Oswego and George, and built Fort Ticonderoga.
1757	Jun–Sep	British expedition to attack Louisburg led by Lord Loudoun failed.
1758		A fourfold attack on the French planned.
	Jul	Fort Duquesne and Louisburg captured by Amherst; but Abercromby's attack on Fort Ticonderoga failed.
	Sep	Forts Frontenac, Oswego and Duquesne taken from the French.
1759	Jul	Fort Niagara fell to British expedition.
	Aug	Ticonderoga and Champlain captured.
	Jun–Sep	Attack on Quebec by Wolfe and Saunders. The French led by Montcalm were defeated in battle before **Quebec** 13 Sep, after Wolfe had scaled the Heights of Abraham. Quebec surrendered 18 Sep.
1760	Sep 8	Marquis de Vaudreuil surrendered Montreal, and with it French Canada.

(c) Naval and Minor Operations

1755	Jun 8	Boscawen captured two French ships carrying reinforce-

ments to Canada, although the rest escaped. There was a general attack on French shipping.

1756	Jun 28	Minorca fell to the French. Admiral Byng, who had failed to relieve it after an inconclusive naval battle 20 May, was executed.
1757	Sep	Failure of a raid on Rochefort.
1758	Feb	Commodore Holmes captured Emden.
		Attacks on the French coast: Cherbourg taken in Jun, but expedition against St Malo repulsed in Sep.
		All French factories on the West African coast captured.
1759	May	Guadeloupe taken from the French.
	Aug 18	Boscawen defeated the French Mediterranean fleet off Lagos.
	Nov 20	Hawke destroyed Brest squadron in battle of **Quiberon Bay.**
1760	Feb	French expedition to Ireland surrendered at Kinsale.
1761	Jun	Dominica and Belle Île captured from French.
1762	Jan 4	England declared war on Spain, and seized Havana in Aug, and Manila in Oct. A British army led by Lord Tyrawley helped the Portuguese to resist a Spanish invasion.
		Rodney forced the surrender of Martinique, Grenada, St Vincent and St Lucia.
		St John's, Newfoundland was lost to the French.

(d) **Treaty of Paris, 10 Feb 1763**

Signed by Britain, France, Spain and Portugal. Principal points:

France ceded to Britain Canada, Nova Scotia, Cape Breton and all lands east of the Mississippi, except New Orleans; she retained fishing rights on the Newfoundland banks.

England restored to France the islands of Guadeloupe, Martinique, St Lucia and Maria Galante. France evacuated territories of Hanover, Hesse, Brunswick and Prussia. Minorca exchanged for Belle Île.

Britain restored Havana to Spain, in exchange for Florida. Spain had been compensated for this in the secret Treaty of San Ildefonso 3 Nov 1762 by receiving from France New Orleans and all Louisiana west of the Mississippi. Spain recovered Manila, and evacuated Portugal and Portuguese colonies.

In Africa, Britain kept Senegal and restored Goree to France.

INDIA

1746	Sep	Madras fell to the French, led by Dupleix and Admiral de la Bourdonnais, who had driven off Commodore Peyton in a naval engagement at Negapatam in Jul.
	Nov	French began unsuccessful siege of Fort St George; ended on arrival of Admiral Boscawen in Apr 1748.
1748	Aug–Oct	Dupleix successfully defended Pondicherry against Boscawen.
	Oct	At the Treaty of Aix-la-Chapelle Madras was restored to Britain, in exchange for Louisburg.
1751		Chanda Sahib, Nawab of the Carnatic, besieged British garrison at Trichinopoly. As a diversion Robert Clive captured Chanda Sahib's capital, Arcot, and withstood a 50-day siege Sep–Nov.
		Clive then defeated the French and their allies at Arni in Nov 1751 and **Covrepauk** in Feb 1752.
1754	Aug	Dupleix relieved of his post. His successor, Godeheu, made peace with the British in the Carnatic.
1756	Jun 20	Surajah Dowlah, Nawab of Bengal, captured Calcutta, and imprisoned 146 Europeans in the 'Black Hole', where 123 died.
1757	Jan 2	Robert Clive and Admiral Watson recaptured Calcutta.
	Jun 23	Clive routed Surajah Dowlah at **Plassey**.
1758		French force under Comte de Lally-Tollendal reached Pondicherry, and captured Fort St David in Jun.
Dec 1758–Feb 1759		Lally unsuccessfully besieged Madras.
1760	Jan 22	Eyre Coote defeated Lally at **Wandiwash**.
1761	Jan 15	Lally's surrender at Pondicherry marked the end of the French bid for power in India.

PRINCIPAL BATTLES, 1688–1763

I Land

Battle	Date	Campaign	Combatants	Strength of armies	Commanders	Casualties
ALMANZA	25 Apr 1707	War of the Spanish Succession	French and Spanish	25 000	Marshal Berwick	4000
			British, Portuguese, Dutch and Germans	15 000	Lord Galway and Marqués das Minas	
AUGHRIM	12 Jul 1691	War of the English Succession	British and allies	25 000	General de Ginkel	700
			French and Irish		General St Ruth	7000
BAHUR	26 Aug 1752	British Conquest of India	British	2500	Major Lawrence	80 out of 400 British
			French	2500	M. Kirjean	
BERGEN	13 Apr 1759	Seven Years' War – Germany	French	30 000	Duc de Broglie	1800
			Allies	24 000	Ferdinand of Brunswick	2500
BLENHEIM	13 Aug 1704	War of Spanish Succession	Allies	56 000	Marlborough and Eugène	12 000
			French and Bavarians	60 000	Marshals Tallard and Marsin, and Elector of Bavaria	29 000 (+ 11 000 prisoners)
BOYNE	11 Jul 1690	War of English Succession	English	36 000	William III	500
			Irish	25 000	James II	1500
BRIHUEGA	10 Dec 1710	War of Spanish Succession	French	20 000	Duc de Vendôme	1800
			British	2500	Earl of Stanhope	500 (+ 2000 prisoners)

Battle	Date	Campaign	Combatants	Strength of armies	Commanders	Casualties
COVREPAUK	14 Feb 1752	British Conquest of India	British	1700	Robert Clive	70
			French	2400	Joseph Dupleix	350
CULLODEN	16 Apr 1746	Jacobite Rebellion	Royalists	9000	Duke of Cumberland	250
			Jacobites	5000	Prince Charles Edward	1000
DENAIN	24 Jul 1712	War of Spanish Succession	French	24 000	Marshal Villars	500
			Allies	10 500	Earl of Albermarle and Prince Eugène	8000
DETTINGEN	27 Jun 1743	War of Austrian Succession	Allies	40 000	George II	2500
			French	60 000	Marshal the Duc de Noailles	6000
DONAUWÖRTH	2 Jul 1704	War of Spanish Succession	British and Imperialists	50 000	Marlborough	5374
			French and Bavarians	12 000	Count D'Arco	—
FLEURUS	1 Jul 1690	War of the Grand Alliance	French	45 000	Marshal Luxembourg	2500
			British, Spanish, German	37 000	Prince of Waldeck	6000 (+ 8000 prisoners)
FONTENOY	11 May 1745	War of Austrian Succession	French	52 000	Marshal de Saxe	7000
			Allies	46 000	Duke of Cumberland	7000
HASTENBECK	26 Jul 1757	Seven Years' War – Germany	French	60 000	Marshal d'Estrées	2350
			Allies	36 000	Duke of Cumberland	1300

Battle	Date	War	Sides	Strength	Commander	Losses
KILLIECRANKIE	17 Jul 1689	Jacobite Rebellion	Jacobites	2500	Dundee	900
			Royalists	3400	General Mackay	2500
KLOSTER KAMP	23 Jun 1758	Seven Years' War – Germany	Allies	7500	Erbprinz of Hesse-Cassel	1600
			French	7000	Marquis de Castries	3000
LAUFFELD	2 Jul 1747	War of Austrian Succession	French	120000	Marshal de Saxe	14000
			Allies	90000	Duke of Cumberland	5600
MALPLAQUET	11 Sep 1709	War of Spanish Succession	Allies	90000	Marlborough and Eugène	20000
			French	90000	Marshal Villars	12000 (+500 prisoners)
MINDEN	1 Aug 1759	Seven Years' War – Germany	Allies	42500	Ferdinand of Brunswick	2700
			French	54000	Marquis de Contades	4900
MONONGAHELA RIVER	9 Jul 1755	Anglo-French struggle for North America	French, Indians	900	Captains Beaujeu and Dumas	65
			British, Virginians	1400	General Braddock	900
NEERWINDEN	29 Jul 1693	War of the Grand Alliance	French	80000	Marshal Luxembourg	9000
			English	50000	William III	19000
OUDENARDE	11 Jul 1708	War of Spanish Succession	Allies	80000	Marlborough and Eugène	7000
			French	85000	Duke of Burgundy and Vendôme	6000 (+9000 prisoners)
PLASSEY	23 Jun 1757	Seven Years' War – India	British	3000	Robert Clive	65
			Bengal	60000	Surajah Dowlah	500

Battle	Date	Campaign	Combatants	Strength of armies	Commanders	Casualties
PRESTONPANS	21 Sep 1745	Jacobite Rebellion	Jacobites Royalists	2500 2300	Prince Charles Edward Sir John Cope	140 400
QUEBEC	13 Sep 1759	Seven Years' War – Canada	British French	5000 4500	General Wolfe Marquis de Montcalm	660 1400
RAMILLIES	23 May 1706	War of Spanish Succession	Allies French	60000 60000	Marlborough Marshal Villeroi	5000 8000 (+7000 prisoners)
ROUCOUX	11 Oct 1746	War of Austrian Succession	French Allies	120000 80000	Marshal de Saxe Prince Charles of Lorraine	5000 5000
SHERIFFMUIR	13 Nov 1715	Jacobite Rebellion	Royalists Jacobites	4000 9000	Duke of Argyll Earl of Mar	600 500
VELLINGHAUSEN	15–16 Jul 1761	Seven Years' War – Germany	Allies French	65000 92000	Ferdinand of Brunswick Prince de Soubise and the Duc de Broglie	1400 5000
WANDIWASH	22 Jan 1760	Seven Years' War – India	British French	4400 3600	Colonel Coote Comte de Lally-Tollendal	190 out of 1900 Europeans 600 out of 2300 Europeans
WARBURG	31 Jul 1760	Seven Years' War – Germany	Allies French	35000	Ferdinand of Brunswick Chevalier du Muy	1200 2000

II Sea

Battle	Date	Campaign	Combatants	Number of ships engaged	Commanders	Ships lost
BEACHY HEAD	30 Jun – 10 Jul 1690	War of the Grand Alliance	French	78	Admiral de la Jonquière	
			British and Dutch	73	Lord Torrington	7
CAPE FINISTERRE	3 May 1747	War of Austrian Succession	British	16	Admiral Anson	
			French	9	Admiral de la Jonquiere	10
CAPE FINISTERRE	14 Oct 1747	War of Austrian Succession	British	14	Admiral Hawke	
			French	9	Admiral de l'Etanduere	4
CAPE PASSARO	11 Aug 1718	War of the Quadruple Alliance	British	21	Admiral Byng	
			Spanish	22	Don Antonio Castañeta	15
LAGOS	27– 28 Jun 1693	War of the Grand Alliance	French	71	Admiral de Tourville	
			Dutch and British	23 (+ 400 convoy ships)	Sir George Rooke	3 (+ 100 merchant ships)
LA HOGUE	29 May– 3 Jun 1692	War of the Grand Alliance	Dutch and British	96	Admirals Russell and Almonde	
			French	44	Admiral de Tourville	15
MALAGA	24 Aug 1704	War of Spanish Succession	British and Dutch	45	Sir George Rooke	0
			French	53	Admiral Comte de Toulouse	0
QUIBERON BAY	20 Nov 1759	Seven Years' War	British	23	Admiral Hawke	2
			French	21	Marshal de Conflans	5

STRENGTH AND COST OF THE BRITISH ARMY, 1689–1763

	Total supplies granted for the Army (£)	Subsidies and pay of foreign troops (£)	Numbers of men voted	Numbers of officers and men in army according to Mutiny Act
1689	2 244 610			
1690	2 413 384			
1691	2 380 698		69 636	
1692	1 825 015		64 924	
1693	1 879 791	162 738	54 562	
1694	2 319 808		83 121	
1695	2 357 076	159 429	87 702	
1696	2 297 109		87 440	
1697	2 297 109		87 440	
1698	1 803 014		35 875	
1699	1 350 000		12 725	
1700	365 000		12 725	
1701	562 033		22 725	
1702	1 261 517	194 517	52 396	
1703	1 590 778	237 464	63 396	
1704	2 115 381	504 190	70 475	
1705	2 456 669	611 166	71 411	
1706	2 694 584	712 797	77 345	
1707	3 054 156	863 547	94 130	
1708	3 030 894	683 462	91 188	
1709	4 016 025	860 669	102 642	
1710	4 002 908	874 619	113 268	
1711	2 864 812	785 730	138 882	
1712	3 397 078	798 958	144 650	
1713	1 146 553	9301	24 400	
1714	1 153 060		16 347	
1715	1 274 907		18 851	
1716	1 520 083		Not stated	
1717	1 523 911	250 000	Not stated	
1718	919 731		16 347	
1719	809 637		17 866	
1720	926 644		19 500	14 294 (home) 5546 (abroad)
1721	904 174	72 000	19 840	12 434
1722	844 472		19 840	16 449
1723	941 990		23 840	16 449
1724	923 300		23 810	16 449
1725	912 968		23 810	16 087
1726	976 034	75 000	23 772	24 013
1727	1 391 730	270 000	32 058	22 950
1728	1 370 184	305 924	28 501	22 955
1729	1 352 099	316 259	28 882	17 709
1730	1 195 712	266 259	23 836	17 709
1731	1 196 060	247 509	23 756	17 709
1732	934 381	22 694	23 756	17 709
1733	907 593		23 756	17 704
1734	980 887		25 634	25 744
1735	1 149 228	56 250	34 354	17 704
1736	1 004 020	56 250	26 314	17 704
1737	1 039 199	42 187	26 314	17 704
1738	961 743		26 896	17 704

	Total supplies granted for the Army (£)	Subsidies and pay of foreign troops (£)	Numbers of men voted	Numbers of officers and men in army according to Mutiny Act
1739	1 021 494	70 583	26 896	35 963
1740	1 268 429	58 333	40 859	46 288
1741	1 703 195	295 752	53 395	46 284
1742	1 809 145	293 263	51 044	51 519
1743	2 546 487	265 195	51 696	51 936
1744	3 071 907	585 200	53 358	55 425
1745	3 028 535	933 219	53 128	74 187
1746	3 354 635	1 266 402	77 664	59 776
1747	3 191 432	1 364 707	61 471	61 489
1748	3 997 326	1 743 316	64 966	18 857
1749	1 730 477	213 991	28 399	18 857
1750	1 238 707	60 985	29 194	18 857
1751	1 077 345	30 000	29 132	18 857
1752	1 041 554	52 000	29 132	18 857
1753	1 069 235	52 000	29 132	18 857
1754	1 068 185	52 000	29 132	18 857
1755	1 139 548	52 000	31 422	34 263
1756	2 174 540	468 946	47 488	49 749
1757	2 516 119	355 639	68 791	53 777
1758	4 173 890	1 475 897	88 370	52 543
1759	4 882 444	1 968 178	91 446	57 294
1760	6 926 490	1 844 487	99 044	64 971
1761	8 615 293	2 091 659	105 221	67 776
1762	7 810 539	1 023 583	120 633	17 536
1763	4 877 139	321 907	120 419	17 532

Source *Parliamentary Papers, 1868–69*, vol. XXXV, pp. 693–703; C. M. Clode, *The Military Forces of the Crown*, vol I, pp. 398–9.

ANNUAL PARLIAMENTARY VOTES FOR THE NAVY, 1689–1763

	Number of seamen and marines voted	Numbers borne (inc marines on shore)	Total grant £
1689	21 695	22 322	1 198 648
1690	27 814	31 971	1 612 976
1691	29 970	35 317	1 791 694
1692	30 000	40 274	1 575 890
1693	33 010	43 827	1 926 516
1694	40 000	47 710	2 500 000
1695	40 000	48 514	2 382 712
1696	40 000	47 677	2 516 972
1697	40 000	44 743	2 372 197
1698	10 000	22 519	1 539 122
1699	15 000	15 834	1 296 383
1700	7000	7754	956 342

	Number of seamen and marines voted	*Numbers borne (inc marines on shore)*	*Total grant £*
1701	30 000	22 869	1 380 000
1702	45 000	33 363	2 209 314
1703	45 000	40 805	2 209 314
1704	45 000	40 433	2 080 000
1705	48 000	43 081	2 230 000
1706	48 000	46 125	2 234 711
1707	48 000	45 055	2 210 000
1708	48 000	44 529	2 210 000
1709	48 000	47 647	2 200 000
1710	48 000	46 493	2 200 000
1711	48 000	46 735	2 200 000
1712	48 000	38 106	2 260 000
1713	20 000	21 636	1 200 000
1714	10 000	13 098	1 068 700
1715	8000*	13 475	1 146 748
1716	10 000*	13 827	984 473
1717	10 000*	13 086	947 560
1718	10 000*	15 268	910 174
1719	13 500*	19 611	1 003 133
1720	13 500*	21 188	1 397 734
1721	10 000*	16 746	789 250
1722	7000*	10 122	1 607 894
1723	10 000*	8078	736 389
1724	10 000*	7037	734 623
1725	10 000*	6298	547 096
1726	10 000*	16 872	732 181
1727	20 000*	20 697	1 239 071
1728	15 000*	14 917	1 495 561
1729	15 000*	14 859	996 026
1730	10 000*	9686	863 787
1731	10 000*	11 133	742 034
1732	8000*	8360	698 885
1733	8000*	9682	748 283
1734	20 000	23 247	2 452 670
1735	30 000	28 819	1 768 914
1736	15 000*	17 010	1 037 436
1737	10 000*	9858	799 201
1738	20 000*	17 668	1 292 886
1739	16 890	23 604	856 689
1740	41 930	37 181	2 157 688
1741	46 550	47 121	2 718 786

	Number of seamen and marines voted	Numbers borne (inc marines on shore)	Total grant £
1742	51 550	44 283	2 765 574
1743	51 550	49 865	2 653 764
1744	51 550	53 754	2 521 085
1745	51 550	53 498	2 567 084
1746	51 550	58 021	2 661 535
1747	51 550	58 508	3 780 911
1748	51 550	50 596	3 640 352
1749	17 000*	18 602	5 179 878
1750	10 000*	12 040	1 021 521
1751	8 000*	9 972	1 056 559
1752	10 000*	9 771	1 794 561
1753	10 000*	8 346	810 207
1754	10 000*	10 149	910 889
1755	22 000*	33 612	1 714 289
1756	50 000*	52 809	3 349 021
1757	66 419	63 259	3 503 939
1758	74 845	70 694	3 874 421
1759	84 845	84 464	5 236 263
1760	88 355	86 626	5 609 708
1761	88 355	80 954	5 594 790
1762	89 061	84 797	5 954 252
1763	34 287	38 350	5 128 977

*No marines voted in these years.
Source   Parliamentary Papers 1868–69, vol XXXV, pp. 693–5.

COMMANDERS 1688–1763

AMHERST, JEFFREY AMHERST, BARON 1717–97

Ensign in the Guards 1731. ADC to Ligonier and Cumberland in Austrian Succession. Maj-Gen 1758, and given command of expedition against French in Canada. Chief command in America Sep 1758 after capture of Louisburg, and led attack on Ticonderoga 1759. Governor-General of British North America 1760–3. Privy Councillor and Lt-Gen of the Ordnance 1772. C-in-C of the army 1772–95 (except 1782–3). Baron 1776. General 1778. Field Marshal 1796.

ANSON, GEORGE ANSON, BARON 1697–1762

Entered navy 1712. Captain 1724. Given command of Pacific squadron, and carried out circumnavigation 1740–4. Rear-Admiral 1744. Promoted to

Board of Admiralty 1745. Vice-Admiral, and command of Channel Fleet 1746. Defeated French off Cape Finisterre May 1747, and created Baron. First Lord of the Admiralty 1751–6 and 1757–62, carrying out important administrative reforms. Admiral of the Fleet 1761.

BOSCAWEN, EDWARD 1711–61

Entered navy 1726. Took part in attacks on Porto Bello 1739 and Cartagena 1741. MP for Truro 1741. Fought in battle off Cape Finisterre May 1747. Made C-in-C of forces in East Indies 1747. Vice-Admiral 1755. Second-in-command of fleet under Hawke 1757. Admiral 1758, and cooperated with Amherst and Wolfe in capture of Louisburg. Privy Councillor, and command of Mediterranean fleet 1759. In the battle of 18 Aug off Lagos he disrupted French plans for invading Britain. General of Marines 1760.

BRADDOCK, EDWARD 1695–1755

Ensign in Coldstream Guards 1710. Served in Holland at siege of Bergen-op-Zoom 1747. Maj-Gen 1754, and appointed to command in North America. He mounted an expedition to attack Fort Duquesne, but his force was destroyed in an ambush after crossing the Monongahela 9 Jul 1755. He himself was wounded, and died 13 Jul.

BURGOYNE, JOHN 1723–92

Cornet in 13th Light Dragoons 1740. Took part in raids on Cherbourg 1758, and St Malo 1759. Raised a light cavalry regiment and commanded it in Portugal 1762. MP for Midhurst 1761, and for Preston 1768. Maj-Gen 1772. Sent to Boston 1774, then to Canada as second-in-command to Carleton. Led an expedition from Canada 1777, but was forced to surrender his whole force at Saratoga 17 Oct. C-in-C in Ireland 1782–3.

CLIVE, ROBERT CLIVE, BARON 1725–74

Sent to Madras in service of East India Company 1743. Fought a duel and twice attempted suicide. Taken prisoner when Madras fell in 1746, but escaped to Fort St David. In Sep 1751 he seized Arcot to distract Chanda Sahib from the siege of Trichinopoly, and followed this with victories at Arni and Covrepauk. In England 1753–5. Returning to Madras, he led the expedition which retook Calcutta Jan 1757, and defeated Surajah Dowlah at Plassey in June. Governor of Bengal 1757–60. Returned to England 1760. Baron in Irish peerage 1762. Knighted 1764. MP for Shrewsbury 1761–74. During his second period as Governor and C-in-C of Bengal 1765–7 he carried out important administrative reforms. Acquitted of corruption in India before Parliamentary Committees 1772–3. Committed suicide 22 Nov 1774.

COOTE, SIR EYRE 1726–83

Entered army at an early age, and served in Germany in Austrian Succession and against Jacobites 1745. In India 1754–62. Played important part in victory at Plassey 1757. Defeated French at Wandiwash 1760. In the following year he captured Pondicherry, and was given command of East India Company forces in Bengal. MP for Leicester 1768. Made C-in-C in Madras Presidency 1769, but quarrelled with the Governor and returned to England 1770. Knighted 1771. Maj-Gen 1775. Lt-Gen 1777. Returned to India as C-in-C 1779, and defeated Hyder Ali. Died at Madras 28 Apr 1783.

CUMBERLAND, WILLIAM AUGUSTUS, DUKE OF 1721–65

Second surviving son of George II. Colonel of Coldstream Guards 1740. Maj-Gen 1742. Lt-Gen 1743. Wounded at Dettingen 1743. C-in-C of the allied army 1745; defeated at Fontenoy. Recalled to put down the Jacobite Rebellion; defeated the rebels at Culloden 1746 and earned the nickname 'Butcher'. Returned to Flanders 1747, and defeated by Saxe at Lauffeld. On outbreak of Seven Years' War he was defeated at Hastenbeck Jul 1757, and signed the Convention of Kloster-Seven for the evacuation of Hanover. As a result he resigned in disgrace Oct 1757.

GAGE, THOMAS 1721–87

Lieutenant in 48th Foot 1741. Fought in Flanders in Austrian Succession, and at Culloden. Sent to America 1754, and wounded in Braddock's expedition 1755. Organised a Light Infantry Regiment (80th) 1758, and commanded light infantry in attack on Ticonderoga. Governor of Montreal 1760. Maj-Gen 1761. Lt-Gen 1770. C-in-C in North America 1763–72. Governor of Massachusetts Bay 1774. Sent force to seize arms at Concord, and fought battle of Bunker Hill 1775. Appointed C-in-C in North America Aug 1775, but resigned Oct. General 1782.

GRANBY, JOHN MANNERS, MARQUIS OF 1721–70

Eldest son of Duke of Rutland. MP for Grantham 1741–54 and Cambridgeshire 1754–70. Colonel of a Regiment raised in 1745 to suppress Jacobites; served as a volunteer on Cumberland's staff. Served in Flanders 1747. Maj-Gen 1755. Colonel of Royal Horse Guards 1758. Lt-Gen 1759. Succeeded Sackville in command of British forces 1759, and defeated French at Warburg 1760. Master-General of the Ordnance 1763. C-in-C of the Army 1766–70.

HAWKE, EDWARD HAWKE, BARON 1705–81

Entered navy 1720. Captain 1734. Took part in action at Toulon 1744. Rear-Admiral and second-in-command of Channel Fleet 1747, commanding it from Sep due to Sir Peter Warren's ill-health. He defeated French off Cape Finisterre Oct 1747, and was knighted. MP for Portsmouth 1747–76. Vice-Admiral 1748. Succeeded to Warren's command 1748–52. Command of western squadron 1755. Sent to relieve Byng in the Mediterranean 1756. Admiral 1757, and led naval force in unsuccessful expedition to Rochefort. Command of western squadron 1759; defeated French at Quiberon Bay 20 Nov. First Lord of the Admiralty 1766–71. Admiral and C-in-C of the Fleet 1768. Baron 1776.

HOWE, RICHARD HOWE, EARL 1726–99

Entered navy 1739. Post Captain 1746. MP for Dartmouth 1757–82. Succeeded as viscount in Irish peerage 1758. Commanded ships in raids on French coast 1758, and played important part in battle of Quiberon Bay 1759. A Lord of the Admiralty 1763–5. Treasurer of Navy 1765–70. Rear-Admiral 1770. Vice-Admiral 1775. Command of North America Station 1776–8. Admiral, viscount and command of Channel Fleet Apr 1782; relieved Gibraltar in autumn. First Lord of the Admiralty Jan–Apr 1783, and Dec 1783–Aug 1788. Baron and Earl 1788. Command of Channel Fleet May–Dec 1790, and 1793–7; defeated French off Ushant 1794. Admiral of the Fleet and General of Marines 1796. Helped pacify mutineers at Spithead 1797.

HOWE, WILLIAM HOWE, VISCOUNT 1729–1814

Cornet in Cumberland's Light Dragoons 1746. MP for Nottingham 1758–80. Commanded 58th Foot Regiment at siege of Louisburg 1758, and leading a newly formed light infantry battalion, took part in capture of Quebec 1759 and Montreal 1760. Maj-Gen 1772. Lt-Gen 1775. Sent to Boston as second-in-command and led left wing in battle of Bunker Hill. Succeeded Gage in supreme command Oct 1775. Resigned 1778. Lt-Gen of the Ordnance 1782–1803. General 1793. Held home commands 1793 and 1795. Succeeded to viscountcy on death of his brother Admiral Lord Howe 1799. Governor of Plymouth 1805.

LIGONIER, JOHN LIGONIER, EARL 1680–1770

Born at Castres in France of Huguenot parents who took refuge in Ireland 1697. Served under Marlborough 1702–11. Lt-Governor of Fort St Philip, Minorca 1712. Colonel of 7th Dragoon Guards 1720. Maj-Gen 1739. Lt-Gen 1743. Staff officer to George II; commanded second division at Dettingen and the Foot at Fontenoy. C-in-C in Netherlands 1746–7. MP for Bath 1748. Lt-Gen of the Ordnance 1748–56. Viscount in Irish peerage 1757. C-in-C of the army 1757–9, and military adviser to Pitt. Master-General of the Ordnance 1759–62. Baron 1763. Field Marshal and Earl 1766.

MARLBOROUGH, JOHN CHURCHILL, 1ST DUKE OF 1650–1722

Born at Ashe in Devon. Commission in Foot Guards 1667. Served in Tangier garrison 1668–70. Captain 1672. Fought at battle of Sole Bay 28 May 1672, then joined English contingent fighting with the French against the Dutch. Baron Churchill in Scottish peerage 1682 (English peerage 1685). Colonel of the 1st Royal Dragoons 1683. Second-in-command under Lord Feversham of army which defeated Monmouth at Sedgemoor 1685. His defection to William of Orange ensured James II's downfall in 1688. Created Earl of Marlborough and given command of expeditions in Flanders and Ireland. Losing royal favour, he was sent to the Tower suspected of treason in 1692. He was released but did not return to Court until 1695. On accession of Queen Anne, an intimate friend of the Marlboroughs, in 1702, Marlborough was made Captain-General of the Forces and Master-General of the Ordnance. He went to Holland on 15 May 1702 and in the next seven years defeated the French in four great battles: Blenheim 1704, Ramillies 1706, Oudenarde 1708 and Malplaquet 1709. In 1711 he was recalled by the Tory government and relieved of his commands.

RODNEY, GEORGE BRYDGES RODNEY, BARON 1718–92

Entered navy 1732. Post Captain 1742. Took part in Hawke's victory off Cape Finisterre Oct 1747. Governor and C-in-C of Newfoundland 1749–52. MP for Saltash 1751, and for Northampton 1768. Served in expedition against Rochefort 1757, and at capture of Louisburg 1758. Rear-Admiral 1759. Raided transport ships on French coast 1759–60. C-in-C of Leeward Islands station 1761–3. Vice-Admiral 1762. Baronet 1764. Governor of Greenwich Hospital 1765–70. Jamaica command 1771–4. Admiral 1778. C-in-C of Leeward Islands 1779–82. Ordered to relieve Gibraltar on his way to the West Indies, he defeated the Spanish and captured a convoy Jan 1780. Defeated French at the battle of the Saints 1782, and created a baron.

SACKVILLE, GEORGE SACKVILLE, VISCOUNT 1716–85

Known from 1720–70 as Lord George Sackville, and from 1770–82 as Lord George Germain.

Third son of Duke of Dorset. Captain in 6th Dragoon Guards 1737. Distinguished service in Austrian Succession; wounded at Fontenoy. MP for Dover 1741–61, Kent 1761–8, and East Grinstead 1768–82. Involved in Irish affairs 1750–6. Maj-Gen 1755. Lt-Gen of the Ordnance 1757–9. Took part in attack on Saint Malo 1758. Given command of British contingent in Germany Oct 1758. Court-martialled for refusing to charge at Minden 1759. Colonial Secretary 1775–82. Viscount 1782.

WOLFE, JAMES 1727-59

Second lieutenant in Marines 1741. Transferred as Ensign to 12th Foot 1742. Fought at Dettingen 1743, against Jacobites at Falkirk and Culloden 1745-6, and was wounded at Lauffeld 1747. Garrison duty in Scotland and England 1749-57. Quartermaster-general in attack on Rochefort 1757. Served under Amherst in expedition against Cape Breton 1758, and was largely responsible for capture of Louisburg. Given command as a Major-General of expedition against Quebec; killed in battle of Heights of Abraham 13 Sep 1759 which led to the capture of the city.

10 THE COLONIES

MAIN TERRITORIES UNDER BRITISH RULE BY 1763

Territory	Original entry into British rule and status in 1763
Antigua	Colony (1663)
Bahamas	First settled 1646: colony (1783)
Barbados	First settled 1627: colony (1662)
Bengal	Ceded by France (1763)
Bermuda	First settled 1609; colony (1684)
Bombay	Ceded by France (1763)
British Honduras	First settled 1638
Canada	Ceded colonies from 1713 onwards.
Cayman, Turks and Caicos Islands	Ceded (1670)
Connecticut	Permanently settled 1635
Delaware	Permanently settled 1683
Dominica	Colony (1763)
Gambia	Settlement began 1618
Georgia	First settled 1733
Gibraltar	Ceded colony (1713)
Gold Coast	Settlement began 1750
Grenada	Ceded colony (1763)
Hudson's Bay Company	Ceded by France (1713)
India	Settlement began 1601
Jamaica	Colony (seized 1655 and ceded 1670)
Madras	Ceded by France (1763)
Maryland	First settled 1634
Massachusetts	First settled 1620
Minorca	Seized from Spain 1708
Montserrat	First settled (1642) as colony
Newfoundland	Settlement began 1623
New Hampshire	First settled 1623
New Jersey	First settled 1664

New York	First settled 1614
North Carolina	First settled 1650
Nova Scotia	Ceded by France (1713)
Pennsylvania	First settled 1682
Quebec	Ceded by France (1713)
Rhode Island	First settled 1636
St Christopher (St Kitts) and Nevis	Colony (1625)
St Helena	Administered by E. India Co. 1673
St Vincent	Ceded colony (1763)
South Carolina	First settled 1670
Virginia	First settled 1607
Virgin Islands	Colonies (1666)
Windward Isles	Colonies (1763)

CHRONOLOGY OF BRITISH COLONIAL EXPANSION, 1688–1760

1689   William and Mary recognise old Charters of colonies.

1690   East India Company makes peace with Mogul Empire; factory at Calcutta established.

1691   Revolution settlement of the New England colonies; new charter granted to Massachusetts; Governor and other officials to be appointed by the Crown.

1693   Carolina divided into North and South Carolina.

1695   Formation of Company of Scotland for trade with Africa and the Indies.

1696   Establishment of Board of Trade and Plantations.

1697   Under Treaty of Ryswick, Hudson's Bay company reduced to only one factory (Fort Albany). Publication of Dampier's *New Voyage Round the World*.

1698   Major attack on old East India Company in new legislation with Act creating New East India Company. Erection of Fort William to protect Calcutta; first Darien expedition by Company of Scotland.

1699   Second Darien expedition also fails.

1702   Delaware becomes separate Crown Colony; French portion of St

Kitts captured at outbreak of the War of the Spanish Succession; merger agreed of rival East India Companies.

1703 Methuen Treaty with Portugal.

1704 English capture Gibraltar.

1708 Capture of Minorca.

1709 Fusion of rival East India Companies completed. New body entitled United Company of Merchants of England trading to the East Indies.

1710 Capture of Nova Scotia.

1711 Formation of South Sea Company.

1713 Treaty of Utrecht signed. France ceded whole of Hudson's Bay, French St Kitts, the Newfoundland settlements and Nova Scotia (except for Cape Breton Island). Spain ceded Gibraltar and Minorca. The Asiento (the monopoly of supplying slaves to Spanish American colonies) also abandoned (granted to the South Sea Company).

1729 Dispute over government of Carolina resolved and divided into North and South Carolina by Act of Parliament.

1732 Proprietary grant to General James Oglethorpe of Georgia.

1733 New colony of Savannah founded by Oglethorpe.

1739 War of Jenkins' Ear; capture of Porto Bello by Admiral Vernon.

1740 Expedition of Commodore George Anson to attack Spanish colonies on Pacific coast of South America. Oglethorpe from Georgia makes unsuccessful attack on Florida.

1741 Attack on Cartagena by Vernon and Wentworth; Dupleix appointed Governor of Pondicherry.

1742 Unsuccessful attack on Cuba.

1744 Capture of Annapolis (in Nova Scotia) by the French marks beginning of Anglo-French struggle over the colonies.

1745 British capture Louisburg; William Shirley (the Governor of Massachusetts) and William Pepperell, leader of the force, both received baronetcies.

1746 French capture of Madras by La Bourdonnais.

1747 Decisive naval victories by Anson at Cape Finisterre and Hawke at Belle Île. Unsuccessful French attacks on Fort St David (Cuddalore).

1748 Peace of Aix-la-Chapelle; mutual restoration of colonies. Four disputed islands (St Lucia, Dominica, St Vincent and Tobago) declared neutral. Formation of the Ohio Company (followed by the Loyal Company and Greenbriar Company).

1749 Dupleix's unauthorised war in India; Chanda Sahib adopted by Dupleix as Nawab of the Carnatic; Chanda Sahib victorious at Battle of Ambur. Marquis de Bussy power behind the throne in the Deccan; foundation of Halifax in Nova Scotia.

1750 British settlement begins on Gold Coast.

1751 British support for Mohammed Ali; Clive successfully attacked Arcot (capital of the Carnatic). Subsequent victory for Clive at Battle of Arni.

1752 Georgia becomes a Crown Colony; relief of siege of Trichinopoly; Mohammed Ali now the effective Nawab.

1753 Dupleix recalled (he received the order in 1754). French in effective control of Ohio, establishment of Fort Duquesne.

1755 Defeat of General Edward Braddock's march to attack Fort Duquesne. Deportation of 6000 French ('Arcadians') from Nova Scotia. Construction of Fort Edward on the east of the Hudson.

1756 Outbreak of Seven Years' War. Initial French successes included fall of Minorca (Admiral Byng subsequently shot) and advances by Montcalm in Canada. Nabob of Bengal imprisons British in 'Black Hole' of Calcutta.

1757 Further French successes in Canada; fall of Fort William Henry to Montcalm. British forced back to upper waters of the Hudson. Battle of Plassey gives Clive mastery of Bengal.

1758 Repulse of Abercrombie before Ticonderoga; capture of Louisburg. Capture of Forts Duquesne and Frontenac.

1759 Capture of Forts Niagara and Ticonderoga. General Wolfe captures Quebec after battle of the Heights of Abraham.

1760 Surrender of Montreal and Canada to British. Battle of Wandiwash breaks French power in India.

IRELAND, 1688–1760

1688 Irish troops dispatched to England (Oct). Londonderry refuses to accept Catholic garrison (Dec).

1689   Landing of James II at Kinsale in Ireland (12 Mar); joined by Tyrconnell and enters Dublin (24 Mar). Siege of Protestants at Londonderry opens (20 Apr). Irish Parliament issues an Attainder, confiscating the land of 2000 of William's adherents (May). Siege of Londonderry lifted (28 Jul) by Kirke and defeat of Catholic forces at Newton Butler (28 Jul). William III sends Marshal Schomberg with 10 000 troops to Belfast (August).

1690   7000 French troops arrive at Kinsale to support James (Mar). William lands in Ireland (14 Jun). William defeats James's forces at Battle of the Boyne (1 Jul) and James flees to France while his forces retreat to the west. First siege of Limerick repulsed (Aug); Cork and Kinsale taken by William's forces.

1691   Fall of Athlone (30 Jun) and defeat of James's forces at Battle of Aughrim by Ginkel (12 Jul). Second siege of Limerick which surrenders on 3 October. Treaty, or pacification of Limerick offers free transportation to all Irish officers and soldiers desiring to go to France. Irish Catholics to have same religious liberties as enjoyed under Charles II and the right to carry arms and practise their professions. 1 000 000 acres of 'rebel' estates confiscated.

1692   Meeting of Irish Parliament (Oct). William and Mary recognised as rulers. Catholics prevented from sitting in Parliament and laws passed to limit their worship, ownership of property and education in defiance of Treaty of Limerick. Parliament prorogued for refusing to pass money bill (Nov).

1693   Irish Parliament dissolved (Jun).

1695   Irish Parliament passes bills prohibiting Catholics from sending children abroad to be educated and preventing them bearing arms.

1697   Irish Parliament banishes all Roman Catholic bishops and monastic clergy. Treaty of Limerick ratified but modified to incorporate penal laws against Catholics.

1699   Irish export woollen trade restricted.

1703   Act passed determining conditions of Catholic worship; priests required to register name and parish in order to celebrate mass or face imprisonment or execution.

1704   Act prevents land being passed on to Catholics. Protestant dissenters excluded from office.

1709   Catholic clergy required to take Oath of Abjuration of Stuart pretender. Refused by 1000 Catholic priests.

1710   Linen Board set up to supervise linen industry.

1713   Duke of Shrewsbury appointed Lord Lieutenant.

1714   Schism Act extended to Ireland.

1719   Law-suit of Sherlock v. Annesley leads to Act for better securing of the dependency of the Kingdom of Ireland upon the Crown of Great Britain, declaring that the British Parliament had full authority to make laws 'of sufficient force and validity to bind the kingdom and people of Ireland' and denying the status of the Irish House of Lords as a Court of Appeal. Act of Toleration granted religious freedom to Protestant dissenters, but Test Acts retained.

1720   Irish cotton industry restricted by British Parliament. Jonathan Swift publishes anonymously a pamphlet supporting Irish manufacturers against British.

1721   Duke of Grafton appointed Lord Lieutenant.

1722   Grant to William Wood, a Wolverhampton ironmaster, of a patent to coin money for Ireland (Jul) arouses controversy.

1723   Irish Parliament protests against 'Wood's halfpence' (Sep) and refuses to transact further business.

1724   Lord Carteret replaces Grafton as Lord Lieutenant. Swift publishes first of *Drapier's Letters* (Feb), attacking the new coinage and the constitutional relationship between Britain and Ireland.

1725   British government reduces amount of currency to be issued by Wood from £108 000 to £40 000. Attempt to prosecute printer of *Drapier's Letters* fails and government withdraws Wood's patent completely.

1727   Irish Catholics deprived of the vote.

1727–30   Series of poor harvests leads to widespread famine.

1731   Duke of Dorset becomes Lord Lieutenant. Dublin Society set up to encourage agriculture and the arts.

1740–1   Serious famine leads to between 80 000 and 400 000 deaths.

1745   Earl Chesterfield becomes Lord Lieutenant and begins suspension of penal laws against Catholics.

1746   Irish forbidden to export glassware.

1747   Charles Lucas begins to publish the *Citizen's Journal*. John Wesley makes first of 42 visits to Ireland; first Methodist church established in Dublin.

1750   Roman Catholics admitted to lower grades of the army.

1753   Irish Parliament defeats money bill to dispose of Irish budget surplus to defray English national debt. Henry Boyle, Speaker of Irish Commons, dismissed as Chancellor of Exchequer. Widespread rejoicing in Dublin. Parliament prorogued.

1755   Marquess of Hartington appointed Lord Lieutenant to secure compromise on money bill. Boyle given earldom and other officials reinstated.

1759   Crowds invade Parliament on rumour of union with England. Henry Flood enters Parliament and leads 'patriots'. Restrictions on export of Irish cattle to England lifted.

NORTH AMERICA, 1688–1760

1689   On news of 'Glorious Revolution' in England, James II's appointee as president of New England, Sir Edmund Andros, seized and imprisoned in Boston (18 Apr). Assembly of representatives meets at Boston. Proclamation of William and Mary.

King William's War sees operation of French with Indian support against the colonists.

1690   Sir William Phipps captures Port Royal (Apr) but fails in attack on Quebec.

1692   New charter issued for Massachusetts and appointment of Sir William Phipps as governor. The charter of the colony included the provinces of Maine, Nova Scotia and all land north of the St Lawrence. The Crown to appoint the governor and vested in him the right of calling, proroguing and dissolving the general court, appointing military officers and law officers and of vetoing acts of the legislature and appointments made by it. The electoral franchise was extended to all freeholders with a yearly income of 40 shillings and all inhabitants having personal property to the amount of £40. Religious liberty granted to Roman Catholics.

Beginning of the Salem witch craze (Feb). Twenty persons executed by October.

Construction of Fort William Henry in Maine.

College of William and Mary in Virginia.

1693   Penn dismissed from government of Pennsylvania.

1696   French capture fort at Pemaquid.

1697   At Peace of Ryswick both sides restore each others' conquests.

1699	French settle Louisiana.
	First Scottish settlement at Darien.
1701	William Penn obtained a new charter for Pennsylvania.
	Yale College founded at New Haven, Connecticut.
1702	War of Spanish Succession leads to renewed fighting between France and Britain.
1703	Pennsylvania divided into the province and the territories with separate assemblies.
1704	French with Indian support defeat Deerfield, but Colonel Church leads expedition on the French settlements in New England.
1706	French and Spanish invade Carolina but repulsed.
1710	English fleet captures Port Royal and renamed Annapolis.
1711	Tuscaroras and other tribes attack colonists in Carolina, but eventually crushed by Barnwell.
1713	Treaty of Utrecht results in cession of Hudson Bay and Straits of Nova Scotia, Newfoundland, and St Christopher to England.
	Treaty with eastern Indians at Portsmouth. Rectification of the boundary between Massachusetts and Connecticut.
1715	Yamassees and allied tribes attack Carolina, but repulsed.
1718	Captain Wood Rogers, governor of New Providence, suppressed the buccaneers in the West Indies and extirpates the pirates on the coast of Carolina.
1719	Beginning of discontent of colonists against the proprietary government in Carolina. The colonists' assembly refused to be dissolved and elected a new governor, resisting the old governor with arms.
1720	Prohibition of trade between Indians and French in New York.
1721	Royal Council declares Charter of Proprietors of Carolina forfeit and establishes a provisional royal government.
1722	In New York, governor Burnet opens negotiations with the Iroquois confederacy at Albany and establishes a trading-house at Oswego.
1724	Indian hostilities in New England with Abinakis.
1725	Yamassees assault English colonists in Carolina from Spanish Florida.

1726 Governor of Massachusetts, Shute, obtains from the Crown the power to suppress debate and limited power of adjournment by the representatives.

In New York, a treaty brings new Indian tribes under English protection.

1728 Boundary between Virginia and North Carolina surveyed and settled.

1729 Agreement reached with proprietors of Carolina. Seven sold their titles and property, an eighth retained his property but lost his proprietary power. The Crown assumed the right of nominating governors and councils. The province was divided into North and South Carolina.

1731 Settlement of boundary between New York and Connecticut.

1733 Settlement of Georgia under James Oglethorpe and 20 other trustees for the Crown. Liberty of worship granted to all except Roman Catholics. First settlement established at Savannah.

1738 Foundation of Princeton College, New Jersey.

1739–48 War between Britain and Spain.

1740 Oglethorpe leads unsuccessful expedition against Florida.

Expedition against Cartagena fails.

1741 Colonists attack Cuba.

1742 Spanish expedition against Georgia repulsed.

1744–8 War with France.

1745 Siege and capture of French fort of Louisburg on Cape Breton Island by colonial troops under William Pepperell.

1746 Projected attack on Canada by the colonists frustrated by the arrival of a French fleet, under D'Anville.

1747 Rioting in Boston against impressment of sailors.

1748 Treaty of Aix-la-Chapelle between England, France and Spain leads to reciprocal surrender of conquests in North America.

Formation of the Ohio Company under a charter from the English Crown.

1750 Disputes between French and English over boundaries of Arcadia.

1751 Governor Clinton, of New York, in association with South Carolina,

Massachusetts and Connecticut concludes a peace with the 'Six Nations' Indian confederacy.

1752   Trustees of Georgia give up their Charter and Georgia is placed on the same footing as the other royal colonies. Introduction of Gregorian calendar in the colonies.

1753   George Washington despatched from Virginia to remonstrate with the French on the Allegheny and the Ohio for encroachments on Virginian territory.

1754   Virginia sends a force to the Ohio, part commanded by Washington, but he is captured and forced to withdraw. Conference of colonial delegates at Albany with the Six Nations. Benjamin Franklin draws up a plan for the union of all the colonies under a president appointed by the crown, with an elected grand council of delegates, with a right of legislation subject to the veto of the president and the approval of the crown. Connecticut, objecting to the veto power, refused to sign the proposal, which was later rejected both by the colonies and the crown.

1756–63 War between England and France. Braddock sent from England to command forces in North America. Colonial governors and Braddock decide to mount three expeditions: against Fort Duquesne; against the fort at Niagara; and against Crown Point in New York. Meanwhile, 3000 troops from Massachusetts captured forts Beausejour and Gaspereaux in Nova Scotia (June).
For the further events of the Seven Years' War in North America, see p. 162.

PRINCIPAL COLONIAL GOVERNORS

ANTIGUA

1682	Nathaniel Johnson
1689	General Codrington
1698	Colonel John Yeamans (Lieut-Gov)
1698	Christopher Codrington
1704	Sir William Matthew
1706	Colonel Parke
1710	Col John Yeamans (Lieut-Gov)
1710	Gen Hamilton
1711	Walter Douglas
1715	General Hamilton
1721	John Hart

1728   Lord Londonderry
1730   William Matthew
1752   Sir George Thomas

BAHAMAS

1687	Bridges	1717	Woodes Rogers
1690	Cadwallader Jones	1721	George Phenny
1694	Trott	1728	Woodes Rogers
1694	Nicholas Webb	1733	Richard Fitzwilliam
1700	Elias Hasket	1738	John Tinker
1700	Ellis Lightfoot	1759	William Shirley
1704	Birch		

BARBADOS

1685	Edwin Stede (Deputy)	1720	Samuel Cox (President)
1690	James Kendall	1722	Henry Worsley
1694	Francis Russell	1731	Samuel Barwick (President)
1696	Francis Bond (President)	1733	James Dotin (President)
1698	Ralph Grey	1733	Lord (Viscount) Scroop Hov
1701	John Farmer (President)	1735	James Dotin (President)
1703	Sir Bevill Granville	1739	Hon Robert Bing
1706	William Sharpe (President)	1740	James Dotin (President)
1707	Metford Crowe	1742	Sir Thomas Robinson
1710	George Willington (President)	1747	Hon Henry Grenville
1711	Robert Lowther	1753	Ralph Weeks (President)
1720	John Frere (President)	1756	Charles Pinfold

BENGAL (Presidents)

1700   Sir Charles Eyre
1701   John Beard
1705–10 Vacant: members of council presided in rotation
1710   Anthony Weltden
1711   John Russell
1713   Robert Hedges
1718   Samuel Feake
1723   John Deane
1726   Henry Frankland
1728   John Deane
1732   John Stackhouse
1739   Thomas Braddyll
1746   John Forster
1748   William Barwell

1749	Adam Dawson	1760	John Z. Holwell
1752	William Fytche	1760	Henry Vansittart
1752	Roger Drake	1764	John Spencer
1758	Col Robert Clive		

BERMUDA

1687	Sir R. Robinson	1721	Sir J. Bruce Hope
1691	Isaac Richier	1727	Capt J. Pitt
1692	Capt Goddard	1737	Alured Popple
1698	Samuel Day	1745	William Popple
1700	Capt Bennett	1764	G. J. Bruere
1713	Henry Pullein		

BOMBAY (Governors)

1681	Sir John Child	1729	Robert Cowan
1690	Bartholomew Harris	1734	John Horne
1694	Sir John Gayer	1739	Stephen Law
1704	Sir Nicholas Waite	1742	William Wake
1708	William Aislabie	1750	Richard Bourchier
1715	Charles Boone	1760	Charles Crommelin
1722	William Phipps		

CONNECTICUT

1683	Robert Treat	1742	Jonathan Law
1698	FitzJohn Winthrop	1751	Roger Wolcott
1708	Gordon Saltonstall	1754	Thomas Fitch
1725	Joseph Talcott		

GEORGIA

1733	James Edward Oglethorpe	1754	John Reynolds
1750	William Stephens	1757	Henry Ellis
1750	Henry Parker		

GIBRALTAR

1704–6	Georg von Hessen-Darmstadt
1707–11	Roger Elliott
1711–13	Thomas Stanwix
1713–20	E of Portmore
1720–7	Richard Kane
1727–30	Jasper Clayton
1730–8	Joseph Sabine

1738–9	Francis Columbine
1739–49	William Hargrave
1749–52	Humphry Bland
1752–6	Thomas Fowke
1756	E of Tyrawley
1756–8	E of Panmure
1758–61	Earl Home

HUDSON'S BAY COMPANY

1670	Prince Rupert	1700	Stephen Evance
1683	James Stuart	1712	Bibye Lake
1685	John Churchill	1743	Benjamin Pitt
1691	Stephen Evance	1746	Thomas Knapp
1696	William Trumbull	1750	Atwell Lake

JAMAICA

1687	D of Albemarle	1722	D of Portland
1690	E of Inchiquin	1728	Maj-Gen Hunter
1702	William Selwyn	1735	H. Cunningham
1710	Ld A. Hamilton	1738	G. Trelawney
1716	Peter Heywood	1752	Charles Knowles
1718	Sir N. Lawes	1758	George Haldane

MADRAS (Governors)

1687	Elihu Yale	1725	James Macrae
1692	Nathaniel Higginson	1730	George Morton Pitt
1698	Thomas Pitt	1735	Richard Benyon
1709	Gulston Addison	1744	Nicholas Morse
1709	Edmund Montague (Acting)	1746	John Hinde
1709	William Fraser (Acting)	1747	Charles Floyer
1711	Edward Harrison	1750	Thomas Saunders
1717	Joseph Collet	1755	George Pigot
1720	Francis Hastings (Acting)	1763	Robert Palk
1721	Nathaniel Elwick		

MARYLAND

1684	William Joseph	1709	Edward Lloyd
1691	Lionel Copley	1714	John Hart
1693	Thomas Lawrence	1720	Charles Calvert
1694	Francis Nicholson	1726	Benedict Leonard Calvert
1698	Nathaniel Blackistone	1731	Samuel Ogle
1703	John Seymour	1732	Charles Calvert

1735	Samuel Ogle	1752	Benjamin Taskar
1742	Thomas Bladen	1753	Horatio Sharpe
1747	Samuel Ogle		

MASSACHUSETTS

1686	Edmund Andros	1728	William Burnett
1689	Simon Bradstreet	1729	William Dummer
1692	William Phipps	1730	William Tailer
1694	William Stoughton	1730	Jonathan Belcher
1699	E of Bellomont	1741	William Shirley
1700	William Stoughton	1749	Spencer Phips
1702	Joseph Dudley	1753	William Shirley
1715	William Tailer	1756	Spencer Phips
1716	Samuel Shute	1757	Thomas Downal
1723	William Dummer		

MINORCA

Governors (since seizure from Spain, 1708)

1708	James Stanhope	1718	George Forbes
1711	Duke of Argyll	1730	Richard Kane
1713	Earl of Peterborough	1737	Earl of Hertford
1714	Duke of Argyll (again)	1742	Earl of Stair
1716	George Carpenter	1747	Earl of Tyrawley (to 1756)

NEWFOUNDLAND

Governors

1729	Capt Osborne	1750	Capt Drake
1737	Capt Vanburgh	1753	Capt Bonfoy
1740	Lord G. Graham	1755	Capt Dorril
1741	Hon J. Byng	1757	Capt Edwards
1744	Sir C. Hardy	1760	Capt Webb
1749	Lord Rodney		

NEW HAMPSHIRE

Governors*

1692	John Usher	1715	George Vaughan
1697	William Partridge	1717	John Wentworth
1699	office vacant until 1703	1730	David Dunbar
1703	John Usher (again)	1741	Benning Wentworth

*Up to 1692, known as Presidents of the Council, from 1692 to 1741 as Lieutenant-Governors, then Governors.

NEW JERSEY*

Governors

1703	Baron Cornbury	1732	William Cosby
1708	John Lovelace	1736	John Hamilton
1709	Richard Ingoldsby	1738	Lewis Morris (third term)
1710	Robert Hunter	1746	John Hamilton (again)
1719	Lewis Morris	1747	Jonathan Belcher
1720	William Burnet	1757	Thomas Pownall
1728	John Montgomerie	1757	John Reading
1731	Lewis Morris (again)	1758	Francis Bernard

*Prior to 1703, divided into East Jersey and West Jersey

NEW PLYMOUTH*

1686	Edmond Andros
1689–92	Thomas Hinckley

*See under Massachusetts after 1692

NORTH CAROLINA

1689	Philip Ludwell	1714	Charles Eden
1691	Thomas Jarvis	1722	Thomas Pollock (again)
1694	John Archdale	1722	William Reed
1696	John Harvey	1724	George Burrington
1699	Henderson Walker	1725	Richard Everard
1704	Robert Daniel	1731	George Burrington (again)
1705	Thomas Cary	1734	Gabriel Johnston
1706	William Glover	1752	Nathaniel Rice
1708	Thomas Cary (again)	1753	Matthew Rowan
1711	Edward Hye	1754	Arthur Dobbs
1712	Thomas Pollock		

NOVA SCOTIA

1749	Hon E. Cornwallis	1754	C. Lawrence
1752	V. Hopson	1756	A. Moulton

PENNSYLVANIA

1688	John Blackwell	1703	Edward Shippen
1690	Thomas Lloyd	1704	John Evans
1693	William Markham	1709	Charles Gookin
1699	William Penn	1717	William Keith
1701	Andrew Hamilton	1726	Patrick Gordon

1736	James Logan
1738	George Thomas
1747	Anthony Palmer
1748	James Hamilton

1754	Robert Hunter Morris
1756	William Denny
1759	James Hamilton

RHODE ISLAND

1686	Edmond Andros
1689	John Coggeshall
1690	Henry Bull
1690	John Easton
1695	Caleb Carr
1696	Walter Clarke
1698	Samuel Cranston
1727	Joseph Jencks
1732	William Wanton
1734	John Wanton

1740	Richard Ward
1743	William Greene
1745	Gideon Wanton
1746	William Greene
1747	Gideon Wanton
1748	William Greene
1755	Stephen Hopkins
1757	William Greene
1758	Stephen Hopkins

SOUTH CAROLINA

1686	James Colleton
1690	Seth Sothel
1692	Philip Ludwell
1693	Thomas Smith
1694	Joseph Blake
1695	John Archdale
1696	Joseph Blake
1700	James Moore
1703	Nathaniel Johnson
1709	Edward Tynte
1710	Robert Gibbes

1711	Charles Craven
1717	Robert Johnson
1719	James Moore
1721	Francis Nicholson
1724	Arthur Middleton
1729	Robert Johnson
1735	Thomas Broughton
1737	William Bull
1743	James Glen
1756	William Henry Lyttelton

11 LAW AND ORDER

LEGAL OFFICE HOLDERS

CHIEF JUSTICES (KING'S BENCH)

1689   Sir John Holt
1710   Sir Thomas Parker (Ld Macclesfield)
1718   Sir John Pratt
1725   Sir Robert Raymond (Ld Raymond)
1733   Sir Philip Yorke (Ld Hardwicke)
1737   Sir William Lee
1754   Sir Dudley Ryder (Ld Ryder)
1756   Lord Mansfield

CHIEF JUSTICES (COMMON PLEAS)

1689   Sir Henry Pollexfen (died, June 1690)
1692   Sir George Treby
1701   Lord Trevor (removed, October 1714)
1714   Sir Peter King
1725   Sir Robert Eyre
1736   Sir Thomas Reeve
1737   Sir John Willes
1762   Sir Charles Pratt (Ld Camden)

CHIEF BARONS OF THE EXCHEQUER

1686   Sir Edward Atkyns (resigned October 1694)
1695   Sir Edward Ward
1714   Sir Samuel Dodd
1716   Sir Thomas Bury
1722   Sir James Montague
1723   Sir Robert Eyre
1725   Sir Geoffrey Gilbert
1726   Sir Thomas Pengelly
1730   Sir James Reynolds
1738   Sir John Comyns
1740   Sir Edmund Probyn
1742   Sir Thomas Parker

MASTER OF THE ROLLS

1689	Sir Henry Powle
1693	Sir John Trevor
1717	Sir Joseph Jekyll
1738	Hon John Verney
1741	William Fortescue
1750	Sir John Strange
1754	Sir Thomas Clarke

MAJOR DEVELOPMENTS IN PUBLIC ORDER

THE GAME LAWS

The taking of game by all except propertied landowners was forbidden by a succession of statutes at least from 1 James I, c. 27, and the property qualification for taking game was further increased by 7 James I, c. 11. Under 22 and 23 Car. II, c. 25 only persons who possessed freehold estate of at least £100 per annum or a leasehold estate of at least £150 a year, or were the son or heir-apparent of an esquire or person of higher degree were entitled to take game. The game laws also exposed crops to the damage of hunters and hounds during the hunting season. Further restrictions were introduced under 4 W. and M., c. 23, while the 'Black Act' of 1723 made into felonies a large number of poaching and related offences which had hitherto been considered misdemeanours. The severity of the law was further increased by Acts subsequent to 1760, notably in 1770, 1800 and 1816.

THE RIOT ACT, 1715

The Riot Act (1 Geo. I, st. 2, c. 5) was passed in June 1715 in the wake of serious rioting following the accession of George I. The statute *supplemented* the existing Common Law offence of riot committed when three or more assembled together to achieve a common purpose by violence or tumult, by making more serious riots automatically a felony when previously they would normally be considered as misdemeanours. Earlier statutes such as I Mar. st. 2 c. 12 (1553) and I Eliz. c. 16 had taken steps in a similar direction, but only for the duration of the reign. The Act of 1715 made it a felony for twelve or more persons riotously to assemble and not to disperse within an hour after the proclamation requiring them to disperse; to oppose the making of such a proclamation and not to disperse within an hour after the making of the proclamation had been opposed; unlawfully to assemble to the disturbance of the public peace and when so assembled unlawfully and with force to demolish or pull down any church, chapel or other building for religious worship, or any dwelling-house, barn, stable or outhouse. It also empowered magistrates to call on the assistance of all able-bodied persons to put down riots and indemnified them for any injuries caused.

The Riot Act greatly strengthened the law against rioters by automatically making it a felony to remain assembled an hour after the reading of the Act, even if no further violent action was taken. By making such offences a felony, it provided for capital punishment in the case of serious riots, and permitted the use of lethal force to disperse them. However, there was a common misapprehension that an hour should be allowed to elapse before any action was taken against rioters whereas, in fact, reasonable force could be employed to disperse rioters at any time under the existing common law of riotous offences. The hesitancy of both magistrates and military to act was demonstrated on a number of occasions, notably in the case of the Gordon Riots of 1780.

WESTMINSTER WATCH ACT, 1735

An Act was passed enabling the householders of Westminster to pay for their own regular watchmen by means of a regular rate. Other metropolitan parishes adopted a similar system in subsequent years to provide a more reliable and responsible system of street patrols, often recruited from fit, army veterans of good character.

THE BOW STREET POLICE OFFICE, 1739

Sir Thomas De Veil, a former army colonel, was the first of a line of distinguished and active magistrates in Westminster. In 1739 he moved to a house in Bow Street from which he conducted business as a magistrate until 1746. In 1749 Henry Fielding took over his position, followed in 1754 by his blind half-brother John. These magistrates dispensed justice daily from the office and were noted for their lack of corruption. In 1753 Henry Fielding proposed, and had accepted by the Duke of Newcastle, a group of paid thief-takers to work under his direction. The 'Bow Street Constables' continued to be used throughout the century and were called in by provincial magistrates to assist with serious crimes.

LONDON HORSE PATROLS, 1752

In 1752 Henry Fielding organised a system of horse patrols to protect travellers on the roads surrounding the metropolis, but its expense led to it being discontinued by 1754. From 1756 a more limited system of patrol was organised by John Fielding. It was later supplemented (c. 1763) by a Foot Patrol financed by £4000 from the Civil List.

THE MILITIA ACT, 1757

The Elizabethan militia was a much decayed and little-used force by the mid-eighteenth century. The crisis of the Seven Years' War and the need to counter a possible invasion threat and replace the regular forces of the crown while they guarded the coasts or went abroad led, in 1757, to the creation of a militia for England and Wales (it did not apply to Scotland). The Militia Act envisaged a body of 60 000 men organised on a county basis, the bulk of whom were to be found by quotas levied on each county and filled by a ballot of all able-bodied men between 18 and 50 years of age. Militia service was for three years, although it was permitted to find a substitute or pay a fine of £10. The force was to train every Sunday between February and October and drill for a few days at Whitweek. When embodied it was to receive army pay and come under normal army discipline. Officers were selected according to property qualifications. Service overseas was not envisaged, although it could involve any part of the British Isles.

The introduction of the Act led to widespread rioting because of misplaced fears of service overseas and resentment that the rich could escape the ballot by paying the fine or buying a substitute. Although the full complement of militia took some time to embody, in the half century after 1757 it was to become, with supplementary legislation, an important domestic peace-keeping force.

POPULAR DISTURBANCES IN BRITAIN
(excluding Ireland)

1688	Sep–Nov	Attacks on Catholic property in London, York, Newcastle, Bristol, Norwich, Cambridge and Oxford.
	Dec	Following the flight of James II from London further attacks on Catholic property in London and upon the embassies of Catholic powers. Similar attacks in the country and in Edinburgh a crowd sacks Holyrood Chapel.
1693–5		Food riots in the Severn Valley, Thames Valley, Northamptonshire, Essex and Suffolk.
1695		Election riots at Oxford, Exeter, Westminster and elsewhere.
1697	June	Anti-enclosure riots at Epsworth, Lincolnshire.
1698		Election riots at Westminster.
1699		Drainage works destroyed by crowds at Deeping Fen, Lincolnshire.

1702		Attacks on dissenting meeting houses at Newcastle-under-Lyme.
1703–4	Dec–Feb	Anti-prelate and anti-government riots in Edinburgh.
1705		Election riots at Coventry, Chester, Salisbury and Honiton.
1707		Riots at Edinburgh and Dumfries against the Act of Union.
1709		Food disturbances at Kingswood, Tyneside, Essex and North Wales.
1710	Mar	Pro-Sacheverell disturbances at Oxford, Exeter, Hereford, Barnstaple, Gainsborough, Frome, Cirencester, Sherborne, Walsall, West Bromwich, Ely, Bridgnorth, York, Canterbury, Norwich, Nottingham, Northampton, Taunton, Liverpool, Chester, Northwich, Marlow, Whitchurch, Coventry, Chippenham, Newark and London.
		Framebreaking in London by Spitalfields weavers.
1713		Bristol election riot.
1714	Sep	Pro-Hanoverian disturbances in Bristol.
1715	Jun–Aug	Attacks upon dissenting meeting houses in over 30 towns, especially in Manchester and the Midlands.
1716	May	Political disturbances in Cambridge.
	Jul	'Mug-house' riots in London between Whigs and Tories. Five rioters hanged.
1717		Disturbances amongst the cloth workers in Taunton and Exeter during industrial dispute.
1719	May	Disturbances during keelmen's strike in Newcastle.
	Jun	Weavers' disturbances in Norwich and Colchester.
		Attacks on women wearing calicoes in London by Spitalfields weavers.
1720	May	Further silk-weavers disturbances in London.
		Riots in Tiverton against imported Irish worsted.

1722	Jul	Pro-Jacobite disturbance at Leicester.
1723		Widespread poaching and other disturbances in Windsor Forest led to the Black Act.
1725		Anti-malt tax riots in Edinburgh.
		Weavers' riots in Crediton.
1726		Riots in Lincoln because of work on the cathedral towers.
	Nov	Riots in Wiltshire and Somerset by woollen workers.
1727		Anti-turnpike riots near Bristol.
1727–9		Food riots in Cornwall and North Wales.
1731		Anti-turnpike riots in Gloucestershire.
1732	Apr–Oct	Riots at the Mayoral elections in Chester.
1734	Mar–Apr	Widespread election riots.
1735		Anti-enclosure riots in Forest of Dean.
1736	Jul–Aug	Disturbances in London against the Gin Act and against Irish workmen.
	Sep	Porters riot in Edinburgh.
1737		Food riot in Penryn.
1738–40		Riots in West Country during dispute in woollen industry.
1740–1	Apr–Jan	Extensive food riots in England and Wales; Newcastle Guildhall sacked.
1743	May & Oct	Attacks upon Methodists in Wednesbury.
1744	Apr	Attacks upon Methodists at St Ives, Cornwall.
1746	Apr–May	Attacks on Catholic chapels in Liverpool. Also attacks on Catholic property in Bath and Sunderland.
	Oct	Attacks on the houses of Jacobites in Manchester.
1749	Jul–Aug	Turnpikes demolished around Bristol.
1750	Mar–May	Disturbances during keelmen's strike in the north-east.

1751	May	Two suspected witches killed by mob at Tring.
1754		Disturbances at the Oxford election. Election and anti-enclosure riots at Leicester.
1756–7	Aug–Dec	Over 140 food riots in England and Wales.
1757	Aug–Sep	Widespread riots against the operation of the Militia Act, especially in Yorkshire, Lincolnshire, Nottinghamshire, Bedfordshire, Hertfordshire, Cambridgeshire, Norfolk and Huntingdonshire.
1758	Jun	Anti-enclosure riots at Shaw Hill, Wiltshire.
1759		Anti-militia riots in Huntingdonshire.

12 SOCIAL DEVELOPMENTS

ESTIMATES OF THE POPULATION OF ENGLAND AND WALES, 1700–1760
(in millions)

	Rickman[1]	Finlaison[2]	Farr[3]	Brownlee[4]	Griffith[5]	Tranter[6]
1700–1	5.5	5.1	6.1	5.8	5.8	5.8
1710–11	5.2	5.1	6.3	6.0	6.0	6.0
1720–1	5.6	5.4	6.3	6.0	6.1	6.0
1730–1	5.8	5.7	6.2	6.0	6.0	6.1
1740–1	6.1	5.8	6.2	6.0	6.0	6.2
1750–1	6.5	6.0	6.3	6.1	6.3	6.5
1760–1	6.7	6.5	6.7	6.6	6.7	6.7

Sources:

[1] J. Rickman, *Observations on the Results of the Population Act, 41 Geo. III,* p. 9 (in *State Papers,* 1802, vii).
[2] J. Finlaison – 1831 census, *Enumeration Abstract,* P. x/v.
[3] W. Farr – 1861 census, *General Report,* p. 22.
[4] J. Brownlee, 'History of the birth and death rates in England and Wales', in *Public Health* (June and July, 1916).
[5] G. Talbot Griffith, *Population Problems in the Age of Malthus* (Cambridge, 1926), p. 18.
[6] N. L. Tranter, *Population since the Industrial Revolution: the case of England and Wales* (London, 1973), p. 41.

ESTIMATES OF THE POPULATION OF IRELAND, 1687–1767
(in thousands)

1687	2167	1725	3042	1754	3191
1712	2791	1726	3031	1767	3480
1718	2894	1732	3018		

Source K. H. Connell, *The Population of Ireland, 1750–1845* (Oxford, 1950), p. 25.

ESTIMATES OF THE POPULATION OF SCOTLAND, 1650–1800

1650	1 000 000	1725	1 100 000	1775	1 375 000
1700	1 040 000	1750	1 250 000	1800	1 500 000

Source J. Babuscio and R. Minta Dunn, *European Political Facts,
1648–1789*, (London, 1985), p. 340.

PRINCIPAL URBAN POPULATIONS

ENGLISH CITIES

Cities	1650	1700	1750
London	400 000	550 000	675 000
Liverpool	1500	5500	22 000
Manchester	4500	8000	18 000
Birmingham	3500	7000	23 500
Bristol	15 000	20 000	40 000
Plymouth	5000	7000	14 000
Norwich	20 000	30 000	36 000
Sheffield	2500	3500	12 000
Bath	1000	2500	6500
Portsmouth	3000	5000	10 000
Leeds	4000	6000	11 000
Nottingham	5000	7000	12 000
Newcastle	12 000	15 000	25 000
Hull	3500	6000	11 000
Sunderland	3000	5000	9000
Leicester	3500	5500	9000
Exeter	12 000	14 000	15 000
York	10 000	10 500	12 000
Coventry	7000	7000	12 000
Chester	7500	9000	11 000
Yarmouth	10 000	11 000	12 000
Oxford	8500	9000	10 000
Worcester	8000	8500	9500
Colchester	9500	10 000	9500
Cambridge	8500	9000	9500
Canterbury	7000	7500	8000
Salisbury	7000	7000	7000
Edinburgh	25 000	35 000	57 000 (1755)
Glasgow		12 000	25 000

Source European Political Facts, 1648–1789, op. cit., p. 341.

MAJOR SOCIAL LEGISLATION

1691   Register of parishioners in receipt of poor relief to be kept.

1694   Wartime tax on births, marriages, and deaths, at 2s, 2s 6d, and 4s respectively. Higher duties for the wealthy.

1697   Settlement Act. Strangers were allowed to enter a parish provided that they possessed a settlement certificate showing that they would be taken by their old parish if they required poor relief. Paupers and their families were to wear a capital 'P' on their clothing. Punishment for disobeying the instruction could be loss of relief, imprisonment, hard labour and whipping.

1722–3   Parishes encouraged to build or rent workhouses and allowed to contract out their maintenance and supervision. Parishes allowed to form unions to set up viable workhouses.

1736   Gin Act. Required retailers to take out a licence of £50 and pay a duty of £1 on every gallon sold.

1747   Master and servant. Disputes between master and servant might be referred to the Justices. Apprentices' indentures could be cancelled in cases of ill-treatment.

1752   Gregorian Calendar introduced. Eleven days, 3–13 September, were removed from the calendar in order to bring the existing calendar in conformity with the Gregorian. Year to start from 1 January instead of from March.

1754   Hardwicke's Marriage Act. This declared that marriages could only be solomnised after the publication of banns which were to be recorded in the marriage register or in a separate book.

SOCIAL STRUCTURE OF THE POPULATION

GREGORY KING'S ESTIMATE OF THE POPULATION AND WEALTH OF ENGLAND AND WALES, CALCULATED FOR 1696

Rank	Number of families	Persons	Yearly income per family £	Yearly expenditure per family £	Total income of group £
Temporal Lords	160	6400	2800	2400	448 000
Spiritual Lords	26	520	1300	1100	33 800
Baronets	800	12 800	880	816	704 000
Knights	600	7800	650	498	39 000

Esquires	3000	30 000	450	420	1 350 000
Gentlemen	12 000	96 000	280	268	3 360 000
Clergy, superior	2000	12 000	60	54	120 000
Clergy, inferior	8000	40 000	45	40	360 000
Persons in the Law	10 000	70 000	140	119	1 400 000
Sciences and Liberal Arts	16 000	80 000	60	57.10s.	960 000
Persons in Offices (higher)	5000	40 000	240	216	1 200 000
Persons in Offices (lower)	5000	30 000	120	108	600 000
Naval Officers	5000	20 000	80	72	400 000
Military Officers	4000	16 000	60	56	240 000
Common Soldiers	35 000	70 000	14	15	490 000
Freeholders (better sort)	40 000	280 000	84	77	3 360 000
Freeholders (lesser)	140 000	700 000	50	45.10s.	7 000 000
Farmers	150 000	750 000	44	42.15s.	6 600 000
Labouring people and servants	364 000	1 275 000	15	15.5s.	5 460 000
Cottagers and Paupers	400 000	1 300 000	6.10s.	7.6.3d.	2 600 000
Artizans, Handicrafts	60 000	240 000	40	38	2 400 000
Merchants by sea	2000	16 000	400	320	800 000
Merchants by land	8000	48 000	200	170	1 600 000
Shopkeepers, Tradesmen	40 000	180 000	45	42.15s.	1 800 000
Common Seamen	50 000	150 000	20	21.10s.	1 000 000
Vagrants		30 000	2	3	60 000

HOSPITAL FOUNDATIONS, 1688–1760

1696	St Peter's, Bristol
1708	French Protestant
1713	Bethel (Norwich)
1720	Westminster
1726	Guy's
1734	St George's, London
1738	Bath General
1739	Queen Charlotte's
1740	London Hospital
1745	Durham, Newcastle-upon-Tyne and Northumberland Infirmary
1745	Gloucester Infirmary
1745	Liverpool Royal Infirmary
1745	Middlesex
1745	Shrewsbury Infirmary
1746	Middlesex County
1746	Worcester Royal Infirmary

1746   London Lock

1750   City of London Maternity

1751   St Luke's, London

1752   Manchester Royal Infirmary

1753   Devon and Exeter

1758   Magdalen

EDUCATION

1690   Haberdashers Askes school founded.

1697   Appleby Parva school (Leics) founded.

1698   The Society for the Propagation of Christian Knowledge begins to set up schools for the poor.

1700   Battersea Grammar School founded.

1702   Chair of Organic Chemistry created at Cambridge.

1704   Watford Grammar School founded.
Chairs of Astronomy and Experimental Philosophy created at Cambridge.

1705   Dame Allan's School, Newcastle.

1707   Chair of Anatomy set up at Cambridge.

1714   Worcester College, Oxford founded.
Radcliffe Library, Oxford founded.

1716   Building of Codrington Library, All Souls, Oxford, commenced (completed 1756).

1724   Regius Chair of Modern History created at Cambridge.

1725   Allan Ramsay starts Edinburgh Circulating Library.

1728   Chair of Botany founded at Cambridge.

1729   Doddridge founds dissenting academy. Dr Williams Library founded in Cripplegate, London.

1732   Portsmouth Grammar School founded.

1733   Bayley's School, Warwickshire, founded.

1737   Bancroft's School, Woodford Green, founded.

1740   Circulating Library established in the Strand. Cawthorn and Hutt's 'British Library' a circulating library, is founded.
Hertford College, Oxford founded.

1748   Kingwood School, Somerset founded.
Thomlinson Library, Newcastle, founded.

1749   St Edmund's School, Canterbury, founded.
St Olave's School, Orpington, founded.
Chairs of Astronomy and Geometry founded at Cambridge.

1753   Library of Sir Hans Sloane purchased for the nation and forms basis of the British Museum. Harleian Collection purchased by the British Museum.

1755   Signet Library, Edinburgh, founded.

1757   Circulating Library opened in Birmingham.

1758   Liverpool Lyceum founded.

1759   British Museum opened at Montague House, London.

1760   Warrington Library founded.

NEWSPAPERS

Foundation Dates of Newspapers and Periodicals, 1688–1760

1690   Worcester Journal

1695   Stamford Mercury

1702   Bristol Post Boy

1702   Daily Courant

1708   Norwich Postman

1710–11 Nottingham Guardian (Journal)

1711   North Mail
Newcastle Journal

1712   Norwich Gazette
Liverpool Courant

1714   Exeter Mercury

1720   Northampton Mercury

1726   Weekly Lloyd's List

1734   Daily Lloyd's List

1737   Belfast Newsletter

1739   Gentleman's Magazine
        The Scot's Magazine

1741   Coventry Standard
        Birmingham Gazette

1748   Aberdeen Press and Journal

1754   Yorkshire Post

1759   Public Ledger (London)

13 ECONOMY AND FINANCE

PRICE OF WHEAT, 1688–1760
(*Shillings per Winchester quarter*)

	Exeter	Eton College	Winchester College
1688	20.50	20.17	18.95
1689	24.36	28.47	29.30
1690	28.01	26.58	23.40
1691	39.65	33.47	37.18
1692	43.29	42.67	45.92
1693	43.46	61.51	57.67
1694	24.56	34.36	34.59
1695	38.69	56.78	53.98
1696	57.68	44.33	49.24
1697	55.29	54.00	56.74
1698	41.25	55.04	55.55
1699	36.67	39.49	37.53
1700	33.40	30.59	32.59
1701	27.20	25.52	24.87
1702	24.90	23.76	26.52
1703	27.97	40.25	38.49
1704	N.A.	26.89	26.52
1705	25.79	21.75	22.29
1706	28.01	20.92	23.03
1707	32.93	24.70	26.91
1708	55.27	47.00	48.36
1709	59.47	74.10	69.52
1710	38.63	45.92	44.98
1711	34.12	45.39	40.81
1712	37.02	30.60	35.26
1713	45.40	50.76	48.89
1714	30.29	30.07	31.11
1715	34.35	39.50	43.56
1716	32.08	37.46	38.07
1717	29.60	35.41	34.96
1718	27.80	27.57	25.04
1719	39.12	29.53	31.55

1720	36.39	31.42	31.55
1721	29.36	28.56	25.81
1722	30.69	27.94	28.77
1723	29.05	29.00	27.99
1724	34.57	32.25	36.15
1725	41.04	43.13	38.07
1726	30.72	31.03	29.55
1727	46.78	41.18	44.37
1728	N.A.	42.08	44.22
1729	N.A.	32.64	30.22
1730	N.A.	28.16	29.96
1731	20.00	23.87	22.74
1732	24.46	22.06	22.94
1733	29.22	24.70	24.68
1734	36.53	33.01	31.10
1735	34.67	34.41	33.19
1736	28.50	32.42	26.91
1737	27.68	29.83	25.94
1738	28.50	27.94	26.50
1739	40.84	34.73	36.39
1740	50.74	48.73	50.20
1741	29.34	28.16	26.64
1742	24.11	22.74	20.92
1743	22.00	19.49	18.13
1744	22.50	20.16	18.55
1745	28.97	28.77	26.22
1746	33.16	29.38	28.03
1747	29.45	27.64	26.98
1748	29.08	29.83	28.58
1749	29.80	27.80	26.78
1750	31.92	26.96	27.61
1751	37.84	37.76	34.93
1752	36.75	35.20	34.59
1753	31.15	32.70	33.19
1754	28.69	25.52	25.94
1755	36.39	29.23	30.40
1756	51.91	49.17	42.12
1757	36.77	43.52	42.12
1758	30.39	34.67	31.24
1759	29.40	29.17	29.00
1760	34.12	27.41	28.59

Source   B. R. Mitchell and P. Deane, *Abstract of British Historical Statistics*, 2nd edn (Cambridge, 1971), pp. 486–7.

OVERSEAS TRADE – ENGLAND AND WALES, 1697–1760
(£000)

	Imports	Exports	Re-exports
1697	3344	2295	1096
1698	4608	3582	1608
1699	5621	3655	1570
1700	5840	3731	2081
1701	5796	4049	2192
1702	4088	3130	1144
1703	4450	3888	1622
1704	5329	3723	1804
1705			
1706	4064	4142	1447
1707	4267	4173	1602
1708	4699	4404	1495
1709	4511	4406	1507
1710	4011	4729	1566
1711	4686	4088	1875
1712			
1713	5811	4490	2402
1714	5929	5564	2440
1715	5641	5015	1908
1716	5800	4807	2243
1717	6347	5384	2613
1718	6669	4381	1980
1719	5367	4514	2321
1720	6090	4611	2300
1721	5908	4512	2689
1722	6378	5293	2972
1723	6506	4725	2671
1724	7394	5107	2494
1725	7095	5667	2814
1726	6678	5001	2692
1727	6799	4605	2670
1728	7569	4910	3797
1729	7541	4940	3299
1730	7780	5326	3223
1731	6992	5081	2782
1732	7088	5675	3196
1733	8017	5823	3015
1734	7096	5403	2897
1735	8160	5927	3402

1736	7308	6118	3585
1737	7074	6668	3414
1738	7439	6982	3214
1739	7829	5572	3272
1740	6704	5111	3086
1741	7936	5995	3575
1742	6867	6095	3480
1743	7802	6868	4442
1744	6363	5411	3780
1745	7847	5739	3333
1746	6206	7201	3566
1747	7117	6744	3031
1748	8136	7317	3824
1749	7918	9081	3598
1750	7772	9474	3225
1751	7943	8775	3644
1752	7889	8226	3469
1753	8625	8732	3511
1754	8093	8318	3470
1755	8773	7915	3150
1756	8962	8632	3089
1757	9253	8584	3755
1758	8415	8763	3855
1759	8923	10079	3869
1760	9833	10981	3714

Source   B. R. Mitchell and P. Deane, *Abstract of British Historical Statistics* 2nd edn (Cambridge, 1971), pp. 279–80.

THE COAL TRADE, 1668–1760

	Shipped coastwise from Newcastle (thousands of Newcastle chaldrons, 1 chaldron = 53 cwt)	Shipped coastwise from Sunderland	Imported into London (thousands of London chaldrons, 1 chaldron = 25½ cwt)
1688	231		
1689	168		
1690	137		
1691	177		
1692	156		
1693	180		

Year			
1694	160		
1695	171		
1696	151		
1697	181		
1698	211		
1699	221		
1700	205		335
1701	245		400
1702	153		243
1703	170		301
1704	198		
1705	182		
1706	163		
1707	151		
1708	193		361
1709	211		
1710	168		328
1711			
1712			
1713			346
1714			414
1715			388
1716			412
1717			440
1718			412
1719			420
1720			425
1721			459
1722			460
1723	262		458
1724	253		451
1725	266		471
1726	286		508
1727	276		496
1728	247		453
1729	293		494
1730	277		455
1731	311		475
1732	269		451
1733	291		496
1734	274		448
1735	282		503
1736	297		512
1737	276		476

1738	271		491
1739	288		442
1740	321		563
1741	263		453
1742	270		457
1743	298		478
1744	273		468
1745	295		471
1746	303		487
1747	259		469
1748	271	147	450
1749	299	135	504
1750	288	162	458
1751	343	129	539
1752	308	177	508
1753	301	167	508
1754	305	166	527
1755	294	174	479
1756	311	175	550
1757	274	179	503
1758	240	187	452
1759	302	187	552
1760	285	180	499

Source   B. R. Mitchell and P. Deane, *Abstract of British Historical Statistics* (Cambridge, 1971), pp. 108–10, 122.

OUTPUT OF WOOLLEN CLOTH IN THE WEST RIDING, 1726–60
(*thousand pieces*)

	Broad cloth	Narrow cloth
1727	29.0	
1728	25.2	
1729	29.6	
1730	31.6	
1731	35.6	
1732	35.5	
1733	34.6	
1734	31.1	
1735	31.7	

1736	38.9	
1737	42.3	
1738	42.4	
1739	43.1	58.8
1740	41.4	58.6
1741	46.4	61.2
1742	45.0	62.8
1743	45.2	63.5
1744	54.6	63.1
1745	50.5	63.4
1746	56.6	68.8
1747	62.5	68.4
1748	60.8	681.
1749	60.7	68.9
1750	60.4	78.1
1751	61.0	74.0
1752	60.7	72.4
1753	58.4	71.6
1754	56.1	72.4
1755	57.1	763.
1756	33.6	79.3
1757	55.8	77.1
1758	60.4	66.4
1759	51.9	65.5
1760	49.4	69.6

Source   Report of the Select Committee on the Woolen Manufacture, State Papers, 1806, p. 25.

OUTPUT OF SILK, CALICOES AND LINENS, 1713–60
(in thousand yards)

1713	2028	1723	3064	1733	2925
1714	2580	1724	2886	1734	2793
1715	1840	1725	2760	1735	3005
1716	2503	1726	2898	1736	2630
1717	2654	1727	2861	1737	3057
1718	2689	1728	2216	1738	3150
1719	2841	1729	2684	1739	3224
1720	1699	1730	2279	1740	3125
1721	1048	1731	2123	1741	3027
1722	1535	1732	2427	1742	2766

1743	3064	1749	3997	1755	4932
1744	3037	1750	4417	1756	4206
1745	2629	1751	4224	1757	4184
1746	2729	1752	4208	1758	5134
1747	3527	1753	4230	1759	5698
1748	3220	1754	4388	1760	6359

[z] Silks, Linens, Calicoes and stuffs charged with duty.

Source   B. R. Mitchell and P. Deane, *Abstract of British Historical Statistics*, 2nd edn (Cambridge, 1971), p. 184.

EXPORTS OF SILK AND LINEN FROM ENGLAND AND WALES, 1697–1760

	Silk (thousands of lb)	Linen (thousands of yards)
1697	41	145
1698	55	285
1699	48	245
1700	38	181
1701	39	141
1702	28	138
1703	33	145
1704	32	147
1705		
1706	42	139
1707	44	171
1708	52	323
1709	57	348
1710	54	304
1711	46	427
1712		
1713	44	287
1714	52	293
1715	58	363
1716	47	324
1717	62	381
1718	71	576
1719	40	448

1720	41	412
1721	38	497
1722	43	601
1723	44	451
1724	49	471
1725	86	672
1726	50	575
1727	37	632
1728	45	742
1729	43	810
1730	58	741
1731	42	748
1732	47	707
1733	45	610
1734	36	645
1735	45	955
1736	47	1040
1737	46	778
1738	47	1176
1739	49	1238
1740	40	1523
1741	58	2201
1742	62	2120
1743	71	1690
1744	46	1354
1745	40	1423
1746	50	3031
1747	56	2667
1748	54	2990
1749	60	4068
1750	63	4068
1751	23	3868
1752	92	4025
1753	90	5004
1754	85	4802
1755	91	3324
1756	89	4528
1757	93	5982
1758	118	7116
1759	173	8389
1760	198	10 494

Source B. R. Mitchell and P. Deane, *Abstract of British Historical Statistics*, 2nd edn (Cambridge, 1971), pp. 201, 209.

RAW COTTON IMPORTS AND RE-EXPORTS, 1697–1760
(*in 1000 lbs*)

	Imports	Re-exports		Imports	Re-exports
1697–8	1266	404	1730	1545	77
1699	1349	60	1731	1473	172
1700	1396	313	1732	1605	199
1701	1976	208	1733	1918	134
1702	1505	125	1734	1478	170
1703	757	173	1735	2198	168
1704	1446	420	1736	2296	460
1705			1737	1679	153
1706	461	95	1738	2537	169
1707	499	27	1739	2246	82
1708	2800	16	1740	1546	82
1709	907	35	1741	1680	109
1710	714	51	1742	1933	169
1711	675	62	1743	1268	65
1712			1744	2032	17
1713	1798	849	1745	1635	86
1714	1755	471	1746	2408	33
1715	1762	101	1747	2325	35
1716	2161	205	1748	5258	385
1717	2034	320	1749	1837	357
1718	2082	125	1750	2318	64
1719	1489	147	1751	2977	74
1720	1968	159	1752	3496	86
1721	1513	71	1753	4278	176
1722	2103	98	1754	3181	145
1723	2144	102	1755	3820	155
1724	977	76	1756	3089	375
1725	1841	103	1757	2706	888
1726	1523	115	1758	2225	237
1727			1759	2552	343
1728	1561	87	1760	2359	618
1729	1182	94			

Source   B. R. Mitchell and P. Deane, *Abstract of British Historical Statistics*, 2nd edn (Cambridge, 1971), p. 177.

OUTPUT OF TIN AND COPPER, 1688–1760

	White tin[1] (in thousand tons)	Copper ore[2] (in thousand tons)
1688	1.4	
1689	1.5	
1690	1.3	
1691	1.3	
1692	1.2	
1693	1.3	
1694	1.2	
1695	1.3	
1696	1.2	
1697	1.1	
1698	1.3	
1699	1.4	
1700	1.4	
1701	1.4	
1702	1.1	
1703	1.6	
1704	1.5	
1705	1.4	
1706	1.5	
1707	1.5	
1708	1.5	
1709	1.4	
1710	2.2	
1711	1.4	
1712	1.4	
1713	1.4	
1714	1.1	
1715	1.2	
1716	1.1	
1717	1.7	
1718	1.6	
1719		
1720	1.5	
1721	1.2	
1722	1.4	
1723	1.4	
1724	1.6	
1725	1.7	

1726	1.5	5.0
1727	1.6	6.7
1728	1.5	6.8
1729	1.6	6.9
1730	1.6	6.9
1731		7.0
1732	1.9	7.3
1733	1.6	7.0
1734	1.8	6.0
1735	1.8	5.2
1736	1.6	8.0
1737	1.7	9.0
1738	1.4	10.0
1739	1.8	11.0
1740	1.7	5.0
1741	1.6	5.5
1742	1.8	6.1
1743	1.9	7.0
1744	1.9	7.2
1745	1.7	6.7
1746	1.9	7.0
1747	1.8	4.9
1748	2.0	6.0
1749	1.1	7.2
1750	2.9	9.4
1751	2.3	11.0
1752	2.6	12.1
1753	2.5	13.0
1754	2.7	14.0
1755	2.8	14.2
1756	2.8	16.0
1757	2.8	17.0
1758	2.7	15.0
1759	2.6	16.7
1760	2.7	15.8

[1] Tin paying coinage dues.
[2] Copper ore sold at public ticketings in Cornwall and Devon.

Source   B. R. Mitchell and P. Deane, *Abstract of British Historical Statistics*, 2nd edn (Cambridge, 1971), pp. 153–4, 156.

EXPORTS OF TIN, COPPER AND LEAD, 1697–1760

	Tin blocks (thousand tons)	Copper and brass (tons)	Lead and shot (thousand tons)
1697	0.9	72	8.0
1698	1.3	130	13.2
1699	1.2	130	11.6
1700	1.4	169	11.6
1701	1.3	137	12.9
1702	0.9	97	9.2
1703	1.0	98	11.1
1704	0.9	75	10.2
1705			
1706	1.2	62	13.0
1707	0.9	60	14.7
1708	1.4	186	14.1
1709	1.1	70	10.6
1710	3.4	100	12.9
1711	0.5	96	14.1
1712	0.5	96	14.1
1713	0.7	166	11.6
1714	1.2	209	17.6
1715	1.3	207	10.8
1716	0.7	213	12.1
1717	1.1	236	13.6
1718	1.1	179	8.3
1719	1.8	182	10.7
1720	1.0	158	7.4
1721	1.0	155	10.0
1722	0.9	174	10.6
1723	1.3	207	9.1
1724	1.2	227	9.9
1725	0.8	269	9.4
1726	1.3	243	10.2
1727	1.4	239	12.5
1728	1.2	320	10.6
1729	1.3	372	12.3
1730	1.4	436	11.4
1731	1.2	429	12.5
1732	1.5	404	15.1
1733	1.3	404	15.1

1734	1.4	344	11.7
1735	1.6	442	12.7
1736	1.1	505	11.8
1737	1.5	535	12.0
1738	1.4	688	12.1
1739	1.4	584	13.4
1740	1.4	502	14.5
1741	1.5	678	14.0
1742	1.5	769	11.8
1743	1.2	930	16.2
1744	1.4	794	9.7
1745	1.5	626	11.9
1746	1.8	817	12.8
1747	1.6	786	11.0
1748	1.5	953	11.2
1749	1.6	1206	12.6
1750	1.8	1378	14.0
1751	1.8	1094	13.6
1752	1.9	1051	10.9
1753	1.6	1462	15.8
1754	1.8	1281	13.6
1755	1.7	1086	12.4
1756	1.6	1165	14.9
1757	1.6	1150	13.0
1758	1.6	1128	12.0
1759	1.7	1287	12.3
1760	1.9	1570	12.0

Source B. R. Mitchell and P. Deane, *Abstract of British Historical Statistics*, 2nd edn (Cambridge, 1971), pp. 161, 164, 169.

PUBLIC INCOME AND EXPENDITURE IN GREAT BRITAIN, 1688–1760

	Total net income (£,000)	Total net expenditure (£,000)
1688–91[1]	8613	11543
1692[2]	4111	4255
1693	3783	5576
1694	4004	5602

1695	4134	6220
1696	4823	7998
1697	3298	7915
1698	4578	4127
1699	5164	4691
1700	4344	3201
1701	3769	3442
1702	4869	5010
1703	5561	5313
1704	5394	5527
1705	5292	5873
1706	5284	6692
1707	5471	8747
1708	5208	7742
1709	5206	9160
1710	5248	9772
1711	5179	15 142[3]
1712	5748	7864
1713	5780	6362
1714	5361	6185
1715	5547	6228
1716	5582	7076
1717	6514	5885
1718	6090	6534
1719	6026	6152
1720	6323	6002
1721	5954	5873
1722	6150	6978
1723	5993	5671
1724	5773	5438
1725	5960	5516
1726	5518	5543
1727	6103	5860
1728	6741	6504
1729	6294	5711
1730	6265	5574
1731	6080	5347
1732	5803	4974
1733	5522	4595
1734	5448	6360
1735	5652	5852
1736	5762	5793
1737	6077	5129
1738	5716	4725

1739	5820	5210
1740	5745	6161
1741	6244	7388
1742	6416	8533
1743	6567	8979
1744	6576	9398
1745	6451	8920
1746	6249	9804
1747	6961	1145[3]
1748	7199	1194[3]
1749	7494	12 544[3]
1750	7467	7185
1751	7097	6425
1752	6992	7037
1753	7338	5952
1754	6827	6030
1755	6938	7119
1756	7006	9589
1757	7969	11 214
1758	7946	13 200
1759	8155	15 382
1760	9207	17 993

[1] 5 November 1688 to 29 September 1691.
[2] Years to 1752 ending 29 September, thereafter 10 October.
[3] Contains debt items consolidated from previous years.

Source B. R. Mitchell and P. Deane, *Abstract of British Historical Statistics* 2nd edn (Cambridge, 1971), pp. 386–7, 389–80.

NATIONAL DEBT, 1691–1760
(£000 000)

1691	3.1[1]	1702	14.1	1711	22.4
1692	3.3	1703	13.6	1712	34.9
1693	5.9	1704	13.4	1713	34.7
1694	6.1	1705	13.0	1714	36.2
1695	8.4	1706	13.0	1715	37.4
1696	10.6	1707	14.5	1716	37.9
1697	16.7	1708	15.2	1717	39.3
1700	14.2	1709	19.1	1718	39.7
1701	14.1	1710	21.4	1719	41.6

1720	54.0	1735	49.3	1748	76.1
1721	54.9	1736	49.7	1749	77.8
1722	52.7	1737	48.5	1750	78.0
1723	53.6	1738	47.5	1751	78.1
1724	53.8	1739	46.9	1752	76.9
1725	52.7	1740	47.4	1753	75.0
1726	52.9	1741	48.8	1754	72.2
1729	52.1	1742	51.3	1755	72.5
1730	51.4	1743	53.5	1756	74.6
1731	51.7	1744	57.1	1757	77.8
1732	50.1	1745	60.1	1758	82.1
1733	50.0	1746	64.9	1759	91.3
1734	49.1	1747	69.4	1760	101.7

[1] Year ending 29 September to 1752, thereafter 10 October.

Source B. R. Mitchell and P. Deane, *Abstract of British Historical Statistics* 2nd edn (Cambridge, 1971), pp. 401–2.

COMPANY FOUNDATIONS, 1688–1760

1688   Cooke, Troughton & Simms, London (Scientific instruments)
        Lloyd's, London (Insurance)
        A. Mackintosh, Cambridge (Ironmongers)

1690   *Berrow's Worcester Journal*, Worcester (Newspapers)
        Merryweather & Sons, London (Fire-engineering)

1692   Coutt's Bank, London (Banking)

1694   Bank of England, London (Banking)

1695   Richard Austie, Devizes (Tobacco)
        Bank of Scotland, Edinburgh (Banking)
        Henekeys, London (Wine merchants)
        H. Tiffin & Son, London (Pest control)
        Stamford Mercury, Stamford (Newspapers)

1696   Hand-in-Hand Fire Office, London (Insurance)
        Lloyd's News, London (Newspapers)

1697   *Old Moore's Almanack*, London (Almanacs)

1698   Society for the Promotion of Christian Knowledge, London
        (Printing and charity work)

1699   Berry Brothers & Rudd, London (Wine merchants)

1700   Englefields, London (Pewterers)
        D. & S. Radford, London (Tobacco)
        Charlie Richards & Company, London (Wine merchants)

1702   *Bristol Post Boy*, Bristol (Newspapers)
        Daily Courant, London (Newspapers)
        Silk Hill, Derby (Silk Manufacture)

1703   Norman Society, London (Friendly Society)
        Society for the Mutual Help of Swiss in London, (Friendly Society)

1704   Bristol City Line of Steamships (Shipping)

1706   Crosse & Blackwell, London (Food manufacturing)
        R. Twining & Co., London and Andover (Tea merchants)

1707   Fortnum and Mason, London (Food retailing)
        W. B. Gurney & Son, London (Shorthand writers)

1708   *Norwich Postman*, Norwich (Newspapers)

1709   Coalbrookdale Company, Coalbrookdale, Shropshire (Iron manu-
        facture and engineering)

1710   William Dalton & Sons, London (Pest Control)
        Nottingham Guardian-Journal, Nottingham (Newspapers)
        Perrotts (Nicol & Peyton), London (Textiles)
        Sun Insurance Company, London (Insurance).

1711   *Newcastle Journal*, Newcastle (Newspapers)
        Nottingham Journal, Nottingham (Newspapers)
        C. & J. Rivington, London (Printing)
        Scotts' Shipbuilding & Engineering Company, Greenock (Ship-
        building)

1712   *Liverpool Courant*, Liverpool (Newspapers)
        Norwich Gazette, Norwich (Newspapers)
        Portals, Haverstock, Hampshire (Papermaking)

1714   *Exeter Mercury*, Exeter (Newspapers)
        Union, or Double Hand-in-Hand, Fire Office, London (Insurance)

1715   Allen & Hanburys, London (manufacturing Chemists)

1717   Austin & McAslan, Glasgow (Seeds)
        Drummonds Bank, London (Banking)
        Westminster Fire Office, London (Insurance)

1718   Joseph Bryant, Bristol (Ropes)
        Cooke, Troughton & Simms, York (Scientific instruments)

1719   Pike, Spicer & Company's Brewery, Portsmouth (Brewing)
        York Mercury, York (Newspapers)

1720   Brock's Fireworks, Sanophar, Scotland (Fireworks)
        Fribourg & Treyer, London (Tobacco)
        London Assistance (Insurance)
        Northampton Mercury, Northampton (Newspapers)
        Royal Exchange Assurance (Insurance)

1722   Thomas Andrews, Comber, Northern Ireland (Flour-milling)

1723   Tollemach & Cobbold, Ipswich (Brewing)
        Stephen Mitchell and Son, Linlithgow, Scotland (Tobacco)

1724   Longmans, Green & Company, London (Printing and publishing)

1725   Charles Davis (Hatters)
        Dring & Fage, London (Scientific Instruments)
        Drivers Jonas, London (Auctioneers)
        Mary Tuke (later Rowntrees), York (Cocoa)

1727   Royal Bank of Scotland (Banking)

1728   John Broadwood & Sons, London (Musical instruments)
        Ellis's bookshop, London (Booksellers)
        J. S. Fry & Sons, Bristol (Cocoa)

1730   Floris, London (Perfume)
        Taylor, Walker & Company, London (Brewing)

1731   Royal Dublin Society, Dublin (Agricultural Shows)

1733   Epworth Press, London (Printing and publishing)

1734   *Lloyd's List*, London (Newspapers)

1736   Gourock Ropework Company, Glasgow (Ropes)

1739   J. R. Phillips & Company, Bristol (Wine merchants)
        Scots Magazine (Newspapers)

1740   E. & W. Austie, Devizes (Tobacco)
        Booth's Distilleries, London (Gin distilling)
        Thwaites & Reed, London (Clockmaking)

1741   *Birmingham Gazette*, Birmingham (Newspapers)
        Coventry Standard, Coventry (Newspapers)
        Stephen Mitchell's Snuff-mill, Waukmilton, Scotland (Tobacco)

1742   Lagavulin Distillery, Islay, Scotland (Whisky)
        Whitbreads Brewery, London (Brewing)

1743   Bushmill's Distillery, Bushmills, Northern Ireland (Whisky)

1744   Cluttons, London (Auctioneers)
              King & Company, Kingston-upon-Hull (Ironmongers)
              Sotheby's, London (Auctioneers)
              Worthington, Burton-on-Trent (Brewing)

1746   British Linen Bank, Edinburgh (Banking)
              Glenochil Distillery, Stirling, Scotland (Whisky)

1747   Bottesford Friendly Society, Leicestershire (Friendly Society)
              J. &. N. Phillips & Company, Manchester (Cotton)

1748   Joseph Gardner & Sons, Liverpool (Timber)
              Press and Journal, Aberdeen (Newspapers)

1749   Finney's, Newcastle (Seeds)
              Justerini & Brooks, London (Wine merchants)
              William Younger & Company, Edinburgh (Brewing)

1750   Alloa Glass Works, Alloa, Scotland (Glass-making)
              Benskin's Cannon Brewery, Watford (Brewing)
              Bouchard Aine, London (Wine merchants)
              Brusna Distillery, Kilbeggan, Ireland (Whisky)
              Coalport China Company, Stoke-on-Trent (Pottery)
              Crosses & Heatons, Bolton (Cotton)
              Dollond & Aitchinson, London (Opticians)
              Eaden Lilley, Cambridge (Retailing)
              Harrison & Sons, London (Painting)
              Parker Gallery, London (Art dealers)
              Arthur Reader, London (Art dealers)
              Royal Crown Derby Porcelain Company, Derby (Pottery)
              C. Shippan, Chichester (Food manufacturing)
              Woodhouse, Carey & Browne, London (Sugar-brokers)

1751   Beatson, Clark & Company, Rotherham (Glassmaking)
              Culter Mills Paper Company, Aberdeenshire (Papermaking)
              Vacher & Son, London (Printing)
              Worcester Royal Porcelain Company, Worcester (Pottery)

1752   Clokie & Company, Castleford (Pottery)
              George Waterson & Sons, Edinburgh (Stationers)

1753   Glyn Mills, London (Banking)

1754   Royal Society of Arts, London (Agricultural shows)
              Yorkshire Post, Leeds (Newspapers)

1755   Brecknockshire Agricultural Society (Agricultural shows)

1756   Bradford & Sons, Yeovil (Timber)
         James Latham, London (Timber)

1757   Charrington's Anchor Brewery, London (Brewing)
         Thomas Street Distillery, Dublin (Whisky)

1758   Fawcett Preston & Company, Liverpool (Engineering)
         Showerings, Shepton Mallet, Somerset (Cider)

1759   Carron Company, Falkirk, Scotland (Iron manufacture and
         engineering)
         Dreweatt, Watson & Barton, Newbury, Berkshire (Auctioneers)
         Guinness Brewery, Dublin (Brewing)
         James Lock & Company, London (Hatters)
         William Playne & Company, Minchinhampton, Gloucestershire
         (Woollen manufacture)
         Public Ledger, London (Newspapers)
         Wedgwood, Barlaston, Staffordshire (Pottery)

1760   Baxter, Payne & Lepper, Beckenham, Kent (Auctioneers)
         John Burgess & Son, London (Food manufacture)
         W. Drummond & Sons, Stirling (Seeds)
         Zachary & Company, Cirencester (Wine merchants)

PARLIAMENTARY ENCLOSURE ACTS, 1688 to 1760 (BY COUNTY)

County	Place	Area enclosed (acres)
Bedford		
1742	Sutton	2200
1760	Aspley Guise	na
Berkshire		
1724	Sunninghill	1190
1743	Aston Tirrold	423
1746	Inkpen	na
1758	Upton	1800
Buckinghamshire		
1738	Ashenden	1300
1742	Wotton Underwood	1668
1744	Shipton	640

Derbyshire

1727	Scarcliffe and Palterton	970
1756	Weston cum Membris and Sawley	na
1760	Mackworth	na

Dorset

1733	Buckland Newton	1600
1736	West Stafford	600

Gloucester

1726	Little Rissington	na
1727	Cherrington	2200
1729	Wich Risington	2000
1731	Prestury	na
1731	Upper and Lower Slaughter	2845
1739	Shipton, Moyle and Dovel	800
1744	Westonbirt	350
1753	Eastlechmartin	1863
1753	Quennington	3000
1755	Hawling	881
1759	Little Barrington	1860
	Preston upon Stower	900

Hampshire

1740	Andover	na
1741	Chawton	na
1743	Dunmer	1760
1749	East Woodhay and Hollington	1300
1757	Barton Stacey	2507
1757	Earlstone	488
1759	Bishop's Waltham	205
1760	Folkesworth	510
1760	Fletton	na

Huntingdon

1727	Overton, Longville and Botolph's Bridge	1515

Leicester

1730	Horninghole	916
1734	Little and Great Claybrooke	430

1744	Langton	na
1749	Norton juxta Twycross	1744
1752	Narborough	1050
1755	Knighton	1680
1757	Wymeswold	1440
1758	Great Glen	1000
1759	Breedon	1336
1759	Belgrave	1000
1759	Desford and Peckleton	1010
1759	Evington and Stoughton	1000
1759	Hoton	1100
1759	Loughborough	na
1759	Oadby	1800
1759	Sileby	2200
1760	Barrow upon Soar	2250
1760	Frisby upon the Wreake	1500
1760	Hoby	1000
1760	Hinckley	2000
1760	Melton Mowbray	2000
1760	Somerby	1400
1760	Seagrave	na

Lincoln

1731	Biscathorpe	na
1734	Wollesthorpe	240
1736	Stallingborough	3642
1751	Dunsly (Dunsby)	1500
1752	Wytham on the Hill	1370
1754	Normanton	3000
1757	Baumber (Banborough)	2048
1757	Stragglethorpe	287
1758	Hareby	451
1759	Coleby	na
1759	Fillingham	2800
1759	Harmston	2528

Norfolk

1755	Brancaster	2350
1755	Swanton, Morley and Worthing	1400
1760	Litcham	600

Northampton

1727	Grafton	318
1733	Chipping Warden	1964
1743	Great Brington	4000
1745	Faxton	1170
1749	Wakerly and Wittering	na
1750	Nether Hoyford, Stow with Nine Churches and Bingbrooke	1365
1751	Farthingstone	1662
1752	Drayton	1487
1753	Hinton	1050
1754	Welton	2520
1755	Norton by Daventry	901
1756	Boughton and Pitford	2993
1758	Upper and Lower Boddington	3000
1758	Helmdon	1550
1758	Woodford	1067
1759	Ecton	3605
1759	Slapton	1330
1760	Blakesley	2000
1760	West Garndon	700
1760	Marston St Lawrence	1680
1760	Sulgrave	2485

Northumberland

1740	Gunnerton Ingrounds	2300
1757	West Matfen	300

Nottingham

1759	Barton and Clifton	1500
1759	Everton	2000
1759	Staunton	na
1760	Costock or Corthingstoke	710
1760	Broughton Sulney	2000
1760	Coddington	1780
1760	Clifton	na
1760	Hawksworth	na
1760	Hayton	1260
1760	Nusson	3760

Oxford

1730	Mixbury	2400

1757	Burchester	1200
1757	Piddington	1060
1758	Northleigh	2160
1759	Neithrop and Wickham	2109

Rutland

1756	Egleton or Edgeton	844
	Tinwell	1013
1758	Edith Weston	1200
1759	Thistleton	1380

Suffolk

1736	Ixworth	1300

Warwickshire

1726	Bobenhull	1000
1730	Lillington	na
1730	Welsbourne Hastings	na
1731	Bishop's Tachbroke	688
	Nuneaton and Attleborough	2670
1732	Little Kinneton	1617
1733	Barston	400
	Westbourne Hastings and Newbold Pacy	1400
1739	Pailton	900
1740	Stichall	600
1741	Brinklow	1700
1742	Aston Cantlow	4067
1744	Wolfamcoat	1690
1753	Kilmorton	569
1755	Churchover	1120
1755	Great Harbarow	945
1755	Kenilworth	1100
1756	Clifton upon Dunsmore	700
1756	Radway	1277
1756	Sow	1400
1757	Loxley	647
1757	Morton Morrell	1225
1757	Prior's Hardwicke	770
1757	Prior's Marston	3800
1757	Wolfamcoat	1800
1758	Geydon	1470

1758	Wilmcote	na
1759	Honington	1365
1759	Willoughby	1500
1760	Barford	1733
1760	Southam	2200

Wiltshire

1726	Compton Bassett	na
1732	Staunton	800
1741	Sherston Magna	1000
1748	Badbury	na
1749	Broad Blumsden	700

Worcester

| 1733 | Aston Magna | na |
| 1736 | Alderminster | na |

Yorkshire, West Riding

1729	Thurnscoe	500
1757	Bishopsthorpe	1000
1759	Bolton upon Dearne	1000
1760	Adwicke in the Street	1000
1760	Calton	na

Yorkshire, East Riding

1731	Catwicke	1760
1740	Bewholm	1600
1741	Great and Little Driffield	3800
1746	Kelfield	600
1755	Nunburnholme	na
	Stillingfleet	800
1757	Fulford	780
1757	Pocklington	na
1758	Ottringham	2400
1758	Skirpenbeck	1980

Yorkshire, North Riding

1748	Faceby in Cleveland	1600
1755	Marsk and Redcar	1400
1755	Slingsby	na
1756	Sutton in the Forest	3000

1756	Warthill	800
1758	Brompton and Sawden	na
1759	East Cotham	800

Adapted from G. Slater, *The English Peasantry and the Enclosure of Common Fields* (London, 1907), Appendix B.

RIVER AND CANAL IMPROVEMENTS

1705 (*c.*)	Yorkshire Derwent navigation opened.
1710	River Itchen navigation opened.
1714 (*c.*)	River Nene navigation opened.
1717	River Tone navigation opened.
1723	River Kennet navigation opened.
1727	Bristol Avon navigation opened.
1732	River Weaver navigation opened.
1736	Mersey and Irwell navigation opened.
1742	River Douglas navigation opened. Newry Canal (Ulster) opened.
1750	Upper Medway navigation opened.
1751	River Don navigation opened.
1757 (*c.*)	River Blyth navigation opened.
1757	St Helens Canal, the Sankey navigation, opened.

14 LOCAL GOVERNMENT

THE COUNTY

ADMINISTRATIVE DIVISIONS

County for the purposes of administration England and Wales were divided into 52 counties (40 and 12 respectively), two of which, Lincolnshire and Yorkshire were subdivided into 'parts' or 'ridings'. Scotland was divided into 33 counties.

County Corporate By 1689 there were 19 cities and boroughs styled 'counties in themselves' by royal charter (viz. Bristol, Canterbury, Carmarthen, Chester, Coventry, Exeter, Gloucester, Haverford West, Hull, Lichfield, Lincoln, London, Newcastle, Norwich, Nottingham, Poole, Southampton, Worcester, York). These were exempt from control by the county sheriff, but most remained within the military jurisdiction of the Lord Lieutenant.

County Palatine By 1689, those counties in which the prerogatives exercised by the Crown had been claimed by a great earl or a Bishop (Lancashire, Cheshire, Durham and the Isle of Ely) largely conformed to the more general county organisation of England and Wales. Elements of Palatinate prerogative, largely formal in character, were to remain until the nineteenth century in Durham and Lancashire.

Hundred (or Wapentake, Ward, Lathe, Rape) an administrative subdivision of the county under a group of justices and a High Constable for matters of law, order and rate collection.

Parish (see also p. 241) smallest administrative unit, into which hundreds were subdivided; under a Petty Constable for matters of law, order and rate collection.

COUNTY ADMINISTRATION

Function designed to enable central government to extract from the county its service to the State – not to encourage establishment of local self-government; but a large proportion of adult males, all unpaid, were involved in the structure of local government as jurymen or officials at parish level.

236

CONTROLS EXERCISED BY CENTRAL GOVERNMENT

(1) All major officers (except coroners) appointed and dismissed by the monarch.

(2) The Court of King's Bench could overrule the justices of the peace by taking cases out of their hands or quashing their verdicts if a mistake had been made.

(3) All civil officers required to present themselves at the Assizes before the King's judges to give an account of the maintenance of law and order within the county.

(4) The Privy Council could issue orders at any time for immediate implementation of statutes and common law.

SERVICES DEMANDED BY CENTRAL GOVERNMENT AND EXECUTED BY
COUNTY OFFICIALS

(1) Military service: either the *posse comitatus* (against internal rebellion) or the *militia* (for national defence).

(2) Taxes: aids, subsidies, land tax, ship money, etc.

(3) Maintenance of the peace.

(4) Upkeep of main bridges and gaols.

COUNTY OFFICERS

Lord Lieutenant office dated from mid-sixteenth century; its holder was normally chosen from among the greatest noblemen and appointed for life; he presided over the whole county. One man could hold office for more than one county. From 1689 the office was often combined with that of Custos Rotulorum (Keeper of the Rolls of the Peace). Responsible for organising the county militia and nominating justices of the peace; frequently a member of Privy Council.

Deputy Lieutenants controlled the militia during absences of the Lord Lieutenant; normally nominated by the latter (subject to royal approval) from amongst the ranks of the lesser nobility or greater gentry.

Custos Rotulorum a civil officer, keeper of the county rolls; from the sixteenth century the office was increasingly combined with that of Lord Lieutenant.

High Sheriff appointed for one year, normally from amongst the minor nobility; service was obligatory. The office had declined in importance since the Middle Ages. Responsible for the County Court, control of Parliamentary elections, nomination of jurymen and ceremonial duties for judges of Assize.

Under Sheriff   a professional appointed for one year by the High Sheriff to undertake all but his ceremonial duties; responsible for execution of all writs and processes of law, for suppression of riots and rebellions, and for holding the County Court.

High Bailiff   appointed by the High Sheriff to execute his instructions in the hundred.

Foot Bailiff (or Bound Bailiff)   appointed by the High Sheriff or Under Sheriff to carry messages or search our individuals for the execution of justice.

Clerk of the Peace   a professional officer receiving fees for his services to individuals; appointed for life by the Custos Rotulorum. *Duties*: to draft formal resolutions of the justices at Quarter Sessions and to advise them on matters of law. Duties often performed by a Deputy Clerk (a leading solicitor in the county town).

Coroner   a professional officer earning fees from his service; between two and 12 elected for life by freeholders of the county from amongst their own number (in certain liberties the traditional right of appointment held by an individual or group – e.g. the Dean of York in the Liberty of St Peter, York; holders of office then known as **franchise coroners**). *Duties*: to hold inquests on (1) suspicious deaths, committing to trial anyone whom the Coroner's Jury find guilty of murder; (2) treasure trove, pronouncing on rightful ownership.

High Constable   appointed normally for one year by Quarter Sessions; service was obligatory; assisted by petty constables in each parish. *Duties*   to execute instructions of the justices in the hundred; towards the end of the seventeenth century also responsible for collecting the county rate assessed at Quarter Sessions and for repair of bridges and gaols.

Justices of the Peace   gradually, under the Tudors and Stuarts, took over from the great officers the government of the county, both judicial and administrative, executing statutes issued from central government. *Qualifications for office*   had to be a £20 freeholder resident in the county; to receive the sacraments in accordance with the Anglican rite; to have sworn the oaths of allegiance and supremacy; and to have (in theory) some knowledge of law and administration. The Justices Qualification Act of 1744 laid down that each justice had to have an estate or freehold, copy hold, or customary tenure of the value of £100. Nominated by the Lord Lieutenant and appointed by the monarch, normally for life, from amongst the noblemen and gentry. *Duties*   'to keep and cause to be kept all ordinance and statutes for the good of our peace' and 'to chastise and punish all persons that offend' against such statutes. Commission revised in 1590 to enable justices to act in three ways: individually; jointly, with colleagues in a division; collectively, as a General Sessions of the County

Court of Quarter Sessions   a General Sessions of the Peace for the whole county to be held four times a year; all justices of the peace summoned to attend under the theoretical chairmanship of the Custos Rotulorum; also summoned were the Sheriff, high bailiffs, high constables, coroners and petty constables, who were required to report offences from within their areas. *Juries in attendenace*: one Jury of Inquiry from each hundred; a Grand Jury and petty juries from the county at large.

Functions

(1)   to try private individuals for breaches of the law;
(2)   to hear presentments against parishes or hundreds (or against individual officers) for failure to carry out their duties;
(3)   to carry out routine administration – e.g. licensing of traders, maintenance of gaols and bridges, regulation of wages and prices, supervision of houses of correction, etc; and
(4)   to hear appeals against decisions by local justices.

Private or Special Sessions   Divisional Sessions, usually based on the hundred and meeting in many cases at monthly intervals. *Summoned to attend*: justices from the division; local parish and hundred officials. Empowered by Privy Council Order (1605) to deal with all matters not requiring juries (e.g. vagrancy, poor relief, etc.).

Petty Sessions   various legislation empowered any two justices sitting together to appoint local overseers of the poor and surveyors of the highways, to supervise accounts of parochial officials, to make rates, to license alehouses, to make orders for maintenance of illegitimate children and removal of paupers, to try and punish certain categories of offenders (e.g. poachers, unlicensed ale-keepers, rioters, etc.) and to hear and commit to Quarter Sessions more serious cases (e.g. larceny, assault, etc.).

The Quorum Clause   the Commission required that, where only two justices were sitting, one should be a justice who had been 'named' in the Commission (i.e. who possessed real knowledge of the law). By the end of the seventeenth century, this clause was scarcely valid, because all justices were named as the quorum.

Justices acting individually   each justice had the power

(1)   to commit suspects to the county gaol to await trial;

(2)   to require a person by summons to appear at the next Quarter Sessions;
(3)   to punish by fine or stocks those guilty of profane oaths, drunkenness, non-attendance at church, breaking the Sabbath, rick-burning or vagrancy; and
(4)   to present at Quarter Sessions any parishes or parish officers failing in their responsibilities for highway maintenance and poor relief.

County Court   although by the seventeenth century most of its dealings had been taken over by Quarter Sessions, etc., it still met under the High Sheriff (or, in practice, the Under Sheriff).

Functions

(1)   to recover civil debts under 40s;
(2)   to witness the High Sheriff's return of the writs requiring election of a Coroner and of two knights of the shire to represent the county in Parliament and
(3)   to assess, with the help of a jury, matters of compensation (for road-widening etc.).

Grand Jury (or Grand Inquest)   composed of between 12 and 24 men, usually drawn from landowners, merchants, manufacturers, clergy and other professional people. An Act of 1692 laid down that a juror should possess freehold, copyhold or life tenure land worth at least £10 per year. An Act of 1730 added leaseholders of £20 a year. An Act of 1696 provided for lists of jurors to be compiled by constables and presented to Quarter Sessions. Summoned by the High Sheriff to attend for one or two days at Quarter Sessions or Assizes; verdicts and presentments valid if at least twelve members agreed.

Functions

(1)   to consider criminal bills of indictment; then as 'true bills' (if a *prima facie* case had been established) or to reject them with the endorsement 'ignoramus';
(2)   to consider presentments of parishes and hundreds (or individual officers) for neglect of their duty, and to return a 'true bill' (as above) if case established;
(3)   to make a formal presentment for repair of the county gaol, county hall, bridges or houses of correction before county funds were released for these purposes by the justices; and
(4)   to express county opinion on matters of common concern in petitions to Parliament or presentments at Quarter Sessions or Assizes (e.g. over unlawful assemblies, vagrancy, etc.)

Hundred Jury (or Petty Jury or Inquiry) each hundred and borough would have its own Petty Jury, composed of between 12 and 24 men and summoned by the High Sheriff through the high bailiffs. Unanimity not required in verdicts or presentments, if at least 12 members agreed. *Functions*: to make a presentment at Quarter Sessions of any public nuisances (especially concerning rivers, bridges, roads) or any local officials neglectful of duties. By the end of the seventeenth century these juries were falling into disuse: tasks taken over by high constables and petty constables.

Traverse or Felons' Juries formed from a panel of petty jurymen summoned by the High Sheriff from the county as a whole; used to decide issues of fact in criminal trials.

THE PARISH

ADMINISTRATIVE FUNCTION

By the seventeenth century the parish was both the ecclesiastical division (in which a priest performed his duties to the inhabitants) and a unit of local government within the larger area of a hundred. By employing unpaid amateurs as parish officers, supervised by justices of the peace, the central government succeeded in collecting its dues and enforcing its statutes even at the remotest local level.

NATURE OF PARISH OFFICE

Terms of Office service unpaid, compulsory, one year's duration (or until a replacement appointed).

Qualification for Office no property or religious qualification: in some parishes all males serviced in rotation, in others holders of certain units of land served in rotation.

Exemptions from Office peers, clergy, Members of Parliament, barristers, justices of the peace, revenue officers, members of the Royal College of Physicians, aldermen of the City of London; exemption could also be gained by paying a fine or finding a substitute.

Responsibilities officer personally responsible to the justices or to the Bishop (in the case of churchwardens), not to the parish, duties were arduous, time-consuming and often unpopular.

PARISH OFFICERS

Churchwardens   usually between two and four appointed annually. Method of appointment varied considerably: by methods described above, by election at an open or close meeting of the Vestry, by nomination of retiring churchwardens, by appointment by the incumbent – or by a combination of these. Sworn in by the Archdeacon. Responsible for

(1)   maintenance and repair of church fabric;
(2)   provision of materials required for services;
(3)   allocation of seats in church;
(4)   maintenance of churchyard;
(5)   annual report to the Bishop on the progress of the incumbent, condition of the fabric and moral state of the parish;
(6)   assistance to the Constable and surveyors of highways in civil duties within the parish;
(7)   assistance to overseers of the poor in relief of poverty, lodging of the impotent poor, apprenticing of children; and
(8)   levying a church rate on all parishioners when required for poor-law purposes, and maintaining proper accounts.

Constable   established in office by two justices (or, occasionally, by surviving manorial Court Leet): responsible to justices of the peace, working under High Constable for the hundred; expenses paid by a 'constable's rate' on the parish or by fees for specific duties. Duties:

(1)   to deal with grants according to the law;
(2)   to supervise alehouses;
(3)   to call parish meetings as required;
(4)   to apprehend felons;
(5)   to place minor trouble-makers in the stocks;
(6)   to attend the justices in Petty and Quarter Sessions, making presentments on law-breakers, etc; and
(7)   to levy the county rate in the parish.

Surveyor of the Highways   established by statute in 1555; formally appointed by the Constable and churchwardens after consultation with other parishioners; responsible to the justices of the peace for giving a regular report on state of the roads, for receiving instructions on work to be done and for rendering his accounts.

Duties

(1)   to direct 'statute labour' as required on local roads (wealthier inhabitants to send men, oxen and horses; ordinary parishioners to offer six days' personal labour);

(2)   to collect fines from defaulters and commutation fees from those who bought exemption;

(3)   to order the removal of obstructions from the highways (e.g. overgrown hedges and trees, undrained ditches, etc); and

(4)   to collect a highway rate, if authorised at Quarter Sessions, and any fines imposed on the parish for failure to maintain its highways.

In 1691 the law was altered whereby the justices chose a surveyor from a list of those eligible provided by the inhabitants. The surveyor was obliged to survey the highways three times a year and organise the statute labour provided by landowners to repair the roads or collect money in lieu.

Overseers of the Poor   established by statute in 1597; between two and four appointed for each parish by the justices to whom they were responsible. *Duties* (in co-operation with churchwardens):

(1)   to relieve destitute people;

(2)   to remove paupers without settlement rights to their former parish;

(3)   to make provision for illegitimate children;

(4)   to apprentice destitute children;

(5)   to assess and collect the poor rate;

(6)   to prepare accounts for the justices.

MINOR PAID OFFICES

Parish Clerk	Hogwarden
Sexton	Pinder
Bellringer	Beadle
Scavenger	Dog Whipper
Town Crier (or Bellman)	Vestry Clerk
Hayward	

Parish Vestry   a parish meeting held in church at Easter, and at other times if necessary.

Functions

(1)   to elect usually one churchwarden;

(2)   to decide on a church rate to defray the churchwarden's expenses and to cover repairs to the fabric;

(3)   to make any new by-laws for the parish; and

(4)   to administer the pound and common pasture.

MUNICIPAL CORPORATIONS

By 1689 there were approximately 200 boroughs in England and Wales which had received the privilege of incorporation through royal charter and possessed some or all of the powers listed below.

POWERS OF THE CORPORATION

(1) To own, administer and sell property and land.
(2) To administer the common meadow and wasteland.
(3) To control trade; to hold markets and fairs.
(4) To return burgesses to sit in Parliament.
(5) To create a magistracy for the purpose of holding borough Petty Sessions and borough Quarter Sessions.
(6) To formulate by-laws.
(7) To levy local taxes and tolls.

OBLIGATIONS OF THE CORPORATION

(1) To collect the King's revenue and to execute his writs.
(2) To maintain the King's peace; to enforce his laws; to organise the nightly watch.
(3) To support financially the borough's burgesses in Parliament.
(4) To repair walls, bridges and streets.
(5) To administer charitable trusts for schools, hospitals, poor people, etc.

MEMBERSHIP OF THE CORPORATION

Method of gaining membership, seldom stipulated in the Charter, varied considerably. Qualifications required for gaining 'freedom' included at least one of the following:

(1) ownership of freehold within the borough (in some cases only the owners of certain specified burgages would qualify);
(2) working an apprenticeship under a freeman of the borough (usually for seven years);
(3) birth (i.e. sons of freeman) or marriage (i.e. husbands of freeman's widow or daughter);
(4) membership of local guilds or trade companies;
(5) co-option by gift, redemption or purchase;
(6) membership of the Governing Council (i.e. no freemen outside). Freemen were normally admitted to membership by formal presentment of a local jury. Freemen could also be disfranchised for breach of duty, misdemeanour, etc.

MINOR OFFICIALS OF THE CORPORATION

Responsible to the chief officers; often salaried or collecting fees; possessing uniform or staff of office.

Agricultural Officials   haymakers, pound-keepers, woodwards, pasture-masters, common-keepers, mole-catchers, swineherds, etc.

Market Officials   bread-weighers, butter-searchers, ale-tasters, searchers and scalers of leather, searchers of the market, fish and flesh searchers, coalmeters, cornprizers, etc.

Order and Maintenance Officials   water bailiffs, bridge-keepers, Serjeant-at-Mace or Beadle. Town Crier or Bellman, Scavenger or Street Warden, Cleaner of the Castle Walks. Cleaner of the Water Grates, Sweeper of Streets, Weeder of Footpaths, etc.

CHIEF OFFICERS OF THE CORPORATION

Mayor (or Bailiff, Portreeve, Alderman, Warden)   named in the charter as head of the Corporation; with wide powers. Presided at all meetings of the Council; responsible for the management of Corporate estates; always a justice of the peace, presided at the borough Quarter Sessions; responsible for courts under the Corporation's jurisdictions; usually acted as Coroner and Clerk of Market; sometimes acted as Keeper of Borough Gaol and Examiner of Weights and Measures; appointed minor officials.

Bailiffs   status varied considerably – in 40 boroughs they were heads of the Corporation, in about 100 they were minor officials, in about 30 they were chief officers. Normally two bailiffs. As chief officers, responsible for summoning juries, accounting for fines, collection of rents, etc; sometimes acted also as Treasurer, Coroner, Keeper of Borough Gaol, Clerk of Market; often, as justices of the peace, sat as judges on borough courts; occasionally undertook duties of Sheriff within the borough. Usually elected by the Council.

Recorder   a lawyer; legal adviser to the Corporation. President at some of the borough courts, administered oath of office to Mayor; as a justice of the peace, sat at the Borough Court of Quarter Sessions; usually received an attendance fee or nominal stipend.

Chamberlain (or Treasurer, Receiver)   the treasurer of the Corporation, usually appointed by the Council.

Town Clerk   usually appointed by the Council, but not a member of it. Responsible for a wide range of administration; often Clerk of the Peace, Clerk of the Magistrates and clerk of all the borough courts; sometimes Coroner, Keeper of the Records, Deputy Recorder, president of the borough court.

Aldermen

Known usually as the Mayor's Brethren, sometimes responsible for ensuring that by-laws were enforced in a particular ward of the borough; but principally a permanent and select consultative council (always part of the Common Council). Also collectively performed some judicial functions (licensing alehouses, making rates, appointing constables, etc.); tenure was normally for life.

Councillors

Usually 12, 24 or 48 in number; had no specific functions other than to form the Court of Common Council (together with the aldermen and chief officers).

COURTS OF THE CORPORATION

Court of Record (or Three Weeks' Court, Court of Pleas or Mayor's Court)   a court of civil jurisdiction consisting of one or more of the specified judges (usually, Mayor, Bailiff, Recorder, Town Clerk, aldermen, etc.); often met every three weeks. Jurisdiction limited to suits arising within the borough; usually personal actions for debt or concerning land.

Court Leet   right to hold court normally granted in the Charter; responsible for minor criminal jurisdiction, making of by-laws, control of commons and wastes, appointment of officers and admission of new tenants and freeholders. Administrative functions gradually taken over by the administrative courts during the latter part of the seventeenth century.

Borough Court of Quarter Sessions   gradually took over criminal jurisdiction from the Court Leet; normally only six justices of the peace, all of whom held particular positions (e.g. Mayor, Recorder, High Steward, Common Clerk, Coroner, etc.); often sat monthly or even weekly to hear a great variety of offences and complaints and to pass administrative orders.

Court of Pie Powder   held by Mayor or deputy to deal summarily with offenders at the market or fair.

Court of Orphans held by Mayor or deputy to administer estates of minors.

Court of Conservancy held by Mayor or deputy to enforce rules concerning the river.

Court of Admiralty held by Mayor or deputy to deal with matters concerning harbours, fishing or shipping.

Court of Common Council an administrative court consisting of aldermen, councillors and chief officers; members fined for absence, sworn to secrecy and obliged to wear their gowns of office; committees appointed to deal with particular functions; by the seventeenth century had acquired wide powers of administration.

LORD LIEUTENANTS OF COUNTIES*

Cheshire

1727	Vt Malpas (3rd E of Cholmondeley)
1771	4th E (1st M) of Cholmondeley

Cornwall

1740	Hon Richard Edgcumbe (1st Ld)
1761	Ld Edgcumbe (Vt later E of Mount-Edgcumbe)

Cumberland

1759	Sir James Lowther (later E of Lonsdale) (until 1802)

Derbyshire

1756	4th D of Devonshire
1764	M of Granby

Devonshire

1751	D of Bedford
1771	Earl Poulett

Dorset

1733	4th E of Shaftesbury
1771	Ld (E) Digby

* In the absence of definitive lists of the Lords Lieutenants this table is not comprehensive. It also uses some sources whose accuracy could not be checked.

Durham

1689	E of Scarborough
1712	Ld Crewe (Bp of Durham)
1715	E of Scarborough
1721	William Talbot (Bp of Durham)
1754	1st E of Darlington
1758	2nd E of Darlington
1792	3rd E of Darlington (D of Cleveland)

Essex

1675	D of Albemarle
1714	E of Suffolk and Bindon
1719	E of Suffolk
n.a.	E of Thomond
1741	Earl Fitzwalter
1756	E of Rochford
1781	Earl Waldegrave

Gloucestershire

1754	Ld Ducie
1761	Ld Chudworth

Herefordshire

1690	E (D) of Shrewsbury
1704	E (D) of Kent
1715	Ld Coningsby
1727	D of Chandos
1741	Charles Hanbury Williams
1747	Vt Bateman
1802	E of Essex

Hertfordshire

1689	E of Shrewsbury (during minority of E of Essex)
1691	E of Essex
1711	E of Salisbury
1714	Earl Cowper
1764	E of Essex

Huntingdonshire

1739	D of Manchester
1762	4th D of Manchester

Kent

1687	Ld Tenham
1692	E of Westmoreland and Vt Sidney (jointly)
1702	E of Nottingham and Winchilsea
1705	1st E of Rockingham
1724	E of Leicester
1737	2nd E of Rockingham
1746	3rd E of Rockingham
1746	1st D of Dorset
1766	2nd D of Dorset

Leicestershire

1721	3rd D of Rutland
1779	4th D of Rutland

Lincolnshire

1742	3rd D of Ancaster and Kesteven
1778	4th D of Ancaster and Kesteven

Middlesex

1714	D of Newcastle
1762	E (D) of Northumberland

Monmouthshire

1715	John Morgan
1720	William Morgan
1728	Sir William Morgan
1732	Thomas Morgan
1771	D of Beaufort

Norfolk

1757	E of Orford
1792	Marquess Townshend

Northamptonshire

1749	E of Halifax
1771	E of Northampton

Northumberland

1753	E (3rd D) of Northumberland
1786	4th D of Northumberland

Nottinghamshire

1763	D of Kingston

Oxfordshire

1760	4th D of Marlborough

Rutland

1751	9th E of Exeter
1779	E of Winchilsea and Nottingham

Shropshire

1761	E of Bath

Somerset

1711	1st Earl Poulett
1744	2nd Earl Poulett
1764	E of Thomond

Staffordshire

1755	Earl Gower (M of Stafford)

Suffolk

1763	Ld (Vt) Maynard

Sussex

1677	E of Dorset
1705	D of Somerset
1754	E of Ashburnham
1757	E of Abergavenny
1759	In commission
1762	E of Egremont

Westmorland

1758	Sir James Lowther (E of Lonsdale) (until 1802)

Worcestershire

    1751   6th E of Coventry (until 1808)

Yorkshire

    1740   E of Holderness
    1751   M of Rockingham

LORD MAYORS OF LONDON, 1688–1760
(*Years ending 9 November*)

1688	Sir John Shorter (d.)	1718	Sir William Lewen
	Sir John Eyles	1719	Sir John Ward
1689	Sir John Chapman	1720	Sir George Thorold
	Sir Thomas Pilkington	1721	Sir John Fryer
1690	Sir Thomas Pilkington	1722	Sir William Stewart
1691	Sir Thomas Pilkington	1723	Sir Gerard Conyers
1692	Sir Thomas Stamp	1724	Sir Peter Delme
1693	Sir John Fleet	1725	Sir George Mertins (or Martyns)
1694	Sir William Ashurst	1726	Sir Francis Forbes
1695	Sir Thomas Lane	1727	Sir John Eyles
1696	Sir John Houblon	1728	Sir Edward Beecher
1697	Sir Edward Clarke	1729	Sir Robert Baylis
1698	Sir Humphrey Edwin	1730	Sir Richard Brocas
1699	Sir Francis Child	1731	Sir Humphrey Parsons
1700	Sir Richard Levett	1732	Sir Francis Child
1701	Sir Thomas Abney	1733	John Barber
1702	Sir William Gore	1734	Sir William Billers
1703	Sir William Dashwood	1735	Sir Edward Bellamy
1704	Sir John Parsons	1736	Sir John Williams
1705	Sir Owen Buckingham	1737	Sir John Thompson
1706	Sir Thomas Rawlinson	1738	Sir John Barnard
1707	Sir Robert Bedingfield	1739	Micajah Perry
1708	Sir William Withers	1740	Sir John Salter
1709	Sir Charles Duncombe	1741	Sir Humphrey Parsons (d.)
1710	Sir Samuel Garrard, bt		Daniel Lambert
1711	Sir Gilbert Heathcote	1742	Sir Robert Godschal (d.)
1712	Sir Robert Beachcroft		George Heathcote
1713	Sir Richard Hoare	1743	Robert Willimot (or Willmot)
1714	Sir Samuel Stanier	1744	Sir Robert Westley
1715	Sir William Humphreys	1745	Sir Henry Marshall
1716	Sir Charles Peers	1746	Sir Richard Hoare
1717	Sir James Bateman	1747	William Benn

1748	Sir Robert Ladbroke	1754	Edward Ironside (d.)
1749	Sir William Calvert		Thomas Rawlinson
1750	Sir Samuel Pennant (d.)	1755	Stephen Theodore Jansen
	John Blachford	1756	Slingsby Bethell
1751	Francis Cockayne	1757	Marshe Dickinson
1752	Thomas Winterbottom (d.)	1758	Sir Charles Asgill
	Robert Alsop	1759	Sir Richard Glyn, bt
1753	Sir Crispe Gascoyne	1760	Sir Thomas Chitty

D1348682

OXFORD MEDIEVAL TEXTS

General Editors

J. W. BINNS   D. D'AVRAY

M. S. KEMPSHALL   R. C. LOVE

CHRONICON ANONYMI CANTVARIENSIS

The Chronicle of Anonymous of Canterbury

1346–1365

CHRONICON ANONYMI
CANTVARIENSIS

The Chronicle of Anonymous of Canterbury
1346–1365

EDITED AND TRANSLATED BY
CHARITY SCOTT-STOKES
and
CHRIS GIVEN-WILSON

CLARENDON PRESS · OXFORD

BIRKBECK
LIBRARY
COLLEGE

OXFORD
UNIVERSITY PRESS

Great Clarendon Street, Oxford OX2 6DP

Oxford University Press is a department of the University of Oxford.
It furthers the University's objective of excellence in research, scholarship,
and education by publishing worldwide in

Oxford New York

Auckland Cape Town Dar es Salaam Hong Kong Karachi
Kuala Lumpur Madrid Melbourne Mexico City Nairobi
New Delhi Shanghai Taipei Toronto

With offices in

Argentina Austria Brazil Chile Czech Republic France Greece
Guatemala Hungary Italy Japan Poland Portugal Singapore
South Korea Switzerland Thailand Turkey Ukraine Vietnam

Oxford is a registered trade mark of Oxford University Press
in the UK and in certain other countries

Published in the United States
by Oxford University Press Inc., New York

© Charity Scott-Stokes and Chris Given-Wilson 2008

The moral rights of the authors have been asserted
Database right Oxford University Press (maker)

First published 2008

All rights reserved. No part of this publication may be reproduced,
stored in a retrieval system, or transmitted, in any form or by any means,
without the prior permission in writing of Oxford University Press,
or as expressly permitted by law, or under terms agreed with the appropriate
reprographics rights organization. Enquiries concerning reproduction
outside the scope of the above should be sent to the Rights Department,
Oxford University Press, at the address above

You must not circulate this book in any other binding or cover
and you must impose this same condition on any acquirer

British Library Cataloguing in Publication Data

Data available

Library of Congress Cataloging in Publication Data

Data available

Typeset by Anne Joshua, Oxford
Printed in Great Britain
on acid-free paper by
Biddles Ltd., King's Lynn, Norfolk
ISBN 978-0-19-929714-6

1 3 5 7 9 10 8 6 4 2

PREFACE

THE idea for a new edition of this chronicle came from CSS, who, while working on an unrelated manuscript in the Cranston Library at St Mary's Parish Church in Reigate (Surrey), learnt of the existence of another manuscript listed in that Library as item number 1117 and realized that it contained both an earlier and a fuller version of the chronicle published by James Tait in 1914 under the title of *Chronicon Anonymi Cantuariensis*. In fact, she was not the first person to have noticed this: no more than a decade or so after Tait's edition appeared, J. P. Gilson had added a handwritten note to this effect to the entry for Stephen Birchington in the *Dictionary of National Biography* in the British Library's Department of Manuscripts, but for the next eighty years or so no one followed this up. Given that the manuscript from which Tait edited the chronicle (Lambeth Palace Library MS 99) had a lacuna of nearly seven years in its text (May 1357–January 1364), this is perhaps a bit surprising. It means, at any rate, that the text printed here is very much fuller for those years than Tait's edition, and accounts in large part for the alacrity with which CGW seized the chance to become involved in the preparation of a new edition when asked by CSS to do so. The division of responsibilities has been broadly as follows: CSS prepared the text, *apparatus criticus*, and index; CGW took principal responsibility for the translation and compiled the historical footnotes; the introduction was written jointly.

One of the more pleasant tasks in reaching the conclusion to an undertaking of this kind is to thank those who have helped us or in various ways afforded us the benefit of their expertise. We are very grateful to the trustees of the Cranston Library, and especially to Martin Roth and Hilary Ely, for drawing our attention to their manuscript and for their interest, support, hospitality, and patience during the preparation of this edition. The trustees deposited the manuscript at Cambridge University Library for several months in two successive years, enabling us to study it in detail. We are also grateful to the staff in the Cambridge University Library manuscripts reading room for looking after the manuscript during these periods. We would also like to thank the trustees for permission to use their

manuscript as the base manuscript for this edition; the trustees of
Lambeth Palace Library for permission to print variants and an
appendix from Lambeth Palace Library MS 99; and the President
and Fellows of Magdalen College, Oxford, and the British Library,
London, for permission to print variants from Magdalen College MS
200 and British Library MS Cotton Julius B. iii. Among those to
whom we are also grateful are Linne Mooney, who examined the
handwriting of the manuscript; Julian Luxford, who examined its
marginal illustrations; Richard Emms, who examined the binding;
and Nigel Ramsay, for information on related manuscripts. During
the copy-editing phase we received invaluable scholarly, editorial, and
administrative support from Bonnie Blackburn; among other things,
she contributed the bibliography. Anne Joshua not only undertook
the typesetting with great speed and expertise when the moment
came; she also gave preliminary advice on text preparation and layout,
which greatly eased our task. CGW would also like to express his
thanks to the Arts and Humanities Research Council for making it
possible for the University of St Andrews to grant him an additional
semester of research leave in 2006 in which to bring this edition to
completion.

                                                           CSS
                                                           CGW

June 2007

CONTENTS

ABBREVIATIONS

Brut	*The Brut or Chronicles of England*, ed. F. Brie (2 vols., Early English Text Society; London, 1906, 1908)
CPR	*Calendar of Patent Rolls Preserved in the Public Record Office*
DNB	*Dictionary of National Biography* (65 vols., London, 1885–1903)
Foedera	*Foedera, Conventiones, Literae et Cuiuscunque Acta Publica*, ed. T. Rymer (7 vols., Record Commission; London, 1819–69)
Gransden, *Historical Writing* i	A. Gransden, *Historical Writing in England, c.550 to 1307* (London, 1974)
Gransden, *Historical Writing* ii	A. Gransden, *Historical Writing in England II, c.1307 to the Early Sixteenth Century* (London, 1982)
HBC	*Handbook of British Chronology*, ed. E. B. Fryde, D. E. Greenway, S. Porter, and I. Roy (3rd edn., Royal Historical Society, London, 1986)
Historia Anglicana	*Thomae Walsingham Historia Anglicana*, ed. H. T. Riley (2 vols., Rolls Series; London, 1863–4)
K. G.	Knight of the Garter
NS	New Series
n.s.	new style dating (i.e. with the year beginning on 1 January rather than 25 March)
OMT	Oxford Medieval Texts
Oxford DNB	*Oxford Dictionary of National Biography* (60 vols., Oxford, 2004)
Polychronicon	*Polychronicon Ranulphi Higden Monachi Cestrensis*, ed. C. Babington and J. R. Lumby (9 vols., Rolls Series; London, 1865–86)
TNA: PRO	The National Archives (Public Record Office), Kew, London

INTRODUCTION

THE chronicle edited in this volume was written during the third quarter of the fourteenth century and covers English political, military, and diplomatic history during the years 1346 to 1365 (with, in some manuscripts, a continuation to 1367). The first scholar to take a serious interest in it was Henry Wharton (1664–95), who made a transcription of the chronicle from the only manuscript of it available to him: his transcription is still to be found in the British Library, London, where it is catalogued as Harley MS 4321. For reasons which he explained elsewhere, Wharton believed the author of the chronicle to have been Stephen Birchington, a monk at Christ Church, Canterbury who died in 1407—despite the fact (of which Wharton was aware) that Birchington did not become a monk at the cathedral until 1382.[1] In his preface to the first (and hitherto only) printed edition of the chronicle, published in 1914, James Tait effectively disposed of the idea of Birchington's authorship, preferring to refer to the chronicle as that of 'Anonymous of Canterbury', by which title, or something like it, it has generally been referred to ever since.[2]

The principal manuscript from which Wharton transcribed and Tait printed their texts of the chronicle is London, Lambeth Palace Library, MS 99. As Tait pointed out, this must have been a copy— and, in one respect at any rate, a rather careless copy—of an earlier manuscript, for it has a lacuna which omits nearly seven years of the nineteen over which the chronicle extends, that is, from May 1357 to January 1364. The present edition is based on Reigate (Surrey), Cranston Library, Item 1117, a manuscript unknown to either Wharton or Tait, but which includes the portion of the text omitted

[1] Wharton made his transcription of the chronicle under the title 'Stephani Birchington Monachi Cantuariensis Historia de Regibus Anglie post Conquestum'; this occupies fos. 108–57 of the Harley MS, with the text edited here on fos. 148–57. His ascription of the authorship of the chronicle to Birchington was based in part on his belief that he had also written the 'Lives of the Archbishops of Canterbury' in the same manuscript, which he printed under the title 'Stephani Birchingtoni Historia de Vitis Archiepiscoporum Cantuariensium', in *Anglia Sacra sive Collectio Historiarum*, ed. H. Wharton (2 vols., London, 1691), i, pp. xix–xx, 1–48.

[2] *Chronica Johannis de Reading et Anonymi Cantuariensis 1346–1367*, ed. J. Tait (Manchester, 1914), pp. 63–8; cf. *Oxford DNB*, 'Birchington, Stephen', article by N. Ramsay.

from the Lambeth manuscript, and which thus appears to be both the earliest and the only complete copy of the chronicle to have survived.[3] As will be seen, the Cranston manuscript also raises, although it does not resolve, questions about the authorship of the chronicle.

I. THE MANUSCRIPTS

The chronicle of Anonymous of Canterbury has survived in four manuscripts: two copies of a full version and two abbreviated versions. With the exception of the seven-year lacuna noted above and an extra paragraph at the end, the two copies of the full version are very similar to one another. The two abbreviated versions are very different, however, and were clearly made independently of one another. These manuscripts will be referred to as follows:

C Reigate, Parish Church of St Mary, Cranston Library, Item 1117 (full version)
L London, Lambeth Palace Library, MS 99 (full version, with lacuna and extra paragraph)
J London, British Library, MS Cotton Julius B. iii (abbreviated version)
M Oxford, Magdalen College, MS 200, also listed in the College as MS lat. 200 (abbreviated version)

These manuscripts will be described in turn and compared.

C (Cranston Library Item 1117) is the base manuscript for the present edition. It was catalogued by Ker and Piper,[4] but has otherwise received little scholarly attention. A codex of 279 folios, it dates from around 1370, and its main contents are as follows:

Front flyleaf: fo. 1^{r-v}. Folios 2–10 are missing from the MS.

Catalogue of Popes, with continuations down to Clement V (d. 1314) and then to 1359 (beginning and end now missing): fos. 11^r–124^v.[5]

[3] A handwritten note added by J. P. Gilson (d. 1929) to the entry under 'Birchington, Stephen' in a set of the (old) *DNB* in the British Library's Department of Manuscripts records the existence of the two copies of the full version and correctly reported Cranston Library Item 1117 to be older than Lambeth Palace Library MS 99. We are grateful to Nigel Ramsay for this reference.
[4] N. R. Ker and A. J. Piper, *Medieval Manuscripts in British Libraries* (5 vols., Oxford, 1969–1992), iv. 199–201.
[5] The MS also lacks fo. 23.

Chronicle of the Roman Emperors to 1346, ending with the election of Charles IV in 1346–7: fos. 125^r–141^r.

Lives of the Archbishops of Canterbury to 1366, with brief further addition to 1368: fos. 142^r–174^v.

First part of *Brut* chronicle, ending shortly after William II's accession in 1087: fos. 176^r–207^r.[6]

Second part of *Brut* chronicle, resuming differently with William I in 1066 and ending with the chronicle of Anonymous of Canterbury, 1346–65: fos. 208^r–273^r. The Canterbury chronicle (the text edited here) begins halfway down fo. 252^r.

Gesta Scotorum contra Anglicos, a chronicle of Anglo-Scottish affairs from 1066 to 1346, with inset satirical *Passio Scotorum Periuratorum*, 1306–7: fos. 274^r–279^v.[7]

Minor additions to the manuscript are found on the front flyleaf, fo. 1^r. These comprise: a note regarding the foundation in 1281 of a chapel of St Katherine in Knockholt, Kent, in the diocese of Rochester; a reference to a statute of 1282; the beginning of a detailed and accurate alphabetical index to the Catalogue of Popes; and the name 'Elysabeth'; all of these in late medieval hands. There is also a record of the gift of the manuscript to the Cranston Library on 7 June 1701 by William Jordan of Gatwick. The Jordans were well-known property owners in north-west Kent and Sussex, but nothing is known of their acquisition of the manuscript. On the back of the front flyleaf, fo. 1^v, is the Apostles' Creed. At the end of the manuscript, in space left blank at the end of the Scottish chronicle, a fifteenth-century hand added an extract from the beginning of the Revelations of St Bridget (fo. 279^v). This text has been crossed out, presumably at the Reformation.

The front pastedown contains a partially illegible copy of satirical verses on the friars and their views on Christ's poverty and use of material goods. The legible phrases make it possible to recognize that the text belongs to the 'verse warfare' tradition flourishing in London around 1357 between the friars and their opponents, and to surmise that the author of this satirical piece belonged to the opponents'

---

[6] The *Brut* begins on fo. 176^r with one paragraph entitled 'De principio mundi et etatibus eiusdem'.

[7] For an account, with transcription and translation, of the *Passio*, see the Marquess of Bute, 'Notice of a Manuscript of the Latter Part of the Fourteenth Century, entitled *Passio Scotorum Perjoratorum*', *Proceedings of the Society of Antiquaries of Scotland*, NS vii (1885), 166–92.

camp.[8] The hands of these pastedown verses and the accompanying rubrics are the same as those found on fo. 137^{r-v}.

In addition to confirming that the manuscript was written during the third quarter of the fourteenth century, palaeographical evidence also suggests the following conclusions regarding the manuscript as a whole and the continuations of the major texts: first, that it was written by several hands, some amateur and some professionally trained; secondly, that a single hand appears to be responsible for the rubrics, including running titles, headings, and marginal subheadings and glosses; thirdly, that this number of hands, some amateurish, yet well supervised overall, points to the scriptorium of a house of monks or friars, or to a school or college; fourthly, that the peachy-yellow tint of the parchment may indicate some association with Oxford[9] (the strong evidence that the author was a man of Kent, and the clear associations of three of the four manuscripts with the south-east, makes it most unlikely that C was actually written in Oxford; however, it is possible that the scribes used parchment from Oxford, or that they were working in the ambience of one of the Oxford masters who held high ecclesiastical office in Kent, such as William Rede); fifthly, that at least one of the scribes was apparently elderly, or suffering from some infirmity causing shakiness.

The shaky and tremulous hand(s), designated here as Hand D/E, wrote fos. 121^r–124^v, fo. 125^{r-v}, fo. 129^{r-v} line 22, fos. 140^r–141^r, fos. 142^r–148^r, fos. 169^r–173^v, and fos. 241^r–279^v line 21.[10] Since the material ascribed to this hand on palaeographical grounds includes all three original continuations—that is, the continuation of the Catalogue of Popes, beginning with the pontificate of John XXII in 1316 (fos. 121^r–124^v); of the Lives of the Archbishops (fos. 169^r–173^v);[11] and the chronicle of Anonymous of Canterbury (fos. 252^r–273^r)—

---

[8] Cf. P. R. Szittya, *The Antifraternal Tradition in Medieval Literature* (Princeton, 1986), p. 192.

[9] We are grateful to Linne Mooney for examining the handwriting of C on our behalf. Professor Mooney provided the palaeographical and codicological information in this paragraph and the preceding one (personal communication, 2004).

[10] Professor Mooney identified the hand of fos. 121^r–124^v and fo. 125^v as D, and that of fo.125^r as E, but noted that E may be the same as D, with a lighter brown ink. From then on she referred to D/E. In the opinion of the present editors it is likely that D/E signifies one shaky and tremulous hand, varying slightly from time to time, sometimes lacking in control of the script, perhaps owing to cold, or cramp, age, or illness, but always in control of the content.

[11] The account of Simon Langham's archiepiscopate (1366–8) and the accession of William Whittlesey in 1368 are in a different hand (fos. 173^v–174^v). The 'Lives of the Archbishops' ends abruptly at the top of fo. 174^v.

there is a strong possibility that this is the hand of the author of all three of these continuations, and thus that the manuscript is the author's autograph. Although there are some errors in transcription from lengthy documents incorporated into the chronicle, notably in the Treaty of Brétigny and the Statutes of 1362, and occasional indications of faltering attentiveness towards the end of the chronicle, the continuations are otherwise almost entirely free from the kind of scribal error attributable to copying from an exemplar. Such errors are, however, found in the other three manuscripts, most strikingly in the occurrence of L's seven-year lacuna.

A distinctive feature of C as compared with the other three manuscripts is the marginal sketches which accompany the texts. These often draw attention to English kings and saints, or to matters of finance and property relevant to England: for instance, to the payment of Peter's Pence (fo. 53^r), a controversial topic for which J contains an entire separate inventory. Not surprisingly, the sketches and marginal notes in C become more frequent in the continuations. In the continuation of the Lives of the Archbishops, the marginalia draw attention to the death and succession of archbishops, and to the plague and mortality which led to the succession of John Offord, Thomas Bradwardine, and Simon Islip within one year, 1348–9. They also draw attention to Simon Islip's selling of trees belonging to Christ Church, Canterbury in order to establish Canterbury Hall in Oxford (fo. 173^v).

An active early reader of C added to these attention-signalling marginals, sometimes repeating the first scribe's headings; he also underlined many items in the texts. From fo. 245^r, when the scribe abandoned the *Brut* and began to use Adam Murimuth's chronicle as his base text (which he did for the years 1326–42),[12] the number of marginalia and underlinings increase. Like the marginal sketches, the items underlined usually refer to people or places; occasionally they highlight dates, or natural disasters such as the plague or the great wind of 1362. The sketches are unsophisticated,[13] and the underlinings do not improve the appearance of the script, yet both indicate a lively interest in the content of the text on the part of both the scribe/compiler and early reader.

---

[12] For his use of Murimuth, see below, p. xx.
[13] We are grateful to Julian Luxford for examining the marginal sketches. Dr Luxford concluded that there is very little of art-historical interest in the manuscript (personal communication, 2004).

The binding of C is of late medieval wooden boards, now covered with modern leather. By the time the manuscript was bound, the first ten folios (the beginning of the Catalogue of Popes, possibly preceded by 'ex-libris' information and/or a list of contents) had already been lost.[14]

L (Lambeth Palace Library MS 99) was written in the late fourteenth century, perhaps soon after 1378, the latest date of extensions to its histories. It shares the following material with C:

Catalogue of Popes, extended to December 1370 to include the accession of Gregory XI.

Chronicle of the Roman Emperors, to the death of Charles IV in 1378.

Lives of the Archbishops of Canterbury, to the accession of William Whittlesey in 1368.

Brut chronicles, ending with the chronicle of Anonymous of Canterbury to 1365, extended to include the battle of Nájera in 1367; but with a lacuna from May 1357 to January 1364.

Gesta Scotorum contra Anglicos, extended to 1368, but without the inserted *Passio Scotorum Periuratorum* found in C.

L also contains further substantial items, often with some bearing on English history, especially ecclesiastical history. These are: a list of English bishoprics; a life of St Modwenna, being an abbreviated version of Geoffrey of Burton's *Life and Miracles of St Modwenna*;[15] an account of the controversy between Canterbury and York; the *Cosmographia* attributed to Roger, monk of Chester, from the *Polychronicon*; a catalogue of English saints; *Ymago mundi* of Honorius of Autun, ending imperfectly; and a tractate and three epitaphs on William the Conqueror.

L is shown to be later than C by the fact that its continuations of the Catalogue of Popes, the Chronicle of the Emperors of Rome, and the Chronicle of Anonymous of Canterbury (on fos. 51^r–56^v) extend further than do the texts in C. Moreover, whereas the last paragraph of the chronicle in C (para. 112) looks like a late addition to the text, being preceded by double underlining, which probably marked the

---

[14] We are grateful to Richard Emms for examining the physical appearance of the manuscript. He pointed out that there is worming in the flyleaf, not matched by any worming in the text itself. Were it not for the loss of the first ten leaves, this would suggest that there was no connection between the flyleaf and the original compilation.

[15] Cf. Geoffrey of Burton: *Life and Miracles of St Modwenna*, ed. R. Bartlett (OMT, 2002), p. xlii.

end of the author's original continuation, in L this is integrated as part of the main text and then followed by a further extension. Generally speaking, L looks much neater and tidier than C, but a fair number of careless errors, and, above all, the seven-year lacuna, show that at least one of the two scribes, though professionally trained and skilled, did not always pay attention to what he was writing.

L was almost certainly compiled in the Benedictine cathedral priory of Christ Church, Canterbury. Some time after the Reformation it belonged for a while to St George's Chapel, Windsor, but by 1690 at the latest—when Henry Wharton read it—it had reached Lambeth Palace.[16]

J (British Library MS Cotton Julius B. iii) has been dated to the fifteenth century, but a date around 1380 seems more likely, since the compilation is associated with the noted theologian and astronomer William Rede, who died in 1385. It contains abbreviated versions of some of the material common to C and L, such as the Catalogue of Popes, the Chronicle of the Roman Emperors (to the death of Ludwig of Bavaria in 1347), the Lives of the Archbishops of Canterbury (to the accession of William Whittlesey in 1368), and the *Brut* chronicles, ending with Anonymous of Canterbury and including the additional paragraph about the battle of Nájera in 1367, as found in L but not C (the abbreviation of the Canterbury Chronicle is to be found on fos. 109^v–115^r). J also contains further items relevant to ecclesiastical administration: a list of the sees in the province of Rome, from the Iberian peninsula to Arabia, and an inventory of Peter's Pence for the provinces of Canterbury and, in part, York.[17]

On fo. 3^r, there is a note in the lower margin in a medieval hand stating that this book was compiled by Master William Rede, third bishop of Chichester: 'istum librum compilauit magister Guillelmus Rede tercius episcopus Cicestrensis'.[18] Rede was archdeacon of

---

[16] *Chronica Johannis de Reading et Anonymi Cantuariensis*, pp. 63–73; N. R. Ker, *Medieval Libraries of Great Britain* (Royal Historical Society; London, 1964), pp. 202–3.

[17] Cf. *Chronica Johannis de Reading et Anonymi Cantuariensis*, pp. 72–5.

[18] Rede was also described as the 'third' bishop of Chichester in a marginal note in another manuscript which belonged to him, a collection of tracts on surgery given by him to Merton College: 'ex dono uenerabilis patris domini Willelmi tercii episcopi Cicestrensis' (Oxford, Bodleian Library, MS E. Mus. 19, fo. 1^v). What was evidently meant by this was that he was the third man called William to hold the see of Chichester: his immediate predecessor was William Linne or Lenn, and in 1088 the see had been held briefly by one Godfrey, who, however, was also (mistakenly) called William in some sources (*HBC*, p. 238). Describing Rede as the third bishop William was a way of distinguishing him from his predecessor.

Rochester from 1359, provost of Wingham College near Canterbury from 1363, and bishop of Chichester from 1368 until his death in 1385. The information that the compilation was made by him is repeated in a list of contents added later, in a post-medieval hand, on fo. 2ᵛ. It is not clear what exactly was meant by 'compilauit'. Some scholars have taken it to mean that the abbreviated version of the chronicles was made by Rede, but this has not been accepted by recent scholars.[19] He is known to have owned some historical books, including this one, but his own extant writings were largely of a scientific nature. He made an important astronomical calculation in 1357 regarding the conjunction of Jupiter and Saturn in 1364; there is no mention of the calculation or the conjunction in the chronicle of Anonymous of Canterbury, even though both years fall within the period it covers.

Perhaps 'compilauit' implied the same sort of process of acquisition, writing, and commissioning that Rede's secretary, Walter Robert, described with relation to another of Rede's manuscripts:

The book of Master William Rede, bishop of Chichester, part of which he had by gift of the reverend lord, his master, Nicholas of Sandwich, part of which he bought from the executors of the reverend father lord Thomas of Bradwardine, archbishop of Canterbury, part of which he bought from the executors of Master Richard Camsall, part of which Master William wrote himself, and part of which he had written.[20]

Rede certainly seems to have owned the book—further strengthening the evidence of early transmission of the chronicle in the southeast of England. In addition to the evidence of the marginalia, the front flyleaf, once used as binding pastedown, contains an extract from Rede's household accounts, while the end pastedown contains

---

[19] It was accepted by C. L. Kingsford in the (old) *DNB*, and by A. B. Emden, *A Biographical Register of the University of Oxford* (3 vols., Oxford, 1957), iii. 1556–60; but not by J. North in the new *Oxford DNB* ('Rede, William') or by R. Sharpe, *A Handlist of the Latin Writers of Great Britain and Ireland before 1540* (Turnhout, 1997), pp. 802–3. L. M. Matheson, *The Prose Brut: The Development of a Middle English Chronicle* (Tempe, Ariz., 1998), p. 42, points out that Rede owned several historical books by writers such as Bede, Henry of Huntingdon, and Aelred of Rievaulx, as well as several saints' lives, but regarding his authorship of this chronicle concludes that 'without corroborating evidence, the attribution to Bishop Rede must remain possible but not proven'.

[20] 'Liber magistri Willelmi Reed episcopi Cicestrensis, cuius partem habuit ex dono reuerendi domini sui magistri Nicholai de Sandwyco, partem emit de executoribus reuerendi patris domini Thome de Bradewardina archiepiscopi Cantuariensis, partem emit de executoribus magistri Ricardi Camsale, partem ipse magister Willelmus scripsit, et partem scribi fecit' (Oxford, Bodleian Library, MS Digby 176, fo. 1ᵛ).

items of episcopal administration. In the early seventeenth century J was owned by the Oxford scholar and book collector Thomas Allen, from whom it passed 'with other cartularies, chronicles, saints' lives and materials relating to England' to Sir Robert Cotton, and thence eventually to the British Library.[21]

M (Oxford, Magdalen College, MS 200 or lat. 200) was written in the late fourteenth or early fifteenth century, as indicated in the Magdalen College Library catalogue. It is made up of two distinct parts, written in different hands, the first of which contains Bonaventure's *Via Salutis*, Robert Grosseteste's *Liber de Venenis eorumque Remediis*, and the *Brut* chronicles with the abbreviated chronicle of Anonymous of Canterbury, but only to January 1362 (at fos. 72^{v}a–73^{v}b). The second part contains biblical material: a fragment of the Proverbs of Solomon, Ecclesiastes, Song of Songs, the Book of Wisdom, and Ecclesiasticus.

The catalogue notes that the later chronicle text agrees 'verbatim' with the chronicle of Murimuth, also found in Magdalen College Library (MS 53), but this ends in 1343, while Murimuth's chronicle continued to 1346. Entries on the front flyleaf of MS 200 and on fo. 56^v, ascribed in both cases to James Tyrrell, mistakenly list the chronicle as continuing only to the year 1346. Since the contents of M, apart from the chronicles, are of a homiletic or biblical nature, it is likely that the compilation was made for a religious house. However, no details of its provenance are known, and this is the only one of the four manuscripts to have no known link with the south-east of England. It is one of fourteen manuscripts, bound in smooth brown calf, largely with historical contents, given in 1614 to Magdalen College by Samuel Foxe, and still in the college library.[22] Samuel Foxe had presumably inherited the manuscripts from his father, John Foxe the martyrologist. Both father and son were Magdalen men.

J and M are clearly independent abbreviations of the texts. J tends to abbreviate by omitting passages, sometimes whole years, but such

---

[21] A. G. Watson, 'Thomas Allen of Oxford and his manuscripts', in *Medieval Scribes, Manuscripts and Libraries: Essays Presented to N. R. Ker* (London, 1978), pp. 279–313, especially p. 300, and, for the complex details of transmission in the seventeenth century, n. 84.

[22] R. Hanna, 'An Oxford library interlude: The manuscripts of John Foxe the martyrologist', *Bodleian Library Record*, xvii (2000–2), 314–26. We are grateful to Professor James Carley for this reference, and for alerting us to the fact that the manuscript belongs to this group.

text as is retained is largely unaltered. M may do the same, but quite frequently there is an attempt to summarize, rather than simply omit material.

To conclude: there is every reason to believe that C was the author's autograph, and that L was copied directly from it and M abbreviated directly from it. It is more difficult to be certain about the exemplar used by the scribe of J, for while he included the final paragraph on the battle of Nájera in 1367 (found in L but not C), he omitted the extensions of some of the other historical works included in L. Since C, L, and J all seem to have been associated with Canterbury or its vicinity, it is possible that J was copied partly from C and partly from L.

II. THE CHRONICLER'S SOURCES

Returning to the Cranston Library MS (C), the base manuscript for this edition, it is clear that from fo. 246^v, by which point the author had reached the beginning of the reign of Edward III (1327–77), to fo. 252^r, on which he began his account of the Crécy campaign, the author was essentially copying the *Continuatio Chronicarum* of Adam Murimuth. He is unlikely to have encountered much difficulty in getting hold of this, since Murimuth had extensive connections with Canterbury.[23] Yet he did not copy the latter slavishly: he omitted, for example, most of the documents which Murimuth inserted into his chronicle, and made a few brief additions of his own, though none of any significance; nevertheless, the framework of his narrative for these years, and much of his actual phraseology, was undoubtedly derived from Murimuth, down at least to his notice of the Dunstable tournament of February 1342. From this point he abandoned Murimuth (which is very full for the years 1342–6),[24] and disposed of the next four and a half years in one sentence, explaining that although the Anglo–French truce had been maintained from 1342 to 1346 (which was not in fact true), the two countries had been unable

[23] Murimuth acted both as the archbishop's vicar-general and as the chapter's proctor at the Roman Curia on several occasions between about 1310 and 1340; he also received a pension from the chapter: *Oxford DNB*, 'Murimuth, Adam', article by W. Childs.

[24] Murimuth's narrative of these four years covers nearly 100 pages in the Rolls Series edition of his chronicle: the Dunstable tournament is described on pp. 123–4; the Latin text ends (with the battle of Neville's Cross) on p. 219: *Adae Murimuth Continuatio Chronicarum. Robertus de Avesbury de Gestis Mirabilibus Regis Edwardi Tertii*, ed. E. M. Thompson (Rolls Series; London, 1889).

to agree a treaty of peace.[25] Following this, he launched straight into his account of the Crécy campaign, the beginning of his independent narrative and of the text edited here.

'Independent narrative' is, however, almost invariably a term that requires some qualification. Like most chronicles, that of Anonymous of Canterbury was constructed through the interweaving of written sources, oral reports, and the eyewitness evidence of the author himself. His written sources included certain documents which he copied out, sometimes in full, and others which he abridged or summarized or from which he merely lifted a sentence or two. The following either certainly or probably fall into the former category:

(a) A list of the dead and captured on the French side at the battle of Poitiers (paras. 30–3).
(b) Two papal bulls from Innocent VI to the Black Prince, written on 3 and 6 October 1356 (paras. 35–6).
(c) A list of Edward III's war captains at the outset of the Reims campaign in November 1359 (para. 59).
(d) A list of the English killed by French raiders at Winchelsea on 15 March 1360 (para. 65).
(e) The entire text of the Anglo–French treaty agreed at Brétigny on 8 May 1360 (para. 76).
(f) The texts of the various oaths to uphold the Treaty of Brétigny–Calais sworn by the French and English kings, the Black Prince, and various other lords in October 1360 (paras. 77–81).
(g) A translation into Latin of the first four clauses of the Statute of 36 Edward III, issued following the parliament of October 1362, followed by an abridgement of some of the subsequent clauses (paras. 92–101).
(h) A list of the dead and captured on Charles de Blois's side at the battle of Auray in September 1364 (para. 109).
(i) The Appendix also includes a list of the dead and captured on the Trastámaran side at the battle of Nájera in April 1367.

Documents copied out *in extenso* are naturally easier to identify than those which the chronicler summarized or abridged, but in this case written sources can certainly be shown to have been used for parts of the narrative, especially of the English campaigns abroad. For

[25] 'Item ab anno Domini supradicto usque ad annum Domini millesimo trecentisimo quadragesimo sexto semper de anno in anno continuata fuit treuga inter Anglie et Francie reges sine aliqua expedicione uel faccione pacis effectualiter faciende' (C, fo. 252ʳ).

Edward III's 1346 campaign and the battle of Crécy, for example, our chronicler employed at least two and probably three written sources, although only one of them was used extensively: this is the letter which the king's confessor, Richard de Winkley, wrote from 'between Boulogne and Wissant' to the London Dominican convent on 2 September, and which is reproduced in full in the chronicle of Adam Murimuth. It describes the progress of the English army from the capture of Caen (26 July) until the day of Crécy (26 August), and evidently circulated widely, for it was also used to a greater or lesser degree by Robert of Avesbury, John of Reading, Henry Knighton, and the authors of the *Brut* and Lanercost chronicles.[26] However, although our chronicler copied out the greater part of this letter (paras. 5–12), he did not simply reproduce it verbatim; rather, he frequently adjusted Winkley's syntax, omitted occasional clauses, and added the odd word or phrase designed (for the most part) to show the French king in a worse light. For example, he stated that King Philip broke the bridge over the Seine at Rouen out of fear of Edward ('regem Anglie metuens'), that he 'foolishly' ('uecorditer') ordered all the bridges around Paris to be broken, and that the Black Prince launched the English vanguard against the French army at Crécy 'with vigour' ('uiriliter'). He also, perhaps carelessly, omitted the phrase 'per uiam maritagii' from Winkley's account of the negotiations between Edward III and the cardinal-legates at Lisieux, the implication of which was that the additional incentive being offered to Edward III if he would agree to peace was an Anglo–French marriage alliance.

For the first two weeks of the campaign, before he began using Winkley's letter, our chronicler selected a few sentences from a second newsletter, written by Edward III to his council from Caen on 29 July,[27] but otherwise he relied either on oral information or

---

[26] *Adae Murimuth Continuatio Chronicarum*, pp. 215–7 (Murimuth), 362–3 (Avesbury); *The Chronicle of Lanercost 1272–1346*, ed. H. Maxwell (Glasgow, 1913), pp. 326–8; *Knighton's Chronicle*, pp. 58–60; *Chronica Johannis de Reading et Anonymi Cantuariensis*, p. 100 (followed by the author of the *Brut*, ii. 298). One phrase employed by Winkley which seems particularly to have caught the chroniclers' imagination is his description of Caen being 'usque ad nudos parietes spoliata'; his use of this phrase is the only evidence that John of Reading saw this letter.

[27] This letter is commonly referred to as Edward's letter to the archbishop of York, but the recent discovery of a complete version of the letter demonstrates that it was in fact addressed by the king to his 'chancellor, treasurer and others of our council remaining in London': K. A. Fowler, 'News from the front: Letters and despatches of the fourteenth century', in P. Contamine, C. Giry-Deloison, and M. H. Keen, eds., *Guerre et Société en*

written sources which have since perished. The first paragraph of the chronicle—an introduction to the campaign which begins by setting out the justification for Edward's invasion—includes the fact that Robert Bertrand was the commander of the force deputed to marshal the French resistance to the landing at La Hougue, which is confirmed by several French sources but mentioned in only one other English chronicle.[28] Paragraphs 2 and 3, which summarize very briefly the march from La Hougue to Caen and the capture of the latter, are based loosely on Edward III's letter of 29 July, but paragraph 4 is an apparently unique description of the difficulties of the terrain through which the English army passed after leaving Caen; the fact that our chronicler claimed here to be retailing the evidence of 'many knights who were captured then' indicates that this may have been information which he received by word of mouth.

Paragraphs 5–12 of the chronicle were, as already noted, based on Richard de Winkley's letter, which our chronicler also used for his brief notice of Crécy itself, although he seems to have used a different list of the French slain at the battle (para. 14): the fact that he knew the see of the second bishop allegedly killed at Crécy (Noyon), and his awkward description of the count of Alençon as 'frater eius Philippi de Valesio', suggests that he used (and garbled) the same list as that used by the Lanercost chronicler and the author of the *Anonimalle Chronicle*,[29] but he abbreviated the list so drastically that it is difficult to be sure. He ended his account of Crécy by recording the portent which was said to have predicted French defeat: the sight, shortly before the battle began, of some 'very black birds' circling over the French army. A similar story also appears in the *Eulogium Historiarum*, where it is said that there were more than a thousand ravens which were 'seen more by the French than the English',[30] and,

---

France, en Angleterre et en Bourgogne, XIV—XV Siècles (Lille, 1991), pp. 63–92, at 83–4. This letter was also used in the *Chronicle of Lanercost* (pp. 326–7) and the *Anonimalle Chronicle* (pp. 19–20).

[28] C. Rogers, *War Cruel and Sharp: English Strategy under Edward III, 1327–1360* (Woodbridge, 2000), p. 219 nn. 10, 12; *Chronica Johannis de Reading et Anonymi Cantuariensis*, pp. 356–7. Bertrand is also mentioned in the 'Acta Bellicosa', a chronicle fragment printed in J. Moisant, *Le Prince Noir en Aquitaine, 1355–1356, 1362–1370* (Paris, 1894), p. 159.

[29] *Chronicle of Lanercost*, p. 329; *Anonimalle Chronicle*, p. 23; an account of the campaign printed by Thompson (*Chronicon Galfridi le Baker*, p. 254) from London, British Library MS Cotton Cleopatra D. vii, fo. 79, also includes the bishops of Sens and Noyon and 'le comte Dalysoun, frere au roy de France' among its list of the slain.

[30] *Eulogium Historiarum*, iii. 211.

somewhat later, in the *Historia Anglicana* of Thomas Walsingham, who claimed that when, shortly before the battle, the blind king of Bohemia was told that flocks of ravens, crows, jackdaws, and 'other scavengers of corpses' ('aliae cadaverum sectatrices') could be seen flying above the French army, he declared that they were a bad omen, signifying that the French would be slaughtered ('significant exercitum fore mactandum').[31] The differences between these various versions of this story suggest that it is unlikely to have circulated in written form, but was simply one of those rumours or anecdotes about notable events which came to the ears of a number of independent chroniclers.

From the battle of Crécy to the battle of Poitiers, the attenuated nature of our chronicler's reportage makes it very difficult to know what written sources, if any, he was relying upon. Tait thought that his account of the battle of Neville's Cross (paras. 16–17) 'seems to be based partly upon that of Murimuth', but the verbal coincidences are so slight that this seems unlikely.[32] The chronologically inverted accounts of the attempted recapture of Calais by Geoffrey de Charny in January 1350 (para. 24), and of the capture of Guines by John of Doncaster two years later (para. 20), share some of their information with other contemporary accounts—although the former also includes details not provided in any other source—and while it is by no means unlikely that either or both of them are based on newsletters, these seem neither to have come to the attention of other chroniclers nor to have survived.[33]

The account of the Black Prince's French expedition of 1355–6 is so brief as to preclude any meaningful discussion of sources (para. 28), but the list of captures and casualties at Poitiers was almost certainly derived ultimately from the well-known letter sent by

[31] *Historia Anglicana*, i. 268.

[32] *Chronica Johannis de Reading et Anonymi Cantuariensis*, p. 358; *Adae Murimuth Continuatio Chronicarum*, pp. 218–19. Tait also observed that our chronicler's account of the Roman Jubilee 'has some verbal similarity to that in the [so-called] continuation of Murimuth', but these entries are really too brief to permit any deductions about their mutual reliance: cf. *Adami Murimuthensis Chronica sui Temporis cum eorundem Continuatio a Quodam Anonymo*, ed. T. Hog (London, 1846), p. 182.

[33] Geoffrey le Baker's accounts of both episodes are so detailed that they must surely have been derived from newsletters, while Robert of Avesbury and John of Reading clearly used the same source for their accounts of Charny's venture. For noteworthy accounts of these exploits, see *Chronicon Galfridi le Baker*, pp. 102–5 (Charny) and 116–18 (Doncaster); *Adae Murimuth Continuatio Chronicarum* (for Avesbury), pp. 408–10 (Charny), and 414–15 (Doncaster); *Anonimalle Chronicle*, pp. 30–1 (Charny); *Chronica Johannis de Reading et Anonymi Cantuariensis*, pp. 107–8 (Charny); and *Historia Anglicana*, i. 273–4 (Charny).

Bartholomew Lord Burghersh to Sir John Beauchamp, undated but clearly written within weeks if not days of the battle (paras. 30–3).[34] Robert of Avesbury reproduced almost exactly the same list, in the same order, as also did Henry Knighton, writing some decades later. It may be doubted, however, whether either Avesbury or Anonymous of Canterbury drew directly from Burghersh's letter, for each of them added (the same) six names of prisoners to the thirty-one given by Burghersh: thus it seems either that they both used some intermediate source based on the Burghersh letter (perhaps some semi-official list circulated by a government clerk) or that our chronicler had access to Avesbury's chronicle and copied his list. Given that Avesbury was employed as registrar to the archbishop of Canterbury, and that his chronicle was known to others within a few years of his death in 1359, the latter is not impossible, although the former is perhaps the more probable.[35]

The one piece of apparently unique information which our chronicler was able to provide about the battle of Poitiers was his enumeration of the 'banners and pennons' in each of the four divisions of the French army: there were, he claimed, eighty in the first, 180 in the second, fifty-five in the third, and eighty-seven in the fourth, the division commanded personally by King John (para. 29). Where he got these figures from is unknown (as is their reliability); it is tempting to suggest some garbled or third-hand descent from the very much longer account of Poitiers given by Geoffrey le Baker, who recorded that at the outset of the battle the French army contained 8,000 fighting men and a very large number of sergeants under 'quater viginti et septem vexillis'—that is, eighty-seven banners, the same figure which our chronicler gave for the division under the French king.[36] Yet there is nothing else to suggest that our chronicler had seen the source used by le Baker, and the coincidence in numbers may be purely fortuitous.

The account of King John's reception by the Londoners on 24 May 1357, the most detailed and vivid to have survived (paras. 39–40),

---

[34] This letter is printed in *Le Prince Noir, poème du héraut d'armes Chandos*, ed. F. Michel (London and Paris, 1883), pp. 336–8, and *The Black Prince: An Historical Poem by Chandos Herald*, ed. H. O. Coxe (Roxburghe Club; London, 1842), pp. 369–70. The original is in Oxford, Bodleian Library, MS Ashmole 789, fo. 149ʳ. There is a translation in C. Rogers, *The Wars of Edward III: Sources and Interpretations* (Woodbridge, 1999), pp. 163–4.

[35] F. Bériac-Lainé and C. Given-Wilson, *Les Prisonniers de la Bataille de Poitiers* (Paris, 2002), pp. 74–6; Gransden, *Historical Writing* ii, pp. 67, 105.

[36] *Chronicon Galfridi le Baker*, p. 143.

may well be based on a written source. Such events were certainly made the subject of newsletters, as witness the (much longer) account of Henry V's *joyeuse entrée* to London a month after Agincourt, which was reproduced by the author of the *Gesta Henrici Quinti*.[37] There are some striking verbal similarities between the accounts of King John's reception given by our chronicler and by the author of the *Anonimalle Chronicle*, most notably their descriptions of the guild members all dressed in their individual liveries and of the two 'very beautiful' girls sprinkling gold and silver leaf on the riders below. However, there are also some significant differences of phraseology between the two accounts, most notably in describing the dress and deportment of the French king: according to our chronicler, he was 'dressed in a robe of black motley lined with miniver in the manner of an archdeacon or other secular clerk', whereas the *Anonimalle Chronicle* described him as 'dressed in a surcoat of coloured cloth like an aged chaplain or an old physician'.[38] Nevertheless, it seems likely that some sort of written source lay behind the two accounts, and the same is probably true of our chronicler's brief but valuable summary of the terms of the 'First Treaty of London' of May 1358, despite the fact that he (probably inadvertently) doubled the size of King John's ransom from four to eight million florins (para. 49). He was apparently the only English chronicler to have gained access to this draft treaty, and it is not impossible that he saw a copy of it in the possession of one or other of the cardinal-legates as they made their way back to the Continent a few months later.[39]

For Edward III's so-called 'Reims campaign' of 1359–60 and the subsequent Treaty of Brétigny–Calais, our chronicler employed a variety of written sources, which may be conveniently listed as follows:

---

[37] *Gesta Henrici Quinti*, ed. and trans. F. Taylor and J. Roskell (OMT, 1975), pp. 100–12.

[38] *Anonimalle Chronicle*, 41. Geoffrey Martin suggested in his edition of *Knighton's Chronicle* (p. xxxv) that Knighton too may have used a newsletter for his account of John's entry to London, but this cannot have been the same one as our author might have used, for Knighton's account is much briefer and less vivid than the other two.

[39] For a fuller draft, see Rogers, *Wars of Edward III*, pp. 170–1. One source of potential confusion which can usefully be cleared up is Tait's note (*Chronica Johannis de Reading et Anonymi Cantuariensis*, p. 363) that our chronicler's account indicates that 'some step in the ratification of the treaty was taken on 4 June'. This is a misreading based on scribal error (due to abridgement) in L: the words 'quarto die Iunii' at the end of the paragraph describing the treaty (ibid. 208) should in fact form the opening words of the next paragraph, describing King John's arrival at Canterbury in 1360. This is clarified by the fact that C has several pages of narrative between the two paragraphs.

(a) A list of English captains with the number of fighting men which each of them commanded (para 59: noted above), presumably derived from a muster or retinue roll of the English army.

(b) A newsletter describing the progress of the army through France from 4 November 1359, the day that the host marched out of Calais, until 10 May 1360, the day on which the dauphin swore at Paris to uphold the peace provisionally agreed at Brétigny. The formal opening to paragraph 60—'On Monday the fourth of November in the year of Our Lord 1359'—probably indicates the point at which our chronicler began using this newsletter, while the statement that 'the people of France too were absolutely overjoyed', which concludes paragraph 64, appears to mark the end of his use of it. This seemingly lost source does not correspond verbally to the more substantial accounts of the campaign (also based on newsletters) to be found in the *Anonimalle Chronicle* and Knighton's chronicle, or to the narrative in the *Scalachronica* of Thomas Gray, which was based on the author's personal experiences in the army,[40] but even so it can be surmised that our chronicler abridged his source, for newsletters describing campaigns tended to include more detailed information than is provided here about the itinerary of the army and military engagements en route.

(c) A newsletter about the skirmish at Faveril in Normandy, which probably took place in early March 1360, which our chronicler inserted into (b) above at what he took to be its correct chronological place (para. 63). Henry Knighton used the same newsletter, and seems to have been equally confused as to whether it was John Bigot or Baudrain de la Heuse who was being referred to as 'the marshal'.[41]

(d) A newsletter recounting the raid on Winchelsea on 15 March 1360 (paras. 65–7, possibly including the retaliatory English raid in para. 68), which also contained the list (noted above) of the inhabitants of the town killed by the French. The detailed personal and topographical information provided here strongly suggests that this report was written by someone who lived in or

---

[40] *Anonimalle Chronicle*, pp. 44–50, 167; *Knighton's Chronicle*, pp. 168–78; Sir Thomas Gray, *Scalacronica*, ed. A. King (Surtees Society Publications, ccix; Woodbridge, 2005), pp. 170–88. Each of these accounts is independent, and they complement each other well, Knighton obtaining most of his news from the duke of Lancaster while Gray was with the division commanded by the Black Prince.

[41] *Knighton's Chronicle*, pp. xxxv, 174. See below, pp. 56–7.

near Winchelsea. It is, at any rate, unique to this chronicle, and is the most important surviving source for the raid.

(e) The entire text of the terms agreed at Brétigny on 8 May 1360 (para. 76). These are presented as if they were the terms finally ratified at Calais on 24 October 1360, a rather careless mistake on the part of our chronicler, who gave no sign of knowing about the changes made to the treaty before ratification. This is nevertheless the only English chronicle to include a complete copy of either the draft or the final treaty.

(f) The texts of the oaths to uphold the treaty sworn by the French and English kings, their sons, and other nobles at Calais and Boulogne in October 1360 (paras. 77–81). Presumably our chronicler acquired copies of these from royal clerks on their way to or from Calais, and the only change he made was to put the oaths taken by Edward III and King John in the third rather than the first person.

Having relied so extensively on written sources to assemble the third quarter of his chronicle, our chronicler largely abandoned this practice for the final quarter, relying instead on such information about major events as reached his ears and on his location on the main route from London to the Continent to monitor the comings and goings of princes or their ambassadors, mainly to the royal court and back—although he did, as already noted, make use of two further documents. His interest in the statute roll for the parliament of 1362 evidently arose principally from its enactment of the 'Great Statute of Purveyors'—purveyance being a subject which particularly concerned him. Thus, although he only included a brief summary of the clause prescribing the use of the English language for legal pleas—the clause which most other chroniclers found especially noteworthy[42]—he copied out the first four clauses of the statute, which regulated purveyance, in full (paras. 92–101). It is also worth noting that he seems to have undertaken his own (not totally successful) translation of the statute from Anglo-Norman into Latin, which he had not bothered to do with the Treaty of Brétigny or its accompanying oaths. The final written source used by our chronicler was the list of those killed or captured at the battle of Auray in September 1364 (para. 109), a list which seems to have circulated quite widely in England, for it is demonstrably the same as

---

[42] Cf. e.g. *Eulogium Historiarum*, iii. 230; *Scalacronica*, p. 200; *Brut*, ii. 315.

that used in the *Anonimalle Chronicle* and by John of Reading, although no two of these chroniclers provided exactly the same list.[43]

The extent to which our chronicler made use of oral sources is difficult to know. Doubtless he had informants in London who were able to tell him about such matters as the progress of King John's illness in the spring of 1364, or the jousts of 1362 and their dire consequences, for after all the archbishop of Canterbury's palace was at Lambeth and there must have been regular comings and goings of messengers and servants. He may also have acquired information from Dover (and, by extension, from Calais) via the monks or servants of St Martin's priory at Dover, which was a cell of Christ Church. On the whole, though, it may be doubted whether there was—or needed to be—anything very systematic about his news-gathering process. Canterbury must surely have hosted enough pilgrims, messengers, and other passers-by on a regular basis to make that unnecessary. He picked up a few of the anecdotes and fashionable prejudices which circulated among his contemporaries, but others passed him by or left him unmoved. For example, he complained (along with John of Reading, who was followed by the continuators of the *Polychronicon* and the *Brut*) about the predilection of English plague widows for marrying foreigners following the second pestilence of 1361,[44] but was one of the few chroniclers writing between the 1340s and the 1360s not to rail against the new and allegedly immodest fashions in dress which were sweeping the country;[45] he knew about the ravens said to have hovered over the French army at Crécy, but not apparently about the exploit of Sir Thomas Colville a few days beforehand, which again was widely reported by the chroniclers.[46]

III. SUBJECT MATTER AND APPROACH

Given that his chronicle covers the years 1346 to 1365, it is scarcely surprising that Anonymous of Canterbury, like every other English chronicler of his time, chose to devote his narrative very largely to war and its handmaiden, diplomacy. From Edward III's Normandy

---

[43] For detailed discussion of these lists, see the notes to para. 109 below.

[44] *Chronica Johannis de Reading et Anonymi Cantuariensis*, p. 150; *Polychronicon*, viii. 411; *Brut*, ii. 314.

[45] For these, and the comments of chroniclers, continental as well as English, see S. M. Newton, *Fashion in the Age of the Black Prince* (Woodbridge, 1980), pp. 6–13, 53–6.

[46] For the ravens, see above, pp. xxiii–xxiv. For Colville's exploit, see C. Given-Wilson, *Chronicles: The Writing of History in Medieval England* (London, 2004), pp. 105–7.

landing of July 1346, with which his independent account opens, to
the despatch of English ambassadors to Flanders in October 1364,
with which it closes,[47] it was the great Anglo–French conflict of the
middle years of the fourteenth century which provided his narrative
with its principal storyline. Whether he was—like Geoffrey le Baker,
or Thomas Gray, or Robert of Avesbury—truly interested in the
practice of warfare, may perhaps be doubted. Except on those
occasions when he was employing a newsletter, he tended to pass
fairly rapidly over the particulars of military engagements; and when
he did use newsletters which could have provided his readers with
more detail about battles or *chevauchées*, he generally chose to abridge
them. Diplomacy, by contrast, was a subject which he seldom
skimped: embassies, ambassadors, the proposals advanced or rejected
on each side, and the protocols surrounding the making of peace were
matters about which he seems to have been eager to pass on as much
information as he could gather, as a result of which he was able to
provide previously unknown details about, for example, the treatment
of the prisoners taken at Poitiers, the peace mission to England of the
cardinal-legates Hélie Talleyrand and Niccolo Capoci in the summer
of 1357, and the Anglo–Flemish negotiations of October 1364. His
chronicle has also for long been recognized as the most important
surviving source for the terms of the (lost) 'First Treaty of London'
of May 1358, and is the only English chronicle to reproduce the text
of the Treaty of Brétigny in its entirety, along with its accompanying
oaths.

The standpoint from which he viewed the Anglo–French conflict
was, it need hardly be said, unashamedly patriotic. His belief in
Edward III's right to the throne of France—clearly expressed in the
opening sentence of the chronicle—appears to have been unquestion-
ing, and he scrupulously forbore from describing either Philip VI
(1328–50) or John II (1350–64) as king of France, choosing instead to
refer to them as 'self-styled king of France', 'Lord Philip de Valois',
'John of France', 'the adversary', and so forth[48]—until, that is, John's
arrival in England in May 1357, when, grasping the new diplomatic
reality consequent upon the French king's capture at the battle of

---

[47] The last paragraph (para. 112), about the departure of the Black Prince to Aquitaine,
was evidently a later addition: see above, pp. xvi–xvii.

[48] Both Adam Murimuth (whose chronicle Anonymous of Canterbury had used) and
Geoffrey le Baker did the same; Baker, for example, consistently referred to Philip VI as
'the tyrant' and John II as 'the crowned one': cf. *Chronicon Galfridi le Baker*, p. 111.

Poitiers, he promptly began to style him 'king of France'; this he continued to do until John's death, when he also allowed the regnal style to his successor, Charles V. Not that his suspicions about Charles were in any way assuaged: no sooner had he recorded the new king's coronation than he proceeded to accuse him of summoning his 'parliament' to Paris, 'so that hostile plans might be made against the English' (para. 108). On the other hand, not all French kings were equally damnable. For Philip VI, he had not a good word to say: the first Valois was cowardly, stubborn, foolish, deceitful, and incompetent: despite the overwhelming numerical superiority of his army at Crécy (much inflated by our chronicler) he still managed to lose the battle before ignominiously fleeing the field. John II, however, fared significantly better at his hands, perhaps because circumstances rendered him an object to be pitied rather than feared, perhaps because our chronicler probably had the opportunity to meet—or at least see—the French king in person when he passed through Canterbury in July 1360, where he 'devoutly' made generous offerings at Becket's shrine and the image of the Blessed Virgin. He may well have seen him again in January 1364, when 'the noble prince Lord John, king of France' passed through Canterbury once more on his final journey to London, and his description of John's terminal illness and death does not lack a degree of compassion. He also probably saw either the French king's corpse or his coffin on its final journey back to France in April 1364 (paras. 72, 105–7).

Yet if circumstances had contrived to minimize the threat from one French king, there was little doubt in our chronicler's mind that falsity, faint-heartedness, and subterfuge were as innate to the French character as courage and decency were to the English. That Louis of Anjou should have broken his parole and slunk away from Calais 'like a fugitive and a perjuror', despite having given his word to serve as a hostage for his father's ransom, was no more than should be expected of a prince of the fleur-de-lis (para. 103): the French habitually broke their word, just as they habitually fled from battles which they had tried, out of cowardice, to avoid in the first place. The French raid on Winchelsea in March 1360, of which our chronicler provided a suitably vivid account, showed them at their brutish worst, slaughtering civilians, pillaging and burning indiscriminately, raping women, and even eating meat despite the fact that it was Lent (paras. 65–7). The Scots were no better: allied to the French 'because of their hatred for the king of England', they too committed atrocities and fled

battlefields, only daring to launch a raid into England when they believed resistance would be at its weakest—although it is worth noting that our chronicler seems to have been happy to refer to David Bruce as 'king of Scotland', once again, presumably, acknowledging the new diplomatic reality following David's capture at Neville's Cross (paras. 16–17).

The English, by contrast, were courageous and resourceful, qualities epitomized by their ever-victorious king: Edward III was munificent, gracious, humane, personally brave, and above all honourable in his dealings with friend or foe—as witness, for example, his patience and generosity towards foreign envoys, or his consideration for the dying King John. If some of his subjects occasionally slipped a little from their customary high standards, Edward nevertheless remained blameless: the 'English' routiers who terrorized France in the late 1350s, for example, did so, according to our chronicler, 'without the knowledge of the king of England'; the fact that Guines was captured in time of truce (in January 1352) was conveniently forgotten. When English armies spread fire and slaughter through France, this was no more than its people deserved—although it was done, naturally, in the cause of peace, which was at all times the English king's overriding aim (paras. 5, 20, 50).[49]

That Edward III acted as the instrument of a *Deus irritatus*, and that He was on the side of the English, admitted of little doubt. It was God's work that the English king was doing, 'unleashing His terror' on the perfidious French, and vigilance and protection were his reward. God it was who saved the English army from the snares of the French in 1346, and who 'preserved the king of England and his people' from the malevolence of Charles V following the latter's accession in 1364; God it was to whom victory at Crécy, Poitiers, and Auray was ultimately due (paras. 1, 14, 30, 108–9). Satan and his evil spirits also intervened directly in earthly affairs, hurling fire and

---

[49] One Englishman about whom our chronicler may, however, have felt a little ambivalent was the Black Prince: despite the prince's military triumphs, there are notes of criticism detectable in, for example, the account of his marriage to Joan of Kent, the leading part which he played in the Smithfield jousts of May 1362, and his failure to feast the expectant London dignitaries at the time of the French king's arrival in the capital in May 1357 (paras. 41, 87, 90). Our chronicler also omitted to say—perhaps deliberately, perhaps not—that the prince as well as the king and queen were exempted from the restrictions placed on purveyance in the statute of 1362 (para. 94; cf. *Statutes of the Realm*, i. 371). It is, of course, possible that it was the controversial Princess Joan, who as countess of Kent in her own right must have been known in and around Canterbury, to whom the chronicler objected.

tempest at their terrified victims when their 'pomp and vainglory' over-reached itself with the holding of tournaments in the early months of 1362 (paras. 88, 90). Yet, fearsome as these warnings were, it is worth noting that only one other portent is recorded in the chronicle, the 'very black birds' which circled over the French army 'as if hungering after their corpses and foretelling the death of Frenchmen' just before Crécy (para. 14). Nor are any prophecies cited, dreams interpreted, astrological conjunctions noted, or miracles attested; generally speaking, in fact, this is not, by comparison with many others, a chronicle in which the supernatural plays an especially prominent part. Even the weather, not infrequently seen by chroniclers as a portent or at least a 'sign', is ignored apart from the great wind of January 1362.

Nor is our chronicler's evident antipathy to the jousts of early 1362 replicated elsewhere in his chronicle. There is no indication that the glitzy St George's Day jousts of 1358, widely reported at the time to have been unprecedented in their splendour, met with his disapproval, despite the fact that the duke of Lancaster was seriously wounded there; nor, it seems, did the tournaments held at Smithfield to celebrate the wedding of John of Gaunt to Blanche of Lancaster in May 1359. Banquets, ostentatious display, and lavish gift-giving provoked no adverse comment—indeed, the chronicle displays a mild fascination with food and feasting. 'Court notices'—the births, marriages, and deaths of princes and nobles—were reported quite briefly and calmly, without flattery, censure, or obituaries.[50] This was, after all, like most chronicles, a chronicle of royal and aristocratic lives, written from the point of view of the landholding establishment. This is not to say that our chronicler was unaware of, for example, the contribution made by archers or valets to the English war effort, but his social viewpoint was fundamentally that of an ecclesiastical landlord or beneficed priest hoping for preferment—as witness, for example, his comment that the Black Death left many churches unserved, 'and those who remained alive were utterly deprived of servants and labourers' (para. 19).

He was, nevertheless, a man who wore his prejudices lightly. His Francophobia, immoderate as it might appear nowadays, was standard fare in English chronicles of the fourteenth and fifteenth centuries, and at least some of his chauvinistic rhetoric was copied

---

[50] Except for the comments on Archbishop's Islip's qualms of conscience regarding the marriage of the Black Prince and Joan of Kent mentioned in the previous footnote.

verbatim from the newsletters which circulated at this time.[51] Towards the pope and his legates, frequently vilified by other English chroniclers for sacrificing their duty of impartial mediation on the altar of French interests, he seems to have borne no animosity; even when Urban V refused a dispensation to allow Edmund of Langley to marry Margaret of Flanders—often seen as one of the most blatant instances of the Avignon papacy's pro-French bias—our chronicler simply recorded the fact without comment (para. 111).[52] Towards the friars, similarly, he seems to have been free from the prejudice so common in other chroniclers (especially monastic chroniclers), or at least unwilling to express it except in an oblique fashion; he noted, for example, that the consequence of Queen Isabella's decision to bequeath her mortal remains and a £1,000 legacy to the Newgate Franciscans was that her body was 'secretly' spirited away to their house immediately following her death (para. 52), but he held back from the kind of antifraternal vitriol which her actions provoked in a chronicler such as John of Reading.[53] Parliamentary taxation, so often the butt of chroniclers' hostility, receives not a mention, while the one instance of papal taxation which he cites was recorded in an entirely neutral manner (para. 45). One issue which does seem to have concerned him was purveyance: as already noted, his principal purpose in copying out sections of the 1362 Statute Roll was to record the measures passed against purveyors in the parliament of that year, and his report on the activities of royal purveyors in Kent in the autumn of 1359 describes them as 'seizing food and other things everywhere, whatever they could get hold of', so that the king and queen's presence in the county for upwards of two months was 'a great burden on the whole area round about' (para 56).[54]

Apart from his dislike of the 1362 jousts, however, this is about as close as our chronicler came to expressing an opinion on a matter of domestic policy. He was a recorder rather than a commentator, more annalist than analyst. Whether it was because he considered it inappropriate or irrelevant, or because he was—as he comes across—of a cautious and nonjudgemental disposition, he allowed

---

[51] For his use of newsletters, see above, pp. xx–xxvii.

[52] There is, however, a suggestion that the cardinals were complicit with the French in putting off the confirmation of the First Treaty of London in 1358 (para. 49).

[53] *Chronica Johannis de Reading et Anonymi Cantuariensis*, pp. 13, 128–9.

[54] If his omission of the Black Prince's name from the statute of 1362 was deliberate (see n. 49 above), then he was also clearly interested in the question of who could and who could not exercise the right of purveyance.

very little of himself to intrude into his chronicle, and left few clues as to his identity.[55] He liked, when he could be, to be precise with his facts: to record, for example, not just the day of the week or the month, but the hour of the day at which events occurred, the daily stages of an itinerary, the names of those who made up an embassy. When he had access to lists—of French casualties, of those killed during the raid on Winchelsea, of witnesses to the Treaty of Brétigny—he usually copied them out in full. All this makes his chronicle a generally discreet but reliable source.

IV. DATING, STRUCTURE, AND LOCATION

There is, on the other hand, no doubt that the levels of chronological accuracy and attention to detail which characterize the first few pages of the narrative (the coverage of the years 1346–55) are noticeably less impressive than in the remainder of the chronicle. His use of news-letters for Edward III's 1346 campaign meant that our chronicler was able to launch his narrative with a relatively accurate sequence of dates for the expedition, but his record of the French casualties at Crécy is a disappointingly scant abridgement of what must have come to him as a more substantial list, and the same is true of his list of Scots 'killed' at Neville's Cross (paras. 14, 17). He managed to provide a fairly accurate date for the arrival of the Black Death in England, but for the following six or seven years (paras. 20–6) his chronology is characterized by brevity, hesitancy, and at times gross inaccuracy. Where year dates are given, they are usually wrong: the capture of Guines in January 1352 is placed out of order, the impression being given that it occurred some time in 1349–50; the death of Philip VI of France is placed in the wrong year, 1351 rather than (August) 1350; and the major English embassy to Avignon of 1354–5 is dated a year too early, as is, by implication, the death of the bishop of Norwich, one of the English ambassadors. There is, in general, a sense of uncertainty about the chronology of these years, with events being described as occurring 'from year to year' ('de anno in annum') or 'some time after this' ('post hec', 'postmodum'): our chronicler may have known the day of the month (4 January) on which Geoffrey de Charny attempted to recapture Calais, but whether he knew the correct year (1350) is another matter (he placed it after the death of Philip VI). In fact, the only year date which he managed to get

---

[55] Although more can be ascertained about him from his 'Lives of the Archbishops': see below, pp. xxxix–xlvii.

right between 1348 and 1355 was that of the Jubilee in Rome, which, considering that Jubilees took place at fifty-year intervals, cannot really be accounted a triumph.

The account of the Black Prince's expedition of 1355–6 and the battle of Poitiers is again very brief but, although our chronicler shows little interest in recording the details of either the campaigns or the battle, the fact that he now copied out in full the list of French dead and captured, along with two of the bulls which Pope Innocent VI sent to the prince in the weeks following his victory, suggests a new desire on his behalf to maintain a more complete and ordered record of contemporary events. The remainder of the chronicle bears out this suggestion: from May 1357, when King John arrived in London, until October 1364, when the English ambassadors crossed from Dover to Calais hoping to finalize arrangements for the Anglo–Flemish marriage, Anonymous of Canterbury is an important—and surely contemporary—source. He was, it is true, sparing with what he chose to record, and he rarely wasted words, but his chronology is almost impeccable. Apart from a few slips of the pen,[56] the only event which he misdated by more than a day or two was the wedding of the Black Prince to Joan of Kent, which he gave as 27 October rather than 10 October (1361), and the only event which he placed out of chronological order was the death of William de Bohun, earl of Northampton, on 16 September 1360 (which he recorded twice, on each occasion tagging it on to another obituary notice, which suggests that, rather than inadvertently inserting it in the wrong place, he was simply grouping his obituary notices together for ease of reference, as chroniclers often did: paras. 70–1, 85–6).

All this naturally has implications for any attempt to work out when our chronicler began composing his chronicle, and what it suggests is that he began to write it in the summer of 1357—inspired, perhaps, by the arrival at Canterbury of papal legates and high-ranking French envoys on their way to London, or simply by great events such as Poitiers and the capture of the French king—but that, having also gained access to material describing the *annus mirabilis* of 1346–7, he decided to take his narrative back a decade to cover Crécy and Neville's Cross as well, and to fill in the intervening years as best he could from an imperfect memory and such scraps of information as he could gather. It is worth noting that disordered chronology and

[56] For example, *Iunii* for *Iulii* (para. 72); *Ianuarii* for *Februarii* (para. 75); and *Septembris* for *Octobris* (para. 77).

extensive lacunae are characteristic of several English chroniclers' coverage of the years between 1348 and 1355—for example, those of Geoffrey le Baker, John of Reading, the *Anonimalle Chronicle*, and the *Eulogium Historiarum*[57]—and it is not difficult to guess why that might have been. Whether or not the Black Death actually occasioned the deaths of chroniclers themselves, it certainly caused extensive dislocation: communication would have been interrupted, and historical writing—especially in monasteries, perhaps, which were hit hard by the plague—might not have been seen as a priority. Indeed, very little contemporary historiography was being undertaken in England in the early 1350s, although by the latter part of the decade it seems to have resumed.[58] In this sense, then, our chronicle seems to fit into a pattern: the chronological accuracy of the narrative from 1357 to 1364 makes it highly likely that he was writing contemporaneously with the events he recorded, concluding in or very shortly after October 1364.[59] The fact that the birth of Edward of Angoulême (in early 1365) is included in a final paragraph which contains gross chronological errors such as dating the grant of the duchy of Aquitaine to the Black Prince in 1360 rather than 1362 suggests (as does the evidence of the manuscript) that this final paragraph must have been added several years after the rest of the chronicle was completed.

As to his location, the internal evidence suggests that our chronicler resided in or close to Canterbury. The language which he employed to describe visitors to Canterbury was consistent in this respect: Cardinal Capoci in July 1357, King John of France in July 1360, the king of Cyprus in October 1363, King John again in January 1364, and both the count of Flanders and the English ambassadors in October of the same year all 'came to' or 'entered' ('uenit', 'intrauit', 'accessit') Canterbury and then 'departed' or 'continued onwards' ('recessit', 'iter arripuit', 'de hinc continuando') in the direction of either London

---

[57] Geoffrey le Baker placed events which took place in 1346 and 1348 *after* Charny's raid on Calais in January 1350; John of Reading made numerous errors, amply illustrated by Tait; Galbraith described the *Anonimalle Chronicle*'s chronology during the early 1350s as 'very confused'; while the *Eulogium* records nothing whatsoever between 1350 and 1355: *Chronicon Galfridi le Baker*, pp. 107–8; *Chronica Johannis de Reading et Anonymi Cantuariensis*, pp. 116–17, 252 ff.; *Anonimalle Chronicle*, p. 163; *Eulogium Historiarum*, iii. 214–15.

[58] It was from 1359, for example, that John of Reading's chronology also became much more accurate, suggesting either that he actually began writing his chronicle in that year or that he (or some other Westminster monk) began to keep a journal which he later used as the basis of his chronicle: *Chronica Johannis de Reading et Anonymi Cantuariensis*, pp. 32–3.

[59] The fact that he wrote 'The year of Our Lord 1357' as a sort of 'running head' in the upper margin of his annal for 1357 might also suggest that this was the moment at which his composition became strictly contemporary (para. 45).

or Dover. Their precise times of arrival and departure were often recorded, as were details of their visits, such as the fact that King John made generous gifts to the cathedral and then hunted in the archbishop's park of Crudeswood (in Wingham hundred) in 1360, that Cardinal Talleyrand lodged at St Augustine's in 1357, or that Louis de Mâle, John of Gaunt, and Edmund of Langley made a joint pilgrimage to Becket's shrine on 17–18 October 1364 (paras. 44, 72, 104–5, 110). At times, our chronicler reveals a slight degree of 'inside knowledge' of archiepiscopal affairs, such as the fact that the cardinal-legates would not allow Simon Islip to bear his cross in their presence when they entered London on 3 July 1357, or the latter's comment that he was 'coerced against his conscience' into agreeing to marry the Black Prince and Joan of Kent in October 1361. It is also worth noting that he dated the arrival of the Black Death in England by reference to the death of Archbishop Stratford on 23 August 1348 (paras. 19, 44, 87).

Gazing, Janus-like, both eastwards to France and westwards to London, our chronicler's principal axis of communication extended from England's capital city to its most recent continental acquisition, Calais. He sometimes picked up quite detailed information about events in London: for example, he provided the most vivid surviving account of King John's entry to the city in May 1357, and knew that the Black Prince had disappointed a delegation of Londoners to whom he had apparently promised a banquet; he knew that the 'cardinal of Rouen' had 'travelled by river to the Savoy, directing his retinue to pass through the city' a month later; and he had heard about the aeronautical exploits of Brother John de Sutton in London during the great wind of January 1362 (paras. 39–40, 43, 89). He could also act as an independent conduit of information from Calais: his accounts of Geoffrey de Charny's abortive raid on the town in January 1350 and of the escape of Louis of Anjou in the autumn of 1363 both include details apparently unknown to other chroniclers. Naturally enough, his sources of information also extended more widely through Kent, as witness his knowledge of the king's and queen's movements in the county (as well as the impact of the royal purveyors there) during the preparations for the Reims campaign in the autumn of 1359, and of course his access a few months later to the unique and valuable account of the French raid on Winchelsea, just over the border in Sussex.

Beyond this London–Kent–Calais axis, however, our chronicler knew next to nothing that was not common knowledge, and not a great deal even of that. Events to the north or west of London barely

touched his consciousness; Scotland is mentioned only in the context of a fairly perfunctory description of the battle of Neville's Cross, and Wales not at all.[60] For English expeditions to France and the engagements that resulted from them, he relied on newsletters, lists, or brief and simple reports, although his comments on the difficulties of the terrain through which the English army had to march in 1346 ('in the opinion of many knights who were captured then') might indicate that he had spoken to some of the French prisoners brought back to England following the sack of Caen (para. 4). There is nothing to suggest that he travelled far from his base, except perhaps to Dover or London, although even this is far from certain, for he could just as easily have relied on reports gleaned from those who passed through Canterbury. As so often with chroniclers, his geographical location determined the boundaries of his evidential base and thus the scope of his narrative.

V. AUTHORSHIP

In attempting to determine the location and authorship of the chronicle, however, there is also the evidence of the Cranston manuscript as a whole to consider. As already noted, it seems likely that C was the author's autograph, and that whoever wrote the chronicle edited here was also the author of the fourteenth-century continuations of the Catalogue of Popes, the Chronicle of the Emperors of Rome, and the Lives of the Archbishops of Canterbury. This, indeed, was the assumption made by both Wharton and Tait, on the basis of similarities in style and subject matter as well as the strong evidence pointing towards contemporary composition in the texts to be found in L—and, as noted above, the palaeographical evidence of C reinforces their conclusions.[61] Common authorship is clearly of importance, since the study of authorial characteristics, attitudes, and values across a wider range of works makes it possible to gain a stronger impression of Anonymous of Canterbury than can be gleaned from the chronicle alone.

There are notable similarities of both subject matter and phraseology between our chronicle and several of the other works in C. For example, the opening few sentences of the chronicle, describing the

---

[60] There is, naturally, much more about Scotland (up to 1346) in the Scottish chronicle at the end of the manuscript, and some information about successions to Welsh bishoprics in the Lives of the Archbishops.

[61] *Chronica Johannis de Reading et Anonymi Cantuariensis*, p. 66; and see above, pp. xiv–xv.

launch of Edward III's 1346 campaign to France, bear a strong resemblance to the corresponding passage in the continuation of the Lives of the Archbishops—a passage which, on palaeographical grounds, is also attributable to our author:

Lives of the Archbishops (C, fos. 169ᵛ–170ʳ)	Anonymous of Canterbury (C, fo. 252ʳ)

Lives of the Archbishops
(C, fos. 169^v–170^r)

Anonymous of Canterbury
(C, fo. 252^r)

Qualiter rex applicuit apud Hoges in Norman'. Anno Domini millesimo trecentisimo quadragesimo sexto, Edwardus rex Anglie, pro recuperacione iuris sui quod ad regnum et in regno Francorum ex successione hereditaria obtinet, septima decima die mensis Iulii cum exercitu suo applicuit apud Hoges in Normannia. Et in eodem portu de Hoges presens erat Bertrandus marescallus Francie, qui sub pena capitis sui erga dominum Philippum de Valesio, dicentem se tunc regem Francie, manuceperat quod cum ducentis uiris armatis dictum portum de Hoges uiriliter custodiret ne rex Anglie cum suo exercitu terram Francie ibidem intraret. Vnde ipse marescallus tam dictum portum quam iuxta apud Barflete cum palis sicut potuit obturauit, ad resistendum regi Anglie cum potencia et manu armata mille equites adminus et ultra sex milia peditum congregauit. Sed ab illo periculo ipsum regem Anglie Dei potencia liberauit. . . .

De applicacione regis apud Hoges. Anno Domini millesimo trecentisimo quadragesimo sexto, aduertens rex Anglie multa uerba Francorum pacifica in dolo, quodque ius suum quod in regno et ad regnum Francie successione hereditaria obtinet recuperare non potuit nisi in gladio undique considerans, septimo decimo die mensis Iulii eodem anno cum exercitu suo applicuit apud Hoges in Normannia. Et in dicto portu de Hoges presens erat marescallus Francie Bertrandus, qui sub pena capitis sui erga dictum Philippum, regem Francie se dicentem, manuceperat ut cum ducentis uiris armatis dictum portum saluum custodiret, ne rex Anglie cum suo exercitu intraret terram Francie quouismodo. Vnde prefatus marescallus portum de Hoges et apud Barflete cum palis sicut potuit obturauit, et ad resistendum regi Anglie cum potencia et armata manu mille equitum adminus et ultra sex milia peditum exercitum congregauit. Sed ab illo periculo ipsum regem Anglie Dei potencia liberauit. . . .

From this point the two texts diverge, with the Lives of the Archbishops going on to explain how Archbishop Stratford made strenuous efforts to promote good government so that the king might rejoice in peace,[62] while the chronicle continues with Edward's

---

[62] 'Quibus sic peractis, idem Iohannes Cantuarien' archiepiscopus circa bonum regimen regni Anglie, ut rex pace gauderet, totis uiribus laborabat.'

military campaign. The Catalogue of Popes also includes striking similarities of wording to the chronicle, as, for example, in its description of the visit of the two cardinals to England in 1357, their response to the archbishop of Canterbury's elevation of his cross in their presence, and the burden on the clergy imposed by the financing of the cardinals' stay in England:

Catalogue of Popes
(C, fo. 124^r)

De cardinalibus uenientibus Anglie
Anno Domini millesimo trecentisimo quinquagesimo septimo, post capcionem domini Iohannis regis Francie, duo cardinales, uidelicet Taylerandus episcopus Albanen' et Nicolaus tituli sancti Vitalis presbiter, pro reformacione pacis inter Anglorum et Francorum reges, dieque Mercurii in uigilia Apostolorum Petri et Pauli idem episcopus Albanen' apud Cantuar', et die Sabbati prima die Iulii idem presbiter cardinalis, ciuitatem intrauerunt Cantuar', et illico uersus Lond' recesserunt. Die autem Lune sequente ipsi cardinales intrarunt ciuitatem London'. Quibus obuiam dedit dominus princeps Wallie ac dominus Simon Cant' archiepiscopus cum aliis magnatibus et populi multitudine copiosa. Et quia idem Cant' archiepiscopus crucem suam ante se fecerat baiulari, ipsi propter hoc grauiter offensi, archiepiscopus ab eorum presencia se retraxit.

Et per dictos cardinales exposita regi Anglie eorum causa aduentus, eos rex benigne audiuit et deliberauit super expositis per eosdem.

Anonymous of Canterbury
(C, fo. 257^{r-v})

De aduentu cardinalium in Angliam.
Die autem Mercurii in uigilia Apostolorum Petri et Pauli, dominus Talairandus, episcopus Albanen', intrauit ciuitatem Cantuarien' et fuit hospitatus in abbatia Sancti Augustini Cantuari', et die Iouis in festo Apostolorum Petri et Pauli uersus London' arripuit iter suum. Die uero Sabbati prima die Iulii, dominus Nicolaus tituli Sancti Vitalis presbiter cardinalis uenit de Douor' Cant', et illo eodem die recessit uersus London' festinanter. Et ambo cardinales predicti tercio die dicti mensis Iulii intrarunt ciuitatem London'. Quibus dominus princeps Wallie cum magna multitudine ciuium London' et dominus Symon, Cant' archiepiscopus, et alii domini solempniter obuiam dederunt, sed dicti cardinales nolebant permittere dictum Cant' archiepiscopum crucem suam in eorum presencia baiulare. Dictique cardinales cum honore ciuitatem London' intrauerunt, et dictus dominus Petragoricen' in manso Lincolnien' episcopi, et idem dominus Nicolaus cardinalis in manso Cicestren' episcopi, London' hospitati fuerunt. Deinde, exposita per eos causa aduentus eorum ad Angliam domino regi Anglie, ipse eos benigne

Et a tempore aduentus dictorum Cardinalium in Angl' ipsi circa reformacionem pacis huiusmodi occupati nichil in effectu fecerunt, nisi dum taxat treugas inter ipsa regna usque ad festum Nat' Sancti Johannis auctoritate apostolica inierunt.

audiuit et deliberauit super responsione eis danda. Et habitis multis tractatibus pacis, et multis et uariis hinc inde petitis, nichil efficaciter erat factum. Postmodum, die Martis proximo ante festum Sancti Laurencii, dicti duo cardinales, uidelicet Petragoricen' et Vrgelen', comederunt cum rege Anglie apud Westm', et ipse fecit eis magnum conuiuium tunc ibidem.

Quattuor denarii de marca
Et per dictos cardinales receptis duabus procuracionibus de clero quattuor uidelicet de marca pro mora eorum in Anglia fere per biennium. . . .

De anno Domini millesimo trecentisimo quinquagesimo septimo. Dispensaciones cardinalium. Et habuerunt dicti cardinales septendecim gracias, uidelicet conferendi beneficia uacatura et alias dispensaciones, a domino Innocencio tunc papa. Et dicti cardinales habuerunt a clero regni Anglie quattuor denarios de marca pro procuracionibus suis in Anglia.

Many further such textual coincidences could be cited from the manuscript: for instance, the description of the battle of Neville's Cross in the *Gesta Scotorum contra Anglicos* is paralleled word for word in the chronicle, with the addition in the former of one further sentence explaining that the Scottish king and the earls of Fife and Menteith were taken to the Tower of London where they remained for a long time.[63]

The sense of contemporary composition and personal knowledge is strong in all these texts: in the close and usually accurate recording of dates, times of day, and days of the week; in detailed itineraries of royalty, magnates, prelates, soldiers, papal legates, and other messengers; and in the identification of individuals, including at times their relationships with one another, functions, and responsibilities. Contemporary familiarity is especially evident in the Lives of the Archbishops in matters pertaining to the brief incumbency of Thomas Bradwardine as archbishop of Canterbury (1348–9) and to that of Simon Islip (1349–66), which extended over most of the period

---

[63] C, fo. 279ᵛ. Cf. paras. 16, 17.

covered by the chronicle. For example, the account of Bradwardine's itinerary on his return to England in 1349 is embellished by precise details of days of the week, dates, festivals, and locations.[64] The author also records the burial place within the cathedral of archbishop John Stratford, the first of three archbishops to die in the plague year of 1348–9,[65] and the time, manner, and place of burial of his successor, John Offord.[66] The account in the Catalogue of Popes of the accession to the archbishopric of Simon Islip in 1349 notes the date (16 November) on which the provision was published in the church of Canterbury—a detail surely most likely to be thought worthy of mention by a member of a local community.[67]

The Lives of the Archbishops also include comments of a more subjective nature. For example, the author recounts how Islip at the beginning of his incumbency carried out a visitation of his diocese of Canterbury and proceeded 'with rigour' against 'certain ecclesiastical persons', before visiting the adjoining sees of Rochester and Chichester and 'unwittingly fatiguing' further persons by summoning them to his manors.[68] A more damning account, and one strongly suggestive of personal knowledge, is given of the payments which Islip succeeded in exacting in his province, and particularly in the diocese of Canterbury, which were larger than authorized by the

---

[64] 'idem archiepiscopus iter suum uersus Angliam arripiens, die Mercurii undeuicesimo die mensis Augusti applicuit Dovorr', et eodem die apud Eastri fuerat hospitatus, et deinde progrediens apud Chertham, et continuatis dietis uenit apud Derteford die Veneris proximo tunc sequente. Et die Sabbati in crastino, uidelicet in uigilia Assumpcionis beate Marie, idem archiepiscopus regem Anglie apud Eltham inueniens, ibidem liberacionem temporalium suorum habebat. Et eodem die accessit London', et ad mansum episcopi Roffen' iuxta Lambeth hospitatus fuit ibidem die Dominica in festo Assumpcionis beate Marie, die Lune et die Martis sequente et die Mercurii, quo die idem archiepiscopus ibidem diem suum clausit extremum. Et die Sabbati, in festo decollacionis Sancti Iohannis Baptiste, in ecclesia Cant' est humatus' (C, fo. 171ʳ).

[65] 'Die autem Martis in crastino Natiuitatis beate Marie eodem anno, corpus ipsius archiepiscopi in ecclesia Cantuar' iuxta summum altare in parte australi honorifice traditur sepulture' (C, fo. 170ʳ).

[66] 'Hic autem Cant' electus circa cessacionem mortalitatis huiusmodi in uigilia sancti Augustini, Anglorum episcopi, mensis Maii apud Totenhale diem suum clausit extremum, et septimo die mensis Iunii anno Domini millesimo trecentisimo quadragesimo nono secrete post matutinas in ecclesia Christi Cantuar' iuxta locum ubi sanctus martirizatus fuerat est sepultus' (C, fo. 170ᵛ).

[67] 'Cui successit magister Simon de Islep' per prouisionem apostolicam, cuius prouisio fuit publicata in ecclesia Cantuar' sexto decimo die Novembris dicto anno' (C, fo. 123ᵛ).

[68] 'Hic uisitauit dioc' suam Cantuar', in qua certas personas ecclesiasticas priuauit et cum rigore processit. Et deinde dioceses Roffen' et Cicestren' perfunctorie uisitauit, postmodum in suis maneriis commorando, et per citaciones ipsos, ut creditur, inscio multipliciter fatigando' (C, fo. 171ᵛ).

papal letters, due to the 'astuteness' of certain of his clerks, whose exposition of them to the clergy of Canterbury diocese was not in accordance with their tenor.[69] Islip was also roundly criticized for his sale in 1362 to Richard, earl of Arundel, for 240 marks, of ancient rights which belonged to the church at Canterbury and the manor of Slindon, contrary to his own undertakings regarding the non-alienation of ecclesiastical property and without consulting the pope.[70] Equally stringent was the author's criticism of the dealings involved in Islip's 'sumptuous' foundation of Canterbury Hall at Oxford, when, in order to establish the college in 1363 as a monastic foundation, the archbishop acquired property in Oxford damaged by the great wind of 1362, planned to appropriate churches (although he died before the plans could be fully implemented), and sold trees which belonged to the church of Canterbury and which no individual archbishop had the right to sell.[71]

[69] 'Hic siquidem literas impetrauit apostolicas pro communi subsidio in relevamen suorum onerum concedendo eidem per dioc' et prouinciam Cant', uidelicet quattuor denarios de marca: sed per astutiam quorundam clericorum suorum, dictis literis apostolicis alio modo quam continebatur in illis clero Cant' dioc' expositis, totalem decimam sic extorsit; et ab aliis prouincie Cant' quattuor denarios de marca habuit iuxta decimarum exigenciam habendarum' (C, fo. 171ᵛ). It is worth noting that when these texts were copied into L, the phrase 'ut creditur inscio' was omitted from the first passage (previous footnote) and 'dictis literis apostolicis alio modo quam continebatur in illis clero Cant' dioc' expositis totalem' was omitted from the second. The scribe of L (a Christ Church monk) did not often abbreviate the text, and may perhaps at this point have consciously wished to soften the criticism of Islip.

[70] 'Anno domini millesimo trecentisimo sexagesimo secundo apud Lamheth', sexto die mensis Ianuarii, hic dominus Simon Cantuarien' archiepiscopus uendidit annuum redditum, ab antiquo ecclesie Cantuarien' et ad manerium de Slyndoun pertinentem notorie, uidelicet tredecim damas uel ceruos tempore pinguedinis, et alias tredecim damarum uel ceruas tempore de ffermeson, percipiendas annuatim a nemoribus, forestis, seu chaceis comitis Arondell et soluendas in manerio de Slyndoun annuatim, ad duos anni terminos ad opus domini Cant' episcopi, qui pro tempore fuerit: et dimisit ac concessit imperpetuum nobili uiro domino Ricardo comiti Arondell et Surr' pro ducentas et quadraginta marcas sterlingorum. Et ille redditus fuit habitus et possessus ab archiepiscopis Cant' qui erant pro tempore de feris bestiis habendis usque ad tempus alienacionis eiusdem redditus sic facte contra iuramentum suum prefatum, Romano pontifice inconsulto. Et quia tractatus solempnis et diligens in ea parte qui in talibus concessionibus perpetuis super alienacionibus rerum ecclesiasticarum exigitur, non fuit habitus iuxta iura, huiusmodi uendicio et concessus annui redditus non poterit de iure subsistere nec debebit; presertim cum urgens necessitas uel euidens utilitas, quare hoc fieri debuit, non subesset' (C, fo. 173ʳ).

[71] 'Circa idem tempus idem Simon archiepiscopus sumptuose fecit fieri unam aulam scolarium Oxon', in parochia ecclesie beate Sancte Marie Oxon', quam uocari uoluit Aulam Cantuarien', et quasdam aulas Oxon' ad terram per uentum horribilem dirutas perquisiuit, pro scolaribus inhabitantibus ibidem. In qua quidem Aula Cantuarien' scolares in iure civili et canonico et in arte dialetica studere debentes sub regimine unius magistri communiter uiuere disposuit, et eisdem scolaribus ecclesias de Pageham et de Ivechirche

As far as the authorship of the chronicle is concerned, the evidence assembled so far points largely in one direction: here was a man who seems to have lived a sedentary lifestyle in or close to Canterbury; who apparently had the resources of a scriptorium to call upon; and who took a personal interest in the activities of his contemporary archbishops of Canterbury, grounded both in personal knowledge of their activities and in his concern for the well-being of the cathedral as a perpetual corporation; all of which might well be thought to point to the conclusion that the author was, as both Tait and Wharton assumed,[72] a monk at Christ Church, Canterbury. This may well have been the case. It is, however, worth considering briefly such evidence as there is which might point to a different conclusion.

It is apparent, for example, from some of the extracts cited above, that the author's knowledge and concern extended not just to the church of Canterbury but also to the archbishop's activities within his province more generally, especially in the neighbouring dioceses of Rochester and Chichester. At times, the manuscript reveals a certain familiarity with the affairs of Rochester in particular. The entry in the Catalogue of Popes regarding the vacancy at Rochester in 1352 and the provision of the former prior, John Sheppey, is unusual, in the context of the Catalogue, in suggesting a degree of sympathy, a human touch, in its treatment of the aged and feeble Hamo Hethe, 'by God's grace bishop of Rochester, broken with age and impotence'.[73] It may also be of significance that John Sheppey, who replaced Hethe, headed the author's list of bishops struck down by the plague of 1360–2 (although this may also have been because he was the first of them to have died: para. 84). The continuation of the Lives of the Archbishops in C also records the subsequent election of William Whittlesey to the see of Rochester in terms which suggest personal knowledge of the proceedings, stating that he was elected 'amicably' by the prior and chapter: 'per eleccionem prioris et capituli

---

patronatus sui appropriari uoluit et uniri. Sed morte preuentus, huiusmodi opus imperfectum dimisit.

Vendicio de Droueden'. Alienacio. Idem etsi archiepiscopus uendidit arbores in et super terris tenencium suorum in walda crescentes uocat' Drouedennes ad ecclesiam Cantuarien' ab antiquo pertinentes: et alienauit de facto ampliando redditus huiusmodi tenencium suorum ex hac causa' (C, fo. 173ᵛ).

[72] *Chronica Johannis de Reading et Anonymi Cantuariensis*, pp. 67–8; Wharton, i. xix–xx.

[73] 'Eodem anno prouidit Roffen' ecclesie de fratre Iohanne Shapeye, priore Roffen', de episcopatu Roffen', uacante per cessionem fratris Hamonis, Dei gracia episcopi Roffen', senio et inpotencia confracti.'

Roffen' in episcopum concorditer electus'. (This phrase is omitted from L, a manuscript known to have been compiled at Canterbury.) The manuscript of C also shows evidence of a Rochester connection, for example in the flyleaf, which contains an account of the foundation in 1281 of Knockholt chapel, in Rochester diocese. Of course, it is quite likely that a monk of Canterbury would be reasonably well informed about affairs at neighbouring Rochester, but then it could equally well be argued that a monk of Rochester would be likely to be well informed about affairs at his metropolitan cathedral at Canterbury. The monks of Rochester were also, of course, similarly well placed to observe the movements of prelates, kings, and French prisoners along the road from London to Dover, as demonstrated by William Dene's account of prior John Sheppey's skill in surviving the lean years at Rochester, when he benefited from familiarity with the French hostages, the count of Eu, and chamberlain Tancarville, and through them came to enjoy the friendship and favour of the pope and the king of France.[74]

Yet should it necessarily be assumed that Anonymous of Canterbury was a monk? He was noticeably free of the antifraternal prejudice characteristic of so many monastic chroniclers. No animosity against the friars is evident in the account of the conflict between the Franciscans and Richard Fitzralph, archbishop of Armagh, with which the Catalogue of Popes ends in C,[75] or, as already noted, in the chronicle's account of Queen Isabella's burial at the London house of the Franciscans.[76] Indeed, there is, on the whole, a striking even-handedness in the author's treatment of the religious orders. Marginal headings and sketches accompanying the Catalogue of Popes draw attention to the founding of the Carthusian order, the Cistercians, the Premonstratensians, the Templars, and both the Dominicans and the Franciscans; the confirmation of the Dominican, Franciscan, and Carmelite orders is highlighted, as are the measures undertaken against the Templars.[77] It is also, perhaps, a little surprising that a monk of Canterbury (or Rochester) would have omitted to mention the general chapter of the Benedictine order

---

[74] 'Historia Roffensis', in *Anglia Sacra*, ed. Wharton, i. 356–377, at p. 376.

[75] C, fo. 124[r–v].

[76] For a violently antifraternal blast on the latter subject, see *Chronica Johannis de Reading et Anonymi Cantuariensis*, pp. 128–9; Thomas Walsingham of St Albans was another Benedictine who made no attempt to hide his dislike of the friars: Gransden, *Historical Writing* ii, p. 130.

[77] C, fos. 67[r], 69[v], 70[r–v], 81[v], 87[v], 115[r].

which met at Northampton under the presidency of the abbot of St Albans early in 1364, as noted by both John of Reading and the St Albans chronicler.[78] Also suggestive is the particular interest which the author demonstrates in diplomacy: in the personnel and comings and goings of ambassadors and intermediaries, for example, and in the terms negotiated with the French in 1358 and 1360 (including, of course, the copying out of the Treaty of Brétigny and its accompanying oaths) and with the count of Flanders in October 1364. Was the author involved in some of these negotiations? If so, he is more likely to have been a secular clerk than a monk.

The clear association of J (apparently the earliest abridgement of several of the texts in C) with William Rede raises further possibilities. Before his provision to the see of Chichester in 1368, Rede was successively archdeacon of Rochester (1359–63) and then provost of Wingham College, six miles east of Canterbury (1363–8). Crudeswood park, where the Black Prince entertained King John of France with a 'fine hunt for wild beasts' on 5 July 1360, is in Wingham hundred. Like the archbishops Thomas Bradwardine and Simon Islip, Rede was an Oxford graduate and a noted scholar, and, as already indicated, the parchment used for C might have come from Oxford. If our author was a clerk in Rede's circle, then Rede would presumably have known his works, and may well have had them abridged for his own compilations.

This is not of course to argue that he *was* a secular clerk in Rede's circle. The most likely conclusion remains that he was a monk at Christ Church. Nevertheless, the evidence both of C itself and of its relationship to L and J does invite some probing of previously held assumptions about who exactly 'Anonymous of Canterbury' was.

VI. HISTORICAL VALUE AND THE CANTERBURY CONTEXT

One thing at any rate is fairly clear: whoever Anonymous of Canterbury was, it would be hard to describe him as an ambitious chronicler. Situated where he was, he must surely have heard and seen a great deal more than he cared to note down; it is difficult not to wonder what Thomas Walsingham or Henry Knighton might have made of such an opportunity. Nevertheless, it has always been acknowledged, and rightly, that he does, usually in small ways but occasionally in

[78] *Chronica Johannis de Reading et Anonymi Cantuariensis*, pp. 159–60, 315.

larger ones, make a far from negligible contribution to the sum total
of our knowledge of the years about which he wrote, and it may be
useful at this point to provide a list, in chronological order, of those
details which he furnishes which are not recorded by other chroniclers, and which have therefore traditionally been regarded as
marking the measure of his contribution to English historiography
even before the publication of the full text of his chronicle:[79]

(a) The identification of Amerigo de Pavia as master of the king's
     galleys at the time of Charny's raid on Calais in January 1350, as
     well as the probable date of the raid (para. 24).

(b) The list of 'banners' and 'pennons' under which the French
     divisions were marshalled at Poitiers (para. 29).

(c) The account of King John's reception by the Londoners in May
     1357 (paras. 38–40).

(d) The attempt by the 'cardinal of Rouen' to secure a private
     interview with King John in the summer of 1357 (para. 43).

(e) The terms of the 'First Treaty of London' of May 1358 (para.
     49).

(f) The date of the Black Prince's crossing to France on 11 August
     1360 (para. 74).

(g) The names of the magnates who in October 1360 took the oath
     along with King John of France to uphold the Treaty of
     Brétigny–Calais (para. 78).

(h) Archbishop Islip's claim to have been 'coerced' into marrying the
     Black Prince and Joan of Kent in October 1361 (para. 87).

(i) Louis of Anjou's 'French leave' from Calais in the autumn of
     1363, and the identification of John de Cobham as having charge
     of the princes of the lily (para. 103).

(j) King John's itinerary from Dover to London in January 1364,
     and the names of his entourage (para. 105).

(k) Details of the return of the French king's corpse from London,
     via Canterbury, to France in April 1364 (para. 107).

(l) The list of dead and captured at the battle of Auray in September
     1364 (para. 109).

(m) Details of the negotiations with the count of Flanders in October
     1364, including his visit to Becket's shrine (para. 110).

---

[79] For assessments of his contribution which mention the following points, see *Chronica
Johannis de Reading et Anonymi Cantuariensis*, pp. 66–70, 361–9; Gransden, *Historical
Writing* ii, pp. 109–10.

(n) The (alleged) fact, recorded in the extension in L but not in C, that King Pedro of Castile promised to make the Black Prince his heir in return for help to restore him to his throne (Appendix).

Since the appearance in 1914 of Tait's edition, the originality of one or two of these points has, naturally, been found to be less exclusive: for example, the full text of the *Anonimalle Chronicle*, first published in 1927, included the same list of casualties at Auray and a similar description of King John's reception by the Londoners in May 1357. There can be no doubt, however, that this is more than counter-balanced by the discovery of the missing portion of the Canterbury chronicle for the years 1357–64. Unsurprisingly, the compilers of J and M included some of the more interesting items of information in their abridgements of the chronicle, but among those which they omitted are the following, which should now be added to the foregoing list:

(a) The dates of departure from England of Cardinals Talleyrand and Capoci in September/October 1358 (para. 51).

(b) The movements of the king and queen in Kent in the autumn of 1359, prior to the invasion of France in November (para. 57).

(c) Although our chronicler's account of the 1359–60 campaign (paras. 60–4) is less detailed than some others, and is sometimes inaccurate, it does include a few items of information not noted elsewhere, such as the story of the two newly created French knights sent out from Paris, one of whom was captured and the other killed.

(d) The account of the French raid on Winchelsea on 15 March 1360, together with the list of inhabitants of the town killed; some of the details of the retaliatory English raid on the Normandy coast and its abandonment on the king's orders; and the fact that Edward III landed at Rye in order to inspect the damage at Winchelsea; all add considerably to our knowledge of this event, for which they constitute the most valuable surviving source (paras. 65–9).

(e) The (alleged) date of John Winwick's death on 24 June 1360 (para. 70).

(f) The story of what happened to Brother John Sutton during the Great Wind of 15 January 1362 (para. 89).

(g) Additional details about the jousts at Smithfield and fire at Clerkenwell priory in May 1362: for example, the involvement

of the Black Prince and the destruction of supplies gathered for the jousts (para. 90).

(h) The dates of arrival and departure of King Peter of Cyprus in October/December 1363, and some of the information about his discussions with Edward III in London (para. 104).

Two factors combine to enhance the value of the chronicle of Anonymous of Canterbury. First, he copied no other chronicle; of course, as already seen, he used newsletters and other documents, but there is no doubt that from 1346 onwards his chronicle was essentially an independent compilation. Secondly, he wrote at a time when the composition of contemporary history in England reached, in Tait's words, 'perhaps its lowest ebb before the fifteenth century'.[80] This is especially true of the years 1357–64 (when, as we have seen, our chronicle becomes increasingly valuable), as a brief review of English chronicles of the 1350s and 1360s will help to illustrate. The chronicles of those voracious war correspondents Robert of Avesbury and Geoffrey le Baker both ended in 1356; the *Chronique* of Jean le Bel and the *Scalacronica* of Thomas Gray may have continued until 1361 and 1363 respectively, but neither of them had much to say about England's domestic history at this time (although each of them contains a good deal of valuable information about Edward III's wars and about European affairs more generally, and, in Gray's case, about Scottish affairs). The same is true of Chandos Herald's *Vie du Prince Noir*, which concentrates almost exclusively on the Crécy, Poitiers, and Nájera expeditions. Jean Froissart, despite residing in England for much of the 1360s, employed an anecdotal and emotive style which was ill suited to the humdrum task of recording domestic history, an undertaking for which he in any case showed little interest at this time.[81] The continuations of the *Polychronicon* and the *Brut* which cover the 1350s and 1360s were not, for the most part, either original or contemporary compilations; nor were the later histories written by Thomas Walsingham and Henry Knighton, both of whom cover this period to a greater or lesser degree. The *Anonimalle Chronicle* and the *Eulogium Historiarum* include some full accounts of the English expeditions to France in 1355–6 and 1360, but neither has a great deal to tell us about English political or diplomatic history

---

[80] *Chronica Johannis de Reading et Anonymi Cantuariensis*, p. 8; cf. J. Taylor, *English Historical Literature in the Fourteenth Century* (Oxford, 1987), p. 82.

[81] Although he later became a valuable source for certain episodes of Richard II's reign.

during the early 1360s. The Wigmore chronicle, although it has 'some slight value' for national history at this time, was conceived primarily as a history of the Mortimer family, the aristocratic circle in which they moved, and the region of Herefordshire around their *caput honoris* at Wigmore.[82]

This leaves the chronicle of John of Reading, a monk of Westminster, which covers the years 1346 to 1367, was written contemporaneously (probably from 1359 onwards), and is without doubt the single most important narrative source for English political history between 1356 and 1367—a fact which seems to have been rapidly recognized by his contemporaries, for within a decade or so of its completion his chronicle had been used as the basis, sometimes at second or third hand, of continuations of the *Polychronicon* and the *Brut*, as well as for the retrospective sections of the chronicles compiled by Thomas Walsingham and others at St Albans.[83] It was, of course, John of Reading's chronicle which Tait edited in the same volume as his edition of Anonymous of Canterbury, and, even allowing for the discovery of the 1357–64 section of the latter, it would be difficult to argue with his verdict on the relative merits of these two principal chronicles of this period.[84] Reading's chronicle is manifestly fuller (although not, obviously, by as much as Tait, working from L and J, supposed); it is also more colourful, which makes it more enjoyable to read but may not always be to the historian's advantage; it is littered with wonders and prodigies, which Tait regarded as a mark of credulity but can also be seen as evidence of serious historical purpose;[85] and it is a more personal and subjective chronicle than that of our chronicler. On the other hand, argued Tait, the Canterbury chronicler, despite producing 'a slighter, more ill-digested and less interesting performance' than Reading, nevertheless demonstrates little of the latter's 'prejudice and superstition', 'tells a straightforward tale grammatically and intelligibly' (compared to Reading's extravagant and at times ungrammatical Latin), and is 'almost pedantically accurate with dates'. One or two of Tait's points of comparison might, naturally, be qualified a little following the discovery of C—for example, the slightness of our

[82] The Wigmore chronicle is discussed and printed by Taylor, *English Historical Literature*, pp. 285–300.

[83] *Chronica Johannis de Reading et Anonymi Cantuariensis*, pp. 8–9.

[84] For the following points and quotations, see *Chronica Johannis de Reading et Anonymi Cantuariensis*, pp. viii, 17, 70.

[85] For the latter view, see Given-Wilson, *Chronicles*, pp. 21–56.

chronicler's scope, or, given his comments on the 1362 jousts, the attention which he paid to portents—but it would be hard to argue that any of them are fundamentally wrong. With the exception of a few important items of information which appear to be unique to the Canterbury chronicle, such as his knowledge of the Winchelsea raid or of the terms of the First Treaty of London, it is in the precision and detail which he added to known events that the primary value of Anonymous of Canterbury's chronicle lies.

It was to a considerable extent, as already noted, his location at or very near to Canterbury which provided our chronicler with the opportunity to furnish details of this kind, and it is, in the light of this, a little surprising that, by comparison with, say, Westminster or St Albans, Canterbury was not more prominent as a centre of national historiography during the later Middle Ages. It had not always been thus: from the late eleventh century to the early thirteenth—the period encompassing Osbern's Life of St Dunstan, Eadmer's *Historia Novorum* and Life of St Anselm, several early lives of Thomas Becket, and the chronicle of Gervase of Canterbury, which extends to 1210— Canterbury could rightly claim to figure among England's foremost centres of historiography, even if much of the history written there had a decidedly particularist flavour.[86] During the thirteenth century, which witnessed the florescence under Roger of Wendover and Matthew Paris of the St Albans school of historiography and, towards the end of the century, that of Westminster abbey, Canterbury fell somewhat behind its rivals. This is not to deny that a continuous tradition of contemporary historical writing was maintained there: Gervase's chronicle was extended from 1207 to 1327 in a compilation written partly at the cathedral and partly at its cell of St Martin's priory in Dover,[87] and it is a source which, although often localized in its subject matter and at times disappointingly brief, nevertheless includes plenty of interesting and independent information, especially for the baronial wars of the 1260s and again during the 1290s. Like our chronicler sixty years later, the author of the narrative of the 1290s was capable of putting his location to good use: in one passage which bears a striking resemblance to our chronicle, for example, he

[86] For these works, see Gransden, *Historical Writing* i, pp. 127–42, 253–60, 296–308.

[87] Gervase had brought his chronicle down to 1210, but his successor briefly retraced some of the events of 1207–10 before continuing. This continuation is discussed and printed in *The Historical Works of Gervase of Canterbury*, ed. W. Stubbs (2 vols., Rolls Series 73; London, 1880), ii, pp. xvii–xxviii, 106–324. Cf. also Gransden, *Historical Writing* i, pp. 422–3, 448–9.

carefully recorded the arrival at Dover on 25 June 1295 of the cardinal-bishops of Albano and Palestrina, charged by Pope Boniface VIII with securing a peace between England and France; their progress the following day to Canterbury, where, tactfully, one stayed at the cathedral and the other at St Augustine's abbey, perhaps in recognition of the fact that they had been greeted at the seashore by the prior of the former and the abbot of the latter, 'and by no other prelate of the whole realm'; their visit to Becket's shrine on 27 June, followed by their departure to Harbledown, where Archbishop Winchelsea met them and there was the usual commotion about whether or not he might bear his cross in their presence; and their onward journey from there via Ospringe, Newington, and Gillingham to London, where the king awaited them. Four years later the chronicler similarly noted that Princess Margaret of France arrived at Dover on 8 September 1299 and came on to Canterbury on 9 September, where that same day the archbishop celebrated her betrothal to Edward I 'at the door of the church giving on to the cloister, next to the door of St Thomas the martyr; and subsequently [that is, the next day], he celebrated the wedding mass at the altar of St Thomas's shrine'.[88]

Other histories, in both Latin and Anglo-Norman, were also being written at the cathedral at this time. The so-called *Polistorie*, a substantial Anglo-Norman national and local history which began with the story of Brutus and continued until 1313, was compiled in the early fourteenth century by a Canterbury monk called John and dedicated to another John, presumably one of the more senior monks at the cathedral. It has virtually no value as an original source, with considerable parts of its thirteenth- and early fourteenth-century material being based on the continuation of Gervase, but it is noteworthy for the wide range of sources used (or often simply copied).[89] Given that the cathedral had one of the best-stocked libraries in England at this time, with Prior Henry Eastry's catalogue of the late 1320s listing no fewer than 1,831 books, this is by no means surprising.[90] As for Latin histories, the manuscripts which preserve

[88] *Historical Works of Gervase of Canterbury*, ii. 311–12, 317. Edward and Margaret were married on 10 September: M. Prestwich, *Edward I* (Berkeley, 1988), p. 521.

[89] The *Polistorie* is discussed by Stubbs in *Historical Works of Gervase of Canterbury*, ii, pp. xxxiv–xxxvii, and by Dominica Legge, *Anglo-Norman Literature and its Background* (Oxford, 1963), pp. 291–3.

[90] Nigel Ramsay, 'The cathedral archives and library', in P. Collinson, N. Ramsay, and M. Sparks, eds., *A History of Canterbury Cathedral* (Oxford, 1995), pp. 341–407, at 355–6.

the chronicle of Anonymous of Canterbury are themselves evidence that attempts were made to preserve some sort of continuous historical record, although the *Brut* histories which these manuscripts contain are almost entirely unoriginal.

Some years after Anonymous of Canterbury laid down his pen in the autumn of 1364, one or more of his fellows made a half-hearted effort to carry the chronicle forward by recording events such as the removal of the Black Prince to Aquitaine and the battle of Nájera, but this quickly petered out. Canterbury men continued to write chronicles of national importance during the later fourteenth and early fifteenth centuries, although they were not Christ Church men: the most noteworthy were the continuation of the *Eulogium Historiarum* from the mid-1360s to 1413, which was probably written by a Franciscan based at the Greyfriars at Canterbury, and the *Liber Metricus de Henrico Quinto* of Thomas Elmham, who was a monk at St Augustine's, Canterbury until 1414 (although he probably did not reside there at the time when he wrote the *Liber Metricus*, for in 1415 he was appointed vicar-general of the Cluniacs in England and Scotland, and also served as a chaplain to the king).[91] Both of these are sources of real importance for English history in the later fourteenth and early fifteenth century. By contrast, the best that Christ Church could produce in the fifteenth century was the chronicle compiled by the Canterbury monk John Stone for the years 1415–71, which is much more concerned with local history, and especially the liturgical history of the cathedral, than with any attempt to write national history. Of course, Christ Church was not alone among English monastic houses in witnessing a decline in both the scope and the quality of its contemporary historiography in the later Middle Ages, especially during the fifteenth century. As Dobson has pointed out, the fact that 'by the beginning of the fifteenth century the writing of narrative history at Canterbury had atrophied beyond repair . . . exemplifies only too well the familiar theme of the decline and fall of the monastic chronicle towards the end of the middle ages'.[92] The chronicle of Anonymous of Canterbury, in conclusion, is not just a source of considerable importance for the

---

[91] For these two chronicles, see *Eulogium Historiarum*, iii. 333–421, and *Memorials of Henry the Fifth*, ed. C. A. Cole (Rolls Series; London, 1858), 79–166. See also Gransden, *Historical Writing* ii, pp. 158 n. 5, 206–10.

[92] Barrie Dobson, 'The monks of Canterbury in the later Middle Ages', in Collinson, Ramsay and Sparks, eds., *A History of Canterbury Cathedral*, pp. 69–153, at 113.

years 1346–64 (and especially, in its full version, for 1357–64); it is also, if it is indeed a product of Christ Church, something of a swansong, the last major and contemporary national history to be written during the Middle Ages at one of England's greatest ecclesiastical centres.

VII. EDITORIAL CONVENTIONS

As already noted, the text edited here is drawn from C (Reigate, Parish Church of St Mary, Cranston Library, Item 1117) as base manuscript. Significant variants from J (London, British Library, MS Cotton Julius B. iii), L (London, Lambeth Palace Library, MS 99), and M (Oxford, Magdalen College, MS 200 or lat. 200) are recorded in the apparatus.

Throughout the Latin and Anglo-Norman texts and apparatus, lower case *u* and *v* are given as *u* (except in the case of roman numerals and folio numbering); upper case *U* and *V* are given as *V*. Lower case *i* and *j* are given as *i*; upper case *I* and *J* are given as *I*. Abbreviations are expanded throughout, except that in the case of names where there are two or more feasible expanded forms, the abbreviated form has been retained, with a mark of suspension. This is particularly frequent with commonly used English place names such as *Lond'*, *London'*, *Cant'*, *Cantuar'*, where the expanded forms could include *Londoniis*, *Londoniensis*, *Cantuarie*, *Cantuariensis*, etc. Roman numerals are spelt out in the Latin and Anglo-Norman texts, but the mixture of numerals and spelt-out forms found in the manuscripts is retained in the apparatus.

Personal names have been anglicized in the translation, but not in the footnotes: for example, the two kings of France who feature most prominently in the narrative are referred to as Philip and John in the translation, but Philippe (VI) and Jean (II) in the footnotes. Capitalization is modernized throughout. Punctuation is modernized in the Latin and Anglo-Norman texts, and largely brought into line with the punctuation of the modern English translation, in order to facilitate comparison between text and translation.

For ease of reference, corresponding paragraph numbers have been introduced into the text and translation. Italics indicate rubricated headings in the base manuscript, C. The headings are incorporated into the body of the edited text, although they rarely occur in this position in the manuscript. Usually they are in the lateral margins.

Some occur in the top margin, and may run right across the top margin of two facing folios. Where this is the case, it is noted in the apparatus. Headings are rare in the other manuscripts; where they occur, they are noted in the apparatus. Marginal sketches in the base manuscript C are noted in the apparatus. They do not occur in the other manuscripts. An early, near-contemporary reader added further marginalia to the base manuscript C, and underlined many items of particular interest, such as names, dates, numbers, instances of French perfidy, and occurrences of the plague. These additions are not recorded in text or apparatus.

Editorial emendation of the Latin and Anglo-Norman texts occurs where there is reasonable certainty of authorial/scribal error or omission. Angled brackets ⟨ ⟩ are used to indicate editorial additions. Asterisks *** are used to indicate a lacuna in the text. Error is most frequent when the author is copying from newsletters, statutes, or the draft treaty of Brétigny. In all cases of emendation and editorial addition, the manuscript reading is recorded in the apparatus.

SIGLA

C   Reigate, Parish Church of St Mary, Cranston Library, Item 1117, fos. 252^r–273^r

J   London, British Library, MS Cotton Julius B. iii, fos. 109^v–115^r

L   London, Lambeth Palace Library, MS 99, fos. 51^r–55^v

M   Oxford, Magdalen College, MS 200 (or MS lat. 200), fos. 72–73

TEXT AND TRANSLATION

1. *De applicacione regis apud Hoges.* Anno Domini millesimo trecentisimo quadragesimo sexto, aduertens rex Anglie multa uerba Francorum pacifica in dolo,^{a} quodque ius suum quod in regno et ad regnum Francie successione hereditaria obtinet recuperare non potuit nisi in gladio undique considerans, septimo decimo die mensis Iulii eodem anno ^{b}cum exercitu suo^c applicuit apud Hoges in Normannia.$^{d\,1}$ Et ^{c}in dicto portu de Hoges presens^c erat^f marescallus Francie Bertrandus, qui sub pena capitis sui erga ^{g}dictum Philippum,^{g} regem Francie ^{h}se dicentem,$^{h\,2}$ manuceperat ut cum ducentis uiris armatis dictum portum saluum^i custodiret, ^{j}ne rex Anglie cum suo exercitu intraret terram Francie quouismodo. Vnde prefatus marescallus^j portum ^{k}de Hoges et apud^k Barflete cum palis ^{l}sicut potuit^l obturauit, et ad resistendum regi Anglie cum ^{m}potencia et armata manu^m mille equitum adminus^n et ultra sex milia peditum exercitum congregauit.^{3} Sed ^{o}ab illo periculo ipsum regem Anglie Dei potencia liberauit, inmittens terrorem suum qui irruit super eos et omnes habitatores terre, ita ut fugerent, nemine persequente, scilicet communiter omnes de ciuitatibus ac uillis magnis et paruis et patria in circuitu^o a uiginti miliaribus ubi^p transitus regis fuit per totam Normanniam, Franciam et Picardiam,^{q} preterquam in locis paucis, de quibus in subsequentibus^r apparebit.^{4}

2. ^{s}Primum^t quidem die Martis ante festum Sancte Margarete,
uidelicet ^{u}duodeuicesimo die mensis Iulii,^{v} | dominus Edwardus rex Anglie cum exercitu suo mouebat se de Hoges iuxta Barflete in Normannia, et cepit^w uillam et castrum^x de Valoigns, et pontem de Eu qui fractus fuerat^y per hostes fecit celeriter reparari, et transiens ibidem cepit castrum ^{z}et uillam^z de Garenten';^{5} et deinde progrediens

---

^{a} M breaks off ^{b} M resumes ^{c} om. JLM ^{d} J breaks off $^{e-e}$ om. M
^{f} fuit LM $^{g-g}$ om. M $^{h-h}$ om. M ^{i} om. M $^{j-j}$ et dictum M
$^{k-k}$ usque M $^{l-l}$ om. M $^{m-m}$ om. M ^{n} om. M $^{o-o}$ omnes fugerunt in aduentu regis Anglie M ^{p} om. M ^{q} M breaks off ^{r} sequentibus L
^{s} heading De bello de Cressy written across top marg. of fo. 252v C; heading more appropriate at top of fo. 253r, where it also occurs ^{t} primo L ^{u} J resumes ^{v} add. uidelicet die Sancte Margarete J ^{w} add. etiam J ^{x} J breaks off ^{y} fuit L $^{z-z}$ om. L

---

^{1} Edward III's landing at St-Vaast-la-Hougue, on the Cotentin peninsula of Normandy, in fact occurred on the morning of 12 July. The chronicler may have misread 'xii' as 'xvii', or he may have been confused by the fact that the English army remained there for a further five days, setting off for Valognes on 18 July: Rogers, *War Cruel and Sharp*, pp. 238–40.
^{2} Philippe VI, the first Valois king of France (1328–50).

1. *The king's landing at La Hougue.* In the year of Our Lord 1346, the king of England, perceiving the many deceitfully conciliatory words of the French, and realizing that he would not be able to make good his right which he possesses by hereditary succession in and to the French kingdom except by widespread use of the sword, landed at La Hougue in Normandy on 17 July that same year with his army.[1] Waiting in the said port of La Hougue was Bertrand, marshal of France, who had undertaken on pain of his head to the aforesaid Philip, self-styled king of France,[2] that he would guard the said port safely with two hundred men-at-arms so that the king of England and his army would not under any circumstances be able to enter the land of France; for which reason the aforesaid marshal blocked up the port of La Hougue and that at Barfleur, insofar as he could, with stakes, and gathered together an army of at least one thousand mounted men and more than six thousand foot soldiers in order to resist the king of England with might and force of arms.[3] But the power of God delivered the said king of England from this danger, unleashing His terror, which engulfed them and all the inhabitants of the land, so that throughout the whole of Normandy, France, and Picardy everyone in the cities and towns, large or small, and the country-dwellers within a radius of twenty miles from wherever the king passed through—apart from a few places, as will become clear from what follows—generally fled, without anyone pursuing them.[4]

2. First, then, on Tuesday before the feast of St Margaret, namely 18 July, Lord Edward king of England advanced with his army from La Hougue, close to Barfleur in Normandy, and he captured the town and castle of Valognes, and ordered the bridge of Eu, which had been broken by the enemy, to be rapidly repaired, and after crossing there he captured the castle and town of Carentan;[5] then, moving on from

[3] Robert Bertrand, lord of Bricquebec and marshal of France, probably had about 300 men-at-arms and about 700 local troops with him at La Hougue, but he fled after an assault led by the earl of Warwick (Rogers, *War Cruel and Sharp*, pp. 218–9, 241–2).

[4] For a 'perfect itinerary' of Edward's 1346 campaign, see the notes and map provided by Thompson in his edition of *Chronicon Galfridi le Baker*, pp. 252–7. Modern works which also provide detailed accounts with maps are Rogers, *War Cruel and Sharp*, pp. 238–72, and J. Sumption, *The Hundred Years War*, i: *Trial by Battle* (London, 1990), pp. 500–34.

[5] Barfleur was also plundered by the English, on 14 July. Valognes, nine miles south-west of La Hougue, surrendered to Edward on 18 July, but was still burned the next day. The 'bridge of Eu' must be the bridge over the Douve at St-Côme-du-Mont, which was

uersus uillam de Sancto Ludouico, inuenit pontem de Herberd fractum, quem fecit concito reparari, et uillam de Sancto Ludouico cepit.[6]

3. *De Cadamo.* Et deinde inimici regis Anglie in Cadamo se ad resistendum fortiter parauerunt, sed statim dicti regis potencia quasi tota[a] milicia Normannie extitit captiuata uel gladio trucidata; ubi captus fuerat[b] constabularius[c] Francie, comes de Eu, et camerarius de Tankeruille, qui ante alium conflictum Francie marescallus fuerat proclamatus; ceteri autem capti uel[d] cesi sunt usque ad magnum numerum, et qui poterant fugam turpiter inierunt, ita quod in dicta ciuitate de Cadamo nullus remansit et dicta uilla fuit usque ad nudos parietes spoliata.[7]

4. Deinde in progressu regis Anglie paludes plurime, aque profundissime, nemora densissima[e] et uie strictissime multiplicauerunt pericula grauia et inmensa, in quibus locis centum armati contra centum milia hominum passum et transitum custodissent, iudicio multorum militum tunc captorum. Sed ab hiis periculis ipsum regem et exercitum suum Dei gracia liberauit, terrens hostes fugam celerem unanimiter capientes.

5. De Cadamo uero, postquam sic[f] capta fuerat, idem rex uersus Rothomagum iter suum dirigens, occurrerunt sibi domini[g] Anibaldus de Cetano et Stephanus Alberti, sancte[h] Romane ecclesie cardinales, in ciuitate Lexon', ipsum regem ad pacem plurimum exhortantes.[8] Quibus per regem curialiter receptis, responsum fuit eis quod rex Anglie, semper pacem desiderans, quesiuit eam omnibus uiis racionabilibus quibus sciuit et potuit, et pro ea habenda obtulit uias multas, licet in sui iuris magnum preiudicium, quodque adhuc paratus erat pacem admittere dummodo uia sibi racionabilis offeratur.

ᵃ add. potencia *L*   *ᵇ* fuit *L*   *ᶜ add.* comes *L*   *ᵈ* et *L*   *ᵉ* densissime *L*
ᶠ si *L*   *ᵍ* dominus *L*   *ʰ* sancti *L*

---

repaired by the English on the night of 19 July, enabling them to reach Carentan the following day; Carentan also surrendered, but was also sacked and burned (Sumption, *Trial by Battle*, pp. 504–6).

[6] St-Lô briefly resisted the English army, but the French soon fled and the town was sacked and burned on 22 July (ibid. 506).

[7] The assault on Caen took place on 26 July. There may have been as many as 6,000 French troops in the town, under the nominal command of the bishop of Bayeux but in practice commanded by Raoul de Brienne, count of Eu and Guines and constable of France (d. 1350), Robert Bertrand the marshal, and Jean de Melun, chamberlain of Tancarville (d. 1347), who had also been proclaimed a marshal of France earlier that same day. The English

there towards the town of St-Lô, he found the bridge at ⟨Pont⟩ Hébert broken, which he quickly had repaired, and captured the town of St-Lô.[6]

3. *Caen.* Whereupon the enemies of the king of England in Caen prepared themselves to resist him, but within a short time almost all the fighting men of Normandy were either captured or put to the sword by the might of the said king. The constable of France, the count of Eu, was captured there, along with the chamberlain of Tancarville, who before a previous engagement had been proclaimed marshal of France; and a large number of others were captured or killed, and those who could do so shamelessly took flight, so that nobody remained in the said city of Caen, and the said city was stripped clean down to its walls.[7]

4. From there onwards, numerous marshes, very deep rivers, dense woods, and narrow roads along the king of England's route greatly increased the gravity and enormity of the dangers; in these places, in the opinion of many knights who were captured then, one hundred armed men could have held the passage and crossing against one hundred thousand men. But the grace of God delivered the said king and his army from these dangers, terrifying their enemies, all of whom fled in haste.

5. After Caen had thus been taken, as the said king was making his way from there towards Rouen, Lords Annibaldus de Ceccano and Stephen Aubert, cardinals of the holy Roman church, came to meet him in the city of Lisieux, pleading strongly with the king to make peace.[8] They were graciously received by the king, who replied to them that the king of England, desirous of peace as ever, sought it by every reasonable way which he could or knew, and had made numerous offers in order to achieve it, even though they were greatly prejudicial to his rights, and that he was still prepared to make peace provided that a reasonable offer was made to him.

army remained at Caen until 31 July, and the plunder and slaughter in the town were extensive, with at least 2,500 French killed and possibly as many as 5,000. Eu and Tancarville were shipped to England to be ransomed (Rogers, *War Cruel and Sharp*, pp. 246–8; Sumption, *Trial by Battle*, p. 510).

[8] Edward III was at Lisieux on 2 and 3 August, and it was on one of these days that the two cardinal-bishops came to speak with him. Ceccano was cardinal-bishop of Tusculum and former archbishop of Naples; Aubert was bishop of Clermont-Ferrand from 1340, and a cardinal from 1342. Their subsequent fates were very different: Ceccano died mysteriously, probably poisoned, following a riot in Rome during the 1350 jubilee; Aubert was elected Pope Innocent VI in 1352: Diana Wood, *Clement VI* (Cambridge, 1989), pp. 75, 96, 128.

6. Dicti autem cardinales, habita responsione huiusmodi, ad dominum Philippum de Valesio redeuntes et ipsum super*ᵃ* hiis apud Rothomagum presencialiter allocuti, ad regem Anglie redierunt sibique ducatum Aquitanie sicut illum pater suus tenuit obtulerunt, et spem dederunt plura*ᵇ* habendi si tractatus pacificus haberetur,⁹ sed quia ista uia eidem regi non placuit, nec *ᶜ*ipsi cardinales dictum Philippum*ᶜ* tractabilem inuenerunt, desperati de bono fine simpliciter recesserunt.

7. *ᵈ*Rex autem Anglie, deinde progrediens continue,*ᵉ* uillas omnes*ᶠ* grossas per quas*ᵍ* transiuit obtinuit, nemine resistente;*ʰ* Deus enim inimicos regis ita terruit ut uiderentur corda sua totaliter perdidisse. Castra insuper et municiones | paucis inuadentibus, licet fortissima essent, impulsu*ⁱ* leuissimo ipse cepit.

fo. 253ʳ

8. *De bello de Cressy.ʲ* Philippus uero de Valesio, aduersarius*ᵏ* regis Anglie,*ˡ* existens in ciuitate Rothomagen' magnum exercitum congregauit ibidem, et licet essent in multitudine graui idem Philippus, regem Anglie*ᵐ* metuens, pontem Secane frangi fecit. Ipse Philippus regem Anglie ex aduerso ex una parte Secane diebus singulis sequebatur, diruens omnes pontes et muniens ne ad eum pateret transitus quouismodo.¹⁰ Et licet continue ibidem spolia fierent et incendia ad latitudinem uiginti miliarium in circuitu et ad unum miliare iuxta dictum aduersarium, ipse tamen aduersarius noluit nec audebat in defensionem*ⁿ* populi sui *ᵒ*et regni,*ᵒ* cum potuisset, aquam transire.

9. *De Pussiaco.* Deinde idem rex Anglie uenit apud Pussiacum, ubi pontem fractum inuenit, et dictus aduersarius, pre timore fugiendo, citra Parisius non quieuit sed ordinauit mille equites et duo milia peditum cum balistis ad custodiam dicti pontis de Pussiaco ut reparari non posset, et omnes pontes in circuitu Parisius per quos posset esse transitus uecorditer frangi fecit. Sed protensis tribus uel quatuor

---

ᵃ de *L*   *ᵇ* plurima *L*   *ᶜ⁻ᶜ* ipsum Philippum dicti cardinales *L*   *ᵈ* *J resumes*
ᵉ om. *J*   *ᶠ* rep. *L*   *ᵍ* add. intrauit et *JL*   *ʰ* J breaks off   *ⁱ* pulsu *L*
ʲ heading across top marg. *C*   *ᵏ* inimicus *L*   *ˡ* add. et aduersarius *L*   *ᵐ* om. *L*
ⁿ defencione *L*   *ᵒ⁻ᵒ* om. *L*

---

⁹ Philippe VI had arrived at Rouen on 31 July. The additional incentive with which he hoped to dissuade Edward from continuing his campaign was, according to the newsletter which the chronicler was using at this point, an offer of a marriage alliance between England and France, a point which he rather surprisingly omitted (*Adae Murimuth Continuatio Chronicarum*, p. 215).

6. The said cardinals, having received this reply, returned to Lord Philip de Valois at Rouen and immediately told him about these matters, then returned once more to the king of England and offered him the duchy of Aquitaine in the same manner as his father held it, as well as giving him hope of gaining more if a treaty of peace were to be agreed;[9] but because this offer was not to the liking of the said king, and nor did the said cardinals find the said Philip willing to be flexible, they despaired of a successful outcome and simply withdrew.

7. The king of England, continuing his progress from there, seized all the major towns through which he passed, encountering no resistance, for God had so terrified the king's enemies that it seemed as if they had entirely lost heart. In addition, he seized castles and fortresses with small numbers of attackers and only minimal effort, even though they were very strong.

8. *The battle of Crécy.* Philip de Valois, however, the king of England's adversary, who was in the city of Rouen, collected a great army there and, although he had large numbers, the said Philip, being afraid of the king of England, ordered the bridge over the Seine to be broken. Day by day this Philip followed the king of England along the opposite bank of the Seine, destroying and securing all the bridges to make sure that there was no way that he would be able to cross.[10] And, although ⟨the English⟩ continually pillaged and burned there along a twenty-mile front all around, and up to within a mile of the said adversary, nevertheless this adversary neither wanted nor dared to cross the river to defend his people and his kingdom, as he could have done.

9. *Poissy.* From there the said king of England came to Poissy, where he found the bridge broken; and the said adversary, fleeing in fear, did not remain before Paris, but ordered a thousand mounted men and two thousand infantry with crossbows to guard the said bridge at Poissy so that it could not be repaired; and he foolishly ordered all the bridges around Paris by which it might be possible to cross to be broken. Nevertheless, by laying three or four timbers over the

---

[10] The English army reached the Seine at Elbeuf on 7 August. For the next five days, while they moved systematically east along the south bank of the river towards Paris, Philippe VI with his army moved simultaneously along the north bank, either guarding securely or breaking the bridges at Pont de l'Arche, Vernon, Mantes, and Meulan. By 12 August, Philippe had moved his army to the outskirts of Paris (Sumption, *Trial by Battle*, pp. 514–15).

trabibus ultra dictum pontem de Pussiaco fractum, aliqui ex Anglia sagittarii transierant, licet pauci, et de parte Francie secundum estimacionem hominum interfecti fuerunt mille uel circiter, et ceteri uersi sunt in fugam omnino.[a][11]

10. Dominus autem rex Anglie, reparato dicto ponte de Pussiaco, fecit per Picardiam transitum suum et semper a latere aduersarium sequebatur,[12] et fractis pontibus undequaque per regem Francie, uia aliqua regi Anglie ⟨nisi⟩[b][13] inter Croteye et Abbeuille non patuit quouismodo. In reflexu uero maris ibidem totus exercitus Anglie transiuit illesus, licet in loco illo a populo illius terre nesciretur esse tutum uadum, nisi[c] strictissimum ubi sex uel decem potuissent transire simul. Tamen gentes[d] regis Anglie indifferenter quasi in omni loco, sicut in uado tutissimo, transierunt, quod mirabile est in occulis omnium qui nouerant locum illum.

11. Philippus uero de Valesio ordinauit mille equites et quinque milia peditum uel circiter pro custodia illius passagii ad resistendum fortiter regi Anglie, sed per comitem Northamptoun et Reginaldum de Cobeham, cum centum armatis et aliquibus sagittariis precedentes[e] exercitum, hostes uiriliter sunt repulsi, et interfectis eodem die de parte Francie [f]duobus milibus uel ultra, ceteri fugerunt ad Abbeuille ubi rex Francie[f] cum exercitu suo fuit.[14]

12. De illo autem loco, [g]die Sabbati uicesimo sexto die mensis Augusti [h]anno Domini millesimo trecentisimo quadragesimo sexto,[h] processit idem rex Anglie [i]uersus Cressy ubi suo occurrit[j] aduersario Philippo de Valesio in campo magno.[15]

---

[a] omnis L   [b] nisi edd.; om. CL   [c] ubi L   [d] gens L   [e] procedentes L
[f-f] om. L   [g] J resumes die autem   [h-h] om. J   [i] M resumes; preceded by sed fregerunt pontes per omnem transitum regis Anglie sed omnes reparauit et transiuit   [j] occurrit edd.; occurrens CJLM

---

[11] Philippe had ordered the bridge at Poissy to be broken on 12 August, but the stumps had been left standing in the river, and on 13 August the English began laying timbers across them. By the time that French forces arrived on the north bank to try to prevent them crossing, enough English had crossed to be able to drive them off; at least 200 French soldiers were killed (Rogers, War Cruel and Sharp, pp. 255–6; Sumption, Trial by Battle, pp. 516–18).

[12] Having moved his army across the Seine at Poissy on the morning of 16 August, Edward moved rapidly northwards. Philippe did not leave the Paris area in pursuit of him until later the same day, but by means of forced marches overtook the English army near Beauvais on 18 August, reaching the Somme on 20 August. By the time that Edward arrived at Airaines, five miles south of the Somme, on 21 August, all the bridges over the Somme apart from those within major walled towns had been broken (Sumption, Trial by Battle, p. 521).

aforementioned broken bridge at Poissy, some of the English archers got across, albeit only a few, and according to what men reckoned a thousand men or thereabouts were killed on the French side, while the rest, to a man, turned in flight.[11]

10. The lord king of England, however, having repaired the said bridge at Poissy, made his way through Picardy, keeping continually to his adversaries' flank;[12] and with the bridges broken on every side by the king of France, there was no other way at all accessible to the king of England ⟨except⟩[13] between Le Crotoy and Abbeville. At low tide there, however, the whole English army crossed unscathed, even though the local population at that place did not consider it to be a safe fording point, except at the narrowest point where six or ten persons might cross together. Nevertheless, the king of England's men crossed without exception at almost every point, as if it were the safest of fords—a remarkable thing in the view of all those who knew that place.

11. In fact, Philip de Valois ordered one thousand mounted men and five thousand foot soldiers or thereabouts to guard that crossing, in order to resist the king of England by force, but the enemy was driven off manfully by the earl of Northampton and Reginald Cobham, who with a hundred men-at-arms and a number of archers went on ahead of the army; and two thousand or more were killed that day on the French side, while the rest fled to Abbeville, where the king of France was with his army.[14]

12. On Saturday 26 August in the year of Our Lord 1346, the said king of England advanced from there towards Crécy, where he came up against his adversary Philip de Valois on a large piece of ground.[15]

[13] Richard de Winkley's newsletter included the word 'nisi' at this point, which was clearly omitted in error by our chronicler, since the English army in fact crossed at the ford of Blanchetaque, which is between Le Crotoy and Abbeville (*Adae Murimuth Continuatio Chronicarum*, p. 216).

[14] The English army's crossing of the ford at Blanchetaque, which occurred on the morning of 24 August, was indeed a remarkable feat, for the north bank of the Somme estuary was defended by some 3,500 French troops under the experienced Godemar du Fay, bailli of Vermandois. However, William de Bohun, earl of Northampton, and Reginald Cobham of Sterborough (who would become a peer in 1347) were two of Edward III's finest commanders, and the English army managed to wade and fight their way across just before the main French army under King Philippe arrived at the southern end of the ford. On 25 August, the French army regrouped at Abbeville (Sumption, *Trial by Battle*, pp. 522–5).

[15] The English army had taken up position between the villages of Crécy and Wadicourt, about ten miles north of the Somme, on gently rising ground with the forest of Crécy-

13. *Numerus bellancium Francorum.* Qui quidem aduersarius habuit exercitum magnum ualde, uidelicet secundum estimacionem homi-num[a] duodecim milia[b] galeatorum et aliorum armatorum adminus sexaginta milia hominum.[16]

14. *Cressy.* Ipse uero aduersarius, intendens specialiter personam regis Anglie inuadere, posuit se in prima acie exercitus sui Francorum, | cui dominus Edwardus princeps Wallie, qui primam aciem exercitus Anglorum habuit, uiriliter se obiecit.[17] Et habito[c] adinuicem conflictu fortissimo [d]et diutino[d] bis idem aduersarius est repulsus, et tertio, congregatis uiribus et exercitu suo, fortiter pugnauerunt cum exercitu regis Anglie, [e]tandemque, [f]cooperante manu Dei, in illo conflictu[f] ceciderunt in gladio apud Cressy dominus rex Boemie, [g]rex Malorg',[g] archiepiscopus Senonen' et[h] episcopus Nouien',[i] [j]ac dux Lorengie, comites Dallason, et frater eius Philippi de Valesio,[j] et multi alii nobiles [k]et magnates[k] regni Francie dicto die Sabbati interfecti fuerunt,[l] sed ipse[m] Philippus de Valesio cum [n]multis aliis[n] nobilibus tunc fugerunt, multis de exercitu dicti regis Anglie insequentibus per totam noctem taliter fugientes.[o] [18] Et antequam

fo. 253[v] (margin, beside paragraph 14)

---

[a] om. *J*   [b] *add.* hominum *J*   [c] rex Francorum repulsus est *M*; *M breaks off*
[d-d] om. *J*   [e] *M resumes:* tandem   [f-f] om. *M*   [g-g] *in marg.* C; om. *JLM*
[h] om. *J*   [i] om. *M*   [j-j] Romeren' *M*   [k-k] om. *M*   [l] sunt *JLM*   [m] om. *M*
[n-n] aliis multis *JLM*   [o] *J breaks off*

Grange behind them. The French army arrived at the battlefield around midday, but the engagement did not begin until about five in the afternoon. The battle is the subject of an extensive literature: the most detailed recent study is Andrew Ayton and Philip Preston, eds., *The Battle of Crécy, 1346* (Woodbridge, 2005).

[16] Chroniclers give very different figures for the sizes of the two armies: it seems likely that the French host, which probably numbered between 20,000 and 25,000 in total, was about twice as large as Edward III's army: Sumption, *Trial by Battle*, p. 526; Rogers, *War Cruel and Sharp*, p. 265.

[17] Edward, the Black Prince, did indeed command the English vanguard, despite being only 16 years old, although he had the experienced earls of Warwick and Northampton to help him. However, King Philippe did not command the vanguard but the rearguard of the French army, just as King Edward commanded the English rearguard. The battle began with an attack by the French vanguard, composed largely of Genoese crossbowmen, rather than an English charge.

[18] This list of the 'slain' is very brief and in most respects wrong. Jean of Luxembourg, the blind king of Bohemia, was indeed killed (his reckless courage and death is perhaps the best-known incident of the battle), but Jaume III—who was by now only titular king of Mallorca, his kingdom having been conquered by Pere IV of Aragon in 1343—fled the field of Crécy, only to die trying to reconquer Mallorca in 1349. Neither Guillaume de Melun, archbishop of Sens, nor Bernard le Brun, bishop of Noyon, was killed at the battle, although it is not surprising that several chroniclers stated that they had been, since a report of the battle written by the king himself includes them, as well as the king of Mallorca, among the

13. *The number of French fighting men.* This adversary had a very large army, that is to say, according to what men reckoned, twelve thousand knights and at least sixty thousand other men under arms.[16]

14. *Crécy.* The adversary himself, specifically planning to attack the person of the king of England, placed himself in the vanguard of his French army, against which Lord Edward, prince of Wales, who commanded the vanguard of the English army, launched himself with vigour.[17] An extremely fierce and prolonged conflict ensued on each side, in which the said adversary was twice driven back, and on the third occasion, his forces and army having rallied, they fought bravely with the English king's army; eventually, however, through the intervention of God's hand, there fell by the sword in that battle at Crécy the lord king of Bohemia, the king of Majorca, the archbishop of Sens, and the bishop of Noyon; the duke of Lorraine, the counts ⟨*recte* count⟩ of Alençon—who was also the brother of the said Philip de Valois—and many other nobles and magnates of the French kingdom were also slain that Saturday, but Philip de Valois himself, with many other nobles, fled at that time, pursued by many of the said king of England's army throughout the night as they fled in this manner.[18] And before the aforesaid armies of England and France

slain: Rogers, *The Wars of Edward III*, p. 131. Richard de Winkley's newsletter, which our chronicler used up to this point, said that he was not certain whether or not the king of Mallorca had been killed, but our chronicler evidently decided to abandon such equivocation (*Adae Murimuth Continuatio Chronicarum*, p. 216). It is, however, worth noting that the scribe of the Lambeth manuscript of our chronicle (as well as those of the later abbreviations) omitted the king of Mallorca from his list, further evidence that it was compiled after the Cranston manuscript, by which time the confusion had presumably been cleared up (*Chronica Johannis de Reading et Anonymi Cantuariensis*, p. 191). Raoul, duke of Lorraine, was actually killed the following morning (27 August), when, arriving late for the battle and unaware of the outcome, several thousand French troops under his command stumbled across the battlefield and were promptly massacred or routed by the earls of Warwick and Northampton. The 'comites' of the manuscript indicates that the chronicler abbreviated a longer list of French counts killed at Crécy (at least seven counts and viscounts died that day), while the ungainly 'et frater eius Philippi de Valois' (which makes it sound as if the author thought that the French king had also been killed, although that was probably not the sense that he intended to convey) also suggests abridgement. Charles, count of Alençon and Perche, the French king's younger brother, probably died quite early in the battle; his premature cavalry charge has sometimes been seen as a factor contributing to the French defeat. The bodies of 1,542 French knights were identified as having been slain at Crécy, and the fatalities among the foot soldiers were undoubtedly considerably higher. King Philippe himself fought bravely but was eventually persuaded by Jean of Hainault to leave the field: he spent the night in a village a few miles from the battlefield and reached Amiens, some thirty miles away, the next morning (Sumption, *Trial by Battle*, pp. 526–33; Rogers, *War Cruel and Sharp*, pp. 266–70).

dicti exercitus *^a*Anglie et Francie*^a* sic more guerrino adinuicem dimicassent, uisi*^b* fuerant*^c* aues nigerimi*^d* in aere uolantes super*^e* exercitum Francorum quasi captantes eorum cadauera et prenosticantes mortem Francorum. *^f*Sicque illo die Sabbati idem rex Anglie de hostibus suis,*^g* assistente sibi*^h* manu Dei, in campo de Cressy reportauit triumphum.

15. *Caleys.*ⁱ *^j*Anno Domini millesimo trecentisimo quadragesimo sexto,*^j* dicto bello de Cressy sic peracto, idem*^k* rex Anglie cum exercitu suo per terram et mare obsidebat castrum et uillam de Kaleys *^l*supra mare,*^l* et durauit obsidio huiusmodi*^m* *ⁿ*a die Sancti Rufi usque ad annum completum,*ⁿ* sicque tandem*^o* dicta*^p* uilla *^q*de Kaleys, una cum castro,*^q* domino*^r* regi Anglie reddita fuerat*^s* manu forti.*^t* [19]

16. Dum autem idem*^u* rex Anglie *^v*fuerat in obsidione*^v* uille de Kaleys, de consilio Francorum, quibus Scoti alligati existunt in odium regis Anglie, Dauid le Bruys, *^w*rex Scocie,*^x* et comites ac*^w* magnates regni*^y* Scocie, terram Anglie latenter ingressi*^z* *^a*cum magna multitudine armatorum,*^{aa}* credentes in regno Anglie, propter absenciam regis et magnatum Anglie apud Kaleys existencium, aliquam resistenciam non habere, *^{bb}*depredaciones, homicidia et incendia ac*^{bb}* multa mala fecerunt. [20]

17. *De capcione David le Bruys et aliorum de Scocia.* Quibus dominus Willelmus la*^{cc}* Zouche archiepiscopus Ebor',*^{dd}* clerus et populus illarum partium, *^{ee}*dictis Scotis in manu fortissima occurrentes,*^{ee}* quodam die Martis, uidelicet septimo decimo die mensis Octobris *^{ff}*anno Domini millesimo trecentisimo quadragesimo sexto,*^{ff}* *^{gg}*tempore Clementis pape sexti anno quinto,*^{gg}* prope ciuitatem Dunelmen' adinuicem fortiter*^{hh}* pugnauerunt, [21] in quo quidem conflictu *ⁱⁱ*Dauid rex Scocie, comes de Meneth, comes de Fyf et *^{jj}*alii multi*^{jj}* nobiles

---

^{a–a} Francie et Anglie *L*   *^b* uise *L*   *^c* sunt *L*; erant *M*   *^d* nigerini *L*
^e supra *L*   *^f* *J resumes*   *^g* om. *LM*   *^h* sic *L*   *ⁱ* *marg. sketch of tower of Calais*
C   *^{j–j}* om. *J*   *^k* om. *J*   *^{l–l}* om. *M*   *^m* om. *J*; huius *M*   *^{n–n}* usque ad annum
completum a festo Sancti Rufi *M*   *^o* om. *M*   *^p* om. *J*   *^{q–q}* et castrum *M*
^r om. *M*   *^s* add. in *J*; fuerant *M*   *^t* om. *J*   *^u* om. *M*   *^{v–v}* in obsidione
fuerat *M*   *^{w–w}* et *M*   *^x* Scotus *L*   *^y* om. *M*   *^z* ingressam *J*   *^{aa–aa}* om. *M*
^{bb–bb} om. *M*   *^{cc}* om. *L*   *^{dd}* add. et *J*   *^{ee–ee}* om. *M*   *^{ff–ff}* om. *J*   *^{gg–gg}* om. *JM*
^{hh} om. *M*   *^{ii–ii}* rex et nobiles Scocie capti sunt *M*   *^{jj–jj}* *word order reversed L*

---

[19] In fact, Edward did not leave Crécy until 28 August, and probably arrived before Calais on 3 September (for the date, see Rogers, *War Cruel and Sharp*, p. 272 and n. 192). The town was surrendered to him on 3 August 1347, exactly eleven months later.

fought in this warlike fashion with each other, some very black birds were seen flying in the sky above the French army as if hungering after their corpses and foretelling the death of Frenchmen; and thus, on that Saturday, the said king of England, aided by the hand of God, won victory on the field of Crécy.

15. *Calais.* In the year of Our Lord 1346, the aforesaid battle of Crécy having thus taken place, the said king of England and his army laid siege by land and sea to the castle and town of Calais by the sea, and this siege lasted for a whole year from the day of St Rufus ⟨27 August⟩, until at length the said town of Calais, together with its castle, was surrendered by force to the lord king of England.[19]

16. While the said king of England was besieging the town of Calais, however, at the prompting of the French, to whom the Scots were allied because of their hatred for the king of England, David Bruce, king of Scotland, and the earls and magnates of the Scottish kingdom, having secretly entered English territory with a great multitude of armed men—believing that, on account of the absence of the king and magnates of England, who were at Calais, they would not meet with any resistance in the kingdom of England—committed acts of depredation, killing, burning, and many other evils.[20]

17. *The capture of David Bruce and others from Scotland.* Lord William la Zouche, archbishop of York, and the clergy and people of those parts went out to confront the aforesaid Scots in great force, and on a Tuesday, that is to say, 17 October in the year of Our Lord 1346, in the fifth year of the time of Pope Clement VI, the two sides fought a fierce battle near to the city of Durham,[21] in which battle David, king of Scotland, the earl of Menteith, the earl of Fife, and many other nobles of the Scottish kingdom were captured, while others, that is to

---

[20] David II of Scotland (1329–71), the son of Robert Bruce, led the Scottish invasion force (which probably consisted of some 2,000 well-armed troops and several thousand more untrained men) across the border on 7 October 1346; marching via Carlisle and Hexham, with considerable devastation en route, they arrived before Durham on 16 October. For a recent detailed study of the campaign and battle of Neville's Cross, see David Rollason and Michael Prestwich, eds., *The Battle of Neville's Cross 1346* (Stamford, 1998).

[21] The battle of Neville's Cross was fought on 17 October, a mile or so to the west of Durham (the actual site is difficult to determine for sure). The English forces, which perhaps numbered 6,000, were commanded by William la Zouche, archbishop of York (1342–52), whose principal captains were Henry Lord Percy, Ralph Lord Neville, and John Lord Mowbray.

regni Scocie capti fuerunt;[ii] [a]ceteri, uidelicet comes de Patrik, comes de Morif, comes de Ros, senescallus Scocie aliique nobiles et populares regni Scocie ibidem tunc interfecti fuerunt.[a] [22]

18. Idem autem[b] rex Anglie, post reddicionem uille de Kaleys, capta treuga cum Francis [c]ad eorum rogatum,[c] rediit in Angliam cum gloria et honore.[23]

19. *De pestilencia et mortalitate gencium.* Anno Domini millesimo trecentisimo quadragesimo octauo, mortuo Iohanne archiepiscopo Cant',[24] cito post incepit pestilencia et mortalitas hominum per totam Angliam tanta[d] [e]et talis[e] quod uix quinta pars uiuencium |
fo. 254r hominum remanebat in uita, et tanta raritas[f] presbyterorum et aliorum seruientium[g] erat quod multe ecclesie inofficiate remanebant,[h] et uiuentes in carne seruientibus et laborariis ex toto carebant, adeo quod terre[i] inculte pro[j] parte maxima remanserunt[k] ubique.[25]

20. *Capcio de Gisnes.* Postmodum uero per unum ualettum Iohannem de Doncastre anglicum, apud[l] Gynes per Gallicos incarceratum,[26] captum fuit castrum de Gynes de nocte subtiliter per prudenciam [m]et astuciam[m] ipsius Iohannis[n] in manum domini[o] regis Anglie, dormientibus ipsius castri [p]de Gynes[p] custodibus;[q] captisque per eundem Iohannem Doncastre spoliis, et quibusdam[r] interfectis ibidem, et quibusdam[s] maioribus captis et in carcere detentis, donec cum consilio regis Anglie quid de taliter captis ageretur, deliberaretur ad plenum. De quo quidem facto idem Iohannes Doncastre magnam reportauit laudem, tam a rege Anglie quam a magnatibus regni sui.

[a–a] *om. M* [b] *om. L* [c–c] de eorum rogatu *L* [d] *om. JLM* [e–e] *om. J* [f] caritas *corrected by later hand to* scarcitas *L* [g] operancium *M* [h] erant *M* [i] *om. M* [j] *om. J* [k] *J breaks off* [l] in *M* [m–m] *om. M* [n] *add.* et *M* [o] *om. M* [p–p] *om. M* [q] *M breaks off* [r] quibus *L* [s] quibus *L*

[22] The chronicler has reported correctly those who were captured: King David II remained a prisoner for eleven years; John Graham, earl of Menteith, was executed for treason on 6 March 1347; Duncan, earl of Fife, was condemned to death for treason but pardoned because of his kinship to Edward III. The list of 'killed' is, however, mostly incorrect: only John Randolph, earl of Moray, was indeed slain at the battle. William, earl of Ross, attended the muster of the army at Perth but then departed before even crossing the border (*Complete Peerage*, xi. 146), while Patrick, earl of Dunbar and March, and Robert the Steward (the future King Robert II) both fled the battle, for which they were much ridiculed by the English (see the comments of Alexander Grant, 'Disaster at Neville's Cross', in Rollason and Prestwich, eds., *The Battle of Neville's Cross 1346*, pp. 15–35).

[23] Edward III returned to England on 12 October 1347 (*HBC*, p. 39). An Anglo-French truce had been agreed on 28 September, to last until 24 June 1348 (*Chronicon Galfridi le Baker*, pp. 92–5, where the text of the truce is given).

say, the earl of Patrick, the earl of Moray, the earl of Ross, the steward of Scotland, and other nobles and commoners of the Scottish kingdom were killed there at that time.[22]

18. Following the surrender of the town of Calais, the aforesaid king of England, having made a truce with the French at their request, returned in glory and honour to England.[23]

19. *The plague and mortality of men.* In the year of Our Lord 1348, shortly after the death of John, archbishop of Canterbury,[24] a plague and mortality of men broke out throughout England to such an extent that scarcely one-fifth of those men who were living remained alive, and there was such a scarcity of priests and other servants that many churches were left unserved, and those who remained alive were utterly deprived of servants and labourers, as a result of which lands for the most part remained untilled everywhere.[25]

20. *The capture of Guines.* Some time after this, the castle of Guines was cunningly captured one night by an English valet, John of Doncaster, who had been imprisoned by the French at Guines;[26] it was delivered into the hands of the lord king of England through the intelligence and acuity of the said John while those who were guarding the said castle of Guines were sleeping; spoil was also seized by the said John of Doncaster, and some persons were killed there and other important persons captured and detained in prison until such time as the king of England's council could deliberate more fully as to what should be done with those who had been captured in this way. The said John of Doncaster was greatly praised for this action, both by the king of England and by the magnates of his kingdom.

[24] John Stratford, archbishop of Canterbury since 1333, died on 23 August 1348 (*HBC*, p. 233).
[25] The Black Death in fact probably arrived in England a month or two before Stratford's death on 23 August. The resultant mortality, although not as extensive as our chronicler suggests, may well have reached 50 per cent (R. Horrox, ed., *The Black Death* (Manchester, 1994), pp. 3, 62–64), and one recent estimate puts it over 60 per cent (O. J. Benedictow, *The Black Death, 1346–1353: The Complete History* (Woodbridge, 2004), pp. 342–83).
[26] This incident is out of chronological order: it occurred on 6 January 1352, when John of Doncaster, an esquire from Lincolnshire serving in the garrison at Calais, managed to take the castle of Guines (six miles south of Calais) by stealth, killing or expelling the French garrison. Although this was a clear violation of the truce, Guines was so strategically valuable that Edward III, with the advice of parliament, decided not to return it to the French: for the full story, see J. Sumption, *The Hundred Years War*, ii: *Trial by Fire* (London, 1999), pp. 88–90. Belief in Doncaster's low social status seems to have been common: le Baker described him as an archer: *Chronicon Galfridi le Baker*, p. 116.

21. *"Item, a tempore reddicionis uille de Kaleys, semper de anno in annum habitis diuersis tractatibus pacis^b inter Anglicos et Gallicos, habitis^c tam in uilla ^{d}de Kaleys^d quam ad calcetum eiusdem,^{27} et continuatis treugis sub spe pacis, nichil^e effectuale quo ad pacem aliquam erat factum.

22. *De anno iubileo.* Anno Domini millesimo trecentisimo quinquagesimo, anno uidelicet iubileo apud Romanam urbem, totus^f populus confluebat undique pro plena remissione peccaminum consequenda, et ad uisitandum limina Beatorum Petri et Pauli Rome, et aliis peregrinacionibus inibi^g faciendis.$^{h\,28}$

23. *De morte P. Valoys.* ^{i}Anno Domini millesimo trecentisimo quinquagesimo primo, mortuus est Philippus de Valesio,^{j} et apud Remens' ^{k}Iohannes de Francia eius filius^k coronatus est ^{l}in regem Francie de facto,^{l} non obstante uendicacione regni Francie per regem Anglie hereditario iure facta.$^{m\,29}$

24. Post hec dominus Galfridus Charny, tunc senescallus Francie, habuit priuatum tractatum et dolosum cum domino Emerico Pauye et fratre suo Ianuen', magistris galearum regis Anglie, super uendicione^n ^{o}castri de Caleys pro septem milibus scutis, et, concessa uendicione^o dicti castri de conniuencia^p regis Anglie, et tandem, quodam die Lune prima ebdomoda mensis Ianuarii, uenit idem dominus Galfridus Charny ante portam uille de Caleys cum exercitu suo pro capcione dicte uille, sed ipse per^q regem Anglie et principem ac comites de Warewyk et Suffolk et exercitum suum captus fuit et London' incarceratus, et tandem pro magna peccunie summa redemptus.^{30}

---

^{a} *J resumes* ^{b} pro pace *J* ^{c} omnes *JL*; habitis *possibly rep. in error* C $^{d-d}$ *om.* L ^{e} *om.* L ^{f} *om.* J ^{g} in illi *J* ^{h} *J breaks off* ^{i} *M resumes* ^{j} *marg. sketch of crowned and bearded head and shoulders* C; *add.* rex Francie *LM* $^{k-k}$ eius filius Iohannes de Francia *LM* $^{l-l}$ *om.* M ^{m} *M breaks off* ^{n} uendicacione *L* $^{o-o}$ *om.* L ^{p} conueniencia *L* ^{q} G. *L*

^{27} The first major Anglo-French conference to be held at Calais following its capture was from late September to mid-November 1348, when it was agreed to extend the truce until 1 September 1349. On 2 May 1349, it was further prolonged until Whitsun 1350 (*Chronicon Galfridi le Baker*, pp. 98–100, 269–71). The 'causeway' was the raised road which crossed the marshy ground from the western gate of the town to the bridge at Nieulay (*Chronica Johannis de Reading et Anonymi Cantuariensis*, p. 358). There was another raised road from Boulogne to Gravelines, above the marshes which stretched out to the south of Calais, passing about half a mile south of the town, and to the south of this there was a 'patch of open ground to the north of Guines which was to serve for many years as the traditional meeting place of the ambassadors of the two realms' (Sumption, *Trial by Fire*, pp. 15–16).

21. Also, from the time of the surrender of the town of Calais, various peace talks were always being held from year to year between the English and the French, both in the town of Calais and on its causeway; and although the truces were extended in the hope of peace, nothing leading to any sort of peace was agreed.[27]

22. *The jubilee year.* In the year of Our Lord 1350, the year of the Jubilee at the city of Rome, all the people converged from all parts in order to obtain full remission of sins and to visit the basilicas of the Blessed Peter and Paul at Rome and make other pilgrimages there.[28]

23. *The death of Philip de Valois.* In the year of Our Lord 1351 ⟨recte 1350⟩, Philip de Valois died, and his son, John of France, was crowned as de facto king of France at Reims, notwithstanding the claim by hereditary right to the kingdom of France put forward by the king of England.[29]

24. Following this, Geoffrey de Charny, then steward of France, had a secret and treacherous discussion with the Genoese Lord Amerigo de Pavia and his brother, masters of the king of England's galleys, concerning the sale of the castle of Calais in return for seven thousand écus, and—the sale of the said castle having been confirmed, with the connivance of the king of England—at length, on a certain day, the Monday of the first week of January, the said Lord Geoffrey de Charny arrived before the gate of the town of Calais with his army in order to seize the said town, but he himself was captured by the king of England and the prince and the earls of Warwick and Suffolk and their army, and imprisoned in London, eventually being ransomed for a large sum of money.[30]

---

[28] Pope Clement VI (1342–52) was not of course based in Rome at this time, but in Avignon, but he proclaimed a jubilee in Rome in 1350 in part as a response to requests from the Romans, and because he did not want to be seen as 'a mere bishop of Avignon'. To qualify for the jubilee indulgence, pilgrims had to visit the Lateran basilica as well as those of St Peter and St Paul: Wood, *Clement VI*, pp. 91–5.

[29] Philippe VI of France died on 22 August 1350; his son Jean II (1350–64) was crowned on 26 September and made his formal entry to Paris on 17 October.

[30] There are varying accounts of this incident. Geoffroi de Charny, although one of the most celebrated knights of his age, was not steward of France; his attempt to take Calais occurred early in January 1350, possibly on the morning of 2 January, possibly (as stated by our chronicler) on Monday 4 January. Amerigo de Pavia, who had been Edward III's galley-master at Calais since April 1348, probably intended to betray Charny from the start, and according to one report had been promised as much as 20,000 écus; his brother Dominic may also have been involved in the double-cross. At any rate, Edward III and the Black Prince, having hastened across the Channel when informed of the plot, were waiting for the

25. *Nuncii ad Romanam curiam destinati.* Anno Domini millesimo trecentisimo quinquagesimo tertio, ad tractandum super reformacione pacis inter Francie et Anglie reges, missi fuerunt ad Romanam curiam dux Lancastrie, comes Arondellie, dominus Willelmus episcopus Norwyc', dominus Michael de Northburgh et alii ex parte regis Anglie, et*a* habitis multis tractatibus cum ambassatoribus Francie sine expedicione pacis ad Angliam diuerterunt.[31]

26. *De morte Willelmi episcopi Norwicen'.* Et die Epiphanie Domini eodem anno, mortuus est ipse*b* dominus Willelmus Norwycens' episcopus in curia et sepultus.[32]

fo. 254ᵛ **27.** *c*Anno Domini millesimo trecentisimo quinquagesimo*d* quinto, Edwardus*e* rex Anglie,*f* pro recuperacione iuris sui in regno Francie ex*g* successione hereditaria matris sue, *h*domini Philippi Pulcri, quondam regis Francie,[33] filie et heredis,*h* destinauit Edwardum filium suum primogenitum,*i j*tunc principem Wallie etatis uiginti quinque annorum et amplius,*j* [34] tanquam capitaneus in Vasconiam, una cum comitibus de Warewyk et Saresbirien',[35] *k*domino Reginaldo*k* Cobham, domino Stephano de Cosyntoun,[36] militibus, et aliis*l* regni Anglie cum nauigio et exercitu magno ualde,*m* ad debellandum*n* contra *o*dominum Iohannem dicentem se regem Francie.*o* Et applicuit *p*idem princeps Wallie*p* apud Burdegalen' et ibidem mansit per totum annum sequentem, et*q* habuit cum delphino de Vienna, *r*filio dicti regis Francie,*r* *s*et cum magnatibus regni Francie,*s* *t*diuersos conflictus*t* in Vasconia et alibi

---

a om. L   *b* om. L   *c* JM resume   *d* .xl. L   *e* om. M   *f* add. distinauit filium suum primogenitum E. M   *g* pro L   *h–h* om. J   *i* om. M   *i–j* et fuit E. .xxv. annorum M   *k–k* et militibus aliis M   *l* add. de J   *m* alii L   *n* bellandum M   *o–o* dominum Iohannem regem Francie dicentem se J; dominum Iohannem se regem Francie dicentem L; regem Francie Iohannem M   *p–p* om. M   *q* add. diuersos conflictos M   *r–r* dicti regis Francie filio JL   *s–s* om. JL   *t–t* om. M

French when they entered the town, and killed about 200 of them and captured thirty others, including Charny himself and Eustace de Ribemont. Charny was released in July 1351; in July 1352 Amerigo de Pavia had the misfortune to fall into his hands at the capture of Frethun, and Charny put him to a very painful death: Sumption, *Trial by Fire*, pp. 60–2, 93; *Chronica Johannis de Reading et Anonymi Cantuariensis*, pp. 239–42.

[31] It was in the autumn of 1354 that this powerful English embassy made its way to Avignon. Henry of Grosmont, duke of Lancaster, and Richard Fitzalan, earl of Arundel, were its leaders, although William Bateman, bishop of Norwich, and Michael Northburgh, who had recently been elected bishop of London, spent longer at the Curia on this occasion. Despite lengthy and complex negotiations over the winter of 1354–5, all that was agreed was a three-month extension of the truce, to 24 June 1355. Lancaster arrived back in London on

25. *Messengers sent to the Roman Curia.* In the year of Our Lord 1353 ⟨*recte* 1354⟩, the duke of Lancaster, the earl of Arundel, Lord William, bishop of Norwich, Lord Michael Northburgh, and others were sent to the Roman Curia on behalf of the king of England for negotiations concerning the establishment of peace between the kings of France and England, but having held numerous talks with the French ambassadors without agreeing peace terms, they returned to England.[31]

26. *The death of William, bishop of Norwich.* And on the day of the Lord's Epiphany that year ⟨6 January, *recte* n.s. 1355⟩, the said Lord William, bishop of Norwich, died at the Curia and was buried.[32]

27. In the year of Our Lord 1355, Edward king of England, in order to enforce his right to the kingdom of France through hereditary succession from his mother, the daughter and heiress of Lord Philip the Fair, former king of France,[33] dispatched his first-born son Edward, then prince of Wales and aged 25 years or more,[34] to be his captain in Gascony, together with the earls of Warwick and Salisbury,[35] Lord Reginald Cobham, Lord Stephen Cossington,[36] knights, and others from the kingdom of England, with a very large army and navy, in order to make war against Lord John, the self-styled king of France. So the said prince of Wales landed at Bordeaux and remained there for the whole of the following year, and he fought several battles in Gascony and elsewhere with the dauphin of Vienne, the son of the said king of France, and with the magnates of the

28 March: K. Fowler, *The King's Lieutenant: Henry of Grosmont, First Duke of Lancaster 1310–1361* (London, 1969), pp. 134–47.

[32] Bateman's death is dated one year too early, although on the correct day. He was buried before the high altar in Avignon cathedral, and succeeded by Thomas Percy, who was provided to the see on 4 February 1355 (*HBC*, p. 262; *Chronica Johannis de Reading et Anonymi Cantuariensis*, p. 359).

[33] Philippe IV 'le Bel' (1285–1314) was survived by three sons and a daughter, Isabelle, who married Edward II of England and was the mother of Edward III. Philippe's three sons in turn became king of France, as Louis X (1314–16), Philippe V (1316–22), and Charles IV (1322–28), but none of them left male issue to inherit the realm, which allowed Edward III to put forward his claim to the throne of France.

[34] Edward, the Black Prince, was born on 15 June 1330.

[35] Thomas Beauchamp, earl of Warwick (1329–69); William Montague, earl of Salisbury (1349–97); the earls of Oxford and Suffolk also accompanied the prince.

[36] Reginald Lord Cobham of Sterborough, Knight of the Garter and a close associate of the prince, served as marshal of the prince's army at Poitiers; Sir Stephen Cossington, also close to the prince, fought in his personal bodyguard and was generously rewarded after the battle. Both were knights of Kent, and therefore presumably known to the chronicler: Bériac-Lainé and Given-Wilson, *Les Prisonniers de la Bataille de Poitiers*, pp. 46, 201–4, 369.

primo anno aduentus sui ad partes illas;*a* cui Deus de inimicis suis in multis locis dedit uictoriam et triumphum, licet aliqui*b* de suo exercitu perierunt.[37]

28. *Bellum de Peytiers.*c* De gentibus armorum principis Wallie.* Anno Domini millesimo trecentisimo quinquagesimo*d* sexto, die Lune uidelicet undeuicesimo die mensis Septembris, *e*anno etatis dicti principis uicesimo sexto,*e* inter eundem principem et dominum Iohannem dicentem se regem Francie, in campo extra Peytiers magnus*f* belli conflictus diutissime*g* habebatur. In quo quidem bello idem princeps habuit in acie sua tria milia homines armorum*h* et mille sagittarios et mille*i* seruientes dumtaxat.*j* [38]

29. *De hominibus regis Francie.* Rex uero Francie habuit quatuor bella. Et*k* in acie sua prima fuerunt*l* octoginta uexilla et pyncelli.[39] Et in acie delphini *m*de Vienna,*m* filii*n* dicti regis Francie,*o* ibi fuerunt centum octoginta*p* uexilla et pyncelli. *q*Et in acie tercia domini ducis Burboun fuerunt quinquaginta quinque uexilla et pyncelli.*q* Et in acie quarta *r*dicti regis Francie*r* cum duobus marchionibus*s* fuerunt octoginta septem*t* uexilla *u*et pyncelli.*u* [40]

30. In quo quidem bello de Peytiers, post multam stragem hominum, terga uerterunt multi magnates de Francia et fugerunt, uidelicet delphinus de Vienna et dominus Willelmus Douglas cum aliis *v*multis Scotis.*v* [41] Et, solius Dei assistente potencia, idem princeps in dicto

---

a illos *L*   *b* aliquo *L*   *c* *heading in top marg. fo. 254v C*   *d* .xl. *L*   *e-e* *om. M*
f *om. M*   *g* *om. M*   *h* armatorum *JLM*   *i* .c. *M*   *j* *om. M*   *k* *om. L*
l fuerat *M*   *m-m* *om. J*   *n* filius *L*   *o* *add.* de *M*   *p* *add.* septem *J*   *q-q* *3rd and 4th battles in reverse order LM*   *r-r* *om. J*   *s* marchionibus *CJLM; for marescallis?*   *t* *om. J*   *u-u* *om. M*   *v-v* uiribus Scotie *M*

---

[37] The Black Prince's army left Plymouth on 9 September 1355 and arrived at Bordeaux on 20 September. October and November were devoted to a *chevauchée* through Languedoc, and the early months of 1356 mainly to military operations against French enclaves along the valleys of the Dordogne and Garonne. The dauphin, however, was not involved in these engagements. For details of the prince's campaigns, see H. J. Hewitt, *The Black Prince's Expedition of 1355–1357* (Manchester, 1958).

[38] The battle of Poitiers was fought about eight kilometres to the south-east of the city of Poitiers, more or less on the site of the modern village of Nouaillé-Maupertuis. The army commanded by the Black Prince probably amounted to about 6,000 men (3,000 men-at-arms, 2,000 archers, and 1,000 Gascon infantry).

[39] 'Vexilla' were the square banners borne by knights banneret; 'pyncelli' were the tapered pennons borne by 'simple' knights.

[40] The chronicler is a little confused here. The total strength of the French army at

French kingdom, during the first year following his arrival in those parts; and God gave him victory and triumph over his enemies in numerous places, although some of his army perished.[37]

28. *The battle of Poitiers. The men-at-arms of the prince of Wales.* On Monday 19 September in the year of Our Lord 1356, when the said prince was in his twenty-sixth year, a very fierce and prolonged battle was fought between the said prince and Lord John, self-styled king of France, in a field outside Poitiers, in which battle the said prince had only three thousand men-at-arms, one thousand archers, and one thousand sergeants in his host.[38]

29. *The men of the king of France.* The king of France, however, had four divisions. In his first division there were eighty banners and pennons;[39] in the division of the dauphin of Vienne, the son of the said king of France, there were 180 banners and pennons; in the third division, that of the lord duke of Bourbon, there were fifty-five banners and pennons; and in the fourth division, that of the said king of France with the two ⟨marshals⟩, there were eighty-seven banners and pennons.[40]

30. And in this battle of Poitiers, after a great number of men had been killed, many of the French magnates turned their backs and fled, that is to say, the dauphin of Vienne and Lord William Douglas, along with many other Scots.[41] And thus, aided by the power of the one God, the said prince gained victory in that battle, and in addition

Poitiers was probably around 11,000 men, with about 8,000 men-at-arms and 3,000 infantry. They were organized in three principal lines or 'battles'. The first was at least nominally commanded by Charles, duke of Normandy, the dauphin, although since he was only 18 years old he was assisted by more experienced commanders such as Pierre, duke of Bourbon, and William Lord Douglas (who commanded a detachment of Scots fighting with the French); the second was under the command of Philippe, duke of Orléans, the king's brother; King Jean himself commanded the third. All the men in these three battles fought dismounted. There was also a fourth 'battle', smaller than the others but consisting entirely of cavalry and led by the two marshals of France, Jean de Clermont and Arnoul d'Audrehem: this was the first 'battle' to engage the prince's army, the intention being to use the cavalry to break up the formations of English archers.

[41] This is a little unfair to both Douglas and the dauphin: Douglas was badly wounded before departing the field, while the young dauphin was probably escorted from the field at the order of his father the king after his 'battle' had been driven back. It is surprising that the chronicler does not mention the duke of Orléans, whose decision to lead his division from the field without engaging the enemy was widely criticized in France in the aftermath of the defeat. His later insistence that he had been ordered by the king to depart did little to save his reputation: Bériac-Lainé and Given-Wilson, *Les Prisonniers de la Bataille de Poitiers*, p. 42.

bello uictoriam*a* reportauit, et preter multos qui de exercitu dicti regis
Francie occisi erant ibidem,*b* capti fuerunt uidelicet:*c* [42]

fo. 254*va*   *dCapcio regis Francorumd*

Dominus Iohannes rex Francie[43]
 Regales
Philippus filius eius iunior[44]
*Iacobus de Burboun,*e* comes Pontiui
Comes de Ew*f* [45]
Comes de Abbeuille,*g* filius domini Roberti d'Artoys[46]

fo. 254*vb*   *Comites Francie*
Comes de Tankeruille[47]
Comes de Ventedour[48]
Comes de Salesbrigg'[49]
Comes de Ventdoyne[50]
Comes de Russy[51]
Comes de Vaudemont[52]
Comes Damartyn[53]
Comes de Nesshowe*h* [54]

fo. 255*ra*   *Clerici capti*
Archiepiscopus Senonen'[55]
Castellanus d'Enpost', familiaris pape et bene dilectus ab eo[56]
 iDomini de Francia capti i
Vicecomes Narbonen'[57]
Vicecomes de*j* Beaumond[58]
Marescallus d'Audenham[59]
Filius comitis d'Ausure[60]
Frater comitis de Vendome[61]

---

a *om.* L *b* *add.* et *JM* *c* in bello de Peyteyrs *M* *d-d* Capti in bello de
Peyters *L* *e-e* *om.* M *f* *add.* et xiiij alii comites et domini multi *M*; *M breaks off*
g Abbeuille *CJL; for* Longeuille? *h* *in bottom marg. in English* Erles 10 *C* *i-i* Occisi
in eodem bello *JL* *j* *om.* J

---

[42] This is one of many lists provided by contemporary writers of those captured or
alleged to have been captured at the battle of Poitiers. The identifications which follow are
taken from Bériac-Lainé and Given-Wilson, *Les Prisonniers de la Bataille de Poitiers*,
pp. 345–61 and *passim*.

[43] Exactly who captured the French king remained a matter of dispute. Denis de
Morbecque, a disaffected knight from Artois fighting on the English side, and Bernard du
Troy, a Gascon esquire, both claimed to have received his surrender. Edward III later
claimed Jean as his own prisoner and compensated both parties pending a decision between
them, but they both died before the dispute could be settled: Bériac-Lainé and Given-
Wilson, *Les Prisonniers de la Bataille de Poitiers*, pp. 183–7.

[44] Philippe 'the Bold', count of Touraine, later duke of Burgundy, youngest son of the
French king.

to the many in the army of the said king of France who were killed there, the following were captured:[42]

The capture of the king of the French.

Lord John, king of France[43]

Princes

Philip, his younger son[44]

James of Bourbon, count of Ponthieu

The count of Eu[45]

The count of ⟨Longueville⟩, son of Lord Robert of Artois[46]

Counts of France

The count of Tancarville[47]

The count of Ventadour[48]

The count of Saarbrücken[49]

The count of Vendôme[50]

The count of Roucy[51]

The count of Vaudémont[52]

The count of Dammartin[53]

The count of Nassau[54]

Churchmen captured

The archbishop of Sens[55]

The castellan of Amposta, a familiar of the pope, and much loved by him[56]

Lords of France captured

The viscount of Narbonne[57]

The viscount of Beaumont[58]

Marshal d'Audrehem[59]

The son of the count of Auxerre[60]

The brother of the count of Vendôme[61]

---

[45] Jean d'Artois, count of Eu, son of Robert, count of Artois (see following note).

[46] Charles d'Artois, brother of the count of Eu (see previous note).

[47] Jean de Melun, count of Tancarville.   [48] Bernard, count of Ventadour.

[49] Jean, count of Saarbrücken.   [50] Bouchard VI, count of Vendôme.

[51] Robert, count of Roucy.

[52] Henri de Joinville, count of Vaudémont.

[53] Charles de Trie, count of Dammartin.   [54] Jean, count of Nassau.

[55] Guillaume de Melun, archbishop of Sens.

[56] Juan Fernandez de Heredia, castellan of Amposta.

[57] Aimery de Lara, viscount of Narbonne.

[58] Jean II de Brienne, viscount of Beaumont.

[59] Arnoul d'Audrehem, marshal of France.

[60] Imbert de Chalon, son of Jean III de Chalon, count of Auxerre, also captured at Poitiers.

[61] Pierre de Vendôme, brother of Bouchard VI, count of Vendôme.

Dominus de Rochefolcaud[62]
Dominus de Montagu[63]
Dominus de Seynt Tyger[64]
Dominus d'Amboyse[65]
Senescallus de Seyntoge[66]
Dominus Gychardus d'Ars
Dominus Mauritius de[a] Mauynet, capitaneus de Peytiers
Dominus de la Tour[67]
Dominus de Derual[68]
Germanus domini de Craoun[69]
Dominus Alanus de Montandre
Dominus Villehernald[70]
Dominus de Mangeler[71]
Dominus Iohannes de Blanco
Dominus d'Aubeney[72]
Dominus de Sully[b][73]

Et preter prescriptos,[c] captiuati fuerunt duo milia [d]homines armorum,[d] milites et alii.[e]

31. *Mortui et interfecti in bello eodem de Peytiers. Occisi in bello de Peytiers*[74]

Dominus de Burboun[75]
Dominus Robertus[f] Duras[76]
Dux Attenuens', constabularius Francie[77]
     Clerici
Episcopus de Chalons[78]

---

[a] *om. J*   [b] *interlinear in English* Lordes 22 *C*; *M resumes:* Occisi sunt in eodem bello .xlv. (*over erasure*) domini   [c] premissos *M*   [d–d] armatorum *L*; *add.* mortui in eodem bello *JL*   [e] *M breaks off*   [f] Rogerus *J*

---

[62] An Aymer de La Rochefoucauld was killed at Poitiers and buried among the victims in the church of the friars at Poitiers, but another lord de La Rochefoucauld was taken prisoner at Poitiers and later appointed as one of the conservators of the truce (Bériac-Lainé and Given-Wilson, *Les Prisonniers de la Bataille de Poitiers*, pp. 83, 108, 403). According to Père Ansèlme, *Histoire généalogique et chronologique de la maison royale de France* (9 vols., Paris, 1726–33), iv. 422–3, Aymer III de La Rochefoucauld, the head of the family at this time, lived until 1362, when he was buried in the Carmelite church at Rochefoucauld, so presumably it was he who was taken prisoner. Ansèlme also notes that he had a younger brother, also called Aymer, of whom nothing is known, so it is possible that he was the one who was killed at Poitiers (it may be significant that the man buried at Poitiers by the friars was not called 'Lord', but simply 'Aymer de La Rochefoucault').

[63] Gilles Aycelin II, lord of Montaigu.

[64] Jean III, lord of St-Dizier.   [65] Ingerger, lord of Amboise.

The lord of ⟨La⟩ Rochefoucauld[62]
The lord of Montaigu[63]
The lord of St-Dizier[64]
The lord of Amboise[65]
The seneschal of Saintonge[66]
Lord Guichard d'Ars
Lord Maurice of Mauvinet, captain of Poitiers
The lord of La Tour[67]
The lord of Derval[68]
The brother of the lord of Craon[69]
Lord Alan of Montendre
Lord Villehernal[70]
The lord of Maignelay[71]
Lord Jean of Blanche
Lord d'Aubigny[72]
The lord of Sully[73]
And in addition to the aforementioned, two thousand men-at-arms, knights, and others were captured.

31. *The dead and killed in the said battle of Poitiers. Those slain in the battle of Poitiers*[74]
The lord of Bourbon[75]
Lord Robert Duras[76]
The duke of Athens, constable of France[77]
    Churchmen
The bishop of Châlons[78]

---

[66] Guichard d'Angle, seneschal of Saintonge; however, our chronicler may have meant to indicate that Guichard d'Ars, next on the list, was seneschal of Saintonge, a mistake made by some other chroniclers (Bériac-Lainé and Given-Wilson, *Les Prisonniers de la Bataille de Poitiers*, pp. 346–7).

[67] Bertrand IV, lord of La Tour.   [68] Bonnabé de Rougé, lord of Derval.

[69] Probably an error for Pierre de Craon (Bériac-Lainé and Given-Wilson, *Les Prisonniers de la Bataille de Poitiers*, p. 350).

[70] Unidentified—listed by le Baker as 'dominus de la Ville, Ernaldus' (Bériac-Lainé and Given-Wilson, *Les Prisonniers de la Bataille de Poitiers*, p. 360).

[71] 'Jean dit Tristan', lord of Maignelay.

[72] Renaud, lord of Aubigny.   [73] Louis, lord of Sully.

[74] As with the prisoners taken at Poitiers, there are several contemporary lists of those said to have been killed at Poitiers: for the following identifications, see Bériac-Lainé and Given-Wilson, *Les Prisonniers de la Bataille de Poitiers*, index and *passim*.

[75] Pierre I, duke of Bourbon.

[76] Robert of Durazzo, a cadet of the house of Anjou.

[77] Gautier de Brienne, duke of Athens and constable of France.

[78] Renaud Chauveau, bishop of Châlons-sur-Marne.

⟨Domini⟩*a*

Marescallus de Clermont*b* 79

'Vicecomes d'Auny80

Vicecomes de Brusso81

Vicecomes de Rocheward82

Dominus R. de Pouns

Dominus Galfridus Charny83

Dominus Galfridus Mathas84

Dominus de Landas85

Dominus Eustachius de Riplemont*d*

Dominus Andreas de*e* Chany*f* 86

Dominus Iohannes de Lidle

Dominus Guillelmus de Noyre87

Dominus Robertus Haungest88

Dominus de Castro Vyleyn89

Dominus de Mount Iohan90

Dominus de Argeyntyn91

Dominus de Sansure92

Dominus Ludouicus de Bruce*g*

Filius domini de*h* Montagu93

*i*Et preter predictos dominos*j* occisos, ⟨mille⟩*k* octingenti homines et persone, de quibus fuerunt mille homines*l* armorum,*m* milites et ualetti."*n* 94

---

a Domini *edd.; subheading required because following names not of churchmen*
b Chermount *L*   *c* Occisi in bello de Peytiers *at end of fo. 255ra, rep. top of fo. 255rb C*   *d* Ripmoundre *J*   *e om. L*   *f* Charny *J*   *g* Druse *JL*   *h om. J*
i M resumes   *j om. M*   *k* mille *edd., from correction in L:* .d.ccc. *corrected to* m.d.ccc.; *om. CJM*   *l om. J*   *m* armatorum et *J*   *n marg. sketch of hand pointing C*

79 Jean de Clermont, marshal of France.
80 This name does not appear on other lists, and cannot be identified with certainty.
81 André III de Chauvigny, viscount of Brosse.
82 Jean, viscount of Rochechouart.
83 For Geoffroi de Charny, who bore the *oriflamme* at Poitiers and fought in the division commanded by the king, see also n. 30 above.
84 According to le Baker, Geoffroi de Charny was 'dominus de Matas', although he is not otherwise known to have held this title (*Chronicon Galfridi le Baker*, pp. 103, 276). This does, however, make it highly likely, as suggested by Thompson and Tait, that this is an instance of two men being made out of one (*Chronica Johannis de Reading et Anonymi Cantuariensis*, pp. 265–6, and see the previous note).
85 Jean Mortagne, lord of Landas.

Lords

The marshal of Clermont[79]
The viscount of Aulnay[80]
The viscount of Brosse[81]
The viscount of Rochechouart[82]
Lord R⟨enaud⟩ of Pons
Lord Geoffrey Charny[83]
Lord Geoffrey Matha[84]
The lord of Landas[85]
Lord Eustace of Ribemont
Lord Andrew of Chany[86]
Lord John of Lisle
Lord William of Noyre[87]
Lord Robert Hangest[88]
The lord of Châteauvillain[89]
The lord of Montjean[90]
The lord of Argenton[91]
The lord of Sancerre[92]
Lord Louis de Brosse
The son of the lord of Montaigu[93]
And in addition to the aforesaid lords who were slain, ⟨so were⟩ another one thousand eight hundred men and persons, among whom were one thousand men-at-arms, knights, and valets.[94]

[86] Probably André de Chauvigny, lord of Levroux, who should be distinguished from his namesake André III de Chauvigny, viscount of Brosse, who also died at Poitiers (see above).

[87] Probably Guillaume de Nielle.

[88] Aubert de Hangest, lord of Henqueville.

[89] Jean de Thil-en-Auxois, lord of Châteauvillain.

[90] Briant, lord of Montjean.

[91] Unidentified—his name does not appear on other lists.

[92] Jean, lord of Sancerre, to be distinguished from Jean de Nevers, count of Sancerre, who was captured at Poitiers.

[93] Probably Gautier, son of the Gilles Aycelin, lord of Montaigu, listed among the captured.

[94] The manuscript used by Tait (*Chronica Johannis de Reading et Anonymi Cantuariensis*, p. 199) gives 1,800, although Tait noted that the 'M' for 'one thousand' was added in a later hand, and that it is probable that the scribe omitted another 'M' and should in fact have recorded a figure of 2,800. For other contemporary estimates of the number of dead at Poitiers, see Bériac-Lainé and Given-Wilson, *Les Prisonniers de la Bataille de Poitiers*, pp. 68–9.

32. *Capcio ante bellum de Peytiers.* Item, die Sabbati ante dictum bellum [a]de Peytiers,[a] [95] fuerunt capti:
Comes de Iuny[96]
Comes de Ausoire[97]
Marescallus de Burgoyne[98]
Et cum ipsis captiuatis,[b] fuerunt occisi ducenti quadraginta homines armorum.[c]

33. Item, die[d] quinta decima ante dictum bellum, capti fuerunt in castro de Romeynt': [99] Dominus de Croune[e] [100] Dominus Brusygaudus, miles[101]
Et cum ipsis captiuatis[f] in dicto castro, occisi fuerunt octoginta homines armorum.[g]

fo. 255v 34. Postquam uero[h] dictum bellum [i]de Peytiers tam graciose fuerat sic[j] peractum, idem[i] Edwardus princeps Wallie [k]cum exercitu suo[k] duxit secum dominum[l] Iohannem, dicentem se regem Francie, et [m]dominum Philippum[m] filium suum[n] iuniorem, [o]una cum ceteris captiuatis regni Francie,[o] apud[p] Burdegalen' in Vasconia, et[q] sub secura custodia [r]posuit eos ibidem in[s] quodam fortalicio, et erga eos idem[t] princeps humaniter se[u] habebat.[r] [102] Et dum idem rex sic[v] erat ibidem[w] in custodia detentus,[x] dominus papa Innocencius sextus scripsit eidem domino[y] principi[z] sub hac forma:[103]

35. *Bulla pape.*[aa] 'Innocencius episcopus, seruus seruorum Dei,[bb] dilecto filio, nobili uiro Edwardo, primogenito carissimi in Christo filii Edwardi regis Anglie illustris, principi Wallie, salutem et apostolicam benedictionem. Quamquam, fili, ex tuorum felicitate[cc]

[a–a] *om. J* [b] captiuis *J* [c] armatorum *M* [d] *om. L* [e] Canne *J* [f] captis *M* [g] armatorum *M* [h] factum est *M* [i–i] *om. M* [j] *om. JL* [k–k] *om. M* [l] *om. M* [m–m] *om. M* [n] eius *M* [o–o] et alios captiuos *M* [p] usque *M* [q] *om. M* [r–r] *om. M* [s] *om. L* [t] ibidem *J* [u] *om. JL* [v] *om. M* [w] *om. M* [x] *om. M* [y] *om. M* [z] *add.* ut ipse fauorabiliter habebat erga dominum Iohannem regem Francie *J*; *J breaks off* [aa] *heading* Bulla pape missa principi Wallie *L* [bb] etc *M*; *M breaks off* [cc] felicitatis *C*

[95] The skirmish at La Chaboterie, to which the chronicler refers, took place on Saturday 17 September about 7–8 kilometres east of Poitiers (ibid. 37).

[96] Jean de Noyers, count of Joigny. [97] Jean III de Chalon, count of Auxerre.

[98] The marshal of Burgundy was Géraud de Thurey, but whether he was in fact captured is open to doubt: R. Delachenal, *Histoire de Charles V* (5 vols., Paris, 1909–31), i. 207, thought that the third major figure taken at La Chaboterie was Jean de Chastillon-sur-Marne, grand master of the king's household.

[99] The castle of Romorantin, on the river Sauldre some sixty kilometres south of Orléans, was taken by assault on Saturday 3 September, sixteen days before Poitiers.

32. *The capture before the battle of Poitiers.* Also, on the Saturday before the said battle of Poitiers,[95] the following were captured:

The count of Joigny[96]

The count of Auxerre[97]

The marshal of Burgundy[98]

And in addition to those who were captured, 240 men-at-arms were slain.

33. Also, on the fifteenth day before the said battle, the following were captured in the castle of Romorantin:[99]

The lord of Craon[100]

Lord Boucicaut, knight.[101]

And in addition to those who were captured in the said castle, eighty men-at-arms were slain.

34. Thereafter, following this most happy outcome to the said battle of Poitiers, the aforesaid prince of Wales with his army took Lord John, the self-styled king of France, and Lord Philip his younger son, together with the other captives from the French kingdom, with them to Bordeaux in Gascony, where they placed them under safeguard in a certain fortress; and the said prince behaved in a humane fashion towards them.[102] And while the aforesaid king was thus detained in custody there, the lord pope, Innocent VI, wrote as follows to the said lord prince:[103]

35. *A papal bull.* 'Innocent the bishop, servant of the servants of God, to our beloved son, the noble Edward prince of Wales, first-born son of our most dear son in Christ, Edward the illustrious king of England, greetings and apostolic benediction. Although it is likely,

---

[100] Amaury IV, lord of Craon.

[101] Jean I le Meingre, called Boucicaut, marshal of France.

[102] The Black Prince and his army, with the French king and some of the more valuable prisoners, marched directly back to Bordeaux after Poitiers. The prince's army entered Bordeaux on 2 October, although (according to the *Eulogium Historiarum*, iii. 226) the prince himself and King Jean remained at Libourne for a further two weeks or so to give the city time to prepare a suitable welcoming ceremony for them. The prince and the king were quartered for the winter at the cathedral of St-André.

[103] For Étienne Aubert, elected Pope Innocent VI in 1352, see above, n. 8. The distrust in which he was held by at least some Englishmen is reflected in the (probably fictitious) story told in the *Anonimalle Chronicle* (p. 39) that the first report which he received of the battle of Poitiers was of a French victory, whereupon he ordered joyful celebrations to be held in Avignon. Michel, *Le Prince Noir*, pp. 338–9, printed a third letter from Innocent VI to the Black Prince, dated 20 October 1356, similarly urging him to shun pride in his victory and make peace with the French king.

successuum cum mundo senciens ut probabiliter glorieris, tenemus
tamen indubie quod, sicut Deo es deuotus et ex deuotis parentibus es
editus, triumphorum gloriam et uictoriarum*a* honorem ad Deum*b*
creatorem tuum, a quo est omnis uictoria omnisque triumphus, cum
reuerencia multa refers. Tenemus quod in eis effusionem cruoris
humani consideras; tenemus quod animarum pericula intueris, et
quod*c* proinde in conspectu ipsius Dei tui eo te humilias amplius quo,
sicut circumspectus et prudens, plane perpendas debere te illi pro hiis
referre graciam pro hiis ab eo ueniam deprecari. Licet enim idem ipse
Deus, prout uult distribuens bona sua, te uictoriarum titulis et
triumphorum pompa fecerit gloriosum, testatur tamen*d* plebis sue
stragem, nec regnancium rancorem an*e* odium, ius uel iniuriam,
compensari uult excidio fidelium et innocencium populorum. Quod
nos attenta meditacione pensantes, non reuocamus in dubium, immo
uerisimiliter illud*f* scimus, quod cum quanto de manu Domini
prosperiora te suscepisse cognoscis, tanto quod*g* ad pacem sis
promptior, tanto ad concordiam fauorabiliter inclineris, maxime*h*
cum ea sit consuetudo potencium imitancium*i* pietatem ut plus eos
ad clemenciam cotidie prosperitas excitet, plus ad mansuetudinem
felicitas indesinenter inducat. Numquam enim pietas in aliquo, nisi
cum possit seuire, perpenditur, numquam dulcedo mansuetudinis,
nisi cum possit rigide, innotescit. Dat igitur potencia occasionem
clemencie, dat etsi*j* pietati. Hanc igitur occasionem, hanc causam, a te
cum exhibere possis exigimus, et pro pace inter carissimum in Christo
filium nostrum Iohannem, regem Francorum*k* illustrem, quem ad
carcerem tuum bellicus euentus adduxit, et te, auctore Domino,
reformanda,*l* nobilitatem tuam confidenter adimus, illam quanta
possumus affeccione rogantes, et per uiscera misericordie Dei
obsecrantes attentius, quatinus gratitudinis uicem Domino Deo tuo
fo. 256*r*   pro hiis que tribuit ipse tibi, ad pacem et concordiam*m* | habilites
animum, cor prepares,*n* disponas et mentem. Nosti enim quod ille rex
pacificus, per quem uiuis et regnas, pacem diligere precipit, et ut

---

a uictoriam *L*   *b* dominum *L*   *c* om. *L*   *d* tum *L*   *e* aut *L*   *f* ibi *C*
g quo *L*   *h* maxima *L*   *i* mittancium *L*   *j* et *L*   *k* Francie *L*
l reformando *L*   *m* add. te *L*   *n* preparas *C*

my son, that you may glory, as is the manner of the world, in the happiness of your successes, we nevertheless know for certain that, since you are devoted to God and sprung from parents devoted to Him, you will with all reverence credit the glory of your triumphs and the honour of your victories to God, your creator, from whom comes all victory and every triumph. We know that you are aware of the shedding of human blood in them; we know that you think about the perils of souls, and that you therefore humble yourself in the sight of God himself, your God, to the same degree that, as a sage and prudent person, you can perceive clearly that you owe it to Him to offer thanks for these and to beg pardon from Him for them. For although this same God, distributing his gifts as he pleases, may have made you glorious with the renown of victories and the pomp of triumphs, nevertheless he abominates the slaughter of his people, and would not wish to see the enmity and hatred, rights and wrongs, of those who rule to be weighed in the balance against the destruction of faithful and innocent people. Considering such matters with deep meditation, we do not in the least doubt, indeed we know it to be true, that you, to the same extent that you are aware of having received greater favours from the hand of the Lord, will be correspondingly more promptly inclined towards peace and more favourably inclined towards concord, especially since it is the custom among powerful men who practice piety that prosperity encourages them more every day towards mercy, while success leads them unceasingly towards gentleness. For compassion is never esteemed in any person, except when he has the power to be cruel, while the sweetness of clemency passes quite unnoticed except when one has the power to act with severity. Power therefore provides the occasion for mercy and for compassion. We exhort you therefore to take this opportunity, to seize this moment, when you are in a position to do so, and, with the help of God, to establish peace between our most dear son in Christ, John, the illustrious king of the French, whom the vicissitudes of war have delivered into your captivity, and yourself; we address this to your nobility with confidence, begging you with as much good will as we can, and beseeching you most earnestly by the bowels of God's mercy, that, displaying in turn your gratitude to your Lord God for those things which he has granted to you, you might accommodate your soul, prepare your heart, and incline your mind towards peace and concord. For you must know that the King of peace, by whom you live and reign, commands you to cherish peace, and takes up his

concordium cordium incolatum resurgit; et ne longis sermonibus diffusius extendamus epistolam, precibus nostris adimus, ut que uenerabilis frater noster Talairandus, episcopus Albanensis, et dilectus filius noster Nicolaus, tituli Sancti Vitalis presbyter cardinalis, apostolice sedis nuncii,[104] uel alter eorum, tibi ex parte nostra per se uel per alios retulerint, aut literis nostris indicauerint, credas indubie; illaque paratis operum fructibus pia uelis prosecucione complere. Data Auinion', quinto nonas Octobris, pontificatus nostri anno quarto.'

36. *Alia bulla exhortatoria directa domino Edwardo principi Wallie.* 'Innocencius episcopus, seruus seruorum Dei, dilecto filio, nobili uiro Edwardo, primogenito carissimi in Christo filii Edwardi regis Anglie illustris, principi Wallie, salutem et apostolicam benedictionem. Venerabilis frater noster Talairandus, episcopus Albanen', apostolice sedis nuncius, per suas literas scripsit nobis quod tu, nobilitatem quam diriuas ex genere confirmans et amplians*a* generositate animi ac operacione uirtutum, tantis eum es prosecutus honoribus, tantis et fauoribus, quantis filium in Christo patri decuit exhibere, animum tuum curialiter ad omnia preparans, nulla es successuum prosperitate elatus, sed in conspectu Domini Dei tui semper humilior, ei omnia deputans a quo omnia suscepisti, carissimo in Christo filio nostro Iohanni, regi Francorum illustri, quem ad carcerem tuum bellicus euentus adduxit, honorificenciam que tanto principi conuenit, benignius iam impendis. Super quo, nobilitatem tuam intentis laudibus prosequentes, speramus indubie quod omnipotens Dominus, qui humilia respicit et alta a longe cognoscit, in te proinde uberius et copiosius graciam sue benediccionis infundit. Nobilitatem tuam attente rogamus, tibi paternis*b* affectibus suadentes, quatinus hiis, fili, semper inniteris*c* operibus, hiis actibus impliceris, uerba pacis libenter audias, audita fauorabiliter prosequaris. Pax enim bonarum arcium decora mater, bonorum nutrix est studiorum, et cuncta parens fecunda uirtutum. Data Auinion', secundo nonas Octobris, pontificatus nostri anno quarto.'

a *add.* ex L   *b* protinus L   *c* miteris L

[104] Hélie Talleyrand de Périgord, cardinal-bishop of Albano, and Niccolo Capoci, bishop of Urgel in Aragon and cardinal-priest of St Vitalis; Talleyrand was said in the *Anonimalle Chronicle*, p. 39, to have been a 'special friend' of the king of England and the Black Prince, but other reports claimed that it was partly through distrust of him that the prince refused to continue the attempts at mediation on the eve of the battle of Poitiers. For their attempts to broker a peace between England and France in 1357–8, see below, pp. 38–47.

dwelling in the hearts of those who live in harmony. And in order not to prolong this epistle with long and diffuse discourse, we add to our prayers that whatever things our venerable brother Talleyrand, bishop of Albano, and our dear son Nicholas, cardinal priest of the title of St Vitalis, legates of the papal see,[104] or either one of them, whether in person or through others, might tell you on our behalf or make known to you by our letters, you should without hesitation believe, and that you should be willing to accomplish such things with pious duty, once the results of your labour have been secured. Dated at Avignon, on the fifth before the nones of October, in the fourth year of our pontificate ⟨3 October 1356⟩.'

36. *Another bull of exhortation sent to the Lord Edward, prince of Wales.*
'Innocent the bishop, servant of the servants of God, to our dear son, the noble Edward, prince of Wales, first-born son of our most dear son in Christ, Edward, the illustrious king of England, greetings and apostolic benediction. Our venerable brother Talleyrand, bishop of Albano, legate of the apostolic see, told us by his letters that you, confirming and displaying the nobility which you derive from birth by generosity of soul and the exercise of virtues, have shown him such honours and such favours as it befits a son to extend to his father in Christ, graciously accommodating your soul to all eventualities, and that, being in no way puffed up by the achievement of your successes, but ever more humble in the sight of your Lord God, attributing all things to Him from whom you have received everything, you do now most graciously extend to our most dear son in Christ, John, the illustrious king of the French, whom the vicissitudes of war have delivered into your captivity, the honourable treatment which befits so great a prince. On which account, in sending to your nobility the praise which you have deserved, we most fervently hope that Almighty God, who esteems the humble but knows the proud from afar, will therefore bestow upon you more abundantly and copiously the grace of his benediction. We earnestly beseech your nobility, urging you with fatherly pleas, O son, that you constantly incline yourself to these matters, embrace these actions, willingly listen to words of peace, and graciously act upon what you have heard. For peace is the fitting mother of good occupations, the nurturer of good desires, and the wholly fruitful progenitor of virtues. Dated at Avignon, the second before the nones of October, in the fourth year of our pontificate ⟨6 October 1356⟩.'

37. *ª*Quibus quidem*ᵇ* literis apostolicis*ᶜ* per dictum*ᵈ* principem Wallie intellectis, ipse*ᵉ* *ᶠ*eas misit ad Angliam*ᶠ* patri suo,*ᵍ* et *ʰ*a tempore capcionis dicti regis Francie*ʰ* continue morabatur apud Burdegalen' cum *ⁱ*dicto rege Francie, erga quem ualde *ʲ*humaniter et curialiter*ʲ* se habebat.*ⁱ*

38. *De aduentu regis Francie London'.*ᵏ* Anno Domini *ˡ*millesimo trecentisimo quinquagesimo septimo,*ˡ* mense Maii, parato*ᵐ* per dictum principem Wallie latenter magno nauigio et nauali exercitu, idem rex Francie *ⁿ*cum aliis captiuatis*ⁿ* ductus fuit *ᵒ*per mare*ᵒ* uersus Angliam, et *ᵖ*die Mercurii in festo Inuencionis Sancte Crucis*ᵖ* |

fo. 256ᵛ applicuerunt*q* *ʳ*omnes naues cum dicto rege Francie et aliis captiuatis in portu de*ʳ* Plomouth *ˢ*in Deuon' circa horam terciam dicti diei.*¹⁰⁵* Et de*ᵗ* illo loco per continuas dietas idem princeps Wallie conduxit dictum regem Francie per ciuitates et*ˢ* loca populosa *ᵘ*regni Anglie*ᵘ* uersus London', et *ᵛ*intrauit ciuitatem London' cum dicto rege Francie, domino*ʷ* Philippo filio suo iuniore, et aliis captiuatis regni Francie usque ad numerum tredecim personarum magnatum.*ᵛ*

39. *Londonienses.* *ˣ*Die Mercurii, uidelicet uicesimo quarto die dicti mensis Maii, et extra dictam ciuitatem London', Henricus Picard maior eiusdem*¹⁰⁶* et ciues, aldermanni et alii de communitate dicte ciuitatis processerunt*ʸ* obuiam dicto principi Wallie ac Iohanni regi Francie ac aliis cum eis captiuatis,*ˣ* uidelicet, de quolibet artificio dicte ciuitatis Lond' magnus equitancium numerus, uariis indumentorum apparatibus*ᶻ* nouiter propterea indutus, in multitudine copiosa. Et gens cuiuslibet artificii Lond' ordinatim*ᵃᵃ* precedebat*ᵇᵇ* dictum regem Francie et alios captiuatos per totam ciuitatem London' cum *ᶜᶜ*magno iocunditatis aspectu.*ᶜᶜ* *ᵈᵈ*Et *ᵉᵉ*pro mirabili*ᶠᶠ* facto,*ᵉᵉ* in conductu*ᵍᵍ* London' *ʰʰ*uinum erat*ʰʰ* positum omnibus potare uolentibus habundanter.*ⁱⁱ* Et in medio de*ʲʲ* Chepe London', circa aurifabros per eos ordinate, fuerunt due iuuencule pulcherrime*ᵏᵏ* in quadam

ª *J*M resume   *ᵇ* *om. M*   *ᶜ* *om. M*   *ᵈ* *om. M*   *ᵉ* *om. M*   *ᶠ⁻ᶠ* misit eas Angl' *J*; misit eas *M*   *ᵍ* in Angliam *M*   *ʰ⁻ʰ om. M*   *ⁱ⁻ⁱ* omnibus captiuis usque ad annum Domini .mccclvi. *M*   *ʲ⁻ʲ* curialiter et humaniter *JL*   *ᵏ marg. sketch of king of France, across chest* rex Francie *C*   *ˡ⁻ˡ* .mccclvi. *M*   *ᵐ om. JL*; et *M*   *ⁿ⁻ⁿ om. M*   *ᵒ⁻ᵒ om. M*   *ᵖ⁻ᵖ om. M*   *q* applicuit *M*   *ʳ⁻ʳ* apud *M*   *ˢ⁻ˢ* et sic ductus fuit per *M*   *ᵗ* ab *L*   *ᵘ⁻ᵘ om. M*   *ᵛ⁻ᵛ* fuerunt capti cum eo et Lond' ducti .xiii. magnat' *M*   *ʷ om. JL*   *ˣ⁻ˣ* et tota communitas London' et omnes artific' cum diuersa secta uestamentorum equitarunt ei obuiam *M*; *M breaks off*   *ʸ* proceres *J*   *ᶻ* apparitibus *J*; operantibus *L*   *ᵃᵃ* ordinatum *L*   *ᵇᵇ* precedebant *J*   *ᶜᶜ⁻ᶜᶜ* magna iocunditate *JL*   *ᵈᵈ M resumes*   *ᵉᵉ⁻ᵉᵉ om. M*   *ᶠᶠ* miraculi *L*   *ᵍᵍ* eodem *J*   *ʰʰ⁻ʰʰ* erat uinum *M*   *ⁱⁱ marg. sketch of hand pointing C*   *ʲʲ om. M*   *ᵏᵏ* pulcre *M*

37. And when the aforesaid prince of Wales had understood these apostolic letters, he sent them to his father in England; and from the time of the capture of the aforesaid king of France he remained continuously at Bordeaux with the said king of France, towards whom he behaved in an exceedingly humane and courteous fashion.

38. *The arrival of the king of France in London.* In the year of Our Lord 1357, in the month of May, after the aforesaid prince of Wales had secretly assembled a large fleet and naval force, the same king of France was taken across the sea with the other captives to England, and on Wednesday the feast of the Discovery of the True Cross ⟨3 May⟩, all the ships landed with the said king of France and the other captives in the port of Plymouth in Devon, at about the third hour of the said day.[105] And from there the said prince of Wales conducted the said king of France successively, day by day, through cities and well-populated places in the kingdom of England to London, and he entered the city of London with the said king of France, lord Philip his younger son, and the other captives from the realm of France to the number of thirteen magnates.

39. *The Londoners.* On Wednesday, namely the twenty-fourth day of the same month of May, Henry Picard, mayor of the city of London,[106] with citizens, aldermen, and others from the commonalty of the said city, went forth outside the said city in order to meet the said prince of Wales and John, king of France, and the others captured with them; that is to say, a multitude of people on horseback came from each craft guild of the said city of London, variously decked out in costumes newly made for the occasion, in great numbers. And the people of each London guild in turn preceded the said king of France and the other captives through the whole city of London, making good cheer; and as the procession passed through London wine was offered in abundance to all who wanted to drink, on account of the amazing spectacle. And in the middle of London's Cheapside, near to the goldsmiths' quarter and at their instigation, two very beautiful young girls were set up on a kind of platform

---

[105] The Black Prince left Bordeaux with King Jean on 11 April and probably arrived at Plymouth on 1 May, although the chroniclers give various dates for his arrival: Bériac-Lainé and Given-Wilson, *Les Prisonniers de la Bataille de Poitiers*, p. 113.

[106] Picard, one of the wealthiest and most influential Londoners of his generation, was a vintner, royal financier, and shipowner; he was alderman of Bishopsgate from 1348 to 1361 (when he died) and mayor of London in 1357 (*Oxford DNB*, 'Picard, Henry', article by R. Axworthy).

catasta *cum certis* cordis artificiose posita ex* parte aurifabrorum usque ad partem selariorum,* dicteque iuuencule sparserunt folia aurea et argentea super capita ibidem equitancium* in conspectu dictorum regis Francie et principis Wallie et aliorum equitancium tunc ibidem, propter quod factum mirabile plurimi applaudebant.[107]

40. Et episcopus London'[108] ac totus clerus* ecclesie London' dederunt eis obuiam in porta cimiterii ecclesie Sancti Pauli London' processionaliter,* et de hinc per Ludgate et Fletebrugge progrediebant omnes taliter equitantes* uersus Westmon', *et intrarunt* palacium regis Anglie apud Westm' hora uesperarum dicte diei Mercurii. *Et idem rex Francie dum sic equitabat per ciuitatem London' indutus erat una roba de nigra mixtura furrata* de minuto* uario more archidiaconi uel alterius clerici secularis.*

41. *Die autem Iouis* in crastino dicti diei Mercurii, *in festo uidelicet Sancti Aldelmi Episcopi,* credentes Londonienses quod idem princeps Wallie magnum eis conuiuium fecisset in maiori aula Westmon', ibidem* ab hora prima *dicte diei* usque post horam nonam[109] sederunt ad mensas *ibidem sine cibo uel potu,* respicientes parietes *et fenestras; sicque ieuuni frustrati a proposito ad propria recesserunt. Et pauci⟨s⟩* quidem ex illis qui paruam

fo. 257^r   intrarunt | aulam Westm' egredi non permiserunt aulici quouismodo absque diligenti exploracione qui et quales fuerant sic intrantes.*

42. *Post hec uero* idem rex Francie* hospitatus fuit apud Saueye* London' in hospicio domini Henrici ducis Lancastrie, ipso duce tunc in Britannia circa obsidionem* uille de Reyns in Britannia existente.[110]

---

a–a om. M   *b* serii *J*   *c* interlinear C; marg. sketch of kerchiefed woman's head C   *d* M breaks off   *e* chorus C   *f* processionabiliter *J*   *g* add. per Flete strete *JL*   *h–h* intraueruntque *JL*   *i* marg. sketch of hand pointing C   *j* furratre *JL*   *k* minnito L   *l* *J breaks off*   *m* M resumes   *n* L breaks off; om. M   *o–o* om. M   *p* om. M   *q–q* om. M   *r–r* om. M   *s–s* om. M   *t* paucis edd.; pauci C   *u* *J* resumes   *v* om. M   *w* om. M   *x* M breaks off   *y* obsidione *J*

---

[107] The triumphal entry to London on 24 May of the Black Prince with his captive King Jean was an event much enjoyed by the chroniclers and doubtless by the Londoners too. For an account which confirms much of what our chronicler says, see *Anonimalle Chronicle*, p. 41, in which King Jean is described as 'dressed in a surcoat of coloured cloth like an aged chaplain or an old physician'. According to this chronicle, the two 'very beautiful and comely' girls had their heads uncovered so that their shining hair hung down over their shoulders, and were 'cleverly and marvellously' suspended on ropes of serge. Our author

cunningly rigged up with some ropes leading from the goldsmiths' quarter to that of the saddlers, and these girls sprinkled gold and silver leaf on the heads of the riders below, while the king of France and the prince of Wales and the others who were riding there looked on; on account of which, many people applauded this amazing scene.[107]

40. And the bishop of London[108] and the entire clergy of the church of London came in procession to meet them at the gate to the cemetery of St Paul's church in London, and from there they all proceeded in this fashion on horseback by way of Ludgate and Fleet bridge towards Westminster, and they entered the king of England's palace at Westminster at the hour of vespers on that same Wednesday. And as the king of France rode through the city of London he was dressed in a robe of black motley lined with miniver in the manner of an archdeacon or other secular clerk.

41. On the next day, Thursday, following that Wednesday, namely on the feast of St Aldhelm the bishop ⟨25 May⟩, the Londoners, believing that the said prince of Wales had prepared a banquet for them in the Great Hall at Westminster, sat there at the tables from the first hour of the said day until after the ninth hour[109] without food or drink, gazing at the walls and the windows, and then went home hungry and frustrated in their purpose. A few of them who penetrated to the Lesser Hall at Westminster were not permitted by the courtiers to leave under any circumstances without a thorough investigation of who and what sort of men these intruders were.

42. After this the king of France was lodged at the Savoy in London, in the house of lord Henry duke of Lancaster, who at the time was occupied in Brittany, besieging the city of Rennes in Brittany.[110]

---

may have inadvertently written 'certis' in place of 'cericis' ('silken') in describing these ropes.

[108] Michael Northburgh, bishop of London 1354–61 (*HBC*, p. 258).

[109] The 'ninth hour' of the day may have been intended to indicate noon, or it may have indicated 3 o'clock in the afternoon. The former was the more common meaning at this time.

[110] The Savoy palace, on the north bank of the Thames to the west of the city of London, had recently been built by Henry, duke of Lancaster (d. 1361), apparently with the loot that he had plundered from the siege of Bergerac in 1345 (*Knighton's Chronicle*, p. 188). Lancaster besieged Rennes for nine months, from 2 October 1356 to 5 July 1357, although one of the conditions of the truce of 23 March 1357 had been that he should raise the siege immediately. For the story of the siege, see Fowler, *King's Lieutenant*, pp. 161–5.

43. *Cardinalis Rothomag' consiliarius regis Francie.* Postmodum in uigilia Natiuitatis Sancti Iohannis Baptiste, circa solis occasum, apud Douorr' applicuit dominus Petrus, nuper archiepiscopus Rothomag', cancellarius Francie et principalis consiliarius dicti regis Francie, presbiter*a* cardinalis *b*tituli basilice Sanctorum Duodecim Apostolorum nouiter creatus.*b* Et cum eo uenerunt ad Angliam dominus*c* archiepiscopus Senonen', comes de Tankeruille, germanus eius, et comes de Vendoyne, regni Francie captiuati.[111] Et uolebat idem cardinalis latenter cum dicto rege Francie habuisse tractatum; transiuit per aquam uersus Saueye, dimittens famulam suam per ciuitatem Londonien' transire, sed in aduentu suo ibidem non habuit liberum colloquium ut uolebat cum rege Francie antedicto.*d*

44. *De aduentu cardinalium in Angliam.* Die autem Mercurii in uigilia Apostolorum Petri et Pauli, dominus Talairandus, episcopus Albanen', intrauit ciuitatem Cantuarien' et fuit hospitatus in abbatia Sancti Augustini Cantuari', et die Iouis in festo Apostolorum Petri et Pauli uersus London' arripuit iter suum. Die uero Sabbati prima die Iulii, dominus Nicolaus tituli*e* Sancti Vitalis presbiter cardinalis uenit de Douor' Cant', et illo eodem die*f* recessit uersus London' festinanter.[112] Et ambo cardinales predicti tercio die dicti*g* mensis Iulii intrarunt*h* ciuitatem London'. Quibus dominus princeps Wallie cum magna multitudine ciuium London' et dominus Symon,*i* Cant' archiepiscopus, et alii domini solempniter obuiam dederunt, sed dicti cardinales nolebant permittere dictum*j* Cant' archiepiscopum crucem suam in eorum presencia baiulare. Dictique cardinales cum honore ciuitatem London' intrauerunt, et dictus dominus Petragoricen' in manso*k* Lincolnien' episcopi, et idem dominus Nicolaus cardinalis in manso*l* Cicestren' episcopi, London' hospitati fuerunt.[113] Deinde, exposita per eos causa aduentus eorum ad Angliam domino regi Anglie, ipse eos benigne audiuit et deliberauit super responsione eis danda. Et habitis multis tractatibus pacis, et multis et uariis hinc inde

---

a om. *J*   *b–b* om. *J*   *c* domini *J*   *d* om. *J*   *e* ecclesie *J*   *f* om. *J*
g om. *J*   *h* intrauerunt *J*   *i* om. *J*   *j* dominum *J*   *k* mansio *J*   *l* mansio *J*

---

[111] The 'cardinal of Rouen' was Pierre de la Forêt, former archbishop of Rouen, who had been chancellor to King Jean before his elevation to cardinal in 1356; for his visit to England (safe-conduct dated 15 June 1357), see W. E. Lunt, *Financial Relations of the Papacy with England, 1327–1534* (Cambridge, Mass., 1962), p. 656. Unlike the other two cardinals mentioned below, he came to England not as a papal legate but as one of the French ambassadors, along with Guillaume de Melun, archbishop of Sens, Jean de Melun, count of Tancarville, and Bouchard VI, count of Vendôme. For the two cardinals, see n. 104 above.

43. *The cardinal of Rouen, counsellor of the king of France.* Thereafter, on the vigil of the Nativity of St John the Baptist ⟨23 June⟩, around sunset, lord Peter, previously archbishop of Rouen, chancellor of France and principal councillor of the said king of France, newly created titular cardinal-priest of the Basilica of the Twelve Apostles, landed at Dover. With him to England came the lord archbishop of Sens, his brother the count of Tancarville, and the count of Vendôme, French captives.[111] The cardinal, wanting to hold secret discussions with the said king of France, travelled by river to the Savoy, directing his retinue to pass through the city of London, but on his arrival there he was not able to converse freely with the aforesaid king of France as he had wished.

44. *The arrival of cardinals in England.* On Wednesday, the vigil of the Apostles Peter and Paul ⟨28 June⟩, lord Talleyrand, bishop of Albano, entered the city of Canterbury and lodged in the abbey of St Augustine at Canterbury, and on Thursday, the feast of the Apostles Peter and Paul ⟨29 June⟩, he continued his journey towards London. On Saturday the first day of July, lord Nicholas, titular cardinal-priest of St Vitalis came from Dover to Canterbury, and left again on the same day, hastening towards London.[112] And the two aforementioned cardinals entered the city of London on the third day of the said month of July. The lord prince of Wales with a great multitude of London citizens and lord Simon, archbishop of Canterbury, and other lords came out to meet them formally, but the said cardinals would not allow the said archbishop of Canterbury to bear his cross in their presence. The said cardinals entered the city of London with honour; and in London the said lord of Périgord lodged in the residence of the bishop of Lincoln, and lord cardinal Nicholas in the residence of the bishop of Chichester.[113] Then, when they had explained the reason for their coming to England to the lord king of England, he graciously listened to them and considered what answer should be given to them. And after many peace negotiations

---

[112] Safe-conducts were issued to the two cardinals to enter England on 1 June 1357. The same two cardinals had attempted to reconcile the Black Prince and the French king on the eve of the battle of Poitiers, and it was in their names that the truce of 23 March 1357 had been proclaimed at Bordeaux: Bériac-Lainé and Given-Wilson, *Les Prisonniers de la Bataille de Poitiers*, pp. 36–9, 101; *Foedera*, iii (1), pp. 348, 357.

[113] The English prelates mentioned here were Simon Islip, archbishop of Canterbury 1349–66; John Gynwell, bishop of Lincoln 1347–62; and Robert Stratford, bishop of Chichester 1337–62.

petitis, nichil efficaciter erat factum. Postmodum, die Martis proximo ante festum Sancti Laurencii, dicti duo cardinales, uidelicet Petragoricen' et Vrgelen', comederunt*a* cum rege Anglie apud Westm', et ipse fecit eis magnum conuiuium tunc ibidem.*b*

45. *De anno Domini millesimo trecentisimo quinquagesimo septimo.*[114] *Dispensaciones cardinalium.* Et habuerunt dicti cardinales septendecim gracias, uidelicet conferendi beneficia uacatura et alias dispensaciones, a domino Innocencio tunc papa. **Et dicti cardinales habuerunt a clero

fo. 257ᵛ regni Anglie quattuor denarios de marca | pro procuracionibus suis in Anglia.[115] Et ipsi cardinales contulerunt beneficia ecclesiastica uacancia taxacionis septem marcarum dumtaxat, et dispensarunt super defectu natalium cum centum personis de soluto genitis et soluta,[116] et cum octoginta matrimonialiter coniunctis in tercio et quarto consanguinitatis et affinitatis gradibus ignoranter; et cum sacerdotibus matrimonia clandestina et prohibita celebrantibus; et super uiolenta manuum inieccione*d* in clericos, citra mortem uel mutilacionem membrorum, et super aliis multis causis, iuxta priuilegia apud eis indulta.

46. Et dicti cardinales tractarunt tam cum consilio regis Francie quam cum consilio regis Anglie, pro reformacione pacis inter eos, pro qua fuerant ad Angliam destinati. Cum autem dominus Iohannis rex Francie a die Mercurii, uidelicet uicesima quarta mensis Maii anno Domini millesimo trecentisimo quinquagesimo septimo usque ad diem Lune, uidelicet duodeuicesimum diem mensis Septembris, per sedecim ebdomadas et quatuor dies apud Saueye, in hospicio domini Henrici ducis Lancastrie, apud London' continue remansisset, et interim inter dictos reges per cardinales eosdem habitis multis tractatibus pacis et finalis concordie; *^e*et quia ipsi*f* reges de certa uia pacis habenda*g* non poterant concordare adinuicem;*h* idem rex *i*Francie cum aliis captiuatis regni Francie*i* missus fuit ad castrum de

---

a comedere *J*   *b* *J breaks off*   *c* *M resumes* Et postea uenerunt duo cardinales ad tractandum de pace et habuerunt .iiii. denarios de marca; *M breaks off*   *d* *marg.* C   *e* *M resumes*   *f* *add.* duo *M*   *g* *om. M*   *h* *om. M*   *i-i* *om. M*

---

[114] These words, placed in the top margin of fo. 257v, just above this point, in fact occur in the middle of the chronicler's annal for 1357, which began with 'The arrival of the king of France in London' (above, p. 34).

[115] For the dispensations granted to the two cardinals by Innocent VI, see *Calendar of Entries in the Papal Registers Relating to Great Britain and Ireland*, ed. W. H. Bliss *et al.* (10 vols., London, 1893–1915), iii (1342–62), 580–1, 624–5. They included the power to

had been held, and many different requests had been made on the subject, nothing of any consequence was done. Subsequently, on the Tuesday before the feast of St Laurence ⟨8 August⟩, the said two cardinals, namely of Périgord and of Urgel, dined with the king of England at Westminster, and he entertained them there very lavishly on that occasion.

45. *The year of Our Lord 1357.*[114] *The dispensations of the cardinals.* And the said cardinals had seventeen graces, namely, for conferring benefices falling vacant and other dispensations, from the lord Innocent then pope. And these cardinals received from the clergy of the kingdom of England 4 pence in the mark for their expenses in England.[115] And the same cardinals conferred vacant ecclesiastical benefices assessed for taxation at no more than 7 marks, and they granted dispensations from illegitimacy to a hundred persons begotten of man and woman,[116] and to eighty persons unwittingly joined in marriage within the third and fourth degrees of consanguinity and affinity, and to priests celebrating clandestine and forbidden marriages, and concerning the violent casting of hands on clergymen, short of death or mutilation of limbs, and concerning many other issues, in accordance with the privileges granted to their discretion.

46. And the said cardinals conducted negotiations both with the council of the king of France and with the council of the king of England, to make peace between them, for which purpose they had been sent to England. However, when lord John king of France had been staying in London at the Savoy, the residence of lord Henry duke of Lancaster, continuously for sixteen weeks and four days, from Wednesday the twenty-fourth day of the month of May to Monday the eighteenth day of September in the year of Our Lord 1357, and during that time many negotiations for peace and final concord had taken place between the said kings through the cardinals, and because the said kings had not been able to come to any agreement on secure terms of peace satisfactory to both sides, then the king of France with the other captives from the realm of France

appoint notaries and to allow persons to choose confessors. The cardinals twice raised procurations of 4 pence in the mark from the spiritualities and temporalities of the English church, both within three months of their arrival (Lunt, *Financial Relations 1327–1534*, pp. 651–5; and, for the unfavourable comments of one chronicler, see *Knighton's Chronicle*, pp. 152, 158).

[116] That is, to allow such persons to take holy orders, from which their illegitimacy would normally bar them.

Wyndesore, ibidem sub custodia moraturus.[a] [117] Et cum dicto rege Francie, ut premittitur, missi fuerunt apud Wyndesore dominus Philippus, filius dicti regis iunior, comes de Vendoyne, comes de Iugny, comes d'Aunsoir et comes Daumartyn, ut premittitur, captiuati. Et dominus Iacobus de Burboun apud Rokyngham, et comes de Tankeruille apud Norwicum, et comes de Ew et frater eius ad castrum de Marleburgh; et comes de Ventadour ad ciuitatem Eboracen', et comes d'Aunsoir ad turrim London', et comes de Salebrug' ad castrum de Notyngham, et marescallus d'Audenham ad castrum de Gloucestre, et dominus Deryual ad castrum Wynton', et dominus de Craon ad castrum de Deuyses, et dominus d'Aubeneye[b] ad uillam Northamptoun missi fuerunt, sub salua custodia moraturi.[118] Post hec autem, multis et uariis tractatibus pacis inter dictos reges et regna habitis, procurantibus cardinalibus antedictis, nulla uia pacis ad utriusque regni honorem potuerat inuenire, dicto rege Francie apud Wyndesore interim reman⟨en⟩te.[c]

47. *De rotunda tabula.*[d] Item, [e]anno Domini[f] millesimo trecentisimo quinquagesimo octauo, in festo Sancti Georgii Martiris,[g] dominus Edwardus rex Anglie[h] fecit [i]fieri solempne[i] conuiuium [j]ac etiam
fol. 258r rotundam tabulam[j] | quod[k] a tempore regis[l] Arthuri [m]nusquam in regno Anglie actum erat,[m] in quo [n]quidem conuiuio siue rotunda tabula[n] erant [o]dicti duo Francorum et Anglorum reges,[o] et tres regine, uidelicet [p]domina Isabella[p] mater dicti[q] regis Anglie, domina[r] Philippa [s]tunc regina Anglie,[s] et domina Iohanna regina Scocie, [t]soror[u] dicti regis Anglie,[t] [119] et [v]quasi tocius Anglie proceres et magnates.[v]

[a] *M breaks off* [b] d'Aubeneye *edd.*; de Daubeneye *C* [c] remanente *edd.*; remante *C* [d] *heading in top marg., fo. 258r* De rotunda tabula *C* [e] *M resumes* [f] *om. M* [g] *om. M* [h] *add.* magnum *M* [i–i] *om. M* [j–j] de rotunda tabula *M* [k] *om. M* [l] *om. M* [m–m] non fuit factum *M* [n–n] *om. M* [o–o] illi duo reges Anglie et Francie *M* [p–p] regina Anglie *M* [q] *om. M* [r] et *M* [s–s] uxor eius *M* [t–t] *om. M* [u] soror *edd.;* sorore *C* [v–v] *om. M*

[117] King Jean probably did not remain at Windsor for long after 18 September; he spent most of the first two years of his captivity at the Savoy, before being moved to Hertford in April 1359, to Somerton in Lincolnshire in August 1359, and back to London in March 1360: Bériac-Lainé and Given-Wilson, *Les Prisonniers de la Bataille de Poitiers*, pp. 133–41.

[118] The prisoners mentioned here had all been captured either at Poitiers itself or at the skirmishes at Romorantin and La Chaboterie which preceded the battle. They were as follows: Philippe de France 'le Hardi', youngest son of the French king, count of Touraine and future duke of Burgundy; Bouchard VI, count of Vendôme; Jean de Noyers, count of Joigny; Jean III de Chalon, count of Auxerre; Charles de Trie, count of Dammartin;

was sent to Windsor castle, there to remain in custody.[117] Also sent to Windsor with the said king of France, as noted above, were the lord Philip his younger son, the count of Vendôme, the count of Joigny, the count of Auxerre, and the count of Dammartin, captives, as before mentioned. And lord James of Bourbon was sent to Rockingham, the count of Tancarville to Norwich, the count of Eu and his brother to Marlborough castle, the count of Ventadour to the city of York, the count of Auxerre to the Tower of London, the count of Saarbrücken to Nottingham castle, marshal d'Audrehem to Gloucester castle, lord Derval to Winchester castle, the lord of Craon to Devizes castle, and lord d'Aubigny to the town of Northampton, there to remain in safe custody.[118] After this, many and various peace negotiations were held between the said kings and kingdoms through the aforementioned cardinals as negotiators, but no way to a peace honourable to both kingdoms could be found; during this time the king of France stayed at Windsor.

47. *The round table.* Also, in the year of Our Lord 1358, on the feast of St George the martyr ⟨23 April⟩, Lord Edward king of England held a solemn banquet and round table such as had never been held in England since the time of King Arthur, at which banquet or round table there were present the said two kings, of the French and the English, and three queens, namely, Lady Isabella, mother of the said king of England, Lady Philippa, then queen of England, and Lady Joan, queen of Scotland, sister of the said king of England,[119] as well as virtually all the nobility and magnates of England.

Jacques de Bourbon, count of Ponthieu; Jean de Melun, count of Tancarville; Jean d'Artois, count of Eu; his brother Charles d'Artois, count of Longueville; Bernard, count of Ventadour; Jean II, count of Saarbrücken; Arnoul d'Audrehem, marshal of France; Bonnabé IV de Rougé, lord of Derval; Amaury IV, lord of Craon; and Renaud, lord of Aubigny. The chronicler appears to repeat the name of the count of Auxerre ('Daunsoir'); one of these may be an error for Jean III de Nevers, count of Sancerre, another of the French captives. This passage adds significantly to what is known of the treatment of the French prisoners during their period of captivity in England from 1357 to 1360, suggesting as it does that they were dispersed to different strongholds as early as the autumn of 1357. Previously, it had been thought that this dispersal only took place in March 1360. On the other hand, the captive French lords certainly did not remain incarcerated in their respective castles throughout the next three years, and many of them were permitted to cross to France on parole during this period in order to raise their ransoms or take part in the continuing negotiations for peace: Bériac-Lainé and Given-Wilson, *Les Prisonniers de la Bataille de Poitiers*, pp. 133–55, 397–400.

[119] Isabella of France, widow of Edward II, whom she had married in 1308; Philippa of Hainault, who had married Edward III in 1328; and Joan 'of the Tower', who had married David II of Scotland in 1328.

48. De hastiludiis Wyndesore. ^aFecitque idem rex Anglie comitum, baronum, magnatum et quasi tocius milicie Anglicane ibidem fieri^a hastiludia inaudita,^b ad que ueniebant^c dux Brabancie et multi magnates de diuersis nacionibus^d undequaque; duraruntque dicta hastiludia per duos dies, in quibus dominus Henricus dux Lancastrie per infortunium erat lesus, sed penes Anglicos uictoria huius hastiludii ex toto remansit.[120]

49. Tractatus pacis. ^ePost hec uero,^f die Martis in rogacionibus, uidelicet septimo^g die Maii anno Domini millesimo trecentisimo quinquagesimo octauo,[121] apud Wyndesore, presentibus tunc ibidem domino Willelmo,^h episcopo Wynton', tunc Anglie cancellario, domino Edwardo, principe Wallie, ac comitibus Arondellie et Warewyk et aliis de priuato consilio regis Anglie,[122] inter dictos dominos Francorum et Anglorum reges tractatu pacis habito, tandem dicti reges ⁱadinuicem osculati fuerantⁱ sub certa forma pacis hinc inde ut sequitur obtinende:[123] uidelicet, quod idem rex Anglie totam Vasconiam,^j Aquitaniam et^k Agenen', necnon uillam de Rochel, sine homagio, tributo uel seruicio alicui faciendis, pro se et heredibus suis imperpetuum, haberet libere^l et teneret, ac etiam uillam de Caleys, de Gisnes et quedam loca alia per ipsum alias^m equitata; quodque pax huiusmodi per dominum papam, magnates, proceres utriusque regni ⁿcum omni securitate que fieri potuit firmaretur; quodque idem rex Francie, antequam exiret Angliam, daret sufficientes obsides regniⁿ Francie ad obseruandum premissa; et preter hec sua redempcione octo miliones florenorum scutorum regi^o Anglie solueret; et sic terram Francie in pace teneret. Cui quidem tractatui^o pacis Francigene noluerant consentire, prorogando de

^{a–a} ibi fuerunt M   ^b om. M   ^c uenit M   ^d M breaks off   ^e J resumes   ^f om. J   ^g octauo J   ^h om. J   ^{i–i} osculati fuerunt adinuicem J   ^j add. et J   ^k add. etiam J   ^l om. J   ^m om. J   ^{n–n} om. J   ^o regni J   ^p tractatu J

[120] The St George's Day jousts of 1358 were widely reported in the chronicles, with general agreement that they were unusually splendid. The author of the *Eulogium Historiarum* said that Lancaster was wounded in the leg or shin ('in crure'), but Thomas Gray in his *Scalacronica* said that 'as he jousted with a knight, another struck across him, hitting him in the side with his lance very dangerously, but he recovered'. John of Reading, however, stated that his ability henceforth to perform feats of arms was diminished by his wound: Gray, *Scalachronica*, p. 151; *Eulogium Historiarum*, iii. 227; *Chronica Johannis de Reading et Anonymi Cantuariensis*, p. 130; cf. *Knighton's Chronicle*, p. 158.

[121] Rogation Tuesday in fact fell on 8 May in 1358.

[122] The lords mentioned here were William Edington, bishop of Winchester 1345–66;

48. *Jousts at Windsor.* The king of England also held unprecedented jousts there with the earls, barons, magnates, and virtually all the knights of England, to which came the duke of Brabant and many magnates from diverse nations and places; and these jousts lasted for two days, during which time Lord Henry, duke of Lancaster, was unfortunately wounded, although overall in this jousting the English were victorious.[120]

49. *A treaty of peace.* After this, on the Tuesday in Rogationtide, namely the seventh day of May in the year of Our Lord 1358,[121] at Windsor, in the presence there of Lord William, bishop of Winchester, then chancellor of England, Lord Edward, prince of Wales, and the earls of Arundel and Warwick and others of the privy council of the king of England,[122] a treaty of peace having been agreed between the aforesaid two lord kings of the French and the English, the said kings kissed each other under the terms of the peace, which were as follows.[123] Namely, that the said king of England should freely have and hold in perpetuity, for himself and his heirs, the whole of Gascony, Aquitaine, and the Agenais, together with the town of La Rochelle, without performing homage, tribute, or service to anybody, and also the towns of Calais and Guines and certain other places elsewhere which he claimed; and that this peace was to be confirmed by the lord pope and by the magnates and nobles of each kingdom with every possible safeguard; and that the said king of France, before leaving England, should hand over a sufficient number of hostages from the kingdom of France to ensure compliance with these undertakings; and, furthermore, that he would pay for his ransom eight million florins of the shield to the king of England; then he could hold his land of France in peace. The French, however, would not agree to this treaty of peace, and, together with the cardinals who were in

Richard Fitzalan, earl of Arundel 1330–76; and Thomas Beauchamp, earl of Warwick 1329–69.

[123] This account of the terms of the so-called 'First Treaty of London' of 8 May 1358 is one of the most important pieces of evidence that we have concerning the treaty, the full text of which has not survived. For what is apparently a draft of the treaty, see Rogers, *Wars of Edward III*, pp. 170–1. Broadly speaking, the chronicler reported the main terms of the treaty quite accurately, although he doubled the size of the French king's ransom from four to eight million florins. (These were presumably 'florins d'or à l'écu', or 'écus d'or', 6 of which were reckoned as equivalent to one pound sterling.) For the evidence concerning the treaty and the significance of the evidence of this chronicle, see J. Le Patourel, 'The Treaty of Brétigny, 1360', *Transactions of the Royal Historical Society*, 5th ser., x (1960), 19–39; and C. Rogers, 'The Anglo-French Peace Negotiations of 1354–1360 Reconsidered', in J. S. Bothwell, ed., *The Age of Edward III* (Woodbridge, 2001), pp. 193–213.

diebus in dies, una cum cardinalibus tunc London' existentibus, stabilimentum pacis huiusmodi ordinate.*[124]

50. *De strage in Francia.* Pendente uero dicto tractatu pacis, inscio domino rege Anglie, multi uiri bellicosi de Anglia et alii regnum Francie manu armata hostiliter inuadentes, strages ⟨et⟩[b] depreda-ciones in ciuitate Paris' et alibi in regno Francorum fecerunt, sibique uillas et opida subiugarunt, et circumquaque ceperunt multa mala et dampna facientes ibidem.[125]

51. *Recessus cardinalium ab Anglia.* Post hec dominus Tailerandus, cardinalis Petragoricen', die Sancti Firmini Episcopi anno Domini millesimo trecentisimo quinquagesimo octauo, et dominus Nicholas, cardinalis Vrgelen', die Sanctarum Vndecim Milia Virginum dicto anno, a rege Anglie licenciati, uersus Romanam curiam ab Anglia recesserunt, cum treuga inter Francorum et Anglorum regna usque ad festum Natiuitatis Sancti Iohannis Baptiste tunc finaliter pro-rogata. Sed quo ad pacem aliquam, pro quo uenerant, nichil aliud dicti fecerunt cardinales in regno Anglie supradicto.[126]

fo. 258ᵛ **52.** *De morte regine.* ᶜAnno Domini millesimo trecentisimo quinqua-gesimo octauo,ᵈ die Mercurii in octauis Assumpcionis Beate Marie, circiter horam primam dicti diei, apud Hertfort, domina Isabella, nuper regina Anglie, mater domini Edwardi tunc regis Anglie, obiit; statimque eius corpus secrete deportatum erat London' ad domum fratrum minorum ibidem, et ibidem in terra positum antequam exequiarum suarum solempnitas erat acta. Et ut fratres minores anime ipsius regine haberent memoriam, ipsa legauit eis mille libras sterlingorum.

53. *De exequiis ipsius.* Postmodum autem, circa festum Sancti Martini Episcopi proximo tunc futurum, dominus Edwardus rex Anglie ipsius matris sue solempnitatem exequiarum fecit fieri cum pontifi-cibus, abbatibus et prioribus regni Anglie ac toto clero eiusdem, una

---

ᵃ *add.* quarto die Iunii *J; J breaks off*   ᵇ *et* edd.; *om.* C   ᶜ *M resumes, and condenses this paragraph:* Eodem anno obiit Isabella regina Anglie et apud fratres minores Lond' est sepulta et eis legauit mille libras ad rogandum pro ea; *M breaks off*   ᵈ *marg. sketch of coifed and crowned woman's head* C

---

[124] In fact there still seem to have been hopes as late as November 1358 that the treaty might be implemented, but the failure of the French to produce the first instalment of their king's ransom, due on 1 November, determined Edward III to prepare for war again (for references, see the previous note).

[125] These were the 'routiers' who would shortly become known as the Great Companies,

London at that time, kept on from day to day putting off confirmation of the peace thus properly agreed.[124]

50. *Massacre in France.* While the peace treaty was pending, and without the knowledge of the king of England, many warlike Englishmen and others invaded the kingdom of France with an armed force in hostile fashion, committing massacres and depredations in the city of Paris and elsewhere in the French kingdom, subjugating towns and cities and perpetrating evil acts and causing damage on all sides there.[125]

51. *The departure of the cardinals from England.* After this, Lord Talleyrand, cardinal of Périgord, on the feast of St Firmin the bishop ⟨25 September⟩ in the year of Our Lord 1358, and Lord Nicholas, cardinal of Urgel, on the feast of the Eleven Thousand Holy Virgins ⟨21 October⟩ in the same year, left England, with the permission of the king of England, and returned to the Roman court, with the truce between the French and English kingdoms eventually having been extended until the feast of the Nativity of St John the Baptist ⟨24 June 1359⟩. But as to any peace, which was the reason why they had come, the said cardinals achieved nothing else in the aforesaid kingdom of England.[126]

52. *The death of the queen.* In the year of Our Lord 1358, on the Wednesday in the octave of the Assumption of the Blessed Virgin Mary ⟨22 August⟩ around the hour of prime, Lady Isabella, former queen of England and mother of Lord Edward then king of England, died at Hertford; and her body was immediately taken secretly to London to the house of the Franciscans and buried there, before her solemn exequies had taken place. And she left one thousand pounds sterling to the Franciscans so that they would remember her soul.

53. *Her exequies.* Following this, around the feast of St Martin the bishop ⟨11 November⟩, Lord Edward king of England had his mother's solemn exequies performed—at which the bishops, abbots, priors, and all the clergy of the kingdom of England, together

and whose depredations plagued France through the 1360s. For a detailed account of their activities, see K. Fowler, *Medieval Mercenaries*, i: *The Great Companies* (Oxford, 2001), pp. 2–4 and *passim*.

[126] The cardinals had spent some fifteen months in England without achieving a settlement between the French and English sides. Royal licences for them to leave the realm were issued on 10 September; another source says that the cardinal of Périgord left on 22 September: *Foedera*, iii (1), pp. 406–7, 413.

cum fratribus mendicantibus London' in magna multitudine congregatis, et prima die in prioratu Sancte Trinitatis London', secundaque die in ecclesia Sancti Pauli London', et tercia die in domo fratrum minorum London', cum processionibus solempnibus per Chepe London' factis, ad honorem corporis dicte matris.[127]

54. *De maritagio inter comitem Richemond et filiam ducis Lancastrie.* Post hec autem, die Dominica in festo Sancti Dunstani Episocopi anno Domini millesimo trecentisimo quinquagesimo nono, apud Radynge, dominus Robertus, Sar' episcopus, matrimonium inter dominum Iohannem de Gaunt, comitem Richemond, et dominam Blanchiam, filiam ducis Lancastrie, attingentes se in quarto consanguinitatis gradu, ex dispencacione sedis apostolice, celebrauit, et in crastino nupciarum hicque, primo apud Radinge et deinde London', hastiludia magna fiebant in memoriam premissorum.[128]

55. *De rege Francie incarcerato.* [a]Eodem autem[b] anno, dominus[c] rex Anglie, finitis treugis inter [d]Francie et Anglie[d] regna [e]initis, dominum Iohannem[e] regem Francorum cum filio suo captiuato[f] ac[g] paucis familiaribus suis[h] apud castrum de Somertoun in partibus[i] Lincoln' destinauit, [j]moraturum ibidem ad tempus.[j] Et fecit [k]London' et alibi publice[k] proclamari quod omnes Francigene alii[l] absque arcubus, sagittis[m] et armis, sub pena capitis plectendi, regnum Anglie exirent, [n]quodque parati essent Douor' uel alibi ad transfretandum die Sancti Iacobi Apostoli proximo tunc futuro;[n] quod [o]et ita factum est.[o] [129]

56. *De aduentu prouisorum.* [p]Deinde uero idem rex Anglie, pro recuperacione iuris sui uersus partes Francie se dirigens, misit seruitores suos in Canciam ad faciendum suam prouidenciam et exercitus sui, sicut per consilium extitit ordinatum. Erantque in Cancia dicti prouisores per totum autumpnum, capientes de

[a] *M resumes*   [b] *om. M*   [c] *om. M*   [d–d] duo *M*   [e–e] *om. M*   [f] *om. M*   [g] et *M*   [h] *om. M*   [i] *om. M*   [j–j] *om. M*   [k–k] rex *M*   [l] *om. M*   [m] *om. M*   [n–n] *om. M*   [o–o] est factum est *M*   [p–p] Et rex Anglie se transtulit uersus Franc' et incepit nauigare apud Sandwy' *M*

---

[127] Although the *Oxford DNB* article on Isabella (by J. C. Parsons) states that she died on 23 August 1358, the chronicler's date of 22 August seems to be confirmed by a number of sources, including the evidence of Isabella's own final wardrobe account (London, British Library, MS Cotton Galba E. xiv, fo. 24). She was buried at the Franciscan friary at Newgate, of which she was a patron, on 27 November, with Archbishop Islip officiating (*Eulogium Historiarum*, iii. 227; and see *Foedera*, iii (1), p. 411, for orders dated 20 November to prepare the city for the arrival of her corpse).

[128] The bishop of Salisbury was Robert Wyvil (1330–75), although the actual wedding

with the mendicant friars of London, were all gathered together in great numbers—at the priory of the Holy Trinity in London on the first day, at St Paul's church in London on the second day, and in the London house of the Franciscans on the third day, with solemn processions along London's Cheapside in honour of his said mother's corpse.[127]

54. *The marriage between the earl of Richmond and the daughter of the duke of Lancaster.* After this, on Sunday the feast of St Dunstan the bishop ⟨19 May⟩ in the year of Our Lord 1359, at Reading, Lord Robert, bishop of Salisbury, by dispensation of the papal see, officiated at the marriage between Lord John of Gaunt, earl of Richmond, and Lady Blanche, daughter of the duke of Lancaster, who were related to each other in the fourth degree of consanguinity; and on the day after the wedding great tournaments were held to commemorate these events, first at Reading and subsequently in London.[128]

55. *The king of France imprisoned.* In this same year, after the truce arranged between the kingdoms of France and England had expired, the lord king of England had Lord John, king of the French, together with his captive son and a few members of his household, sent to Somerton castle in Lincolnshire, to remain there for the time being. And he had it publicly proclaimed in London and elsewhere that all other Frenchmen, under pain of capital punishment, should quit the kingdom of England, leaving behind their bows, arrows, and arms, and that they should be ready to cross from Dover or elsewhere on the feast of St James the Apostle next following ⟨25 July⟩; and this is what happened.[129]

56. *The arrival of purveyors.* Then the said king of England, having decided to go to France in order to recover his rights, sent his servants into Kent in order to make purveyances for himself and his army, as had been decreed by the council. And these purveyors remained in Kent throughout the whole autumn, seizing food and

ceremony, which took place on 20 May, was performed by Thomas de Chynham, clerk of the queen's chapel. The subsequent tournament in London was held on 27–9 May, at Smithfield: A. Goodman, *John of Gaunt: The Exercise of Princely Power in Fourteenth-Century Europe* (London, 1992), pp. 34–5. It was through his marriage to Blanche that Gaunt, Edward III's third surviving son, acquired his title of duke of Lancaster in 1362, following Duke Henry's death in 1361.

[129] The Anglo–French truce expired on 24 June 1359. The French king and his son Philippe reached Somerton on 4 August (see n. 117 above).

uictualibus et rebus aliis, quicquid capere poterant, undequaque,*p* *a*tantusque populus uirorum bellancium erat iuxta Sandwicum et alibi in partibus Cancie quod uix illos tota patria capere poterat,*a* tantusque exercitus ibi fuerat quod prius non erat uisus *b*ibidem. Et*b* in portu de Sandwico erant circiter mille naues*c* et nauiculi pro transitu dicti regis et exercitus sui ad transfretandum parate.

57. *De aduentu regis in Canciam.* Die autem Veneris ante festum Sancti Bartholomei Apostoli et anno Domini millesimo trecentisimo quinquagesimo nono, idem rex Anglie cum hospicio suo uenit in Canciam, et fuit hospitatus apud Thorne in Thaneto, et per uices eundo | apud Ledes, ubi regina Anglie tunc erat, et redeundo ad diuersa loca in Cancia, usque ad diem Lune in festo Apostolorum Simonis et Iude per duos menses et amplius, ad graue onus tocius patrie undequaque. Die Sancti Firmini Episcopi eodem anno, dominus Henricus, dux Lancastrie, cum suo exercitu in Franciam transfretauit; et subsequenter dominus Rogerus, comes Marchie, cum suo exercitu applicuit apud Caleys.[130]

fol. 259^r

58. *Aduentus regis apud Calais.* *d*Deinde die Lune in festo Apostolorum*e* Simonis et Iude *f*proximo tunc sequente, dominus rex Anglie cum suo exercitu naues ingrediens apud Sandwicum, et, prospero uento nauigans, eodem die*f* applicuit apud*g* Caleys, ibidem*h* per ebdomadam commorando. *i*Et die Lune sequente, uidelicet quarto die Nouembris,*i* rex*j* ordinatis aciebus *k*bellorum suorum,*k* uillam de Caleys fortiter tunc*l* exiuit.*m* [131]

59. *Exercitus Anglorum. Nomina dominorum cum rege Anglie in Franciam pro guerra proficentes:*[132]
Dominus Edwardus rex Anglie cum mille hominibus armatis et mille quadringentis sagittariis;
Dominus Edwardus princeps Wallie cum sexagentis hominibus armatis et octingentis quadraginta sagittariis;
Dominus Leonellus comes Vlnestre cum centum octoginta hominibus armatis et centum sagittariis;
Dominus Iohannes comes Richemond cum ducentis hominibus armatis et quadringentis sagittariis;

---

^{a–a} om. M   ^{b–b} quia M   ^c M breaks off   ^d M resumes   ^e om. M
^{f–f} om. M   ^g om. M   ^h et ibi M   ^{i–i} om. M   ^j add. uero M   ^{k–k} om. M
^l om. M   ^m M breaks off

---

[130] According to Fowler, *King's Lieutenant*, pp. 201–2, Lancaster arrived at Calais 'around 1 October', while Roger Mortimer, earl of March (who would die on 26 February

other things everywhere, whatever they could get hold of, and there were so many soldiers around Sandwich and in other parts of Kent that the whole area could hardly contain them, for no army of such magnitude had ever been seen there before. And in the port of Sandwich there were around a thousand ships and small boats waiting to make the crossing in order to transport the king and his army.

57 *The arrival in Kent of the king.* The king of England himself arrived in Kent with his household on the Friday before the feast of St Bartholomew the Apostle ⟨23 August⟩ in the year of Our Lord 1359, and he stayed at Thorne in Thanet, coming and going on occasion to Leeds, where the queen of England was at the time, and to various other places in Kent, for two months and more, until Monday the feast of the Apostles Simon and Jude ⟨28 October⟩, which was a great burden on the whole area round about. On the feast of St Firmin the bishop ⟨25 September⟩ in the same year, Lord Henry, duke of Lancaster, crossed with his army to France, and subsequently Lord Roger, earl of March, landed with his army at Calais.[130]

58. *The arrival of the king at Calais.* Then on Monday the feast of the Apostles Simon and Jude next following ⟨28 October⟩, the lord king of England embarked with his army at Sandwich and, sailing with a favourable wind, landed that same day at Calais, where he stayed for a week. And on the Monday following, namely the fourth day of November, having drawn up his troops in battle order, the king set forth in might from Calais.[131]

59. *The army of the English. The names of the lords who set out with the king of England for war in France.*[132]
Lord Edward king of England with 1,000 men-at-arms and 1,400 archers;
Lord Edward prince of Wales with 600 men-at-arms and 840 archers;
Lord Lionel earl of Ulster with 180 men-at-arms and 100 archers;
Lord John earl of Richmond with 200 men-at-arms and 400 archers;

1360, while the campaign was still in progress), crossed to France 'six days in advance of the king', that is, on 22 October.

[131] The chronicler's dates for Edward III's arrival at and departure from Calais at the start of the so-called 'Reims Campaign' are correct. Edward had assembled one of the largest English armies of the Hundred Years' War, the wage bill for which amounted to £133,820 (TNA: PRO E101/393/11, fos. 79–117).

[132] For a fuller list of the principal retinue leaders of Edward's army in 1359–60 and the sums paid to each of them for their wages of war, see TNA: PRO E101/393/11, fos. 3–4.

Dominus Edmundus de Langele cum sexaginta hominibus armatis et octoginta sagittariis;

Dominus Iohannes dux Britannie cum quindecim hominibus armatis et quadraginta sagittariis;

Dominus Henricus dux Lancastrie cum quindecim milibus hominibus bellicosis;

Dominus Willelmus comes Northamptoun, constabularius Anglie, cum centum hominibus armatis et centum uiginti sagittariis;

Dominus Rogerus comes Marchie, marescallus Anglie, cum trecentis quinquaginta hominibus armatis et sexcentis sagittariis;

Dominus Thomas comes Warewyk cum centum quadraginta hominibus armatis et centum sexaginta sagittariis;

Dominus Robertus comes Suffolk cum trecentis uiginti lanceis ⟨et⟩*ᵃ* trecentis sexaginta sagittariis;

Dominus Willelmus comes Sar' cum nonaginta hominibus armatis et centum sagittariis;

Dominus Radulphus comes Stafford cum ducentis lanceis et quadringentis sagittariis;

Dominus Guido Brian, senescallus regis, cum quadraginta hominibus armatis et octoginta sagittariis;

Dominus Iohannes Cherletoun, camerarius regis, cum decem hominibus armatis et centum decem sagittariis;

Dominus Iohannes Chandoys cum ***.*ᵇ*

Senescallus et camerarius principis;[133]

Soldarii extranei cum quindecim mille hominibus bene pugnantibus;

*ᶜ*Cariagium regis cum trecentis quadraginta lanceis et ducentis sexaginta sagittariis, et

*ᵈ*Summa totium*ᵈ* hominum armatorum, lancearum, sagittariorum et uirorum bellicosorum triginta milia trecenti quadraginta.*ᵉ* Et omnes alii magnates, barones cum milicia Anglie, sagittariis et aliis bellicosis.[134]

60. *Egressus regis de Calais.* Die Lune quarto die Nouembris anno Domini millesimo trecentisimo nono et quintagesimo, dominus Edwardus rex Anglie cum toto exercitu suo, uillam de Caleys exiens in Franciam, illa nocte in foresta de Fiens in Picardia, inter Boloun et Gisnes, pausauit; et in crastino idem dominus rex ulterius progrediens uenit ad abbatiam de Wast' ordinis Cisterciensis;[135] et

---

ᵃ et *edd.; om.* C   *ᵇ* *space for number left blank* C   *ᶜ* M *resumes* Et cariagis; *statements of king's baggage train and sum total in reverse order* M   *ᵈ⁻ᵈ* cum M   *ᵉ* M *breaks off*

Lord Edmund of Langley with sixty men-at-arms and eighty archers;

Lord John duke of Brittany with fifteen men-at-arms and forty archers;

Lord Henry duke of Lancaster with 15,000 warlike men;

Lord William earl of Northampton, constable of England, with 100 men-at-arms and 120 archers;

Lord Roger earl of March, marshal of England, with 350 men-at-arms and 600 archers;

Lord Thomas earl of Warwick with 140 men-at-arms and 160 archers;

Lord Robert earl of Suffolk with 320 lances and 360 archers;

Lord William earl of Salisbury with ninety men-at-arms and 100 archers;

Lord Ralph earl of Stafford with 200 lances and 400 archers;

Lord Guy Brian, the king's steward, with 40 men-at-arms and 80 archers;

Lord John Charlton, the king's chamberlain, with ten men-at-arms and 110 archers;

Lord John Chandos, with . . . ⟨blank⟩;

The steward and chamberlain of the prince;[133]

Foreign soldiers with 15,000 good fighting men;

The king's baggage train with 340 lances and 260 archers.

The sum total of men-at-arms, lances, archers, and fighting men was 30,340. And in addition, all the other magnates and barons with the soldiery of England, the archers, and other fighting men.[134]

60. *The king's departure from Calais.* On Monday the fourth of November in the year of Our Lord 1359, Lord Edward king of England, setting out from the town of Calais into France with his whole army, halted for the night in the forest of Fiennes in Picardy, between Boulogne and Guines; and, proceeding further the next day, the same lord king reached the Cistercian abbey of Wastine,[135] and,

---

[133] Edmund Wauncy was the Black Prince's steward, Nigel Loryng was his chamberlain: T. F. Tout, *Chapters in the Administrative History of Medieval England* (6 vols., Manchester, 1920–33), v, p. 432.

[134] In fact, the figures given above total a minimum of 38,655, which would make this the largest army ever known to have been assembled by an English king during the Middle Ages, but the figures of 15,000 'warlike men' with the duke of Lancaster and another 15,000 with the 'foreign soldiers' should be treated with scepticism. Rogers, *War Cruel and Sharp*, pp. 401–2, reckoned that Lancaster's 'combined forces can hardly have exceeded six thousand men'.

[135] Wastine abbey, a little to the east of St-Omer.

dietas suas de hinc ulterius continuans, tandem uenit ad capud aque de Somme in Francia cum exercitu suo saluo.

fo. 259ᵛ **61. *Progressus regis in Francia*.** Et ibidem rex diuisit exercitum suum in tres acies bellorum, et progrediens ulterius tandem uenit Attrebatum, et ibidem infra triduum redditum fuit sibi castrum.[136] Et rex deinde, per Chalons et loca alia transiens, demum uenit ante uillam Remen', et ibidem totus exercitus iacuit tempore Natalis Domini, et rex deprope fuerat hospitatus. Et post idem festum rex Anglie mouebat se uersus insulam de Bars et iacuit super aquam de Marles prope castrum de Vitriaco.[137] Et de hinc per Burgundiam transiens, dux Burgundie occurrit regi Anglie, soluens sibi pre manibus tributum ut in pace terram suam dimitteret per quinquennium tunc futurum.[138] Dum autem rex in Burgundia morabatur, uenerunt ad eum legati missi ex parte domini pape, uidelicet abbas Cluniacen' et alii, pro reformacione pacis inter regna Francie et Anglie, ut dicebant, et exposito negotio huiusmodi recedebant.[139] Rex uero, de Burgundia transiens, iuit per aquam de Leyre ueniens per ciuitatem Ourelianen', et per medium foreste ibidem; rex autem Anglie ante ciuitatem Paris' semper exspectando bellum cum Francis habere, sed ipsi pugnare non audebant. Miserunt tamen extra Paris' duos iuuenes creatos milites, quorum unus statim occisus per Anglicos et alius extitit captiuatus.[140] Et idem rex, de hinc transiens, uenit per Normanniam, ubi redierunt dicti legati exponentes pacis habende negocium iterato, sed adhuc nichil effectuale proficiebant in hac parte.[141]

[136] The itinerary given here for Edward III's army contains a number of inaccuracies, although it preserves the route followed by the king in its essentials. For detailed descriptions of the campaign see Delachenal, *Histoire de Charles V*, ii. 149–93; Fowler, *King's Lieutenant*, pp. 202–11; and Rogers, *War Cruel and Sharp*, pp. 402–16 (the latter two include maps). The 'headwaters of the Somme' presumably refers to St-Quentin, which was reached on 28–9 November, by which time the army had already been divided into three 'battles', headed by Edward III, the Black Prince, and the duke of Lancaster, for some three weeks, in order to facilitate the gathering of supplies. Arras was passed (by the battle led by the king) before reaching St-Quentin, not after, and no attempt was made to take it.

[137] Châlons-sur-Marne was not reached until after the siege of Reims, which lasted from 4 December until 11 January 1360. During the siege the king lodged for most of this time at the abbey of St-Basle at Verzy, some twenty kilometres to the south-east of Reims; Châlons-sur-Marne is a further twenty-five kilometres to the south-east. Vitry-la-Ville is close to the confluence of the Marne with the Moivre and the Guenelle. The 'island of Bar' is presumably the county of Bar (later the duchy, around modern Bar-le-Duc), with the people of which (according to Thomas Gray in his *Scalacronica*, p. 175) Edward III made a treaty.

[138] Edward III reached Guillon in Burgundy on 19 February (Ash Wednesday), and remained there until about 20 March, before marching west and then north to Paris. On 10 March he agreed the 'Treaty of Guillon' with representatives of the duke of Burgundy, Philippe de Rouvre (who was still a minor, having been born in 1346); the duke agreed to

continuing his daily marches onwards from there, he eventually reached the headwaters of the Somme in France with his army intact.

61. *The king's progress in France.* And there the king divided his army into three lines of battle, and proceeding further finally reached Arras, and within three days the castle was surrendered to him.[136] Then, passing through Chalons and other places, the king finally arrived before the city of Reims, and there the whole army remained during the Christmas season, while the king lodged nearby. And after this feast the king of England moved on towards the island of Bar and stayed above the water of Marles near the castle of Vitry.[137] And as the king of England was passing from there through Burgundy, the duke of Burgundy hastened to meet him, offering payment of a tribute to him, cash in hand, if he would leave his territory in peace for the next five years.[138] While the king was still in Burgundy, however, legates sent by the lord pope came to him, namely the abbot of Cluny and others, to try to make peace between the kingdoms of France and England, so they said; and when they had declared their business they departed.[139] But the king, passing on from Burgundy, moved along the river Loire and came to the city of Orléans, and through the middle of the forest there; and all the time the king of England expected to join battle with the French before the city of Paris, but they did not dare to fight; however, they did send out from Paris two young men who had been created knights, one of whom was immediately killed by the English and the other taken captive.[140] Then the king, moving on from there, entered Normandy, where the aforesaid legates returned, reiterating their proposals for making peace, but they were still unable to achieve anything in this regard.[141]

pay a ransom of 200,000 moutons (£40,000), and to support Edward as king of France should he succeed in having himself crowned at Reims, in return for a promise from Edward to leave his lands in peace for three years.

[139] André de la Roche, abbot of Cluny, and Hugues de Genève, lord of Anthon, were commissioned by Pope Innocent VI on 4 March to try to reconcile the English and French; an initial conference was held between representatives of the two sides in the leper house at Longjumeau (about twenty kilometres south of Paris) on 3 April, Good Friday, but the talks were abandoned after one day.

[140] Edward remained close to Paris, firing the suburbs and taunting the dauphin and his captains to come out and join battle, for some two weeks, from 31 March to 12 April. On 13 April he marched south-west, past Chartres, to Chateaudun, and then east to Tournoisis, about twenty kilometres from Orléans, as close as he got to the city.

[141] Although the abbot of Cluny had visited the English camp a second time on 10 April, while it was still outside Paris, serious negotiations only began again on 1 May, at the hamlet of Brétigny, just east of Chartres. The Treaty of Brétigny, which brought the first phase of the Hundred Years War to an end, was agreed on 8 May, and later ratified at Calais.

62. *De morte Rogeri comitis Marchie.* Prima autem ebdomada quadragesime, in Burgundia mortuus est dominus Rogerus comes Marchie in lecto suo, corpusque eius in Angliam delatum extitit et apud Wiggernor' sepultum.[142]

63. *De strage Francorum.* Et tunc, inter Anglicos et Francos conflictu habito, capti et deuicti fuerunt dominus Laurencius Harecourt, locum tenens ducis Normannie, dominus Iohannes Bigot marescallus, dominus Baldewinus de la Hese cum duobus fratribus suis, dominus de Brakemont et frater suus, balliuus de Caux et unus baro consanguineus suus, et dominus Willelmus de Martell'. Et ⟨preter⟩[a] dictos captiuatos, alii milites et armigeri ad numerum centum triginta tres interfecti fuerunt.[143]

64. *Capcio treuge per legatos pape.* [b]Post hec, rege Anglie apud Chartres [c]in Normannia existente,[c] per dictos[d] legatos pape [e]cum ipso rege ex una parte[e] et dalphino[f] de Vienna regente[g] regnum Francie [h]ex altera, uariis tractatibus habitis, hinc et inde, tandem condescendebant[h] in [i]unam certam formam[i] pacis, [j]et apud Sourse, ante uillam de Chartres, capte fuerunt treuge usque ad certum terminum durature et tam in regnis Francie quam Anglie solempniter proclamate; et statim super reformacione pacis huiusmodi, interuenientibus dictis legatis,[j] quibusdam articulis pacis deliberate conceptis et in scriptis redactis.[144] Idem dalphinus de Vienna [k]primo et principaliter, in presencia domini principis Wallie in ciuitate Paris',[k] iurauit [l]super corpus Christi, ibidem consecratum, et[l] super sancta Dei euangelia, dictos[m] articulos [n]pacis quatenus ad se attinent in omnibus et per omnia[n] obseruare [o]et facere obseruari,[o] unde tam tota ciuitas Paris' quam incole Francie ingenti gaudio exultabant.[145]

[a] preter *edd.; om.* C   [b] M *resumes, preceded by* Et sic processit in Franciam et quotquot ei resistebant iugulauit   [c-c] existente in Normannia M   [d] *om.* M   [e-e] *om.* M   [f] delphinum M   [g] tunc regentem M   [h-h] concordatum est M; *last word* condenscebant C   [i-i] una certa forma M   [j-j] *om.* M   [k-k] *om.* M   [l-l] *om.* M   [m] eos M   [n-n] *om.* M   [o-o] *om.* M

---

[142] Roger Mortimer, earl of March, died on 26 or 27 February, apparently after having been wounded in a foraging raid at Rouvray (Delachenal, *Histoire de Charles V*, ii. 165 n. 2; Fowler, *King's Lieutenant*, p. 20), although it is possible, as the chronicler implies, that he died of natural causes; Thomas Gray, *Scalacronica*, p. 175, said that he died of a fever; his death was at any rate very sudden. Wigmore in Herefordshire was the principal seat of the Mortimer family in the Welsh March. The Wigmore Chronicle (printed in Taylor, *English Historical Literature*, p. 290) gives his date of death as 'IV kalendas marcii', which, since this was a leap year, should have indicated 27 February.

[143] This skirmish took place at Faveril, near Honfleur in Normandy, probably in early March. According to Thomas Gray in his *Scalacronica*, p. 177, about 450 French soldiers

62. *The death of Roger, earl of March.* During the first week of Lent, Lord Roger earl of March died in his bed in Burgundy, and his body was taken to England and buried at Wigmore.[142]

63. *Massacre of the French.* And then, following a fight between the English and the French, Lord Laurence ⟨*recte* Louis⟩ Harcourt, lieutenant of the duke of Normandy, Lord John Bigot, Lord Baudrain de la Heuse, the marshal, along with two brothers of his, the lord of Bracquemont and his brother, the bailiff of Caux, and a nobleman who was one of his kinsmen, and Lord William de Martel were defeated and captured. And ⟨in addition to⟩ these men being taken captive, 133 other knights and men-at-arms were killed.[143]

64. *A truce established by the papal legates.* Following this, while the king of England was staying at Chartres in Normandy, various negotiations having been arranged at various places by the aforesaid papal legates between the king of England, on the one hand, and the dauphin of Vienne, regent of the kingdom of France, on the other, they finally hammered out secure terms of peace; and at Sours, outside the city of Chartres, a truce was agreed for a fixed period of time and solemnly proclaimed in the kingdoms of both France and England. Whereupon, with the aforesaid legates acting as intermediaries, certain articles of peace concerning the establishment of peace were promptly drawn up through discussion and set down in writing.[144] Then, in the city of Paris, in the presence of the lord prince of Wales, the dauphin of Vienne first and foremost swore upon the body of Christ, consecrated there, and by the holy gospels of God, that he would observe and cause to be observed the said articles of peace inasmuch as they pertained to him, in all ways and by all means; whereupon not only the whole city of Paris but the people of France too were absolutely overjoyed.[145]

and about 140 English were involved (note that 'xl' is here mistranslated as 'sixty'). Knighton said that the English were led by Sir Thomas Fogg (*Knighton's Chronicle*, 174). The French were led by Louis d'Harcourt, lieutenant general of Normandy, and le Baudrain de la Heuse, marshal of Normandy and admiral of France. Renaud de Bracquemont and Guillaume Martel were both Norman lords, but it has not been possible to identify Jean Bigot (in *Knighton's Chronicle*, pp. 175 and 568, he is identified as marshal of Normandy, but 'the marshal' in the text must refer to le Baudrain de la Heuse, who in fact held that post): Delachenal, *Histoire de Charles V*, ii. 176–9.

[144] The chronicler is referring here to the negotiations held during the first week of May which led to the Treaty of Brétigny on 8 May. Edward was staying at the time at Sours, about ten kilometres from Chartres and two from Brétigny.

[145] The dauphin (the future Charles V) swore an oath to uphold the Treaty of Brétigny on 10 May in Paris, in the presence of six English knights, although the Black Prince was

65. *Combustio uille de Wynchelse.* Dum autem rex Anglie*ᵃ* sic in Francia*ᵇ* morabatur, quidam de Francia, dominus uidelicet Iohannes de Neuille, constabularius Francie, *ᶜ*dominus de Fiens, dominus Hugo Chasteleyn, dominus Henricus de May, dominus Pepinus de Essaunts, dominus Rislardus, bastardus Flandrie, et dominus de Cay, cum quadraginta militibus et hominibus armatis*ᶜ* ad summam sex*ᵈ* milium, apud Wynchelse cum nauigio, triginta sex nauibus *ᵉ*et nauiculis,*ᵉ* die Dominica in medio*ᶠ* quadragesime, *ᵍ*uidelicet quinto decimo die Martii,*ᵍ* circa horam nonam *ʰ*dicti diei,*ʰ* applicantes latenter et transeuntes per quendam mariscum uocatum le Vothere*ⁱ* in parochia de Pecte, distantem a Wynchelse per duo miliaria et amplius, *ʲ*inter duos montes uocatos Hochknok', et sic per uillam de Iklesham incedentes, armati dictam uillam de Wynchelse in tribus aciebus hostiliter intrauerunt,*ʲ* et omnes quos*ᵏ* poterint neci*ˡ* crudeliter tradiderunt,*ᵐ* quorum nomina sunt hec:¹⁴⁶

Iohannes Vynch, mercator

Iohannes Dighere, draperus

Robertus Wikham, armiger

Iohannes Waryn, draperus

Iohannes Ewell, draperus

Iohannes Rode, pistor

Iohannes Gibbe, tannarus

Henricus Vynch, mercator

Henricus de Felde, sutor

Robertus Smyth, de Tad'

Thomas Sted, carnifex

ᵃ Franc' *M*   *ᵇ* Anglia *M*   *ᶜ⁻ᶜ* et alii *M*   *ᵈ* .vii. *M*   *ᵉ⁻ᵉ om. M*   *ᶠ om. M*   *ᵍ⁻ᵍ om. M*   *ʰ⁻ʰ om. M*   *ⁱ* Voyde *M*   *ʲ⁻ʲ om. M*   *ᵏ add.* inuenire *M*   *ˡ om. M*   *ᵐ* occiderunt *M; M breaks off*

not there; the prince's oath to abide by the treaty was sworn in the church of Notre-Dame at Louviers in Normandy on 15 May, in the presence of six French knights: Delachenal, *Histoire de Charles V*, ii. 207–10.

¹⁴⁶ Although the raid on Winchelsea on 15 March 1360 was reported in some detail by several of the chroniclers, this account includes substantially more local knowledge than any other, most notably of the terrain around Winchelsea (the 'mariscum uocatum le Vothere' must refer to the marshy land around the estuary of the western arm of the River Rother, later known as Pett marsh) and the names of the townsmen slain or captured by the French, the latter being unique to this chronicle. The raid was originally planned by Louis d'Harcourt and le Baudrain de la Heuse, apparently as an attempt to liberate the French king from his English prison, but following their capture at Faveril in early March (above, n. 143), leadership passed to Jean de Neuville, nephew and lieutenant of Arnoul

65. *The burning of the town of Winchelsea.* While the king of England remained thus in France, certain Frenchmen, namely Lord John of Neuville, the constable of France, the lord of Fiennes, Lord Hugh Chastelain, Lord Henry de May, Lord Pippin des Essars, Lord Rifflard, bastard of Flanders, and Lord de Cay, with forty knights and a total of six thousand men-at-arms, secretly landing with a fleet of thirty-six ships and small boats at Winchelsea on the Sunday in mid-Lent, that is the fifteenth of March (n.s. 1360), around the hour of noon on the same day, and traversing a marsh called the ⟨R⟩other in the parish of Pett, two miles and more from Winchelsea, then passing between two hills called Hochknock and through the town of Icklesham, descended in arms and with hostile intent in three battle lines upon the town of Winchelsea, and cruelly put to death all of those whom they could, the names of whom are as follows:[146]

John Finch, merchant

John Dyer, draper

Robert Wickham, esquire

John Warren, draper

John Ewell, draper

John Rode, baker

John Gibb, tanner

Henry Finch, merchant

Henry de Feld, cobbler

Robert Smith of Tad'

Thomas Stead, butcher

d'Audrehem, marshal of France, who had been captured at Poitiers and was in English captivity at the time. The fleet departed from le Crotoy at the mouth of the Somme at the beginning of March. Normans, Picards, Flemings, and Parisians took part: the Flemings were led by Rifflard, bastard brother of the count of Flanders, the Parisians by Pépin des Essars, who had been involved in the assassination of Étienne Marcel, leader of the revolutionary Paris estates in 1358. The count of St-Pol, Gui de Châtillon, also took part: this may be whom the chronicler meant by 'Hugh Chastelain', although he may have meant the Hue de Châtillon who was later grand master of the French crossbowmen: F. Autrand, *Charles V: Le Sage* (Paris, 1994), p. 616. Robert de Fiennes, constable of France, also took part, but it has not been possible to identify Henri de May or 'Lord de Cay'. Estimates of the number of French invaders varied, but Delachenal thought the true figure to be around 1,200 men-at-arms and 800 crossbowmen. The inhabitants of Winchelsea were apparently surprised while attending mass (15 March being a Sunday), and the English chroniclers did not stint their accounts of the violence and cruelty of the French, Walsingham even claiming that they repeatedly ravished one beautiful young woman in the church until she died of her injuries. One French source states that 160 inhabitants of Winchelsea died in the raid (*Scalacronica*, p. 179; *Historia Anglicana*, i. 287–8; Delachenal, *Histoire de Charles V*, ii. 176–82).

Stephanus Storfast, barbitonsor
Iohannes Goutherst, sutor
Thomas atte Fontes
Margir' uxor eius
Philippus, barbitonsor
Petrus Glouere, piscator
Dominus Robertus Brembre
Rector ecclesie Sancti Egidii uille de Wynchelse.[147]

66. Et alie parte *a*ad estimacionem centum uiginti*b* tunc ibidem interfecti fuerunt. Et per totum illum diem Dominicam dicti Franci apud Wynchelse morabantur, depredando, comburendo et mala que poterant faciendo, mulieres opprimendo et, non obstante tempore quadragesimali, carnes comedendo.

67. Die uero Lune in crastino, Henricum Vynch, Robertum Shipman, Ricardum Corteys, Iohannem Gibbe et Henricum Hokere de Wynchelse ad naues eorum ducentes, ipsos ibidem interfecerunt in mari, sed *c*ipsi Francigene,*c* cum spoliis ad naues suas*d* festinantes, ad estimacionem centum quadraginta *e*ibidem in mari submersi fuerunt.*e* Quibus proactis, dicti Franci qui uico remanserant leuatis uelis uersus Depe in Normannia nauigarunt, Roberto Arnold, maiore dicte uille, auxilio duorum presbitrorum ab eorum manibus liberato. Et isti Franci antequam recesserant uiginti quattuor naues et nauiculas in portu de Wynchelse combusserunt.[148]

68. *f*Quibus quidem Francorum maleficiis*g* statim per Angliam diuulgatis, timor inhabitantibus iuxta mare incussit.*f* Sed maiores London', una*h* cum priore Sancti Iohannis Ierusalem *i*London' et cum domino Iohanne de Bokyngham, clerico domini regis Anglie, ad resistendum illis manu forti in casu quo applicare in Angliam uoluerant, se audaci animo parauerunt et,*i* paratis nauibus, mare intrauerunt, *j*uersus Depe in Normannia nauigantes, ad obuiandum si

---

a M resumes   *b* M breaks off   *c–c* M resumes: alii Francorum   *d* om. M *e–e* sunt in mare obuisi M; remainder of paragraph largely illegible M   *f–f* om. M *g* marg. hand pointing C   *h* om. M   *i–i* om. M   *j–j* ad uindicandum se de illis Francis set M

---

[147] On 18 May 1359, Robert Brember was granted licence by the king, at the request of John de Scarle, late parson of the church of St Thomas, Winchelsea, to amortise to Robert,

Stephen Storfast, barber
John Goudhurst, cobbler
Thomas atte Fontes
Margery his wife
Philip the barber
Peter Glover, fisherman
Lord Robert Brember
The rector of the church of St Giles in the town of Winchelsea.[147]

66. And in addition an estimated 120 more were killed there at that time. And for the whole of that Sunday the said Frenchmen remained in Winchelsea, plundering and burning and doing whatever harm they could, ravishing women, and eating meat regardless of the fact that it was Lent.

67. On the next day, Monday, they took Henry Finch, Robert Shipman, Richard Curteis, John Gibb, and Henry Hooker from Winchelsea to their ships and killed them there in the sea, although an estimated 140 of those same Frenchmen, hurrying with booty to their ships, were themselves drowned in the sea there. Then, having perpetrated these deeds—and once Robert Arnold, mayor of the said town, had been liberated from their grasp with the help of two priests—those Frenchmen who were still there hoisted their sails and crossed to Dieppe in Normandy. Before they departed, however, these same French burnt twenty-four ships and small boats in the port of Winchelsea.[148]

68. News of these misdeeds of the French spread throughout England at once, striking fear into the inhabitants along the coast. The mayors of London, however, together with the prior of St John of Jerusalem in London and Lord John of Buckingham, a clerk of the lord king of England, in order to resist them by force if they tried to land in England, boldly got themselves ready and, having prepared some ships, set out to sea, heading for Dieppe in Normandy in order

parson of the church of St Giles, Winchelsea, a messuage adjoining the churchyard at St Giles, 'to make a manse for the stay and habitation of the parson' (*CPR 1358–61*, p. 207).

[148] Some of the English chroniclers claimed that the French escaped without loss of life, but it seems more likely that some of them were indeed killed when the townsmen and other local forces, including some led by the abbot of Battle, rallied and pursued them to their ships—although Knighton's figures of 4,000 French dead out of a total force of 20,000 are a wild exaggeration. Thomas Gray said that they lost two ships and 300 men (*Scalacronica*, p. 179; *Chronica Johannis de Reading et Anonymi Cantuariensis*, p. 279; *Knighton's Chronicle*, p. 174; *Polychronicon*, viii. 351). They in fact returned to Boulogne rather than Dieppe.

possent dictis Francorum malefactoribus et ad pugnandum hostiliter cum eisdem. Et cum ipsi de Anglia apud Witsand, Depe et alibi in Francia et Normannia ac locis ibidem maritimis maleficiis factis per illos de Francia apud Wynchelse recompensando pro uiribus obuiasse et mala que poterant peregisse,^j superuenit eis mandatum domini regis Anglie propter treugas captas de supersedendo contra Francos omnino.^{a 149}

fo. 260^v **69.** *Aduentus regis in Angliam.* Dum hec ^bin Anglia fierent,^{b c}conceptis et formatis^c articulis^d pacis ^einter Francie et Anglie regna et in scriptis autenticis deliberate redactis,^e rex Anglie uersus^f Angliam^g se disposuit, et die Lune in uigilia Sancti Dunstani apud Rye, ut uideret que mala fiebant apud Wynchelse dum sic in regno Francie morabatur, applicuit, et per totam illam noctem uersus London' equitando, die Martis in festo Sancti Dunstani anno Domini millesimo trecentisimo sexagesimo uenit rex London',¹⁵⁰ et die Lune sequente tenuit consilium suum London' super pace huiusmodi concordata.

70. *De morte I. Wynewyk.* Deinde London', in festo Natiuitatis Beati Iohannis Baptiste proximo tunc sequente, moriebatur dominus Iohannes Wynewyk, portitor priuati sigilli regis, cui successit in officio dominus Iohannes de Bokyngham, clericus regis.¹⁵¹

71. *De morte comitis Northamptoun.* Et die Mercurii in festo Sancte Edithe Virginis eodem anno, dominus Willelmus de Boum, comes Northamptoun, apud Rocheford diem suum clausit extremum.¹⁵²

72. *Recessus regis Francorum de Anglia.* ^hQuarto die Iunii ⁱanno Domini millesimo trecentisimo sexagesimo, ^jdominus Iohannes^j rex

^a *om. M*   ^{b–b} agerentur in Anglia *M*   ^{c–c} *om. M*   ^d articule *M*   ^{e–e} future ordinate sunt et *M*   ^f uenit ad *M*   ^g *M breaks off*   ^h *marg. sketch of crowned male head C; M resumes*   ⁱ *J resumes*   ^{j–j} *om. M*

¹⁴⁹ This retaliatory English raid seems to have been organized by the chancellor, Bishop William Edington of Winchester, rather than by John Buckingham, a former keeper of the wardrobe who would in July 1360 be appointed keeper of the privy seal. About 3,000–5,000 men and 160 ships seem to have been involved, and financial contributions were received from merchants such as John Wesenham of Lynn and Henry Picard, former mayor of London, as well as through the raising of local subsidies (see n. 106 above for Picard, and n. 285 below for Wesenham). The English forces, led by John Pavely, prior of the Hospitallers (for whose appointment as admiral on 26 March see *Foedera*, iii (1), p. 479), arrived off the French coast at the end of April, seized the fortress of Leure on the north bank of the Seine estuary, and invested Harfleur, but following the cessation of hostilities agreed at Brétigny on 8 May, they were obliged to raise the siege. Edward III used this fleet

to catch up with the said French malefactors if they could and attack them. And when the men of England had done their best to avenge the evils done at Winchelsea by the French, and had done as much damage as they could in Wissant, Dieppe, and elsewhere in France and Normandy and in other places along the coast, a mandate reached them from the lord king of England to cease all action against the French because of the truce that had been negotiated.[149]

69. *The arrival of the king in England.* While these things were going on in England, and once articles of peace between the kingdoms of France and England had been composed and formulated and clearly and unambiguously set down in formal documents, the king of England set out towards England, landing on Monday the vigil of St Dunstan ⟨18 May⟩ at Rye so that he could inspect the damage done at Winchelsea while he was still in France; and he rode all through that night towards London, where he arrived on Tuesday the feast of St Dunstan ⟨19 May⟩ in the year of Our Lord 1360;[150] and on the following Monday ⟨25 May⟩ he held a council at London to discuss the aforesaid peace agreement.

70. *The death of John Winwick.* Subsequently, on the feast of the Nativity of St John the Baptist following ⟨24 June⟩, Lord John Winwick, keeper of the king's privy seal, died in London and was succeeded in office by Lord John de Buckingham, a royal clerk.[151]

71. *The death of the earl of Northampton.* Also, on Wednesday the feast of St Edith the Virgin ⟨16 September⟩ in the same year, Lord William de Bohun, earl of Northampton, breathed his last at Rochford.[152]

72. *The departure of the king of the French from England.* On 4 June ⟨*recte* July⟩ in the year of Our Lord 1360, Lord John king of the

---

to return to England ahead of his army, embarking at Honfleur on 19 May (Sumption, *Trial by Fire*, pp. 444–8; *Chronica Johannis de Reading et Anonymi Cantuariensis*, pp. 280–1; Delachenal, *Histoire de Charles V*, ii. 184).

[150] TNA: PRO E101/393/11, fo. 40, confirms that Edward III landed at Rye (East Sussex) on 18 May.

[151] According to the *Oxford DNB* ('Winwick, John', article by S. L. Waugh), Winwick died on 20 June 1360, but in the 1359–60 royal wardrobe account he was paid out of court expenses until 12 July. The same account indicates that Buckingham took up office as keeper of the privy seal on 1 July (TNA: PRO E101/393/11, fo. 64).

[152] The date is correct. Rochford is in Essex, and Bohun was buried at Walden abbey, also in Essex (*Oxford DNB*, 'Bohun, William de', article by W. M. Ormrod). His death is reported again below, pp. 102–3.

*a*Francorum, postquam in Anglia a festo Inuencionis Sancte Crucis*a* *b*anno Domini millesimo trecentisimo quinquagesimo septimo fere*b* captiuatus per triennium remanserat,*c* in*d* transitu suo uersus Caleys una cum domino*e* principe Wallie apud*f* *g*Cant' uenit,*g* et ibidem ad feretrum Sancti Thome unum iocale pulcherrimum*h* ad ducentas marcas *i*et amplius*i* appreciatum *j*deuote obtulit,*j* et deinde *k*in criptis*k* ad ymaginem Beate Marie*l* unum nouche aureum pro oblacione dimisit,*m* lapidibus preciosis ornatum. Et per*n* totum illum diem idem rex in prioratu Cant' morabatur, et die Dominico in crastino ualde mane ipse rex, una cum domino principe Wallie, de Cant' recedens in eundo uersus Douorr', transiuit per parcum de Crodeswode, quod est archiepiscopi*o* Cant', et habuit ibidem pulcrum deductum ferarum bestiarum, et fuit illa nocte in domo Dei Douorr' hospitatus.*p*

73. *De conuiuio principis apud Douorram.* Et die Lune in crastino, idem princeps Wallie fecit eidem regi Francie in castro Douor' tam de carnibus quam de piscibus magnum festum,*q* et die Martis sequente in festo translacionis*r* Sancti Thome Martyris, post horam nonam dicti diei, idem Iohannes rex Francie apud Douorr' mare ingrediens, hora uesperarum dicti diei applicuit apud Caleys, ibidem *s*consilium exspectando et interim*s* cum *t*consilio suo Francie super articulis pacis deliberate tractando.*t* [153]

74. *De aduentu regis apud Calays.* Postmodum in crastino Sancti Laurencii eodem anno, dominus princeps Wallie, dominus Henricus dux Lancastrie una cum domino Willelmo episcopo Wynton', cancellario Anglie,[154] proceribusque*u* et magnatibus ac clericis in iure peritis regni Anglie, apud Douorr' accedentes applicuerunt apud Caleys, tractantes usque aduentum regis Anglie cum rege Francie et consilio suo*v* tunc existente apud Caleys super articulis pacis huiusmodi prelocute. *w*Idemque rex Anglie, *x*die Veneris*x* *y*in festo*y* Sancti Dionisii eodem anno *z*de Sandwico nauigans, illo die applicuit apud Caleys. Et ibidem dicti reges, cum magnatibus et

---

a-a om. M   *b-b* om. JM   *c* fuerat M   *d* om. JM   *e* om. JM   *f* om. JM
g-g uenit Cant' M   *h* pulchrum M   *i-i* om. M   *j-j* om. JM   *k-k* om. JM
l add. in cryptis JM   *m* M breaks off   *n* om. J   *o* archiepiscopo J   *p* om. J
q conuiuium J   *r* om. J   *s-s* M resumes: et sic transit uersus Caleys
t-t magnatibus suis loquebatur tractantes usam ad domini regis Anglie M; M breaks off
u proceribus J   *v* om. J   *w* M resumes: Et   *x-x* om. JM   *y-y* in die festo J
z-z uenit ad Caleys et M

---

[153] It was in fact on 8 July that King Jean arrived at Calais. For the date of his arrival at Canterbury, the chronicler clearly meant to write 4 July (a Saturday) rather than 4 June; the

French, having remained as a prisoner in England for about three years since the feast of the Discovery of the Holy Cross ⟨3 May⟩ in the year of Our Lord 1357, passed through Canterbury on his way to Calais together with the lord prince of Wales, where he devoutly offered up a most beautiful jewel worth two hundred marks and more at the shrine of St Thomas, as well as making an offering of a golden ornament decorated with precious stones to the image of the Blessed Virgin Mary in the crypt. And throughout that day this king remained at Canterbury priory, and very early the following morning, a Sunday, the same king together with the lord prince of Wales left Canterbury on his way to Dover, and passed through the park of Crudeswood, which belongs to the archbishop of Canterbury, where he enjoyed a fine hunt for wild beasts, and that night he was entertained in the Maison Dieu at Dover.

73. *The banquet of the prince at Dover.* On the following day, the Monday, the said prince of Wales held a great banquet including both meat and fish dishes for the said king of France in Dover castle, and after the hour of noon on the next day, which was Tuesday the feast of the Translation of St Thomas the Martyr ⟨7 July⟩, the said King John of France embarked at Dover, landing at Calais at the hour of vespers that same day to meet his council there and spend some time with his council of France carefully discussing the articles of peace.[153]

74. *The arrival of the king at Calais.* Following this, on the morrow of the feast of St Laurence ⟨11 August⟩ in the same year, the lord prince of Wales, Lord Henry duke of Lancaster, and Lord William bishop of Winchester, chancellor of England,[154] along with nobles and magnates and clerks learned in the law from the kingdom of England, sailed from Dover to Calais and held extended discussions there with the king of France and his council, who were at that time at Calais, concerning the aforesaid articles of peace, until the arrival of the king of England, who sailed from Sandwich on Friday the feast of St Denis ⟨9 October⟩ in the same year, arriving at Calais the same day. And there the said kings, together with their magnates and councils from each kingdom, held negotiations with each other concerning the

king had only left the Tower of London on 30 June (Delachenal, *Histoire de Charles V*, ii. 219; Bériac-Lainé and Given-Wilson, *Les Prisonniers de la Bataille de Poitiers*, pp. 140–1). The Maison Dieu at Dover was the hospital of St Mary.

[154] The bishop of Winchester was William Edington, chancellor of England 1356–63.

consiliis suis utriusque regni, super reformacione pacis perpetue inter regna Francorum et Anglorum habende tractantes*z* adinuicem, *ª*tan-
fo. 261*r* dem ipsi in unam certam | formam pacis imperpetuum habende*b* unanimiter*ª* concordarunt, *c*et eam per manum publicam redigi fecerunt in scriptis.*c* 155 Et deinde, soluta regi Anglorum certa quantitate*d* scutorum, *e*iuxta ordinacionem in hac parte habitam,*e* et obsidibus Francie*f* in Angliam missis, idem rex Francie in Franciam et rex Anglie in Angliam libere recesserunt.156

75. *Parliamentum regis Anglie.* *g*Deinde rex Anglie, parliamentum suum apud Westm' *h*proximo Conuersionis*h* Sancti Pauli conuo-cans,157 in eodem coram prelatis et proceribus regni Anglie articulos pacis huiusmodi, in uerbis gallicis conceptos, mandauit publice recitari, et die Dominica, uidelicet ultima*i* die Februarii eodem anno, in ecclesia Westm' ad altare Sancti Edwardi regis per dominum Simonem, tunc Cantuar' archiepiscopum, missa solempniter decan-tata in presencia dicti regis, prelatorum,*j* procerum et magnatum, fecit dictos articulos solempniter publicari.*k* 158

76. Quorum *l*articulorum pacis*l* tenor talis est:

*Articuli pacis.*159 Edward, aisne filx au noble roi de France et d'Engleterre,*m* prince de Gales, ducs de Cornwaille et conte de Cestre, a toux ceux qi cestes lettres uerront, salutz. Nous uous faisons sauoir qe, de touz les debaz, descordes qecumqes, meux et desmenez entre nostre tresdouce seignour et piere le roi de France et d'Engleterre d'une part, et noz cosyns le roi, son filx ainsne, le regent le Realme de France, d'autre part, pour bien de pais est

---

a–a pro pace perpetua M   *b* add. et J   *c–c* om. M   *d* summa M   *e–e* om. M
f Francorum M   *g* M condenses this paragraph: Et postea articule pacis per prelatos et magnates Anglie London' London' [sic] sunt promulgate   *h–h* post Conuersionem J
i ultimo J   *j* prelatum J   *k* J breaks off   *l–l* tractorum M   *m* add. etc. M; M breaks off

---

155 Edward III remained at Calais from 9 October until 1 November 1360; the Treaty of Brétigny–Calais was ratified on 24 October.
156 The payment of an initial 600,000 écus (out of the total of three million, worth £500,000 sterling, agreed for King Jean's ransom), and the handing over of forty French hostages as pledges for payment of the remainder, were stipulated in articles 14 and 15 of the terms agreed at Brétigny as the conditions for King Jean's release from captivity: see below, pp. 80–3.
157 This parliament was indeed summoned to meet on 24 January, although since this was a Sunday its first session was probably not held until 25th; it lasted until 18 February: W. M. Ormrod (ed.), 'Edward III: Parliament of 1361, Introduction', in *The Parliament Rolls of Medieval England (PROME)*, ed. C. Given-Wilson et al. (16 vols., Woodbridge, 2005), v. 133.

establishment of a perpetual peace between the kingdoms of the French and the English, and eventually they came to a unanimous agreement on a secure form of perpetual peace, and they had it set down in writing by public authority.[155] Subsequently, once a certain quantity of écus had been handed over to the king of the English, as had been agreed on this point, and hostages from France had been sent to England, the French king returned freely to France, and the English king to England.[156]

75. *The parliament of the king of England.* Then the king of England, having summoned his parliament to meet at Westminster shortly before the feast of the Conversion of St Paul ⟨25 January, n.s. 1361⟩,[157] ordered that these articles of peace, composed in French, be publicly recited there in the presence of the prelates and nobles of the kingdom of England; and on the last day of February ⟨*recte* January⟩ that same year, which was a Sunday, once a solemn mass had been sung in the church of Westminster in the presence of the said king, the prelates, nobles, and magnates at the altar of St Edward the king ⟨the Confessor⟩ by Lord Simon, who was at that time archbishop of Canterbury, he ordered the said articles to be solemnly published.[158]

76. The tenor of which articles of peace is as follows.
The articles of peace.[159] Edward, the eldest son of the noble king of France and England, prince of Wales, duke of Cornwall, and earl of Chester, greets all those who will see these letters. We would have you know that, concerning all the disagreements and disputes whatsoever which have occurred and been conducted between our dearest lord and father the king of France and England on the one hand, and our cousins the king and his eldest son, regent of the realm of France, on the other hand, agreement has been reached for the sake

---

[158] Simon Islip, archbishop of Canterbury 1349–66. John of Reading said that a mass of the Trinity was sung by Islip on Sunday 31 January; Edward III and his sons were there, as were the French king's sons (being by now hostages for their father), and all those who had not yet sworn to uphold the treaty did so: *Chronica Johannis de Reading et Anonymi Cantuariensis*, p. 148.

[159] Despite what the chronicler says, the version of the Treaty of Brétigny–Calais given here is the draft agreed at Brétigny on 8 May 1360, rather than the final terms ratified at Calais on 24 October. This treaty, which marked the end of the first phase of the Hundred Years War, has attracted a considerable amount of comment from both sides of the Channel: see especially Delachenal, *Histoire de Charles V*, ii. 193–265; Le Patourel, 'The Treaty of Brétigny'; and Rogers, *War Cruel and Sharp*, pp. 385–422.

accorde le uitisme jour de mai l'an de grace mille treis centz sessant a Bertigny deles Chartres en la manere qe s'ensuit:

Primus articulus. De Peytiers, de Peytou, de Xaintes, d'Agen,[a] *Pierecort, Lymosyn, Caturcen, d'Engolisme.* Premerement, qe le roi d'Engleterre, auec ce qu'il tient en Guyene et en Gascoigne, aura pour lui et pour ces heirs, perpetuelment a touz jours, touz les choses qe s'ensuent, a tenir par la manere qe le roi de France ou son filx ou ascun de ces ancestres rois de France les tindrent. C'est a sauoir, ce q'en souereinte, en souereynte, ce que en demeyne, en demeyne, et par les temps et maneres a desouz esclaritz. La citee, le chastel et la contee de Peytiers, et tote la terre et le pais de Peytou, ensemble les fiez de Thouar' et la terre de Belleuille; la cite et le chastel de Xaintes et tote la terre et le pais de Xantonge, par decea et par dela la Charante; la cite et le chastel d'Agen[b] et la terre et le pais d'Agennois; la cite et le chastel e tote le contee de Pirregort et tote la terre et le pais de Pierreguiz; la citee e le chastel de Lymoges et la terre e le pais de Lymosyn; la citee et le chastel de Caours, la terre et le pais de Caourcyn;[160] la citee et le chastiel et le pais de Tarbe; la terre et le pais et la conte de Bygorre; la contee, terre et le pais de Gaure; la citee et le chastel' d'Engolisme et la conte, la terre e le pais d'Angolmeys; la citee et le chastel de Rodeys et les terres et le pais de Rouergue. Et s'il a ascuns seignurs, come le conte de Foys, le conte d'Armygnak, le conte de l'Ile, le conte de Pierregort, le visconte de Lymoges, ou fo. 261ᵛ autres qe tiegnent ascuns terres ou lieux dedeyntz | les metes des ditz lieux, ils ferront hommage au roi d'Engleterre, et touz autres seruices et deuoirs duwes a cause de lour terres ou lieux, en la manere q'ils ont faite en temps passe.

Secundus articulus. Item, aura le roi d'Engleterre tot ce qe le roy d'Engleterre ou ascun des rois d'Engleterre anxiement tyndrent en la uille de Montstroil sour la mier et les appourtenances.[161]

Tercius articulus. De comitatu Pontiui. Item, aura le roy d'Engleterre tote la conte de Pontieu toute entierement, sauf et excepte qe si ascuns choses ont este alienes par le rois d'Engleterre qi ont est⟨e⟩[c] pour le temps de la dite contee et aportenances et a autres persones qe au rois de France, le roi de France ne serra pas tenutz de les rendre as rois d'Engleterre, et si les ditz alienacions ont este faites as rois de

---

[a] Agen *edd.;* Angou C   [b] Agen *edd.,* Angen C   [c] este *edd.;* est C

of peace on the eighth day of May in the year of grace 1360 at Brétigny near Chartres in the following manner:

The first article. Poitiers, Poitou, Saintes, Agen, Périgord, Limousin, Caoursin, Angoulême. Firstly, that the king of England, together with what he already holds in Guienne and Gascony, shall have for himself and for his heirs, perpetually for all time, all the things which follow, to hold in the manner in which the king of France or his son or any of his ancestors the kings of France held them: that is to say, what was held in sovereignty, in sovereignty, and what in demesne, in demesne, for the time and in the manner specified below. The city, castle, and county of Poitiers, and all the territory and land of Poitou, together with the fief of Thouars and the territory of Belleville. The city and castle of Saintes and all the territory and land of Saintonge, on both sides of the river Charente. The city and castle of Agen and the territory and land of Agenais. The city and castle and all the county of Périgord and all the territory and land of Périgueux. The city and castle of Limoges and the territory and land of Limousin. The city and castle of Cahors; the territory and land of Caoursin.[160] The city and castle and land of Tarbe. The territory and land and county of Bigorre. The county, territory, and land of Gaure. The city and castle of Angoulême and the county and territory and land of Angoumois. The city and castle of Rodez and the territory and land of Rouergue. And if there are any lords, such as the count of Foix, the count of Armagnac, the count of L'Isle, the count of Périgord, the viscount of Limoges, or others who hold any lands or places within the bounds of the said places, they shall do homage to the king of England, along with all the other services and dues owing on account of their lands or places, in the same manner as they have done in time past.

The second article. Also, the king of England shall have everything that the king of England or any of the kings of England held in ancient times in the town of Montreuil-sur-Mer and its appurtenances.[161]

The third article. The county of Ponthieu. Also, the king of England shall have the whole county of Ponthieu in its entirety, saving and except that if anything in the said county and appurtenances has been alienated by former kings of England to persons other than the kings of France, the king of France shall not be obliged to restore them to the king of England; and if such alienations have been made to former

---

[160] Also known as Quercy.
[161] Montreuil-sur-Mer, in the county of Ponthieu (the subject of the next article).

France qi ont este pour le temps santz ascun myen, et le roi de France les tiegne a present en sa mayn, il les lessera au roi d'Engleterre entierement, excepte qe si le rois de France les ont eu par eschange a autres terres, le roi d'Engleterre deliurera au roi de France ce qe hon en a ehu par eschange, ou il li lessera les choses ensi alienetz. Mais si les rois d'Engleterre qi ont este pour le temps en auoient alienez ou transportez ascuns choses en autres persones qe as rois de France, et depuis soient uenutz es mayns du roi de France, ou aussi par partage, le roi de France ne serra pas tenutz de les rendre. Aussi, si les choses dessusdites deiuent hommages, le roi les baillera autre qi enferra hommage au roi d'Engleterre, et se il ne deiuent hommage, le roi de France baillera un tenant qi li enferra le deuoir dedens un an procheyn apres ce q'il serra partiz de Caleys.

Quartus articulus. De Caleys, de Merk', de Sandgate, de Colnes. Item, le rei d'Engleterre aura le chastel et la uille de Caleys, le chastel, la uille et seignurie de Merk'; les uilles et les chasteux et seignuries de Sandgate, Collignes, Hammes, Wale et*ᵃ* Oyes auec terres, boys, marreys, riuieres, rentes, seignuries, adueisons d'esglises et totes autres appurtenances et lieux entregisantz dedenz les metes et bondes qi s'enficient. C'est assauoir, de Caleys iusqes au fil de la riuere par deuant Grauelinges, et aussi par la fil de mesme la riuere, *ᵇ*tout entour Langle, et auxi par la riuere qe ua par dela Poil, et auxi par mesme la riuer*ᵇ* qi chiest ou grant lay de Gisnes iusqes a Fretun, et deleuc par la ualee entour la montaigne de Calkuly, encloant mesme la montaigne, et aussi iusqes a la mier, auec Sandgate et toutes ces apportenances.¹⁶²

Quintus articulus. De comitatu de Gisnes, de Caleys. Item, le dit roi d'Engleterre aura le chastel et la uille et toute entierement la conte de Gisnes, auec toutes les terres, uilles, chasteux, forteresces, lieux, homes, hommages, seignuries, boys, fiez, forestz,*ᶜ* droitures d'icelles aussi entierement come le conte de Gisnes derrenement mort les tient au temps de sa mort,¹⁶³ et obeiront les esglises et les bons gentz estantz dedans les limitacions du dit contee de Gisnes, de Caleys et de Merk' et des autres lieux dessusdits, au roi d'Engleterre aussi come ils

---

ᵃ interlinear C   *ᵇ⁻ᵇ lower marg. C*   *ᶜ interlinear C*

¹⁶² For identification of the places mentioned in this article, see 'Some documents regarding the fulfilment and interpretation of the Treaty of Brétigny (1361–1369)', ed. P. Chaplais, *Camden Miscellany*, xix (London, 1952), pp. 16–17. La Walle was in the hamlet of St-Blaise, Langle between St-Omer and Gravelines; Poil was also known as Polder.

¹⁶³ Raoul de Brienne, count of Eu and Guines, had been executed by King Jean in 1350

kings of France without any intermediary, and the king of France holds them at present in his hand, he shall restore them in their entirety to the king of England, except that if the king of France had them by exchange for other territories, the king of England shall hand over to the king of France either whatever was received in exchange, or he shall leave the things which were alienated as they are. But if former kings of England had alienated or transferred anything to persons other than the kings of France, and these have subsequently come into the hands of the king of France, or been partitioned, the king of France shall not be obliged to restore them. Also, if the aforementioned items owe homage, the king will deliver them to another person who will do homage for them to the king of England; and if they do not owe homage, the king of France will deliver them to a tenant who will perform what is due to him within a year of his departure from Calais.

The fourth article. Calais, Marck, Sangatte, Coulogne. Also, the king of England shall have the castle and town of Calais; the castle, town, and lordship of Marck; the towns and castles and lordships of Sangatte, Coulogne, Hammes, La Walle, and Oye with the territories, woods, marshes, rivers, rents, lordships, advowsons of churches, and all other appurtenances and places lying within the following limits and bounds: that is to say, from Calais up to the channel of the river before Gravelines, and also along the course of the same river, right around Langle, and also along the river which runs on the other side of Poil, and also along the same river which opens into the great lake of Guines as far as Frethun, and from there along the valley around the hill of Coquelles, including the hill; and also as far as the sea, including Sangatte and all its appurtenances.[162]

The fifth article. The county of Guines, Calais. Also, the said king of England shall have the castle and town and the entirety of the county of Guines, with all the territories, towns, castles, fortresses, places, men, homages, lordships, woods, fiefs, forests, and associated rights as entirely as the recently deceased count of Guines had them at the time of his death;[163] and the churches and good people living within the limits of the said county of Guines, and those of Calais and Marck and the other places aforementioned, shall obey the king of England

---

(Delachenal, *Histoire de Charles V*, i. 67–9). Thompson (*Chronicon Galfridi le Baker*, p. 286), noted that Raoul left no heir of his body, but that Gautier de Brienne, duke of Athens, married his sister Jeanne, and may have adopted the title before being killed at Poitiers, in which case it is possible that he is being referred to here.

obeissoient au roi de France et au conte de Gisnes qi fuit pour le temps; toutes les quieles choses de Merk' et de Caleys contenues en ce

present article et en | l'article prochein precedent le roi d'Engleterre tendra en demayne, excepte le heritage des eglises qi demouront aus dites esglises entierement, quelque part q'ils soient assis.ᵃ Et aussi excepte les heritages des autres gentz des pais de Merk' et de Caleys assis hors la uille de Caleys iusqes a la ualue de cent libres de terre par an de la monoye currante en pais et au desouz, les quielx heritages leur demouront iusqes a la ualue dessusdite et au desoux, mais les habitacions et heritages assises en la dite uille de Caleys auec leurs appourtenances demourront en demayne au roi d'Engleterre, pour en ordeiner a sa uolente. Et aussi demourront aus habitanz en la conte, uille et terre de Gisnes toutz leurs demaynes entierement, et y reuendront pleinement, sauf ce qu'est dit des confrentacions, metes et bondes en le article prochein precedent.

Sextus articulus. Item, accorde est qe le dit roi d'Engleterre et ces heirs auront et tendront totes les isles adiacentz aus terres, pais et lieux auantnomez, ensemble auecqes totes les autres isles les quelx le dit roi d'Engleterre tient a present.

Septimus articulus. De hommagio regi reddendo et aliis. Item, est accorde qe le dit roi de France et son ainsnez filz, le regent, pour eulx et pour toutez lour heirs et successours, a pluis tost qe s'en porra sanz fraude et sanz mal engin, et a pluis tart dedans la feste seynt Michel proscheyn uenant en un an, rendront, bailleront et deliuereront au dit roy d'Engleterre et a touz ces heirs et successours, et transporteront en eaux, toutz les honurs, obediences, hommages, ligeances, uassalx, fiez, seruices, recoignissances, droitures, meer et mixte empire, et toutes maneres des iurisdiccions hautes et basses, ressors, et sauues gardes, aduoesons et patronages d'esglises, et toutes maneres desᵇ seigneuries et souerayntez et tout le droit qu'il auoient ou pouoient auoir, appartenoient, appartiennent et poent appartenir par qecumque cause, tiltre ou colour de droit a eulz, aus rois et la coroune de France, pur cause des citez, contez, chasteaux, uilles, terres, pais, isles et lieux auantnomez, et de toutz leurs appourtenances et appendances, quel part q'il soient, et chascune d'ycelles, santz rienz y retenir a eaux, a leurs heirs ne successours aus roys ne a la coroune de France. Et aussi manderont le dit roi et son ainsnez filx, par leurs

---

ᵃ *marg. heading* De Calais *rep.* C   ᵇ *interlinear* C

just as they used to obey the king of France and former counts of Guines; all of which things pertaining to Marck and Calais contained in this present article and in the immediately preceding article the king of England will hold in demesne, except for the inheritance of churches which will remain entirely to the said churches, wherever they are situated, and also except for the inheritances of other people of the lands of Marck and Calais situated outside the town of Calais up to the value of 100 pounds of land per year in the present currency of the country and below, which inheritances shall remain to them up to and below the aforesaid value; but the dwellings and inheritances situated within the said town of Calais with their appurtenances shall remain in demesne to the king of England, for him to do with according to his will. And also the inhabitants of the county, town, and territory of Guines shall retain in entirety all their demesnes, and shall freely return to them, except for what is said regarding demarcations, limits, and bounds in the immediately preceding article.

The sixth article. Also, it is agreed that the said king of England and his heirs will have and hold all the islands adjacent to the aforesaid territories, lands, and places, together with all the other islands which the said king of England holds at present.

The seventh article. The rendering of homage and other things to the king. Also, it is agreed that the said king of France and his eldest son, the regent, on behalf of themselves and all their heirs and successors, as soon as possible without fraud and deceit, and at the latest by the feast of Michaelmas next year ⟨29 September 1361⟩, will restore, hand over, and deliver to the said king of England and to all his heirs and successors, and will transfer to them, all the honours, obediences, homages, allegiances, vassals, fiefs, services, obligations, rights, pure and mixed authority, and all manner of jurisdictions high and low, as well as ressorts, safeguards, advowsons and patronages of churches, and all manner of lordships and sovereignties and all the right that they had or could have, or that belonged or belong or could belong by whatever cause, title, or colour of right to them, to the kings or to the crown of France, by reason of the aforesaid cities, counties, castles, towns, territories, lands, islands, and places, and all their appurtenances and appendages, and each of them, wherever they may be, without retaining anything from them for themselves, or for their heirs or successors, or for the kings or the crown of France. And also the said king and his eldest son will, by their letters patent, order all

letres patentes, a totes archeuesqes, euesqes et autres prelatz de sainte
esglise, et aussi as contes, viscontes, barons, nobles, citoiens et autres
qecumqes des cites, contez, terres, pais, isles et lieux auantnomez,
q'ils obeisont au roi d'Engleterre et a ces heirs, et a leur*a* certain
comandement, en la manere q'ils ont obeiez au rois et a la coroune de
France, et, par mesmes les letres, leur quiteront et absoudreront a
mieux q'il se porra faire de toutz hommages, foi et serementz,
obligacions, subieccions et promesses faitz par ascun d'eulx aus rois
et a la coroune de France en quecumqes maneres.

    *Octauus articulus. Quod rex Anglie habebit ciuitates, castra et loca
prenominata perpetuo et hereditarie.* Item, accorde est qe le roi
d'Engleterre aura les citez, contes, chasteaux, | terres, pais, isles et
lieux auantnomez, auec toutes leur appurtenances et appendances
quelque part q'il soient, a tenir a lui et a touz ces heirs et successours
heritablement et perpetuelment, en demaine ce qe le rois de France y
auoient en demayne, et aussi en fiez, seruices, soueraintez ou resort ce
qe les rois de France y auoient par tiele manere, sauf tant com est dit
par desus en le article de Caleys et de Merk'. Et si*b* des citez, contez,
chasteux, terres, pais, isles et lieux auantnomez, soueraintez, droitz,
meer et mixte impire, iurisdiccions et profitz qecumqes qe tenoit
ascun roi d'Engleterre illoeqes, et en leur appartenances et appendances quecomqes, aucuns alienacions, donacions, obligacions ou
charges ont este faites par ascun des rois de France qi ont estez
pour le temps puis setante auns en cea, par quelez fourme ou cause qe
ce soit, touz tiels donacions, alienacions, obligacions et charges sont
desores et serront de tout repelletz, cassees et anulles, et toutes choses
aussi donez, alienez ou charges serront realment et de fait rendues et
baillez au dit roi d'Engleterre ou a ses deputez espescialx, a mesme
l'anterte q'il furont au roi de Engilterre*c* depuis setante ans en cea, a
pluis tost qe l'en porra santz mal engin, et a pluis tard dedanz la feste
Seynt Michel procheyn uenant en un an, a tenir au dit roy
d'Engleterre et a touz ces heirs et successours, perpetuelment et
hereditablement, par manere qe desus est dit. Excepte ce q'est dit par
dessus en l'article de Pontieu, qi demorra en sa force, et sauf et
excepte toutes les choses donez et alienees aus esglises, qi leur
demorront paisiblement en touz les pais et lieux cy desus et desoutz
nomez, si qe les persones des dites esglises priont diligentement por

fo. 262*v*

---

   a leur *edd.;* leux, *by association with* lieux *directly above?* C   *b* *over erasure* C
  c *over erasure* C

the archbishops, bishops, and other prelates of holy church, as well as the counts, viscounts, barons, noble citizens, and all other persons of the aforesaid cities, counties, territories, lands, islands, and places, that they shall obey the king of England and his heirs, and be at their command, in the same manner as they have obeyed the kings and the crown of France; and, by the same letters, they will acquit and absolve them as best they can from all homages, fealty and oaths, obligations, submissions, and promises made by any of them to the kings and the crown of France in whatever manner.

The eighth article. That the king of England shall hold the aforesaid cities, castles and places perpetually and heritably. Also, it is agreed that the king of England shall have the aforesaid cities, counties, castles, territories, lands, islands, and places, with all their appurtenances and appendages wherever they may be, to hold for himself and all his heirs and successors by heredity and in perpetuity, holding in demesne whatever the kings of France held in demesne, and as fiefs, services, sovereignties, or ressorts whatever the kings of France held in such manner, saving what is said above in the article concerning Calais and Marck. And if from the aforesaid cities, counties, castles, territories, lands, islands, and places, sovereignties, rights, pure and mixed authority, jurisdictions, and profits of any sort which any king of England held there, along with all their appurtenances and appendages, any alienations, donations, obligations, or charges have been made by any of the kings of France during the last seventy years, in whatever form or for whatever reason, all such donations, alienations, obligations, and charges are from now on and shall be entirely repealed, cancelled, and annulled, and all the things which have thus been granted, alienated, or burdened with charges shall be restored and delivered in reality and in effect to the said king of England or to his special deputies, to the full level that they belonged to the king of England during the last seventy years, as soon as possible without deceit, and at the latest by the feast of Michaelmas next year ⟨29 September 1361⟩, to be held by the said king of England and all his heirs and successors perpetually and by heredity in the manner stated above; except for what is said above in the article regarding Ponthieu, which shall remain in force; and saving and except for all the things given and alienated to churches, which they shall retain in peace in all the lands and places named above and below, so that the parsons of the said churches may pray diligently for

les ditz rois come pour leur foundeours, sour qoi leur consciences ent serront chargeez.

Nonus articulus. Item, accorde est qe le roi d'Engleterre toutz les citez, contez, chastealx, pais dessusnomez qi anxiement n'ont estez des roi d'Engleterre aura et tendra en l'estat et aussi come les rois de France ou ces filx les tienent a present.

Decimus articulus. Item, est accorde qe si dedanz les meetes des ditz pais qe furent anxienement des roys d'Engleterre, auoit ascuns choses qe autrefetz n'eussent estez des roys d'Engleterre, dont le roi de France estoit en possession le jour de la bataille de Poytiers,^{a} qe fuit le disneuime jour de septembre l'an de grace mille treis centz cinquante six, elles serront et demourront au roi d'Engleterre et a ces heirs par manere qe dessus est dit.

Undecimus articulus. Quod rex Francie liberabit regi Anglie regalitatem, obedienciam, homagium de locis prenominatis. Item, accorde est qe le dit roi de France et son ainsnez filx, le regent, pour eaux et pour leur heirs et pour touz les rois de France et leurs successours a toutz jours, a pluis tost q'il se porra faire santz mal engyn, et au pluis tard fol. 263^r dedans la feste saint Michel procheyn uenant en un | an, rendront et bailleront au dit roy d'Engleterre et a toutz ces heirs et successours, et transporteront en eux, toutz les honurs, regaltetz, obediences, hommages, ligeances, uassalx, feez, seruices, recognissances, serementz, droitures, meer et mixte impire, toutes maneres des iurisdiccions hautes et basses, ressortz, sauues gardes et seignuries et soueraintez qi appartenoient, appartiennent ou pourroient en ascun manere appartenir aus rois et a la coroune de France ou a ascun autre persone a cause du roi et de la coroune de France en qecumque temps, es citez, contez, chasteaulx, terres, pais, isles et lieux auantnomez, ou en ascun de eaux et en leurs appartenances et appendances qecumqes, ou es persones, uassaulx ou subgitz quecomqes d'yceux,^{164} soient princes, ducs, contes, viscontes, arceuesqes, euesqes et autres prelatz de sainte esglise, barons, nobles et autres quecomqes; santz riens a eaux, leurs heirs et successours ou a la Coroune de France ou autre qe ce soit, retenir ne reseruer en yceux,

---

^{a} *marg. hand pointing* C

^{164} When the treaty came to be ratified at Calais in October, clause 11 ended at this point, with the remainder of it, as well as the whole of clause 12, being omitted and set out in a separate schedule to be ratified later. These two clauses thus became known as the 'Renunciations Clauses', and have attracted a considerable amount of comment, since, as it turned out, they never were ratified, and it was this fact which enabled Charles V to hear

the said kings as for their founders, which they will be charged to do upon their conscience.

The ninth article. Also, it is agreed that the king of England shall have and hold all the aforesaid cities, counties, castles, and lands which have not previously belonged to the kings of England in the same state and manner as the king of France or his sons hold them at present.

The tenth article. Also, it is agreed that if within the bounds of the said lands which anciently belonged to the kings of England, there are any things which did not formerly belong to the kings of England, of which the king of France held possession on the day of the battle of Poitiers, namely the nineteenth day of September in the year of grace 1356, they should belong and remain to the king of England and his heirs in the manner specified above.

The eleventh article. That the king of France will deliver the regality, obedience, and homage of the aforesaid places to the king of England. Also, it is agreed that the said king of France and his eldest son, the regent, on behalf of themselves and their heirs and all the kings of France and their successors for ever, as soon as possible and without deceit, and at the latest before the feast of Michaelmas next year ⟨29 September 1361⟩, shall restore and deliver to the said king of England and all his heirs and successors, and transfer to them, all the honours, regalities, obediences, homages, allegiances, vassals, fees, services, obligations, oaths, rights, pure and mixed authority, all manners of jurisdictions high and low, ressorts, safeguards, lordships, and sovereignties which belonged, belong, or might in any manner or at any time belong to the kings and to the crown of France or to any other person by reason of the king and crown of France, in the aforesaid cities, counties, castles, territories, lands, islands, and places, or in any of them or any of their appurtenances and appendages, or in any of their persons, vassals, or subjects whatsoever,[164] be they princes, dukes, counts, viscounts, archbishops, bishops, or other prelates of holy church, barons, nobles, or any others; without retaining or reserving in them anything for themselves, their heirs and successors, or the crown of France or any other

---

appeals from various Gascon lords against the Black Prince in the winter of 1368–9, which led to the renewal of the war in the following year. For discussion of these events, see Delachenal, *Histoire de Charles V*, ii. 242–50; Le Patourel, 'The Treaty of Brétigny'; and 'Some documents regarding the fulfilment and interpretation of the Treaty of Brétigny', ed. Chaplais.

pour qoi ils ne leurs heirs et successors et autres rois de France, ou autre qe ce soit au cause du roy et de la coroune de France, ascune chose y pourront chalenger ou demander en temps auenir sour le roy d'Engleterre, ces heirs et successours, ou sour ascuns des uassaulx et subgitz auantditz par cause des pais et lieux auantnomez; ainssi qe toutz les auantnomez persones et leurs heirs et successours perpetuelment serront hommes lieges et subgietz au roi d'Engleterre et a touz ces heirs et successours, et qe le dit roi d'Engleterre, ces heirs et successours toutz les persones, citez, contez, terres, pais, isles, chasteaux et lieux auantnomez, et toutz leur appartenances et appendances, tendront et auront, et a eux demorront pleinement, perpetuelment, franchement en leur seignurie, souerainte, obeisance, ligeance, et subjection, come le rois de France les auoient et tenoient en ascun temps passe; et qe le dit roy d'Engleterre, ces heirs et successours, auront et tendront perpetuelment toutz les pais auant nomez, auec leur appartenances et appendances et les autres choses auant nomez, en toute franchise et liberte perpetuele, com seignur, souereins et lieges et come ueysins au roi et au roialme de France, santz y recognaistre souerayn⟨te⟩,[a] ou faire ascune obedience, homage, resort, subieccion, et santz faire en ascun temps auenir ascune seruice ou recognissance aus roys ne a la coroune de France des citez, contez, chasteaux, terres, pais, isles, lieux et persones auantnomez, ou pour ascune de ycelles.

Duodecimus articulus. De renunciationibus faciendis. [b]*Renunciacio nominis regis Francie et corone.*[b] *Renunciacio facienda de Normannia et Flandria.* Item, est accorde qe le roi de France et son ainsne filx renounceront expressement aus ditz ressortz et soueraintez, et a tout le droit q'il ont et pouent auoir en toutez les choses qe par ce present traitie doyuent appurtenir au rei d'Engleterre; et semblablement le roy | d'Engleterre et son ainsne filx renounceront expressement a toutes les choses qe par ce present traicte ne deiuont estre baillez ou demourrer au roi d'Engleterre, et a toutes les demandez q'il faisoit au roy de France, et par especial au noun et au droit de la coroune et du roialme de France,[c] a le homage, souerainte et demayne du duche de Normandie, du duche de Thouraine, des contez d'Angeu et de Maine, et la souerainte, hommage du duche de Britaigne, a la souerainte et hommage du conte et pais de Flandres, et au toutes autres demandes qe le roi d'Engleterre fesoit ou faire pourroit au roy

fol. 263ᵛ

---

[a] soueraynte *edd.;* souerayn C   [b–b] *upper marg., underlined and bracketed C; sketch of fleur–de–lis and leaf spray linked, left upper marg.* C   [c] *marg. hand pointing* C

person, whereby either they or their heirs and successors or other kings of France, or any other person acting on behalf of the king and crown of France, might in future be able to claim or demand anything there against the king of England, his heirs and successors, or against any of his aforesaid vassals and subjects by reason of the aforesaid lands and places; so that all the aforesaid persons and their heirs and successors in perpetuity shall be the liegemen and subjects of the king of England and all his heirs and successors, and that the said king of England and his heirs and successors shall have and hold all the aforesaid persons, cities, counties, territories, lands, islands, castles, and places together with all their appurtenances and appendages, and these will remain fully, freely, and perpetually in their lordship, sovereignty, obedience, allegiance and subjection, in the same way that the kings of France had and held them at any time in the past; and that the said king of England, his heirs and successors shall have and hold in perpetuity all the aforesaid lands, along with their appurtenances and appendages and the other things mentioned above, in complete freedom and perpetual liberty, as sovereign and liege lords and as neighbours to the king and kingdom of France, without acknowledging any sovereignty, or doing any obedience, homage, ressort, or subjection, or performing at any time to come any service or obligation to the kings or to the crown of France for the aforesaid cities, counties, castles, territories, lands, islands, places, or persons, or for any of them.

The twelfth article. The renunciations to be made. The renunciation of the name and crown of the king of France. The renunciation to be made of Normandy and Flanders. Also, it is agreed that the king of France and his eldest son shall expressly renounce the aforesaid ressorts and sovereignties, together with all the right that they have or could have in all the things which by this present treaty ought to pertain to the king of England; and similarly the king of England and his eldest son shall expressly renounce all the things which by this present treaty should not be delivered to or remain with the king of England, along with all the demands that he has made to the king of France, and especially the title and right to the crown and realm of France, to the homage, sovereignty, and demesne of the duchy of Normandy, the duchy of Touraine, and the counties of Anjou and Maine, the sovereignty and homage of the duchy of Brittany, the sovereignty and homage of the county and land of Flanders, and to all the other demands which the king of England has made or could make to the

de France pour qecumqe cause qe se soit, ultre ce *et except'*ᵃ qe par
cest present traite doit demorer ou estre baillez au dit roi d'Engleterre et a ces heirs; et transporteront, cesseront et delaisseront li uns
rois a l'autre perpetuelment tout le droit qe chescun de eaux a ou
poet auoir en toutes les choses qi par cest present traitie deiuent
demorer ou estre balliez a chescun de eaux. Et dou temps et lieu ou
et quant les ditz renunciacions se ferront, parleront et ordeineront
les deux roys a Caleys ensamble.

ᵇ *Tertius decimus articulus.* Item, est accorde, a fyn qe ceste present
traitee puis estre plus briefment acompli, qe le roi d'Engleterre ferra
amener le roi de France a Caleys dedans trois simaignes apres la
Natiuite seint Iohan le Baptistre procheyn a uenir, cessant tote iuste
enpeschement, au despais du roi d'Engleterre, hors les fiez de l'ostel
du dit roi de France.ᵇ ¹⁶⁵

*Quartus decimus articulus. De tribus milionibus florenis regi Anglie
soluendis.* Item, est accorde qe le roi de France paiera au roy
d'Engleterre trois milions d'escuz d'or, dont les deux ualent un
noble de la monye d'Engleterre, et ent serront paiez au dit roi
d'Engleterre ou a ces deputez six centz mille escutz a Calays
dedans qatre moys a compter depuis qe le roy de France serra
uenutz a Caleys,¹⁶⁶ et dedanz l'an deslors procheyn ensuant, ent
serront paiez qatre centz mille escuz tielx come dessus en la cite de
Londres en Engleterre, e deslors chescun an procheyn ensuant qatre
centz mille escuz, tielx come deuant en la dite cite, iusqes a tant qe les
ditz trois milions serront parpaiez.

*Quintus decimus articulus. De liberacione uille de Rochel. De ostagiis
reddendis regi Anglie.* Item, est accorde qe par paiant les ditz sis centz
mille escutz a Caleys, et par baillant les hostages cy dessouz nomez,
et deliurant au roi d'Engleterre dedanz les quatre mois a compter
depuis qe le roi de France serra uenutz a Caleys, come dit est, la
uille et les forceresses de la Rochele et les chasteux et forceresses et
uilles de la conte de Guynes, auec touz leur appartenances et
appendances, la persone dou dit roy serra tout deliure de prison
et porra partir franchement de Caleys et uenir en son roialme sanz

---

ᵃ⁻ᵃ *interlinear C*   ᵇ⁻ᵇ *lower marg. C*

---

¹⁶⁵ As noted above, Edward III kept his word on this: King Jean was brought to Calais on
8 July.
¹⁶⁶ An English noble was worth 6 shillings and 8 pence. Thus King Jean's ransom was
worth £500,000 sterling in total. In fact only 400,000 of the stipulated 600,000 écus for the
first instalment could be collected by the time King Jean was released in late October.

king of France for any reason whatsoever, apart from and except for what ought by this present treaty to remain with or be delivered to the said king of England and to his heirs; and each king shall transfer, cede, and release to the other in perpetuity all the right which each of them has or could have in all the things which by this present treaty ought to remain with or be delivered to each of them. And the two kings together at Calais shall discuss and make arrangements concerning the time and place where and when the aforesaid renunciations ought to be performed.

The thirteenth article. Also, it is agreed, in order that this present treaty may be more speedily effected, that in the absence of any lawful impediment the king of England will have the king of France brought to Calais within three weeks of the next feast of the Nativity of St John the Baptist ⟨24 June 1360⟩, at the expense of the king of England, apart from the costs of the said king of France's household.[165]

The fourteenth article. The three million florins to be paid to the king of England. Also, it is agreed that the king of France will pay to the king of England three million écus d'or, two of which are worth one noble in English money, of which 600,000 écus shall be paid to the said king of England or to his deputies at Calais within four months from the time of the king of France's arrival at Calais;[166] and then within a further year after that, 400,000 écus will be paid in the same manner in the city of London in England, and each year after that a further 400,000 écus, in the same manner and in the same city, until such time as the aforesaid three millions have been paid.

The fifteenth article. The handing over of the town of ⟨La⟩ Rochelle. The hostages to be delivered to the king of England. Also, it is agreed that in return for the payment of the said 600,000 écus at Calais, and for delivering the hostages named below, and for handing over to the king of England within four months from the time of the king of France's arrival at Calais, as aforesaid, the town and fortress of La Rochelle and the castles and fortresses and towns of the county of Guines, together with all their appurtenances and appendages, the person of the said king shall be released entirely from prison and permitted to depart freely from Calais and enter his kingdom without

Edward III nevertheless agreed to let him go, and the French king drew up a new schedule agreeing to pay the outstanding 200,000 in two equal instalments at Christmas 1360 and Candlemas (2 February) 1361: Delachenal, *Histoire de Charles V*, ii. 228. For the whole story of the payment of King Jean's ransom, see 'The ransom of John II, King of France, 1360–1370', ed. D. Broome, *Camden Miscellany*, xiv (London, 1926).

ascun enpeschement. Mais il ne se purra armer ne ces gentz contre le roi d'Engleterre iusqes a tant q'il ait acompli ce q'il tenutz de faire par ceste presente traitie. E toute les ostages qi demorront pour le roi de France ceux qe s'ensuent. C'est assauoir:[167]

Monsire le conte d'Angou[168]

Le conte de Poitiers[169]

Le ducs de Orliens[170]

Le duc de Bourbon[171]

Le conte de Bloys ou son frere[172]

Le conte d'Alencon ou monsire Piers d'Alencon son frere[173]

fo. 264ʳ Le conte | de saint Pol[174]

Le conte de Harecourt[175]

Le conte de Porcien[176]

Le sire de Coucy[177]

Le sire de Fienles[178]

Le conte de Valentinoys[179]

Le sire de Preaux[180]

Le sire de Seint Venant[181]

Le sire de Carenteres[182]

Le conte de Breus[183]

Le conte de Waudemont[184]

Le uisconte de Beaumont[185]

Le dauphin d'Auuerne[186]

Le sire de Hanget[187]

Le sire de Montmorency[188]

Le conte de Foees[189]

Monsire Guillaume de Craon

Monsire Loys de Harecourt

Monsire Iohan Lygny.

[167] Although clause 17 below, along with other copies of the treaty, give the number of hostages for King Jean's ransom as forty, in fact forty-one names are given here.

[168] Louis, count (later duke) of Anjou, the French king's son.

[169] Jean, count of Poitiers (later duke of Berri), the French king's son.

[170] Philippe, duke of Orléans, the king's brother.

[171] Louis, duke of Bourbon.

[172] Gui de Châtillon, count of Blois, in fact replaced his brother Louis as a hostage for the king and remained in England until 1367.

[173] Charles, heir to the county of Alençon, entered holy orders (and became archbishop of Lyon), thus his brother Pierre 'the Noble', mentioned here, became count of Alençon.

[174] Gui de Châtillon, count of St-Pol (not to be confused with the count of Blois, mentioned above), died while still a hostage in England in 1363.

[175] Jean, count of Harcourt.

[176] Jean, count of Porcien.

any hindrance. But he may not arm himself or his men against the
king of England until such time as he has accomplished what he is
bound by this present treaty to do. And here follow all the hostages
who will remain on behalf of the king of France, that is to say:[167]

My lord the count of Anjou[168]
The count of Poitiers[169]
The duke of Orléans[170]
The duke of Bourbon[171]
The count of Blois or his brother[172]
The count of Alençon or my lord Peter of Alençon, his brother[173]
The count of St-Pol[174]
The count of Harcourt[175]
The count of Porcien[176]
The lord of Coucy[177]
The lord of Fiennes[178]
The count of Valentinois[179]
The lord of Préaux[180]
The lord of St-Venant[181]
The lord of Garencières[182]
The count of Braisne[183]
The count of Vaudémont[184]
The viscount of Beaumont[185]
The dauphin of Auvergne[186]
The lord of Hangest[187]
The lord of Montmorency[188]
The count of Forez[189]
My lord William of Craon
My lord Louis of Harcourt
My lord John of Ligny.

[177] Enguerrand, lord of Coucy, who adapted so well to life in England that in 1365 he
married Isabella, daughter of Edward III, became a Knight of the Garter, and switched to
the English allegiance: Bériac-Lainé and Given-Wilson, *Les Prisonniers de la Bataille de
Poitiers*, pp. 162–3.

[178] Robert de Fiennes, constable of France.
[179] Aymar de Poitiers, count of Valentinois.
[180] Pierre, lord of Préaux.
[181] Robert de Wavrin, lord of St-Venant.
[182] Yon, lord of Garencières.
[183] Simon de Roucy, count of Braisne.
[184] Henri de Joinville, count of Vaudémont.
[185] Jean de Brienne, viscount of Beaumont.
[186] Beraud, dauphin of Auvergne.
[187] Rabache, lord of Hangest.
[188] Charles, lord of Montmorency.
[189] Louis, count of Forez.

Ces sont les nouns de prisoners qi furent pris en la bataille de Poytiers:

Monsire Philippe de France[190]

⟨Le⟩[a] conte de Eu[191]

Le conte de Longeuille[192]

Le conte de Pontieu[193]

Le conte de Tancaruille[194]

Le conte de Ioigny[195]

Le conte de Saunsuerre[196]

Le conte de Dampmartyn[197]

Le conte de Vendadour[198]

Le conte de Salubruge[199]

Le conte d'Aussuerre[200]

Le sires de Craon[201]

Le sire de Deruall[202]

Le marescal d'Odenehem[203]

Le sire d'Aubigny,[204] et

Le conte de Vandesme.[205]

Sextus decimus articulus. Quod captiuati reddent se carceri regis. Item, est accorde qe les ditz seze[b] prisoners[206] uendront demourer en ostage pour le roi de France, come dit est, et serront par my ce deliures de leurs prisons santz paier ascun raensons pour temps passez s'il n'ount este a accort de certaine ranceon par couenant faite par auant les tiers iours de may drainerement passe.[207] Et si ascun de eux est hors d'Engleterre et ne se rent a Caleys en ostage dedanz le premier mois apres le ditz trois simaignes de la saint Iohan,[208] cessant iuste enpeschement il ne serra pas quite de la prisoun mais serra constreint par le roi de France a retourner en Engleterre come prisoner ou a paier la peyne par lui prouise et encourree par defaute de son retour.

Septimus decimus articulus. De ostagiis. Item, est accorde qe en lieu des ditz ostages qi ⟨ne⟩[c] uendront a Caleys, ou qi mouerront, ou se

---

[a] Le *edd.*; *om.* C   [b] seze *edd., from* Foedera *iii (1),* 490; seignurs C   [c] ne *edd.,* *from* Foedera *iii (1),* 490; *om.* C

[190] Philippe, count of Touraine (later duke of Burgundy), the king's youngest son.
[191] Jean d'Artois, count of Eu.
[192] Charles d'Artois, count of Longueville.
[193] Jacques de Bourbon, count of Ponthieu.
[194] Jean de Melun, count of Tancarville.   [195] Jean de Noyers, count of Joigny.
[196] Jean de Nevers, count of Sancerre.   [197] Charles de Trie, count of Dammartin.
[198] Bernard, count of Ventadour.   [199] Jean, count of Saarbrücken.
[200] Jean de Chalon, count of Auxerre.   [201] Amaury, lord of Craon.

These are the names of the prisoners who were taken at the battle of Poitiers:

My lord Philip of France[190]

The count of Eu[191]

The count of Longueville[192]

The count of Ponthieu[193]

The count of Tancarville[194]

The count of Joigny[195]

The count of Sancerre[196]

The count of Dammartin[197]

The count of Ventadour[198]

The count of Saarbrücken[199]

The count of Auxerre[200]

The lord of Craon[201]

The lord of Derval[202]

Marshal d'Audrehem[203]

The lord of Aubigny,[204] and

The count of Vendôme.[205]

The sixteenth article. That those who were captured should hand themselves over to the king's prison. Also, it is agreed that the aforesaid ⟨sixteen⟩ prisoners[206] shall, as noted above, come and remain as hostages for the king of France, and as a result shall be released from their prisons without paying any ransoms for time past as long as they have not agreed a fixed ransom by covenant made before the third day of May last past.[207] And if any of them is out of England and fails to deliver himself up as a hostage at Calais within one month after the aforesaid three weeks ⟨after the feast⟩ of St John ⟨24 June⟩,[208] unless he can show lawful impediment he shall not be released from prison but will be constrained by the king of France to return to England as a prisoner or pay the penalty promised and incurred by him for failing to return.

The seventeenth article. The hostages. Also, it is agreed that in place of any of the said hostages who do not come to Calais, or who die, or

---

[202] Bonnabé de Rougé, lord of Derval.

[203] Arnoul d'Audrehem, marshal of France.

[204] Renaud, lord of Aubigny.

[205] Bouchard, count of Vendôme.

[206] That is, the last sixteen named in the previous clause.

[207] That is, the day on which a draft of the Treaty of Brétigny–Calais was first agreed. For the background to this clause, see Bériac-Lainé and Given-Wilson, *Les Prisonniers de la Bataille de Poitiers*, pp. 156–7.

[208] That is to say, by mid-August 1360.

departirent santz conge hors du pouair del roi d'Engleterre, le roi de France serra tenu de en bailler autres de semblable estat, au pluis pres q'il porra estre fait, dedans quatre moys procheyn apres qe le baillif de Amyens ou le maire de Seynt Omer en serra sour ce par letres du dit roi d'Engleterre certefiez. Et pourra le roi de France a son departir de Caleys amesner en sa compaignie, tielx come les deux rois accorderont, dys des hostages, et souffira qe de nombre de quarante dessusditz en demorriront iusqes a nombre de trente.[209]

Duodeuicesimus articulus. De ostagiis Paris' et aliis locis Francie reddendis regi Anglie. Item, est accorde qe le roi de France, dedenz trois mois apres ce q'il serra departiz de Caleys, rendra a Caleys en ostage quatre persones de la uille de Paris et deux persones des chascun des uilles dont les nouns s'ensuent, c'est assauoir, de Saint Omer, Arraz, Amyens, Beauuez, Lyle, Doway, Tournay, Reyns, Chaalons, Troies, Chartres, Toulouse, Lyons, Orliens, Champaigne, Rouan, Caen, Tours, Brugges, pluis suffisauntz des ditz uilles por l'acomplissement de ce present traitie.[210]

Item, est accorde qe le roi de France serra amene d'Engleterre a
fo. 264ᵛ Caleys | et demourra a Caleys par quatre mois apres sa uenue, mais il ne paiera rien por le premier moys par cause de sa garde, et pour chascun des autres moys ensuiantz q'il demourra a Caleys par defaute de lui ou de cezᵃ gentz, il paiera pour ses gardes dys mille roialx tielx come courrent au present en France auant son departir de Caleys, et ainsi au fuer du temps qu'il y demourra.[211]

Undeuicesimus articulus. Quod Iohannes de Monford habebit comitatum de Montfort. Item, est accorde qe, a pluis tost qe faire se pourra dedans l'aan proschein apres ce qe le roi de France serra partitz de Caleys, monsire Iohan, counte de Montfort, ᵇaura le conte de Montfortᵇ auec toutz ces appurtenances, en faisant hommage lige au roi de France, et deuoir et seruice en toutz cas tielx come bons et loialx uassaux liges doient faire a son seignur lige a causeᶜ de la dite contee,[212] et aussi lui serront rendutz ces autres heritages qe ne sont

---

ᵃ cez *edd.*; centz *by association with* gentz *immediately following? C*   ᵇ⁻ᵇ *repeated, rep. cancelled C*   ᶜ *interlinear C*

---

[209] In fact, King Jean was eventually allowed to take with him not ten but fourteen of the sixteen prisoner-hostages when he left Calais: the two excluded from this agreement were the counts of Longueville and Dammartin: Bériac-Lainé and Given-Wilson, *Les Prisonniers de la Bataille de Poitiers*, p. 157.

[210] The remainder of this clause was subsequently removed and made into a separate

who remove themselves without permission from the power of the king of England, the king of France will be obliged to deliver to him others of similar rank, or as close as possible thereto, within four months of the bailiff of Amiens or the mayor of St-Omer being informed of this by letters of the said king of England. And at his departure from Calais the king of France may take with him any ten of these hostages, those that shall be agreed between the two kings, and it will suffice that thirty of the aforementioned figure of forty shall remain.[209]

The eighteenth article. Hostages from Paris and other places in France to be delivered to the king of England. Also, it is agreed that the king of France, within three months following his departure from Calais, shall deliver to Calais as hostages four persons from the town of Paris and two persons from each of the following towns: that is to say, from St-Omer, Arras, Amiens, Beauvais, Lille, Douai, Tournai, Reims, Châlons, Troyes, Chartres, Toulouse, Lyon, Orléans, Compiègne, Rouen, Caen, Tours, Bourges—the most worthy persons from the said towns for the accomplishment of this present treaty.[210]

Also, it is agreed that the king of France shall be brought from England to Calais and shall remain at Calais for four months following his arrival, but he shall pay nothing for his keep for the first month, and for each of the following months that he remains at Calais through the fault of him or his men, he will pay for his keep ten thousand royals of the current coin of France until he departs from Calais, for the cost of the time that he stays there.[211]

The nineteenth article. That John de Montfort shall have the county of Montfort. Also, it is agreed that, as soon as possible within a year following the departure of the king of France from Calais, my lord John, count of Montfort, will have the county of Montfort with all its appurtenances, performing liege homage for it to the king of France, together with duty and service in all cases such as a good and loyal liege vassal ought to do to his liege lord in respect of the said county;[212] and his other inheritances which are not part of the duchy

clause when the treaty was ratified at Calais, with each of the remaining clauses being successively renumbered.

[211] The 'roial' or royal is probably being used here as shorthand for the florin or 'royal florin', a term commonly used to describe various currencies in fourteenth-century France: P. Spufford, *Handbook of Medieval Exchange* (Royal Historical Society Publications; London, 1986), p. 172.

[212] The county of Montfort lay in the heart of the Île-de-France, roughly halfway between Paris and Chartres; for Jean de Montfort, see the following footnote.

mie de la duchee de Britaigne, en faisant hommage et autre deuoir qe
appendra. Et s'il ueut ascune chose demander en ascun des heritages
qe sont de la dite duchee hors du pais de Britaigne, bone et brief
raison lui serra fait par la court de France.

*Vicesimus articulus. De questione Britannie terminanda per reges
Francie et Anglie. De Britannia minore.* Item, sur la question du
demayne de la duchie de Bretaigne, qi entre le dit monsire Iohan de
Montfort d'une parte, monsire Charles de Bloys d'autre part,[213]
accorde est qe les deux rois, appelletz par deuant eulx ou leur deputez
les parties principales de Bloys et de Montfort, par eulx et par leurs
deputez especialx se enfourmeront du droit des parties, et s'efforceront de mettres les dites parties en accord sur tote ce q'est en debat
entre eulx a pluis tost qe ils purront. Et en cas qe le ditz rois, par eulx
ne par leurs ditz deputez, ne les purront accorder dedans un an
proschein apres qe le roi de France serra arriuetz a Caleys,[214] les amys
d'une part et d'autre se enfourmeront diligentement du droit des
parties par manere qe dessus est dit, et s'efforceront de mettres les
dites parties a accord a mielx qe faire se pourra a pluis tost q'il
porront. Et si ne les puent mettre a accord dedantz demi aan donke
proscheyn ensuiant, ils rapporteront aus ditz rois ou a leurs deputez
tot q'ils en auront trouez sour le droit des parties susdites et sour qoi
le debat demourra entre les ditz parties, et adonke les deux rois, par
eux et par leurs deputez especialx, a pluis tost q'ils pourront les ditz
parties mettront a accord, ou dirront leurs final auys sour le droit
d'une partie et d'autre, et ce serra executez par les deux rois; et en cas
fo. 265ʳ q'ils ne les pourront ffaire dedanz demi an deslors | proschein
ensuiant, adonqe les deux parties principals de Bloys et de Montfort
ferront ce qe mielx lour semblera, et les amys d'une part et de autre
aideront quelqe part qe lour plerra, santz enpeschement des ditz rois
et santz auoir en ascun temps auenir damage, blasme ne reproeche par
ascun des ditz rois pour la cause dessusdite. Et si aussi estoit qe la une
partie des dites parties ⟨ne⟩ᵃ uousist comparier suffisantesment
deuant les ditz rois ou leur ditz deputez au temps qe lui serra

---

ᵃ ne *edd.; om.* C

---

[213] Jean de Montfort and Charles de Blois were, respectively, the English- and French-
sponsored claimants to the duchy of Brittany, which had been in dispute between them and
their supporters, and thus in a state of civil war, since the death of Duke Jean of Brittany in
1341. Charles de Blois claimed the duchy through his wife, Jeanne de Penthièvre, while
Jean de Montfort, who was born only in 1340, and subsequently brought up at the English
court, inherited the claim of his father (also Jean, d. 1345) as the nearest heir in the male

of Brittany shall also be restored to him, performing homage and other appropriate duties. And if he wishes to claim anything in any inheritances belonging to the said duchy which are outside the land of Brittany, a good and speedy answer will be given to him by the Court of France.

The twentieth article. The question of Brittany to be decided by the kings of France and England. Lesser Brittany. Also, on the question of the demesne of the duchy of Brittany, which is ⟨disputed⟩ between the said Lord John de Montfort on the one hand ⟨and⟩ Lord Charles de Blois on the other,[213] it is agreed that the two kings, having summoned before them or their deputies the principal parties of Blois and Montfort, shall inform themselves, in person or through their special deputies, about the right of the parties, and will endeavour to bring the said parties to agreement on all the matters which are disputed between them as soon as possible. And if it happens that the said kings, in person or through their said deputies, cannot make them reach an agreement within a year following the arrival of the king of France at Calais,[214] friends from each side will inform themselves diligently about the right of the parties in the aforesaid manner, and will endeavour, in the shortest time possible, to make the said parties reach the best agreement that can be made. And if they cannot bring them to agreement within half a year following, they shall report to the said kings or to their deputies concerning everything which they have discovered about the right of the aforesaid parties and the reasons for the continuing dispute between them, whereupon the two kings, in person or through their special deputies, shall as soon as possible bring the said parties to agreement or deliver their final advice concerning the right of each party, and this will be enforced by the two kings; and if they are unable to do this within the next half a year, then the two principal parties of Blois and Montfort shall do what seems best to them, and the friends of each side may help whichever side they wish, without hindrance from the said kings and without at any time in the future being punished, blamed, or reproached on this account by either of the said kings. And if it should happen that one of the said parties does not wish to appear in an appropriate fashion before the said kings or their said deputies at

line. The wording of this clause reveals something of the intractability of the Breton problem, which in fact was only settled following the death of Charles de Blois at the battle of Auray in 1364.

[214] That is, by July 1361.

establez, et aussi en cas qe les ditz rois ou leurs deputez en auroient ordinez ou declarez qe les ditz parties fuissent a accorder, ou q'il auroient dit lour auys pour le droit d'une partie, et ascun des ditz parties ne se uoudroit accorder a ce ne obeir a la dite declaracion, adonqes les ditz rois serront encontre luy[a] de tot leur poair et a aide del autre qe se uoudroit accorder et obeir. Mais en nul cas les deux rois, par leurs propres persones ne par autres, ne purront faire ne contrerendre guerre l'un a l'autre par la cause dessusdite, et touz jours demourra la souerainte et hommage de la dite duchie au roi de France.

Vicesimus primus articulus. Item, qe totes les terres, pais, uilles, chasteaux et autres lieux baillez au ditz rois serront en tielx libertes et franchises come elles sont a present, et serront confermez par les ditz seignurs rois ou par leurs successours et par chascun de eux totes les foez q'il en serront sour ce duement requis.[215]

Vicesimus secundus articulus. Quod rex Francie faciet liberari domino Philippo de Nauarra hereditatem suam. Item, le roi de France rendra et ferra rendre et restablir de fait a monsire Phelippe de Nauarre, a toutz ces adherentz,[216] en appert, a pliis tost qe l'en pourra, santz mal engin, et a pliis tard dedanx un an prochein apres qe le roi de France serra partitz de Caleys, totes les uilles, chasteaux, forceresces, seignuries, droitz, rentes, profitz, iurisdiccions et lieux qecumque qe le dit monsire Phelippe, tant par cause de lui comme par cause de sa femme, ou ces ditz adherentz, tindront ou doiuont tenir ou roialme de France; ne leur ferra jammes le dit roi de France reprosche, dammage ne enpeschement pour ascun chose fait auant ces heures, et leur pardonrra totes offenses et mesprises du temps passe par cause de la guerre, et sour ce auront ces letres bones et suffisantz, et qe le dit monsire Phelippe et ces auantditz adherentz retournent en son hommage, et lui facent les deuoirs et lui soient bons et leaux uassaux.

Vicesimus tertius articulus. Quod rex Anglie possit dare terras domini G. Harecourt. Item, est accorde qe le roi d'Engleterre pourra doner, ceste foiz tant soulement, a qi lui plerra, en heritage totes les terres et heritages qe furent de feu monsire Godefray de Harecourt, a tenir

---

[a] *interlinear* C

[215] Other copies of the treaty include here the words 'provided that they are not contrary to this present agreement' (cf. *Foedera*, iii (1), p. 491).

[216] Philippe of Navarre was the brother of Charles II 'the Bad', king of Navarre. In 1356, following King Jean's imprisonment of Charles the Bad and execution of several Navarrese lords at Rouen, Philippe renounced his allegiance to the French king, seized control of

the appointed time, or if it should happen that the said kings or their deputies shall have ordained or announced that the said parties should reach an agreement, or that they have declared their advice in favour of the right of one party, but one or other of the said parties does not wish to agree to or obey the said declaration, then the said kings shall go against him with all their power, so as to help the other one who is willing to agree and to be obedient. But under no circumstances shall the two kings, either in their own persons or through others, make or undertake war against each other on this account; and the sovereignty and homage of the said duchy will remain for ever to the king of France.

The twenty-first article. Also, that all the territories, lands, towns, castles, and other places delivered to the said kings shall continue to have the liberties and franchises which they do at present, and these will be confirmed by the said lord kings and by each of their successors on each occasion when they shall be duly required to do this.[215]

The twenty-second article. That the king of France will order Lord Philip of Navarre's inheritance to be delivered to him. Also, the king of France shall restore, and order to be restored, and indeed return to my lord Philip of Navarre and to all his adherents,[216] openly, as soon as possible, without deceit, and at the latest within one year following the departure of the king of France from Calais, all the towns, castles, fortresses, lordships, rights, rents, profits, jurisdictions, and places whatsoever which the said Lord Philip, in his own right or through his wife, or his aforesaid adherents, held or ought to hold in the kingdom of France; nor will the said king of France ever blame, punish, or harm them for anything which has been done up until this time, and he will pardon them all offences and trespasses committed in the past on account of the war; and on this point they will receive good and sufficient letters from him; and the said Lord Philip and his aforesaid adherents shall return to his homage, and will do their duty and be good and loyal vassals to him.

The twenty-third article. That the king of England may grant out the lands of Lord G⟨odfrey⟩ d'Harcourt. Also, it is agreed that the king of England may grant heritably, for this one time only, to whomsoever he pleases, all the lands and inheritances which belonged to my lord

much of Normandy, and allied himself with Edward III, who appointed him as his lieutenant in Normandy: these well-known events are summarized in Rogers, *War Cruel and Sharp*, pp. 333–4.

fo. 265ᵛ du duc | de Normandie ou des autres seignurs des quilles ils doiuent estre tenutz par raison parmi les hommages et seruices anxienement acustumez.[217]

Vicesimus quartus articulus. Item, est accorde qe nul homme ne pais qe ait este en le obeissance de l'une partie et uendra par cest accord a le obeissance de l'autre part ne serra enpesche pour chose fait en temps passez.

Vicesimus quintus articulus. De bannitis et adherentibus quod non grauentur. Item, est accorde qe les terres des bannes et adherentz de l'une partie et de l'autre, et aussi des esglises de l'un roailme et del autre, qe touz ceux qe sont desheritez ou ostez de leurs terres ou heritagez, ou chargees de ascun pension, taille ou re⟨de⟩uance[a] ou autrement greuez en qecumque manere qe ce soit par cause de ceste guerre, soient restituez entierement en mesme les droitz et posses-sions q'ils eurent deuant la guerre commence, et qe toutz maneres forfeitures, trespas et misprisions faitz par eux ou a ascun de eux en miene temps soient de tout pardonez, et qe ces choses soient faites a pluis tost qe l'en pourra bonement, et au pluis tard[b] dedans un an[c] proschein apres qe le roi de France serra partitz de Caleys; excepte ce q'est dit en le article de Caleys, de Merk' et des autres lieux nomez en le dit article, et excepte aussi le uiconte de Frunsac et monsire Iohan de Galart,[218] les queux ne serront pas compris en ceste article, mais demoureront leurs bien et heritages en l'estat q'il estoient par deuaunt ceste presente traitee.

Vicesimus sextus articulus. Item, est accorde qe le roi de France deliuerera au rei d'Engleterre a pluis tost q'il porra bonement, et au pluis tard dedans la feste seint Michel proscheyn uenant en un an apres son departir de Caleys, toutz les citez, uilles, pais et autres lieux dessuznomez qe par ceste presente traite doiuent ester baillez au roi d'Engleterre.

Vicesimus septimus articulus. Quod rex Anglie faciet liberari fortalicia in Francia capta. Item, est accorde q'en baillant au rei d'Engleterre, ou a autre pour lui, par especial deputez, les uilles, forteresces et toute

---

    ᵃ redeuance *edd.;* reuance *C*   ᵇ *interlinear C*   ᶜ *interlinear C*

---

[217] Godfroi d'Harcourt was one of the most powerful supporters of the English cause in Normandy; having done homage to Edward III and recognized him as king of France as early as 1346, he subsequently rejoined the French allegiance, but once again renounced his homage to King Jean after the latter's imprisonment of Charles of Navarre in April 1356. He was killed in a skirmish at Brévands (Manche) on 11 November 1356, leaving several of his lands including St-Sauveur to Edward III: Rogers, *War Cruel and Sharp*, pp. 238, 333–

Godfrey d'Harcourt, deceased, to be held from the duke of Normandy or from the other lords from whom they ought to be held by reason of the ancient and accustomed homages and services.[217]

The twenty-fourth article. Also, it is agreed that no man or land that has been under the obedience of one party and changes as a result of this agreement to the obedience of the other party shall be punished for anything done in the past.

The twenty-fifth article. Those who are banished, or adherents ⟨of others⟩ are not to be ill-treated. Also, it is agreed that the lands of those who are banished, and the adherents of one party or the other, and the churches of one kingdom or the other, and all those who have been disinherited or ousted from their lands or inheritances, or charged with any pension, tax, or imposition, or otherwise deprived in any manner whatsoever as a result of this war, shall be fully restored to the same rights and possessions which they had before the war began, and that all kinds of forfeitures, trespasses, and misprisions committed by them or to any of them in the meantime shall be pardoned in full, and that these things shall be done in good faith and as soon as possible, and at the latest within one year following the departure of the king of France from Calais; except for what is said in the article concerning Calais and Marck and the other places mentioned in that article, and except for the viscount of Fronsac and my lord John de Galard,[218] who are not to be included in this article, but rather their goods and inheritances are to remain in the state that they were before the making of this present treaty.

The twenty-sixth article. Also, it is agreed that the king of France shall deliver to the king of England as soon as he can, and at the latest before the feast of Michaelmas next within a year after his departure from Calais ⟨29 September 1361⟩, all the aforementioned cities, towns, lands, and other places which ought by this present treaty to be handed over to the king of England.

The twenty-seventh article. That the king of England should ensure that captured fortresses in France are handed over. Also, it is agreed that upon delivery to the king of England, or to another person on his

---

4, 387; Delachenal, *Histoire de Charles V*, i. 265–6. The duke of Normandy mentioned here was the dauphin, the future Charles V.

[218] Jean Galard, lord of Limeuil on the Dordogne, had defected to the English cause in April 1356: Rogers, *War Cruel and Sharp*, pp. 328–30; according to Sumption, it was the fifth time that he had changed sides in ten years. Raymond of Fronsac, whose *vicomté* was close to the confluence of the Dordogne and the Garonne, a little to the north-east of Bordeaux, had gone over to the French side in June 1351: Sumption, *Trial by Fire*, pp. 78, 193.

la conte de Pontieu, les uilles et forteresces et tote la conte de Montfort, la cite et le chastel de Xaintes, les chasteux, uilles et forteresces et tout ce qe le roi tient en demaine ou pais de Xantege deca et dela la Charente, le chastel et la cite d'Engelesme et les chasteux et les forteresces et uilles qe le roi de France tient en demaine ou pais d'Angelesmes, auec letres et mandementz de delaissement des fees et hommages, le roi d'Engleterre, a ces propres cous et frez, deliuerera totes les forteresces prises et occupez par lui, par ces subgitz, adherentz et allies es pais de France, de Tourayne, d'Auniou, de Mayne, de Berry, d'Ouuergne, de Bourgoigne, de Champaigne, de Picardie et de Normandie, et de toutes les autres

fo. 266ʳ parties, terres et lieux du roialme de France, excepte | celles du duche de Bretaigne et de pais et teeres qi par cest present traicte doiuent appartenir et demorer au rei d'Engleterre.

Vicesimus octauus articulus. Ad deliberandum regi Anglie uillas, ciuites et castra. De uadiis. Item, est accorde qe le roy de France ferra bailer et deliuerer au roi d'Engleterre et a ces heirs ou deputez totes les uilles, chastealx, forteresces et autres terres, pais et lieux auantnomez, auec leur appartenances, aus propres foez et cous*ᵃ* du dit roi de France, et*ᵇ* aussi qe s'il y auoit ascuns rebelles ou desobeisantz de render, bailler ou de restituer au dit roi d'Engleterre ascuns citez, uilles, chastealx, pais, lieux ou forteresces qi par ceste presente traicte li doiuent appartenir, le roi de France serra tenutz de les faire deliurer au roi d'Engleterre a ces despens; et semblablement le roi d'Engleterre ferra deliurer, a ces despens, les forteresces qi par ceste present traictie doiuent appartenir au roi de France; et serront tenutz les ditz rois, lour gentz a eux entreaider quant a ce si requis ent sont, aus gages de la partie qi les requerra, qi serront d'une floryn de Florence par iour pour chiualer,²¹⁹ et demy floryn pur squire, et pour les autres au feor; et dou surpluis des doubles gages, est accorde*ᶜ* qe si les ditz gages sont trop petitz en regard au marche de uiures en pais, il en serra a l'ordenance de quatre chiualers pur ce esluz, c'est assauoir, deux d'une partie et deux d'autre.

Vicesimus nonus articulus. De archiepiscopis, episcopis et de subieccione eorum. Item, est accorde qe touz les arceuesqes, euesqes et autres prelatz de sainte esglise, a cause de leur temperaltez, serront subgitz de celi de deux rois souz q'il tenderont leur temperaltez, et se il ont

---

ᵃ *interlinear extending into marg.* C   ᵇ *interlinear* C   ᶜ *interlinear* C

²¹⁹ A florin of Florence was usually held to be worth 3 shillings sterling at this time.

behalf, through special deputies, the towns, fortresses, and all the county of Ponthieu, the towns, fortresses, and all the county of Montfort, the city and castle of Saintes, the castles, towns, and fortresses and all that the king holds in demesne in the land of Saintonge on both sides of the Charente, the castle and city of Angoulême and the castles, fortresses, and towns which the king of France holds in demesne in the land of Angoumois, with letters and mandates of quittance of fees and homages, the king of England, at his own cost and expense, will deliver all the fortresses captured and occupied by him, his subjects, adherents, and allies in the land of France, in Touraine, Anjou, Maine, Berry, Auvergne, Burgundy, Champagne, Picardy, Normandy, and all the other regions, territories, and places in the kingdom of France, except for those in the duchy of Brittany and the lands and territories which by this present treaty ought to belong and remain to the king of England.

The twenty-eighth article. The handing over to the king of England of towns, cities, and castles. Wages. Also, it is agreed that the king of France shall ensure the handover and delivery to the king of England and to his heirs or deputies of all the aforesaid towns, castles, fortresses, and other territories, lands, and places, together with their appurtenances, at the king of France's own cost and expense, and also that if there are any rebellious or disobedient persons who will not hand over or restore to the said king of England any cities, towns, castles, lands, places, or fortresses which by this present treaty ought to belong to him, the king of France will be obliged at his own expense to ensure that they are delivered to the king of England; and similarly the king of England shall ensure the delivery, at his expense, of the fortresses which by this present treaty ought to belong to the king of France; and the two kings and their men shall be obliged to help each other in this if required to do so, at the wages of whichever party requires them, which will be at the rate of a florin of Florence per day for a knight,[219] half a florin for an esquire, and corresponding sums for others; and as to any increase on double wages, it is agreed that if the aforesaid wages are too low in relation to the cost of provisions in the land, this matter will be determined by four knights chosen for this purpose, namely, two from each side.

The twenty-ninth article. Archbishops, bishops, and to whom they are subject. Also, it is agreed that all the archbishops, bishops, and other prelates of holy church, by reason of their temporalities, shall be subject to the king under whom they hold their temporalities,

temperalte souz touz les deux rois, ils serront subgitz de chescun de deux rois pour la temperalte q'il tendront souz chascun de ceulx.

Tricesimus articulus. Item, est accorde qe bones alliances, ameistez et confederacions soient faites entre les deux rois de France et d'Engleterre et leurs roialmes, en gardant l'amour et la conscience de l'un roi et de l'autre, non obstantz qecumqes confederacions q'il auoit de ca et de la auec quecumqes persones, soit il d'Escoce, de Flandres ou d'autre pais qecumque.

Tricesimus primus articulus. Quod duo reges recedent de alligacionibus Scotorum et aliorum. Contra Fla⟨n⟩dren',ᵃ ne fiat cum eis alligacio. Item, est accorde qe le dit roi de France et son ainsne filz, le regent, pour eux et pour leur heirs rois de France, si auant come il porra estre fait, se deslairont et departeront de tout des alliances q'il ont auec les Escoz, et promettront, si auant come faire se purra, qe iammes eux ne leurs heirs ne les rois de France qi pour le temps serront ne dourront ne ferront au roi ne a realme d'Escoce, ne a subgitz de celui presentz ⟨ou⟩ᵇ auenir, aide, confort ne fauour contre le roi d'Engleterre ne contre ces heirs et successours, ne contre son roialme ne contre ces subgitz en qecumque manere, et q'ils ne ferront autres alliances auec les ditz Escoz en ascun temps auenir en contre les ditz rois et roialme d'Engleterre. Semblablement, si auant come faire se purra, | le roi d'Engleterre et son ainsne filz se deslaieront et departiront de tout des alliances q'il ont auec les Flammengs, et promettront qe eux ne leur heirs, ne le rois d'Engleterre qi pur le temps serront, ne dorront ne ferront as Flamencs, presentz ou auenir, aide, confort ne fauour contre le roi de France, ces heirs et successours, ne contre son reialme ne contre ces subgitz en qecumque manere, et q'ils ne ferront autres alliances auec les Flammencs en ascun temps auenir contre les rois et roialme de France.²²⁰

Tricesimus secundus articulus. De collacionibus beneficiorum, quod stent in suo robore. Item, accorde est qe les collacions et prouisions faitez d'une part et d'autre des benefices uacantz tant come la guerre ad duree tiegne et soit uallable, et qe les fruitz, issues et reuenues resceuez et leuez des qecumqes benefices et autres choses temporales qecumqes es ditz roialmes de France et d'Engleterre par une partie et par autre durantz les ditz guerres soient quites de une part et d'autre.

fo. 266ᵛ

ᵃ Flandren *edd.;* Fladren C   ᵇ ou *edd.; om.* C

²²⁰ The Franco–Scottish and Anglo–Flemish alliances had first become a significant factor in Anglo–French relations in the 1290s; the Franco–Scottish alliance was renewed by Charles IV of France and Robert Bruce, king of Scotland, in 1326, while an Anglo–Flemish

whichever of the two it may be; and if they hold temporalities under both kings, they shall be subject to each of the two kings for the temporalities which they hold under each of them.

The thirtieth article. Also, it is agreed that a firm alliance, friendship, and confederation shall be established between the two kings of France and England and their kingdoms, saving the love and conscience of each king, notwithstanding any confederations which they have entered into at home or abroad with any persons, be they from Scotland, from Flanders, or from any other land.

The thirty-first article. That the two kings should withdraw from their alliances with the Scots and others. Against the Flemish, that there be no alliance with them. Also, it is agreed that as soon as possible the said king of France and his eldest son, the regent, on behalf of themselves and their heirs the kings of France, shall renounce and withdraw from any alliances that they have with the Scots, and shall promise, as soon as it can be done, that neither they nor their heirs nor any kings of France in the future shall ever give or furnish to the king or kingdom of Scotland, or to its subjects present or future, any aid, comfort, or favour against the king of England or against his heirs and successors, or against his realm or his subjects in any manner, and that they will not make any other alliances with the aforesaid Scots at any time to come against the said king and kingdom of England. And similarly the king of England and his eldest son shall, as soon as possible, renounce and withdraw from any alliances that they have with the Flemings, and shall promise that neither they nor their heirs nor any kings of England in the future will give or furnish to the Flemings, present or future, any aid, comfort, or favour against the king of France, his heirs or successors, nor against his realm or his subjects in any manner, and that they will not make other alliances with the Flemings at any time to come against the king and kingdom of France.[220]

The thirty-second article. That collations to benefices should retain their validity. Also, it is agreed that collations and provisions to vacant benefices made on each side for as long as the war has lasted shall hold firm and remain valid, and that the fruits, issues, and revenues received and raised from any benefices and other temporal sources whatsoever in the said kingdoms of France and England by one party or the other during the said wars shall be acquitted by both parties.

alliance was proclaimed by Edward III in January 1340, at the time when he first formally laid claim to the French throne.

Tricesimus tertius articulus. Item, qe les rois dessusditz serront tenutz de faire confermer toutz les choses dessusdites par nostre saint piere le pape,[221] et serront uallez par serementz *et censures et sentences* du court de Rome et touz autres lieux en la pluis forte manere qe faire ce purra, et serront impetrez dispensacions, absolucions et letres de la dite court de Rome tochantz la perfeccion et complessement de ceste presente traictie.* Et serront baillez as parties a pluis tard dedanz les trois simaignes apres qe le roi de France serra arriuez a Caleys.

Tricesimus quartus articulus. Item, qe touz les subgitz des ditz rois qe uoudront estudier es studez et uniuersitez des roialmes de France et d'Engleterre ioyeront des priuilegez et libertez des ditz estudez et uniuersitez tout aussi com ils poont faire auant ces present guerres et come ils font a present.

Tricesimus quintus articulus. De firmitate pacis facienda per literas sigillandas et iuramenta. Renunciacio guerrarum per utrumque regem. Item, a fin qe les choses desussdites traitez et parlez soient plus fermez, stables et uallables, serront faitez et donez les sermentz qe s'ensuent: c'est assauoir, letres sealez des sealx des ditz rois et de ainsnez filz d'yceux, les meillours q'il purront faire et ordiner par les conssailx des ditz roys, et iureront les deux rois et leurs enfantz ainsnez et autres enfantz, et aussy les autres des linages des ditz seignurs et autres grantzs des realms, iusqe a nombre de uingt de chascune partie, qi tendront et aideront a tenir, pur tant com a chascun de eux touche, les ditz choses traitez et accordez, et acompliront sanz iammes uenir* a contraire, sanz fraude, santz mal engin, et sanz faire nul enpeschement. Et s'il auoit ascun du dit roialme de France ou du roialme d'Engleterre qi fuissent rebelles, ou ne uousist accorder a les choses desussditez, les deux roys ferront tot leur poair, de corps et des biens et amys, de metres les ditz rebelles en uerraie obeisance solonc la fourme et tenour du dite traictie. Et auec ce se souzmettront* les ditz rois et leur heirs et roialmes a cohercion de nostre saint piere le pape, a fin q'il puisse constraindre par sentences, censures d'esglise et autres uoies dehues celi qe serra rebelle, solonc | q'il serra de raison. Et parmi les fermetez et seurtez dessusdites, renonceront les ditz rois et leurs heirs, par foi et par

---

a–a interlinear, extending into marg. C   *b interlinear* C   *c interlinear* C
d souzmettront *edd.;* senzmettront C

The thirty-third article. Also, that the aforesaid kings shall be obliged to have all the aforementioned things confirmed by our holy father the pope,[221] and they shall be guaranteed by oaths and censures and sentences of the Court of Rome and all other places in the strongest manner possible, and dispensations, absolutions, and letters shall be sought from the said Court of Rome touching the performance and implementation of this present treaty; and these shall be delivered to the parties within three weeks following the arrival of the king of France at Calais at the latest.

The thirty-fourth article. Also, that all the subjects of the said kings who wish to study at the schools and universities of the kingdoms of France and England shall enjoy the privileges and liberties of the said schools and universities in the same manner that they could before these present wars and as they do at present.

The thirty-fifth article. The peace to be confirmed by sealed letters and oaths. Renunciation of wars by each king. Also, in order that the aforesaid matters which have been negotiated and discussed should be more firm, settled, and valid, the following oaths will be taken and given. That is to say, letters sealed with the seals of the said kings and their eldest sons, the best that can be made and drawn up by the said kings' councils; and the two kings and their eldest children and other children, as well as others of the lineages of the said lords and other great men of the kingdoms, to the number of twenty from either side, shall swear to uphold and help to uphold the said things which have been negotiated and agreed inasmuch as it touches each of them, and to implement them without ever doing anything to the contrary, without fraud or deceit or any kind of impediment. And if any person in the kingdom of France or the kingdom of England proves to be rebellious, or does not want to agree to the aforesaid things, the two kings will employ all their power, in body or goods or friends, to reduce any such rebels to true obedience in accordance with the form and tenor of the said treaty. And in addition the said kings and their heirs and their kingdoms will submit themselves to the coercion of our holy father the pope, so that he may be able to constrain anyone who rebels by ecclesiastical sentences, censures, and other suitable ways, in accordance with what is reasonable. And among the aforesaid guarantees and assurances, the said kings and their heirs shall renounce, on their faith and by oaths, all war and all process by

[221] Pope Innocent VI (1352–62); for his letters to the Black Prince following the battle of Poitiers, see above, pp. 28–33.

serementz, a tote guerre et as touz proces de fait. Et si par desobeisance, rebellion ou puissance d'ascuns subgitz du roialme de France, ou autre iuste cause, le roi de France ou ces heirs ne poueuent acomplir totes les choses dessusdites, le roi d'Engleterre, ces heirs, ou ascun par eux ne ferront ou doiueront faire guerre contre le dit roi de France, ces heirs, ne son roialme, mais toutz ensemble s'afforceront de metre les rebelles en uerraie obeisance et de accomplir les choses susdites. Et aussi si ascun du roialme et obeisance le roi d'Engleterre ne uouloient rendre ses uilles, chasteaux et forteresces q'il tiegnent en roialme de France et obeir au traitie dessusdit, ou par iuste cause ne purront acomplir ce q'il doit faire par ceste presente traitie, le roi de France ne ces heirs, ou ascun pur eux, ne ferront point de guerre au roi d'Engleterre ne a son roialme, mais tot deux ensemble ferront lour poair de recouerer les chasteaux, uilles et forteresces desussdit, et qe toute obeisance et acomplissement soit fait es traitez dessusdites. Et serront aussi faites et donees d'une partie et d'autre, selonc la nature du fait, totes maneres de fermetetz et seurtez qe l'en saura ou porra diuiser, tant par le pape, collegie et la court de Rome, come autrement, pur tenir et garder perpetuelment la pais et toutz les choses pardesus accordez.

Tricesimus sextus articulus. Item, est accorde par ceste present traitie et accord' qe toutz autres accords, traites ou perlocutions, si ascuns en y a faitz ou purparletz en temps passez, soient nulls et de nulle ualour et de tot mis a neant, et ne s'en purront iammes aider les parties, ne faire a ascun reproche le un contre l'autre par cause d'yceux traitez ou accords, si ascuns en y auoit, com est dit.

Tricesimus septimus articulus. De confirmacione tractatus. Item, qe ceste present traitee serra approue, iure et conferme par les deux rois a Caleys quant ils y serront en leur persones, et depuis qe le roi de France serra partitz de Caleys et serra en son poair, dedans un moys prescheyn ensuant le partiment le dit roi de France, en ferra letres confirmatories et autres necessairs ouertes et les enuoiera et deliuerera a Caleys au dit roi d'Engleterre, ou a ces deputez au dit lieu, et aussi le roy d'Engleterre, enprenant les dites letres confirmatoirs, rebaillera letres confirmatoirs parailles a ycelles du roi de France.

Tricesimus octauus articulus. Quod neutra pars pro guerra grauabit alium. Item, accorde est qe nul des rois ne pro‘cure′ra,[n] ne ferra

[n] prora, *interlinear* cure C

direct action. And if the king of France or his heirs are unable to implement all the aforesaid things as a result of the disobedience, rebellion, or power of any subjects of the kingdom of France, or for some other just cause, the king of England, his heirs, or any of them shall not and ought not to make war against the said king of France, his heirs, or his kingdom, but acting together they should endeavour to reduce those rebels to obedience and to implement the aforesaid things; and similarly if any persons from the kingdom or obedience of the king of England shall refuse to restore the towns, castles, and fortresses which they hold in the kingdom of France and obey the aforesaid treaty, or for some just cause cannot do what they ought to do by this present treaty, neither the king of France nor his heirs, nor anyone acting on their behalf, shall in any way make war upon the king of England or his kingdom, but acting together they shall do everything in their power to recover the said castles, towns, and fortresses and to ensure that the said treaty is fully obeyed and implemented. And in addition each party shall draw up and give to the other, in accordance with what is required, whatever kinds of assurances and guarantees are known or can be devised—whether by the pope, the College or Court of Rome, or in some other manner—in order to maintain and preserve in perpetuity the peace and all the things agreed above.

The thirty-sixth article. Also, it is agreed by this present treaty and agreement that all other agreements, treaties, or negotiations, if any have taken place or been discussed in the past, shall be null and void and cancelled in their entirety; and they shall never be of advantage to either party, nor form the basis of a reproach from one party against the other on account of these treaties or agreements—if, as said above, any have taken place.

The thirty-seventh article. Confirmation of the treaty. Also, that this present treaty shall be approved, sworn, and confirmed by the two kings in person at Calais when they are present there; and afterwards, when the king of France has left Calais and is in his own power once again, within a month following the departure of the said king of France, he will have confirmatory letters and other necessary instruments openly drawn up and will send and deliver them to the said king of England at Calais, or to his deputies there; and the king of England, having received these confirmatory letters, shall send similar confirmatory letters back to the king of France.

The thirty-eighth article. That neither party harass the other on account of war. Also, it is agreed that neither of the kings shall

procurer, par li ne par autre, qe ascuns nouelletez ou griefs se facent par l'esglise de Rome, ou par autres de saint esglise qecumqes y soient, contre cest present traitie, sur ascun des ditz rois, lour coadiutours, adherentz ou allies, queles q'il soient, ne sur leurs terres ne de lour subgitz, pour occasion de la guerre ou pour autre cause, ne pour seruices qe les ditz coadiutours ou allies aient faitz ad dites roys ou a ascun de eux. Et si nostre dit saint piere ou autre le uoloit faire, les deux rois le destorberont solonc ce q'ils purront bonement, sanz mal engyn.

fo. 267ᵛ   ⟨*Tricesimus nonus articulus*⟩.[a] Item, des ostages qi serront baillez au roi d'Engleterre a Caleys, de la manere et du temps de leur departiement, les deux rois en ordineront a Caleys.[222]

Totes les queles choses dessus escriptes,[223] et chascune d'ycelles, furent faites et ordinez depar nostre seignur le roy et par:

Nostre amee cosyn le duc de Lancastre[224]

William conte de Northamptoun[225]

Thomas le conte de Warewyk[226]

Rauf conte de Stafford[227]

William conte de Saresbury[228]

Messire Gautier sire de Mauny[229]

Messire Reynald de Cobeham[230]

Messire Iohan de Beauchamp[231]

Messire Guy de Brienne[232]

Messire Iohan de Greyli, captan de la Busshe[233]

Bartholomeu de Burherss'[234]

Monsire Franc van Hale[235]

---

[a] Tricesimus nonus articulus *edd.*; *om.* C

---

[222] For the arrangements made at Calais with respect to the hostages, see Delachenal, *Histoire de Charles V*, ii. 250–52.

[223] This paragraph is a clumsy attempt to abbreviate the original text of the treaty. The text given in *Foedera*, iii (1), pp. 487–94, lists the councillors and secretaries of the French king first, and then continues 'with the commissioners and deputies of the said king of England named below, that is to say', following which the list of English signatories is given, beginning as here with the duke of Lancaster: hence the confusion at the end of the paragraph.

[224] Henry of Grosmont, first duke of Lancaster (K. G., founder; d. 1361); for his death, see n. 264 below.

[225] William de Bohun, earl of Northampton (K. G.); for his death just four months later, on 16 Sept. 1360, see above, n. 152.

[226] Thomas Beauchamp, earl of Warwick (K. G., founder; d. 1369).

[227] Ralph de Stafford, earl of Stafford (K. G., founder; d. 1372).

[228] William Montague, earl of Salisbury (K. G., founder; d. 1397).

procure, nor cause to be procured, on his own behalf or through another person, the use of any devices or penalties by the Church of Rome, or by any other persons of holy church whatsoever, which are contrary to this present treaty, against either of the said kings, their coadjutors, adherents, or allies, whoever they may be, or against their lands or their subjects, by reason of the war or for any other reason, or for any services which the said coadjutors or allies have performed for the said kings or either of them. And if our said holy father or some other person wishes to do this, the two kings will do their best to prevent him, without deceit.

⟨The thirty-ninth article⟩. Also, concerning the hostages who will be handed over to the king of England at Calais, the manner and time of their departure, the two kings shall ordain at Calais all the matters set out above and each one of them.[222]

All the matters set out above,[223] and each one of them, were done and ordained on behalf of our lord the king and by:

Our beloved cousin the duke of Lancaster[224]
William earl of Northampton[225]
Thomas earl of Warwick[226]
Ralph earl of Stafford[227]
William earl of Salisbury[228]
Lord Walter Mauny[229]
Lord Reginald Cobham[230]
Lord John Beauchamp[231]
Lord Guy Brian[232]
Lord John de Grailly, captal of Buch[233]
Bartholomew Burghersh[234]
Lord Frank van Hale[235]

---

[229] Walter Mauny (K. G., d. 1372), a Hainaulter and one of the most celebrated warriors of the time, consistently supported the English cause.

[230] Reginald Lord Cobham of Sterborough (K. G., d. 1361), for whom see n. 36 above.

[231] John Lord Beauchamp of Warwick (K. G., founder), younger brother of the earl of Warwick; he died seven months later, on 2 Dec. 1360.

[232] Guy Lord Brian, or Bryan (K. G., d. 1390).

[233] Jean de Grailly, Captal de Buch (K. G., founder), was a Gascon, a famous soldier, and one of the foremost supporters of the English in the duchy; he was captured by the French in 1372 and remained in prison in Paris until his death in 1377.

[234] Bartholomew Lord Burghersh (K. G., founder; d. 1369) was a famous soldier and close friend of the Black Prince.

[235] Sir Franc van Halen (K. G., d. 1375), a Brabançon knight who had served Edward III since the mid-1340s (Hugh Collins, The Order of the Garter 1348–1461 (Oxford, 2000), p. 55 n. 94).

Messire William de Grasson[236]

Messire Iohan Chandos[237]

Messire Neel de Loryng[238]

Messire Richard de la Vache,[239] et

Messire Miles de Stapeltoun,[240] cheualers;

Sire Iohan de Wynewyk, tresorer de Euerwyk, chanceller nostre seignur le roy;[241]

Maistre Henry de Asshetoun

Maistre Guillame de Loughtebury, sires de ley;[242]

Maistre Iohan de Branketre

Adam de Hiltoun, et

William de Tiryngtoun[243]

comis et deputez a ce de par nostre dit seignur le roy et la nostre *** [a] auec les comis et deputez.*** [b] [244]

Explicit tractatus pacis inter Francie et Anglie regna.

77. ʿPostmodum uero, die Lune uicesimo sexto die Septembris anno Domini millesimo trecentisimo sexagesimo, celebrante missam[d] Guillelmo, archiepisocopo[e] Senon',[245] in ecclesia Beate Marie Boloine supra mare, dominus [f]Iohannes, rex Francie,[g] intra missarum solempnia iuramentum perfecit[h] sub hac forma:[246]

ʿNous, Iohan, roy de France, promettoms en loialte et parole du roy sacre, et iurons sour le corps Ihesu Crist sacre et les saintz euangelies qe cy sount, a tenir et garder, entreamer et acomplir totes les choses et chescune de ycelles contenutz et escriptes en cestes

[a] *lacuna* C   [b] *lacuna* C   [c] *J resumes*   [d] missa *J; add.* domino *J*
[e] episcopo *J*   [f] *M resumes; preceded by* Et Bolonie fecit   [g] *add.* cum .xii.
magnatibus *M*   [h] praestitit *J; J breaks off;* suum *M; M breaks off*

---

[236] This is presumably the William Grandison to whom Edward III granted an annuity of £50 on 13 May 1359, raised to £60 on 30 April 1361 (*CPR 1358–61*, p. 205; *CPR 1361–64*, p. 10). He is difficult to identify, but must have belonged to the Grandison family of which John de Grandison, bishop of Exeter and Lord Grandison, was at this time the head. He may have been the illegitimate son ('William Bastard') of Sir Otes de Grandison mentioned in the latter's will of 1358. Sir Otes's legitimate son William predeceased him in 1349 (*Complete Peerage*, vi. 66). The William listed here was the only knightly witness to the treaty on the English side who never became a Knight of the Garter.

[237] John Chandos (K. G., founder; d. 1369), was one of the most celebrated knights of his age and an intimate of the Black Prince.

[238] Sir Nigel, or Nele, Loryng (K. G., founder; d. 1386), chamberlain of the Black Prince.

[239] Sir Richard de la Vache (K. G.; d. 1365), chamberlain of the royal household 1363–5.

[240] Sir Miles Stapleton of Bedale in Yorkshire (K. G., founder; d. 1364), to be distinguished from his cousin Sir Miles Stapleton of Haddlesey, who died in 1372 (*Oxford DNB*, 'Stapleton, Miles', article by C. Shenton).

Lord William Grandison[236]
Lord John Chandos[237]
Lord Nigel Loryng[238]
Lord Richard de la Vache,[239] and
Lord Miles Stapleton,[240] knights;
Sir John Winwick, treasurer of York, chancellor of our lord the king;[241]
Master Henry Ashton
Master William Loughborough, men of law;[242]
Master John Brancaster
Adam Hilton, and
William Tirrington[243] committed and deputed for this matter by appointment of our said lord the king and our . . . with the commissioners and deputies . . .[244]

Here ends the treaty of peace between the kingdoms of France and England

77. Following this, that is to say on Monday 26 September ⟨*recte* October⟩ in the year of Our Lord 1360, while William, archbishop of Sens,[245] celebrated mass in the church of the Blessed Mary at Boulogne-on-sea, Lord John, king of France, swore his oath during the solemnities of the mass in the following form:[246]

'We, John, king of France, promise faithfully on the sacred word of a king, and we swear upon the holy body of Jesus Christ and the holy gospels here present, to maintain, uphold, undertake, and implement each and every one of the things contained and written in these

[241] John Winwick was not chancellor but keeper of the king's privy seal, although the great seal was also in his possession at this time (Tout, *Chapters*, iii. 226). He died within two months of the agreement at Brétigny: see above, pp. 62–3.

[242] Henry Ashton was a doctor of laws; William of Loughborough, treasurer of Chichester cathedral, was a doctor of civil law; both were attached to the royal chancery.

[243] John de Brancaster, clerk of the diocese of Norwich, Adam de Hilton, and William Tirrington were all notaries; Hilton and Tirrington were also clerks of the privy seal. Brancaster was apparently the man actually responsible for drafting the treaty (Tout, *Chapters*, iii. 226–7).

[244] For the (lack of) sense of this paragraph, see n. 223 above.

[245] Guillaume de Melun, archbishop of Sens.

[246] The two kings in fact took their oaths on 24 October in the church of St Nicholas at Calais, at a mass celebrated by André de la Roche, abbot of Cluny and papal legate. The main point of the ceremony at Boulogne on 26 October was to allow the heirs to the English and French thrones, Edward the Black Prince and the dauphin, Charles, to swear their oaths in each other's presence there. As noted below, however, King Jean did also repeat his oath and publicly proclaim the peace on 26 October at Boulogne, as did a number of other French magnates, presumably including those listed here immediately following the oath: Delachenal, *Histoire de Charles V*, ii. 252–63.

articles cy nomez par la fourme et en manere comprise es letres ordinez et accordez par nostre consail.'

Item, dominus dux iura les choses iurez par le roy de France.[247]

78. [a]Nomina magnatum [b]regni Francie.[b]

Dominus Edwardus princeps Wallie[c] [248]

Dominus Karolus dux Normannie

Dominus [d]archiepiscopus Remen'[d] [249]

Dominus Petrus [e]archiepiscopus Rothomag'[e] [250]

Dominus Guillelmus archiepiscopus Senonen' [251]

Dominus Ludouicus comes Stanpie[252]

Dominus Egidius episcopus Nouiomen'[253]

Dominus Iohannes, dominus de Garensers

Dominus Arnulphus d'Audenham, marescallus regni Francie

Dominus Willelmus de Recurrour, senescallus Bolonie[f]

79. Eisdem die, loco et anno, post iuramentum dicti domini regis, ut premittitur, prefatum unusquisque istorum dominorum iurarunt sub hiis uerbis:

'Nous, tiel et tiel, iurons sur le corps Ihesu Crist et les saintz euangelies qe cy sont escritz, tenir et garder totes les choses iurez par le roy mon seignur, et noun uenir en countre uous, tant come en nous est, ou il nous poet tocher.'

fo. 268[r] **80.** *Sequitur iuramentum regis Francie.*[254] | *Iuramenta facta per Iohannem regem Francie.*

i. Premierement, il a iure, conferme et approue par serement la paes et tot la accord fait a Bretigny par la manere q'il est escript et depuis corrigie a Caleys, et ycelui es touz ces poyntz et articles, pour tant come luy touche acomplir et enterminer et non uenir en contraire.

---

[a] *J resumes*   [b–b] *ibidem iuratum J*   [c] *add.* dominus H. dux Lancastriae *J*
[d–d] *rep. J*   [e–e] *word order reversed J*   [f] *J breaks off*

[247] The 'lord duke' was presumably the dauphin, Charles, duke of Normandy, mentioned again two lines below. The inclusion of the prince of Wales under the 'magnates of the kingdom of France' was presumably to counterbalance the dauphin, they being the heirs to the two kingdoms. The inclusion in J of the name of Henry, duke of Lancaster, following that of the prince of Wales, may have been because he held lands in France (Fowler, *King's Lieutenant*, pp. 71–2, 172).

[248] The Black Prince did not at this point hold any lands or titles in France; but in addition to counterbalancing the dauphin (see previous note), his inclusion on this list may

articles mentioned here in accordance with the form and manner set out in the letters drawn up and agreed by our council.'

Also, the lord duke swore the things sworn by the king of France.[247]

78. *The names of the magnates of the kingdom of France*
Lord Edward, prince of Wales[248]
Lord Charles, duke of Normandy
The lord archbishop of Reims[249]
Lord Peter, archbishop of Rouen[250]
Lord William, archbishop of Sens[251]
Lord Louis, count of Étampes[252]
Lord Giles, bishop of Noyon[253]
Lord Yon, lord of Garencières
Lord Arnold d'Audrehem, marshal of the kingdom of France
Lord William de Recurrour, seneschal of Boulogne

79. On the same day and year, and in the same place, following this oath of the said lord king, as noted above, each one of the aforesaid lords took an oath in the following words:

'We, such and such, swear upon the body of Jesus Christ and the holy gospels written here to maintain and uphold all the things sworn by my lord the king, and, insofar as it lies in our power, not to do anything contrary to them in any matter which concerns us.'

80. *Here follows the oath of the king of France.*[254] *The oaths taken by John, king of France.*

i. First, he has sworn, confirmed, and approved on oath the peace and all the agreement made at Brétigny in the manner that it was written down and subsequently corrected at Calais, and all the points and articles included in it, insofar as it behoves him to accomplish and implement it and not do anything contrary to it.

have been in anticipation of his grant of the Principality of Aquitaine in 1362 (below, pp. 142–4).

[249] Jean de Craon, archbishop of Reims.

[250] Pierre de la Forêt, 'cardinal of Rouen', who in fact ceased to be archbishop of Rouen in 1356; the see was vacant from 1359 to 1362 (*Chronica Johannis de Reading et Anonymi Cantuariensis*, p. 364).

[251] Guillaume de Melun, archbishop of Sens.

[252] Louis of Evreux, count of Étampes.

[253] Gilles de Lorris, bishop of Noyon.

[254] The oaths sworn by the French and English kings which follow may also be found (in the first rather than the third person), in *Foedera*, iii (2), pp. 520–1, where they are dated 24 October at Calais.

ii. Item, il a iure affaire les renunciacions, cessions et transportz qe sont affaire de sa partie et accordez par son conseil, et ycelles enuoier et deliuerer au roi d'Engleterre ou a ces deputez au iour et lieu contenutz es letres accordez des parties.

iii. Item, il a iure de sesser de user souerainte et ressors quant a les choses qe tient le roi d'Engleterre et qe lui serront baillez et les queles lui deyuont demourer par uertue du dit accord et traitie, par la fourme et manere et iusqe au temps exprimez et contenutz es letres sour ce faitz par les conseils des parties.

iv. Item, il ad iure affaire deliuerer au roi d'Engleterre les chasteux, uilles et terres qe lui doiuent ester baillez, pour fair uoider les forteresses occupez ou roialme de France par le roi d'Engleterre, ces allies, aidantz ou adherentz, par la fourme, manere et solonc la moderacion contenu es letres sour ce faitez.

v. Item, il a iure deliuerer et faire deliuerer, au roi d'Engleterre ou a ces deputez, totes les terres, uilles et pais qe lui doit bailler et deliuerer par le dit accord, pour le temps, fourme et manere accordez par les consailz des parties, et lui baillera ou ferra bailler les letres qe bailler et deliuerer lui doit por la deliuerance des dites terres, et q'il paiera touz les sommes du quel il est tenutz de paier au roi d'Engleterre pour le temps et manere accordez par le consail des partiz.

vi. Item, il a iure renuncier a toute guerre et proces du fait contre le roi d'Engleterre et ces heirs solonc la fourme des letres sour ce accordez.

vii. Item, il a iure les alliances faitz au roi d'Engleterre par la manere qe accordez sont, ouesqe la modificacion q'est faite des Escoz et de Britaigne.

viii. Item, *"il a"* iure faire et accomplir par la manere accordee tout ce q'il doit et est tenutz de faire des ostages q'il doit bailler au roy d'Engleterre.

ix. Item, q'il lerra et deliuera as eglises*ᵇ* tot ce qe a este occupez de lour pour*ᶜ* occasion de la guerre, *ᵈ⟨et pardonnera⟩ᵈ* totes offenses par la manere qe accordez est.

x. Item, qe les seremenz qe sont affaire par ces enfauntz ou autres de sa parte par le dit accord, il les ferra faire au plus tost q'il porra bonementz et delyuera par le dit accord.

---

ii. Also, he has sworn to make the renunciations, cessions, and transfers which need to be made on his part and have been agreed by his council, and to send and deliver them to the king of England or his deputies at the time and place specified in the letters agreed by the parties.

iii. Also, he has sworn to cease exercising sovereignty and ressort with respect to the things which belong to the king of England and which will be handed over to the latter and ought to remain with him by virtue of the said agreement and treaty, in the form and manner and up until the time specified and contained in the letters relating to this drawn up by the councils of the parties.

iv. Also, he has sworn to deliver to the king of England the castles, towns, and territories which ought to be handed over to him in order to end the occupation of the fortresses occupied in the kingdom of France by the king of England, his allies, supporters, or adherents, in the form and manner and in accordance with the conditions contained in the letters drawn up relating to this.

v. Also, he has sworn to deliver, and to ensure the delivery of, to the king of England or his deputies, all the territories, towns, and lands which he ought by the said agreement to hand over and deliver to him, in the time, form, and manner agreed by the councils of the parties, and he will make sure to hand over to him the letters which he ought to hand over and deliver to him for the transfer of the said territories; and that he will pay all the sums which he is obliged to pay to the king of England in the time and manner agreed by the councils of the parties.

vi. Also, he has sworn to desist from all war and direct action against the king of England and his heirs in accordance with the form of the letters agreed on this point.

vii. Also, he has sworn the alliances made with the king of England in the manner that they were agreed, including the conditions agreed concerning the Scots and Brittany.

viii. Also, he has sworn to do and accomplish in the agreed manner everything which he is bound and obliged to do concerning the hostages which he must hand over to the king of England.

ix. Also, that he will hand over and deliver to the churches everything of theirs which has been occupied by reason of the war, and will pardon all offences in the manner that has been agreed.

x. Also, he will ensure the taking of the oaths which by the said agreement are to be taken by his children or others of his party as soon as it can easily be done, and will deliver them in accordance with the said agreement.

⟨xi.⟩[a] Item, qe toutes[b] les letres q'il doit enuoier ou bailler au roy d'Engleterre auant ou apres la deliuerance de sa persone, il baillera et enuoiera, par la fourme, temps et manere accordez entre les parties, et ferra et acomplira tot ce qe faire doit par le dit accord et par manere contenu en ycelle et es letres accordez par les consealx des parties.

81. *Sequitur iuramentum prestitum per dominum regem Anglie. Iuramentum regis Anglie.[c]*

fo. 268ᵛ

i. Premierement, q'il iure, conferme et approue par serment la paes et totes les tretee et accord faitz a Bretigny en manere q'est escrit et corrigie a Caleys, et celui es touz poyntz et article, pur tant come il lui touche acomplir et terminer et nient uenir en contre.

ii. Item, q'il iure affaire les renunciacions, cessions et transportz qe sont affaire de sa partie, et ycelles enuoier et deliuerer au roy de France ou a ces deputez a iour et lieu contenutz es letres accordez des parties.

iii. Item, q'il iura de sesseer de user le noun du roi de France, selonc accord.

iv. Item, q'il iure deliuerer au roi de France les forteresses occupez par engleis en roialme de France, solonc la fourme accordez.

v. Item, qe par serement il renunce a tote guerre et process fait contre le roi de France et ses heirs, solonc la fourme accordez.

vi. Item, q'il iure les alliances faites au roi de France par manere accordee, ouesqe la modificacion qi est faite de Flandres et de Britaigne.

vii. Item, q'il iure la deliuerance de la persone du roi de France par la manere accorde, et des prisons de Poitiers et des dits ⟨ostages⟩[d] qe doiuent aler ouesqe le roi de France.

viii. Item, qe [e]⟨il iure⟩[e] la deliuerance des ostages, et coment ils serront gouerne et demene par la manere qe accorde est.

ix. Item, q'il iure confermer les priuileges des bones uilles qe lui soient baillez par la manere accordee.

x. Item, q'il lerra et deliuerra as esglises totes les terres q'ils ont eux et qe lur serront baillez par le dit accord, par manere traitie.

---

[a] xi. *edd.; om.* C   [b] toutes *edd., from* Foedera iii (*1*), *520;* contre C   [c] *heading* Iuramentum domini regis Anglie *rep. at beg. of new fo.* C   [d] ostages *edd., from* Foedera iii (*1*), *521; om.* C   [e-e] il iure *edd., from* Foedera iii (*1*), *521; om.* C

xi. Also, that he will hand over and send all the letters which he ought to send or hand over to the king of England before or after he is released in person, in the form, time, and manner agreed between the parties, and he will do and accomplish everything which he ought to do by the said agreement and in the manner specified in it and in the letters agreed by the councils of the parties.

81. *Here follows the oath taken by my lord the king of England. The oath of the king of England.*

i. First, that he swears, confirms, and approves by oath the peace and the entire treaty and agreement made at Brétigny in the manner that it was written down and corrected at Calais, and all the points and articles included in it, insofar as it behoves him to accomplish and implement it and not do anything contrary to it.

ii. Also, that he swears to make the renunciations, cessions, and transfers which need to be made on his part, and to send and deliver these to the king of France or his deputies at the time and place specified in the letters agreed by the parties.

iii. Also, he swears to cease using the name of King of France, as agreed.

iv. Also, that he swears to deliver to the king of France the fortresses occupied by the English in the kingdom of France in the agreed manner.

v. Also, that he renounces by oath all war and direct action against the king of France and his heirs, in accordance with the agreed form.

vi. Also, that he swears the alliances made with the king of France in the manner that they were agreed, including the conditions agreed concerning Flanders and Brittany.

vii. Also, that he swears with respect to the release of the king of France's person in the agreed manner, along with the prisoners of Poitiers and the ten hostages who ought to go with the king of France.

viii. Also, ⟨he swears⟩ concerning the handing over of the hostages, and how they are to be looked after and treated in the manner which has been agreed.

ix. Also, that he swears to confirm the privileges of the good towns that will be handed over to him in the agreed manner.

x. Also, that he will hand over and deliver to the churches all the territories which they had and which are to be handed over to them by the said agreement, in the manner of the treaty.

xi. Item, qe les serementz q'il sont affaire par ses enfantz et autres de sa partie par le dit accord, il les ferra faire a plus tost q'il purra bonement.

xii. Item, qe totes les letres q'il doit enuoier ou bailler au roi de France auant ou apres la deliuerance de sa persone, il enuoiera par la manere et forme accordez, et ferra et acomplira tot ce qe faire doit par le dit accord et par la manere contenu en ycelles.

Iuramentum regis Anglie

'Nous, Edward, roi d'Engleterre, promettoms en loiaute et parole du roi faite, et iurons sour le corps Ihesu Crist sacre et les saintz euangelies qe cy sont, tenir, garder, enterminer et acomplir totes les choses et chescune de ycelles contenutz et escritz en ceste role par la fourme et manere comprises es letres ordinez et accordez par nostre consail.'

'Nous, Edward, eisne filz au roi d'Engleterre, prince de Gales, promettons et iurons sour le corps Ihesu Crist sacre et sour les seintz euangelies qe cy sont, tenir, garder, enterminer et acomplir totes les fo. 269ʳ choses et chescune | de yceles par nostre dit seignur et piere roy d'Engleterre iurez et promises, par fourme et manere comprise en le role et es letres ordinez et accordez par le consail nostre dit seignour et piere.'

82. ᵃPost hec, idem dominusᵇ Iohannes, rex Francie,ᶜ de Caleys ad uillam Boloun supra mare transiens, ibidem, in presencia domini principis Wallie et ᵈepiscoporum regni Francie, magnatumque et communitatum dicti regni Francie, tractatum pacis huiusmodi pub-licauitᵈ et iurauit prescriptosᵉ articulos pacis quatenus eum concer-nunt in omnibus obseruare.²⁵⁵ ᶠEt post hec, per dictumᵍ regem Francie missis in Angliam obsidibus prelocutis,ʰ et demum sic inter regna Francie et Anglie pace firmataᶠ sigillis utriusque partis scriptis autenticis roboratis, rex Anglie in Angliam, et idemⁱ rex Francorum in Franciam, ʲubi uolebantʲ libere diuertebant.

83. ᵏDe pestilencia et mortalitate gencium.ᵏ Anno Domini millesimo trecentisimo sexagesimo,ˡ²⁵⁶ per totum orbem terrarum incepit grauis

---

ᵃ *JM resume*   ᵇ *om. J*   ᶜ *add. post iuramentum regis Anglie M*   ᵈ⁻ᵈ *aliorum tractantium pacis promisit M*   ᵉ *scriptos J*   ᶠ⁻ᶠ *om. M*   ᵍ *dominum J*   ʰ *om. J*   ⁱ *om. JM*   ʲ⁻ʲ *om. M*   ᵏ⁻ᵏ *heading written in text C; heading Secunda pestilencia J*   ˡ *remainder of paragraph condensed as follows: fuit secunda pestilencia ad terciam partem hominum M*

²⁵⁵ For the assembly at Boulogne, see n. 246 above.
²⁵⁶ Tait, working from J (which also has 1360), thought that the chronicler must have

xi. Also, that he will ensure the taking of the oaths which by the said agreement ought to be taken by his children and others of his party, as soon as it can easily be done.

xii. Also, that he will send all the letters which he ought to send or hand over to the king of France before or after he is released in person, in the agreed manner and form, and he will do and accomplish everything which he ought to do in accordance with the said agreement and the manner specified in it.

The oath of the king of England.

'We, Edward, king of England, promise faithfully and on the given word of a king, and we swear upon the holy body of Jesus Christ and the holy gospels which are here present, to maintain, uphold, undertake, and implement each and every one of the things included and written in this record, in the form and manner specified in the letters drawn up and agreed by our council.'

'We, Edward, eldest son of the king of England, prince of Wales, promise and swear on the holy body of Jesus Christ and the holy gospels which are here present, to uphold, maintain, undertake, and implement each and every one of the things sworn and promised by our said lord and father the king of England, in the form and manner specified in the record and in the letters drawn up and agreed by the council of our said lord and father.'

82. Following this, the same Lord John, king of France, having left Calais and gone to the town of Boulogne-on-sea, there, in the presence of the lord prince of Wales and the bishops, magnates, and counts of the kingdom of France, publicly proclaimed the aforesaid treaty of peace and swore to observe the said articles of peace insofar as they related to him in all matters.[255] And then, once the aforementioned hostages had been sent over to England by the said king of France, and thus at last peace between the kingdoms of France and England had been confirmed and properly authenticated in writing with the seals of each party, the kings of England and France, free to go wherever they wanted, returned to England and France respectively.

83. *The pestilence and mortality of people.* In the year of Our Lord 1360,[256] a dreadful pestilence and mortality among people broke out

meant to write 1361 here, and emended his text accordingly. Certainly, most of the other English chroniclers dated the outbreak of the 'second plague' to 1361, although the chronicle of the Grey Friars at Lynn agrees with our chronicler that it began in 1360

pestilencia et gentium mortalitas, adeo quod apud Auinion', in Romana curia, circiter septem cardinales et alii prelati existentes ibidem et alii clerici diuersarum nacionum morte subitanea obierunt.^a Et postea in aliis mundi partibus ^bsic efferbuit,^b quod uix tertia pars gencium remansit in uita. Postmodum in Anglia mense Iulii eodem anno incepit dicta pestilencia, in qua primo^c pueri et iuuenes incipiebant mori communiter, et deinde senes, tam religiosi quam^d clerici beneficiati, et alii sine delectu personarum subito ab hoc seculo decesserunt, fixis primitus ^eulceribus et^e maculis et aliis signis mortis in corporibus sic decedentium tunc ubique. Tuncque multe erant ecclesie uacantes et inofficiate pro defectu sacerdotum, ^fet mulieres pro magna parte remanebant superstites, adeo quod multe erant uidue, quarum plures non notis personis sed extraneis et precipue uiris bellicosis de Normannia se ex capite proprio maritari fecerunt.^f

84. De morte episcoporum Anglie.^g Et durauit dicta^h pestilencia per quatuor menses et amplius in partibus anglicanis.ⁱ Et in ipsa pestilencia de prelatis subito mortui fuerunt frater Iohannes de Scapeya, Roffen' episcopus, cui successit magister Willelmus de Witleseye doctor in decretis;²⁵⁷ et frater Iohannes de Lile, Elien' episcopus, cui successit dominus Simon, abbas Westm',²⁵⁸ et dominus Iohannes Trillek, episcopus Herforden', cui successit magister Ludouicus de Cherletoun;²⁵⁹ et dominus Thomas Fastolf, episcopus Meneuen', cui successit magister Adam Hoghtoun;²⁶⁰ et dominus Michael de Northburgh, episcopus London', cui successit magister Simon de Sudbury;²⁶¹ et dominus Reginaldus Brian, Wygorn' episcopus, cui successit magister Iohannes Barnet in

---

^a morierunt J   ^{b-b} om. J   ^c uero J   ^d om. J   ^{e-e} om. J   ^{f-f} om. J
^g marg. sketch of mitred head C   ^h om. J   ⁱ JM break off

('about Michaelmas'). It should also be noted that two of the bishops whose deaths our chronicler ascribed to the plague (see the following paragraph) died in 1360. The exchequer and judicial benches were closed on account of the plague on 10 May 1361, and it lasted with varying intensity in different parts of the country until the autumn of 1362. The mortality suffered during this plague has never been studied in as much detail as it deserves, but the likelihood is that it was around 15 to 20 per cent. Several contemporaries remarked on the fact that it was especially virulent among young people, with both the chronicler of Louth Park Abbey and the Anonimalle Chronicle referring to it as the 'children's plague', although it was also noted, and can to some extent be confirmed from surviving records, that it seems to have hit the aristocracy almost as hard as the Black Death of 1348–50. Walsingham agreed with our chronicler that more men than women died, and John of Reading also commented on the fact that plague widows, showing no shame, rushed to marry foreigners: see Horrox, The Black Death, pp. 85–8;

in all parts of the world, as a result of which, in the Roman Curia at Avignon, about seven cardinals as well as other prelates living there suddenly died, as did other clerics of various nations; following which it spread to other parts of the world, so that scarcely one-third of the population remained alive. In England, it was in the month of July of the same year that this pestilence subsequently broke out, in which generally it was first boys and young men who began to die, followed by old men; monks, beneficed clerks, and others without distinction were suddenly taken from this world, their bodies having first been afflicted by ulcers and blotches and other signs of death in the same way as those who died everywhere at this time. And as a result many churches were left vacant and unserved because of the lack of priests, although women for the most part survived, so that there were numerous widows, several of whom took it into their own heads to marry themselves off, not to people who were known but to foreigners, and especially to warlike men from Normandy.

84. *The death of bishops of England.* This pestilence lasted for four months and more in English parts; and among the prelates who died suddenly in this pestilence were Brother John de Sheppey, bishop of Rochester, who was succeeded by Master William de Whittlesey, doctor of canon law;[257] and Brother John ⟨recte Thomas⟩ de Lisle, bishop of Ely, who was succeeded by Lord Simon ⟨Langham⟩, abbot of Westminster;[258] and Lord John Trilleck, bishop of Hereford, who was succeeded by Master Lewis de Charlton;[259] and Lord Thomas Fastolf, bishop of St David's, who was succeeded by Master Adam Houghton;[260] and Lord Michael Northburgh, bishop of London, who was succeeded by Master Simon de Sudbury;[261] and Lord Reginald Brian, bishop of Worcester, who was succeeded in his bishopric by

A. H. Thompson, 'The pestilences of the fourteenth century in the diocese of York', *Archaeological Journal*, lxxi (1914), 97–154; J. C. Russell, *British Medieval Population* (Albuquerque, 1948), pp. 215–8; *Foedera*, iii (2), p. 616; *Chronica Johannis de Reading et Anonymi Cantuariensis*, pp. 150, 212.

[257] John Sheppey, bishop of Rochester from 1352, died on 19 October 1360; William Whittlesey was bishop of Rochester until 1364 (*HBC*, p. 267).

[258] Thomas de Lisle, bishop of Ely from 1345, died on 23 June 1361; Simon Langham was bishop of Ely until 1366 (*HBC*, p. 244).

[259] John Trilleck, bishop of Hereford since 1344, died on 20 November 1360; Lewis Charlton was bishop of Hereford until 1369 (*HBC*, p. 250).

[260] Thomas Fastolf, bishop of St David's from 1352, died in June 1361; Adam Houghton was bishop of St David's until 1389 (*HBC*, p. 297).

[261] Michael Northburgh, bishop of London from 1354, died on 9 September 1361; Simon Sudbury was bishop of London until 1375 (*HBC*, p. 258).

episcopatu;[262] et frater Thomas Pascal, episcopus Landauen', cui successit frater Iohannes Godrich de ordine minorum.[263]

85. *De morte ducis Lancastrie.* [a]Item, uicesimo tertio die mensis Martii anno Domini millesimo trecentisimo sexagesimo primo, apud Leycestre obiit dominus Henricus, primus dux Lancastrie,[b] et die Martis sexto die Aprilis eodem anno apud Leycestre in domo sacerdotum | quam idem dux ibidem construi fecit honorifice est humatus.[264]

fo. 269ᵛ

86. *De morte comitis Northamptoun.* Die uero Mercurii in festo Sancte Edithe Virginis anno Domini millesimo trecentisimo sexagesimo, apud Rocheford, obiit dominus Willelmus, comes Northamptoun.[265]

87. *De nupciis domini principis Wallie.* [c]Anno Domini millesimo trecentisimo sexagesimo primo [d]die Dominica uidelicet uicesimo septimo die Octobris, dominus[d] Simon, [e]Dei gracia[e] Cantuar' archiepiscopus,[266 f]apud Wyndesore, presentatis sibi literis apostolicis super dispensacione facta quod dominus Edwardus, princeps[f] Wallie, [g]posset in uxorem ducere dominam[g] [h]Iohannam, comitissam Cantie,[h] [i]filiam domini Edmundi nuper comitis Cantie patruelis sui, illo consanguinitatis[i] non obstante [j]defectu, ac etiam non obstante[j] cognacione spirituali[k] quod idem princeps duos filios dicte comitisse prius[l] de sacro fonte leuauit, [m]matrimonium inter ipsos[n] ex huiusmodi dispensacione apostolica[m] idem archiepiscopus contra conscienciam suam,[o] ut dixit, et coactus, [p]solempniter celebrauit.[p] [267]

---

[a] *M resumes*   [b] *M breaks off*   [c] *JM resume*   [d-d] *om. M*   [e-e] *om. M*
[f-f] celebrauit nupcias inter E. principem *M*   [g-g] et *M*   [h-h] cometissam Cancie
Iohannam *J*   [i-i] *om. M*   [j-j] *om. JM*   [k] *add.* uidelicet *M*   [l] *om. M*
[m-m] *om. M*   [n] eos *J*   [o] *om. J*   [p-p] fecit *M*

---

[262] Reginald Brian, bishop of Worcester from 1352, died on 10 December 1361; he was in fact translated to the see of Ely following the death of Thomas de Lisle, but died before his translation could take effect; John Barnet was bishop of Worcester until 1363 (*HBC*, p. 279).

[263] John Paschal, bishop of Llandaff from 1344, died on 11 October 1361; he was in fact replaced by Roger Cradock, who remained bishop of Llandaff until 1382 (*HBC*, p. 293).

[264] Henry of Grosmont, first duke of Lancaster, died on 23 (or possibly 24) March 1361 (according to the usual reckoning of the author, who began the new year on 25 March, this would still have been 1360, but he appears to have made a slight error in this case). Lancaster was buried in the church of the Newarke, or collegiate church of Our Lady, one of several religious houses which he had founded (*Complete Peerage*, vii. 409; *HBC*, p. 468).

[265] This information is repeated from above, pp. 62–3.

[266] Simon Islip, archbishop of Canterbury 1349–66.

[267] The marriage of the prince of Wales and Joan, the 'Fair Maid of Kent', took place on 10 October 1361 at Windsor (27 October was in any case a Wednesday, not a Sunday). The

Master John Barnet;[262] and Brother Thomas ⟨recte John⟩ Paschal, bishop of Llandaff, who was succeeded by Brother John Godrich of the minorite order.[263]

85. *The death of the duke of Lancaster*. Also, on 23 March in the year of Our Lord 1361, Lord Henry, first duke of Lancaster, died at Leicester, and on Tuesday 6 April of the same year he was buried with honour at Leicester in the house of priests which this same duke had built there at Leicester.[264]

86. *The death of the earl of Northampton*. Also, on Wednesday the feast of St Edith the virgin ⟨16 September⟩ in the year of Our Lord 1360, Lord William, earl of Northampton, died at Rochford.[265]

87. *The wedding of the lord prince of Wales*. On Sunday 27 October in the year of Our Lord 1361, Lord Simon, by the grace of God archbishop of Canterbury[266]—following the presentation to him of papal letters granting a dispensation for Lord Edward, the prince of Wales, to be allowed to marry Lady Joan, countess of Kent, the daughter of Edmund, former earl of Kent, his cousin, notwithstanding this impediment of consanguinity, and also notwithstanding their spiritual affinity arising from the fact that this same prince had previously raised from the holy font the two sons of this same countess—as a result of this papal dispensation, the archbishop solemnly celebrated the marriage between them at Windsor, although he said that he was coerced against his conscience.[267]

bull of dispensation from Pope Innocent VI, dated 7 September 1361, mentioned only one of Joan's sons to whom the prince had acted as godfather ('raised from the holy font'), but also stated that they had already contracted a marriage by 'verba de praesenti', and absolved them from any consequences arising from this (*Foedera*, iii (2), pp. 626–7, which also includes Archbishop Islip's solemnization of the marriage). Joan's father Edmund, earl of Kent, had died in 1331, and following the death of her brother John in 1352, she became countess of Kent in her own right. She had already been married twice, to Sir Thomas Holand and William Montague, earl of Salisbury; her marriage to Montague was annulled in 1349 on the grounds that she claimed to have already been married to Holand at the time when she married the earl, a source of scandal at the time which doubtless contributed to Archbishop Islip's reluctance to perform the marriage ceremony (see, for example, *Polychronicon*, viii. 360), although it was principally the fact that the couple shared a common great-grandfather in King Edward I which required a papal dispensation. Despite the fact that Holand had died in 1360, thus leaving Joan free to remarry, William Montague was still alive (he lived until 1397), which was doubtless a further embarrassment. Edward III is said to have disapproved of the match, and Archbishop Islip apparently warned the couple that some people might challenge the legitimacy of any children they might have. See K. P. Wentersdorf, 'The clandestine marriages of the Fair Maid of Kent', *Journal of Medieval History*, v (1979), pp. 203–31.

88. *^aDe hastiludiis in Chepe.^a De uento terribili, inaudito ^bet magno.^b*
Anno Domini millesimo trecentisimo sexagesimo primo, ^cex parte
domini regis Anglie,^c ^dpost nupcias huiusmodi,^d facta^e ^fubilibet
proclamacione publica de hastiludiis^f in Chepe London',^gper diabo-
lum et matrem eius ac septem peccata mortalia figuratiue per infra,
contra quoscumque uenientes per extra, die Lune septimo decimo die
Ianuarii faciendis, diabolus magnus Sathanas per prenosticaciones
malas angelos suos et signa sue malicie premittens,²⁶⁸ die Sabbati ante
hastiludia huiusmodi, uidelicet ^hin festo Sancti Mauri Abbatis, circa
horam uesperarum dicti diei, inceperunt tempestates horribiles
numquam alias uise uel audite et uentorum turbines in Anglia,
adeo quod domus et edificia pro magna parte corruerunt ad terram,
et quedam alia discooperta deformiter per flatum uentorum huius-
modi remanserunt,²⁶⁹ arboresque fructifere in gardinis etⁱ locis aliis, et
arbores alie in nemoribus et alibi existentes, cum magno sonitu a terra
radicitus euulse fuerunt, ^jac si^j dies^k iudicii adueniret, et inhabitantes
terram Anglie timor ac tremor sic exterruit quod nullus sciuit ubi
secure potuit laticare, nam ecclesiarum campanilia, molendina ad
uentum ac mansiones multe ceciderunt ad terram absque magna
^lcorporum lesione.^l Sed multa in ^millis tempestatibus^m stupenda et
prodigia contigisse dicuntur.ⁿ

89. *De fratre Augustini'.* Et inter cetera sic fertur London' contigisse:
nam quidam frater Iohannes de Suctoun ordinis heremitarum con-
uentus London', robustus corpore, uolens clausisse hostium eorum
ibidem, uentus superuenit magnus et terribilis eleuans eum de terra et
transuexit eum per medium unius fenestre usque in gardinum eorum,
et ibidem per malum, ut creditur, spiritum est super quondam absque
lesione dimissus, et multa alia stupenda tam London' quam alibi tunc
casualiter euenisse dicuntur, mansionesque et edificia per dictum
uentum sic diruta pro defectu operariorum irreperata deformiter
remanserunt. Et ecce dictorum hastiludiorum signa pessima et
malorum presagia futurorum.

^{a-a} *heading in text* C; De magno uento J   ^{b-b} *in marg.* C; J *resumes*   ^{c-c} *om.* J
^{d-d} *om.* M   ^e J *breaks off; add.* sunt hastiludia M   ^{f-f} *om.* M   ^g *add.* diabolo
post nupcias illas et propter . . . M; M *ends with this paragraph, becoming increasingly
compressed, and difficult to read*   ^h J *resumes*   ⁱ *add.* in J   ^{j-j} ac si *over erasure* C
^k *om.* J   ^{l-l} lesione corporum J   ^{m-m} illa tempestate J   ⁿ J *breaks off*

²⁶⁸ John of Reading discusses these jousts in similar terms, also noting that they were
much disrupted by the incessant rain that year, and that the jousters were themselves
disguised as the seven deadly sins (*Chronica Johannis de Reading et Anonymi Cantuariensis*,
p. 151). The seven deadly sins were especially associated with jousting, since the church

88. *Jousts in Cheapside. The great, terrible, and unprecedented wind.* In the year of Our Lord 1361 (n.s. 1362), following this wedding, a public proclamation having been issued everywhere on behalf of the king that jousts would be held at Cheapside in London on Monday 17 January (ostensibly against all comers, but inwardly and figuratively through the agency of the devil and his mother and the seven deadly sins), the great devil Satan sending in advance as warnings his evil angels and signs of his malice,[268] on the Saturday before these jousts, namely, on the feast of St Maurus the abbot ⟨15 January⟩, around the hour of vespers on that day, dreadful storms and whirlwinds such as had never been seen or heard before occurred in England, causing houses and buildings for the most part to come crashing to the ground, while some others, having had their roofs blown off by the force of the winds, were left in that ruined state;[269] and fruit trees in gardens and other places, along with other trees standing in woods and elsewhere, were wrenched from the earth by their roots with a great crash, as if the Day of Judgement were at hand, and fear and trembling gripped the people living in England to such an extent that no one knew where he could safely hide, for church towers, wind-mills, and many dwelling-houses collapsed to the ground, although without much bodily injury. Many extraordinary and prodigious stories are told about what happened during those storms.

89. *The Austin friar.* Among them, an incident is said to have occurred in London, when a certain Brother John de Sutton of the London convent of the order of hermits, a strong man, went to close their doors there, and a powerful and violent gust of wind picked him up off the ground and hurled him through the middle of one of the windows into their garden, where—through the agency of an evil spirit, so it is believed—he was eventually left, without having been injured; and many other extraordinary accidents are said to have happened at that time, in London and elsewhere; and the houses and buildings which were thus destroyed by this wind remained ruined and unrepaired because of the lack of workmen. Behold the wretched omens of these jousts, the harbingers of future evils!

stated that they were all committed by those who took part in tournaments: Juliet Barker, *The Tournament in England 1100–1400* (Woodbridge, 1986), p. 95.

[269] The great storm of 15 January 1362 was clearly comparable to the great storm of October 1987, and every bit as remarkable to contemporaries: see e.g. *Knighton's Chronicle*, p. 184; *Historia Anglicana*, i. 296; *Anonimalle Chronicle*, p. 50, which notes especially the collapse of a number of notable bell towers; and *Eulogium Historiarum*, iii. 229, which describes it as 'a dreadful scourging from God'.

fo. 270^r **90.** *De aliis hastiludiis in Smethefeld factis. De igne apud Clerkenwelle per duos dies.* Anno Domini millesimo trecentisimo sexagesimo secundo, per dominum Edwardum, principem Wallie, facta altera uice ubilibet proclamacione publica de aliis hastiludiis in Smethefeld London' die Lune secundo die Maii contra quascumque naciones faciendis, diabolus uolens iterum radicem sue malicie premittere, die Sabbati ante hastiludia huiusmodi ignis prioratum hospitalis Sancti Iohannis Ierusalem de Clerkenwelle London', ac prouidencias pro dictis hastiludiis ibi factas necnon iocalia multa et lectisternia et bona alia usque ad magnam summam et ualorem, inextinguibiliter incendebat, in quo ignis incendio quinque humana corpora perierunt. Et durauit ignis huiusmodi tam uehemens quod dicto die Sabbati et Dominica sequente usque ad horam uesperarum uix extingui potuit, adeo quod totam ciuitatem London' terruit et turbauit.²⁷⁰ Et hiis malis non obstantibus, facta fuerunt hastiludia solempnia inaudita, cum magnis pompis et uana gloria huius mundi, et durarunt per tres dies et amplius dicta hastiludia, in quibus unus miles occisus est et alii multi lesi sunt et mala plurima contigerunt. Et ecce finem dictorum hastiludiorum, in malo et dura presagia futurorum, et de tercio hastiludio est cauendum, et de futuris periculis quod absit contingentibus in eodem!²⁷¹

91. Duodecimo die mensis Septembris, in crastino Sanctorum Prothi et Iacincti, apud Auinion' Innocencius papa sextus mortuus est.²⁷²

92. *Statuta bona edita.*ᵃ Anno regni regis Edwardi tercii a conquestu sexto et tricesimo, idem rexᵇ in parlamento suo in quindena Sancti Michaelis apud Westm' tento, ad honorem et placenciam Dei et ad releuamen oppressionum sui populi et ad peticionem communitatis dicti regni Anglie, per consensum prelatorum, magnatum et procerum dicti regni, concessit pro se et heredibus suis imperpetuum articulos subsequentes:²⁷³

ᵃ *running across top of fols. 270v–271r* De statutis bonis per regem editis C   ᵇ *marg.*
sketch of crowned head and neck C

---

²⁷⁰ The priory of the Knights Hospitallers, St John's, Clerkenwell, founded in about 1144: D. Knowles and R. Hadcock, *Medieval Religious Houses, England and Wales* (Harlow, 1971), p 244.

²⁷¹ John of Reading, followed by Walsingham, says that these jousts were held at Smithfield during the first five days of May 1362; the king and queen were present, along with a great number of English and French knights, and some Spanish, Cypriot, and Armenian knights, who according to John of Reading attended in the hope of persuading some English knights to come and help them to defend their lands against pagan invaders: *Chronica Johannis de Reading et Anonymi Cantuariensis*, pp. 152–3; *Historia Anglicana*, i. 296–7.

90. *More jousts held at Smithfield. A fire at Clerkenwell for two days.* In the year of Our Lord 1362, a public proclamation having once again been issued everywhere by Lord Edward, prince of Wales, of further jousts to be held at Smithfield in London on Monday 2 May against all comers from whatever nation, and the devil wishing once again to demonstrate the root of his malice, on the Saturday before these jousts a fire which could not be extinguished destroyed the priory of the hospital of St John of Jerusalem at Clerkenwell, London, together with the supplies gathered there for the jousts and many jewels and precious cloths and other goods of great worth and value, during which conflagration five human beings perished; and this fire continued with such intensity that neither on that Saturday nor until the hour of vespers on the following Sunday could it be properly put out, which terrified the whole city of London and threw it into turmoil.[270] Yet notwithstanding these evils, the jousts went ahead with unprecedented grandeur, with all the pomp and vainglory of this world, and these jousts lasted for three days and more, during which one knight was killed and many others were wounded and many other evil things happened. Behold the consequence of these jousts, the dire and evil harbingers of things to come! And be wary of a third joust, and God forbid that future perils might result from it![271]

91. On the twelfth day of the month of September, the day following the feast of SS Prothus and Hyacinth, Pope Innocent VI died at Avignon.[272]

92. *Good statutes published.* In the thirty-sixth year of the reign of King Edward the third since the conquest, the same king, in his parliament held at Westminster on the quinzaine of Michaelmas ⟨13 October 1362⟩, to the honour and gratification of God and to relieve the oppression of his people and at the petition of the community of the said realm of England, with the consent of the prelates, magnates, and nobles of the said kingdom, granted in perpetuity for himself and his heirs the following articles.[273]

[272] The date is correct: Innocent VI was elected pope on 18 December 1352 and died on 12 September 1362.

[273] What follows is taken from the Statute Roll for the thirty-sixth year of Edward III's reign, issued following the parliament of October 1362. The first four clauses of the statute are reproduced more or less verbatim, although in Latin rather than the Anglo-Norman in which they occur on the roll. Some of the subsequent clauses are then abbreviated. For comparison, see *Statutes of the Realm*, i. 371–6. The 'Great Statute of Purveyors' of 1362 is discussed in C. Given-Wilson, 'Purveyance for the Royal Household, 1362–1413', *Bulletin of the Institute of Historical Research*, lvi (1983), pp. 145–63.

93. *De magna carta.* *ᵃ*In primis,*ᵃ* ²⁷⁴ quod magna carta et carta de foresta et statuta tam tempore suo quam progenitorum suorum salubriter edita in omnibus obseruentur.

94. *De capcionibus uictualium de prouisoribus non faciendis. De emptoribus regis.* Item,²⁷⁵ pro grauissimis querelis prouisorum uictualium tam hospicii regis et regine Anglie quam aliorum dominorum Anglie sepe factis, rex ex proprio motu suo concessit et ordinauit, pro tranquillitate sui populi, quod extunc nullus nisi rex ipse et regina dumtaxat capcionem uictualium habeat, et preterea ad hec addendo statuit quod pro prouidenciis hospicii dictorum regis et regine fiat prouita solucio super unguem, uidelicet quod de prouisis rebus sicut uenduntur per circuitum in marcatiis, quodque odiosum nomen prouisorum mittetur sub uocabulo emptorum. Et si*ᵇ* huiusmodi emptorum regis de et super nuncius bono modo concordare non poterit cum uenditore, tunc capciones uictualium fiant per uisum et testimonium et appreciacionem dominorum seu balliuorum suorum, constabulariorum et quatuor proborum hominum cuiuslibet uille, et hoc fiat per indenturam inter eosdem emptores ac alios supradictos, continentes quantitatem huiusmodi uictualium et ualorem et inter quas personas, et quod dicte capciones fiant bono modo et absque

fo. 270ᵛ duricia, | uituperio siue minis, et quod empciones uictualium huiusmodi et capciones in locis in quibus maior habetur copia fiant, et hoc in tempore competenti, et plus non capiatur quam sit opus pro hospiciis antedictis, et quod numerus huiusmodi emptorum quatenus bono modo fieri poterit minuetur, quodque huiusmodi emptores sint sufficientes ad respondendum regi et populo, et quod nullus eorum sub se habeat deputatum, eorumque commissiones magno regis sigillentur sigillo, et quolibet dimidio anno dicte commissiones in cancellaria regis restituantur et alie noue fiant, et in dictis commissionibus modus et forma huiusmodi capcionis et empcionis comprehendantur adplenum, et extunc omnes alie commissiones prouisorum penitus reuocentur, quodque nullus aliis dominorum emptoribus obedire nisi uoluerit teneatur, nec huiusmodi emptoribus dictorum hospiciorum regis et regine nisi soluciones uelint facere super

---

ᵃ⁻ᵃ In primis *rep.* C   *ᵇ* *interlinear* C

---

²⁷⁴ This paragraph reproduces clause 1 of the statute, although it should be noted that whereas the statute included the king's eldest son (at this time, the Black Prince) along with the king and queen as being exempt from the prohibition on purveyance, the chronicler either deliberately or otherwise omitted him.

93. *Magna Carta.* First,[274] that Magna Carta and the Charter of the Forest and those statutes which have been granted wisely both in his own time and in his predecessors' time should be observed in all points.

94. *Seizures of victuals not to be made by purveyors. The king's buyers.* Also,[275] on account of the grievous complaints frequently made concerning purveyors of victuals both for the household of the king and queen of England and of other lords of England, the king of his own accord has granted and ordained, for the tranquillity of his people, that henceforward nobody except the king himself and the queen should be allowed to seize victuals; and moreover in addition to this he decreed that for purveyances for the household of the said king and queen payment must be made on the nail, that is to say, that the items purveyed should be sold at the price obtaining in the vicinity of markets; also that the odious name of purveyors should be replaced by the word buyers; and if the agent for the king's buyers is not able to come to an amicable agreement with the seller, then the taking of the victuals should be done by view and testimony and valuation of the lords or their bailiffs, constables, and four honest men of each town, and that it should be done by indenture between these buyers and the aforesaid persons, specifying the quantity and value of the victuals and the persons involved; and that these purchases should be made amicably and without duress, enmity, or threats, and that such purchases and seizures of victuals should happen in places where there is greatest abundance, and at a convenient time, and nor should more be taken than is needed for the said households; also, that the number of these buyers should be reduced by as much as possible, and that these buyers should be accountable to the king and the people, and that none of them should have a deputy under him, and their commissions should be sealed with the king's great seal, and every half-year the said commissions should be returned to the king's chancery and new ones made; and in these commissions the manner and form of such purchases and seizures should be set out in full, and henceforward all other commissions for purveyors should be utterly revoked; and that no one shall be constrained to obey other lords' buyers unless he wishes to, nor the buyers for the said households of the king and queen unless they are prepared to make payment on the

---

[275] The next two paragraphs reproduce clause 2 of the statute.

unguem, et quod nullus propter inobedienciam in ea parte in contemptum ponatur.

95. *De bladis.* Et quod emptores bladorum et brasium pro dictis hospiciis ea mensurari faciant non per cumulum sed per mensuram rasam, et pro cariagio dictorum bladorum et aliarum rerum promptissime satisfiat, et quod plus quam opus fuerit de hoc cariagio non capietur, et si nullus de dictis emptoribus, post nouas commissiones factas, empciones uel capciones cariagii alio modo quam quod in sua contineatur commissione ⟨faciat⟩,[a] habeat puniciones uite et membrorum sicut in statutis aliis de prouisoribus est contentum.

96. *Item de emptoribus uictualium procurantibus ex odio malum.* Item,[276] quod nullus emptor uictualium seu captor cariagii capiat uel recipiat de nullo uel alio pro faciendo desportum, nec grauet aliquem in suo officio, odio, inuidia uel ex mala uoluntate uel procuracione, et si ipse faciat et si sit conuictus ad sectam partis, reddat parti dampna sua ad triplum, et incarceracionem habeat per duos annos et stabit uoluntati Regis, et ipsius curiam abiurabit, et si persona uelit prosequi,[277] contra eum tercium habebit denariorum recuperatum pro labore, et preter hec hic emptor habeat puniciam superius expressatam. Et preterea ordinatum est quod quilibet emptor in compoto suo declaret et distinguat separatim omnes capciones et empciones cuiuslibet comitatus et uille ac singularis persone.

97. *De commissionibus.* Et[278] pro refrenanda emptorum uictualium et captorum cariagii malicia, fiant commissiones duobus bonis hominibus et legalibus cuiuslibet comitatus, et tertia commissio sit facta uni de hospicio regis nominato in dictis commissionibus, ita quod si aliquis de illis tribus non ueniat, duo procedant ad inquirendum super gestu et factis emptorum et captorum huiusmodi, quantumque receperint et emerint et quantum de cariagio in qualibet uilla ceperint seu uillana, ad audiendum et terminandum contemptus, crimina et delicta tam ad sectam regis quam persone alterius cuiuscumque uolentis conqueri de eisdem, et pro informacione facienda iusticie, congregentur senescalli, thesaurarii et contrarotulatores dictorum hospiciorum, et uocari faciant coram eis omnes clericos officiarios

---

[a] faciat *edd.*; *om.* C

[276] This paragraph reproduces clause 3 of the statute.
[277] The author as copyist has slightly garbled the sense of this clause, which says at this point that if the injured party does not wish to sue, a third party may do so, receiving a third of any money recovered for his effort.

nail; and no one shall be charged with disobedience for showing contempt in this regard.

95. *Grains.* Also, that the buyers of grain and malt for the said households should have them measured not by the heaped but by the razed measure, and for the carriage of the said grain and other things they shall make immediate satisfaction, and that no more by way of carriage should be taken than is needed; and if, after the new commissions have been made, any of the aforesaid buyers should make purchases or requisition carriage in any way other than what is specified in his commission, he shall suffer punishment of life and limb as is set out in the other statutes concerning purveyors.

96. *Buyers of victuals who procure evil out of hatred.* Also,[276] that no buyer of victuals or taker of carriage should take or receive anything from anyone for granting exemptions, nor shall he harm anyone while in office, through hate, envy, ill will, or by procurement, and if he does so and is convicted at the suit of the party, he shall pay treble damages to the party and be imprisoned for two years and be at the king's pleasure and abjure his court; and if any person wishes to prosecute,[277] he shall have a third of the money recovered from him for his effort, and in addition the buyer will receive the punishment stated above. Furthermore it is decreed that each buyer shall set out and itemize separately in his account all the seizures and purchases from each county and town and individual person.

97. *Commissions.* And[278] in order to curb the malice of buyers of victuals and takers of carriage, let commissions be made out to two good and loyal men of each county, and a third commission to a named member of the king's household in these commissions, in such a way that if any of these three does not come, the other two shall proceed to inquire into the actions and behaviour of these buyers and takers, how much they received and purchased and what carriage they took in each town or village, so as to hear and determine crimes and offences of contempt either at the suit of the king or another party, whoever it might be, who wishes to complain about them; and in order to gather judicial information, let the stewards, treasurers, and controllers of the said households assemble together, and let all the office-bearing clerks of these households be summoned to their

---

[278] This paragraph reproduces clause 4 of the statute.

eorundem hospiciorum ad uidendum parcellas et recepta in partibus
et in dictis expendita officiis, et quolibet quarterio ⟨uel⟩*a* dimidii anni,
certificent in cancellaria regis parcellas captas in qualibet uilla et de
qualibet persona singulariter, quid et quantum, et cancellarius |
fo. 271ʳ   faciet*b* mandari iusticie assignatis, et si repertum fuerit in partibus per
euidencias quod plus ceperint quam liberarint hospiciis antedictis, et
quod non soluerint pro rebus sic captis, habeant illi puniciam de uita
et membro sicut dictum est supra.

98. *De equis eorum.* Item,[279] quod nullus de dictis hospiciis plures
equos teneat quam sit opus, et cetera. Item,[280] quod nullus alius regni
Anglie dominus exceptis rege et regina faciet capciones uictualium,
sed per suos emere faciant et soluere pro eisdem, et cetera.

99. *De capellanis.*ᶜ Item,[281] statuit de consensu prelatorum quod
capellanus parochialis sex marcas, et celebrans annale quinque
marcas, dumtaxat pro suis salariis sint contenti, et cetera.

100. *De placitando in anglicis linguis.* *d*Item,[282] statuit idem rex,
attentis multis dispendiis et incommodis regno Anglie ex hoc quod
in lingua gallica placitarunt cotidie imminentibus, quod exnunc*e* in
dicto regno Anglie fiant*f* placita in lingua anglicana, ita quod quilibet
incola perpendere poterit de suo comodo *g*et incommodo*g* *h*quid sit*h*
dictum, et sibi de remedio et auxilio quociens et quando opus fuerit
melius prouidere.*i*

101. Preterea idem dominus rex, etatis sue anno quinquagesimo,[283]
qui annus quinquagesimus annus iubileus uel remissiuus interpreta-
tur, uolens graciam communitati regni sui facere, ad peticionem
communitatis eiusdem concessit gracias et perdonaciones transgressionum,[284] malefactorum, negligenciarum ignoranciarum ante dictum

---

a uel *edd.; om.* C   *b* faciet *at end of fo. 270v, rep. top of fo. 271r; first occurrence
deleted* C   *c* *marg. sketch of tonsured head* C   *d* *J resumes; preceded by additional
paragraph:* Anno Domini millesimo trecentisimo sexagesimo tertio circa festum
Assumpcionis Beate Marie dominus Edwardus rex ad utilitatem regni sui prohibuit
antiquam monetam florenorum et ordinauit nouam scilicet majorem florenum de
dimidia marca et minorem de .xl. denariis et minimum de .xx. denariis, et circa idem
tempus idem rex ordinauit escambium monete sue fieri Lond', Cant' et Ebor', uidelicet de
argento unum nobile de .iiii. denariis et alium de duobus denariis, et de antiquis sterlingis
sicut fieri sterlingum paulo minorem   *e* extunc *J*   *f* sciant *J*   *g-g* *om.* *J*
h-h quit sicut *J*   *i* expedire *J; J breaks off*

---

[279] This sentence abridges clause 5 of the statute.
[280] This sentence abridges clause 6 of the statute.
[281] This sentence abridges clause 8 of the statute.

presence in order to view the items and receipts in the country and the expenses in each of those offices; and every half- or quarter-year, let them certify in the king's chancery the items taken in each town, and from each individual person, what and how much, and the chancellor shall have orders sent to those assigned to do justice; and if it is found through this evidence in the country that they took more than they delivered to the said households, and that they did not pay for the things thus taken, they shall suffer punishment of life and limb as set out above.

98. *Their horses.* Also,[279] that no member of the said households should keep more horses than are needed, etc. Also,[280] that no other lord of the kingdom of England apart from the king and queen should have victuals seized, but they should buy them through their men and pay for them, etc.

99. *Chaplains.* Also,[281] he decreed, with the consent of the prelates, that a parish chaplain should be content with 6 marks, and an annual celebrant with no more than 5 marks, for their salaries, etc.

100. *Pleading in the English language.* Also,[282] the same king, considering the great expense and inconvenience in the kingdom of England arising every day from the fact that the French language was being used for legal pleas, decreed that henceforth pleading should be conducted in the English language in the said kingdom of England, so that every inhabitant should be able to weigh up whatever might be said to his advantage or disadvantage and make better provision for remedy and help for himself as and when needed.

101. Moreover, the same lord king, being in his fiftieth year,[283] which fiftieth year is reckoned to be a year of jubilee or remission, wishing to act graciously towards the community of his realm, at the petition of the same community granted graces and pardons for transgressions,[284] wrongdoings, acts of negligence and ignorance committed

---

[282] This sentence abridges clause 15 of the statute. The note about the recoinage with which J resumes at this point is clearly misplaced: this recoinage took place in 1351, not 1363, as the result of an order issued by the king on 20 June of that year: *Foedera*, iii (1), pp. 222–3, and cf. *Chronica Johannis de Reading et Anonymi Cantuariensis*, p. 113, and *Chronicon Galfridi le Baker*, p. 116, both of which give the correct year.

[283] Edward III was born on 13 November 1312; his fiftieth birthday thus fell during this parliament, which was dissolved on 17 November.

[284] From 'transgressionum' onwards, this paragraph is a not entirely successful attempt to translate into Latin a section of the general pardon which appears (in Anglo-Norman) in the margin of the Statute Roll and is reproduced in *Statutes of the Realm*, i. 376–7.

parlamentum factorum, quodque articuli iusticiorum itinerancium
unde puniciones et redempciones aut fines, seu pene peccuniarie,
incarceraciones, amerciamenta communitatum, uillarum aut personarum singularium siue ministrorum regis, fierent uel uenire deber-
ent, et remisit escampas latronum et catalla felonum et fugitiuorum
contingentia a tempore perdonacionis ultime facte non soluta, ita
quod de hiis non inquiretur, nec aliquis de populo grauetur, siue
fuerit minister regis uel alius quiscumque, heres coronatorum,
uicecomitum, escaetorum non delinquens, sed penitus remittantur
omnia supradicta, et super huiusmodi perdonacionibus et aliis
contentis in peticione communitatis Anglie et concessis, fiant carte
regie sine feodo pro sigillo uel alicuicumque petenti, sicut in
huiusmodi peticionibus plenius continetur.

102. Anno Domini millesimo trecentisimo sexagesimo*a* secundo,
dominus Edwardus, rex Anglie, de consilio regni sui, destinauit
quosdam burgenses maiores ciuitatis London' et quosdam alios
ceterarum ciuitatum eiusdem regni ad certum numerum apud
Caleys moraturos ibidem, de quibus quidem burgensibus, Iohannem
Wroth, ciuem London', perfecit maiorem dicte uille de Caleys, et
Iohannem Wesenham maiorem stapule lanarum ibidem, una cum aliis
uiris potentibus et magnatis ad uaria ibidem officia pro secura
custodia dicte uille, qui quidem burgenses de uenditione lanarum
et aliarum rerum fecerunt sua mercimonia, et ceteri deputati ibidem
custodiebant fortiter dictam uillam, sicut per consilium regis Anglie
extitit ordinatum.[285]

103. Item, *b*anno Domini millesimo trecentisimo sexagesimo tertio,
dux*c* d'Angou, unus de principalibus*d* ostagiis *e*regis Francie,*e* *f*Lu-
douicus nomine,*f* et eius filius, Lond' morantibus, | accepta dolose*g*
spaciandi licencia,*h* accessit apud Caleys, causa recreacionis, ut
asseruit, habende et ibidem a domino Iohanne Cobham milite, dicte
uille de Caleys capitaneo, ut*i* causa uenandi extra Caleys parum exire
posset uno dierum accepta licencia, cum suis dolose exiuit, cogitans se

fo. 271*v*

---

a .l. C   *b* J resumes   *c* preceded by erased word C   *d* principibus J
e–e words reversed J   *f–f* in marg. C; phrases reversed et eius filius Lodouicus nomine J
g dolosa J   *h* licenciam J   *i* et J

---

[285] The Calais staple was formally established on 1 March 1363, largely in order to make
the town financially independent of the English crown, and a 'new company' of twenty-six
English merchants was set up to govern the town. John Wroth, a fishmonger who had been
mayor of London in 1360–1, became mayor of the town, and John Wesenham, a merchant,

prior to this parliament, as well as the articles of the justices in eyre, whereby punishments, ransoms, and fines—whether financial penalties, imprisonments, amercements of communities, towns, or individual persons, including ministers of the king—might or ought to occur; and he pardoned escapes of thieves and chattels of felons and things due from fugitives since the time of the last pardon which had not been paid, so that no enquiries should be made about these things, nor should any person be molested, be he a minister of the king or any other person, or the innocent heir of a coroner, sheriff, or escheator, but that all the aforesaid things should be entirely remitted; and concerning these pardons and other matters mentioned in the petition from the community of England which have been granted, let royal charters be drawn up without any fee for the seal or anyone having to petition for them, as is clearly set out in these petitions.

102. In the year of Our Lord 1362 (n.s. 1363), Lord Edward, king of England, with the council of his kingdom, sent certain important burgesses of the city of London and a certain number of others from other cities of the same kingdom to reside at Calais; of these burgesses, he made John Wroth, citizen of London, mayor of the said town of Calais, and John Wesenham mayor of the wool staple there, as well as granting various offices there to other powerful men and magnates for the safe custody of the said town; which burgesses did their business through the sale of wool and other things, and the others who had been sent over guarded the town strenuously, just as had been arranged by the king of England's council.[285]

103. Also, in the year of Our Lord 1363, the duke of Anjou, Louis by name, the son of the king of France and one of the principal hostages for him detained in London, having craftily acquired permission to travel, made his way to Calais—for recreational purposes, so he claimed—and one day while there, having been given licence by Lord John Cobham, knight and captain of the said town of Calais, to go a little way out of Calais in order to go hunting, treacherously left with his men, planning not to return to England, which was contrary to his

shipowner, and financier who during the 1340s especially had been active in raising loans to finance Edward III's wars, became mayor of the staple. Unfortunately the two men fell out and became the leaders of opposing factions at Calais, and within two years the king's scheme for the government of the town collapsed, a governor and treasurer were appointed instead, and Wesenham was briefly imprisoned in the Tower of London: see T. H. Lloyd, *The English Wool Trade in the Middle Ages* (Cambridge, 1977), pp. 210–14, and *Oxford DNB*, 'Wesenham, John', article by T. H. Lloyd.

nolle redire ad Angliam, contra iuramentum suum, quasi uenando, et dum in nemoribus extra Caleys quasi uenando, a conspectu inhabitancium uillam de Caleys, fuisset, latenter aufugit et euasit ad partes Francie quas uoluerat, ibidem congregata multitudine lancearum, ut profugus et periurus scienter tanquam proditor equitando.[a] [286]

104. *Rex Cipra*. Anno Domini millesimo trecentisimo sexagesimo tertio, nobilis princeps dominus Petrus, rex Cipri, applicans Douor', intrauit ciuitatem Cant' cum honorabili comitiua suorum ac balliuorum et burgensium ciuitatis Cant' die Martis uicesima quarta die mensis Octobris, et die Mercurii in crastino, uersus regem Anglie London' existentem, dietas suas continuans in festo Apostolorum Simonis et Iude ciuitatem London' intrauit. Et apud Westm', domino regi Anglie per dictum regem Cipri exposita causa aduentus sui in Anglia, asseruit grauiter querelando qualiter Saraceni et Turci totam terram suam Cipri destruxerant bellicose, quodque eius terra Cipri illis non potuit resistere absque christianorum adiutorio aliorum, requirens humiliter ab eo subsidium pro defensione fidei christiane, addensque quod tunc ad triennium fuit dies belli inter ipsum regem et Saracenos, capta primitus treuga, finaliter assignatus. Quibus per dictum regem Anglie benigne auditis, ipse concessit sibi subsidium gencium Anglie ibidem accedere uolencium, et fecit eum secum morari London' et tam in equis quam aliis sibi donaria magna dedit, et unam magnam nauem nouam apud Sandwicum existentem cum peccunia multa nimis. Et postmodum idem rex Cipri, capta licencia a domino rege Anglie, uersus partes suas Cipri arripuit iter suum, et circa festum Sancte Lucie Virginis apud Douor' transfretauit, et fuit cum domino rege Francie apud Bolon in festo Natalis Domini tunc sequente.[287]

[a] *J breaks off*

---

[286] The story of the escape of Louis, duke of Anjou, is difficult to piece together satisfactorily, but it is certain that our chronicler has got at least some of the details wrong. The son of King Jean of France, Louis was one of the four princes of the blood—the dukes of Berri, Orléans, and Bourbon being the others—with whom Edward III had concluded an agreement in November 1362 which they hoped would advance the date of their liberation. In May 1363 they were moved to Calais, having sworn an oath upon their honour that they would not attempt to escape. According to French sources, Anjou went on a 'pilgrimage' to Notre-Dame of Boulogne, where his wife Marie de Châtillon, whom he had barely seen since their marriage in July 1360, was waiting for him, and they slipped off to the castle of Guise together. Edward III described his flight as 'a shame on his honour and on the reputation of his whole family', but despite the exhortations of both the French king and the dauphin, Louis refused to return to English captivity. Delachenal, *Histoire de Charles V*,

oath; and while he was in the woods outside Calais, out of sight of the inhabitants of the town of Calais and pretending to hunt, he secretly slipped away and escaped into the part of France that he had chosen, where a crowd of lancers had gathered, riding like a fugitive and a perjuror, and knowingly like a traitor.[286]

104. *The king of Cyprus.* In the year of Our Lord 1363, the noble prince Lord Peter, king of Cyprus, having landed at Dover, entered the city of Canterbury on Tuesday 24 October with an honourable company of his own men and officials and burgesses of the city of Canterbury; and on the following day, the Wednesday, he set out towards London, where the king of England was, continuing his journey each day until he arrived in the city of London on the feast of the Apostles Simon and Jude ⟨28 October⟩. And at Westminster, once the said king of Cyprus had told the lord king of England the reason for his coming to England, he explained and complained with a heavy heart how the aggression of the Saracens and Turks had destroyed his whole land of Cyprus, and that his land of Cyprus was unable to resist them without the help of other Christians, humbly begging him for assistance in defence of the Christian faith, and adding that the day for war between the said king and the Saracens had been definitively fixed for three years hence, a truce having been established in the meantime. And when the said king of England had listened patiently to this, he granted him the help of men from England who were willing to go there, and he made him stay with him in London and gave him generous gifts of horses and other things, including a big new ship which was lying at Sandwich as well as a large sum of money. And after this the said king of Cyprus set off with the permission of the lord king of England towards his land of Cyprus, embarking at Dover around the feast of St Lucy the virgin ⟨13 December⟩ and spending the subsequent feast of Christmas with the lord king of France at Boulogne.[287]

---

ii. 346–8, and Sumption, *Trial by Fire*, p. 499, 527, date his escape to early September 1363, but the evidence for this is fragmentary, and the *Dictionnaire de Biographie Française*, xviii (Paris, 1994), p. 571, suggests that it may have taken place in October. John Cobham was not in fact captain of Calais at this time (see previous note), but he had been sent to Calais in May with the hostages (*Chronica Johannis de Reading et Anonymi Cantuariensis*, p. 366).

[287] Pierre I de Lusignan, king of Cyprus (1359–69), left Cyprus in October 1362 partly in order to kindle enthusiasm in the West for a crusade, and took the cross at Avignon in March 1363, along with King Jean of France, who was to lead the projected expedition. Despite Jean's death in April 1364, Pierre remained in the West until June 1365, when he left Venice at the head of a crusading force which attacked Alexandria in October:

105. *De rege Francie.*[a] [b]Eodem anno, nobilis princeps dominus Iohannes, rex Francie, tenens festum [c]Natalis Domini[c] apud Bolon supra mare, applicuit Douor' in uigilia Epiphanie Domini, et in ipso[d] morabatur ibidem.[288] Et die Dominica in crastino, post horam nonam circa uesperas dicti diei, intrauit ciuitatem Cantuar' cum magna comitiua[e] nobilium personarum, uidelicet episcopi Ambianen', dom-inorum[f] ducis Aureliani, germani dicti regis, ducis de Berry filii dicti Regis, comitis de Sancto Paulo ac prioris[g] Sancti Iohannis Ierusalem in Francia, domini electi Cluniacen', domini de Tankeruille, camera-rii dicti regis, Gilberti de Moleyns, thesaurarii, ac Roberti[h] Hoget, burgensis Paris', [i]ac etsi aliorum.[i] [289] Et fuit idem rex per dies Lune et Martis sequentes apud Cant', et die Mercurii sequente fuit apud Osprenge, et de hinc[j] continuando dietas suas uenit London', et apud Saueye ibidem fuerat hospitatus. Et causa aduentus sui in Angliam, ut dixit regi Anglie, fuerat primo propter solucionem milionis, secundo pro ostagiis Francie habendis, et super hoc, per ipsum regem Anglie magnatum conuocato consilio de ostagiis Francie liberandis,[290] de diebus in dies dilacionem deliberacio regis Anglie capiebat. Et interim fo. 272[r] rex Francie apud Saueye[k] | morabatur absque expedicione finali.

106. *Infirmitas regis Francie.* Et per quadragesimam sequentem cepit grauiter infirmari, et semper inualuit infirmitas sua, adeo[l] quod

---

[a] *marg. sketch of crowned head* C   [b] *J resumes*   [c–c] Pasche *J*   [d] ipsa *J*
[e] comitauia *J*   [f] domini *J*   [g] priori *J*   [h] Roberto *J*   [i–i] et al *J*   [j] *L resumes*   [k] *marg. sketch of altar* C   [l] *om.* L

P. Edbury, *The Kingdom of Cyprus and the Crusades 1191–1374* (Cambridge, 1991), pp. 164–6. Tait, in his edition of the *Chronica Johannis de Reading et Anonymi Cantuariensis* (pp. 311–12), states on the evidence of the *Eulogium Historiarum*, iii. 233, that Pierre did not arrive in London until 6 November, but there is no good reason to prefer that date to the first-hand evidence of our chronicler, who evidently saw the Cypriot king pass through Canterbury. His visit to England later became associated with an alleged 'feast of five kings' in London, which in fact did not take place. For evidence relating to this, and some of the English king's gifts to him, see C. L. Kingsford, 'The feast of five kings', *Archaeologia*, lxvii (1915–16), pp. 119–26. Froissart (quoted by Kingsford) said that the ship which Edward III gave to Pierre was called the *Katherine*, but that Pierre never took it away from Sandwich, perhaps because he could not afford to fit it out. According to John of Reading (p. 158), Pierre was robbed by brigands in Kent on his way back from London to Dover in early December. For his celebration of Christmas 1363 with the French king, see the following note.

[288] Although our chronicler was well placed to monitor the French king's movements at this time, he in fact probably landed at Dover on 4 January 1364, having spent Christmas at Hesdin rather than Boulogne: Delachenal, *Histoire de Charles V*, ii. 351–2.

[289] Jean de Cherchemont, bishop of Amiens; Philippe, duke of Orléans; Jean, duke of Berri; Gui de Châtillon, count of St-Pol; Robert de Juilly, grand prior of the Order of St John of Jerusalem in France; the 'elect of Cluny' appears to be an error, for there was no

105. *The king of France.* In the same year, the noble prince Lord John, king of France, after celebrating the feast of Christmas at Boulogne-on-sea, landed at Dover on the vigil of the Lord's Epiphany ⟨5 January, n.s. 1364⟩, remaining there for that feast.[288] On the following day, the Sunday ⟨7 January⟩, after the ninth hour, around the time of vespers on that day, he entered the city of Canterbury with a large company of nobles, namely the bishop of Amiens and the lords the duke of Orléans, the said king's brother, the duke of Berry, the said king's son, the count of St-Pol, and the prior of St John of Jerusalem in France, the lord elect of Cluny, the lord of Tancarville, the said king's chamberlain, Gilbert de Moleyns, treasurer, and Robert Hoget, burgess of Paris, among others.[289] And the said king remained at Canterbury for the following Monday and Tuesday, and on the Wednesday following ⟨10 January⟩ he was at Ospringe, from where he continued his journey day by day until he came to London, where he was accommodated at the Savoy. The reason why he came to England, so he told the king of England, was first for the payment of the million, and secondly to secure the hostages from France,[290] whereupon the said king of England summoned a council of magnates to discuss the liberation of the hostages from France, but the king of England's deliberations were delayed from day to day; and meanwhile the king of France remained at the Savoy without any final decision.

106. *The illness of the king of France.* And during the following Lent he became seriously ill, and his illness kept on getting worse, so that on

vacancy in the abbacy of Cluny at this time, but the chronicler was probably referring to André de la Roche, former abbot of Cluny who was now a cardinal (see Tait's comments in *Chronica Johannis de Reading et Anonymi Cantuariensis*, pp. 296, 367); Jean de Melun, count of Tancarville and chamberlain of France.

[290] The 'million' mentioned here probably refers to the 'first million' of King Jean's ransom, as it was sometimes referred to at the time. It is often assumed that King Jean returned to England in January 1364 out of a sense of honour, his son Louis of Anjou having forfeited his honour by absconding, and it is interesting that our chronicler does not say this, or at least not directly. The French king had announced his intention to return to a meeting of the French Estates at Amiens in late November; Delachenal, *Histoire de Charles V*, ii. 351–2, suggests that his motivation for doing so may well have been much as indicated by our chronicler, that is, to renegotiate the payment dates of his ransom, to try to secure the release of at least some of the principal hostages, and generally to improve Anglo–French relations, which were coming under strain on account of his failure to meet the terms of the Treaty of Brétigny–Calais as well as Louis of Anjou's flight. In an attempt to appease Edward III, Jean handed over 107,000 écus to the English king shortly after his arrival in London on 14 January, money which had been due to be paid as long ago as November 1361 ('The ransom of John II', ed. Broome, pp. x, xv, 10–11).

propter debilitatem corporis sui cibaria carnea et de carnibus sumebat, et illis utebatur sperans reconualescenciam habiturus.

107. De morte regis Francie in Anglia. Rex uero Anglie eundem regem Francie in*ᵃ* infirmitate*ᵇ* iacentem uisitauit sepius, et multum doluit propter eum, et*ᶜ* precepit omnia desiderabilia pro conseruacione*ᵈ* uite et sui sanitate corporis sibi dari, sed mors de diebus in dies dictum regem Francie tam grauiter insultabat, quod ulterius uiuere non potuit ullo modo; die autem Lune uidelicet octauo die mensis Aprilis anno Domini millesimo trecentisimo sexagesimo quarto, circa noctem, mortuus est Iohannes rex Francie in sana memoria atque bona apud Saueye;²⁹¹ et familiares sui corpus dicti regis mortui exinterarunt et cum balsamo parauerunt ad deferendum ad partes Francie in monasterio Sancti Dionisii tumulandum. Et postmodum *ᵉ*corpus eius*ᵉ* ad ecclesiam Sancti*ᶠ* Pauli London' deportatum fuerat, ubi, in presencia regis Anglie et regine, filiorum suorum, comitum et baronum, per*ᵍ* episcopos,*ʰ* abbates et alios religiosos Anglie in multitudine maxima fiebant exequie pro anima dicti regis solempniter inaudite.²⁹² Et post missarum solempnia decantata, familiares dicti regis corpus *ⁱ*dicti regis*ⁱ* deferri fecerunt eodem die apud Derteford de nocte, et die Veneris in crastino de nocte apud Newentoun, et de hinc apud Cant'. Die Sabbati sequente, uidelicet uicesimo die mensis Aprilis, deportatum fuit corpus eius ad ecclesiam Cant' cum solempni processione prioris et capituli ecclesie Cant' et aliorum religiosorum ciuitatis Cant', cleroque et populo eius sequentibus, ubi fiebat pro anima eius cum omni solempnitate officium mortuorum. Et in crastino, die Dominica, celebratis missis, et magna missa in ecclesia Christi Cant' per Ambian' episcopum celebrata *ʲ*pro anima dicti Regis,*ʲ* corpus eius*ᵏ* hora prima dicti diei Dominice a ciuitate Cant' uersus Douorr' cum magna comitiua fuit*ˡ* deportatum. Et die Lune delatum erat in Franciam, in*ᵐ* loco electo per eum ante obitum tumulandum, cuius corpus postmodum, die Lune in festo Sancti Iohannis ante Portam Latinam, erat in monasterio Sancti Dionisii in Francia*ⁿ* honorifice traditum sepulture.²⁹³

ᵃ re *deleted J*   *ᵇ* infirmitatem *JL*   *ᶜ om. J*   *ᵈ add.* et *L*   *ᵉ⁻ᵉ* eius corpus *L*
ᶠ om. L   *ᵍ om. L*   *ʰ add.* et *JL*   *ⁱ⁻ⁱ* eius *JL*   *ʲ⁻ʲ om. JL*   *ᵏ* dicti regis *JL*
ˡ fuerat *JL*   *ᵐ om. J*   *ⁿ* Francie *L*

---

²⁹¹ King Jean seems to have become ill in early March, although the nature of his illness is not known. He died shortly before midnight on 8 April: Delachenal, *Histoire de Charles V*, ii. 361.

²⁹² The requiem mass for King Jean was held in St Paul's cathedral on Thursday 18

account of his bodily weakness he was taking meat and fleshly nourishment and eating them in the hope of making himself well again.

107. *The death of the king of France in England.* The king of England often visited the said king of France as he lay ill, and grieved greatly for him, ordering that whatever was needed in order to preserve his life and bodily health should be given to him, but day by day death assailed the said king of France more insistently, so that in the end there was no way for him to stay alive, and on Monday 8 April in the year of Our Lord 1364, around nightfall, King John of France died, of sound and good memory, at the Savoy;[291] his household servants disembowelled the body of the said king and prepared it with balsam to be taken back to France for burial in the monastery of St-Denis; and then his body was borne to St Paul's church in London, where, in the presence of the king and queen of England, their children, the earls and barons, unprecedented exequies were solemnly performed for the soul of the said king by the bishops, abbots, and other religious of England gathered there in great numbers.[292] And after the masses had been solemnly sung, on that same day, the household servants of the said king had the same king's body conveyed by night to Dartford, and on the following day, the Friday, by night to Newington, and from there to Canterbury. And on the following Saturday, namely 20 April, his body was carried in a solemn procession with the prior and chapter of the church of Canterbury and other religious of the city of Canterbury, with its clergy and people following, to the church of Canterbury, where the office of the dead was performed with due solemnity for his soul. And on the next day, the Sunday, after the celebration of masses including a high mass at Christ Church Canterbury by the bishop of Amiens for the soul of the said king, at the first hour on the said Sunday his body was borne with a great company from the city of Canterbury towards Dover; and on the Monday it was taken over to France, to the place where, before his death, he had chosen to be buried; and afterwards, on Monday the feast of St John before the Latin Gate ⟨6 May⟩, his body was buried with honour in the monastery of St-Denis in France.[293]

April, and it may be that his entrails were buried there following the embalming of his body. The *Anonimalle Chronicle*, p. 50, states that he asked for his entrails to be buried at St Paul's, his heart at Canterbury, and his body at Paris, but see Delachenal, *Histoire de Charles V*, iii. 17–18.

[293] In the will which he made two days before his death, King Jean had requested burial at St-Denis; he was in fact buried there, just to the left of the high altar, on Tuesday 7 May,

108. *Rexᵃ Francie.* Die uero Sancti Dunstani in festo Sancte Trinitatis anno Domini millesimo trecentisimo sexagesimo quarto, apud Reyns, coronatus fuit in regem Francieᵇ dominus Karolus dalphinus Vienne,ᶜ filius dicti Iohannis regis defuncti, per archiepiscopum Remen' solempniter et iniun⟨c⟩tusᵈ more regio coronatus.²⁹⁴ Hic rex post coronacionem suam conuocauit parliamentum suum apud Paris', ad quod fecit uocari omnes pares regni sui et alios qui ad hoc tenerentur uenire, ut ordinaret et statueret, ut asseruit, aliqua utilia regni sui, sed pocius conuicitur ut aliqua contra Anglicos fierent nocitura. Verumptamen Deus omnipotens, qui regem Anglie et gentem suam hactenus saluauit, mentes Francorum a circumuencionibus maliuolis obturauit.

fo. 272ᵛ **109.** Eodem quoque anno ᵉDomini millesimo trecentisimo sexagesimo quarto,ᵉ in festo Sancti Michaelis Archangeli, iuxta castrum de Orey in Britannia minore,ᶠ facta primitus obsidione prediciti castri de Orey, graue prelium fuit inter dominum Karolumᵍ de Bloys ex parte una et dominum Iohannem de Montfort ex alteraʰ racione ducatus Britannie predicte, ipsoⁱ Karolo ad eum iure hereditario ducatum huiusmodiʲ pertinere debere, et ipso Iohanne in contrariumᵏ asserente.²⁹⁵ Ex parte ipsius Karoli mortui et capti fuerunt inferius descripti, ita quod uictoria dicti belliˡ penes eundem Iohannem Montford, domino adiuuante, remansit:²⁹⁶

ᵃ *word erased* C   ᵇ Francorum L   ᶜ *marg. sketch of coronation of* Karolus Rex C
ᵈ iniunctus *edd.;* iniuntus C; inunctus JL   ᵉ⁻ᵉ *om.* J   ᶠ minori JL   ᵍ *om.* J
ʰ *add.* parte J   ⁱ ipse L   ʲ *om.* L   ᵏ contrario J   ˡ *om.* J

high mass having been sung for his soul at Notre-Dame in Paris on 6 May: Delachenal, *Histoire de Charles V,* iii. 19–20.

²⁹⁴ Delachenal, *Histoire de Charles V,* iii. 65–97, has a very detailed account of Charles V's coronation ceremony on 19 May; the archbishop of Reims (1355–73) was Jean de Craon.
²⁹⁵ Auray is on the south coast of Brittany, in the modern département of Morbihan, some ten miles west of Vannes. This battle, which effectively settled the Breton civil war (1341–64), was fought on Sunday 29 September.
²⁹⁶ The list which follows was also used by the author of the *Anonimalle Chronicle* (who carelessly included it twice, at pp. 50–1 and p. 78) and by John of Reading (*Chronica Johannis de Reading et Anonymi Cantuariensis,* pp. 161–2). The *Anonimalle Chronicle* included five further names, two of which are also in Reading's list: the lord of Rochefort and lord William de Angor or Waugo (*Anonimalle Chronicle* and Reading); the lord of Albayn or Seint Albayn, Robert de Vaucoulour, and the count of Maurey (*Anonimalle Chronicle* only). As usual, the English chroniclers mangle these names dreadfully, and it is sometimes difficult to identify them. For example, William de Angor or Waugo may really be William d'Avaugour, who is also listed separately in all three of the lists, a point which our chronicler may have realized and thus decided not to make two men out of one. The

108. *The king of France.* Then, on the feast of St Dunstan, Trinity Sunday ⟨19 May⟩, in the year of Our Lord 1364, Lord Charles, dauphin of Vienne, son of the said deceased King John, was solemnly crowned king of France at Reims by the archbishop of Reims and anointed in the traditional coronation fashion.[294] Following his coronation, this king convened his parliament to Paris, to which he summoned all the peers of his realm along with other persons who ought to attend it; he claimed that this was so that he could ordain and decree various matters beneficial to his realm, but in fact, as became clear, it was so that hostile plans might be made against the English. Notwithstanding this, Almighty God, who up to now has preserved the king of England and his people, has prevented the French from carrying out any malevolent designs.

109. Also, in the same year of Our Lord 1364, on the feast of St Michael the Archangel ⟨29 September⟩, near to the castle of Auray in Brittany, following a siege of this same castle of Auray, a fierce battle was fought between Lord Charles de Blois on the one hand and Lord John de Montfort on the other over the aforesaid duchy of Brittany, for the aforesaid Charles claimed that this duchy ought to belong to him by hereditary right, while the said John argued the contrary.[295] The dead and captured on the side of this Charles have been written out below, and the result was that victory in this battle fell, with God's help, to the aforesaid John de Montfort.[296]

author of the *Anonimalle Chronicle* also, presumably inadvertently, made one or two changes between his first and second lists, such as referring to 'mounsire de Albayn' in the first list and 'le seignur de seint Albayn' in the second. Reading also agrees with the *Anonimalle Chronicle* (in its second list) in stating that 900 knights and esquires—or 'good men' as the latter calls them—died on Charles de Blois's side, and that 1,500 were captured, whereas only seven men died in de Montfort's army, but he seems to have tired of his task and omitted fifteen of the names recorded by the *Anonimalle Chronicle*, simply adding that 'another thirteen nobles' died. It is just possible that Henry Knighton also saw this list, for he too noted that 900 men were killed on the French side (*Knighton's Chronicle*, p. 192). Our chronicler does not distinguish between those who were killed and those who were captured on the Blois side, but other sources confirm that the great majority of those whom he lists were in fact taken alive rather than killed. We are very grateful to Professor Michael Jones of the University of Nottingham for his help in identifying many of those mentioned, several of whom feature in *Letters, Orders and Musters of Bertrand du Guesclin, 1357–1380*, ed. M. Jones (Woodbridge, 2004). Nevertheless, some of the identifications of the names given by our chronicler remain tentative. The fullest contemporary account of the battle is given by Alain Bouchart, *Grandes Chroniques de Brétagne*, ed. M-L. Auger and G. Jeanneau (Paris, 1986), ii. 87–91, who provides a very different list of the dead and captured, as follows: *Dead*: Charles de Blois; his bastard son Jean de Blois; the lord of Léon; the lord of Avaugour; the lord of Lohéac; the lord of Malestroit; the lord of Pont; and the lord of Kergorlay. *Captured*: the count of Auxerre; the count of Joigny; the viscount of Rohan;

fo. 272va   *Mortui*^a

Dominus Carolus de Bloys^b

Comes Dauciers[297]

Comes de Iugny[298]

Dominus de Pyse[299]

Dominus de Brutort[300]

Dominus Bartholomeus de^c Cleukyn, comes de Longeuylle[301]

Dominus comes de Roan[302]

Dominus de Montfort[303]

Dominus de Dynay^d [304]

Dominus de Gregoule[305]

Dominus Petrus de Glaskyn[306]

Dominus de Montbay[307]

Dominus Siluester^e de la Foille[308]

Dominus Guillelmus d'Auagour[309]

Dominus Iohannes^f Comenet[310]

Dominus Henricus de Pledray[311]

Dominus Iohannes Iuch[312]

fo. 272vb   Dominus capitaneus de Fouchiers[313]

---

^a *add.* et capti *JL*   ^b *add.* mortuus *L*   ^c *om. J*   ^d Binay *JL*   ^e Clucstor *JL*
^f *add.* de *J*

Lord Gui de Léon; the lord of Rays; the lord of Rieux; the count of Tonnerre; Lord Henri de Malestroit; Lord Olivier de Mauny; the lord of Rivillie; the lord of Frainville; the lord of Rayneval; and the lord of Rochefort.

[297] Jean IV de Chalon, who succeeded his father Jean III (who had been captured at Poitiers) in 1361; according to the *Grandes Chroniques de Brétagne*, he was captured rather than killed.

[298] Jean de Noyers, count of Joigny; according to the *Grandes Chroniques de Brétagne*, he was captured rather than killed; he had also been captured at Poitiers.

[299] Possibly Girard V Chabot, lord of Rays (d. 1371); if so, he was clearly captured rather than killed, as confirmed by the *Grandes Chroniques de Brétagne*.

[300] Robert de Brucourt, lord of Maisy (Calvados), who was in fact captured rather than killed.

[301] Bertrand du Guesclin, a Breton and one of the foremost French heroes of the fourteenth-century Anglo–French wars, had only recently been created count of Longueville, on 27 May 1364 (Delachenal, *Histoire de Charles V*, iii. 114). He became constable of France in 1370 and was buried in the abbey of St-Denis following his death in 1380. He was effectively joint commander with Charles de Blois of the latter's forces at Auray, where he was captured by an esquire in the retinue of Sir John Chandos; three years later, he would become a prisoner of the English once again at the battle of Nájera.

[302] Jean I, viscount of Rohan (d. 1396); as confirmed by the *Grandes Chroniques de Brétagne*, he was captured rather than killed.

[303] Probably Raoul, lord of Montfort-sur-Meu (d. 1394), to be distinguished from the

The dead

Lord Charles de Blois
The count of Auxerre[297]
The count of Joigny[298]
The lord of ⟨Rays⟩[299]
The lord of Brucourt[300]
Lord Bartholomew ⟨*recte* Bertrand⟩ du Guesclin, count of Long-
ueville[301]
The lord count of Rohan[302]
The lord of Montfort[303]
The lord of ⟨Dinan⟩[304]
The lord of Kergorlay[305]
Lord Peter du Guesclin[306]
The lord of Montauban[307]
Lord Silvester de la Feuillée[308]
Lord William d'Avaugour[309]
Lord John de Coëtménech[310]
Lord Henry de Plédran[311]
Lord John de Juch[312]
The lord captain of Fougères[313]

county of Montfort-l'Amaury, between Paris and Chartres, from which the victor of Auray
took his name.

[304] Probably Lord Charles de Dinan, lord of Montafilant and Châteaubriant, although it
may have been his father Roland who was killed at Auray. If Charles is referred to, he must
have been captured rather than killed, for he lived until 1418.

[305] Jean, lord of Kergorlay (Finistère). The *Grandes Chroniques de Brétagne* confirm that
he was killed at Auray.

[306] Pierre III de Guesclin, lord of Plessis-Bertrand, cousin to Bertrand du Guesclin; he
was captured rather than killed.

[307] Olivier IV, lord of Montauban, died in 1388, so clearly captured rather than killed at
Auray.

[308] Silvestre de la Feuillée; he was captured rather than killed, and later became marshal
of Brittany in 1372 and chancellor in 1384-5, dying around 1395.

[309] Guillaume d'Avaugour was closely related to Jeanne de Penthièvre, the wife of
Charles de Blois; the *Grandes Chroniques de Brétagne* confirm that he was killed at Auray.

[310] Probably a member of the family of vicomtes de Coëtménech, from Ploudier
(Finistère).

[311] Henri de Plédran, who lived until at least 1392, so clearly captured rather than killed
at Auray.

[312] Jean II, lord of Juch (Finistère) died in 1372, so clearly captured rather than killed at
Auray.

[313] It is possible that the chronicler meant it to be understood that Jean de Juch was the
captain of Fougères, but it has not been possible to find evidence which corroborates this,
and it is worth noting that in the list of captured given in the *Anonimalle Chronicle*, p. 51,
based on the same list as that used by our chronicler, the names of Bertrand de St-Père and
Olivier de Mauny appear between 'Jean de Juch' and 'The lord captain of Fougères'.

Dominus Bertrandus de Sancto Petro[314]
Dominus Oliuerus de Mauny[315]
Dominus Herueis *ᵃde Iuch',ᵃ* capitaneus de Nantes[316]
Dominus Guillelmus de Lescot, capitaneus de Dynard*ᵇ* [317]
Capitaneus de*ᶜ* Guyham[318]
Capitaneus de Rocheduryan'[319]
Capitaneus de Lamballe[320]
Dominus Iohannes de la Mote*ᵈ* saint Gile[321]
Dominus Willelmus*ᵉ* de Monteney, capitaneus de Iugoun[322]
cum *ᶠmultis aliis.ᶠ*

110. *ᵍDie autem Sabbati ante festum Sancti Luce Euangeliste eodem*ʰ
anno Domini millesimo trecentisimo sexagesimo quarto, Douor'
⟨uenit⟩*ⁱ* dominus Ludouicus, comes Flandrie,[323] cum multis nobilibus
et magnatibus Flandrie, et in castro Douor' hospitati fuerunt. Et die
Dominica sequente, intrauit rex Anglie dictum castrum dum ipsi
domini Flandrie ibidem erant in cena, et post cenam iidem*ʲ* rex et
comes amicabiliter loquebantur, totam illam noctem in gaudio
deducentes; et fuerunt ibi*ᵏ* dux Lancastrie et dominus Edmundus
de Langele, filii*ˡ* dicti regis.[324] Et diebus Lune, Martis et Mercurii
idem rex Anglie cum ipso comite Flandrie tractarunt de maritagio
inter dictum Edmundum et dominam Iohannam, filiam heredem dicti
comitis,[325] faciendo, et tandem inter se quid et quantum de rege
Anglie*ᵐ* dicti contrahentes amicabiliter concordarunt. Post hec, die
Iouis in uigilia Sancti Luce Euangeliste, accessit idem comes apud

---

*ᵃ⁻ᵃ om. L   ᵇ Dinay JL   ᶜ om. JL   ᵈ Monte L   ᵉ I. JL   ᶠ⁻ᶠ aliis multis
JL; J breaks off; followed by double line, indicating end of text? C   ᵍ add. heading Pro
matrimonio inter Edmundum de Langele, filius regis, et filiam comitis Flandrie L
ʰ om. L   ⁱ uenit edd.; om. CL   ʲ idem L   ᵏ ibidem L   ˡ filius L
ᵐ add. haberent L*

---

[314] Bertrand de St-Père (or St-Pern) died *c.*1389, so clearly captured rather than killed at
Auray.
[315] Olivier de Mauny, lord of Lesnen (Ille-et-Vilaine) was Bertrand du Guesclin's
cousin, and died in 1390, so clearly captured rather than killed at Auray, as confirmed by
the *Grandes Chroniques de Brétagne*.
[316] Hervé du Juch, lord of Pratanroux (d. 1369), younger brother of Jean II (see above),
died in 1369, so clearly captured rather than killed at Auray. The chronicler may have
thought that either he or Guillaume de Lescouët was captain of Nantes.
[317] Guillaume de Lescouët had served with Charles de Blois at Lesneven in 1357. The
chronicler may have thought that he was captain of either Nantes or Dinan.
[318] Guingamp, in northern Brittany, was one of Charles de Blois's most important
centres of power, but the name of its captain in 1364 is not known.
[319] Possibly Geoffroi, lord of Kerimel (d. 1388–9), so clearly captured rather than killed
at Auray.

Lord Bertrand de St-Père[314]
Lord Oliver de Mauny[315]
Lord Hervey du Juch[316]
The captain of Nantes
Lord William de Lescouët[317]
The captain of Dinan
The captain of Guingamp[318]
The captain of Roche Derrein[319]
The captain of Lamballe[320]
Lord John of la Motte de St-Gilles[321]
Lord William of Montenay[322]
The captain of Jugon and many others.

110. Also, on the Saturday before the feast of St Luke the Evangelist ⟨12 October⟩ in the same year of Our Lord 1364, Lord Louis, count of Flanders,[323] ⟨arrived at⟩ Dover with many nobles and magnates from Flanders, and they stayed at Dover castle; and on the following Sunday, the king of England arrived at the said castle while these Flemish lords were dining there, and after dinner the said king and count spoke together in amicable fashion, passing that whole night pleasurably; also present there were the duke of Lancaster and Lord Edmund of Langley, sons of the said king;[324] and on the Monday, Tuesday, and Wednesday the aforesaid king of England discussed with the said count of Flanders the question of arranging a marriage between the said Edmund and Lady Joanna ⟨*recte* Margaret⟩, daughter and heir of the said count,[325] and at length they came to an amicable agreement between themselves as to what and how much those who were to be joined together ⟨should receive⟩ from the king

---

[320] Lamballe, in northern Brittany, was another Blois stronghold, but the name of its captain in 1364 is not known.

[321] Probably Jean de St-Gilles, whose family came from the area around Auray; but he was still alive in the 1390s, so clearly captured rather than killed at Auray.

[322] Guillaume de Montenay, a Norman knight who served with du Guesclin in 1371, so clearly captured rather than killed at Auray.

[323] Louis de Mâle, count of Flanders 1346–84.

[324] John of Gaunt, third surviving son of Edward III, was born in 1340 and created duke of Lancaster on 13 November 1362 (his father's fiftieth birthday); Edmund of Langley, fourth surviving son of Edward III, was born in 1342 and created earl of Cambridge, also on 13 November 1362.

[325] Marguerite de Mâle was her father's only child, and heiress through him and her mother to vast territories in the Low Countries and Burgundy. For these Anglo–Flemish marriage negotiations and their significance in Anglo–French relations during the 1360s, see J. J. N. Palmer, 'England, France, the papacy and the Flemish succession, 1361–9', *Journal of Medieval History*, ii (1976), pp. 339–64.

Cantuar' ad feretrum Sancti Thome peregrinando cum dictis filiis
regis Anglie | et honorabili comitiua. Et in festo Sancti Luce, facta
peregrinacione sua, idem comes post prandium dicti diei recessit de
Cantuar' et uenit illa nocte apud Douor'; et die Sabbati in crastino,
unanimiter de die desponsacionis inter eos, uidelicet die Iouis post
festum Purificacionis Beate Marie proximo tunc futurum, faciendo
apud Bregis in Flandria, si canonicum non obsistat, ⟨concordarunt⟩,ᵃ
die Dominica sequente, mane post gentaculum, in Flandriam trans-
fretauit.³²⁶

III. *Flandria pro maritagio.* Et in uigilia Apostolorum Simonis et
Iude tunc sequente, dominus Simon Sudbury, London' episcopus, et
dominus dux Lancastrie et dominus Edmundus Langele, comes
Grantebrigge, filii domini regis Anglie, uenerunt Cant', et in crastino
recesserunt Douorr', et de hinc apud Caleys transfretarunt ad
faciendum finem de prelocuto matrimonio inter dictum Edmundumᵇ
Langele et filiam dicti comitis Flandrie; sed, obstante dispensacione
papali, nichil tunc de dicto matrimonio erat actum.ᶜ ³²⁷

II2. ᵈ*Transfretacioᵉ principisᶠ in Vasconiam ᵍad morandum.*ᵍ ³²⁸ Post
hec, ʰanno Domini millesimo trecentisimo sexagesimo,ʰ per dominum
Edwardum, regem Anglie, filio suo primogenito domino Edwardo,
principeⁱ Wallie et duce Cornubie, in principem Aquitannie in pleno
parliamento ordinato et facto, idem rex, de consilio tociusʲ regni sui et
pro utilitate eiusdem, ordinauit dictum filium suum primogenitum
morari debere in Vasconia adᵏ gubernandum totam terram Aquitannie ut principem eiusdem;³²⁹ qui, iter suum uersus Vasconiam in
crastino Sanctiˡ Bartholomei Apostoliᵐ ⁿanno Domini millesimo

---

ᵃ concordarunt *edd.; om. C*   ᵇ *add.* de L   ᶜ *followed by renewed double lines to
mark end of text? C*   ᵈ *J resumes with heading*   ᵉ *add.* domini JL   ᶠ *add.* Wallie
JL   ᵍ⁻ᵍ *om. J;* ut dux Vasconie L   ʰ⁻ʰ *om. J*   ⁱ principi J   ʲ *om. JL*
ᵏ *ad edds., from JL;* ac C   ˡ *om. J*   ᵐ *om. JL*   ⁿ⁻ⁿ *om. J; add.* iter suum L

³²⁶ The 'Treaty of Dover', the agreement for a marriage between Marguerite de Mâle
and Edmund of Langley, was dated 19 October at Dover castle; the projected date for the
wedding was in fact the Tuesday after the Purification rather than the Thursday (4 rather
than 6 February 1365): *Foedera*, iii (2), pp. 750–1.

³²⁷ Edmund and Marguerite were related in the fourth degree of consanguinity, which
meant that they required a dispensation from the pope, Urban V (1362–70). On both 18
December 1364 and 16 January 1365, however, Urban twice declared that he would not
grant them a dispensation to marry, although two years later, in March 1367, he granted a
dispensation for Marguerite to marry Philippe 'the Bold', duke of Burgundy, to whom she
was also related in the fourth degree, and in 1369 Philippe and Marguerite were duly
married. This whole episode greatly irritated the English, who were convinced of Urban's

of England; after this, on Thursday the vigil of St Luke the Evangelist ⟨17 October⟩, the aforesaid count came on pilgrimage with the aforementioned sons of the king of England and an honourable company to the shrine of St Thomas at Canterbury; and on the feast of St Luke, having performed his pilgrimage, the said count departed from Canterbury after dinner that day and arrived that night at Dover; and, once they had come to a unanimous agreement on the following day, the Saturday, concerning the day of the espousals to take place between them—that is to say, on the Thursday after the feast of the Purification of the Blessed Virgin Mary next following ⟨6 February 1365⟩ at Bruges in Flanders, barring any canonical impediment—then on the following Sunday ⟨20 October⟩, early in the morning after breakfast, he crossed to Flanders.[326]

III. ⟨*Ambassadors sent to*⟩ *Flanders for the marriage.* And on the vigil of the Apostles Simon and Jude next following ⟨27 October⟩, Lord Simon Sudbury, bishop of London, and the lord duke of Lancaster and Lord Edmund of Langley, earl of Cambridge, the sons of the lord king of England, arrived at Canterbury, and on the following day they departed for Dover, and from there they crossed to Calais in order to finalize the negotiations for the marriage between the said Edmund of Langley and the daughter of the said count of Flanders; but, since no papal dispensation was forthcoming, nothing was subsequently done with regard to this marriage.[327]

112. *The crossing of the prince to reside in Gascony.*[328] Following this, in the year of Our Lord 1360 ⟨*recte* 1362⟩, after the Lord Edward, king of England, had in full parliament made and created his first-born son, Lord Edward, prince of Wales and duke of Cornwall, as prince of Aquitaine, the said king, with the agreement and for the benefit of his entire kingdom, ordered his aforesaid first-born son to go and reside in Aquitaine in order to govern the whole land of Aquitaine as its prince;[329] the latter, having set out on his journey from London to Gascony on the morrow of the feast of St Bartholomew the Apostle

partiality towards the French: see Palmer, 'England, France, the papacy and the Flemish succession'.

[328] This paragraph was almost certainly added as an afterthought, as indicated by the double underlining in the manuscript immediately after the preceding paragraph. Given the seriousness of the chronological errors in this final paragraph, it is likely to have been added some years after the events it describes.

[329] The Black Prince was created prince of Aquitaine on 19 July 1362, although no parliament was sitting at the time; for the text of his charter of creation, and a facsimile of the original, see *Foedera*, iii (2), pp. 667–8.

trecentisimo sexagesimo primo[n] de Lond'[a] arripiens, [b]in ducatu suo Deuonie et Cornubie[b] morabatur [c]usque ad[c] tres ebdomodas [d]ante festum[d] Apostolorum Petri et Pauli; [e]et in die dicti festi[e] applicuit in Vasconia apud [f]castrum de[f] Lormond, distans a Burdegal' per tria miliaria dicte terre.[g] [330] Et[h] postmodum,[i] uicesimo septimo die Ianuarii [j]anno Domini millesimo trecentisimo sexagesimo quarto,[j] in castro de Engolisma Aquitanie,[k] natus est Edwardus primogenitus dicti[l] domini[m] Edwardi, principis Wallie et Aquitanie, de quo ibidem[n] [o]gaudium magnum[o] fuit.[331] [p]Et idem princeps Aquitanie ab omnibus sibi subditis recepit fidelitates et homagia undequaque in Vasconia, apud Burdegalen' et Peytiers, Engolism' per uices et alibi in dicta terra, prout sibi placuit commorando.[p] [332]

---

[a] *add.* uersus Vasconiam *JL*   [b-b] continuatis diebus uenit ad Cornubiam et ibidem in Deuonia *JL*   [c-c] per *JL*   [d-d] et in die *JL*   [e-e] eodem anno *JL*   [f-f] *om. J*
[g] *add.* recipiens ab omnibus suis subditis ibidem fidelitates et homagia undequaque et moram trahens in Vasconia apud Burdegal' et Peitiers et Engelsm' per uices prout placuit sibi circuiendo *JL, occurs later in C; see p–p below*   [h] *om. JL*   [i] *add.* uero *JL*
[j–j] *om. J*   [k] *om. JL*   [l] *om. JL*   [m] *om. J*   [n] *interlinear C*   [o–o] magnum gaudium *J*   [p–p] *this sentence placed prior to birth of Edward in JL; see g above*

---

[330] The chronology here clearly does not make sense. The Black Prince did indeed leave London on 25 August (1362, not 1361), apparently hoping to cross to Aquitaine within a few weeks, but for various reasons ended up spending most of the winter at Restormel castle in his duchy of Cornwall; he eventually set sail from Plymouth, in *Saint Mary Cog* of Ipswich, on 9 June 1363, arriving at Lormont on the Garonne (now a suburb of Bordeaux) on 29 June: R. Barber, *Edward, Prince of Wales and Aquitaine* (London, 1978), pp. 178–9. The text in the *Chronica Johannis de Reading et Anonymi Cantuariensis*, p. 222, also includes chronological errors, although the Latin there makes better sense.

[331] Tait, *Chronica Johannis de Reading et Anonymi Cantuariensis*, p. 324, basing his

⟨25 August⟩ in the year of Our Lord 1361 ⟨recte 1362⟩, remained in his duchy of Devon and Cornwall for three weeks before the feast of the Apostles Peter and Paul ⟨29 June⟩; and on the day of the said feast he arrived in Gascony at the castle of Lormont, which is three miles away from Bordeaux in that land.[330] After this, on 27 January in the year of Our Lord 1364 ⟨n.s. 1365⟩, Edward, the first-born son of the said Lord Edward, prince of Wales and Aquitaine, was born in the castle of Angoulême in Aquitaine, an occasion for great joy there.[331] And the aforesaid prince of Aquitaine received at various times the fealty and homage of all his subjects everywhere in Aquitaine, at Bordeaux, Poitiers, Angoulême, and elsewhere in the said land, according to where it pleased him to reside.[332]

argument principally on the evidence of contemporary chronicles, thought that our chronicler had misdated the birth of Edward 'of Angoulême' by one day, and that he was probably born on 26 rather than 27 January 1365, but Barber has recently suggested that Edward may in fact have been born in early March (the date usually associated with his christening), for, had he been born in January, the tournament which the Black Prince held on 27 April to celebrate the churching of Princess Joan 'would imply an exceptional interval' between birth and purification (Barber, Edward, Prince of Wales and Aquitaine, pp. 184 and 262 n. 18). Edward died in September 1370, opening the way for his younger brother Richard (II) to become king of England in 1377. The text in Chronica Johannis de Reading et Anonymi Cantuariensis, p. 222, places this sentence after rather than before the account of the prince receiving homage, which maintains the correct chronological order.

[332] The prince began taking homage and fealty from his Gascon subjects on 9 July 1363 in the cathedral of St-André at Bordeaux, and continued to do so at regular intervals and in various places throughout his duchy for the next nine months; he did so at Angoulême on 18 August, and at Poitiers in September and October. By 4 April 1364, he had received homage in person from 1,047 of his subjects in the duchy: Barber, Edward, Prince of Wales and Aquitaine, p. 180.

APPENDIX

Continuation of the chronicle in
Lambeth Palace Library MS 99 (L) and
British Library, MS Cotton Julius B. iii (J)

Text from L, the fuller version, with significant variants from J.

Bellum de Nasers in Ispania.[a] [1] Dum dominus Edwardus princeps Wallie in terra Vasconie morabatur, accessit ad eum dominus Petrus, uerus, ut asseruit, rex Ispanie, requirens ab eo cum magna instancia auxilium militare contra Henricum bastardum, qui regnum Ispanie occuparat iniuste,[2] pro eo et ex eo quod idem princeps sibi in sanguine taliter fuerat alligatus. Nam olim Edwardus, rex Anglie, illustris filius Henrici regis Anglie, primo Alianoram filiam quondam regis Ispanie desponsarat, de qua Edwardum[b] Carnaruan' in matrimonio suscitarat, et, ea mortua, de Margareta, filia regis Francie, secunda uxore sua,[3] Thomam de Brotherton' et Edmundum de Wodestoke genuit subsequenter, et ex hac prima causa alligationis sanguinis ipse princeps[c] regem Ispanie iuuare et defendere in suo iure regio tenebatur.[4] Quibus per dictum principem auditis, ipse asseruit se uelle cum domino suo patre, domino Edwardo rege Anglie inclito, deliberare, sibique super | hiis responsum dare pro loco et tempore opportunis.

Anno igitur Domini mille trecentisimo sexagesimo septimo, habita per dictum principem super hiis deliberatione non modica, et pro eo quod idem dominus Petrus, rex Ispanie, post obitum suum dictum principem heredem suum fieri uoluit iure successionis, sicut constanter promisit, idem princeps eidem regi Ispanie totum adiutorium suum cum potentia armata concessit, parans se ⟨de⟩[d] diebus in dies aduersum dictum bastardum ad pugnandum cum eo, ad hoc uiris congregatis undique bellicosis.[5] Et deinde idem princeps, aduertens quod non in multitudine exercitus sed in Dei fortitudine uictoria belli

---

[a] heading om. J   [b] add. de J   [c] add. eum J   [d] de edd., from J; om. L

---

[1] The story of the Black Prince's invasion of Castile in the early months of 1367, and the battle of Nájera, fought on Saturday 3 April, is best told by P. Russell, *The English Intervention in Spain and Portugal in the Time of Edward III and Richard II* (Oxford, 1955), pp. 59–107.

[2] Pedro I 'the Cruel', the legitimate but unpopular king of Castile since 1350, was driven out of his kingdom in 1366 following a rebellion led by his illegitimate half-brother Enrique Trastámara 'the Bastard'. He arrived at Bayonne in Gascony on 1 August 1366, whence he made his way to the Black Prince's court at Bordeaux.

[3] Edward I married Leonor (Eleanor), daughter of King Fernando III of Castile and León, in 1254; Edward II was born of this marriage at Caernarvon in 1284. Following her death, Edward I married Marguerite of France in 1299.

[4] The chronicler omits to say that Edward III and Pedro I had also agreed a treaty of

The battle of Nájera in Spain.[1] While the lord Edward, prince of Wales, was staying in the land of Gascony, he was approached by lord Peter, who claimed to be the rightful king of Spain, and who begged him most urgently to give him military assistance against Henry the bastard, who unlawfully occupied the kingdom of Spain,[2] on account of and by reason of the fact that the aforesaid prince Edward was related to him Peter by blood in the following way: for, some time ago, Edward I, king of England, the illustrious son of King Henry III of England, had married as his first wife Eleanor, daughter of the former king of Spain, by whom he had begotten in wedlock Edward of Caernarvon; and then, after her death, he begat Thomas of Brotherton and Edmund of Woodstock by Margaret, the daughter of the king of France, his second wife;[3] and because of this first connection through blood relationship, the said prince was duty bound to assist and uphold the king of Spain in his royal right.[4] When the aforesaid prince had listened to these arguments, he declared that he wished to consult with his lord and father, the renowned lord Edward, king of England, and that he would give him an answer on these matters when and where it was convenient to do so.

In the year of Our Lord 1367, therefore, once the aforesaid prince had held extensive discussions on these matters, and because the said lord Peter, the king of Spain, wished to make the said prince his heir by right of succession after his death—for so he kept promising—the aforesaid prince agreed to give the said king of Spain all his support by force of arms, and began day by day to ready himself to go against the aforesaid bastard to do battle with him, having summoned fighting men from all parts for this purpose.[5] Thereafter the said prince, understanding that victory in war depends not on the size of an army

---

alliance at London in 1362, in which the English king promised to make troops available to Pedro, to be paid by the Castilian treasury, in just such an eventuality as this: Russell, *English Intervention*, pp. 3–4.

[5] This is the only source to say that Pedro promised to make the prince his heir in return for military assistance, although John of Reading hints at the hereditary rights which an English king might have had in the Castilian throne (*Chronica Johannis de Reading et Anonymi Cantuariensis*, pp. 172, 341). Our chronicler is almost certainly wrong on this point: the prince was to receive some territory and (in theory) a large amount of money, but not the Castilian kingdom: Russell, *English Intervention*, pp. 66–8.

consistit, posuit se et suos in manum solius Dei, et progrediens cum exercitu suo in Ispaniam,[6] tandem uenit deprope ubi dictus bastardus, cum exercitu suo tam fidelium quam infidelium secum existentium, fuerat logiatus. Ex parte dicti principis exploratoribus et insidiatoribus belli praemissis, secundo die Aprilis, anno praedicto, *eidem principi* iuxta Nauerete in Ispania, ubi tentoria sua fixerat, uenerunt noua quod idem bastardus cum exercitu suo fere per duo miliaria a dicto principe super ripam de Nazare,[7] directis belli sui aciebus, placeam ceperant ad pugnandum ibidem, dictum principem expectando. Quibus per dictum principem gaudenter auditis, ipse in crastino, uidelicet die Sabbati in Passione Domini, in festo Sancti Ricardi episcopi Cicestrensis,[8] mouebat se cum armata potentia ad debellandum bastardum eundem.

Et habito hinc inde dicto die Sabbati graui conflictu bellicoso, tandem cum Dei adiutorio idem bastardus cum toto exercitu suo et gratia Dei deuictus fuerat. In quo quidem bello circiter sex milia gentium armatorum, exceptis ienetoriis, pauysoriis et peditibus seruientibus sine numero,[9] in gladio ceciderunt. Quibus sic peractis, idem bastardus fugit cum sedecim personis apud Auinionem ad papam, narrans ei exitum dicti belli.[10] Sed idem princeps nesciuit pro certo ubi ipse bastardus fuerat tempore deuictionis dicti belli. Et post hec princeps ipse ⟨cum⟩*f* rege Ispanie iter suum arripuit uersus Burges ciuitatem, ubi adinuicem nunc morantur.[11]

*Nomina dominorum et comitum*g *captiuorum in bello de Nasers in Ispania*

Dominus Sencho, frater regis Ispanie[12]

---

e-e eidem principi *edd.;* idem princeps *JL*   *f* cum *edd.; om. JL*   *g om. J*

---

[6] The Anglo-Gascon army passed through the Pyrenean kingdom of Navarre by the pass of Roncesvalles and arrived in Castile around the beginning of March 1367. Nájera is less than ten miles from the Navarrese–Castilian border.

[7] In fact, Navarrete and Nájera are about nine miles apart.

[8] Saturday 3 April, the day before Passion Sunday; Richard Wich, saint and bishop of Chichester, had died on 3 April 1253.

[9] For the 'jinetes' or 'genetours', lightly armed horsemen so-called from the jennets or small coursers which they rode, see *Chronica Johannis de Reading et Anonymi Cantuariensis*, p. 353. Each paviser bore a large shield or 'pavis' which he used to protect an archer.

[10] Enrique did indeed flee to France, but not to the pope at Avignon. After briefly taking refuge in Aragon, he went to seek help from Louis of Anjou, brother of Charles V of France, who as governor of Languedoc was residing in Toulouse, and with whom he concluded an alliance in August 1367; a month later he returned to Spain, and in March 1369 he overthrew and murdered King Pedro, seized the throne, and established the Trastámaran dynasty, which was to rule Castile for the next century (Russell, *English Intervention*, pp. 108, 127–48).

but on the power of God, placed himself and his men in the hands of the One God and, advancing with his army into Spain,[6] he at length arrived close to the spot where the said bastard was encamped with his army of Christians and infidels who remained with him. And, after spies had been sent out and ambushes for the war laid on the prince's part, on the second day of April in the aforesaid year, news came to the prince as he was close to Navarrete in Spain, where he had set up his camp, that the said bastard with his army was barely two miles away from the said prince on the bank of the Najerillo,[7] awaiting the said prince, having drawn up his troops for battle and chosen a spot there for the fight. The said prince, hearing these tidings with joy, himself, on the morrow—that is to say the Saturday of the Lord's Passion, the feast of St Richard, bishop of Chichester[8]—advanced with his armed might to do battle with this same bastard.

A great and fierce battle having thus been fought there on the aforesaid Saturday, the said bastard was at length, with the help of God and by the grace of God, defeated along with his whole army; in which battle around six thousand men-at-arms fell by the sword, not counting innumerable light horsemen, pavisers, and foot sergeants.[9] When it was over, the said bastard fled with sixteen followers to the pope at Avignon and told him the outcome of the battle.[10] The aforesaid prince, however, did not know for sure where the bastard himself was at the time of his defeat in this battle; and after this the prince himself travelled with the king of Spain towards the city of Burgos, where both of them are now staying together.[11]

The names of the lords and counts taken prisoner in the battle of Nájera in Spain.

Lord Sancho, brother of the king of Spain[12]

[11] The basis of the chronicler's account of the campaign and battle of Nájera was a letter sent by the Black Prince to his wife, Joan of Kent, on Monday 5 April 1367, the day that he and King Pedro left the battlefield and went to Burgos. From 'on the second day of April in the aforesaid year . . .' he follows this quite closely. The letter was discovered by A. E. Prince and is printed in the *Anonimalle Chronicle*, p. 171. The list of captured and slain which follows was also based on a newsletter of some kind: it was used by John of Reading and by the author of the *Anonimalle Chronicle* as well as by our chronicler.

[12] Sancho, count of Albuquerque, brother of Enrique the Bastard, not Pedro, which makes it a little surprising that he is referred to here as brother of the king. This list of the captured and slain includes many spectacular mistranscriptions and misunderstandings, some of which defy identification. The following sources have been used to try to identify them: *Chronica Johannis de Reading et Anonymi Cantuariensis*, pp. 183–4; *Anonimalle Chronicle*, pp. 54–5; Fernão Lopes, *The English in Portugal 1367–87*, ed. D. W. Lomax and R. J. Oakley (Warminster, 1988), pp. 5–33, 337–9; Russell, *English Intervention*, pp. 83–107.

Comes de Duny[13]
Dominus I. Martius[h] de Lucie
Dominus Iohannes Remers Daurialane[i] [14]
Dominus Bertrandus Cleykin[15]
Episcopus de Rilions
Dominus Philippus de Castro[16]
Petrus Heurik[17]
Petrus Lupis d'Aurial[18]
Diate Lapus, frater suus
Gracy Alberite de Tholeto
Rodeus de Roche
Dominus Bertrandus de Gabaray
Petrus Ferrandus de Blask'
Petrus Gunsalmur de Medasco
Iohannes Senchyse Manuel
Petrus Sermiento'[19]
Sencho Senchisie Moscoste[20]
Abbas Lupus de la Serne
Alphosus Henrik, filius regis Henrici bastardi[21]
Homfigus, magister de Federik[22]
Iohannes Stoner[23]
Comes de Gastenado[24]
Sencho de Tholar[25]
Sencho Lupus Papatus, clericus de Ballamus[26]
Fernandus de Ciuile[27]
Clauiger de Calatraue[28]
Petrus de Malfaleto[29]
Clauiger de la Cant'[30]

[h] Martyn *J*   [i] *J breaks off*

---

[13] Alfonso de Villena, count of Ribagorza and Denia, leader of the Aragonese contingent in Pedro's army. The dispute over his ransom would later cause a political furore in England: E. Perroy, 'Gras profits et rançons pendant la guerre de cent ans: L'affaire du comte de Denia', in *Mélanges d'histoire au Moyen Age dédiés à la mémoire de Louis Halphen* (Paris, 1951), pp. 572–80.   [14] He was lord of Allo.

[15] The famous Breton war captain, for whom see above, p. 138, n. 301.

[16] Castro was Enrique the Bastard's brother-in-law.

[17] Manrique was the *adelantado mayor* of Castile.

[18] Ayala, the celebrated Castilian chronicler, bore the standard of the Order of the Sash (*La Banda*) at Nájera, whose members comprised the elite corps of Enrique's army.

[19] Pedro Rodríguez de Sarmiento.

[20] Moscoco, grand master of Santiago, was captured but, according to Lopes, *English in Portugal*, p. 21, put to death by King Pedro after the battle.

The count of Denia[13]
Lord Juan Martínez of Luna
Lord Juan Ramírez of Arellano[14]
Lord Bertrand du Guesclin[15]
The bishop of Relionus
Lord Felipe of Castro[16]
Pedro Manrique[17]
Pedro López of Ayala[18]
Diego López, his brother
Garci Alvarez of Toledo
Ruy Díaz of Rojas
Lord Beltran of Guevara
Pedro Fernández of Velasco
Pedro González of Mendoza
Juan Sánchez Manuel
Pedro Sarmiento[19]
Sancho Sánchez of Moscoco[20]
Alvar López of Cerna
Alfonso Enríquez, son of King Henry the Bastard[21]
Homfigus, master of Fadrique[22]
John Stoner[23]
Gómez of Castañeda[24]
Sancho of Tovar[25]
Sancho López Hippolytus, clerk of Badajoz[26]
Fernández of Seville[27]
The treasurer of Calatrava[28]
Pedro of Malfaleto[29]
The treasurer of Alcántara[30]

[21] Alfonso, count of Noreña, was himself the bastard son of King Enrique.
[22] This may be a garbled attempt to denote Pedro, son of Don Fadrique, master of Santiago, who, according to Lopes, *English in Portugal*, p. 9, took part in the battle, though he does not say that he was captured.
[23] Possibly García Jofre Tenorio, who, according to Lopes, *English in Portugal*, p. 21, was captured and put to death by King Pedro after the battle.
[24] Gómez González de Castañeda.
[25] Sancho Fernández de Tovar.
[26] For 'Hippolytus', see *Chronica Johannis de Reading et Anonymi Cantuariensis*, p. 184.
[27] Fernández Arias de Seville.
[28] This should probably denote the Master of the Order of Calatrava, the Aragonese Pedro Muñiz de Godoy (Lopes, *English in Portugal*, p. 338).
[29] Unidentified: the *Anonimalle Chronicle*, p. 54, called him 'Petre de Malsoleto'.
[30] Unidentified: the Order of Alcántara was the León branch of the Order of Calatrava. For the Iberian military orders, see Lopes, *English in Portugal*, pp. xxii–xxiv.

Iohannes Romeye[31]

Diegus Remoris la Dyamascant[32]

Petrus Gonys de Porry, eius filius[33]

Rogo Sarus de Siuers[34]

Magister Sancti Iacobi[35]

Magister Hospitalis Hispanie[36]

fo. 56ᵛ Gubernator de Seragos

Marescallus d'Audenham[37]

Dominus I. Remeruk[38]

Dominus Becco de Vileyns[39]

Et alii ad summam duo milium et amplius bonarum gencium.

    Mortui in bello de Nasers

Sencho Lopus d'Euesque[40]

Sencho Senchis de Roches

Garcy Basies[41]

Gonsaluus comes de Siueris

Albarus Fernandus de Bosco

Dominus I. Sermentour[42]

ʲEt aliiᵏ usque ad numerum quinque milium ˡuel sex miliumˡ bonarum gencium armatarum, exceptis ienetoriis, pauisoriis et seruientibus sine numero.

ʲ J resumes   ᵏ *add.* inibi *J*   ˡ⁻ˡ *om. J*

---

[31] Juan Ramírez de Guzman.

[32] The *Anonimalle Chronicle*, pp. 54–5, calls him 'Diego Romers de Diamastaunt'.

[33] The *Anonimalle Chronicle*, p. 55, has 'et son fils' in place of 'eius filius'. Porras was grand prior of the Hospitallers in Castile (Lopes, *English in Portugal*, p. 338), which suggests that the 'master of the Hospital of Spain' three lines below may refer to him.

[34] Unidentified: just possibly Arnoul du Solier, a French mercenary known to have been taken at the battle (Russell, *English Intervention*, p. 128).

[35] Gonzalo Mejía.

[36] Possibly Gómez Pérez de Porras (see three lines above).

[37] Arnoul d'Audrehem, marshal of France, who had also been captured at Poitiers, and

Juan Ramírez[31]
Diego Ramírez of Diamastaunt[32]
Gómez Pérez of Porras and his son[33]
Rogo Sarus of Sivers[34]
The master of Santiago[35]
The master of the Hospital of Spain[36]
The governor of Zaragoza
Marshal d'Audrehem[37]
Lord Juan Ramírez[38]
Lord Bègue of Villaines[39]
and others, to a total of two thousand and more good men.

   Those slain in the battle of Nájera

Iñigo López of Orosco[40]
Sancho Sánchez of Rojas
Garcilaso de la Vega[41]
Gonsalvo Gómez of Siveris
Alvaro Fernández of Bosco
Lord Juan Sarmiento[42]
and others, to a total of five or six thousand good men-at-arms, not
counting innumerable light horsemen, pavisers, and sergeants.

had still not paid his ransom, for which the Black Prince accused him of treason following
his capture at Nájera, but he was acquitted by a jury of twelve knights (Lopes, *English in
Portugal*, p. 23).

   [38] Possibly a repetition of Juan Ramírez de Guzman (see eight lines up).

   [39] Pierre de Villaines, count of Ribadeo, known as 'le bègue' ('the stutterer'), a French
mercenary whom Chandos Herald claimed was killed at Nájera, but it is certain that he was
captured rather than killed (Russell, *English Intervention*, p. 128).

   [40] Iñigo López de Orosco was put to death after the battle by King Pedro, apparently by
the king's own hand: Lopes, *English in Portugal*, p. 21.

   [41] Ancestor of the great *mestizo* historian of the same name, Garcilaso de la Vega El Inca
(d. 1616).

   [42] Juan Rodríguez Sarmiento.

BIBLIOGRAPHY

Primary Sources

Adae Murimuth Continuatio Chronicarum. Robertus de Avesbury de Gestis Mirabilibus Regis Edwardi Tertii, ed. E. M. Thompson (Rolls Series 93; London, 1889).

Adami Murimuthensis Chronica sui Temporis cum eorundem Continuatio a Quodam Anonymo, ed. T. Hog (London, 1846).

Anglia Sacra sive Collectio Historiarum, ed. H. Wharton (2 vols., London, 1691).

The Anonimalle Chronicle 1333–1381, ed. V. H. Galbraith (Manchester, 1927).

The Black Prince: An Historical Poem by Chandos Herald, ed. H. O. Coxe (Roxburghe Club; London, 1842).

BOUCHART, ALAIN, *Grandes Chroniques de Brétagne*, ed. M-L. Auger and G. Jeanneau (Paris, 1986).

Calendar of Entries in the Papal Registers Relating to Great Britain and Ireland, ed. W. H. Bliss *et al.* (10 vols., London, 1893–1915).

Chronica Johannis de Reading et Anonymi Cantuariensis 1346–1367, ed. J. Tait (Manchester, 1914).

The Chronicle of Lanercost 1272–1346, ed. H. Maxwell (Glasgow, 1913).

Chronicon Galfridi le Baker de Swynebroke, ed. E. M. Thompson (Oxford, 1889).

Eulogium Historiarum sive Temporis Chronicon ab Orbe Condita usque ad annum Domini 1366, ed. F. S. Haydon (3 vols., Rolls Series 9; London, 1863).

GEOFFREY OF BURTON: *Life and Miracles of St Modwenna*, ed. R. Bartlett (OMT; 2002).

Gesta Henrici Quinti, ed. and trans. F. Taylor and J. Roskell (OMT; 1975).

GRAY, SIR THOMAS, *Scalachronica*, ed. A. King (Surtees Society Publications, ccix; Woodbridge, 2005).

The Historical Works of Gervase of Canterbury, ed. W. Stubbs (2 vols., Rolls Series 73; London, 1880).

Knighton's Chronicle 1337–1396, ed. G. H. Martin (OMT; 1995).

Letters, Orders and Musters of Bertrand du Guesclin, 1357–1380, ed. M. Jones (Woodbridge, 2004).

Memorials of Henry the Fifth, ed. C. A. Cole (Rolls Series 11; London, 1858).

The Parliament Rolls of Medieval England (PROME), ed. C. Given-Wilson *et al.* (16 vols., Woodbridge, 2005).

Le Prince Noir, poème du héraut d'armes Chandos, ed. F. Michel (London and Paris, 1883).

'The ransom of John II, King of France, 1360–1370', ed. D. Broome, *Camden Miscellany*, xiv (London, 1926).

'Some documents regarding the fulfilment and interpretation of the Treaty of Brétigny (1361–1369)', ed. P. Chaplais, *Camden Miscellany*, xix (London, 1952).

Statutes of the Realm (11 vols., Record Commission, London, 1810–28).

Secondary Sources

ANSÈLME, PÈRE, *Histoire généalogique et chronologique de la maison royale de France* (9 vols., Paris, 1726–33).

AUTRAND, F., *Charles V: Le Sage* (Paris, 1994).

AYTON, ANDREW, and PRESTON, PHILIP, eds., *The Battle of Crécy, 1346* (Woodbridge, 2005).

BARBER, R., *Edward, Prince of Wales and Aquitaine* (London, 1978).

BARKER, JULIET, *The Tournament in England 1100–1400* (Woodbridge, 1986).

BENEDICTOW, O. J., *The Black Death, 1346–1353: The Complete History* (Woodbridge, 2004).

BÉRIAC-LAINÉ, F. AND GIVEN-WILSON, C., *Les Prisonniers de la Bataille de Poitiers* (Paris, 2002).

BUTE, MARQUESS OF, 'Notice of a Manuscript of the Latter Part of the Fourteenth Century, entitled *Passio Scotorum Perjoratorum*', *Proceedings of the Society of Antiquaries of Scotland*, NS vii (1885), 166–92.

COLLINS, HUGH, *The Order of the Garter 1348–1461* (Oxford, 2000).

The Complete Peerage of England, Scotland, Ireland, Great Britain and the United Kingdom, ed. G. E. Cokayne *et al.* (13 vols., London, 1910–59).

DELACHENAL, R., *Histoire de Charles V* (5 vols., Paris, 1909–31).

DOBSON, BARRIE, 'The monks of Canterbury in the later Middle Ages', in P. Collinson, N. Ramsay, and M. Sparks, eds., *A History of Canterbury Cathedral* (Oxford, 1995), pp. 69–153.

EDBURY, P., *The Kingdom of Cyprus and the Crusades 1191–1374* (Cambridge, 1991).

EMDEN, A. B., *A Biographical Register of the University of Oxford* (3 vols., Oxford, 1957).

FOWLER, K., *The King's Lieutenant: Henry of Grosmont, First Duke of Lancaster 1310–1361* (London, 1969).

—— *Medieval Mercenaries*, i: *The Great Companies* (Oxford, 2001).

—— 'News from the front: Letters and despatches of the fourteenth century', in P. Contamine, C. Giry-Deloison, and M. H. Keen, eds., *Guerre et Société en France, en Angleterre et en Bourgogne, XIV—XV Siècles* (Lille, 1991), pp. 63–92.

GIVEN-WILSON, C., *Chronicles: The Writing of History in Medieval England* (London, 2004).

—— 'Purveyance for the Royal Household, 1362–1413', *Bulletin of the Institute of Historical Research*, lvi (1983), pp. 145–63.

GOODMAN, A., *John of Gaunt: The Exercise of Princely Power in Fourteenth-Century Europe* (London, 1992).

GRANT, ALEXANDER, 'Disaster at Neville's Cross', in Rollason and Prestwich, eds., *The Battle of Neville's Cross 1346*, pp. 15–35.

HANNA, R., 'An Oxford library interlude: The manuscripts of John Foxe the martyrologist', *Bodleian Library Record*, xvii (2000–2), 314–26.

HEWITT, H. J., *The Black Prince's Expedition of 1355–1357* (Manchester, 1958).

HORROX, R., ed., *The Black Death* (Manchester, 1994).

KER, N. R., *Medieval Libraries of Great Britain* (Royal Historical Society; London, 1964).

—— and PIPER, A. J., *Medieval Manuscripts in British Libraries* (5 vols., Oxford, 1969–1992).

KINGSFORD, C. L., 'The feast of five kings', *Archaeologia*, lxvii (1915–16), pp. 119–26.

KNOWLES, D. and HADCOCK, R., *Medieval Religious Houses, England and Wales* (Harlow, 1971).

LEGGE, DOMINICA, *Anglo-Norman Literature and its Background* (Oxford, 1963).

LE PATOUREL, J., 'The Treaty of Brétigny, 1360', *Transactions of the Royal Historical Society*, 5th ser., x (1960), 19–39.

LLOYD, T. H., *The English Wool Trade in the Middle Ages* (Cambridge, 1977).

LOPES, FERNÃO, *The English in Portugal 1367–87*, ed. D. W. Lomax and R. J. Oakley (Warminster, 1988).

LUNT, W. E., *Financial Relations of the Papacy with England, 1327–1534* (Cambridge, Mass., 1962).

MATHESON, L. M., *The Prose Brut: The Development of a Middle English Chronicle* (Tempe, Ariz., 1998).

MOISANT, J., *Le Prince Noir en Aquitaine, 1355–1356, 1362–1370* (Paris, 1894).

NEWTON, S. M., *Fashion in the Age of the Black Prince* (Woodbridge, 1980).

PALMER, J. J. N., 'England, France, the papacy and the Flemish succession, 1361–9', *Journal of Medieval History*, ii (1976), pp. 339–64.

PERROY, E., 'Gras profits et rançons pendant la guerre de cent ans: L'affaire du comte de Denia', in *Mélanges d'histoire au Moyen Age dédiés à la mémoire de Louis Halphen* (Paris, 1951), pp. 572–80.

PRESTWICH, M., *Edward I* (Berkeley, 1988).

RAMSAY, NIGEL, 'The cathedral archives and library', in P. Collinson, N. Ramsay, and M. Sparks, eds., *A History of Canterbury Cathedral* (Oxford, 1995), 341–407.

ROGERS, C., 'The Anglo-French Peace Negotiations of 1354–1360 Recon-

sidered', in J. S. Bothwell, ed., *The Age of Edward III* (Woodbridge, 2001), pp. 193–213.

—— *War Cruel and Sharp: English Strategy under Edward III, 1327–1360* (Woodbridge, 2000).

—— *The Wars of Edward III: Sources and Interpretations* (Woodbridge, 1999).

ROLLASON, DAVID, and PRESTWICH, MICHAEL, eds., *The Battle of Neville's Cross 1346* (Stamford, 1998).

RUSSELL, J. C., *British Medieval Population* (Albuquerque, 1948).

RUSSELL, P., *The English Intervention in Spain and Portugal in the Time of Edward III and Richard II* (Oxford, 1955).

SHARPE, R., *A Handlist of the Latin Writers of Great Britain and Ireland before 1540* (Turnhout, 1997).

SPUFFORD, P., *Handbook of Medieval Exchange* (Royal Historical Society Publications; London, 1986).

SUMPTION, J., *The Hundred Years War*, i: *Trial by Battle* (London, 1990); ii: *Trial by Fire* (London, 1999).

SZITTYA, P. R., *The Antifraternal Tradition in Medieval Literature* (Princeton, 1986).

TAYLOR, J., *English Historical Literature in the Fourteenth Century* (Oxford, 1987).

THOMPSON, A. H., 'The pestilences of the fourteenth century in the diocese of York', *Archaeological Journal*, lxxi (1914), 97–154.

TOUT, T. F., *Chapters in the Administrative History of Medieval England* (6 vols., Manchester, 1920–33).

WATSON, A. G., 'Thomas Allen of Oxford and his manuscripts', in *Medieval Scribes, Manuscripts and Libraries: Essays Presented to N. R. Ker* (London, 1978), pp. 279–313.

WENTERSDORF, K. P., 'The clandestine marriages of the Fair Maid of Kent', *Journal of Medieval History*, v (1979), pp. 203–31.

WOOD, DIANA, *Clement VI* (Cambridge, 1989).

INDEX

✓

BIRKBECK COLLEGE

||||||| ||||||||||| ||| ||||||||| |||||

1912643173

822
CHR

![Birkbeck University of London]
Malet Street, London WC1E 7HX
020-7631 6239
Items should be returned or renewed by the latest date stamped below.
Please pick up a Library guide or visit the Library website
http://www.bbk.ac.uk/lib/
for information about online renewals.

1-8-08